Pascal Reference Chart (cont.)

PROGRAM COMPOSITION (PAGE IN TEXT)	EXAMPLE
Variable section (49,72)	

var

Count, I, Number : integer;
Hours, Rate, Wages : real;
DeptCode, FirstInit, SecondInit : char;
OverTime : boolean;
OutFile : text;
Dept : DepartmentName;
EmpCode : Digit;
Product, Item : List;
ProductName : String;
Letters : CapLetterSet;
EmpRec : InfoRecord;
InFile : EmployeeFile;
FirstPtr, TempPtr : ListPointer;

(predefined types)
  integer
  real
  character
  boolean
  text file
(user-defined types)

Subprogram section (141)
  Function definition (141)

function *RoundCents* (*Amount : real*) : *real*;
(∗ Round *Amount* to nearest cent ∗)
begin (∗ *RoundCents* ∗)
  RoundCents := *round*(100 ∗ *Amount*) / 100
end (∗ *RoundCents* ∗);

Procedure definition (152)

procedure *ReadCodes* (**var** *Department,*
                          Employee : char);
(∗ Read department & employee codes ∗)
begin (∗ *ReadCodes* ∗)
  write ('Enter dept. & employee codes: ');
  readln (*Department, Employee*)
end (∗ *ReadCodes* ∗);

Statement part (48,71)

begin (∗ main program ∗)
  statement-1;

      .
      .
      .

  statement-n
end (∗ main progra

**Pascal:
Programming
and
Problem
Solving**

PASCAL
Programming and Problem Solving

Sanford Leestma
Larry Nyhoff

Department of
Mathematics and
Computer Science
Calvin College

Macmillan Publishing Company
NEW YORK

Collier Macmillan Publishers
LONDON

Macmillan Publishing Company
866 Third Avenue, New York, New York 10022

Collier Macmillan Canada, Inc.

Library of Congress Cataloging in Publication Data

Leestma, Sanford.
  Pascal: Programming and Problem Solving.

  Includes index.
  1. PASCAL (Computer program language)   I. Nyhoff,
Larry R.   II. Title.
QA76.73.P2L44   1984   001.64′2   83–11297
ISBN 0–02–369460–2

Printing: 5 6 7 8   Year: 5 6 7 8 9 0 1 2

ISBN   0-02-369460-2

PREFACE

Pascal was developed in the late 1960s and early 1970s by Niklaus Wirth, a Swiss computer scientist at the Eidgenössische Technische Hochschule (ETH) in Zurich, Switzerland. His primary goal was to develop a language that makes it possible "to teach programming as a systematic discipline based on certain fundamental concepts clearly and naturally reflected by the language." The *Pascal User Manual and Report* written by Wirth and K. Jensen and published in 1974 serves as the basic definition of the Pascal language. As the use of Pascal grew, some differences appeared in various implementations. To ensure that Pascal programs written on one system can be executed on another, national and international standards for the language have been formulated. A recent standard is *An American National Standard IEEE Standard Pascal Computer Programming Language,* which was published in 1983 by IEEE (Institute of Electrical and Electronics Engineers). This standard was approved by the IEEE Standards Board and the American National Standards Institute and serves as the basis for this text.

Although this book gives a complete presentation of Pascal, it is more than just a programming manual. It reflects our view that the main reason for learning a programming language is to use the computer to solve problems. Three basic steps in computer-assisted problem-solving are discussed and illustrated in the text: (1) problem analysis and algorithm development, (2) transformation of the algorithm into a program, and (3) program execution and validation. We also feel that an intelligent user of the computer must have some elementary understanding of the manner in which a computer operates, how it stores information, how it processes data, and what some of its capabilities and limitations are. For this reason the text also contains a brief sketch of the history of computers and a simple description of some of the main features of a computer system.

The text also emphasizes the importance of good structure and style in programs. In addition to describing these concepts in general, it contains a large number of complete programs, each of which is intended to demonstrate good algorithm design and programming style. At the end of each chapter a Programming Pointers section summarizes the main points regarding structure and style as well as language features presented and some problems that beginning programmers may experience.

This text is intended for a first course in computing and assumes no previous experience with computers. It corresponds to the recommendations of the Association for Computing Machinery (ACM) for the first two courses CS1 and CS2 in an undergraduate program in computer science. A one-semester introductory programming course can be based on the material in the first eight chapters. Sections that may be omitted without loss of continuity are indicated by an asterisk (*).

Chapter 1 of the text begins with a brief summary of the history of the development of computer systems. We realize that this is usually not included in programming texts, but we feel that some historical perspective is appropriate for a beginning programmer. We also feel that it is appropriate for a beginning programmer to have some idea—albeit naive—of the main components of computer systems and of the manner in which information is represented in a computer. This chapter thus also presents a very elementary introduction to computer systems and data representation. This entire chapter may be omitted or given as an independent reading assignment by those who wish to move immediately to the material more directly related to programming.

Chapter 2 begins with a discussion of the three steps of the problem-solving process listed earlier and illustrates them with two simple examples. The second section of this chapter presents enough basic Pascal so that students can already begin to read and write simple programs. This reflects our feeling that students should begin work with the computer as soon as possible. This chapter closes with a discussion of documentation, program style, program testing and debugging, and program refinement.

Chapter 3 begins the formal presentation of Pascal. It includes a discussion of the standard data types, arithmetic operations and functions, the assignment statement, and elementary input and output operations. The composition of a Pascal program is described and illustrated with several simple but complete examples. The last section introduces syntax diagrams as a convenient method for describing language constructs.

In Chapter 4 the three basic control structures—sequential, repetition, and selection—are described as the basis for structured programming. Compound statements implement sequential structure; **for, while,** and **repeat** statements implement repetition structures; and **if** and **case** statements implement selection structures.

Chapter 5 introduces functions and procedures, including a discussion of scope rules for identifiers. Section 5.5 illustrates random number generation and simulation. The example of Section 5.6 demonstrates top-down design and modular programming. Recursion is introduced in Section 5.7 and the use of functions and procedures as parameters in Section 5.8, which is an optional section.

An expanded treatment of input and output is given in Chapter 6. Since interactive input–output is cumbersome with large data sets and can be rather difficult with some Pascal compilers, text files are introduced in this chapter.

User-defined simple data types are discussed in Chapter 7. Enumerated data types and subrange types are described and illustrated with several examples.

Chapters 8 and 9 introduce the array data type. One-dimensional arrays are described in Chapter 8 and the important applications to sorting and searching data and string processing are described in detail. Multidimensional arrays are considered in Chapter 9.

The other structured data types—sets, records, and files—are discussed in Chapters 10, 11, and 12. Many examples illustrate these data types and include a simple lexical analyzer, searching and sorting lists of records, and updating a file.

Chapter 13 introduces pointer variables and dynamic data structures, and considerable effort is made to make these understandable to the beginning programmer. Linked lists are used to implement stacks, queues, and ordered lists.

The final chapter contains four advanced applications: evaluation of Reverse Polish expressions using stacks; tree-processing using multiply linked structures; the quicksort algorithm for sorting an array of records; and the natural mergesort method for sorting a file.

ACKNOWLEDGMENTS

We express our appreciation and gratitude to all those who have been involved in the preparation of this text: to our colleagues D. Brink, W. Dyksen, and M. Stob, who have used this material in their classes and whose suggestions have strengthened the presentation; to our students who have served as test subjects; to Bob Macek, Ron Harris, and all other Macmillan personnel who initiated, supervised, produced, or in some other way contributed to the finished product; to the several reviewers of the original manuscript, whose comments were encouraging, helpful, and sincerely appreciated; and to Shar, Jeff, Jim, Julie, Joan, Marge, Michelle, Sandy, and Michael, whose patience, love, support, and understanding during the preparation of this text exceeded what we had any right to expect.

S.C.L.
L.R.N.

CONTENTS

1

1.1 History of Computing Systems 1	**Introduction and**
1.2 Computing Systems 12	**History**
1.3 Internal Representation 14	**1**
Exercises 17	

2

2.1 Program Analysis and Algorithm Development 21	**Algorithms and**
2.2 Program Coding 29	**Programs**
2.3 Program Execution 33	**21**
2.4 Program Design, Validation, and Refinement 36	
Exercises 39	

3

3.1 Data Types 45	**Basic Pascal**
Exercises 50	**45**
3.2 Arithmetic Operations and Functions 51	
Exercises 54	
3.3 The Assignment Statement 55	
Exercises 60	
3.4 Input/Output 61	
Exercises 70	
3.5 Program Composition 71	
3.6 An Example 73	
3.7 Syntax Diagrams 76	
Programming Pointers 79	
Exercises 84	

4

4.1 Sequential Structure: Compound Statements; **begin** and **end** 87	**Control Structures**
4.2 Repetition Structure: The **for** Statement 89	**87**
4.3 Boolean Expressions 95	
Exercises 99	
4.4 Repetition Structure: The **while** Statement 99	
4.5 Repetition Structure: The **repeat** Statement 104	
Exercises 106	

4.6 Selection Structure: The **if** Statement   110

4.7 Multialternative Selection Structure: Nested **if** Statements and the **case** Statement   119

Programming Pointers   126

Exercises   132

5

Functions and Procedures 139

5.1 Predefined Functions and Procedures   140

5.2 User-Defined Functions   141

Exercises   148

5.3 User-Defined Procedures; Value Parameters and Variable Parameters   152

Exercises   159

5.4 The Scope of Identifiers   161

5.5 An Example: Random Number Generation   171

Exercises   173

5.6 An Example: Top–Down Design and Modular Programming   177

5.7 Recursion   192

* **5.8** Functions and Procedures as Parameters   200

Programming Pointers   204

Exercises   207

6

Input/Output 211

6.1 Input/Output Procedures   211

Exercises   219

6.2 Introduction to Text Files; the *eof* and *eoln* Functions   222

Programming Pointers   234

Exercises   238

7

Ordinal Data Types: Enumerated and Subrange 243

7.1 The Type Section   244

7.2 Enumerated Data Types   246

7.3 Subrange Data Types   253

Programming Pointers   255

Exercises   256

8

One-Dimensional Arrays and String Processing 259

8.1 Introduction to Arrays and Subscripted Variables   259

8.2 List Processing Using One-Dimensional Arrays   263

8.3 Applications: Class Averages, Sorting, Searching   272

Exercises   284

8.4 String Processing   290

8.5 Application: Text Editing   300

Programming Pointers   305

Exercises   307

9

Multidimensional Arrays 313

9.1 Introduction to Multidimensional Arrays; Multiply Subscripted Variables 313
9.2 Processing Multidimensional Arrays 317
9.3 Application to String Processing 324
9.4 Numeric Applications: Automobile Sales, Matrix Multiplication 328
Programming Pointers 336
Exercises 337

10

Sets 347

10.1 Set Declarations, Set Constants, Set Assignment 348
10.2 Set Operations and Relations 351
10.3 Processing Sets 356
10.4 Examples: Sieve of Eratosthenes, Simple Lexical Analyzer 358
Programming Pointers 365
Exercises 366

11

Records 369

11.1 Introduction to Records and Fields 369
11.2 Processing Records; the **with** Statement 373
11.3 Application of Records: Sorting 383
*__**11.4** Variant Records 389
Programming Pointers 393
Exercises 397

12

Files 401

12.1 Review of Text Files 402
12.2 Files of Other Types 403
12.3 Application: Updating a File 419
Programming Pointers 422
Exercises 423

13

Pointers and Dynamic Data Structures 429

13.1 Pointers; the Procedures *new* and *dispose* 430
13.2 Linked Lists, Stacks, Queues 435
13.3 General Linked Lists, Ordered Lists 444
Programming Pointers 458
Exercises 462

14.1 Application of Stacks: Reverse Polish Notation 468
Exercises 476
14.2 Multiply Linked Structures: Trees 478
Exercises 491
14.3 Quicksort 498
Exercises 506
14.4 External Sorting: Mergesort 507
Exercises 515

**Advanced
Applications
467**

A ASCII and EBCDIC A1

B Reserved Words, Standard Identifiers, and Operators A7

C Syntax Diagrams A11

D Predefined Functions and Procedures A23

E Sample Data Files A25

F Miscellany A35

G Answers to Selected Exercises A45

Index A61

**Pascal:
Programming
and
Problem
Solving**

1

Introduction and History

The modern electronic computer is one of the most important products of the twentieth century. It is an essential tool in many areas including business, industry, government, science, and education; indeed, it has touched nearly every aspect of our lives. The impact of this twentieth-century information revolution brought about by the development of high-speed computing systems has been nearly as widespread as the impact of the nineteenth-century industrial revolution. This chapter gives a summary of the history of computer systems and briefly describes the components that comprise such systems.

1.1 History of Computing Systems

There are two important concepts in the history of computation, *the mechanization of arithmetic* and *the concept of a stored program for the automatic control of computations.* We shall focus our attention on some of the devices that have implemented these concepts.

A variety of computational devices were used in ancient civilizations. One of the earliest, which might be considered a forerunner of the modern computer, is the *abacus* (Figure 1.1), which has movable beads strung on

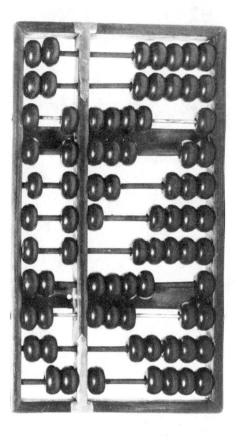

Figure 1.1.
Abacus.

rods to count and make computations. Although its exact origin is unknown, the abacus was used by the Chinese perhaps three to four thousand years ago and is still used today.

The ancient British stone monument *Stonehenge,* located in southern England, was built between 1900 and 1600 B.C. and evidently was an astronomical calculator to predict the changes of the seasons. Five hundred years ago, the Inca Indians of South America used a system of knotted cords called *quipus* to count and record divisions of land among the various tribal groups. In Western Europe, *Napier's bones* and tables of *logarithms* were designed by the Scottish mathematician John Napier (1550–1617) to simplify arithmetic calculations. These led to the subsequent invention of the *slide rule.*

In 1642, the young French mathematician Blaise Pascal (1623–1662) invented one of the first mechanical adding machines. This device used a system of gears and wheels similar to that used in odometers and other modern counting devices. Pascal's adder could both add and subtract and was invented to calculate taxes. Pascal's announcement of his invention reveals the labor-saving motivation for its development:

> Dear reader, this notice will serve to inform you that I submit to the public
> a small machine of my invention, by means of which you alone may, without

(a)

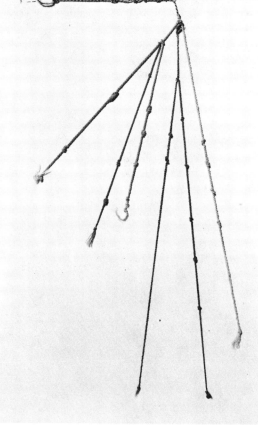

(b)

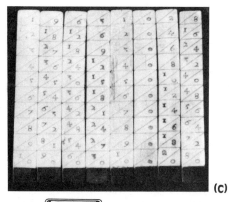

(c)

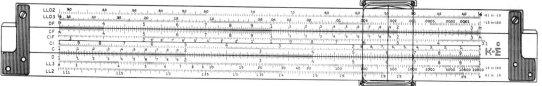

(d)

Figure 1.2.
(a) Stonehenge. (b) Quipus (Courtesy of the American Museum of Natural History).
(c) Napier's bones (Courtesy of the Smithsonian Institution). (d) Slide rule.

any effort, perform all the operations of arithmetic, and may be relieved of the work which has often times fatigued your spirit, when you have worked with the counters or with the pen. As for simplicity of movement of the operations, I have so devised it that, although the operations of arithmetic are in a way opposed the one to the other—as addition to subtraction, and multiplication to division—nevertheless they are all performed on this machine by a single movement. The facility of this movement of operation is very evident since it is just as easy to move one thousand or ten thousand dials, all at one time, if one desires to make a single dial move, although all accomplish the movement perfectly. The most ignorant find as many advantages as the most experienced. The instrument makes up for ignorance and for lack of practice, and even without any effort of the operator, it makes possible shortcuts by itself, whenever the numbers are set down.

Although Pascal built more than fifty of his adding machines, his commercial venture failed, since the devices could not be built with sufficient precision for practical use.

In the 1670s, the German mathematician Gottfried Wilhelm von Leibniz (1646–1716) produced a machine that was similar in design to Pascal's but that was somewhat more reliable and accurate. Leibniz's device could add, subtract, multiply, and divide, as well as calculate square roots.

A number of other mechanical calculators followed that further refined the designs of Pascal and Leibniz. By the end of the nineteenth century, these calculators had become important tools in science, business, and commerce.

As noted earlier, the second idea to emerge in the history of computing was the concept of a stored program to control the calculations. One early example of an automatically controlled device is the weaving loom invented by the Frenchman Joseph Marie Jacquard (1752–1834). This automatic loom, introduced at a Paris exhibition in 1801, used metal cards punched with holes to position threads for the weaving process. A collection of these cards made up a program that directed the loom. Within a decade, eleven thousand

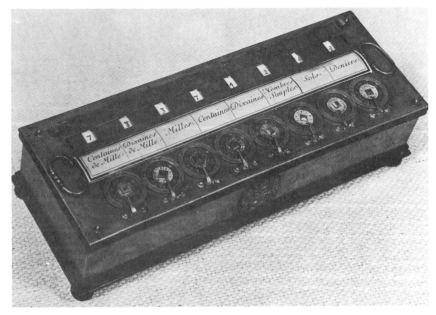

Figure 1.3.
Pascal's adder.
(Courtesy of IBM.)

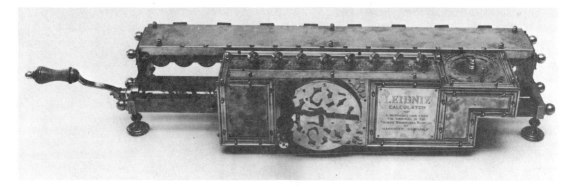

Figure 1.4.
Leibniz's calculator. (Courtesy of IBM.)

of these machines were in use in French textile plants, resulting in what may have been the first incidence of unemployment caused by automation. Unemployed workers rioted and destroyed several of the new looms and cards. Jacquard wrote: "The iron was sold for iron, the wood for wood, and I its inventor delivered up to public ignominy." The Jacquard loom is still used today, although modern versions are controlled by magnetic tape rather than punched cards.

Figure 1.5.
Jacquard loom.
(Courtesy of IBM.)

(a)

Figure 1.6.
(a) Babbage's
difference engine.
(b) Babbage's
analytical engine.
(Courtesy of IBM.)

(b)

INTRODUCTION AND HISTORY

These two concepts of mechanized calculation and stored program control were combined by the English mathematician Charles Babbage (1792–1871), who began work in 1822 on a machine that he called the "Difference Engine." This machine was designed to compute polynomials for the preparation of mathematical tables. Babbage continued his work until 1833 with support from the British government, which was interested in possible military applications of the Difference Engine. But Babbage later abandoned this project since the metal-working technology of that time was not sufficiently advanced to manufacture the required precision gears and linkages. Babbage was not discouraged, however, but designed a more sophisticated machine that he called his "Analytical Engine." This had several special-purpose components that were intended to work together. The "mill" was supposed to carry out the arithmetic computations; the "store" was the machine's memory for storing data and intermediate results; and other components were designed for the input and output of information and for the transfer of information between components. The operation of this machine was to be fully automatic, controlled by punched cards, an idea based on Jacquard's earlier work. In fact, Babbage himself said, "The analogy of the Analytical Engine with this well-known process is nearly perfect." Ada Augusta, Lord George Byron's daughter and the Countess of Lovelace, understood how the device was to work and supported Babbage. Considered by some to be the first programmer, Lady Lovelace described the similarity of Jacquard's and Babbage's inventions: "The Analytical Engine weaves algebraic patterns just as the Jacquard loom weaves flowers and leaves." Although Babbage's machine was not built during his lifetime, it is nevertheless part of the history of computing because many of the concepts of its design are used in modern computers.

A related development in the United States was the census bureau's use of punched-card systems to help compile the 1890 census. These systems, designed by Herman Hollerith, a young mathematician employed by the bureau, used electrical sensors to interpret the information stored on the punched cards. In 1896, Hollerith left the census bureau and formed his own tabulating company, which in 1924 became the International Business Machines Corporation (IBM).

The development of computing devices continued at a rapid pace in the United States. Some of the pioneers in this effort were Howard Aiken, J. P. Eckert, J. W. Mauchly, and John von Neumann. Repeating much of the work of Babbage, Aiken designed a system consisting of several mechanical calculators working together. This work, which was supported by IBM, led to the invention in 1944 of the electromechanical Mark I computer. This machine is the best-known computer built before 1945 and may be regarded as the first realization of Babbage's Analytical Engine.

The best known of the early fully electronic computers was the ENIAC (Electronic Numerical Integrator and Computer), constructed in 1946 by J. P. Eckert and J. W. Mauchly at the Moore School of Electrical Engineering of the University of Pennsylvania. This extremely large machine contained over 18,000 vacuum tubes and 1500 relays and nearly filled a room 20 feet by 40 feet in size. It could multiply numbers approximately 1000 times faster than the Mark I could, though it was quite limited in its applications and was used primarily by the Army Ordnance Department to calculate firing tables and trajectories for various types of shells. Eckert and Mauchly later

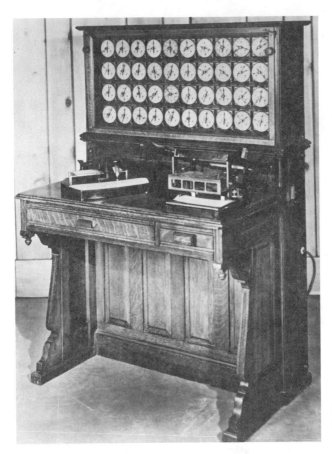

Figure 1.7.
Hollerith equipment.
(Courtesy of IBM.)

Figure 1.8.
Mark I.
(Courtesy of IBM.)

left the University of Pennsylvania to form the Eckert-Mauchly Computer Corporation, which built the UNIVAC (Universal Automatic Computer), the first commercially available computer designed for both scientific and business applications. The first UNIVAC was sold to the census bureau in 1951.

The instructions, or program, that controlled the ENIAC's operation were entered into the machine by rewiring some parts of the computer's circuits. This complicated process was very time-consuming, sometimes taking several people several days, and during this time, the computer was idle. In other early computers, the instructions were stored outside the machine on punched cards or some other medium and were transferred into the machine one at a time for interpretation and execution. A new scheme, developed by the Princeton mathematician John von Neumann and others, used internally stored commands. The advantages of this stored program concept are that internally stored instructions can be processed more rapidly, and more importantly, that they can be modified by the computer itself while computations are taking place. The stored program concept makes possible the general-purpose computers so commonplace today.

The actual physical components used in constructing a computer system are its *hardware*. Several generations of computers can be identified by the type of hardware used. The ENIAC and UNIVAC are examples of *first-generation* computers, which are characterized by their extensive use of vacuum tubes. Advances in electronics brought changes in computing systems, and in 1958, IBM introduced the first of the *second-generation* computers, the IBM 7090. These computers were built between 1959 and 1965 and used transistors in place of vacuum tubes. Consequently, these computers were smaller and less expensive, required less power, generated far less heat,

Figure 1.9.
ENIAC.
(Courtesy of Sperry
Corporation.)

and were more reliable than their predecessors. The *third-generation* computers that followed used integrated circuits and introduced new techniques for better system utilization, such as multiprogramming and time-sharing. The IBM System/360 introduced in 1964 is commonly accepted as the first of this generation of computers. Computers of the 1970s used large-scale integrated circuits on silicon chips and other microelectronic advances to shrink their size and cost still more while enlarging their capability. A typical memory chip is equivalent to many thousands of transistors, is smaller than a baby's fingernail, weighs a small fraction of an ounce, requires only a trickle of power, and costs but a few dollars. Such miniaturization made possible the development of the popular personal computers such as the Apple, Commodore, Radio Shack, and IBM microcomputers (Figure 1.10). One of the pioneers in the development of microcomputers, Robert Noyce, contrasted them with the ENIAC as follows:

> An individual integrated circuit on a chip perhaps a quarter of an inch square now can embrace more electronic elements than the most complex piece of electronic equipment that could be built in 1950. Today's microcomputer, at a cost of perhaps $300, has more computing capacity than the first electronic computer, ENIAC. It is twenty times faster, has a larger memory, consumes the power of a light bulb rather than that of a locomotive, occupies 1/30,000 the volume and costs 1/10,000 as much. It is available by mail order or at your local hobby shop.

The stored program concept was a significant improvement over manual programming methods, but early computers were still difficult to use because of the complex coding schemes required for the representation of programs and data. Consequently, in addition to improved hardware, computer manufacturers began to develop collections of programs known as *system software*

Figure 1.10.
A typical personal computer. (Courtesy of Tandy Corporation.)

to provide easier access to their machines by a larger audience. One of the more important advances in this area was the development of *high-level languages,* which allow users to write programs in a language similar to natural language. A program written in a high-level language is known as a *source program.* For most high-level languages, the instructions that make up a source program must be translated into *machine language,* that is, the language used by a particular computer. This machine language program is called an *object program.* The programs that translate source programs into object programs are called *compilers.* Another part of the system software, the *operating system,* controls the translation of the source program, allocates storage for the program and data, and carries out many other supervisory functions.

One of the first high-level languages to gain widespread acceptance was FORTRAN (FORmula TRANslation). It was developed for the IBM 704 computer by John Backus and a team of thirteen other programmers at IBM over a three-year period (1954–1957). Since that time many other high-level languages have been developed including ALGOL, BASIC, COBOL, Pascal, PL/I, and Ada. In this text we shall discuss the Pascal programming language.

Pascal, named in honor of the French mathematician Blaise Pascal, was designed by Niklaus Wirth at the Eidgenössische Technishe Hochshule (ETH) in Zurich, Switzerland. The first Pascal compiler appeared in 1970, and the first report on the language was published in 1971.[1] A revised user manual and report was published in 1974.[2] The first two paragraphs of the introduction to this report describe Wirth's reasons for developing Pascal:

> The development of the language Pascal is based on two principal aims. The first is to make available a language suitable to teach programming as a systematic discipline based on certain fundamental concepts clearly and naturally reflected by the language. The second is to develop implementations of this language which are both reliable and efficient on presently available computers.
>
> The desire for a new language for the purpose of teaching programming is due to my dissatisfaction with the presently used major languages whose features and constructs too often cannot be explained logically and convincingly and which too often defy systematic reasoning. Along with this dissatisfaction goes my conviction that the language in which the student is taught to express his ideas profoundly influences his habits of thought and invention, and that the disorder governing these languages directly imposes itself onto the programming style of the students.

For Pascal, Wirth used much of the framework of ALGOL-60, a version of ALGOL. Pascal itself has served as the basis for Ada, a more recent programming language.

In summary, the history of computation and computational aids began several thousands of years ago, and in some cases, the theory underlying such devices developed much more rapidly than did the technical skills required to produce working models. Although the modern electronic computer with its mechanized calculation and automatic program control has its roots

---

[1] N. Wirth, "The Programming Language Pascal," *Acta-Informatica 1* (1971):35–63.
[2] K. Jensen and N. Wirth, *Pascal User Manual and Report* (Heidelberg: Springer-Verlag, 1974).

in the midnineteenth-century work of Charles Babbage, the electronic computer is a fairly recent development. The rapid changes that have marked its progression since its inception in 1945 can be expected to continue into the future.

In our discussion of the history of computing, we noted that Babbage designed **Computing** his Analytical Engine as a system of several separate components, each with **Systems** its own particular function. This general scheme was incorporated in many later computers and is, in fact, a common feature of most modern computers. In this section we briefly describe the major components of a modern computing system.

The heart of any computing system is its *central processing unit,* or *cpu.* The cpu controls the operation of the entire system, performs the arithmetic and logic operations, and stores instructions and data. The instructions and data are encoded as sequences of 0's and 1's and are stored in a high-speed *memory unit.* The *control unit* fetches these instructions from memory, decodes them, and directs the system to execute the operations indicated by the instructions. Those operations that are arithmetical or logical in nature are carried out using special registers and circuits of the *arithmetic-logic unit* (*alu*) of the cpu.

Instructions, data, and computed results must be transmitted between the user and the cpu. There are many *input/output devices* designed for this purpose in use today, such as card readers, remote terminals, paper-tape readers, optical scanners, voice input devices, and high-speed printers. The function of these input/output devices is to convert information from an external form understandable to the user to electrical pulses decodable by the cpu, and vice versa.

The cpu memory unit is called the *internal* or *main memory* of the computing system. In older machines this memory usually consisted of magnetic cores, whereas newer machines use metal oxide semiconductors. Although these devices allow for the rapid retrieval of information stored in them, they are rather expensive, and so most computing systems also contain components that serve as *external* or *secondary memory.* Common forms of this type of memory are magnetic disks and magnetic tapes. These provide relatively inexpensive storage for large collections of information, but the rate of transfer of information to and from the cpu is considerably slower than that for internal memory.

The diagram in Figure 1.11 shows the relationship between these components in a computer system, and Figure 1.12 shows these components as they appear in a modern computer system.

In some cases, the user of a computer system enters the instructions and data of a program onto punched cards, using a keypunch. The information from this deck of cards is then entered into the system by means of a card reader. The program is processed, and the output produced is usually printed by a high-speed line printer. This mode of operation in which a job is input to the system and carried through to completion without user interaction is known as *batch mode* operation.

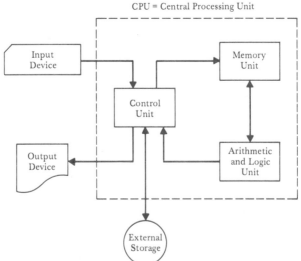

CPU = Central Processing Unit

Input Device

Memory Unit

Control Unit

Output Device

Arithmetic and Logic Unit

External Storage

Figure 1.11.
Major components of a computing system.

Another common mode of operation is known as *time-sharing,* in which several users can interact with the system simultaneously via remote terminals. For example, data may be read from a disk for one user while results are being written at the line printer for another user while the arithmetic-logic unit is performing calculations for yet another user. Typically, however, each

Figure 1.12.
A typical minicomputer system. (Courtesy of Prime Computer Corporation.)

user has the illusion that the entire system is dedicated to him or her alone.

A third mode of operation might be called the *personal* mode, in which a single microcomputer serves an individual user. This mode of operation has become increasingly more common with the development of relatively inexpensive personal microcomputers. Pascal is one of several programming languages commonly available on microcomputer systems.

1.3

As we noted in the preceding section, instructions and data stored in the **Internal** memory of a computer system are encoded as sequences of 0's and 1's. This **Representation** is because the devices that make up the memory unit are two-state devices and hence are ideally suited for storing information that is coded using only two symbols. If one of the states is interpreted as 0 and the other as 1, then a natural scheme for representing information is one that uses only the two symbols 0 and 1.

The number system that we are accustomed to using is a *decimal* or *base-10* number system, which uses the digits 0, 1, 2, 3, 4, 5, 6, 7, 8, and 9. The significance of these digits in a numeral depends on the positions that they occupy in that numeral. For example, in the numeral

$$485$$

the digit 4 is interpreted as

$$4 \text{ hundreds}$$

and the digit 8 as

$$8 \text{ tens}$$

and the digit 5 as

$$5 \text{ ones}$$

Thus, the numeral 485 represents the number four-hundred eighty-five and can be written in *expanded form* as

$$(4 \times 100) + (8 \times 10) + (5 \times 1)$$

or

$$(4 \times 10^2) + (8 \times 10^1) + (5 \times 10^0)$$

The digits that appear in the various positions of a decimal (base-10) numeral thus represent coefficients of powers of 10.

Similar positional number systems can be devised using numbers other than 10 as a base. The *binary* number system uses 2 as the base and has only two digits, 0 and 1. These binary digits are usually called *bits*. As in a decimal system, the significance of the bits in a binary numeral is determined by their positions in that numeral. For example, the binary numeral

$$101$$

can be written in expanded form (using decimal notation) as

$$(1 \times 2^2) + (0 \times 2^1) + (1 \times 2^0)$$

that is, the binary numeral 101 has the decimal value

$$4 + 0 + 1 = 5$$

To avoid confusion about which base is being used, it is common to enclose a nondecimal numeral in parentheses and write the base as a subscript. Using this convention, we would write the binary numeral 101 as

$$(101)_2$$

In a decimal numeral representing a fraction, the digits to the right of the decimal point are also coefficients of powers of 10. In this case, however, the exponents that appear on the base 10 are negative integers. For example, the numeral 0.317 can be written in expanded form as

$$(3 \times 10^{-1}) + (1 \times 10^{-2}) + (7 \times 10^{-3})$$

or equivalently;

$$\left(3 \times \frac{1}{10}\right) + \left(1 \times \frac{1}{100}\right) + \left(7 \times \frac{1}{1000}\right)$$

The point in a binary numeral representing a fraction is called a *binary point,* and the positions to the right of the binary point represent negative powers of the base 2. For example, the expanded form of $(110.101)_2$ is

$$(1 \times 2^2) + (1 \times 2^1) + (0 \times 2^0) + (1 \times 2^{-1}) + (0 \times 2^{-2}) + (1 \times 2^{-3})$$

and thus has the decimal value

$$4 + 2 + 0 + \frac{1}{2} + 0 + \frac{1}{8} = 6.625$$

The two-state devices that comprise the memory unit are organized into groups called *words,* each of which contains a fixed number of these devices. Each of these words can thus store a fixed number of bits. Word sizes vary with computers, but common sizes are 8, 16, and 32 bits. Each word is identified by an *address* and can be directly accessed using this address. This makes it possible to store information in a specific memory word and then retrieve it later.

The fixed word size limits the magnitude of the integers that can be stored internally. For example, consider a computer whose word size is eight bits. Typically, the leftmost bit is used to represent the sign of a number (0 representing +, 1 representing −); thus the largest positive integer that can be stored in such an eight bit word is

$$(01111111)_2$$

which is the binary representation of

$$2^7 - 1 = 127$$

Similarly, the largest positive integer that can be stored in a 16-bit word is

$$2^{15} - 1 = 32767$$

and in a 32-bit word

$$2^{31} - 1 = 2147483647$$

An attempt to store an integer greater than the maximum allowed will result in the loss of some of the bits of its binary representation; this phenomenon is known as *overflow*. This limitation may be partially overcome by using more than one word to store an integer. Although this enlarges the range of integers that can be stored exactly, it does not resolve the problem of overflow, as the range of representable integers is still finite.

A similar problem arises when storing a fraction that does not have a terminating binary representation. Because it is possible to store only a fixed number of bits in a memory word, some of the bits will be lost. For example, suppose that six bits are used to store the decimal fraction 0.7. The binary representation of 0.7 is

$$(0.10110011001100110 \ldots)_2$$

where the block 0110 is repeated indefinitely. If the first six bits are stored and all remaining bits truncated, then the stored representation of 0.7 is

$$(0.101100)_2$$

which in fact has the decimal value 0.6875. If the binary representation is rounded to six bits, then the stored representation for 0.7 is

$$(0.101101)_2$$

which has the decimal value 0.703125. In either case, the stored value is not exactly 0.7. This error can be reduced, but not eliminated, by using a larger number of bits to store the binary representation of fractions.

Computers store and process not only numeric data but also character data and other types of nonnumeric information. The schemes used for storing character data are based on the assignment of a numeric code to each of the characters in the character set. Several standard coding schemes have been developed, such as ASCII (American Standard Code for Information Interchange) and EBCDIC (Extended Binary Coded Decimal Interchange Code). A complete table of ASCII and EBCDIC codes for all characters is given in Appendix A.

Characters are represented internally using these binary codes. A memory word is usually divided into 8-bit segments called *bytes,* each of which can store the binary representation of a single character. For example, the character string HI would be stored in a single 16-bit word with the code for H in the left byte and the code for I in the right byte; with ASCII code, the result would be as follows:

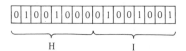

An eight-bit memory word can store one character; 32-bit memory words are usually divided into four bytes and thus can store four characters. Character strings of a length greater than the number of bytes in a word are stored in two or more consecutive memory words.

Exercises

1. Describe the importance of each of the following persons to the history of computing:

   (a) Charles Babbage   (b) Blaise Pascal

   (c) John von Neumann   (d) Herman Hollerith

   (e) Joseph Jacquard   (f) Gottfried Wilhelm von Leibniz

2. Describe the importance of each of the following devices to the history of computing:

   (a) ENIAC   (b) Analytical Engine

   (c) Jacquard loom   (d) UNIVAC

   (e) Mark I

3. Briefly define each of the following terms:

   (a) stored program concept   (b) compiler

   (c) FORTRAN   (d) Pascal

   (e) cpu   (f) bit

   (g) byte   (h) word

   (i) overflow   (j) ASCII

   (k) EBCDIC

4. Convert each of the following binary numerals into base 10:

   (a) 1001   (b) 110010

   (c) 1000000   (d) 111111111111111 (fifteen 1's)

   (e) 1.1   (f) 1010.10101

5. An *octal* numeration system uses a base of 8 and the digits 0, 1, 2, 3, 4, 5, 6, and 7. In an octal numeral such as $(1703)_8$, the digits represent coefficients of powers of 8, and so this numeral is an abbreviation for the expanded form

$$(1 \times 8^3) + (7 \times 8^2) + (0 \times 8^1) + (3 \times 8^0)$$

and hence has the decimal value

$$512 + 448 + 0 + 3 = 963$$

Convert each of the following octal numerals to base 10:

   (a) 123   (b) 2705   (c) 10000

   (d) 77777   (e) 7.2   (f) 123.45

6. A *hexadecimal* numeration system uses a base of 16 and the digits 0, 1, 2, 3, 4, 5, 6, 7, 8, 9, A (ten), B (eleven), C (twelve), D (thirteen),

E (fourteen), and F (fifteen). The hexadecimal numeral $(5E4)_{16}$ has the expanded form

$$(5 \times 16^2) + (14 \times 16^1) + (4 \times 16^0)$$

which has the decimal value

$$1280 + 224 + 4 = 1508$$

Convert each of the following hexadecimal numerals to base 10:

(a) 12   (b) 1AB   (c) ABC

(d) FFF   (e) 8.C   (f) AB.CD

7. Conversion from octal representation (see Exercise 5) to binary representation is easy, as we need only replace each octal digit with its three-bit binary equivalent. For example, to convert $(617)_8$ to binary, replace 6 with 110, 1 with 001, and 7 with 111 to obtain $(110001111)_2$. Convert each of the octal numerals in Exercise 5 to binary numerals.

8. Imitating the conversion scheme in Exercise 7, convert each of the hexadecimal numerals in Exercise 6 to binary numerals.

9. To convert a binary numeral to octal, place the digits in groups of three, starting from the binary point, or from the right end if there is no binary point and replace each group with the corresponding octal digit. For example, $(10101111)_2 = (010\ 101\ 111)_2 = (257)_8$. Convert each of the binary numerals in Exercise 4 to octal numerals.

10. Imitating the conversion scheme in Exercise 9, convert each of the binary numerals in Exercise 4 to hexadecimal numerals.

11. One method for finding the *base-b* representation of a whole number given in base-10 notation is to divide the number repeatedly by b until a quotient of zero results. The successive remainders are the digits from right to left of the base-b representation. For example, the binary representation of 26 is $(11010)_2$, as the following computation shows:

$$
\begin{array}{r}
0 \text{ R } 1 \\
2\overline{)1} \text{ R } 1 \\
2\overline{)3} \text{ R } 0 \\
2\overline{)6} \text{ R } 1 \\
2\overline{)13} \text{ R } 0 \\
2\overline{)26}
\end{array}
$$

Convert each of the following base-10 numerals to (i) binary, (ii) octal, (iii) hexadecimal:

(a) 27   (b) 99   (c) 314   (d) 5280

12. To convert a decimal fraction to its base-b equivalent, repeatedly multiply the fractional part of the number by b. The integer parts

are the digits from left to right of the base-b representation. For example, the decimal numeral 0.6875 corresponds to the binary numeral $(0.1011)_2$, as the following computation shows:

$$
\begin{array}{r|l}
 & .6875 \\
 & \times\,2 \\
\hline
1 & .375 \\
 & \times\,2 \\
\hline
0 & .75 \\
 & \times\,2 \\
\hline
1 & .5 \\
 & \times\,2 \\
\hline
1 & .0 \\
\end{array}
$$

Convert the following base-10 numerals to (i) binary, (ii) octal, (iii) hexadecimal:

(a) 0.5   (b) 0.25   (c) 0.625

(d) 16.0625   (e) 8.828125

13. Even though the base-10 representation of a fraction may terminate, its representation in some other base need not terminate. For example, the following computation shows that the binary representation of 0.7 is $(0.1011001100110011001100110 \ldots)_2$, where the block of bits 0110 is repeated indefinitely. This representation is commonly written as $(0.1\overline{0110})_2$.

$$
\begin{array}{r|l}
 & .7 \\
 & \times\,2 \\
\hline
1 & .4 \\
 & \times\,2 \\
\hline
0 & .8 \\
 & \times\,2 \\
\hline
1 & .6 \\
 & \times\,2 \\
\hline
1 & .2 \\
 & \times\,2 \\
\hline
0 & .4 \\
\end{array}
$$

Convert the following base-10 numerals to (i) binary, (ii) octal, (iii) hexadecimal:

(a) 0.3   (b) 0.6   (c) 0.05   (d) $0.\overline{3} = 0.33333 \cdots = 1/3$

14. Using the tables for ASCII and EBCDIC in Appendix A, indicate how each of the following character strings would be stored in two-byte words using (i) ASCII and (ii) EBCDIC:

     (a) TO   (b) FOUR   (c) AMOUNT

     (d) ETC.   (e) J. DOE   (f) A#*4 − C

     (g) B**2 − 4*A*C

2

Algorithms and Programs

People always get what they ask for; the only trouble is that they never know, until they get it, what it actually is that they have asked for.

ALDOUS HUXLEY

The main reason that people learn programming languages is to use the computer as a problem-solving tool. At least three steps can be identified in the computer-aided problem-solving process:

1. Problem analysis and algorithm development.
2. Transformation of the algorithm into a program.
3. Program execution and validation.

In this chapter we discuss these three phases of the problem-solving process.

2.1 Problem Analysis and Algorithm Development

In this section we consider the first and most difficult part of the problem-solving process, namely, the analysis of the problem and the formulation of a procedure for its solution. It is this phase that requires the most imagination, ingenuity, and creativity on the part of the programmer. The first step in the problem analysis is to carefully review the problem in order to identify what information must be produced to solve it. Next, the programmer must identify those items of information given in the problem that may be useful in obtaining the solution. Finally, a procedure to produce the desired results from the given data must be designed. Since the computer is a machine possessing no inherent problem-solving capabilities, this procedure must be formulated as a detailed sequence of simple steps. Such a procedure is called an *algorithm.* The information supplied to the algorithm is called its *input,* and the information produced by the algorithm is called its *output.*

The solution to a complex problem may require so many steps in the final algorithm that they cannot all be anticipated at the outset. To attack such problems, a *top-down* approach is commonly used. We begin by identifying the major tasks to be performed to solve the problem and arranging them in the order in which they are to be carried out. This step-by-step outline serves as a first description of the algorithm and provides an overview of the main sequence of activities to be performed. Usually, most of the steps in this first outline are incomplete and must be *refined.* Thus we expand the outline, adding more details to these steps, and so we obtain a second outline of the algorithm. Some of the steps of this second outline may still require additional refinement, which then leads to a third description of the algorithm. For complex problems, several *levels of refinement* are often needed before a clear, precise, and complete algorithm can be obtained.

To illustrate the algorithm development phase of the problem-solving process, we consider the following problem:

> Suppose that someone has worked 38.5 hours in a given week and earns $4.50 per hour. The total tax withheld from his paycheck will be 17.5 percent of his gross pay. What will be his gross pay, how much tax will be withheld for this pay period, and what will be his net pay?

The given information that will be used to solve this problem is the number of hours worked, 38.5; the hourly pay rate, $4.50; and the tax-withholding rate, 17.5 percent. The information that must be produced to solve this problem is the gross pay, the dollar amount of tax withheld, and the net pay. In summary, we have the following:

Input	Output
Hours worked: 38.5	Gross pay
Hourly rate: $4.50	Amount of tax withheld
Tax-withholding rate: 17.5%	Net pay

Although this problem is so simple that a complete algorithm for its solution could be given immediately, we shall demonstrate the top-down method of algorithm development and introduce some related techniques. Identifying the three major tasks of obtaining the input data, calculating the desired quantities, and displaying the output, we might develop the following first outline of the algorithm.

Algorithm (Level 1)
1. Obtain values for hours worked, hourly rate, and tax-withholding rate.

2. Calculate gross pay, amount of tax withheld, and net pay.
3. Display gross pay, amount of tax withheld, and net pay.

The structure of an algorithm can be displayed in a *structure diagram* which shows the various tasks that must be performed and their relation to one another. In the first level, the main tasks are displayed in the order in which they are to be performed. Thus the structure diagram for the preceding algorithm might have the following form:

For more complex problems, one or more of these first-level tasks may be divided into subtasks. These subtasks are then placed on a second level of the structure diagram. These subtasks may be divided further into smaller subtasks, resulting in additional levels. An analysis of a complex problem like that considered in Section 5.6 may lead to a structure diagram having several levels.

The details of an algorithm or of part of an algorithm can be displayed using a *flowchart.* A flowchart is a diagram that uses the standard symbols shown in Figure 2.1. Each step of the algorithm is displayed within the appropriate symbol, and the order in which these steps are to be carried out is indicated by connecting them with arrows called *flow lines.* The wage calculation algorithm that we are considering could thus be represented by the following flowchart:

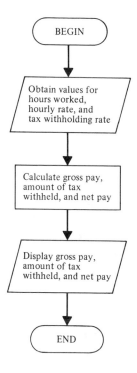

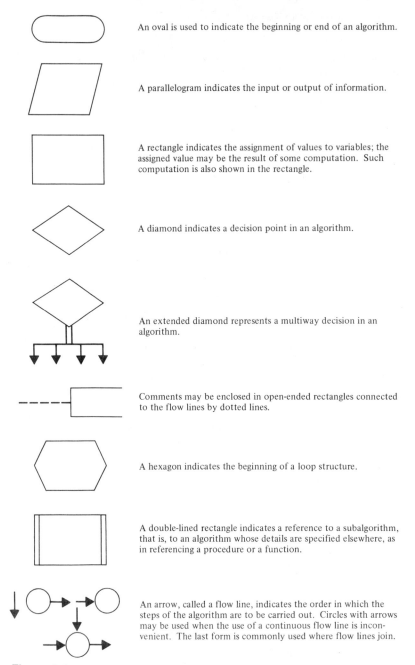

An oval is used to indicate the beginning or end of an algorithm.

A parallelogram indicates the input or output of information.

A rectangle indicates the assignment of values to variables; the assigned value may be the result of some computation. Such computation is also shown in the rectangle.

A diamond indicates a decision point in an algorithm.

An extended diamond represents a multiway decision in an algorithm.

Comments may be enclosed in open-ended rectangles connected to the flow lines by dotted lines.

A hexagon indicates the beginning of a loop structure.

A double-lined rectangle indicates a reference to a subalgorithm, that is, to an algorithm whose details are specified elsewhere, as in referencing a procedure or a function.

An arrow, called a flow line, indicates the order in which the steps of the algorithm are to be carried out. Circles with arrows may be used when the use of a continuous flow line is inconvenient. The last form is commonly used where flow lines join.

Figure 2.1.

In the wage calculation problem, specific values are given for the hours worked, hourly rate and tax rate: 38.5, \$4.50, and 17.5 percent, respectively. The gross pay for this employee can be calculated by multiplying the hours worked by the hourly rate:

$$\text{gross pay} = 38.5 \times 4.50$$

The dollar amount of tax withheld is then calculated by multiplying this gross pay by the tax-withholding rate:

$$\text{tax withheld} = (\text{gross pay}) \times 0.175$$

The net pay can then be calculated by subtracting the amount of tax withheld from the gross pay:

$$\text{net pay} = (\text{gross pay}) - (\text{tax withheld})$$

This solves the wage calculation problem for this employee. It should be clear, however, that this problem is a special case of the more general problem of finding the gross pay, tax withheld, and net pay for any employee. An algorithm for solving the general problem can be used in a variety of situations and is consequently more useful than is an algorithm designed for solving only the original special problem. The information that may be used to solve this more general problem consists of the values for the hours worked, hourly rate, and tax-withholding rate for some employee. The output to be produced remains the same: gross pay, amount of tax withheld, and net pay. The gross pay is calculated by multiplying the number of hours worked by the hourly rate. The amount of tax to be withheld can then be obtained by multiplying the gross pay by the tax rate expressed in decimal form. The net pay is then obtained by subtracting the tax withheld from the gross pay. Refining Step 2 of our Level-1 algorithm to include these three calculations, we obtain

Input: hourly rate, hours worked, tax-witholding rate.
Output: gross pay, tax withheld, net pay.

Algorithm (Level 2)

1. Obtain values for hours worked, hourly rate, and tax-withholding rate.
2. Calculate gross pay, amount of tax withheld, and net pay.
   a. Calculate gross pay by multiplying the hours worked by the hourly rate.
   b. Calculate the amount of tax to be withheld by multiplying the gross pay by the tax-withholding rate.
   c. Calculate the net pay by subtracting the tax withheld from the gross pay.
3. Display the gross pay, amount of tax withheld, and net pay.

Up to now, our algorithm descriptions have been expressed in ordinary English. But programs must be written in a language that can be understood by the computer. It is natural, therefore, to describe algorithms in a language that more closely resembles the language used to write computer programs, that is, in a "pseudoprogramming language," or as it is more commonly called, *pseudocode.*

Unlike high-level programming languages such as Pascal, there is no set of rules that defines precisely what is and what is not pseudocode. It varies from one programmer to another. Pseudocode is a mixture of natural language and symbols, terms, and other features commonly used in one or more high-level languages. Typically one finds the following features in the various pseudocodes that appear in textbooks.

1. The usual computer symbols are used for arithmetic operations: + for addition, − for subtraction, * for multiplication, and / for division.

2. Symbolic names (variables) are used to represent the quantities being processed by the algorithm.
3. Some provision is made for including comments. This is done by enclosing each comment between a pair of special symbols such as (* and *) or { and }.
4. Certain key words that are common in high-level languages may be used; for example, *read* or *enter* to indicate an input operation; *display, print* or *write* for output operations.
5. Indentation is used to indicate certain key blocks of instructions.

The wage calculation algorithm can be expressed in pseudocode as follows:

Algorithm for Wage Calculation

(* This algorithm calculates *GrossPay, Withhold* (dollar amount of tax withheld), and *NetPay* for a given number of hours worked (*Hours*), a given hourly rate (*HourlyRate*), and a given tax-withholding rate (*TaxRate*) expressed in decimal form. *)

1. Enter *Hours, HourlyRate, TaxRate.*
2. Calculate *Gross Pay = Hours * HourlyRate.*
3. Calculate *Withhold = GrossPay * TaxRate.*

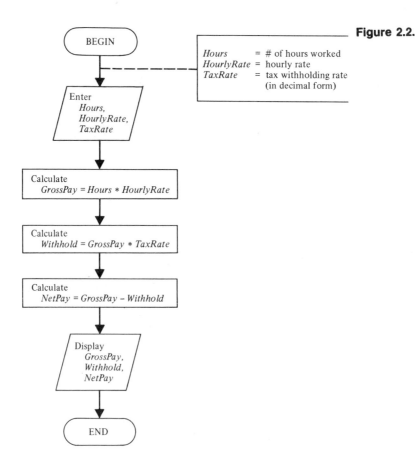

Figure 2.2.

4. Calculate *NetPay* = *GrossPay* − *Withhold.*
5. Display *GrossPay, Withhold, NetPay.*

Figure 2.2 displays the same information in flowchart form.

As another illustration of the problem analysis and algorithm development phase of the problem-solving process, we consider the following problem:

What is the value of the sum

$$1 + 2 + 3 + \cdots + 100?$$

The information given in this problem is that 100 consecutive integers starting with 1 are to be added, and we are required to find their sum. To solve this problem with pencil and paper, we might begin as follows:

$$
\begin{array}{r}
0 \\
+\ 1 \\
\hline
1 \\
+\ 2 \\
\hline
3 \\
+\ 3 \\
\hline
6 \\
+\ 4 \\
\hline
10 \\
+\ 5 \\
\hline
15 \\
\vdots
\end{array}
$$

(Although we might not actually write down the first two lines but rather only "think" them, they are included here for completeness.) We see that the procedure involves two quantities:

(i) a counter that is added at each step and then increased by 1 in the next step and
(ii) the sum of the integers from 1 up to that counter.

$$
\begin{array}{rl}
0 & -\text{sum} \\
+\ 1 & -\text{counter} \\
\hline
1 & -\text{sum} \\
+\ 2 & -\text{counter} \\
\hline
3 & -\text{sum} \\
+\ 3 & -\text{counter} \\
\hline
6 & -\text{sum} \\
+\ 4 & -\text{counter} \\
\hline
10 & -\text{sum} \\
+\ 5 & -\text{counter} \\
\hline
15 & -\text{sum} \\
\vdots &
\end{array}
$$

The procedure begins with 1 as the value of the counter and with 0 as the initial value of the sum. At each stage, the value of the counter is added to the sum, producing a new sum, and the value of the counter is increased by 1. These steps are repeated until eventually we reach

$$\begin{array}{r} \vdots \\ \underline{+100} \\ ???? \\ \underline{+101} \end{array}$$ — counter
???? — sum
+101 — counter Stop!

As soon as the value of the counter exceeds 100, the sum is the desired answer, and the computation stops.

The following pseudocode description summarizes this algorithm:

Algorithm for Summation Problem

(* This algorithm calculates the value of the sum $1 + 2 + \cdots + 100$. It uses the variable *Counter* as a counter and the variable *Sum* for the sum $1 + 2 + \cdots +$ *Counter*. *)

1. Set *Counter* to 1.
2. Set *Sum* to 0.

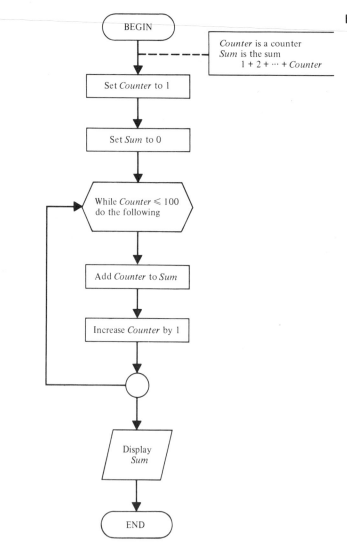

Figure 2.3.

3. While *Counter* ≤ 100 do the following:
  a. Add *Counter* to *Sum*.
  b. Increment *Counter* by 1.
4. Display *Sum*.

Figure 2.3 displays this algorithm in flowchart form.

The second step in using the computer to solve a problem is to express the **Program Coding** algorithm in a programming language. In the first phase, the algorithm may be described in a natural language or pseudocode, but the program that implements that algorithm must be written in the vocabulary of a programming language and must conform to the *syntax,* or grammatical rules, of that language. The major portion of this text is concerned with the vocabulary and syntax of the programming language Pascal. In this section we introduce some elementary features of this language and give an example of a simple Pascal program. These features will be discussed in detail in subsequent chapters.

In the two examples in the preceding section, we used names to identify various quantities. These names are called *variables.* In the first example, the variables *Hours, HourlyRate,* and *TaxRate* represented the hours worked, hourly rate, and tax-withholding rate, respectively. The output in this example was the employee's gross pay, dollar amount of tax withheld, and net pay as represented by the variables *GrossPay, Withhold,* and *NetPay,* respectively. In the second example, the variable *Counter* was used for a positive integer that served as a counter, and the variable *Sum* denoted the sum of the positive integers from 1 through *Counter.*

In Pascal, variable names must begin with a letter, which may be followed by any combination of letters and digits. This allows us to choose names that suggest what the variable represents. For example, *Hours, HourlyRate, TaxRate, GrossPay, Withhold, NetPay, Counter,* and *Sum* are valid Pascal variables. *Meaningful variable names should always be used because they make the program easier to read and understand.*

In the examples we have been considering, two types of numbers are used. The values of *Counter* and *Sum* in the second example are integers, whereas the values of *Hours, HourlyRate, TaxRate, GrossPay, Withhold,* and *NetPay* in the first example are real; that is, they have fractional parts. Pascal distinguishes between these two types of numeric data, and the types of values that each variable may have must be specified. This may be done by placing declarations of the form

var
  list1 : *integer*;
  list2 : *real*;

at the beginning of the program, where *list1* is a list of the variable names of integer type, and *list2* is a list of variable names of real type. Thus, the types of the Pascal variables in the first example can be specified by

var
    Hours, HourlyRate, TaxRate,
    GrossPay, Withhold, NetPay : real;

and those in the second example by

var
    Counter, Sum : integer;

Notice that **var** is shown here in boldface. In this text, the words printed in boldface are *reserved words* in Pascal. They may not be used for any purpose other than those designated by the rules of the language. For example, reserved words may not be used as variable names.

Addition and subtraction are denoted in Pascal by the usual $+$ and $-$ symbols. Multiplication is denoted by $*$ and division by $/$. The assignment operation is denoted by $:=$ in Pascal programs. For example, the statement

    *GrossPay := Hours * HourlyRate*

assigns the value of the expression

    *Hours * HourlyRate*

to the variable *GrossPay*.

In the pseudocode description of an algorithm in the preceding section, we used the words "enter" and "read" for input operations and "display," "print," "write" for output operations. In a flowchart, a parallelogram is used to indicate the input or output of information. One Pascal statement that may be used for input is the *readln* statement. A simple form of this statement is

    readln (list)

where *list* is a list of variables for which values are to be read. For example, the statement

    readln (Hours, HourlyRate, TaxRate)

reads values for the variables *Hours, HourlyRate,* and *TaxRate* from some input device.

A simple output statement in Pascal is the *writeln* statement of the form

    writeln (list)

where *list* is a list of items to be displayed. For example, the statement

    writeln ('Gross wages = ', GrossPay)

displays the label

Gross wages =

followed by the value of the variable *GrossPay.*

Comments can also be incorporated into Pascal programs. They are indicated by enclosing them within (* and *)

(* *comment* *)

or within braces

{ *comment* }

Figure 2.4 shows a Pascal program for the algorithm to solve the wage calculation problem considered earlier in this chapter. The program begins with the *program heading*

program *Wages* (*input, output*);

```
PROGRAM Wages (input, output);                                          Figure 2.4.

(*******************************************************************

   Program to read the hours worked, hourly rate, and a tax
   withholding rate for an employee, then calculate and
   display his/her gross pay, tax withheld, and net pay.

********************************************************************)

VAR
    Hours,            (* hours worked *)
    HourlyRate,       (* hourly pay rate *)
    TaxRate,          (* tax-withholding rate *)
    GrossPay,         (* gross wages *)
    Withhold,         (* amount of tax withheld *)
    NetPay : real;    (* net pay *)

BEGIN
    writeln ('Enter hours worked, hourly rate, and tax rate');
    readln (Hours, HourlyRate, TaxRate);
    GrossPay := Hours * HourlyRate;
    Withhold := GrossPay * TaxRate;
    NetPay := GrossPay - Withhold;
    writeln ('Gross pay = $', GrossPay:6:2);
    writeln ('Amount of tax withheld = $', Withhold:6:2);
    writeln ('Net pay =   $', NetPay:6:2)
END.


Sample run:
==========

Enter hours worked, hourly rate, and tax rate
38.5 4.50 0.175
Gross pay = $173.25
Amount of tax withheld = $ 30.32
Net pay =   $142.93
```

where *Wages* is the name assigned to the program by the programmer, and *input* and *output* indicate that certain information will be input to the program from an external source and that the program will also produce some output.

The first step in the algorithm is an input instruction to enter values for the variables *Hours*, *HourlyRate*, and *TaxRate*:

1. Enter *Hours*, *HourlyRate*, *TaxRate*.

This is translated into two statements in the program:

> *writeln* ('Enter hours worked, hourly rate, and tax rate');
> *readln* (*Hours*, *HourlyRate*, *TaxRate*);

The *writeln* statement is used to prompt the user that the values are to be entered. The *readln* statement actually assigns the three values entered by the user to the three variables *Hours, HourlyRate,* and *TaxRate*. Thus, in the sample run shown, when the user enters

> 38.5   4.50   0.175

the value 38.5 is assigned to *Hours,* 4.50 to *HourlyRate,* and 0.175 to *TaxRate*.

The next three steps in the algorithm

2. Calculate *GrossPay = Hours ∗ HourlyRate*.
3. Calculate *Withhold = GrossPay ∗ TaxRate*.
4. Calculate *NetPay = GrossPay − Withhold*.

translate into the Pascal assignment statements

> *GrossPay* := *Hours ∗ HourlyRate*;
> *Withhold* := *GrossPay ∗ TaxRate*;
> *NetPay* := *GrossPay − Withhold*;

The output instruction

5. Display *GrossPay, Withhold, NetPay*.

is translated into the three Pascal statements

> *writeln* ('Gross pay = $', *GrossPay*:6:2);
> *writeln* ('Amount of tax withheld = $', *Withhold*:6:2);
> *writeln* ('Net pay   = $', *NetPay*:6:2)

As the sample run shows, each *writeln* statement produces one line of output. Each line consists of an appropriate label followed by the value, rounded to two decimal places, of the corresponding variable in a six-space zone:

> Gross pay = $173.25
> Amount of tax withheld = $ 30.32
> Net pay   = $142.93

The end of the program is indicated by the Pascal reserved word **end** followed by a period. Note that the statements in the program are separated by semicolons.

The third step in using the computer to solve a problem is to submit the **Program** program to a computer for execution. This procedure varies with computer **Execution** systems and languages. In this section we present the general procedure for preparing a Pascal program for input. The details regarding your specific computer system can be obtained from your instructor, computer center personnel, or user manuals supplied by the manufacturer.

For some systems, programs and data may be entered using punched cards. These cards are prepared using a *keypunch* which has a typewriterlike keyboard and which codes the information entered from the keyboard by punching holes in a card like the one shown in Figure 2.5.

When a program is to be executed by a computer, special cards called *control cards* must be placed with the deck of program cards. Information concerning these control cards and their use must be obtained from someone familiar with your particular system. Usually, control cards must be placed at the beginning of the deck, at the end of the deck, and between the program cards and the data cards. Figure 2.6 shows the typical arrangement of a complete deck. The information from these cards is then entered into the computer via a card reader, and the results are returned to the user via some output device such as a line printer.

In many computer systems, programs and data can be entered from a typewriterlike terminal. To establish a connection between the terminal and the computer system, some *login* procedure may be required. The details of this procedure vary from one computer system to another, but some general principles are the same for all systems. Usually the first step is to enter some identification information which the system checks to ensure that the person attempting to login is an authorized user. This identification can also be used for accounting purposes. Once the login has been completed, the program must be entered from the terminal. Often, the system's software includes editing packages to help the user enter information and correct errors.

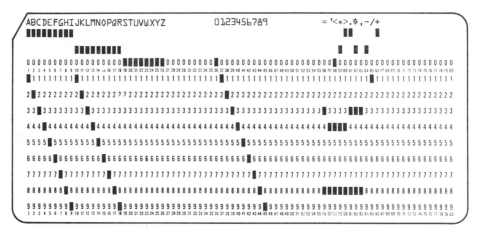

Figure 2.5.
A punched card.

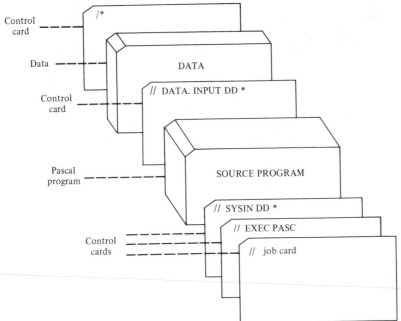

Control card ——— /*

Data ——— DATA

Control card ——— // DATA. INPUT DD *

Pascal program ——— SOURCE PROGRAM

// SYSIN DD *

// EXEC PASC

Control cards ——— // job card

Figure 2.6.
A complete card deck for a computer program.

```
LOGIN S12345
Password?

S12345 (user 72) logged in Thursday, 26 May 83 10:35:05
Welcome to PRIMOS version 19.1.1
Last login Wednesday, 25 May 83 14:34:40

OK, EDPAS
INPUT
PROGRAM Wages (input, output);

(***************************************************************

   Program to read the hours worked, hourly rate, and a tax
   withholding rate for an employee, then calculate and
   display his/her gross pay, tax withheld, and net pay.

   **********************************************************)

VAR
   Hours,            (* hours worked *)
   HourlyRate,       (* hourly pay rate *)
   TaxRate,          (* tax-withholding rate *)
   GrossPay,         (* gross wages *)
   Withhold,         (* amount of tax withheld *)
   NetPay : real;    (* net pay *)

BEGIN
   writeln ('Enter hours worked, hourly rate, and tax rate';
   readln (Hours, HourlyRate, TaxRate)
   GrossPay := Hours * HourlyRate;
   Withhold := GrossPay * TaxRate;
   NetPay := GrossPay - Withhold;
   writeln ('Gross pay = $', GrossPay:6:2);
   writeln ('Amount of tax withheld = $', Withhold:6:2);
   writeln ('Net pay =   $', NetPay:6:2)
END.
```

Login procedure

Using the edit system to create the Pascal program

Figure 2.7.
Entering and executing a program in a time-sharing mode.

Fig. 2.7. (cont.)

```
EDIT
FILE SAMPLE.PASCAL
OK, RUN SAMPLE.PASCAL                                              Attempt to
(   20) ERROR   4: SYMBOL EXPECTED WAS ")"                         execute the
(   22) ERROR   6: UNEXPECTED SYMBOL                               program,
(   23) ERROR 104: IDENTIFIER NOT DECLARED                         but it has
0003 ERRORS (PASCAL-S 1.8) (TIME USED: 1 SECONDS)                  errors.

OK, ED SAMPLE.PASCAL
EDIT
POINT 20
   writeln ('Enter hours worked, hourly rate, and tax rate';
CHANGE /rate'/rate')
   writeln ('Enter hours worked, hourly rate, and tax rate');
NEXT
   readln (Hours, HourlyRate, TaxRate)
APPEND ;
   readln (Hours, HourlyRate, TaxRate);
NEXT 2
   Withhold := GrosPay * TaxRate;
CHANGE /GrosPay/GrossPay
   Withhold := GrossPay * TaxRate;
TOP
PRINT 50
.NULL.
PROGRAM Wages (input, output);

(***************************************************************

   Program to read the hours worked, hourly rate, and a tax
   withholding rate for an employee, then calculate and          Return
   display his/her gross pay, tax withheld, and net pay.         to editor
                                                                 to correct
****************************************************************) errors.

VAR
   Hours,             (* hours worked *)
   HourlyRate,        (* hourly pay rate *)
   TaxRate,           (* tax-withholding rate *)
   GrossPay,          (* gross wages *)
   Withhold,          (* amount of tax withheld *)
   NetPay : real;     (* net pay *)

BEGIN
   writeln ('Enter hours worked, hourly rate, and tax rate');
   readln (Hours, HourlyRate, TaxRate);
   GrossPay := Hours * HourlyRate;
   Withhold := GrossPay * TaxRate;
   NetPay := GrossPay - Withhold;
   writeln ('Gross pay = $', GrossPay:6:2);
   writeln ('Amount of tax withheld = $', Withhold:6:2);
   writeln ('Net pay =   $', NetPay:6:2)
END.
BOTTOM
FILE
SAMPLE.PASCAL

OK, RUN SAMPLE.PASCAL
0000 ERRORS (PASCAL-S 1.8) (TIME USED: 1 SECONDS)

Executing WAGES                                                   Successful
                                                                 compilation,
Enter hours worked, hourly rate, and tax rate                    load, and
38.5 4.50 0.175                                                  execution of
Gross pay = $173.25                                             the program
Amount of tax withheld = $ 30.32
Net pay =   $142.93
```

Fig. 2.7. (cont.)

```
OK, SLIST SAMPLE.PASCAL
PROGRAM Wages (input, output);

(****************************************************************

   Program to read the hours worked, hourly rate, and a tax
   withholding rate for an employee, then calculate and
   display his/her gross pay, tax withheld, and net pay.

****************************************************************)

VAR
    Hours,          (* hours worked *)
    HourlyRate,     (* hourly pay rate *)
    TaxRate,        (* tax-withholding rate *)
    GrossPay,       (* gross wages *)
    Withhold,       (* amount of tax withheld *)
    NetPay : real;  (* net pay *)

BEGIN
    writeln ('Enter hours worked, hourly rate, and tax rate');
    readln (Hours, HourlyRate, TaxRate);
    GrossPay := Hours * HourlyRate;
    Withhold := GrossPay * TaxRate;
    NetPay := GrossPay - Withhold;
    writeln ('Gross pay = $', GrossPay:6:2);
    writeln ('Amount of tax withheld = $', Withhold:6:2);
    writeln ('Net pay =    $', NetPay:6:2)
END.
OK, LOGOUT
S12345 (user 72) logged out Thursday, 26 May 83 11:09:13
Time used: 00h 34m connect, 00m 24s CPU, 00m 21s I/O
OK,
```

A final
clean
listing
of the
program

Logout
procedure

The program is compiled and executed using appropriate system commands, and the results are returned to the user via the terminal and/or some other output device. Figure 2.7 illustrates this procedure in a time-sharing mode.

2.4

Because program development cost is a major part of the cost of using a computer to solve a problem, much effort has gone into developing techniques that assist in designing programs that can be easily read and understood. This is extremely important because many real-world applications involve complex programs that are written by more than one person. Each part of the program must be clearly written so that its function can be easily understood by all members of the programming team. Such programs are usually used for several years and will probably require some modifications as time passes. Because these modifications are often made by someone not involved in the original design, the programs must be easy to understand and modify. In this section we discuss some of the programming practices used in designing such programs. Although some of these practices are not essential to the design of the rather simple program considered thus far, the beginning pro-

Program Design, Validation, and Refinement

grammer should establish good habits that will then be transferred to the design of more complex programs.

Documentation. Documentation refers to information that explains how a program works. It includes diagrams such as structure diagrams and flowcharts that display the logical structure of the program as well as any other documents that describe the input to and output from the program, variables used in the program, the processing carried out by the program, and so on. It is also possible to write the program in such a way that it is at least partially self-documenting. Some programming practices that are useful in this regard are the following:

1. Each variable name should suggest the quantity it represents. For example, the statement

*Distance := Rate * Time*

means more than does

*X7 := R * Zeke*

2. The program should include comments that make it easier to understand. This may include comments at the beginning of the program that identify the author of the program, indicate the date it was written, and briefly describe the variables and the purpose of the program. In addition, comments should be used throughout the program to explain the purpose of the main sections of the program. Such comments should be few and brief. Too many or too detailed comments clutter the program, making it more difficult to read.

Program Style. Other practices can improve a program's physical appearance.

1. Spaces between items in a Pascal statement should be used as needed to improve its readability. For example, the statement

Sum := Sum + Counter;

is more readable and pleasing to the eye than either

Sum:=Sum+Counter;

or

Sum   :=Sum+   Counter;

2. Blank lines may be used to separate program sections.
3. Statements making up a block should be indented to emphasize this relationship.

Program Testing and Debugging. The output produced when we run a program may contain messages indicating errors in the program, messages generated by the computer system to help the user find and correct these errors, or "bugs" (see Figure 2.7). Errors can be detected at various stages of program processing and may cause the processing to be terminated ("aborted"). For example, an incorrect system command or an error in one of the control cards will be detected early in the processing and will usually prevent compilation and execution of the program. Errors in the program's syntax, such as incorrect punctuation or misspelled key words will be detected during compilation of the program and thus are called *compile-time errors*. Severe compile-time errors, sometimes called "fatal" errors, make it impossible to complete the compilation and execution of the program. Less severe errors may generate "warning" messages, but the compilation will be continued and execution of the resulting object program attempted.

Other errors, such as an attempt to divide by zero in an arithmetic expression, may not be detected until the execution of the program has begun. Such errors are called *run-time errors*. The error messages displayed by your particular system can be found in the user manuals supplied by the manufacturer. In any case, the errors must be corrected by replacing the erroneous statements with correct ones, and the modified program must be rerun.

Errors that are detected by the computer system are relatively easy to identify and correct. There are, however, other errors that are more subtle and difficult to identify. These are *logical errors* that arise in the design of the algorithm or in the coding of the program that implements the algorithm. For example, if the statement

$GrossPay := Hours * HourlyRate$

in the program of Figure 2.4 were mistakenly entered as

$GrossPay := Hours + HourlyRate$

with the multiplication symbol ($*$) replaced by the symbol for addition ($+$), the program would still be syntactically correct. No error would occur during the compilation or execution of the program. But the results produced by the program would be incorrect because an incorrect formula would have been used to calculate the gross pay. Thus, if the values 38.5, 4.50, and 0.175 were entered for the variables *Hours, HourlyRate,* and *TaxRate,* respectively, the output produced by the program would be

Gross pay = $ 43.00
Amount of tax withheld = $ 7.52
Net pay = $ 35.48

instead of the correct output

Gross pay = $173.25
Amount of tax withheld = $ 30.32
Net pay = $142.93

as shown in the sample run in Figure 2.4.

Since it may not be obvious whether the results produced by a program are correct, *it is important that the user run a program several times with input data for which the correct results are known in advance.* For the preceding example, it is easy to calculate by hand the correct answer for values such as 10.0, 2.00, and 0.25 for *Hours, HourlyRate,* and *TaxRate,* respectively, to check the output produced by the program. This process of *program validation* is extremely important, as a *program cannot be considered to be correct until it has been validated with several sets of test data.* The test data should be carefully selected so that each part of the program can be checked.

Refinement. Although a program may be documented, nice looking, readable, and correct, it may still have room for improvement. This is often the case when the algorithm developed is not general but is limited to solving only one problem. In such cases the algorithm can often be modified so as to solve a class of problems that includes the given problem. For example, the algorithm given in Section 2.1 to solve the problem

What is the value of the sum

$$1 + 2 + 3 + \cdots + 100?$$

could easily be modified to solve the following class of problems:

For a given value of *Last,* what is the value of the sum

$$1 + 2 + 3 + \cdots + Last?$$

It could also be modified so that several values of *Last* can be processed, in which case some method for halting the computation must be provided. In the following algorithm and in the flowchart representation of it in Figure 2.8, computation terminates when a negative value is entered for *Last.* A general algorithm of this type is obviously more useful than the very limited one given in Section 2.1.

Algorithm for General Summation Problem
(* This algorithm calculates the value of the sum $1 + 2 + \cdots +$ *Last* for several values of *Last.* It uses the variable *Counter* as a counter and the variable *Sum* as a sum. New values of *Last* are called for until zero or a negative value is read. *)

    1. Enter *Last.*
    2. While *Last* > 0 do the following:
       a. Set *Counter* to 1.
       b. Set *Sum* to 0.
       c. While *Counter* ≤ *Last* do the following:
         (i) Add *Counter* to *Sum.*
         (ii) Increase *Counter* by 1.
       d. Display *Last, Sum.*
       e. Enter *Last.*

Exercises

For each of the problems described in Exercises 1 through 8, identify the information that must be produced to solve the problem and the given information that will be useful in obtaining the solution. Then design an algorithm to solve the problem.

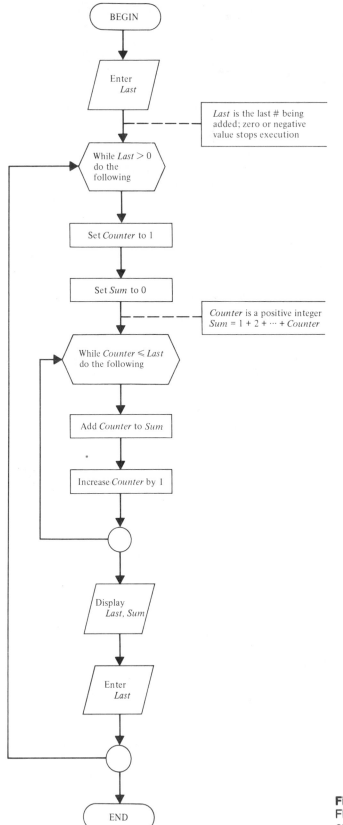

Figure 2.8.
Flowchart for general summation problem.

1. Calculate and display the circumference and area of a circle with a given radius.

2. Two common temperature scales are the Fahrenheit and the Celsius scales. The boiling point of water is 212° on the Fahrenheit scale and 100° on the Celsius scale. The freezing point of water is 32° on the Fahrenheit scale and 0° on the Celsius scale. Assuming a linear relationship ($F = a \cdot C + b$) between these two temperature scales, convert a temperature on the Celsius scale to the corresponding Fahrenheit temperature.

3. The business manager of a certain company desires a program to calculate the wages for the company's employees. This program should accept an employee number, his or her base pay rate per hour, and the number of hours worked. All hours above 40 are to be paid at the overtime rate of 1.5 times the base rate. For each employee, the program should print his or her number, total number of hours worked, base pay rate, and total wages, and it should also print the total of all wages paid by the company.

4. A certain city classifies a pollution index of less than 35 as "pleasant," 35 through 60 as "unpleasant," and above 60 as "hazardous." The city pollution control office desires a program that will accept several values of the pollution index and will produce the appropriate classification for each.

5. Suppose that a professor gave a quiz to her class and compiled a list of scores ranging from 50 through 100. She intends to use only three grades: A if the score is 90 or greater, B if it is below 90 but above or equal to 75, and C if it is below 75. She would like a program to assign the appropriate letter grades to the numeric scores.

6. The "divide and average" algorithm for approximating the square root of any positive number A is as follows: Take any initial approximation X that is positive and then find a new approximation by calculating the average of X and A / X, that is, $(X + A / X) / 2$. Repeat this procedure with X replaced by this new approximation, stopping when X and A / X differ in absolute value by some specified error allowance, such as 0.00001.

7. The quadratic equation $Ax^2 + Bx + C = 0$ has no real roots if the discriminant $B^2 - 4AC$ is negative; it has one real root, $-B/2A$, if the discriminant is zero; and it has two real roots given by the quadratic formula

$$\frac{-B \pm \sqrt{B^2 - 4AC}}{2A}$$

if the discriminant is positive. A program is to be developed to solve several different quadratic equations or to indicate that there are no real solutions.

8. The Rinky Dooflingy Company currently sells 200 dooflingies per month at a profit of $300 per dooflingy. The company now spends $2000 per month on advertising and has a fixed operating cost of $10,000 per month that does not depend on the volume of sales. If the company doubles the amount spent on advertising, its sales will increase by 20 percent. The company president would like to know, beginning with the company's current status and successively doubling the amount spent on advertising, at what point will the net profit "go over the hump," that is, begin to decline.

9. Enter and execute the following short Pascal program on your computer system:

program *Exercise9* (*input, output*);

(* Program to perform various arithmetic
   operations on two numbers X and Y. *)

var
    X, Y, *Sum* : *integer*;

begin
    $X := 214$;
    $Y := 2057$;
    Sum $:= X + Y$;
    writeln ('Sum of', X, Y, ' is', *Sum*)
end.

10. Make the following changes in the program in Exercise 9 and execute the modified program:

(a) Change 214 to 1723 in the statement assigning a value to X.

(b) Change the variable names X and Y to *Alpha* and *Beta* throughout.

(c) Insert the comment

(* Calculate the sum *)

before the statement

Sum $:= Alpha + Beta$;

(d) Insert the following comment and statement before the *writeln* statement:

(* Now calculate the difference *)
Difference $:= Alpha - Beta$;

change the variable declaration to

var
    Alpha, Beta, Sum, Difference : *integer*;

and add the following statement after the *writeln* statement:

writeln ('Difference of', *Alpha, Beta*, ' is', *Difference*)

Note: For the modified program to work correctly, you must also insert a semicolon at an appropriate location.

11. Using the program in Figure 2.4 as a guide, write a Pascal program for the algorithm in Exercise 1.

12. Using the program in Figure 2.4 as a guide, write a Pascal program for the algorithm in Exercise 2.

3

Basic Pascal

Kindly enter them in your note-book.
And, in order to refer to them
conveniently, let's call them A, B, and Z.

THE TORTOISE IN LEWIS CARROLL'S
What the Tortoise Said to Achilles

In language, clarity is everything.

CONFUCIUS

As we noted in Chapter 1, the programming language Pascal was developed in the late 1960s and early 1970s by the Swiss computer scientist Niklaus Wirth. Different versions of Pascal have appeared since its introduction, and for several years the *Pascal User Manual and Report* published by Wirth and Kathleen Jensen in 1974 served as the *de facto* standard for these versions. In 1983 an official standard was prepared by committees of the American National Standards Institute (ANSI) and the Institute of Electrical and Electronic Engineers (IEEE) and was published as the *American National Standard Pascal Computer Programming Language.* This ANSI/IEEE standard is the basis for this text, and in this chapter we begin our study of Pascal by considering several of its basic features.

3.1 Data Types

Computer programs, regardless of the language in which they are written, are designed to manipulate some kind of data. Thus we begin our discussion of the Pascal language by considering the types of data that can be processed in a Pascal program.

Pascal provides four standard types of data:

integer
real
char
boolean

The first two are numeric types and are used to process different kinds of numbers. The *char* type is used to process character data. The *boolean* type is used to process so-called boolean or logical data; such data may have either the value true or the value false.

Constants. *Constants* are quantities whose values do not change during program execution. They may be of numeric, character, or boolean type. An *integer* constant is a string of digits that does not include commas or a decimal point; negative integer constants must be preceded by a negative sign, but a plus sign is optional for nonnegative integers. Thus

        0
      137
    −2516
    +17745

are valid integer constants, whereas the following are invalid for the reasons indicated:

    5,280   (Commas are not allowed in integer constants.)
    16.0   (Integer constants may not contain decimal points.)
    −−5   (Only one algebraic sign is allowed.)
      7−   (The algebraic sign must precede the string of digits.)

Another type of numeric data is the *real* type. Constants of this type may be represented as ordinary decimal numbers or in scientific notation. The *decimal* representation of real constants must include exactly one decimal point, but the constant may not begin or end with a decimal point. As in the case of integer constants, no commas are allowed. Negative real constants must be preceded by a negative sign, but the plus sign is optional for nonnegative reals. Thus

      1.234
    −0.1536
    +56473.0

are valid real constants, whereas the following are invalid for the reasons indicated:

    1,752.63   (Commas are not allowed in real constants.)
       82   (Real constants in decimal form must contain a decimal point.)
      .01   (Real constants may not begin with a decimal point.)
      24.   (Real constants may not end with a decimal point.)

The *scientific* or *floating-point* representation of a real constant consists of an integer or real constant in decimal form followed by the letter E and an integer constant which is interpreted as an exponent on the base 10. For example, the real constant 337.456 may also be written as

$$3.37456E2$$

which means

$$3.37456 \times 10^2$$

or it may be written in a variety of other forms, such as

$$0.337456E3$$

$$337.456E0$$

$$33745.6E-2$$

$$337456E-3$$

A *character* is one of the symbols in the Pascal character set. Although this character set may vary from one Pascal implementation to another, it usually includes digits 0 through 9; upper-case letters A through Z; lower-case letters a through z; usual punctuation symbols such as the semicolon (;), comma (,), and period (.); and special symbols such as $+$, $=$, $>$, and $\uparrow$. In fact, many Pascal implementations allow a character to be any symbol from the character set for that machine. (See Appendix A for two commonly used character sets, ASCII and EBCDIC.)

A *character constant* consists of a character enclosed within apostrophes (single quotes); for example,

'A',   '+',   '3',   ':'

If a character constant is to consist of an apostrophe, then it must appear as a pair of apostrophes enclosed within single quotes (apostrophes):

''''

A sequence of characters is commonly called a *string,* and a *string constant* consists of a string enclosed within single quotes. Thus

'John Q. Doe'

and

'PDQ123-A'

are valid string constants. Again, if an apostrophe is to be one of the characters in a string constant, it must appear as a pair of apostrophes; for example,

'Don''t'

The type *boolean* is named after the nineteenth-century mathematician George Boole, who originated the logical calculus. There are only two *boolean constants, true*

and

false

These constants are called *logical* constants in some programming languages.

Identifiers. *Identifiers* are names given to programs, constants, variables, and other entities in a program. Identifiers may contain any number of letters or digits, but must begin with a letter.[1] *This allows one to choose meaningful identifiers that suggest what they represent.*

Pascal *reserved words* such as **var, begin,** and **end** may not be used as identifiers, since they have a special meaning in Pascal. A complete list of reserved words is given in Appendix B. There are also certain *standard identifiers* in Pascal, such as *integer, real, true, false, read, readln, write,* and *writeln. These identifiers have a predefined meaning, but they are not reserved words. Consequently, they may be redefined by the programmer, but it is not good practice to do so.* A complete list of standard identifiers is given in Appendix B.

Variables. In mathematics, a symbolic name is often used to refer to a quantity. For example, the formula

$$A = l \cdot w$$

is used to calculate the area (denoted by A) of a rectangle with a given length (denoted by l) and a given width (denoted by w). These symbolic names, A, l, and w, are called *variables*. If specific values are assigned to l and w, this formula can be used to calculate the value of A, which then represents the area of a particular rectangle.

Variables were also used in Chapter 2 in the discussion of algorithms and programs. When a variable is used in a Pascal program, the compiler associates it with a particular memory location. The value of a variable at any time is the value stored in the associated memory location at that time. Variable names are identifiers and thus must follow the rules for forming valid identifiers.

The type of a Pascal variable must be one of the four data types described earlier (or one of the other data types discussed later), and the type of each variable determines the type of value that may be stored in that variable. It is therefore necessary to specify the type of each variable in a Pascal program.

Every Pascal program has the general form

program heading
declaration part
statement part.

---

[1] Some implementations of Pascal only recognize the first eight characters of an identifier as significant; thus, *WithholdFederalTax, WithholdSocialSecurity,* and *WithholdStateTax* would all represent the same identifier. In some implementations, other characters such as $ and __ (underline) may be allowed.

Included in the declaration part is a *variable section* in which all variables used in the program are listed and their types are specified. This section begins with the reserved word **var** and has the form

> **var**
> > *variable-list-1* : *type-1*;
> > *variable-list-2* : *type-2*;
> > $\vdots$
> > *variable-list-m* : *type-m*;

where each *variable-list-i* is a single variable or a list of variables separated by commas, and each *type-i* is one of the Pascal data types *integer, real, char,* or *boolean* (or one of the other types discussed later). For example, the variable declaration section

> **var**
> > *EmpNumber* : *integer*;
> > *Hours* : *real*;
> > *Rate* : *real*;
> > *Wages* : *real*;

or equivalently,

> **var**
> > *EmpNumber* : *integer*;
> > *Hours, Rate, Wages* : *real*;

declares that only the four variables *EmpNumber, Hours, Rate,* and *Wages* may be used in the program and that *EmpNumber* is of type *integer,* whereas *Hours, Rate,* and *Wages* are of type *real.*

It is good programming practice to use meaningful variable names that suggest what they represent since this makes the program more readable and easier to understand. It is also good practice to include brief comments that indicate how the variable is to be used. These comments may be included in the variable declaration section. The following illustrates:

> **var**
> > *EmpNumber* : *integer*;   (* employee number *)
> > *Hours*,   (* hours worked *)
> > *Rate*,   (* hourly pay rate *)
> > *Wages* : *real*;

Named Constants.   Certain constants occur so frequently that names are often given to them. For example, the name "pi" is commonly given to the constant 3.14159. . . and "e" to the base 2.71828. . . of natural logarithms. Pascal allows the programmer to assign identifiers to certain constants in the *constant section* of the program's declaration part. This section, if present, must precede the variable section and must begin with the reserved word **const**; it has the form

const
    identifier-1 = *constant-1*;
    identifier-2 = *constant-2*;
            ⋮
    identifier-k = *constant-k*;

For example, the identifiers *pi* and *e* would be associated with the real constants 3.14159 and 2.71828, respectively, by the following constant section:

const
    pi = 3.14159;
    e = 2.71828;

Pascal also includes three predefined constant identifiers: the boolean constant identifiers *true* and *false* and the integer constant identifier *maxint*. The value of *maxint* is the largest integer that can be represented in the particular computer being used. Typical values are 32767 ($2^{15} - 1$) or 2147483647 ($2^{31} - 1$).

Exercises

1. Which of the following are legal Pascal identifiers?

    (a) *XRay*   **(b)** *X−Ray*   **(c)** *Jeremiah*   **(d)** *R2D2*

    (e) *3M*   **(f)** *PDQ123*   **(g)** *PS.175*   **(h)** *x*

    (i) *4*   **(j)** *N/4*   **(k)** *$M*   **(l)** *ZZZZZZ*

    (m) *night*   **(n)** *ngiht*   **(o)** *nite*   **(p)** *to day*

2. Classify each of the following as an integer constant, real constant, or neither:

    (a) 12   **(b)** 12.   **(c)** 12.0   **(d)** '12'

    (e) 8+4   **(f)** −3.7   **(g)** 3.7−   **(h)** 1,024

    (i) +1   **(j)** $3.98   **(k)** 0.357E4   **(l)** 24E0

    (m) E3   **(n)** five   **(o)** 3E.5   **(p)** .000001

    (q) 1.2×10   **(r)** −(−1)   **(s)** 0E0   **(t)** 1/2

3. Which of the following are legal string constants?

    (a) 'X'   **(b)** '123'   **(c)** IS'   **(d)** 'too yet a minute'

    (e) 'DO''ESNT'   **(f)** 'isn''t'   **(g)** 'constant'   **(h)** '$1.98'

    (i) 'DON'T'   **(j)** '12 + 34'   **(k)** '''twas'   **(l)** 'A''B''C'

4. Write variable sections to declare:

    (a) *Item, Number,* and *Job* to be of real type.

    (b) *ShoeSize* to be of integer type.

(c) *Mileage* to be of real type and *Cost* and *Distance* to be of integer type.

(d) *Alpha* and *Beta* to be of integer type, *Code* to be of character type, *Root* to be of real type, and *RootExists* to be of boolean type.

5. For each of the following, write constant sections to name each given constant with the specified name:

(a) 1.25 with the name *Rate.*

(b) 40.0 with the name *RegHours* and 1.5 with the name *Overtime-Factor.*

(c) 1984 with the name *Year,* 'F' with *Female,* and a blank character with *Blank.*

(d) *true* with the name *Exists,* 0 with *Zero,* ∗ with *Asterisk,* an apostrophe with *Apostrophe,* and the string CPSC151A with *Course.*

In the preceding section we considered variables and constants of various types. These variables and constants can be processed by using operations and functions appropriate to their types. In this section we discuss the arithmetic operations and functions that are used with numeric data.

Arithmetic Operations and Functions

In Pascal, addition and subtraction are denoted by the usual plus (+) and minus (−) signs. Multiplication is denoted by an asterisk (∗). This symbol must be used to denote every multiplication; thus to multiply n by 2, we must use $2 * n$ or $n * 2$, not $2n$. There are three other arithmetic operations in Pascal: a division operation denoted by a slash (/) which yields a real result; a division operation denoted by the reserved word **div** which yields an integer result; and the operation denoted by the reserved word **mod** which yields the remainder that results from an integer division. The following table summarizes these arithmetic operations:

Operator	Operation
+	addition
−	subtraction, unary minus
∗	multiplication
/	real division
div	integer division
mod	remainder (modulus) in integer division

For the operators +, −, and ∗, the operands may be of either integer or real type. If both are integer, the result is integer; but if either is of real type, the result is real. For example,

$$2 + 3 = 5$$
$$2 + 3.0 = 5.0$$
$$2.0 + 3 = 5.0$$
$$2.0 + 3.0 = 5.0$$

The division operator / produces a real result, regardless of the type of the operands, for example,

$$7 / 2 = 3.5$$
$$7.0 / 2 = 3.5$$
$$7 / 2.0 = 3.5$$
$$7.0 / 2.0 = 3.5$$

For the operators **div** and **mod,** the operands must both be of integer type, and the result is also of integer type. If x and y are of integer type, then x **div** y produces the integer quotient obtained when x is divided by y, and x **mod** y produces the remainder. For example,

$$7 \textbf{ div } 2 = 3$$
$$7 \textbf{ mod } 2 = 1$$
$$12 \textbf{ div } 3 = 4$$
$$12 \textbf{ mod } 3 = 0$$
$$0 \textbf{ div } 5 = 0$$
$$0 \textbf{ mod } 5 = 0$$

There are two *precedence levels* for these arithmetic operators: high and low. The high-priority operators are *, /, **div,** and **mod,** and the low-priority operators are + and −. When an *expression* containing several of these operators is evaluated, all high priority operations are performed first in the order in which they occur, from left to right, and then all low priority operations are carried out in the order in which they occur, from left to right.

To illustrate, consider the expression

$$7 * 10 - 5 \textbf{ mod } 3 * 4 + 9$$

The leftmost multiplication is performed first, giving the intermediate result

$$70 - 5 \textbf{ mod } 3 * 4 + 9$$

The next high-priority operator encountered is **mod,** which gives

$$70 - 2 * 4 + 9$$

The second multiplication is the final operation of high priority; when it is performed, it yields

$$70 - 8 + 9$$

Next, the low-priority operations are performed in the order in which they occur, from left to right. The subtraction is thus performed first, giving

$$62 + 9$$

and then the addition is carried out, giving the final result

71

The standard order of evaluation can be modified by using parentheses to enclose subexpressions within an expression. These subexpressions are first evaluated in the standard manner, and the results are then combined to evaluate the complete expression. If the parentheses are "nested," that is, if one set of parentheses is contained within another, the computations in the innermost parentheses are performed first.

For example, consider the expression

$$(7 * (10 - 5) \bmod 3) * 4 + 9$$

The subexpression $10 - 5$ is evaluated first, producing

$$(7 * 5 \bmod 3) * 4 + 9$$

Next the subexpression $7 * 5 \bmod 3$ is evaluated in the standard order, giving

$$2 * 4 + 9$$

Now the multiplication is performed, giving

$$8 + 9$$

and the addition produces the final result

$$17$$

Care must be taken in writing expressions containing two or more operations to ensure that they are evaluated in the order intended. Even though parentheses may not be required, they should be used freely to clarify the intended order of evaluation and to write complicated expressions in terms of simpler subexpressions. One must make sure, however, that the parentheses balance, that is, that they occur in pairs, since an unpaired parenthesis results in an error.

The symbols $+$ and $-$ can also be used as *unary operators;* for example, $-x$ and $+(a + b)$ are allowed. But unary operators must be used carefully, since Pascal does not allow two operators to follow in succession. For example, the expression $n * -2$ is not allowed; rather, it must be written $n * (-2)$. These unary operations have low priority, as do the corresponding binary operations.

In summary, the following rules govern the evaluation of arithmetic expressions:

1. The high-priority operators *, /, **div,** and **mod** are performed first. The low-priority operators $+$ and $-$ (both binary and unary) are performed last. Operators having the same priority are evaluated from left to right.
2. If an expression contains subexpressions enclosed within parentheses, these are evaluated first, using the standard order specified in Rule 1. If there are nested parentheses, the innermost subexpressions are evaluated first.

There are also a number of predefined arithmetic functions in the Pascal language, as given in Table 3.1. To use any of these functions, we simply give the function name followed by the constant, variable, or expression to

Table 3.1. Standard Pascal Arithmetic Functions

Function	Description	Type of Parameter	Type of Value
abs(x)	Absolute value of x	Integer or real	Same as argument
arctan(x)	Inverse tangent of x (value in radians)	Integer or real	Real
cos(x)	Cosine of x (in radians)	Integer or real	Real
exp(x)	Exponential function e^x	Integer or real	Real
ln(x)	Natural logarithm of x	Integer or real	Real
round(x)	x rounded to nearest integer	Real	Integer
sin(x)	Sine of x (in radians)	Integer or real	Real
sqr(x)	x^2	Integer or real	Same as argument
sqrt(x)	Square root of x	Integer or real	Real
trunc(x)	x truncated to its integer part	Real	Integer

which the function is to be applied enclosed within parenthesis. Thus, to calculate the square root of 5, we write

$$sqrt(5)$$

and to calculate $\sqrt{b^2 - 4ac}$, we could use

$$sqrt(sqr(b) - 4 * a * c)$$

If the value of the expression $sqr(b) - 4 * a * c$ is negative, an error results because the square root of a negative number is not defined.

Exercises

1. Find the value of each of the following expressions or explain why it is not a valid expression.

   (a) $9 - 5 - 3$

   (b) 2 div 3 + 3 / 5

   (c) 9 div 2 / 5

   (d) 9 / 2 div 5

   (e) 2.0 / 4

   (f) $(2 + 3)$ mod 2

   (g) 7 mod 5 mod 3

   (h) (7 mod 5) mod 3

   (i) 7 mod (5 mod 3)

   (j) (7 mod 5 mod 3)

   (k) 25 * 1 / 2

   (l) 25 * 1 div 2

   (m) 25 * (1 div 2)

   (n) $-3.0 * 5.0$

   (o) $5.0 * -3.0$

   (p) 12 / 2 * 3

   (q) $((12 + 3)$ div 2) / $(8 - (5 + 1))$

   (r) $((12 + 3)$ div 2) / $(8 - 5 + 1)$

   (s) $(12 + 3$ div 2) / $(8 - 5 + 1)$

   (t) sqrt(sqr(4))

   (u) sqrt(sqr(−4))

   (v) sqr(sqrt(4))

   (w) sqr(sqrt(−4))

   (x) trunc(8 / 5) + round(8 / 5)

2. If zwei = 2.0, drei = 3.0, vier = 4, funf = 5, and acht = 8, find the value of each of the following:

(a) *zwei* + *drei* + *drei*   **(b)** *acht* **div** 3

(c) *acht* / 3   **(d)** (*drei* + *zwei*) * *vier*

(e) *acht* **div** *funf* * 5.1   **(f)** *sqr*(*vier*) / *sqr*(*zwei*)

(g) *sqr*(*funf*) / *sqr*(*zwei*)   **(h)** *sqrt*(*zwei* + *drei* + *vier*)

3. Write Pascal expressions to compute the following:

(a) $10 + 5B - 4AC$.

(b) Three times the difference $4 - n$ divided by twice the quantity $m^2 + n^2$.

(c) The square root of $a + 3b^2$.

(d) The real quantity x rounded to the nearest tenth.

The *assignment statement* is used to assign values to variables and has the **The Assignment** form **Statement**

> *variable* := *expression*

where *expression* may be a constant, another variable to which a value has previously been assigned, or a formula to be evaluated. For example, suppose that *xCoord* and *yCoord* are real variables, *Number* and *Position* are integer variables, *Code* is a character variable, and *Done* is a boolean variable as declared by the following variable section:

```
var
    xCoord, yCoord : real;
    Number, Position : integer;
    Code : char;
    Done : boolean;
```

These declarations associate memory locations with the six variables. This might be pictured as follows, where the question marks indicate that these variables are initially undefined:

xCoord	?
yCoord	?
Number	?
Position	?
Code	?
Done	?

Now consider the following assignment statements:

```
xCoord := 5.23;
yCoord := sqrt(25.0);
Number := 17;
Code := 'M';
Done := false;
Position := Number div 3 + 2;
xCoord := 2.0 * xCoord;
```

The first assignment statement assigns the real constant 5.23 to the real variable *xCoord,* and the second assigns the real constant 5.0 to the real variable *yCoord.* The next three assignment statements assign the integer constant 17 to the integer variable *Number,* the character M to the character variable *Code,* and the boolean value *false* to the boolean variable *Done.* Thus the memory locations named by the variables *xCoord, yCoord, Number, Code* and *Done* contain the values 5.23, 5.0, 17, M, and *false,* respectively; the variable *Position* is still undefined.

xCoord	5.23
yCoord	5.0
Number	17
Position	?
Code	M
Done	*false*

This means that until the contents of these memory locations are changed, these values are substituted for the variable names in any subsequent expression containing these variables. Thus, in the sixth assignment statement, the value 17 is substituted for the variable *Number,* the expression *Number* **div** 3 + 2 is evaluated yielding 7, and this value is then assigned to the integer variable *Position;* the value of *Number* is unchanged.

xCoord	5.23
yCoord	5.0
Number	17
Position	7
Code	M
Done	*false*

In the last assignment statement, the variable name *xCoord* appears on both sides of the assignment operator (:=). In this case, the current value 5.23 for *xCoord* is used in evaluating the expression 2.0 * *xCoord*, yielding the value 10.46; this value is then assigned to *xCoord*. The old value 5.23 is lost because it has been replaced with the new value 10.46.

xCoord	10.46
yCoord	5.0
Number	17
Position	7
Code	**M**
Done	*false*

In every assignment statement, the variable to be assigned a value must appear on the left of the assignment operator (:=), and a legal expression must appear on the right. Furthermore, both the variable and the expression must be of the same type. However, *it is legal to assign an integer value to a real variable;* the integer value will be converted to the corresponding real value. *One may not, however, assign a real value to an integer variable.*

The following are examples of invalid Pascal assignment statements. A reason is given for each to explain why it is not valid. The variables in these statements are assumed to have the types specified earlier.

Statement	Error
5 := *Number*	Variable must appear on the left of the assignment operator.
xCoord + 3.5 := 2.7	Arithmetic expressions may not appear on the left of the assignment operator.
Code := 5	Numeric value may not be assigned to a character variable.
Number := '5'	Character constant may not be assigned to a numeric variable.
Number := 3.4	Real value may not be assigned to an integer variable.
Number := '2' + '3'	'2' + '3' is not a legal expression.
Position := *Number* := 1	*Number* := 1 is not a legal expression.
Done := 'F'	'F' is not a boolean expression.

It is important to remember that *the assignment statement is a replacement statement.* Some beginning programmers forget this and write an assignment statement like

$$A := B$$

when the statement

$$B := A$$

is intended. These two statements produce very different results: the first assigns the value of B to A, leaving B unchanged, and the second assigns the value of A to B, leaving A unchanged (see Figure 3.1).

To illustrate further that an assignment statement is a replacement statement, suppose that *Alpha* and *Beta* are integer variables with values 357 and 59, respectively. The following statements interchange the values of *Alpha* and *Beta*, using the auxiliary integer variable *Temp:*

> *Temp* := *Alpha*;
> *Alpha* := *Beta*;
> *Beta* := *Temp*;

Figure 3.2 shows the replacement of values produced by each of these three assignment statements.

As another example, consider the statement

> *Sum* := *Sum* + *Counter*

Such a statement in which the same variable appears on both sides of the assignment operator often confuses beginning programmers. Execution of this statement causes the values of *Sum* and *Counter* to be substituted for these variables to evaluate the expression *Sum* + *Counter*, and the resulting value is then assigned to *Sum*. The following diagram illustrates this for the case in which the integer variables *Sum* and *Counter* have the values 120 and 16, respectively,

Note that the old value of the variable *Sum* is lost because it was replaced with a new value.

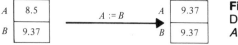

Figure 3.1.
Difference between
$A := B$ and $B := A$.

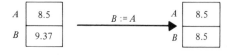

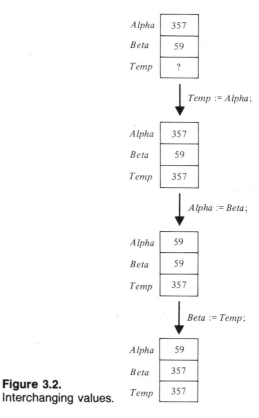

Figure 3.2.
Interchanging values.

Another statement in which the same variable appears on both sides of the assignment operator is

$$Counter := Counter + 1$$

This statement implements the operation "increase *Counter* by 1." When it is executed, the current value of *Counter* is substituted for this variable to evaluate the expression *Counter* + 1, and this new value is then assigned to *Counter*. For example, if *Counter* has the value 16, the value of *Counter* + 1 is 16 + 1 = 17, which is then assigned as the new value for *Counter*:

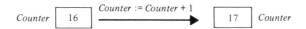

Note once again that the old value of the variable has been lost because it was replaced with a new value.

In a Pascal program, *variables are undefined until their values have been explicitly specified* by an assignment statement or by one of the other statements discussed later. The results of attempting to use undefined variables are unpredictable and depend on the particular Pascal compiler being used.

Exercises

1. Assuming that *Number* is of integer type, *xValue* and *yValue* are of real type, *Grade* is of character type, and *Found* is of boolean type, determine which of the following are valid Pascal assignment statements. If they are not valid, explain why they are not.

   (a) *xValue* := 2.71828   (b) 3 := *Number*   (c) *Grade* := 'B+'

   (d) *Number* := Number+   1   (e) *xValue* := 1   (f) *Grade* := A

   (g) *Number* + 1 := *Number*   (h) *xValue* := 'l'   (i) *Found* := *Grade*

   (j) *yValue* := *yValue*   (k) *xValue* := A   (l) *Grade* := *Grade* + 10

   (m) *Found* := 'true'   (n) *xValue* := *Number*   (o) *Number* := *yValue*

2. Given that *two, tri, four,* and *xCoord* are real variables with *two* = 2.0, *tri* = 3.0, and *four* = 4.0; *acht, funf,* and *zahl* are integer variables with *acht* = 8 and *funf* = 5; and *Numeral* and *Symbol* are character variables with *Numeral* = '2'; find the value assigned to the given variable by each of the following, or indicate why the statement is not valid.

   (a) *xCoord* := (*two* + *tri*) * *tri*

   (b) *xCoord* := (*tri* + *two* / *four*) * 2

   (c) *xCoord* := *acht* / *funf* + 5

   (d) *zahl* := *acht* **div** *funf* + 5

   (e) *xCoord* := sqr(*funf*) / sqr(*acht*)

   (f) *zahl* := sqr(*funf*) / sqr(*acht*)

   (g) *Symbol* := 4

   (h) *Symbol* := *Numeral*

   (i) *Symbol* := '4'

   (j) *Symbol* := *four*

   (k) *two* := 2

   (l) *two* := '2'

   (m) *two* := *Numeral*

   (n) *acht* := *acht* + 2

   (o) *zahl* := 1 + *Numeral*

   (p) *zahl* := round(sqr(*acht* **mod** *funf*) / *four*)

3. Write a Pascal assignment statement for each of the following that calculates the given expression and assigns the result to the specified variable:

(a) *Rate* times *Time* to *Distance.*

(b) $\sqrt{a^2 + b^2}$ to *c.*

(c) $\dfrac{1}{\dfrac{1}{R1} + \dfrac{1}{R2} + \dfrac{1}{R3}}$ to *Resistance.*

(d) Area of a triangle of base *b* and height *h* (one-half base times height) to *Area.*

(e) 5/9 of *Fahrenheit* $-$ 32 to *Celsius.*

4. For each of the following, give values for the integer variables *a*, *b*, and *c* for which the two given expressions have different values.

(a) *a* * (*b* **div** *c*) and *a* * *b* **div** *c*

(b) *a* **div** *b* and *a* * (1 / *b*)

(c) (*a* + *b*) **div** *c* and *a* **div** *c* + *b* **div** *c*

In the preceding section we considered the assignment statement, which en- **Input/Output**
ables us to calculate the values of expressions and store the results of these
computations by assigning them to variables. An assignment statement does
not, however, display these results on some output device, nor does it allow
the user to enter new values during execution. For example, a program to
calculate the wages earned by John Doe, employee #31564, for 38.5 hours
of work at an hourly rate of $8.75 could contain the variable section

```
var
    EmpNumber : integer;      (* employee number *)
    Hours,                    (* hours worked *)
    Rate,                     (* hourly pay rate *)
    Wages : real;             (* total wages *)
```

and the statement part

```
begin
    EmpNumber := 31564;
    Hours := 38.5;
    Rate := 8.75;
    Wages := Hours * Rate
end.
```

The value of *Wages* is calculated as desired but is stored only internally in
the memory location associated with *Wages* and is not displayed to the user.
Moreover, if the same wage calculation is to be done for Mary Smith, employee
#31565, who worked 37.5 hours at an hourly rate of $9.25, the statement
part of the program must be almost completely rewritten as follows:

```
    begin
        EmpNumber := 31565;
        Hours := 37.5;
        Rate := 9.25;
        Wages := Hours * Rate
    end.
```

The output statement that we consider in this section provides a method for easily displaying information. We also consider an input statement to provide a convenient method to assign values from an external source to variables during execution of the program.

Program Heading. Any collection of data to be input to a program or output from a program is called a *file*. There are programs that do not require any input from a file, since all values to be processed are assigned within the program. This is true, for example, in the preceding program segments. All useful programs, however, do produce some output, because the results obtained would not otherwise be displayed to the user.

The program heading in a Pascal program has the form

program *name* (*file-list*);

where *name* is a valid Pascal identifier used to name the program and *file-list* is a list of files used in the program. Two standard files provided by the Pascal language are *input* and *output*. The file *input* refers to a system input device, such as a terminal or a card reader, and the file *output* refers to a system output device, such as a terminal or a line printer. An appropriate program heading for a Pascal program that does not require input could have the form

program *name* (*output*);

A program that requires input and produces output could have a program heading of the form

program *name* (*input, output*);

Output. There are two output statements in Pascal, the *write* and the *writeln* (read "write-line") statements. In this introductory section we consider only the *writeln* statement. (The *write* statement is described in Chapter 6.) A simple form of the *writeln* statement is

writeln (*output-list*)

where *output-list* is a single expression or a list of expressions separated by commas. Each of these expressions can be a constant, a variable, or a formula. Execution of a *writeln* statement displays the values of the items in the output list on the current line and then advances to the next line so that subsequent output will appear on a new line. For example, the statements

writeln (*Alpha, Beta*);
writeln (*Gamma, Delta*)

display the values of *Alpha* and *Beta* on one line and the values of *Gamma* and *Delta* on the next line. Subsequent output would begin on yet another line.

The values of the expressions in the output list of a *writeln* statement are displayed in *fields,* which are zones of consecutive positions in the output line. To illustrate, suppose that *Counter, RealNum, Code,* and *BooleVar* are variables declared by

> **var**
>> *Counter : integer;*
>> *RealNum : real;*
>> *Code : char;*
>> *BooleVar : boolean;*

and consider the following statements:

> *Counter := 16;*
> *RealNum := 123.456;*
> *Code := 'A';*
> *BooleVar := true;*
> *writeln ('Counter');*
> *writeln (Counter);*
> *writeln (Counter, ' is even', Counter + 1, ' is odd');*
> *writeln (RealNum, RealNum / 70000);*
> *writeln (Code, 'B', 'C', '***');*
> *writeln (BooleVar, false)*

These statements produce output similar to the following:

```
Counter
        16
        16 is even        17 is odd
 1.234560000E+02 1.763657143E-03
ABC***
TRUE FALSE
```

The format of the output will vary from one system to another since the field widths used for integer, real, and boolean values are compiler-dependent. For a character or a string value, however, the field width is the number of characters in that value. Note that numeric values are *right-justified* in their fields, that is, they are placed so that the last digit is in the rightmost position of the field, and that real values are displayed in floating-point notation.

In some situations, one or more blank lines in the output improve readability. A blank line is produced by the statement

> *writeln*

in which the output list is empty. Note that the parentheses that normally enclose the output list are also omitted. For example, consider the statements

```
Counter := 16;
writeln (Counter, ' is even', Counter + 1, ' is odd');
writeln;
writeln ('*********');
writeln ('*       *');
writeln ('*********');
writeln;
writeln;
writeln (2 * Counter, ' is even')
```

These statements produce output similar to the following:

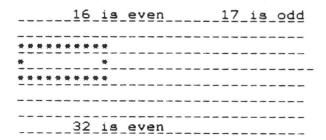

In earlier example in this section we considered the problem of calculating wages for an employee. To display some of the relevant information from this example, we might add several *writeln* statements, as shown in the program in Figure 3.3.

The output produced by the program in Figure 3.3 is not really satisfactory, for two reasons. First, too many spaces are used to display the values, and second, the real values are displayed in floating-point form that is not appropriate for monetary values. These deficiencies can be remedied by specifying the format of the output by appending *format descriptors* to the items in the output list.

A format descriptor can have one of two forms

   :w

or

   :w:d

In both forms, *w* is a positive integer expression that specifies the field width to be used in displaying the corresponding value. For example, in the statement

   writeln (Counter:2, ' is even', Counter + 1 : 5, ' is odd')

the format descriptor :2 specifies that the value of *Counter* is to be displayed in a field of width 2, and the format descriptor :5 specifies that the value of *Counter* + 1 is to be displayed in a field of width 5. If *Counter* has the value 16, the output produced by this statement is

```
16 is even   17 is odd
```

```
PROGRAM WageCalculation (output);

(*********************************************************************

    This program calculates wages as hours * rate for a given number
    of hours worked and a given hourly rate for some employee
    identified by his/her employee number.

 *********************************************************************)

VAR
    EmpNumber : integer;    (* employee number *)
    Hours,                  (* hours worked *)
    Rate,                   (* hourly rate *)
    Wages : real;           (* gross wages earned *)
BEGIN
    EmpNumber := 31564;
    Hours := 38.5;
    Rate := 8.75;
    Wages := Hours * Rate;
    writeln ('Employee #', EmpNumber);
    writeln ('Hours worked:  ', Hours);
    writeln ('Hourly rate:  $', Rate);
    writeln ('Total Wages:  $', Wages)
END.




Sample run:
==========


Employee #   31564
Hours worked:   3.850000000E+01
Hourly rate: $ 8.750000000E+00
Total Wages: $ 3.368750000E+02
```

Figure 3.3.

If *Zone* is an integer variable with value 2, the statement

   writeln (*Counter*:*Zone*, ' is even', *Counter* + 1 : *Zone* + 3, ' is odd')

produces this same output. The statement

   writeln (*Counter*:1, ' is even', *Counter* + 1 : 1, ' is odd')

produces

```
16 is even17 is odd
```

As this last example demonstrates, if a numeric value is too large for
the specified field, then the field is automatically enlarged to accommodate
this value. Thus, because the value 16 of *Counter* has two digits, the field
of size 1 specified for it by *Counter*:1 is enlarged so that both digits are
displayed. But if a field is too small for a character, string, or boolean value,
it is not enlarged, and only the leftmost *w* characters are displayed where
w is the specified field width. Consequently, the output produced by the
statement

writeln (*Counter*:1, ' is even':7, *Counter* + 1 : 1 ' is odd':5)

is

`16_is_eve17_is_o`

If the field width is larger than necessary, the value is *right-justified* in the field. Thus, the output produced by the statement

writeln (*Counter*:5, 'is even':8, *Counter* + 1 : 10, 'is odd':8)

is

`___16_is_even_____17__is_odd`

If a real value is output using the format descriptor :*w*, it is displayed in scientific form. If the usual decimal form for a real value is desired, the format descriptor :*w*:*d* must be used. In this descriptor, *d* is an integer expression specifying the number of digits to be displayed to the right of the decimal point. The value to be displayed is *rounded* to *d* decimal places with zeros added as necessary. To illustrate, suppose that *Alpha* and *Beta* are real variables with the values 3.51 and 123.47168, respectively, and that *Zone* and *NumDigits* are integer variables with the values 8 and 2, respectively. Consider the following statements:

```
writeln (Alpha:4:2);
writeln (Beta:9:5);
writeln;
writeln (Alpha:8:4, Beta:12:6);
writeln;
writeln (Alpha:8:2, Beta:12:3);
writeln (Alpha:8:1, Beta:12:1);
writeln;
writeln (Alpha:3:1, Beta:3:1);
writeln;
writeln (Alpha + 3 : Zone : NumDigits);
writeln (Beta - 1 : Zone + 1 : NumDigits + 1);
```

The output produced by these statements is

```
3.51
123.47168

  3.5100  123.471680

     3.51       123.472
      3.5       123.5

3.5123.5

     6.51
  122.472
```

We remarked earlier that the output produced by the program in Figure 3.3 is not really satisfactory. The program in Figure 3.4 is a modification that uses format descriptors to display the results in a more acceptable format.

Input. There are two input statements in Pascal, the *read* and the *readln* (read "read line") statements. Here we consider only the *readln* statement and restrict our attention to numeric input, since this statement cannot be used for boolean values and the input of character strings is somewhat more complicated.

A simple form of the *readln* statement is

readln (*input-list*)

where *input-list* consists of a single variable or a list of variables separated by commas. A *readln* statement reads values from the standard file *input* and assigns them to the variables in the input list. Recall that the standard file *input* refers to a system input device, such as a terminal in an interactive

```
PROGRAM WageCalculation (output);

(**********************************************************************

    This program calculates wages as hours * rate for a given number
    of hours worked and a given hourly rate for some employee
    identified by his/her employee number.

**********************************************************************)

VAR
    EmpNumber : integer;    (* employee number *)
    Hours,                  (* hours worked *)
    Rate,                   (* hourly rate *)
    Wages : real;           (* gross wages earned *)

BEGIN
    EmpNumber := 31564;
    Hours := 38.5;
    Rate := 8.75;
    Wages := Hours * Rate;
    writeln ('Employee # ', EmpNumber:1);
    writeln ('Hours worked:  ', Hours:7:2);
    writeln ('Hourly rate:  $', Rate:7:2);
    writeln ('Total wages:  $', Wages:7:2)
END.




Sample run:
==========


Employee # 31564
Hours worked:    38.50
Hourly rate:  $    8.75
Total wages:  $ 336.88
```

Figure 3.4.

mode of operation or a card reader in a batch mode of operation. The examples in this text assume interactive input so that data values are entered from the terminal during program execution.

To illustrate, consider the statement

readln (*EmpNumber*, *Hours*, *Rate*)

where *EmpNumber* is an integer variable and *Hours* and *Rate* are real variables. If the data values

31564 38.5 8.75

are entered, the value 31564 is assigned to the variable *EmpNumber*, 38.5 to *Hours*, and 8.75 to *Rate*. Thus this single *readln* statement can replace the three assignment statements

EmpNumber := 31564;
Hours := 38.5;
Rate := 8.75;

used in the program of Figures 3.3 and 3.4. The modified program is shown in Figure 3.5. Note that because the program involves both input and output, the program heading includes both of the standard files *input* and *output*.

Data values entered for the variables in the input list of a *readln* statement must be constants, and the consecutive numbers should be separated by one or more blanks. (An algebraic sign may also be used to separate consecutive numbers.) They must be arranged so that the type of each value agrees with that of the variable to which it is to be assigned. Assignment of a real value to an integer variable is not allowed, although an integer value may be read for a real variable.

Each *readln* statement reads values from a new input line. Consequently, if an input line contains more values than there are variables in the input list, the first data values are read, but all remaining values are ignored.

If there are fewer entries in a line of input data than variables in the input list, successive lines of input data are processed until values for all variables in the input list have been obtained. Thus for the statement

readln (*EmpNumber*, *Hours*, *Rate*)

the values for *EmpNumber*, *Hours*, and *Rate* can all be entered on the same line

31564 38.5 8.75

or on three separate lines

31564
38.5
8.75

or with the value for *EmpNumber* on the first line and the values for *Hours* and *Rate* on the next line

```
PROGRAM WageCalculation (input, output);

(*********************************************************************

    This program calculates wages as hours * rate for an employee
    identified by his/her employee number.  The employee number,
    hours worked, and hourly rate are read during execution.

 *********************************************************************)

VAR
    EmpNumber : integer;   (* employee number *)
    Hours,                 (* hours worked *)
    Rate,                  (* hourly rate *)
    Wages : real;          (* gross wages earned *)

BEGIN
    readln (EmpNumber, Hours, Rate);
    Wages := Hours * Rate;
    writeln ('Employee # ', EmpNumber:1);
    writeln ('Hours worked:  ', Hours:7:2);
    writeln ('Hourly rate:  $', Rate:7:2);
    writeln ('Total wages:  $', Wages:7:2)
END.




Sample run:
==========


31564 38.5 8.75
Employee # 31564
Hours worked:    38.50
Hourly rate:  $   8.75
Total wages:  $ 336.88
```

Figure 3.5.

31564

38.5 8.75

and so on.

In a batch mode of operation, these lines of input data are entered
on data cards. When a *readln* statement is encountered, the values from
these data cards are retrieved automatically and assigned to the variables
in the input list.

In an interactive mode of operation, the values assigned to variables
in an input list are entered from a terminal. In this case, when a *readln*
statement is encountered, program execution is suspended while the user
enters values for all variables in the input list. Program execution then automatically resumes. Because execution is interrupted by a *readln* statement
and because the correct number and types of values must be entered before
execution can resume, *it is good practice to provide some message to prompt
the user when it is necessary to enter data values.* This is accomplished by
preceding *readln* statements with *writeln* statements that display appropriate

```
PROGRAM WageCalculation (input, output);

(************************************************************************

    This program calculates wages as hours * rate for an employee
    identified by his/her employee number.  The employee number,
    hours worked, and hourly rate are read during execution.

*************************************************************************)

VAR
    EmpNumber : integer;    (* employee number *)
    Hours,                  (* hours worked *)
    Rate,                   (* hourly rate *)
    Wages : real;           (* gross wages earned *)

BEGIN
    writeln ('Enter employee number');
    readln (EmpNumber);
    writeln ('Enter hours worked and hourly rate');
    readln (Hours, Rate);
    Wages := Hours * Rate;
    writeln ('Employee # ', EmpNumber:1);
    writeln ('Hours worked:  ', Hours:7:2);
    writeln ('Hourly rate:  $', Rate:7:2);
    writeln ('Total wages:  $', Wages:7:2)
END.




Sample run:
==========


Enter employee number
31564
Enter hours worked and hourly rate
38.5 8.75
Employee # 31564
Hours worked:    38.50
Hourly rate:  $   8.75
Total wages:  $ 336.88
```

Figure 3.6.

prompts. The program in Figure 3.6 illustrates this by prompting the user
when values for *EmpNumber, Hours,* and *Rate* are to be entered; it is a
modification of the program in Figure 3.5.

Exercises

1. Assuming that *Alpha* and *Beta* are real variables with values
   −567.392 and 0.0004, respectively, and that *Rho* is an integer variable
   with a value 436, show precisely the output that each of the following
   sets of statements produces:

   (a) *writeln* (*Alpha*:8:1, *Rho*:5);
       writeln ('Tolerance:', *Beta*:8:5);

(b) *writeln* ('Alpha =', *Alpha*:12:5);
    writeln ('Beta =', *Beta*:6:2, ' ':4, 'Rho =', *Rho*:6);
    writeln (*Alpha* + 4.0 + *Rho*:15:3);

(c) *writeln* ('Tolerance =':8, *Beta*:5:3);
    writeln;
    writeln;
    writeln (*Rho*:2, *Alpha*:4:2);

(d) *writeln* (10 * *Alpha*:8:1, *trunc*(10 * *Alpha*):8,
              round(10 * *Alpha*):8);
    writeln (*sqr*(*Rho* **div** 100):5, *sqrt*(*Rho* **div** 100):5)

2. Assuming that I and J are integer variables with $I = 15$ and $J = 8$, that C and D are character variables with $C = $ 'C' and $D = $ '—', and that X and Y are real variables with $X = 2559.50$ and $Y = 8.015$, show precisely the output that each of the following sets of statements produce:

(a) *writeln* ('New balance =':*I*, *X*:*J*:2);
    writeln (*C*:*I* **mod** 10, *Y*:*J*:*J* − 6);

(b) *writeln* ('I =':*I*, *I*:*I*, 'J =':*J*, *J*:*J*);
    writeln;
    writeln (*I*:*J*, *J*:*I*);
    writeln (*trunc*(*X* / *J*):*J*, *J* − *Y*:*I*:*J*, *D*:*J* **div** 7)

3. Assume that *N1* and *N2* are integer variables with values 39 and −5117, respectively; that *R1* and *R2* are real variables with values 56.7173 and −0.00247, respectively; and that *C* is a character variable with a value F. For each of the following, write a set of output statements that use these variables to produce the given output (where Ƀ denotes a blank):

(a) ƀƀ56.7173ƀƀƀFƀƀƀ39
    −5117PDQ−0.00247

(b) ƀƀ56.717ƀƀƀ−0.0025***39ƀƀF
    ƀƀƀ56.72 ƀƀƀ39−5117

(c) ROOTSƀAREƀƀ56.717ƀANDƀ−0.00247

(d) APPROXIMATEƀANGLES:ƀƀ56.7ƀANDƀ−0.0
    MAGNITUDESƀAREƀƀƀƀ39ƀANDƀƀƀ5117

A Pascal program consists of three parts:

    program heading
    declaration part
    statement part.

Program Composition

These three parts *must* appear in the order shown. The *program heading* is a single statement of the form

> **program** *name* (*file-list*);

as described in the preceding section. The name assigned to the program must be a legal Pascal identifier, distinct from any other identifier used in the program.

The *declaration part* of a Pascal program may contain up to five sections that define various entities used in the program. These sections in the order in which they must appear are

> label section
> constant section
> type section
> variable section
> subprogram section

The *constant section* has the form

> **const**
> $\quad$ *identifier-1* = *constant-1*;
> $\quad$ *identifier-2* = *constant-2*;
> $\qquad \vdots$
> $\quad$ *identifier-k* = *constant-k*;

and is used to assign names to constants, as described in Section 3.1. The *variable section* has the form

> **var**
> $\quad$ *variable-list-1* : *type-1*;
> $\quad$ *variable-list-2* : *type-2*;
> $\qquad \vdots$
> $\quad$ *variable-list-m* : *type-m*;

and is used to declare *all* variables used in the program, that is, to specify their names and types. This also was discussed in Section 3.1. The other sections of the declaration part are discussed later.

The *statement part* of the program has the form

> **begin**
> $\quad$ *statement-1*;
> $\quad$ *statement-2*;
> $\qquad \vdots$
> $\quad$ *statement-n*
> **end**

This part of the program contains the statements that implement the steps of an algorithm. It may include such statements as assignment statements, input/output statements, and other statements considered in subsequent chapters of this book.

Correct punctuation is critical in a Pascal program, and each of the sections must be punctuated exactly as indicated. In particular, the program heading, each constant definition, and each variable declaration must end with a semicolon. In the statement part, the statements are *separated* by semicolons, but there need be no semicolon following the last statement. Finally, note that a period must follow the reserved word **end** that closes the statement part of the program.

We have seen that comments are indicated in Pascal program by enclosing them between (* and *)

(* *comment* *)

or within braces

{ *comment* }

These comments are not program statements and may be placed anywhere in the program, except, of course, in the middle of a reserved word, an identifier, a constant, and so on. As discussed in Section 2.4, comments should be used to explain the use of variables, to explain the purpose of the program or a program segment, and to provide other pertinent information about the program. Such documentation is intended to clarify the purpose and the structure of the program. It is invaluable if revisions and modifications are made to the program in the future, especially if such maintenance is done by persons other than the original programmer.

Suppose that a manufacturing company maintains a fleet of trucks to deliver **An Example** its products. On each trip, the driver records the distance traveled in miles, the number of gallons of fuel used, the cost of the fuel, and the other costs of operating the truck. As part of the accounting process, the comptroller needs to calculate and record for each truck and for each trip the miles per gallon, the total cost of that trip, and the cost per mile. A simple program is to be designed to carry out these calculations.

The input to the program is the miles traveled, gallons of fuel used, fuel cost, and other operating costs, and the output must include the miles per gallon, the total cost of the trip, and the cost per mile. The calculations required to solve this program are quite simple. The miles per gallon is obtained by dividing the number of miles traveled by the number of gallons of fuel used. The total cost is obtained by adding the cost of fuel to the other operating costs. This sum is divided by the number of miles traveled to yield the cost per mile. Figure 3.7 displays this algorithm in flowchart form.

Expressing this algorithm in pseudocode is quite straightforward once we select the appropriate variable names to represent the quantities involved. Selecting names that are somewhat self-documenting, we use the following:

Miles	Total miles traveled
Fuel	Total gallons of fuel used
FuelCost	Total cost of fuel
OperCost	Total of other operating costs
Mpg	Miles per gallon
TotalCost	Total cost of the trip
CostPerMile	Cost per mile

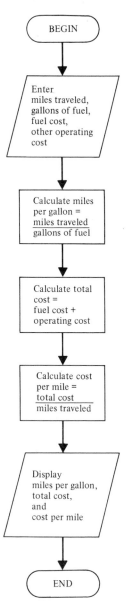

Figure 3.7.

A pseudocode description of the algorithm is the following:

Algorithm to Calculate Truck Costs:
(∗ This algorithm calculates miles per gallon (*Mpg*), total cost of the trip (*TotalCost*), and cost per mile (*CostPerMile*), given the number of miles traveled (*Miles*), gallons of fuel used (*Fuel*), cost of the fuel (*FuelCost*) and other operating costs (*OperCost*). ∗)

    1. Enter *Miles, Fuel, FuelCost,* and *OperCost.*
    2. Calculate *Mpg* = *Miles* / *Fuel.*
    3. Calculate *TotalCost* = *FuelCost* + *OperCost.*

4. Calculate *CostPerMile = TotalCost / Miles.*
5. Display *Mpg, TotalCost,* and *CostPerMile.*

A Pascal program implementing this algorithm with two sample runs using test data to verify its correctness are shown in Figure 3.8.

```
PROGRAM TruckCosts (input, output);

(*********************************************************************

    This program calculates the miles per gallon, total cost, and cost
    per mile for the operation of a vehicle based on the miles traveled,
    fuel consumed, cost of fuel, and other operating costs.

*********************************************************************)

VAR
    Miles : integer;          (* total miles traveled *)
    Fuel,                     (* total gallons of fuel used *)
    FuelCost,                 (* total cost of fuel *)
    OperCost,                 (* total of other operating costs *)
    Mpg,                      (* miles per gallon *)
    TotalCost,                (* total cost of the trip *)
    CostPerMile : real;       (* cost per mile *)

BEGIN
    writeln ('Enter miles traveled, gallons of fuel used,');
    writeln ('total cost of fuel, and total of other costs:');
    readln (Miles, Fuel, FuelCost, OperCost);
    Mpg := Miles / Fuel;
    TotalCost := FuelCost + OperCost;
    CostPerMile := TotalCost / Miles;
    writeln ('Miles per gallon:', Mpg:7:2);
    writeln ('Total cost:       $', TotalCost:7:2);
    writeln ('Cost per mile:  $', CostPerMile:7:2)
END.



Sample runs:
===========


Enter miles traveled, gallons of fuel used,
total cost of fuel, and total of other costs:
10 1 1.50 3.50
Miles per gallon:  10.00
Total cost:      $   5.00
Cost per mile:  $   0.50


Enter miles traveled, gallons of fuel used,
total cost of fuel, and total of other costs:
100 10 15 10
Miles per gallon:  10.00
Total cost:      $  25.00
Cost per mile:  $   0.25
```

Figure 3.8.

Every language has a syntax and semantics. The *syntax* of a language is **Syntax Diagrams** its grammar, that is, the set of rules for forming words and sentences in that language. The interpretation or meaning of the statements in a language is called the *semantics* of the language. A convenient device for describing a language's syntax is the *syntax diagram.* These diagrams are most easily explained by examples, and so we give several in this section.

In Section 3.1 we specified the syntax of a Pascal identifier by stating that it may consist of any number of letters or digits, but it must begin with a letter. This syntax rule is also given by the following syntax diagram:

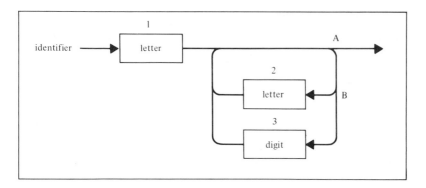

To use this diagram as a syntax rule for forming identifiers, we begin on the left and proceed to the right. Each time we pass through one of the boxes, we record a character of the specified type. At a junction in the diagram, any one of the paths may be followed. When we exit from the right, we will have formed a legal identifier. For example, the identifier *x14a* can be formed as follows: Beginning on the left and passing through the first box, we record the letter *x*. Moving to the right, at Junction A we loop back, passing through Box 3, and record the digit *1*. When we return to Junction A, we loop back again and record the digit *4* when we pass through Box 3. At Junction A we loop back one final time, but this time at Junction B we take the path through Box 2 and record the letter *a*. Finally, at Junction A we proceed to the right and exit, having formed the identifier *x14a*. (We labeled the boxes and junctions of the syntax diagram to facilitate our discussion, though normally such labels are not used.)

A syntax diagram may also be used to specify the syntax of a Pascal statement. For example, a syntax diagram specifying the correct form of an assignment statement is the following:

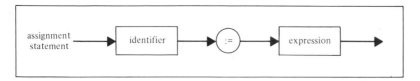

In a syntax diagram such as this one, the rectangular boxes indicate a language construct for which syntax rules must be specified. These syntax rules may also be given by syntax diagrams like that for an identifier. For

example, the following set of syntax diagrams specifies the structure of arithmetic expressions:

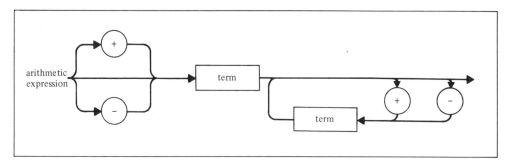

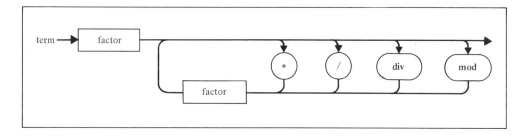

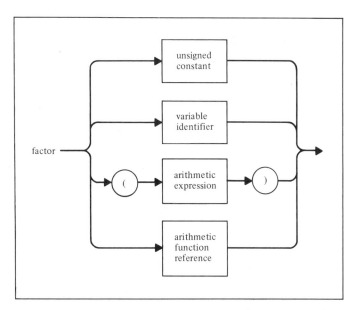

The circles or oval figures in a syntax diagram indicate a symbol or
reserved word in Pascal that must appear exactly as shown. For example,
:= is a symbol that must be used to represent the assignment operator in
an assignment statement, and the reserved word **mod** represents one of the
operators that may be used to combine two factors in a term.

Syntax diagrams may also be used to specify the form of a Pascal
program and its various parts. The basic structure of a Pascal program is
pictured in the following syntax diagram:

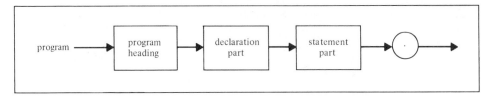

Each of the three parts of a program can also be described by syntax diagrams.
The syntax diagrams

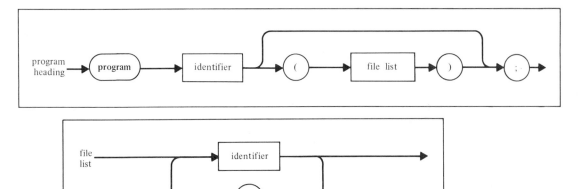

specify the structure of the program heading, and

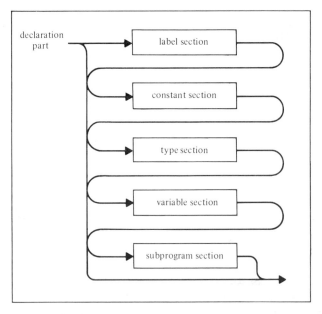

specifies the structure of the declaration part. Syntax diagrams can also be given for the constant section and the variable section in the declaration part.

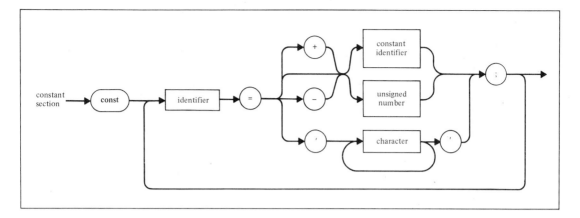

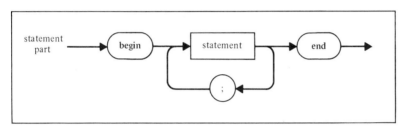

The statement part of a program can be described by the following syntax diagram:

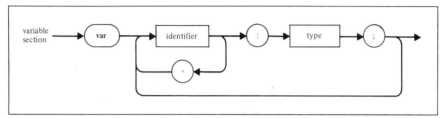

A complete set of syntax diagrams for the various components of a Pascal program is given in Appendix C.

Programming Pointers

In this section we consider some aspects of program design and suggest guidelines for good programming style. We also point out some errors that may occur in writing Pascal programs.

Program Design

1. *Programs cannot be considered correct until they have been validated using test data.* Test all programs with data for which the results are known or can be checked by hand calculations.

2. *Programs should be readable and understandable.*

   - *Use meaningful identifiers.*

For example,

$Wages := Hours * Rate$

is more meaningful than

$W := H * R$

or

$Z7 := Alpha * X$

Also, avoid "cute" identifiers, as in

$BaconBroughtHome := HoursWasted * Pittance$

- *Use comments to describe the purpose of a program or other key program segments.* However, don't clutter the program with needless comments; for example, the comment in the statement

  $Counter := Counter + 1$ (* add 1 to counter *)

  is not helpful and should be omitted.
- *Label all output produced by a program.* For example,

  writeln ('Employee #', *EmpNumber*:5, ' Wages = $', *Wages*:8:2)

  produces more informative output than

  writeln (*EmpNumber*:5, *Wages*:8:2)

3. *Programs should be efficient.* For example, unnecessary computations such as

   $Root1 := (-B + sqrt(B*B - 4*A*C)) / (2*A);$
   $Root2 := (-B - sqrt(B*B - 4*A*C)) / (2*A)$

   should be avoided. It is not efficient to calculate $B*B - 4*A*C$ or its square root twice; calculate it once, assign it to a variable, and then use this variable in these calculations.

4. *Programs should be general and flexible.* They should solve a class of problems rather than one specific problem. It should be relatively easy to modify a program to solve a related problem without changing much of the program. As a simple example, consider the statements

   $Tax := 0.1963 * Wages;$
   $NewBalance := OldBalance + 0.185 * OldBalance$

   Using the specific constants 0.1963 and 0.185 in these statements limits their flexibility; if the tax rate 0.1963 or the interest rate 0.185 is changed, these two statements and others containing these constants must be changed. It is better to associate these constants with constant identifiers

   const
   $TaxRate = 0.1963;$
   $InterestRate = 0.185;$

and then use these identifiers in place of the numeric constants:

Tax := *TaxRate* * *Wages*;
NewBalance := *OldBalance* + *InterestRate* * *OldBalance*

Then only the values of these constant identifiers need be changed when necessary.

Potential Problems

1. *Real constants must have at least one digit before and at least one digit after the decimal point.* Thus, 2. and .1 are not valid real constants.

2. *String constants must be enclosed within single quotes.* If either the beginning or ending quote is missing, an error will result. An apostrophe is represented in a character constant or a string constant as a pair of apostrophes, for example, 'isn''t'.

3. *Parentheses within expressions must be paired.* For each left parenthesis there must be exactly one matching right parenthesis.

4. *Real division is denoted by /, integer division by* **div.** Thus 8 / 5 = 1.6, 8 **div** 5 = 1, 8.0 / 4.0 = 2.0, but 8.0 **div** 4.0 is not a valid expression.

5. *All multiplications must be indicated by* *. For example, 2 * *n* is valid, but 2*n* is not.

6. *A semicolon must appear*
   - *at the end of the program heading.*
   - *at the end of each constant declaration.*
   - *at the end of each variable declaration.*
   - *between statements in a compound statement.*

   For example, the compound statement

   begin
       Sum := *Sum* + *Counter*;
       Counter := *Counter* + 1
   end

   is correct, but

   begin
       Sum := *Sum* + *Counter*
       Counter := *Counter* + 1
   end

   is not. The compound statement

   begin
       Sum := *Sum* + *Counter*;
       Counter := *Counter* + 1;
   end

is valid; the semicolon at the end of the statement *Counter* := *Counter* + 1 produces an *empty statement* between this statement and the reserved word **end.**

7. *Comments are enclosed within* (* *and* *) *or* { *and* }. Each beginning delimiter (* must have a matching end delimiter *). Failure to use these in pairs can produce strange results. For example, in the statement

    > **begin**
    >   (* Read employee data
    >   *readln* (*EmpNumber, Hours, Rate*);
    >   (* Calculate wages *)
    >   *Wages* := *Hours* * *Rate*
    > **end**

    everything from "Read employee data . . ." through "Calculate wages," including the *readln* statement, is a single comment. No values are read for *EmpNumber, Hours* and *Rate,* and so *Hours* and *Rate* are undefined when the statement *Wages* := *Hours* * *Rate* is executed.

8. *There must be a period after the reserved word* **end** *at the end of the program.* Failure to include it usually causes an error.

9. *All identifiers must be declared.* Failure to declare an identifier used in a program is an error.

10. *Pascal does not distinguish between upper-case and lower-case letters except in string constants.* For example, *Sum, sum,* and *SUM* all represent the same identifier. Thus, variable declarations such as

    > **var**
    >   *Sum* : *integer*;
    >   *SUM* : *real*;

    produce an error, since the same identifier is declared more than once.

11. *All variables are initially undefined.* Although some compilers may initialize variables to specific values (e.g., 0 for numeric variables), it should be assumed that all variables are initially undefined. For example, the statement $y := x + 1$ usually produces a "garbage" value for y if x has not previously been assigned a value.

12. *The type of a variable and the type of its value must be the same.* Thus, entering the value 2.7 for the integer variable *Counter* in the statement

    > *readln* (*Counter*)

    may generate an error message such as

*** I/O error while reading input from the terminal.
'.' found where '+', '−', or digit expected.

Similarly, the assignment statement

Counter := 2.7

also is incorrect. An integer value may, however, be assigned to a real variable and is automatically converted to real type.

13. *Reserved words, identifiers, and constants as well as the assignment operator may not be broken at the end of a line nor may they contain blanks, (except, of course, a string constant may contain blanks).* Thus, the statements

EmpNumber := 12345;
writeln ('Employee number is ',
       EmpNumber:5)

are valid, whereas the statements

Emp Number := 12 345;
writeln ('Employee number
      is ', *EmpNumber*:5)

are not valid.

14. *An equal sign (=) is used in constant declarations to associate an identifier with a constant. The assignment operator (:=) is used in assignment statements to assign a value to a variable.* These two operators are not interchangeable; do not confuse them. Also note that := is a single operator; : and = may not be separated by a blank.

Program Style

In the examples in this text, we adopt certain stylistic guidelines for Pascal programs, and you should write your program in a similar style. In this text the following standards are used; others are described in the Programming Pointers of subsequent chapters.

1. *Put each statement of the program on a separate line.*

2. *Put the program heading and the reserved words* **begin, end, const,** *and* **var** *on separate lines.*

3. *When a statement is continued from one line to another, indent the continuation line(s).*

4. *Each* **begin** *and its corresponding* **end** *should be aligned. The statements enclosed by* **begin** *and* **end** *are indented.*

```
begin
    statement-1;
        ⋮
    statement-n
end
```

5. *Indent each constant declaration and each variable declaration; for example,*

```
const
    TaxRate = 0.1963;
    InterestRate = 0.185;
var
    EmpNumber : integer;
    Hours, Rate, Wages : real;
```

6. *Insert a blank line before the* **const** *section, the* **var** *section, the beginning of the statement part of the program, and wherever appropriate in a sequence of statements to set off blocks of statements.*

7. *Use spaces between the items in a statement to make it more readable.*

Exercises

1. Write a program that reads two three-digit integers and then calculates and prints their sum and their difference. The output should be formatted to appear as follows:

```
      456           456
   +  123        -  123
   - - - - -     - - - - -
      579           333
```

2. Write a program that reads two three-digit integers and then calculates and prints their product and the quotient and the remainder that result when the first is divided by the second. The output should be formatted to appear as follows:

```
      739                  61 R    7
   X   12              - - - - -
   - - - - -        12 )  739
      8868
```

3. The shipping clerk at the Rinky Dooflingy Company (Exercise 8 of Section 2.4) is faced with the following problem. Dooflingies are very delicate and must be shipped in special containers. These containers are available in four sizes, huge, large, medium, and small, which can hold 50, 20, 5, and 1 dooflingy, respectively. Write a program that reads the number of dooflingies to be shipped and prints the number of huge, large, medium, and small containers needed to send the shipment in the minimum number of containers. Use constant definitions for the number of dooflingies each type of container can hold. The output should be similar to the following:

Container	Number
Huge	211
Large	2
Medium	1
Small	3

Execute the program for 3, 18, 48, 78, and 10598 dooflingies.

4. Write a program to read the lengths of the two legs of a right triangle, and calculate and print the area of the triangle (one half of the product of the legs) and the length of the hypotenuse (square root of the sum of the squares of the legs).

5. Write a program to read values for the coefficients A, B, and C of the quadratic equation $Ax^2 + Bx + C = 0$, and then find the two roots of this equation by using the quadratic formula

$$\frac{-B \pm \sqrt{B^2 - 4AC}}{2A}$$

Execute the program with several values of A, B, and C for which the quantity $B^2 - 4AC$ is nonnegative including $A = 4$, $B = 0$, $C = -36$; $A = 1$, $B = 5$, $C = -36$; $A = 2$, $B = 7.5$, $C = 6.25$.

6. Write a program to convert a measurement given in feet to the equivalent number of (a) yards, (b) inches, (c) centimeters, and (d) meters. (1 ft = 12 in., 1 yd = 3 ft, 1 in. = 2.54 cm, 1 m = 100 cm) Read the number of feet, and print the number of yards, number of feet, number of inches, number of centimeters, and number of meters, with appropriate labels.

7. Write a program to read values for the three sides a, b, and c of a triangle, and then calculate its perimeter and its area. These should be printed together with the values of a, b, and c, using appropriate labels. Execute the program with several values of a, b, and c for which the sum of any two of the values is greater than the third; sample values are $a = 3$, $b = 4$, $c = 5$; $a = 1$, $b = 1$, $c = 1$; $a = 5.1$, $b = 15$, $c = 10.05$. (For the area, you might use Hero's formula for the area of a triangle:

$$\text{area} = \sqrt{s(s-a)(s-b)(s-c)}$$

where s is one half the perimeter.)

8. Write a program to read a student's number, his or her old GPA (grade point average), and old number of course credits (for example, 31479, 3.25, 66), and then print these with appropriate labels. Finally, read in the course credit and grade for each of four courses; for example, $Course1 = 5.0$, $Grade1 = 3.7$, $Course2 = 3.0$, $Grade2 = 4.0$, and so on. Calculate:

old # of honor points = (old # of course credits) * (old GPA)

new # of honor points = *Course1* * *Grade1* + *Course2* * *Grade2* + $\cdots$
total # of new course credits = *Course1* + *Course2* + $\cdots$

$$\text{current GPA} = \frac{\text{\# of new honor points}}{\text{\# of new course credits}}$$

Print the current GPA with appropriate label. Then calculate

$$\text{cumulative GPA} = \frac{(\text{\# of old honor points}) + (\text{\# of new honor points})}{(\text{\# of old course credits}) + (\text{\# of new course credits})}$$

and print this with a label.

9. Write a program that reads the amount of a purchase and the amount received in payment, (both amounts in cents) and that then computes the change in dollars, half-dollars, quarters, dimes, nickels, and pennies.

10. Angles are often measured in degrees (°), minutes ('), and seconds ("). There are 360 degrees in a circle, 60 minutes in one degree, and 60 seconds in one minute. Write a program that reads two angular measurements given in degrees, minutes, and seconds, and then calculates and prints their sum. Use the program to verify each of the following:

   74°29'13" + 105°8'16" = 179°37'29"
   7°14'55" + 5°24'55" = 12°39'50"
   20°31'19" + 0°31'30" = 21°2'49"
   122°17'48" + 237°42'12" = 0°0'0"

11. Write a program that reads two three-digit integers and then prints their product in the following format:

```
        749
X       381
-------
        749
   5992
 2247
-------
 285369
```

Execute the program with the following values: 749 and 381; −749 and 381; 749 and −381; −749 and −381; 999 and 999.

4

Control Structures

A journey of a thousand miles begins with a single step.

ANCIENT PROVERB

Then Logic would take you by the throat, and force you to do it!

ACHILLES IN LEWIS CARROLL'S
What the Tortoise Said to Achilles

But what has been said once can always be repeated.

ZENO OF ELEA

There are a number of techniques that assist in the design of programs that are easy to understand and whose logical flow is easy to follow. Such programs are more likely to be correct when first written than are poorly structured programs; and if they are not correct, the errors are easier to find and correct. Such programs are also easier to modify, which is especially important, since such modifications are often made by someone other than the original programmer.

In a *structured program,* the logical flow is governed by three basic control structures:

1. Sequential.
2. Repetition.
3. Selection.

In this chapter we consider these control structures and their implementation in Pascal.

4.1 Sequential Structure: Compound Statements; begin and end

Sequential structure, as illustrated in Figure 4.1, refers to the execution of statements in the order in which they appear. The sample programs in Chapter 3 are all "straight-line" programs in which the only control used is sequential. In this section we consider the implementation of sequential structure as a compound statement in Pascal.

87

Figure 4.1.
Sequential structure

A *compound statement* is a sequence of statements preceded by the reserved word **begin** and followed by the reserved word **end.** The statements that make up the compound statement are separated by semicolons. It thus has the form

>**begin**
>>*statement*-1;
>>*statement*-2;
>>⋮
>>*statement-n*
>
>**end**

Execution of the statements in a compound statement proceeds sequentially. For example, the compound statement

>**begin**
>>*writeln* ('Enter two numbers:');
>>*readln* (*Number1, Number2*);
>>*Sum* := *Number1* + *Number2*;
>>*writeln* ('Sum = ', *Sum*)
>
>**end**

first displays a prompt to the user and then reads two numbers whose sum is then calculated and displayed.

CONTROL STRUCTURES

The following syntax diagram displays the form of a compound statement.

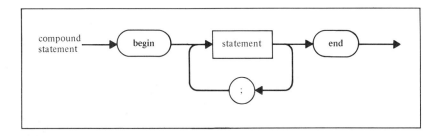

A *repetition structure* or *loop* makes possible repeated execution of one or more statements. This repetition must be controlled so that these statements are executed only a finite number of times. Pascal provides three statements that implement repetition structures: the **for** statement, the **while** statement, and the **repeat** statement. In this section we consider the first of these three statements.

Repetition Structure: The for Statement

The **for** statement has either the form

> **for** *index-variable* := *initial-value* **to** *final-value* **do**
>> *statement*

or

> **for** *index-variable* := *initial-value* **downto** *final-value* **do**
>> *statement*

In these forms, the index variable, the initial value, and the final value must all be of the same type, which may be integer, character, or boolean (or other types as described in Chapter 7). In the examples of this chapter they are always of integer type. The initial value and the final value may be any valid Pascal expressions. The syntax diagram for a **for** statement is

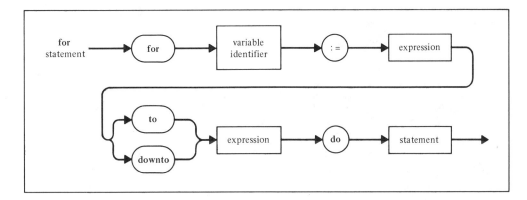

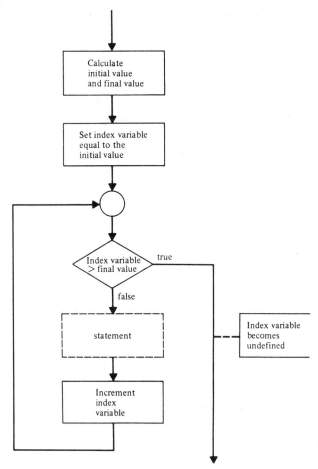

Figure 4.2.
for — **to** Repetition Structure.

A **for** statement of the form

> **for** *index-variable* := *initial-value* **to** *final-value* **do**
>   *statement*

implements the repetition structure shown in Figure 4.2. As the flowchart shows, when a **for** statement of this form is executed, the index variable is assigned the initial value, and the specified statement is executed unless the initial value is greater than the final value. The index variable is incremented, and if this new value does not exceed the final value, the statement is executed again. Thus the specified statement is executed for each value of the index variable from the initial value up to and including the final value.

To illustrate, consider the statement

> **for** *Number* := 1 **to** 10 **do**
>   *writeln* (*Number*:2, *sqr*(*Number*):5)

where *Number* is of integer type. In this statement, *Number* is the index variable, the initial value is 1, and the final value is 10. When this statement is executed, the initial value 1 is assigned to *Number,* and the *writeln* statement is executed. The value of *Number* is then increased by 1, and because this new value 2 is less than the final value 10, the *writeln* statement is executed again. This repetition continues as long as the value of the index variable

Number is less than or equal to the final value 10. Thus, the output produced by this statement is

```
 1    1
 2    4
 3    9
 4   16
 5   25
 6   36
 7   49
 8   64
 9   81
10  100
```

The statement that appears within a **for** statement may be a compound statement. For example, the statements

```
Sum := 0;
for Count := 1 to 5 do
    begin
        readln (Score);
        Sum := Sum + Score
    end (* for *)
```

read five scores and calculate their sum. If the data

```
80
70
83
95
77
```

are entered, the first value read for *Score* is 80. Since the initial value of *Sum* is 0, the statement

```
Sum := Sum + Score
```

within the for loop evaluates the expression $0 + 80 = 80$ and assigns this value to *Sum*. The next value read for *Score* is 70, and the assignment statement then evaluates the expression $Sum + Score = 80 + 70 = 150$ and assigns this value to *Sum*. This process of reading a value for *Score* and adding it to the previous value of *Sum* continues until the value of the index variable *Count* reaches 6, which is greater than the final value 5. Repetition of the *readln* and assignment statements is then terminated, at which time *Sum* has the value 405.

In the second form of the **for** statement

> **for** *index-variable* := *initial-value* **downto** *final-value* **do**
>   *statement*

the index variable is decremented rather than incremented, and repetition continues as long as the value of the index variable is greater than or equal to the final value. This is illustrated in the flowchart in Figure 4.3.

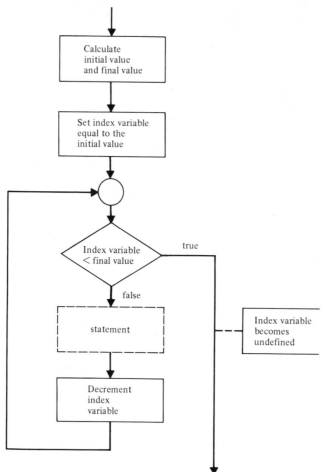

Figure 4.3.
for — downto
Repetition Structure

For example, consider the statement

for *Number* := 10 **downto** 1 **do**
  writeln (*Number*:2, *sqr*(*Number*):5)

The index variable *Number* is assigned the initial value 10, and because this value is greater than the final value 1, the *writeln* statement is executed. The value of *Number* is then decreased to 9, and because this new value is greater than the final value, the *writeln* statement is executed again. This process continues as long as the value of *Number* is greater than or equal to the final value 1. Thus, the output produced is

```
10   100
 9    81
 8    64
 7    49
 6    36
 5    25
 4    16
 3     9
 2     4
 1     1
```

Note that in this form of the **for** statement, **downto** is a single word.

As Figures 4.2 and 4.3 illustrate, the value of the index variable is compared with the final value *before* the specified statement is executed. Thus, in the first form of the **for** statement, if the initial value is greater than the final value, the specified statement is never executed. This is also the case in the second form if the initial value is less than the final value.

The initial and/or final values in a **for** statement may be variables or expressions. To illustrate, consider the statements

> *writeln* ('Enter table size:');
> *readln* (*TableSize*);
> **for** *Number* := 1 **to** *TableSize* **do**
>   *writeln* (*Number*:4, *sqr*(*Number*):8);

The value entered for *TableSize* is the final value in this **for** statement. These statements are used in the program of Figure 4.4 to print a table of squares whose size is read during program execution.

```
PROGRAM TableOfSquares (input, output);

(***********************************************************************

    This program prints a table of integers and their squares.
    The size of the table is entered during execution.

 **********************************************************************)

VAR
    TableSize,          (* number of rows in table *)
    Number : integer;   (* number whose square is calculated *)

BEGIN
    writeln ('Enter table size:');
    readln (TableSize);
    writeln;
    writeln ('Number  Square');
    writeln ('======  ======');
    FOR Number := 1 TO TableSize DO
        writeln (Number:4, sqr(Number):8)
END.

Sample run:
==========

Enter table size:
10

Number  Square
======  ======
   1       1
   2       4
   3       9
   4      16
   5      25
   6      36
   7      49
   8      64
   9      81
  10     100
```

Figure 4.4.

The initial and final values are determined before repetition begins and changing them during execution of the **for** statement does not affect the number of repetitions. Also, the statement within a **for** statement may use the value of the index variable, though *it must not modify the value of the index variable. When execution of the **for** statement is completed, the index variable becomes undefined.* Using this variable before assigning it a value yields unpredictable results.

The statement that appears within a **for** statement may itself be a **for** statement. In this case, one **for** statement is said to be "nested" within another **for** statement. As an example, consider the program in Figure 4.5 that calcu-

```
PROGRAM Products (input, output);

(*******************************************************************

   This program calculates and displays a list of products
   of two numbers.

********************************************************************)

VAR
   X, Y,                (* two numbers being multiplied *)
   LastX, LastY,        (* last values of X and Y, respectively *)
   Product : integer;   (* product of X and Y *)

BEGIN
   writeln ('Enter upper limits for factors of product:');
   readln (LastX, LastY);
   writeln;
   FOR X := 1 TO LastX DO
      FOR Y := 1 TO LastY DO
         BEGIN
            Product := X * Y;
            writeln (X:2, ' *', Y:2, ' =', Product:3)
         END
END.


Sample run:
==========

Enter upper limits for factors of product:
4 4

1 * 1 =   1
1 * 2 =   2
1 * 3 =   3
1 * 4 =   4
2 * 1 =   2
2 * 2 =   4
2 * 3 =   6
2 * 4 =   8
3 * 1 =   3
3 * 2 =   6
3 * 3 =   9
3 * 4 =  12
4 * 1 =   4
4 * 2 =   8
4 * 3 =  12
4 * 4 =  16
```

Figure 4.5.

CONTROL STRUCTURES

lates and displays products of the form $X * Y$ for X ranging from 1 through *LastX* and Y ranging from 1 through *LastY* for integers *LastX* and *LastY*. The table of products is generated by the **for** statement

```
for X := 1 to LastX do
    for Y := 1 to LastY do
        begin
            Product := X * Y;
            writeln (X:2, ' *', Y:2, ' =', Product:3)
        end
```

In the sample run, *LastX* and *LastY* are both assigned the value 4. The index variable X is assigned its initial value 1, and the statement

```
for Y := 1 to LastY do
    begin
        Product := X * Y;
        writeln (X:2, ' *', Y:2, ' =', Product:3)
    end
```

is executed. This calculates and displays the first four products $1 * 1$, $1 * 2$, $1 * 3$, and $1 * 4$. The value of X is then incremented by 1, and the preceding **for** statement is executed again. This calculates and displays the next four products, $2 * 1$, $2 * 2$, $2 * 3$, and $2 * 4$. The index variable X is then incremented to 3, producing the next four products, $3 * 1$, $3 * 2$, $3 * 3$, and $3 * 4$, and finally X is incremented to 4, giving the last four products, $4 * 1$, $4 * 2$, $4 * 3$, and $4 * 4$.

4.3

Boolean Expressions

As noted in the preceding section, Pascal provides three statements to implement repetition structures: the **for** statement, the **while** statement, and the **repeat** statement. In a **while** statement, repetition continues while some boolean expression is true. In a **repeat** statement, repetition continues until some boolean expression becomes true. Consequently, before we can describe the **while** and **repeat** statements, we must explain how boolean expressions are formed and evaluated.

Recall that there are two boolean constants, *true* and *false*, and that boolean variables may have only these values. A boolean variable is declared in the variable section, using the standard type identifier *boolean* to specify its type; for example,

```
var
    Male, Adult, Graduate : boolean;
```

declares that *Male, Adult,* and *Graduate* are boolean variables.

Boolean expressions are formed by combining boolean constants, boolean variables, and other boolean expressions by using the *boolean operators* **not**, **and**, and **or**. These operators are defined as follows:

Boolean Operator	Boolean Expression	Definition
not	**not** *p*	*negation* of *p:* **not** *p* is false if *p* is true; **not** *p* is true if *p* is false.
and	*p* **and** *q*	*conjunction* of *p* and *q: p* **and** *q* is true if *p* and *q* both are true; it is false otherwise.
or	*p* **or** *q*	*disjunction* of *p* and *q: p* **or** *q is true if either p* or *q* or both are true; it is false otherwise.

These definitions are summarized by the following *truth tables,* which display all possible values for *p* and *q* and the corresponding values of the boolean expression:

p	**not** *p*
true	false
false	true

p	*q*	*p* **and** *q*
true	true	true
true	false	false
false	true	false
false	false	false

p	*q*	*p* **or** *q*
true	true	true
true	false	true
false	true	true
false	false	false

In a boolean expression containing several of these operators, the operations are performed in the order **not, and, or.** Parentheses may be used to indicate subexpressions that should be evaluated first. For example, given the boolean variables *Adult, Male,* and *Graduate,* we can form boolean expressions such as

> *Adult* **and** *Male*
> **not** *Male* **and** *Graduate*
> (*Adult* **or** *Male*) **and** *Graduate*

The first expression *Adult* **and** *Male* is true only in the case that *Adult* and *Male* both are true. In the second example, the subexpression **not** *Male* is evaluated first, and this result is then combined with the value of *Graduate,* using the operator **and.** The entire expression is therefore true only in the case that *Male* is false and *Graduate* is true. In the last example, the subexpression *Adult* **or** *Male* is evaluated first, and this result is then combined with the value of *Graduate,* using the operator **and.** Thus the entire expression is true only in the case that *Graduate* is true and either *Adult* or *Male* (or both) is true. This is summarized in the following truth table:

Adult	Male	Graduate	(Adult **or** Male) **and** Graduate
true	true	true	true
true	true	false	false
true	false	true	true
true	false	false	false
false	true	true	true
false	true	false	false
false	false	true	false
false	false	false	false

Boolean expressions may also be formed by using *relational operators* which compare two values of the same type. In Pascal there are six relational operators:

Relational Operator	Definition
<	is less than (or precedes)
>	is greater than (or follows)
=	is equal to
<=	is less than or equal to
>=	is greater than or equal to
<>	is not equal to

These relational operators may be applied to any of the four standard data types: integer, real, boolean, and character. The following are examples of boolean expressions formed using these relational operators:

$$x < 5.2$$
$$sqr(b) >= 4*a*c$$
$$Number = 500$$
$$Initial <> \text{'Q'}$$

For numeric data, the relational operators are the standard ones used to compare numbers. Thus, if x has the value 4.5, the expression $x < 5.2$ is true. If *Number* has the value 400, the expression *Number* = 500 is false.

When using the relational operators = and <> to compare numeric quantities, it is important to remember that *most real values cannot be stored exactly* (see Section 1.3). *Consequently, boolean expressions formed by comparing real quantities with = are often evaluated as false, even though these quantities are algebraically equal.* This is illustrated by the program in Figure 4.14.

For character data, a *collating sequence* is used to establish an ordering for the character set. This sequence varies from one machine to another, but in all cases, letters are in alphabetical order, and digits are in numerical order. Thus

$$'A' < 'F'$$
$$'6' > '4'$$

are true boolean expressions. Comparison of characters and strings is discussed in more detail in Chapter 8.

For boolean values, the constant *false* is less than the constant *true*. Thus,

$$false < true$$
$$true > false$$

are true boolean expressions.

The evaluation of a boolean expression that contains an assortment of arithmetic operators, boolean operators, and relational operators is carried out using the following precedence levels:

Operator	Priority
not	high (performed first)
/, *, div, mod, and	
+, −, or	
<, >, =, <=, >=, <>	low (performed last)

As an example, suppose that we wish to determine whether the value of the real variable x is strictly between 1.0 and the real value $z + 7.0$. The appropriate boolean expression is

$$(1.0 < x) \text{ and } (x < z + 7.0)$$

If the parentheses are omitted, the resulting expression

$$1.0 < x \text{ and } x < z + 7.0$$

is equivalent to the expression

$$1.0 < (x \text{ and } x) < (z + 7.0)$$

since the highest-priority operator **and** is evaluated first. This is clearly not a valid expression because the boolean operator **and** cannot be applied to numeric operands.

Exercises

1. Assuming that a, b, and c are boolean variables, use truth tables to display the values of the following boolean expressions for all possible values of a, b, and c:

   (a) a **or not** b **(b) not**(a **and** b)

   (c) not a **or not** b **(d)** a **and** *true* **or** $(1 + 2 = 4)$

   (e) a **and** (b **or** c)   **(f)** (a **and** b) **or** (a **and** c)

2. Write boolean expressions to express the following conditions:

   (a) x is greater than 3.

   (b) y is strictly between 2 and 5.

   (c) r is negative and z is positive.

   (d) *Alpha* and *Beta* both are positive.

   (e) *Alpha* and *Beta* have the same sign (both are negative or both are positive).

   (f) $-5 < x < 5$.

   (g) a is less than 6 or is greater than 10.

   (h) $p = q = r$.

   (i) x is less than 3, or y is less than 3, but not both.

3. Given the boolean variables a, b, and c, write a boolean expression that is

   (a) true if and only if a and b are true and c is false.

   (b) true if and only if a is true and at least one of b or c is true.

   (c) true if and only if exactly one of a and b is true.

4.4
Repetition Structure: The while Statement

The **for** statement described in Section 4.2 can be used to implement a repetition structure in which the number of iterations is determined before execution of the **for** statement. In some cases a repetition structure is required for which the number of iterations is not known in advance but in which repetition continues while some boolean expression remains true. Such a structure is illustrated in flowchart form in Figure 4.6 and can be implemented in Pascal by using the **while** statement.

The **while** statement has the form

while *boolean-expression* **do**
      statement

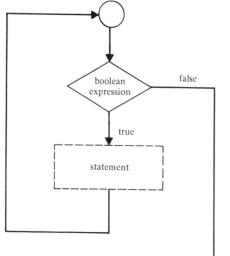

Figure 4.6.
The **while** Repetition
Structure.

Its syntax diagram is

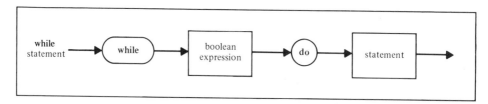

When a **while** statement is executed, the boolean expression is evaluated, and if true, the statement following the **do** is executed. The boolean expression is then reevaluated, and if still true, the statement is executed again. This process of evaluating the boolean expression and executing the specified statement is repeated as long as the boolean expression is true. When it becomes false, repetition is terminated. Note that this means that execution of the statement within the **while** statement must eventually cause the value of the boolean expression to become false, since otherwise repetition would continue *ad infinitum.*

To demonstrate the use of the **while** statement, consider the following problem:

For a given value of *Limit,* what is the smallest positive integer *Number* for which the sum

$$1 + 2 + \cdots + Number$$

is greater than *Limit,* and what is the value of this sum?

The following algorithm solves this problem:

Algorithm
(* Algorithm to find the smallest positive integer *Number* for which the sum $1 + 2 + \cdots + Number$ is greater than *Limit.* *)

1. Enter *Limit.*
2. Set *Number* equal to 0.
3. Set *Sum* equal to 0.
4. While *Sum* ≤ *Limit* do the following:
   a. Increase *Number* by 1.
   b. Add *Number* to *Sum.*
5. Display *Number* and *Sum.*

In the program in Figure 4.7, the repetition structure in Step 4 is implemented by the **while** statement

```
PROGRAM Summation (input, output);

(*********************************************************************

    Program to find the smallest positive integer Number for which
    the sum
                      1 + 2 + ... + Number
    is greater than the value of a specified number Limit.  It also
    displays the value of this sum.

 *********************************************************************)

VAR
    Number,           (* positive integer added to the sum *)
    Sum,              (* 1 + 2 + ... + Number *)
    Limit : integer;  (* limit for sum *)

BEGIN
    writeln ('Enter value that 1 + 2 + ... + ? is to exceed:');
    readln (Limit);
    writeln;
    Number := 0;
    Sum := 0;
    WHILE Sum <= Limit DO
       BEGIN
          Number := Number + 1;
          Sum := Sum + Number
       END (* WHILE *);
    writeln ('1 + ... + ', Number:1, ' = ', Sum:1)
END.



Sample runs:
===========

Enter value that 1 + 2 + ... + ? is to exceed:
10

1 + ... + 5 = 15



Enter value that 1 + 2 + ... + ? is to exceed:
10000

1 + ... + 141 = 10011
```

Figure 4.7.

```
    while Sum <= Limit do
        begin
            Number := Number + 1;
            Sum := Sum + Number
        end (* while *);
```

As Figure 4.6 illustrates, the boolean expression in a **while** statement is evaluated before repetition begins. Thus, if the boolean expression is initially false, the specified statement is not executed. Thus, in the summation program in Figure 4.7, if the value −1 were entered for *Limit,* the **while** statement would cause an immediate transfer of control to the *writeln* statement which would display the value 0 for both *Number* and *Sum.*

As another example which uses a repetition structure in which the number of iterations is not known in advance, we now develop a program to calculate the mean of a set of test scores. The program is to be used with sets of scores from various classes. Since the number of students in each class is not known in advance, the program should count the number of scores being averaged.

In this problem, the input is a set of real scores, one for each student in the class. The output is the number of students in the class and the mean score. An algorithm for solving the problem consists of reading a score, counting it, and adding it to the sum of scores previously read. This must be repeated for each student. In this example, we append to the data an artificial value called a *flag* or *sentinel,* which is distinct from any possible valid data item. As each data item is read, it is checked to determine if it is this end-of-data flag. When the end of data is reached, the repetition is terminated, the mean is calculated, and the desired information is displayed.

Algorithm

(* Algorithm to read a list of scores, count them, and find the mean score (*MeanScore*); *Score* represents the current score read, *NumScores* is the number of scores, and *Sum* is the sum of the scores. Scores are read until the end-of-data flag is encountered. *)

1. Set *Sum* equal to 0.
2. Set *NumScores* equal to 0.
3. Read first *Score.*
4. While *Score* is not the end-of-data flag do the following:
   a. Add 1 to *NumScores.*
   b. Add *Score* to *Sum.*
   c. Read next *Score.*
5. Calculate *MeanScore* = *Sum* / *NumScores.*
6. Display *MeanScore* and *NumScores.*

```
PROGRAM CalculateMeanScore (input, output);

(*************************************************************************

    This program reads in a list of scores, counts them, and
    calculates the mean score.  Any negative number serves as
    an end-of-data flag.

*************************************************************************)
```

Figure 4.8.

CONTROL STRUCTURES

Fig. 4.8. (cont.)

```
VAR
    NumScores : integer;     (* number of scores *)
    Sum,                     (* sum of the scores *)
    Score,                   (* current score being processed *)
    MeanScore : real;        (* mean of the scores *)

BEGIN
    writeln ('*** Enter a negative score to signal the end of input.');
    writeln;
    Sum := 0;
    NumScores := 0;
    writeln ('Score:');
    readln (Score);
    WHILE Score >= 0 DO
        BEGIN
            NumScores := NumScores +1;
            Sum := Sum + Score;
            writeln ('Score:');
            readln (Score)
        END;
    MeanScore := Sum / NumScores;
    writeln;
    writeln (NumScores:1, ' scores with mean = ', MeanScore:5:2)
END.
```

```
Sample runs:
==========

*** Enter a negative score to signal the end of input.

    Score:
    60
    Score:
    70
    Score:
    80
    Score:
    -1

    3 scores with mean = 70.00


    *** Enter a negative score to signal the end of input.

    Score:
    55
    Score:
    86.5
    Score:
    79.5
    Score:
    86
    Score:
    84
    Score:
    55
    Score:
    97.5
    Score:
    100
    Score:
    57
    Score:
    83.5
    Score:
    72
    Score:
    -1

    11 scores with mean = 77.82
```

In the Pascal program in Figure 4.8 that implements this algorithm, a negative score is used as an end-of-data flag, and the repetition structure in Step 4 is implemented as a **while** statement controlled by the boolean expression *Score* >= 0.

Repetition Structure: The repeat Statement

In addition to the **for** and **while** statements, Pascal provides a third statement for implementing repetition structures. Recall that the **for** statement is used when the number of iterations can be determined before repetition begins. The **while** statement implements a repetition structure in which the number of iterations cannot be determined in advance but is instead controlled by a boolean expression. The boolean expression in a **while** statement is evaluated before execution of the specified statement begins. But sometimes it is appropriate to execute a statement or statements before evaluating the boolean expression that controls the repetition. This can be accomplished in Pascal by using the **repeat** statement.

The **repeat** statement has the form

> **repeat**
>   *statement-1*;
>   *statement-2*;
>   ⋮
>   *statement-n*
> **until** *boolean expression*

and implements the repetition structure shown in Figure 4.9. A syntax diagram for this statement is

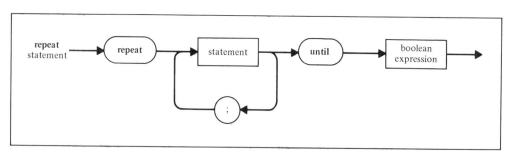

When a **repeat** statement is executed, the specified statements *statement-1, statement-2, . . . , statement-n* are executed, and the *boolean expression* is evaluated. If its value is true, execution continues with the next statement in the program; otherwise, the specified statements are executed again. This repetition continues until the boolean expression becomes true.

To illustrate the **repeat** statement, we reconsider the problem of finding the smallest positive integer *Number* for which the sum $1 + 2 + \cdots + Number$ is greater than some specified value *Limit*. Suppose that the algorithm given earlier is modified as follows:

Algorithm

(* Algorithm to find the smallest positive integer *Number* for which the sum $1 + 2 + \cdots + Number$ is greater than *Limit*. *)

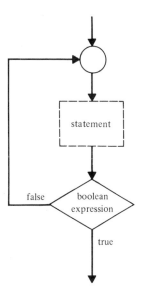

Figure 4.9.
The **repeat–until**
Repetition Structure.

1. Enter *Limit.*
2. Set *Number* equal to 0.
3. Set *Sum* equal to 0.
4. Repeat the following until *Sum* > *Limit.*
   a. Increase *Number* by 1.
   b. Add *Number* to *Sum.*
5. Display *Number* and *Sum.*

For this algorithm, it is appropriate to implement the repetition structure in Step 4 by a **repeat** statement, as shown in the program in Figure 4.10.

```
repeat
    Number := Number + 1;
    Sum := Sum + Number
until Sum > Limit;
```

Any number of statements separated by semicolons may be placed between the reserved words **repeat** and **until.** Since these reserved words clearly mark the beginning and the end of this statement, it is not necessary to use the reserved words **begin** and **end** for this purpose, as was required for the **while** statement.

A more important feature that distinguishes the **repeat** statement from the **while** statement is that the boolean expression is evaluated *after* the specified statements, *not before.* This means that *these statements are always executed at least once.* Thus, for the **repeat** statement

```
repeat
    Number := Number + 1;
    Sum := Sum + Number
until Sum > Limit;
```

in the program in Figure 4.10, the two statements *Number* := *Number* + 1 and *Sum* := *Sum* + *Number* are always executed at least once, regardless of the value of *Limit.*

```
PROGRAM Summation (input, output);

(*********************************************************************

    Program to find the smallest positive integer Number for which
    the sum
                        1 + 2 + ... + Number
    is greater than the value of a specified number Limit.  It also
    displays the value of this sum.

*********************************************************************)

VAR
    Number,             (* positive integer added to the sum *)
    Sum,                (* 1 + 2 + ... + Number *)
    Limit : integer;    (* limit for sum *)
BEGIN
    writeln ('Enter value that 1 + 2 + ... + ? is to exceed:');
    readln (Limit);
    Number := 0;
    Sum := 0;
    REPEAT
        Number := Number + 1;
        Sum := Sum + Number
    UNTIL Sum > Limit;
    writeln ('1 + ... + ', Number:1, ' = ', Sum:1)
END.


Sample runs:
===========

Enter value that 1 + 2 + ... + ? is to exceed:
15
1 + ... + 6 = 21


Enter value that 1 + 2 + ... + ? is to exceed:
10000
1 + ... + 141 = 10011
```

Figure 4.10.

Exercises

1. Assuming that *I, J,* and *K* are integer variables, describe the output
   produced by each of the following program segments:

   (a) for *I* := 1 **to** 3 **do**
         for *J* := 1 **to** 3 **do**
            for *K* := *I* **to** *J* **do**
               writeln (*I*:1, *J*:1, *K*:1);

   (b) *K* := 5;
       for *I* := 1 **to** *K* **do**
           begin
              writeln (*I* + *K*:2);
              K := 2
           end;

(c) K := 5;
    I := -2;
    while I <= K do
        begin
            I := I + 2;
            K := K - 1;
            writeln (I + K:2)
        end;

(d) I := -2;
    repeat
        K := I * I * I - 3 * I + 1;
        writeln (I:3, K:3)
    until I > 2;

2. Write a Pascal statement to

(a) Print the value of *x* and decrease *x* by 0.5 as long as *x* is positive.

(b) Read values for *a*, *b*, and *c* and print their sum, repeating this as long as none of *a*, *b*, or *c* is negative.

(c) Read values for *a*, *b*, and *c*, and print their sum, repeating this until at least one of *a*, *b*, or *c* is negative.

(d) Print the squares of the first 100 positive integers in increasing order.

(e) Print the cubes of the first 50 positive integers in decreasing order.

(f) Print the square roots of the first 25 odd positive integers.

(g) Calculate and print the squares of consecutive positive integers until the difference between a square and the preceding one is greater than 50.

(h) Print a list of points (*x*, *y*) on the graph of $y = x^3 - 3x + 1$ for *x* ranging from -2 to 2 in steps of 0.1.

3. Write a program that uses nested **for** statements to print the following multiplication table:

```
    1   2   3   4   5   6   7   8  9
1   1
2   2   4
3   3   6   9
4   4   8  12  16
5   5  10  15  20  25
6   6  12  18  24  30  36
7   7  14  21  28  35  42  49
8   8  16  24  32  40  48  56  64
9   9  18  27  36  45  54  63  72 81
```

REPETITION STRUCTURE: THE REPEAT STATEMENT

4. Write a program that prints two temperature conversion tables. Use a **while** statement to calculate and print the Celsius equivalents of all Fahrenheit temperatures at 5 degree intervals from 120 to 140 degrees. Use a **repeat** statement to calculate and print the Fahrenheit equivalents to all Celsius temperatures at 3 degree intervals from 50 to −40 degrees. The table columns should be labelled and aligned. (The conversion formula is $F = \frac{9}{5}C + 32$.)

5. Write a program to read data values as shown in the following table, calculate the miles per gallon in each case, and print the values with appropriate labels.

Miles Traveled	Gallons of Gasoline Used
231	14.8
248	15.1
302	12.8
147	9.25
88	7
265	13.3

6. Write a program to read several real values representing miles, convert miles to kilometers (1 mile = 1.60935 kilometers), and print all values with appropriate labels.

7. One method of calculating depreciation is the *sum-of-the-years-digits* method. Suppose that $15,000 is to be depreciated over a five-year period. We first calculate the sum $1 + 2 + 3 + 4 + 5 = 15$. Then 5/15 of $15,000 ($5,000) is depreciated the first year, 4/15 of $15,000 ($4,000) is depreciated the second year, 3/15 the third year, and so on.

   Write a program that reads the amount to be depreciated and the number of years over which it is to be depreciated, for example, 7000 dollars over 10 years. Then for each year number from 1 through the indicated number of years, print the year number and the amount to be depreciated for that year.

8. The Rinky Dooflingy Company (Exercise 8 of Chapter 2) currently sells 200 dooflingies per month at a profit of $300 per dooflingy. The company now spends $2000 per month on advertising and has fixed operating costs of $1000 per month which do not depend on the volume of sales. If the company doubles the amount spent on advertising, sales will increase by 20 percent. Write a program that prints under appropriate headings the amount spent on advertising, the number of sales made, and the net profit. Begin with the company's current status and successively double the amount spent on advertising until the net profit "goes over the hump," that is, begins to decline. The output should include the amounts up through the first time that the net profit begins to decline.

CONTROL STRUCTURES

9. Write a program to read a set of numbers, count them, and calculate and display the mean, variance, and standard deviation of the set of numbers. The *mean* and *variance* of numbers $x_1, x_2, \ldots, x_n$ can be calculated using the formulas

$$\text{mean} = \frac{1}{n} \sum_{i=1}^{n} x_i, \quad \text{variance} = \frac{1}{n} \sum_{i=1}^{n} x_i^2 - \frac{1}{n^2} \left(\sum_{i=1}^{n} x_i \right)^2$$

The *standard deviation* is the square root of the variance.

10. The sequence of *Fibonacci numbers* begins with the integers

1, 1, 2, 3, 5, 8, 13, 21, . . .

where each number after the first two is the sum of the two preceding numbers. In this sequence, the ratios of consecutive Fibonacci numbers (1/1, 1/2, 2/3, 3/5, . . .) approach the "golden ratio"

$$\frac{\sqrt{5} - 1}{2}$$

Write a program to calculate all the Fibonacci numbers smaller than 5000 and the decimal values of the ratios of consecutive Fibonacci numbers.

11. Suppose that at a given time, genotypes AA, AB, and BB appear in the proportions x, y, and z, respectively, where $x = 0.25$, $y = 0.5$, and $z = 0.25$. If individuals of type AA cannot reproduce, then the probability that one parent will donate gene A to an offspring is

$$p = \frac{1}{2} \left(\frac{y}{y + z} \right)$$

since $y/(y + z)$ is the probability that the parent is of type AB and $\frac{1}{2}$ is the probability that such a parent will donate gene A. Then the proportions x', y', and z' of AA, AB, and BB, respectively, in the succeeding generation are given by

$$x' = p^2, \, y' = 2p(1 - p), \, z' = (1 - p)^2$$

and the new probability is given by

$$p' = \frac{1}{2} \left(\frac{y'}{y' + z'} \right)$$

Write a program to calculate and print the generation number and the proportions of AA, AB, and BB under appropriate headings for 30 generations. (Note that the proportions of AA and AB should approach 0, since gene A will gradually disappear.)

12. In an *infinite series* such as $\sum_{k=1}^{\infty} \frac{6}{k^2}$, the nth *partial sum* is the

sum of the first n terms of the series; for example, $\frac{6}{1^2} + \frac{6}{2^2} +$ $\frac{6}{3^2} + \frac{6}{4^2}$ is the fourth partial sum. Write a program to calculate and print the square roots of the first 20 partial sums of this series.

13. The infinite series $\sum\limits_{k=0}^{\infty} \frac{1}{k!}$ converges to the number e. [For a positive integer n, $n!$ (read "n *factorial*") is the product of the integers from 1 through n; $0!$ is defined as 1.] Write a program to calculate and print the first 10 partial sums of this series. (See Exercise 12 for the definition of partial sum.)

14. The infinite series $\sum\limits_{k=1}^{\infty} \frac{1}{k}$ is called the *harmonic series* and diverges to $+\infty$. Write a program to calculate and print n and the nth partial sum (see Exercise 12) until both of the following are satisfied: $n > 50$ and the nth partial sum > 5.

15. Write a program to calculate and print the first 20 partial sums of the *continued fraction*

$$1 + \cfrac{1}{1 + \cfrac{1}{1 + \cfrac{1}{1 + \cfrac{1}{1 + \begin{matrix} \cdot \\ \cdot \\ \cdot \end{matrix}}}}}$$

If S_k is the kth partial sum, then $S_1 = 1$, $S_2 = 1 + \frac{1}{1}$, $S_3 = 1 + \cfrac{1}{1 + \cfrac{1}{1}}$, and so on. (*Hint:* Find a relationship between S_{k+1} and S_k.)

Selection Structure: The if Statement

The *selection structure* makes possible the selection and execution of one of a number of alternative actions. This enables the programmer to introduce decision points in a program, that is, points at which a decision is made *during program execution* to follow one of several courses of action. In this section we consider the simple selection structures in which there are two possible courses of action. These are illustrated in Figure 4.11.

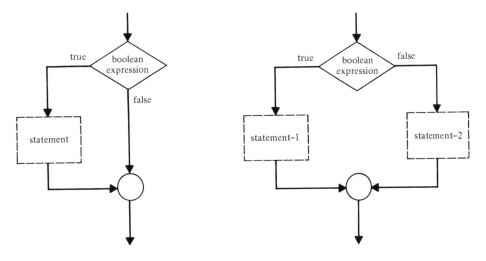

Figure 4.11.

These selection structures are implemented in Pascal using the **if** statement. This statement has one of the forms

> **if** *boolean expression* **then**
> > *statement*

or

> **if** *boolean expression* **then**
> > *statement-1*
> **else**
> > *statement-2*

Both forms are summarized in the following syntax diagram:

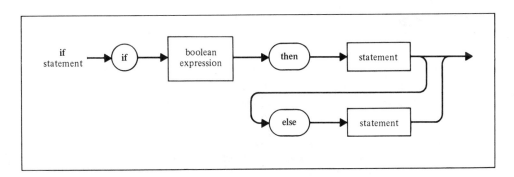

In the first form of the **if** statement, the specified statement is executed if the boolean expression is true; otherwise, it is bypassed, and execution continues with the next statement in the program. The following examples illustrate this simple form of the **if** statement:

```
if Score <= 60 then
    writeln ('F')
if Hours > 40 then
    begin
        Overtime := Hours − 40;
        OvertimePay := 1.5 * Overtime * Rate
    end (* if *)
```

In the first example, the boolean expression *Score* <= 60 is evaluated, and if it is true, the letter F is displayed. Otherwise, the *writeln* statement is bypassed. Similarly, in the second statement, the values of *Overtime* and *OvertimePay* are calculated only in the case that the boolean expression *Hours* > 40 is true.

The second form of the **if** statement allows the programmer not only to specify the statement selected for execution when the boolean expression is true but also to indicate an alternative statement for execution when it is false. If the boolean expression is true, *statement-1* is executed and *statement-2* is bypassed. Otherwise, *statement-1* is bypassed and *statement-2* is executed. In either case, execution continues with the statement following the **if** statement.

To illustrate this form of the **if** statement, consider the following problem of calculating wages: Suppose that a manufacturing company pays its employees an hourly wage, with all hours over 40 paid at 1.5 times the regular hourly rate. A program is to be written to calculate the wages for the company's employees and the total wages for this payroll.

In this problem, the input data are an employee number, his or her hourly rate, and the number of hours that each employee worked. The output to be produced consists of the employees' numbers and wages followed by the total wages for all employees. The algorithm consists of entering the data, calculating the wages, displaying the employee number together with his or her wages, and then adding the wages to the total. This procedure must be repeated for each employee until some termination condition is satisfied. Finally, the total wages for this payroll must be displayed.

Algorithm

(*Algorithm to calculate *Wages* for several employees whose employee number (*EmpNumber*), *Hours* worked, and hourly *Rate* are read; *RegWages* denotes regular wages, *OverWages* are overtime wages paid at 1.5 times the hourly rate for hours over 40. The total company wages for this payroll (*TotalWages*) are also calculated. *)

1. Set *TotalWages* equal to 0.
2. Read *EmpNumber, Hours,* and *Rate* for the first employee.
3. While *EmpNumber* is not the end-of-data flag do the following:
    a. If *Hours* > 40 then calculate
        $RegWages = Rate * 40$, and
        $OverWages = 1.5 * Rate * (Hours − 40)$.
    Else
        calculate $RegWages = Rate * Hours$, and
        set *OverWages* equal to 0.
    b. Calculate $Wages = RegWages + OverWages$.

c. Display *EmpNumber* and *Wages.*

d. Add *Wages* to *TotalWages.*

e. Read *EmpNumber, Hours,* and *Rate* for the next employee.

4. Display *TotalWages.*

A Pascal program to implement this algorithm is given in Figure 4.12. An **if** statement is used to implement the selection structure that selects the method of calculating wages depending on the boolean expression *Hours* > 40. Note the use of the two constant identifiers *OvertimeFactor* and *HoursLimit* in place of the constants 1.5 and 40. These identifiers are defined in the constant section and then used throughout the program. If the program has to be modified to handle overtime paid at a rate different from 1.5 or for hours above some number other than 40, we need change only the definitions of *OvertimeFactor* and *HoursLimit;* the statement part of the program need not be modified.

The statements in an **if** statement may themselves contain other **if** statements. In this case, one **if** statement is said to be "nested" within the other **if** statement. To illustrate, suppose that in the preceding problem, each employee with a number greater than or equal to 1000 is paid weekly an amount equal to his or her annual salary divided by 52 but that all other employees are paid on an hourly basis. The following algorithm solves this problem:

Algorithm

(*Algorithm to calculate wages for several employees. Those with an employee number (*EmpNumber*) 1000 or above are salaried and receive weekly *Wages* of *Salary* / 52. All others are paid according to *Hours* worked at a given hourly *Rate.* For these employees, *RegWages* denotes regular wages, *OverWages* denotes overtime wages paid at 1.5 times the hourly rate for hours above 40. Total company wages (*TotalSalary, TotalHourly*) for each type of employee—salaried, hourly—are also calculated. *)

```
PROGRAM Payroll (input, output);

(*********************************************************************

    Program to calculate wages for several employees whose employee
    number, hours worked, and hourly rate are read in.  Hours above
    HoursLimit are paid at OvertimeFactor times the hourly rate.
    Total wages for this payroll are also calculated.

**********************************************************************)

CONST
    OvertimeFactor = 1.5;    (* overtime multiplication factor *)
    HoursLimit = 40.0;       (* overtime hours limit *)

VAR
    EmpNumber : integer;     (* employee number *)
    Hours,                   (* hours worked *)
    Rate,                    (* hourly pay rate *)
    RegWages,                (* regular wages *)
    OverWages,               (* overtime pay *)
    Wages,                   (* total wages for employee *)
    TotalPayroll : real;     (* total wages for this payroll *)
```

Figure 4.12.

Fig. 4.12. (cont.)

```
BEGIN
    writeln ('*** To terminate, enter an employee number of -999');
    writeln ('*** and any values for hours worked and hourly rate.');
    writeln;
    TotalPayroll := 0;
    writeln ('Enter employee #, hours worked, hourly rate:');
    readln (EmpNumber, Hours, Rate);
    WHILE EmpNumber <> -999 DO
        BEGIN
            IF Hours > HoursLimit THEN
                BEGIN (* Overtime *)
                    RegWages := Rate * HoursLimit;
                    OverWages := OvertimeFactor * Rate * (Hours - HoursLimit)
                END (* Overtime *)
            ELSE
                BEGIN (* No overtime *)
                    RegWages := Rate * Hours;
                    OverWages := 0
                END (* No overtime *);
            Wages := RegWages + OverWages;
            TotalPayroll := TotalPayroll + Wages;
            writeln;
            writeln ('Employee #', EmpNumber:1, '  Wages = $', Wages:4:2);
            writeln;
            writeln;
            writeln ('Enter employee #, hours worked, hourly rate:');
            readln (EmpNumber, Hours, Rate)
        END (* WHILE *);
    writeln;
    writeln ('Total wages = $', TotalPayroll:3:2)
END.
```

```
Sample run:
==========

*** To terminate, enter an employee number of -999
*** and any values for hours worked and hourly rate.

Enter employee #, hours worked, hourly rate:
1234 30.0 10.00

Employee #1234  Wages = $300.00


Enter employee #, hours worked, hourly rate:
1235 45.0 10.00


Employee #1235  Wages = $475.00


Enter employee #, hours worked, hourly rate:
2775 43.5 8.55

Employee #2775  Wages = $386.89


Enter employee #, hours worked, hourly rate:
2884 38.25 9.45

Employee #2884  Wages = $361.46


Enter employee #, hours worked, hourly rate:
-999 0 0

Total wages = $1523.35
```

1. Set *TotalSalary* and *TotalHourly* equal to 0.
2. Read *EmpNumber* for the first employee.
3. While *EmpNumber* is not the end-of-data flag do the following:
   a. If *EmpNumber* ≥ 1000 then   (* salaried employee *)
      (i) Read *Salary.*
      (ii) Calculate *Wages* = *Salary* / 52.
      (iii) Add *Wages* to *TotalSalary.*
    Else   (* hourly employee *)
      (i) Read *Hours* and *Rate.*
      (ii) If *Hours* > 40 then   (* overtime *)
          Calculate *RegWages* = *Rate* * 40, and
          OverWages = 1.5 * *Rate* * (*Hours* − 40).
        Else   (* no overtime *)
          Calculate *RegWages* = *Rate* * *Hours,* and
          set *OverWages* equal to 0.
      (iii) Calculate *Wages* = *RegWages* + *OverWages.*
      (iv) Add *Wages* to *TotalHourly.*
   b. Display *EmpNumber* and *Wages.*
   c. Read *EmpNumber* for the next employee.
4. Display *TotalSalary* and *TotalHourly.*

This pseudocode description of the algorithm clearly shows the selection structure for calculating wages based on the condition *Hours* > 40 nested within the larger selection structure based on the condition *EmpNumber* ≥ 1000. This nested selection structure is implemented in the Pascal program in Figure 4.13 by nested **if** statements.

```
PROGRAM Payroll (input, output);

(*******************************************************************

    Program to calculate wages for several employees.  Each employee's
    number is read.  If this number is greater than WageTypeLine, an
    annual salary for this employee is then read, and wages are
    calculated by dividing this salary by NumPayPeriods.  Otherwise,
    the number of hours worked and the rate per hour are read and wages
    are calculated with hours above HoursLimit paid at OvertimeFactor
    times the hourly rate.  The total of all salaried wages and the
    total of all hourly wages are also calculated and displayed.

 ******************************************************************)

CONST
    WageTypeLine = 1000;     (* dividing-line for salaried & hourly type *)
    NumPayPeriods = 52;      (* number of pay periods *)
    OvertimeFactor = 1.5;    (* overtime multiplication factor *)
    HoursLimit = 40.0;       (* overtime hours limit *)
```

Figure 4.13.

Fig. 4.13. (cont.)

```
VAR
    EmpNumber : integer;        (* employee number *)
    Salary,                     (* annual salary *)
    Hours,                      (* hours worked *)
    Rate,                       (* hourly pay rate *)
    RegWages,                   (* regular wages *)
    OverWages,                  (* overtime pay *)
    Wages,                      (* total wages for employee *)
    TotalSalary,                (* total salaried-wages for this payroll *)
    TotalHourly : real;         (* total hourly-wages for this payroll *)


BEGIN
    TotalSalary := 0;
    TotalHourly := 0;
    writeln ('Enter employee # (-999 to stop):');
    readln (EmpNumber);
    WHILE EmpNumber <> -999 DO
        BEGIN
            IF EmpNumber >= WageTypeLine THEN
                BEGIN (* salaried *)
                    writeln ('Enter salary:');
                    readln (Salary);
                    Wages := Salary / NumPayPeriods;
                    TotalSalary := TotalSalary + Wages
                END (* salaried *)
            ELSE
                BEGIN (* hourly *)
                    writeln ('Enter hours & rate:');
                    readln (Hours, Rate);
                    IF Hours > HoursLimit THEN
                        BEGIN (* Overtime *)
                            RegWages := Rate * HoursLimit;
                            OverWages := OvertimeFactor * Rate
                                            * (Hours - HoursLimit)
                        END (* Overtime *)
                    ELSE
                        BEGIN (* No overtime *)
                            RegWages := Rate * Hours;
                            OverWages := 0
                        END (* No overtime *);
                    Wages := RegWages + OverWages;
                    TotalHourly := TotalHourly + Wages
                END (* hourly *);
            Writeln ('Employee #', EmpNumber:1, '  Wages = $', wages:4:2);
            writeln;
            writeln ('Enter employee #:');
            readln (EmpNumber)
        END (* WHILE *);
    writeln;
    writeln ('Total salaried wages = $', TotalSalary:10:2);
    writeln ('Total hourly wages =    $', TotalHourly:10:2)
END.



Sample run:
==========

Enter employee # (-999 to stop):
12345
Enter salary:
52000
Employee #12345  Wages = $1000.00
```

Fig. 4.13. (cont.)

```
Enter employee #:
375
Enter hours & rate:
42.0 10.00
Employee #375   Wages = $430.00

Enter employee #:
2253
Enter salary:
25900
Employee #2253   Wages = $498.08

Enter employee #:
410
Enter hours & rate:
37.5 8.35
Employee #410   Wages = $313.12

Enter employee #:
-999

Total salaried wages = $   1498.08
Total hourly wages =   $    743.12
```

In a nested **if** *statement, each* **else** *clause is matched with the nearest preceding unmatched* **if.** For example, in the statement

if $x > 0$ **then**
   if $y > 0$ **then**
      $z := sqrt(x) + sqrt(y)$
   else
      $readln (z)$

the **else** clause is associated with the **if** statement containing the boolean expression $y > 0$. Consequently, the *readln* statement is executed only in the case that x is positive and y is nonpositive. If we wish to associate this **else** clause with the outer **if** statement, we can write

if $x > 0$ **then**
   begin
      if $y > 0$ **then**
         $z := sqrt(x) + sqrt(y)$
   end
else
   $readln (z)$

Here the *readln* statement is executed whenever x is nonpositive.

In these examples, note that each **else** clause is aligned with the corresponding **if.** This alignment emphasizes the relationship between each **if** and its associated **else.**

In Section 4.3 we noted that because most real values cannot be stored exactly, boolean expressions formed by comparing two real quantities with the relational operator = are often evaluated as false, even though the two quantities are algebraically equal. The program in Figure 4.14 demonstrates

```
PROGRAM Roundoff (input, output);

(*********************************************************************

          Program to show inexact representation of reals.

**********************************************************************)

VAR
    X,                      (* real number entered *)
    Y : real;               (* Y = X * (1 / X) *)
    Response : integer;     (* user response *)

BEGIN
    REPEAT
        writeln ('Enter real # :');
        readln (X);
        Y := X * (1.0 / X);
        writeln ('X = ', X:7:5, '    Y = X*(1/X) = ', Y:7:5,
                 '    1.0 - Y = ', 1.0 - Y:12);
        IF Y = 1.0 THEN
            writeln ('*** YES ***')
        ELSE
            writeln ('*** NO ***');
        writeln;
        writeln ('More (0 = No, 1 = Yes)?');
        readln (Response)
    UNTIL Response <> 1
END.



Sample run:
==========


Enter real # :
0.5
X = 0.50000    Y = X*(1/X) = 1.00000    1.0 - Y =   0.00000E+00
*** YES ***

More (0 = No, 1 = Yes)?
1
Enter real # :
0.1
X = 0.10000    Y = X*(1/X) = 1.00000    1.0 - Y =   1.42109E-14
*** NO ***

More (0 = No, 1 = Yes)?
1
Enter real # :
0.2
X = 0.20000    Y = X*(1/X) = 1.00000    1.0 - Y =   1.42109E-14
*** NO ***

More (0 = No, 1 = Yes)?
1
Enter real # :
6.39632
X = 6.39632    Y = X*(1/X) = 1.00000    1.0 - Y =   1.42109E-14
*** NO ***

More (0 = No, 1 = Yes)?
0
```

Figure 4.14.

this by showing that for most real values X, the value of $X * (1 / X)$ is not 1.

The selection structure considered in the preceding section involved selecting one of two alternatives. It is also possible to use the **if** statement to design selection structures that contain more than two alternatives. The program for wage calculation in Figure 4.13 is, in fact, an example of a three-way selection structure in which a selection was made from the following three alternatives:

Multialternative Selection Structure: Nested if Statements and the case Statement

1. Salaried wages.
2. Hourly wages with overtime.
3. Hourly wages with no overtime.

This three-way selection structure was implemented with a nested **if** statement of the form

    if *boolean-expression-1* **then**
        statement-1
  else
        if *boolean-expression-2* **then**
          statement-2
      else
        statement-3

A general *n-way selection structure* can be constructed using a nested **if** statement of the form

    if *boolean-expression-1* **then**
        statement-1
  else
        if *boolean-expression-2* **then**
          statement-2
      else
        if *boolean-expression-3* **then**
          statement-3
           .
           .
           .
             else
               statement-n

Such *compound* **if** *statements* may become quite complex, and the correspondence between **ifs** and **elses** may not be clear if indentation is not used properly. When implementing an *n*-way selection structure with a compound **if** statement, we write the statement in the form

```
    if boolean-expression-1 then
        statement-1
    else if boolean-expression-2 then
        statement-2
            ⋮
    else
        statement-n
```

This format clarifies the correspondence between **ifs** and **elses** and also emphasizes that the statement implements an *n*-way selection structure in which exactly one of *statement-1, statement-2, . . . , statement-n* is executed.

As an illustration of multialternative selection, consider the problem of assigning letter grades to test scores, counting the number of A's and the number of F's, and calculating the class average. Letter grades are to be assigned in the following manner:

Numeric Score	Letter Grade
score $\geq$ 90	A
$80 \leq$ score < 90	B
$70 \leq$ score < 80	C
$60 \leq$ score < 70	D
score < 60	F

This selection is implemented in the program in Figure 4.15 with the **if** statement

```
    if Score >= 90 then
        begin
            Grade := 'A';
            Acount := Acount + 1
        end
    else if Score >= 80 then
        Grade := 'B'
    else if Score >= 70 then
        Grade := 'C'
    else if Score >= 60 then
        Grade := 'D'
    else
        begin
            Grade := 'F';
            Fcount := Fcount + 1
        end
```

```
PROGRAM Grader (input, output);

(*******************************************************************

    Program to assign letter grades to integer test scores, count # of
    A's and # of F's, and calculate class average.

 *****************************************************************)
```

Figure 4.15.

CONTROL STRUCTURES

Fig. 4.15. (cont.)

```
VAR
    Grade : char;       (* letter grade *)
    Score,              (* test score *)
    Acount,             (* count of A's *)
    Fcount,             (* count of F's *)
    TotalCount,         (* count of all scores *)
    Sum : integer;      (* sum of scores *)

BEGIN
    writeln ('*** Enter a negative score to signal the end of data.');
    writeln;
    Acount := 0;
    Fcount := 0;
    TotalCount := 0;
    Sum := 0;
    writeln ('Score:');
    readln (Score);
    WHILE Score >= 0 DO

        BEGIN
            IF Score >= 90 THEN
                BEGIN
                    Grade := 'A';
                    Acount := Acount + 1
                END (* IF *)
            ELSE IF Score >= 80 THEN
                Grade := 'B'
            ELSE IF Score >= 70 THEN
                Grade := 'C'
            ELSE IF Score >= 60 THEN
                Grade := 'D'
            ELSE
                BEGIN
                    Grade := 'F';
                    Fcount := Fcount + 1
                END (* ELSE *);
            TotalCount := TotalCount +1;
            Sum := Sum + Score;
            writeln ('Grade = ', Grade);
            writeln;
            writeln ('Score:');
            readln (Score)
        END (* WHILE *);
    writeln;
    writeln ('Number of A''s:  ', Acount:1);
    writeln ('Number of F''s:  ', Fcount:1);
    writeln ('Class average:  ', Sum / TotalCount:3:1)
END.
```

Fig. 4.15. (cont.)

```
Sample run:
==========

*** Enter a negative score to signal the end of data.

Score:
100
Grade = A

Score:
30
Grade = F

Score:
65
Grade = D

Score:
90
Grade = A

Score:
50
Grade = F

Score:
-1

Number of A's:   2
Number of F's:   2
Class average:   67.0
```

We can implement a multialternative structure with the **case** statement:

> **case** *selector* **of**
>   *label-list-1* : *statement-1*;
>   *label-list-2* : *statement-2*;
>   ⋮
>   *label-list-n* : *statement-n*
> **end**

where *selector* is an expression of integer, boolean, or character type (or of enumerated or subrange type, as defined in Chapter 7). Note that the selector may not be of real type. Each *label-list-i* is a list of one or more possible values of the selector. When a **case** statement is executed, the selector is evaluated; if this value is in *label-list-i*, then *statement-i* is executed and execution continues with the statement following the reserved word **end** that marks the end of the **case** statement. It is an error if the selector's value is not in any of the label lists.[1] A syntax diagram for the case statement is

---

[1] Many implementations of Pascal allow execution of a **case** statement to "fall through" if the value of the selector is not in any of the label lists; that is, execution continues with the statement following the **case** statement. Many implementations also allow an **otherwise** clause that is executed if the value of the selector does not appear in any of the label lists.

> **case** *selector* **of**
>   *label-list-1* : *statement-1*;
>   ⋮
>   *label-list-n* : *statement-n*
>   **otherwise**
>   *statement*
> **end**

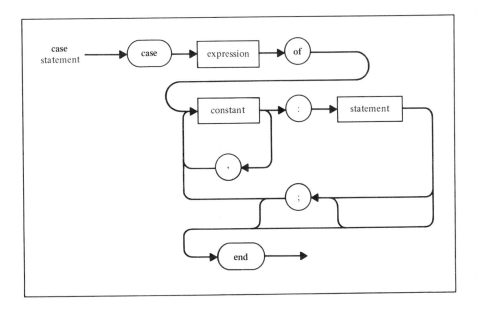

As an application of the **case** statement, consider the problem of converting an integer class code to a class name. If the value of the variable *Class* is 1, 2, 3, or 4, the following **case** statement is appropriate:

case *Class* **of**
    1: *writeln* ('Freshman');
    2: *writeln* ('Sophomore');
    3: *writeln* ('Junior');
    4: *writeln* ('Senior')
end (* **case** *)

To ensure that the value of the selector *Class* is in the range from 1 through 4, an **if** statement may be used:

if (*Class* < 1) **or** (*Class* > 4) **then**
    writeln ('Illegal class code')
else
    case *Class* **of**
        1: *writeln* ('Freshman');
        2: *writeln* ('Sophomore');
        3: *writeln* ('Junior');
        4: *writeln* ('Senior')
    end (* **case** *)

Occasionally, no action is required for certain values of the selector in a **case** statement. In such situations, these values may be placed in a label list for which the corresponding statement is empty. For example, a program to count aces and face cards might use the **case** statement

```
case Card of
            'A': ace := ace + 1;
      'J','Q','K': face := face + 1;
'2','3','4','5','6',
    '7','8','9','T':
end (* case *)
```

The grading program in Figure 4.15 uses a compound **if** statement to implement a multialternative selection structure. The program in Figure 4.16 does the same processing but implements the selection structure using a **case** statement:

```
case Score div 10 of
        9, 10  : begin
                    Grade := 'A';
                    Acount := Acount + 1
                 end;
           8 : Grade := 'B';
           7 : Grade := 'C';
           6 : Grade := 'D';
 0, 1, 2, 3, 4, 5 : begin
                    Grade := 'F';
                    Fcount := Fcount + 1
                 end
end (* case *)
```

```
PROGRAM Grader (input, output);

(*********************************************************************

   Program to assign letter grades to integer test scores, count # of
   A's and # of F's, and calculate class average.

********************************************************************)

CONST
   MaxScore = 100;    (* maximum score *)

VAR
   Grade : char;      (* letter grade *)
   Score,             (* test score *)
   Acount,            (* count of A's *)
   Fcount,            (* count of F's *)
   TotalCount,        (* count of all scores *)
   Sum : integer;     (* sum of scores *)

BEGIN
   writeln ('*** Enter a negative score to signal the end of data.');
   writeln;
   Acount := 0;
   Fcount := 0;
   TotalCount := 0;
   Sum := 0;
   writeln ('Score:');
   readln (Score);
```

Figure 4.16.

Fig. 4.16. (cont.)

```
    WHILE Score >= 0 DO
       BEGIN
          IF Score > MaxScore THEN
             writeln ('*** Illegal Score *** ')
          ELSE
             BEGIN
                CASE Score DIV 10 OF
                           9, 10 : BEGIN
                                      Grade := 'A';
                                      Acount := Acount + 1
                                   END;
                               8 : Grade := 'B';
                               7 : Grade := 'C';
                               6 : Grade := 'D';
                   0, 1, 2, 3, 4, 5 : BEGIN
                                      Grade := 'F';
                                      Fcount := Fcount + 1
                                   END
                END (* CASE *);
                TotalCount := TotalCount +1;
                Sum := Sum + Score;
                writeln ('Grade = ', Grade);
                writeln
             END (* ELSE *);
          writeln ('Score:');
          readln (Score)
       END (* WHILE *);
    writeln;
    writeln ('Number of A''s:  ', Acount:1);
    writeln ('Number of F''s:  ', Fcount:1);
    writeln ('Class average:  ', Sum / TotalCount:3:1)
END.

    Sample run:
    ==========

    *** Enter a negative score to signal the end of data.

    Score:
    100
    Grade = A

    Score:
    30
    Grade = F

    Score:
    65
    Grade = D

    Score:
    90
    Grade = A

    Score:
    50
    Grade = F

    Score:
    -1

    Number of A's:  2
    Number of F's:  2
    Class average:  67.0
```

Programming Pointers

Program Design

1. *All programs can be written using the three control structures considered in this chapter: sequential, repetition, and selection.*

2. *Use constant identifiers in place of specific constants for values that may need to be changed in a later revision of a program.* For example, the statement

    Interest := 0.18 * *Balance*

    is better expressed as

    Interest := *InterestRate* * *Balance*

    where *InterestRate* is a constant defined by

    const
    InterestRate = 0.18;

    In later revisions of the program, only the constant section need be modified; no changes are required in the statement part of the program.

3. *Multialternative selection structures can be implemented more efficiently with a* **case** *statement or a compound* **if** *statement than with a sequence of* **if** *statements.* For example, using the statements

    if *Score* < 60 **then**
        Grade := 'F';
    if (*Score* >= 60) **and** (*Score* < 70) **then**
        Grade := 'D';
    if (*Score* >= 70) **and** (*Score* < 80) **then**
        Grade := 'C';
    if (*Score* >= 80) **and** (*Score* < 90) **then**
        Grade := 'B';
    if *Score* >= 90 **then**
        Grade := 'A';

    is less efficient than

    if *Score* < 60 **then**
        Grade := 'F'
    else if *Score* < 70 **then**
        Grade := 'D'
    else if *Score* < 80 **then**
        Grade := 'C'
    else if *Score* < 90 **then**
        Grade := 'B'
    else
        Grade := 'A';

    In the first case, all of the **if** statements are executed for each score processed, and three of the boolean expressions are compound expressions. In the second case, each boolean expression is simple and not all of them are evaluated for each score; for example, for a score of 65, only the boolean expressions *Score* < 60 and *Score* < 70 are evaluated.

Potential Problems

1. *The index variable, initial value, and final value of a* **for** *statement cannot be modified within the body of the* **for** *statement.* For example, the statements

    $k := 5$;
    for $i := 1$ **to** k **do**
        begin
            writeln (k);
            $k := k - 1$
        end

   produce the output

    5
    4
    3
    2
    1

   The statement

    for $i := 1$ **to** 5 **do**
        begin
            writeln (i);
            $i := i - 1$
        end

   is an error and produces a message such as

    ***An index variable must not be altered in its "FOR" loop.

2. *Parentheses must be used within boolean expressions to indicate those subexpressions that are to be evaluated first.* The precedence of operators that may appear in boolean expressions is

not	—— highest priority (performed first)
*, /, **div**, **mod**, **and**	
+, −, **or**	
<, >, =, <=, >=, <>	—— lowest priority (performed last)

   To illustrate, consider the statement

    if $1 < x$ **and** $x < 10$ **then** *writeln* (x)

   where x is of real type. The first operation performed in evaluating the boolean expression is the **and** operation. However, the subexpression x **and** x is not a valid boolean expression, because boolean operators cannot be applied to numeric quantities; thus an error message such as the following results:

    *** Illegal types of operand(s). Types of operands conflict.

3. *Real quantities that are algebraically equal may yield a false boolean expression when compared with* =, *because most real values are not stored exactly.* For example, even though the two real expressions $x * (1 / x)$ and 1.0 are algebraically equal, the boolean expression $x * (1 / x) = 1.0$ is usually false.

4. *The statement within a* **while** *statement must eventually cause the boolean expression controlling repetition to become false. The statements within a* **repeat** *statement must eventually cause the boolean expression in the* **until** *clause to become true.* An "infinite loop" is the result otherwise. For example, if x is a real variable, the statements

> $x := 0$;
> **repeat**
>   *writeln* $(x:4:1)$;
> $x := x + 0.3$
> **until** $x = 1.0$

produce an infinite loop.

> Output:
> 0.0
> 0.3
> 0.6
> 0.9
> 1.2
> 1.5
> 1.8
>   ⋮

Since the value of x is never equal to 1, repetition is not terminated. In view of Potential Problem 3, the statements

> $x := 0$;
> **repeat**
>   *writeln* $(x:4:1)$;
> $x := x + 0.2$
> **until** $x = 1.0$

may also produce an infinite loop.

> Output:
> 0.0
> 0.2
> 0.4
> 0.6
> 0.8
> 1.0
> 1.2
> 1.4
> 1.6
>   ⋮

Since x is initialized to 0 and 0.2 is added to x five times, x should have the value 1. But the boolean expression $x = 1$ may be false, because most real values are not stored exactly.

5. *In a* **while** *statement, the boolean expression is evaluated before execution of the statement within the* **while** *statement. In a* **repeat** *statement, the boolean expression is evaluated after execution of the statements within the* **repeat** *statement.* Thus, the statement within a **while** statement is not executed if the boolean expression is false, but the statements within a **repeat** statement are always executed at least once.

6. *In an* **if** *statement containing an* **else** *clause, there is no semicolon before the* **else.** A statement such as

> if $x > 0$ then
>   *writeln* (x);
> else
>   *writeln* $(2 * x)$

results in an error. A semicolon following **then** or **else** as in

> if $x > 0$ then;
>   *writeln* (x);

or

> if $x > 0$ then
> $x := abs (x)$
> else;
>   *writeln* (x);

is syntactically correct, but it is almost surely a mistake since it indicates an empty statement. For both of these examples, the statement *writeln* (x) is executed, regardless of whether x is positive or not.

7. *In a nested* **if** *statement, each* **else** *clause is matched with the nearest preceding unmatched* **if.** For example, consider the following statements, which are purposely given without indentation:

> if $x > 0$ then
> if $y > 0$ then
> $z := x + y$
> else
> $z := x + abs (y)$;
> $w := x * y * z$;

With which **if** is the **else** associated? According to the rule just stated, these statements are executed as

> if $x > 0$ then
>   if $y > 0$ then
> $z := x + y$

else
    $z := x + abs\ (y);$
$w := x * y * z;$

where the **else** clause matches the **if** statement containing the boolean expression $y > 0$.

8. *It should be assumed that all subexpressions are evaluated in determining the value of a compound boolean expression.* Suppose, for example, we write the statement

    if $(x >= 0)$ **and** $(sqrt(x) < 5.0)$ **then**
        writeln ('Square root is less than 5')

where the subexpression $x >= 0$ is intended to prevent an attempt to calculate the square root of a negative number when x is negative. Some Pascal compilers may evaluate the subexpression $x >= 0$ and if it is false, not evaluate the second subexpression $sqrt(x) < 5.0$. Other compilers evaluate both parts, and thus an error results when x is negative. This error can be avoided by rewriting the statement as

    if $x >= 0$ **then**
        if $sqrt(x) < 5.0$ **then**
            writeln ('Square root is less than 5')

9. *The* **repeat** *statement controls repetition of all statements between* **repeat** *and* **until,** *but* **for** *and* **while** *statements control repetition of only one statement.* For example, the statements

    Count $:= 1;$
    while *Count* $<= 10$ **do**
        begin
            writeln (*Count*:2, *sqr*(*Count*):5);
            Count $:= Count + 1$
        end (* **while** *)

display a list of the integers from 1 through 10 and their squares. The statements

    Count $:= 1;$
    while *Count* $<= 10$ **do**
        writeln (*Count*:2, *sqr*(*Count*):5);
        Count $:= Count + 1$

produce an infinite loop.

    Output:
      1   1
      1   1
      1   1
      ⋮   ⋮

Program Style

In this text, we use the following conventions for formatting the statements considered in this chapter.

1. *In a* **for** *statement,* **for . . . do** *is on one line, with the body of the loop indented on the next line(s).*

   for . . . do
      statement
   for . . . do
      begin
         statement-1;
            ⋮
         statement-n
      end (* **for** *)

2. *In a* **while** *statement,* **while . . . do** *is on one line, with the body of the loop indented on the next line(s).*

   while . . . do
      statement
   while . . . do
      begin
         statement-1;
            ⋮
         statement-n
      end (* **while** *)

3. *In a* **repeat** *statement,* **repeat** *is aligned with the corresponding* **until** *and the body of the loop indented.*

   repeat
      statement-1;
        ⋮
      statement-n
   until . . .

4. *For an* **if** *statement,* **if . . . then** *is on one line, with its statement indented on the next line. If there is an* **else** *clause,* **else** *is on a separate line, aligned with* **if,** *and its statement indented on the next line.*

   if . . . then
      statement-1
   else
      statement-2
   if . . . then
      begin
         statement-1;
            ⋮
         statement-k
      end (* **if** *)

```
        else
            begin
                statement-k+1;
                    ⋮
                statement-n
            end (* else *)
```

An exception is made when an **if** statement is used to implement a multialternative selection structure. In this case the format used is

```
    if . . . then
        statement-1
    else if . . . then
        statement-2
    else if . . . then
        statement-3
            ⋮
    else
        statement-n
```

5. In **case** statements, **case** is aligned with its corresponding **end,** and the lines within the **case** statement are indented and the colons or the label lists are aligned.

```
    case selector of
        label-list-1  :  statement-1;
                ⋮
        label-list-n  :  statement-n
    end (* case *)
```

Exercises

1. Write a Pascal statement for each of the following:

   (a) If *Code* has the value 1, read values for x and y and calculate and print the sum of x and y.

   (b) If A is strictly between 0 and 5, set B equal to $1/A^2$; otherwise set B equal to A^2.

   (c) Assign true to the boolean variable *LeapYear* if the integer variable *Year* is the number of a leap year. (A leap year is a multiple of 4, and if it is a multiple of 100, it must also be a multiple of 400.)

   (d) Assign the value to *Cost* corresponding to the value of *Distance* given in the following table:

Distance	Cost
0 through 100	5.00
More than 100 but not more than 500	8.00
More than 500 but less than 1000	10.00
1000 or more	12.00

(e) Assign the value true to the boolean variable *Triangle* if *a*, *b*, and *c* could represent sides of a triangle, and false otherwise. (For three numbers to be the lengths of the sides of a triangle, the sum of any two must be greater than the third.)

(f) Display the number of days in the month corresponding to the value of *Month* (1, 2, . . . , 12). Use part (c) to determine the number of days if the value of *Month* is 2, assuming that a value has been assigned to *Year*.

2. Describe the output produced by each of the following poorly indented program segments:

(a) *Number* := 4;
    Alpha := −1.0;
    if *Number* > 0 **then**
        if *Alpha* > 0 **then**
            writeln ('First writeln')
    else
        writeln ('Second writeln');
    writeln ('Third writeln');

(b) *Number* := 4;
    while *Number* > 0 **do**
        Number := *Number* − 1;
        writeln (*Number*:1);
        writeln;
    writeln ('*****');

(c) **for** *Number* := 1 **to** 4 **do**
        writeln (*Number*:1);
        writeln (' squared = ', *sqr*(*Number*):1);
        writeln;

3. Write a program that implements the "divide and average" algorithm for approximating square roots (see Exercise 5 of Section 2.5). It should accept positive real values for the variables *PosReal*, *Approx*, and *Epsilon*, and approximate the square root of *PosReal* by repeatedly replacing *Approx* by the average of *Approx* and *PosReal* / *Approx*, until *Approx* and *PosReal* / *Approx* differ in absolute value by less than *Epsilon*, where the value of *Epsilon* is small. Have the program display each of the successive values of *Approx*.

4. A certain city classifies a pollution index of less than 35 as "pleasant," 35 through 60 as "unpleasant," and above 60 as "hazardous." Write a program that accepts several real numbers representing pollution indices and displays the appropriate classification for each.

5. Write a program that reads one of the numbers 2 through 13 representing a TV channel and then uses a **case** statement to print the call letters of the station that corresponds to that number or some

message indicating that the channel is not used. Use the following channel numbers and call letters:

  2: WCBS
  4: WNBC
  5: WNEW
  7: WABC
  9: WOR
11: WPIX
13: WNET

6. Write a program to check several quadratic equations of the form $Ax^2 + Bx + C = 0$ to see if they have real roots, and if so, find these roots. If there are no real roots, print out an appropriate message. (See Exercise 7 of Chapter 2.)

7. Write a program using the boolean variable *Triangle* of Exercise 1(e) so that if *Triangle* is true, the triangle is classified as equilateral (3 sides equal) or isosceles (2 sides equal) but not equilateral, or scalene (no 2 sides equal).

8. Write a program to read a set of numbers, count them, and find and display the largest and smallest numbers in the list and their positions in the list.

9. Write a program that converts measurements from either minutes to hours, or from feet to meters (1 foot = 0.3048 meters), or from degrees Fahrenheit to degrees Celsius ($C = \frac{5}{9}(F - 32)$). The program should print a *menu* of these options and ask the user to select one; use a repetition structure that allows the user to make as many conversions as desired; verify that the user's responses are valid; and use a **case** statement to decide which option the user selects. The output should be similar to the following:

Do you want to
   1) convert minutes to hours
   2) convert feet to meters
   3) convert degrees Fahrenheit to degrees Celsius
   4) quit

Enter 1, 2, 3, or 4:
3
Enter degrees Fahrenheit:
212
This is equivalent to 100.0 degrees Celsius

Enter 1, 2, 3, or 4:
8
*** 8 is not a valid response ***

Enter 1, 2, 3, or 4:
1
Enter minutes:
360
This is equivalent to 6.0 hours

Enter 1, 2, 3, or 4:
4

10. The proper divisors of an integer n are the positive divisors less than n. A positive integer is said to be a *deficient, perfect,* or *abundant* number if the sum of its proper divisors is less than, equal to, or greater than the number, respectively. For example, 8 is deficient, because its proper divisors are 1, 2, and 4, and $1 + 2 + 4 < 8$; 6 is perfect, because $1 + 2 + 3 = 6$; and 12 is abundant, because $1 + 2 + 3 + 4 + 6 > 12$. Write a program that classifies n as being deficient, perfect, or abundant for $n = 20$ to 30, then for $n = 490$ to 500, and finally for $n = 8120$ to 8130. Extra: Find the smallest odd abundant number.

11. Write a program that accepts a positive integer and gives its prime factorization, that is, expresses the integer as a product of primes or indicates that it is a prime.

12. A wholesale office supply company discounts the price of each of its products depending on the number of units bought and the price per unit. The discount increases as the number of units bought and/or the unit price increases. These discounts are given in the following table.

Number Bought	Unit Price (dollars)		
	0–10.00	10.01–100.00	100.01–
1–10	0%	2%	5%
11–100	5%	7%	9%
101–500	9%	15%	21%
501–1000	14%	23%	32%
1001–	21%	32%	43%

Write a program that reads the number of units bought and the unit price, and then calculates and prints the total full cost, the total amount of the discount, and the total discounted cost. The program should repeatedly process input until the value zero is entered for the number bought.

13. A lumber yard stocks Douglas Fir, Knotty Pine and Redwood in various sizes. However, the yard stocks only certain sizes of each kind of wood; this information is summarized in the following table in which an X indicates that the particular size and kind of wood is in stock.

Size	Douglas Fir	Knotty Pine	Redwood
1 X 2	X	X	X
1 X 4	X	X	X
1 X 6	X	X	
1 X 8		X	
1 X 10		X	
2 X 4	X		X
2 X 6	X		X
2 X 8	X		X
2 X 10	X		
2 X 12	X	X	
4 X 4	X		X
4 X 8			X
4 X 12	X	X	
4 X 16	X		

Write a program that reads a size as two integers, and then determines and prints the kinds of wood of that size in stock. The program should use a nested **case** statement to set boolean variables *Douglas-Fir, KnottyPine* and *Redwood* to true or false depending on whether the particular kind of wood is or is not in stock. The program should repeatedly process input until the value zero is entered for size.

14. An airline vice president in charge of operations needs to determine whether or not their current estimates of flight times are accurate. Since there is a larger possibility of variations due to weather and air traffic in the longer flights, he allows a larger error in the time estimates for them. He compares an actual flight time with an estimated flight time and considers the estimate to be too large, acceptable, or too small, depending on the following table of acceptable error margins.

Estimated Flight Time in Minutes	Acceptable Error Margin in Minutes
0–30	1
31–60	2
61–90	3
91–120	4
121–180	6
181–240	8
241–360	13
361–480	17

For example, if an estimated flight time is 106 minutes, then the acceptable error margin is 4 minutes. Thus, the estimated flight time is too large if the actual flight time is less than 102 minutes, or the estimated flight time is too small if the actual flight time is greater than 110 minutes; otherwise, the estimate is acceptable. Write a program that reads an estimated flight time and an actual flight time, and then calculates and prints whether the estimated time is too large, acceptable, or too small. If the estimated flight time is either too large or too small, the program should also print the amount of the overestimate or underestimate. The program should repeatedly process input until the value zero is entered for the estimated flight time.

5

Functions and Procedures

Great things can be reduced to small things, and small things can be reduced to nothing.

CHINESE PROVERB

Pascal programs are made more flexible through the use of functions and procedures. These are program units or modules that are designed to perform some particular task. These functions and procedures are written only once but may be referenced at several points in a program so as to avoid unnecessary duplication of code.

Another important advantage of functions and procedures is that they enable the programmer to develop programs for complex problems using the top-down approach introduced in Section 2.1. Individual functions and procedures are written to carry out each of the major tasks identified in the analysis of the problem. Because the program units in this modular style of programming are independent of one another, the programmer can write each module and test it without worrying about the details of other modules. This makes it considerably easier to locate an error when it arises, since it often occurs in the module most recently written and added to the program. Programs developed in this manner also are usually easier to understand, since the structure of each program unit can be studied independently of the other program units.

We begin this chapter by describing the Pascal predefined functions and procedures. In the second and third sections, we consider user-defined functions and procedures. Finally, we illustrate the use of functions and procedures in modular programming.

In Chapter 3 we introduced the Pascal *predefined arithmetic functions:*

Function	Description	Type of Parameter	Type of Value
abs(x)	Absolute value of x	Integer or real	Same as argument
arctan(x)	Inverse tangent of x (value in radians)	Integer or real	Real
cos(x)	Cosine of x (in radians)	Integer or real	Real
exp(x)	Exponential function e^x	Integer or real	Real
ln(x)	Natural logarithm of x	Integer or real	Real
round(x)	x rounded to nearest integer	Real	Integer
sin(x)	Sine of x (in radians)	Integer or real	Real
sqr(x)	x^2	Integer or real	Same as argument
sqrt(x)	Square root of x	Integer or real	Real
trunc(x)	x truncated to its integer part	Real	Integer

Recall that to use any of these functions, it is necessary to give only its name and the expression to which it is to be applied. For example, the statements

> *writeln* (*abs(x)*);
>
> *Alpha* := *round*(100 * *Beta*) / 100;
>
> **if** *Number* < 10 **then**
>   *Number* := *sqr(Number)*;

display the absolute value of the variable *x*, assign to *Alpha* the value of *Beta* rounded to the nearest hundredth, and square the value of *Number* if *Number* is less than 10.

Pascal also provides the following *predefined boolean-valued functions:*

Function	Description
odd(x)	The parameter x is of integer type. The value of the function is true if x is an odd integer; otherwise it is false.
eof(f)	The parameter f is a file name. The value of the function is true if the **end of** the file has been encountered, that is, if there are no more data to be read from the file; otherwise, it is false. If the file is *input,* the parameter and the parentheses may be omitted.
eoln(f)	The parameter f is a file name. The value of the function is true if the **end of** the current input line has been reached; otherwise, it is false. If the file is *input,* the parameter and the parentheses may be omitted.

These functions, like the other functions, are referenced by specifying the name of the function and its parameter. Because the values of these functions are of boolean type, they may be used in boolean expressions. For example, the statement

if (*Number* > 1) **and** *odd*(*Number*) **then**
    writeln (*Number*)

displays the value of *Number* if its value is an odd integer greater than 1. The boolean functions *eof* and *eoln* are used with input operations and are described in detail in the next chapter.

Pascal also provides several *predefined procedures.* Like functions, they are designed to carry out certain tasks that occur frequently in programs. In the input/output statements described in Chapter 3, the identifiers *readln* and *writeln* are names of predefined Pascal procedures designed to carry out input and output operations. Since such input/output operations are an important part of most programs and require special attention, we discuss these procedures in more detail in the next chapter. Other predefined procedures are considered in later chapters. A complete list of predefined procedures and their descriptions is given in Appendix D.

In some programs it may be convenient for the user to define functions **User-Defined** different from the standard predefined Pascal functions. Such *user-defined* **Functions** *functions* are possible in Pascal, and once defined, they are used in the same way as are the predefined functions. They are defined in the *subprogram section,* which is the last section in the declaration part of the program (see the syntax diagram in Section 3.7.)

Like a Pascal program, a function consists of a heading, a declaration part, and a statement part. The syntax diagram for a function definition is

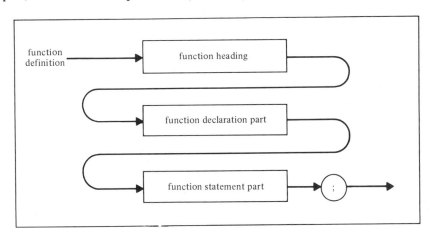

The function heading has the form

function *name* (*formal-parameter-list*) : *result-type*;

Here *name* is the name of the function and may be any legal Pascal identifier. The type of the function value, *result-type,* may be any of the standard Pascal data types (or certain other data types considered later). The *formal-parameter-list* has the form

$$list\text{-}1 : type\text{-}1;\ list\ 2 : type\text{-}2;\ \ldots\ ;\ list\text{-}k : type\text{-}k$$

where *list-i* is usually a single identifier or a list of identifiers separated by commas. These identifiers are called the *formal parameters* of the function. Each *type-i* is an identifier indicating the type of the parameters in *list-i.* The following syntax diagrams summarize this description of the function heading:

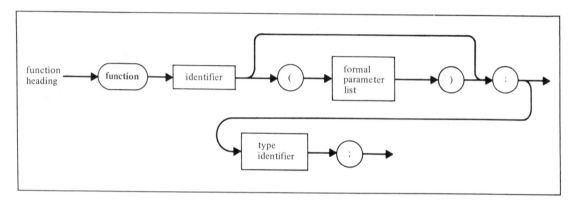

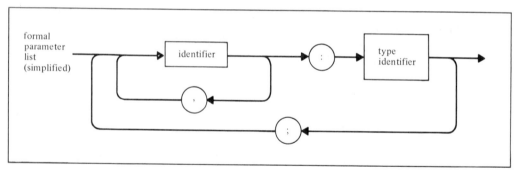

To illustrate, suppose that we wish to define the trigonometric tangent function, which is an important function in mathematics but which is not one of the predefined functions in Pascal. This function has a single formal parameter, which is of real type, and the result type is also real. Thus an appropriate function heading is

function *tan*(*x* : *real*) : *real*;

The formal parameter *x* has no value until the function is referenced by a statement such as

Slope := *tan*(1.5)

The value 1.5 in this function reference is called the *actual parameter,* and it is this value that is assigned to the corresponding formal parameter *x*.

The statement part of a function definition has the same form as the statement part of a Pascal program, except that a semicolon rather than a period follows the reserved word **end** marking the end of the function definition. At least one of the statements in this statement part must assign a value to the identifier which names the function.

The statement part of the function *tan* thus might be

```
begin (* tan *)
    tan := sin(x) / cos(x)
end (* tan *);
```

A complete function definition for *tan* is

```
function tan(x : real) : real;

    (* Function tan returns the tangent
       of x (which is in radians). *)

    begin (* tan *)
        tan := sin(x) / cos(x)
    end (* tan *);
```

Note that a comment is included to describe the function. It is good practice to include such documentation to briefly describe what the function does, what its parameters represent, and other information that explains the function definition.

This function definition is placed after the variable section in the declaration part of a Pascal program. The function *tan* can then be referenced in the statement part of the program in the same manner as are the predefined Pascal functions. The simple program in Figure 5.1 illustrates.

```
PROGRAM TangentTable (input, output);

(*******************************************************************

    Program to print a table of values of the tangent function.

 *******************************************************************)

VAR
    Lower, Upper,   (* bounds on range of values *)
    Step,           (* increment *)
    Theta : real;   (* actual argument *)

FUNCTION tan (x : real) : real;

    (***************************************************************

        Function tan returns the tangent of x (which is in radians).

     ***************************************************************)

    BEGIN (* tan *)
        tan := sin(x) / cos(x)
    END (* tan *);
```

Figure 5.1.

Fig. 5.1. (cont.)

```
BEGIN (* main program *)
   writeln ('Enter range of values and step size:');
   readln (Lower, Upper, Step);
   writeln;
   writeln ('Theta  tan(Theta)');
   writeln ('=====  ==========');
   Theta := Lower;
   WHILE Theta <= Upper DO
      BEGIN
         writeln (Theta:5:2, tan(Theta):10:4);
         Theta := Theta + Step
      END (* WHILE *)
END (* main program *).


Sample run:
==========


Enter range of values and step size:
0 1.5 0.25

Theta  tan(Theta)
=====  ==========
 0.00    0.0000
 0.25    0.2553
 0.50    0.5463
 0.75    0.9316
 1.00    1.5574
 1.25    3.0096
 1.50   14.1014
```

Several of the sample programs in the preceding chapters calculated wages. In these examples, as in most programs involving monetary calculations, the amounts should be rounded to the nearest cent. A function to do this is the following:

> **function** *RoundCents*(*Amount* : *real*) : *real*;
>
> (* Function to round *Amount* to the nearest cent. *)
>
> **begin** (* *RoundCents* *)
>   *RoundCents* := *round*(100 * *Amount*) / 100
> **end** (* *RoundCents* *);

A statement such as

> *GrossPay* := *RoundCents*(*Wages*)

can then be used to reference this function.

As another example, consider a function to find the maximum of two integers. If we name the function *Maximum* and its formal parameters *Number1* and *Number2,* then the function definition is

```
function Maximum (Number1, Number2 : integer) : integer;

   (* Function returns the maximum of two
      integers Number1 and Number2. *)

begin (* Maximum *)
   if Number1 >= Number2 then
      Maximum := Number1
   else
      Maximum := Number2
end (* Maximum *);
```

Some function definitions may require the use of variables other than the formal parameters to calculate the function value. Such variables usually are declared within the function itself, and their types are specified in the variable section of the function's declaration part. For example, consider the operation of exponentiation, which, unfortunately, is not a standard operation in Pascal. The following function can be used to calculate x^n for a real variable x and an integer variable n:

```
function Power(x : real; n : integer) : real;

   (* Function returns the nth power of x for any real value
      x and any integer value n (positive, zero, or negative). *)

var
   i : integer;
   Prod : integer;
begin (* Power *)
   if x = 0 then
      Power := 0
   else
      begin
         Prod := 1;
         for i := 1 to abs(n) do
            Prod := Prod * x;
         if n >= 0 then
            Power := Prod
         else
            Power := 1 / Prod
      end (* else *)
end (* Power *);
```

In this example, the variables x, n, i, and Prod have values only when the function Power is referenced and these values are accessible only within the function. These variables are therefore said to be *local* to the function. The portion of a program in which a variable is accessible is called the *scope* of that variable. Thus the scope of the variables x, n, i, and Prod is the function Power.

One consequence of this scope rule for local variables is that the same variable name can be used without conflict in two different program units. For example, the functions tan and Power can be used in the same program,

even though both use the variable name *x*. When these functions are referenced, the variable *x* in the function *tan* is associated with a different memory
location than is the variable *x* in the function *Power*. Thus, changing the
value of one does not change the value of the other. Similarly, the identifiers
n, i, and *Prod* may be used without conflict elsewhere in the program. The
program in Figure 5.2 illustrates this scope principle for local variables. The
sample run shows that there is no conflict between the variable *x* in the
function *tan* and the variable *x* in the function *Power* and no conflict between
the variable *i* in the main program and the variable *i* in the function *Power*.

```
PROGRAM Sequence (input, output);

(***********************************************************************

    Program prints the first NumTerms terms of the sequence

                       2            3
            tan(Theta), tan (2*Theta), tan (3*Theta), . . .

    for values of Theta and NumTerms entered during execution.

 ********************************************************************** )
VAR
    NumTerms,       (* number of terms *)
    i : integer;    (* index *)
    Theta,          (* angle *)
    Term : real;    (* a term of the sequence *)

FUNCTION tan (x : real) : real;

    (*******************************************************************

        Function tan returns the tangent of x (which is in radians).
        An output statement has been added to display the value of x.

     **************************************************************** )

    BEGIN (* tan *)
        writeln ('   *** In function tan, x = ', x:6:4);
        tan := sin(x) / cos(x)
    END (* tan *);

FUNCTION Power(x : real; n : integer) : real;

    (*******************************************************************

        Function returns the n-th power of x for any real value x and
        any integer value n (positive, zero, or negative).  Output
        statements have been added to display the values of x and i.

     **************************************************************** )

    VAR
        i : integer;    (* index *)
        Prod : real;    (* product of x's *)
```

Figure 5.2.

Fig. 5.2. (cont.)

```
    BEGIN (* Power *)
        writeln ('        **** In function Power, x = ', x:6:4);
        IF x = 0 THEN
            Power := 0
        ELSE
            BEGIN
                Prod := 1;
                FOR i := 1 to abs(n) DO
                    BEGIN
                        writeln ('        **** In function Power, i = ', i:1);
                        Prod := Prod * x
                    END (* FOR *);
                IF n >= 0 THEN
                    Power := Prod
                ELSE
                    Power := 1 / Prod
            END (* ELSE *)
    END (* Power *);

BEGIN (* main program *)
    writeln ('Enter angle and number of terms:');
    readln (Theta, NumTerms);
    FOR i := 1 TO NumTerms DO
        BEGIN
            writeln ('Computing Term # i for i = ', i:1);
            Term := Power(tan(i*Theta), i);
            writeln ('Term is ', Term:5:4);
            writeln
        END (* FOR *)
END (* main program *).
```

```
Sample run:
==========


Enter angle and number of terms:
1.5 3
Computing Term # i for i = 1
    *** In function tan, x = 1.5000
        **** In function Power, x = 14.1014
        **** In function Power, i = 1
Term is 14.1014


Computing Term # i for i = 2
    *** In function tan, x = 3.0000
        **** In function Power, x = -0.1425
        **** In function Power, i = 1
        **** In function Power, i = 2
Term is 0.0203

Computing Term # i for i = 3
    *** In function tan, x = 4.5000
        **** In function Power, x = 4.6373
        **** In function Power, i = 1
        **** In function Power, i = 2
        **** In function Power, i = 3
Term is 99.7251
```

When a function is referenced, the number of actual parameters must be the same as the number of formal parameters, and the types of the actual parameters must be the same as the types of the corresponding formal parameters. One exception is that an actual parameter of integer type may be associated with a formal parameter of real type. Thus, for the function *Power*, if *Alpha* and *Beta* are of real type and *Number* is of integer type, the following are valid function references:

> *Alpha* := *Power*(*Beta* / 3, *Number*);

> *writeln* (*Power*(*Number*, 4));

The following, however, are not valid, for the reasons indicated:

Alpha := *Power*(*Beta*); (The number of actual parameters does not agree with the number of formal parameters.)

Alpha := *Power*(*Number*, *Beta*); (The real parameter *Beta* may not be associated with the integer parameter *n*.)

Exercises

1. Consider the following program skeleton:

> **program** *Demo* (*input, output*);

> **const**
> > *pi* = 3.14159;
> > *two* = 2;

> **var**
> > *Month, Day, Year* : *integer*;
> > *Hours, Rate, Amount* : *real*;
> > *Code* : *char*;

> **function** *f*(*x, y* : *real*; *d* : *integer*) : *real*;
> > ⋮

Determine whether each of the following statements can be used in the statement part of the program. If it cannot be used, explain why.

(a) *Amount* := *f*(*pi, Rate, Month*);

(b) *Rate* := *f*(*Hours, Day, two*);

(c) *writeln* (*f*(0, 0, 0));

(d) *Hours* := *two* * *f*(*pi, Amount*) / (2.71828 * *Rate*);

(e) *Amount* := *f*(*pi* * *Hours*, (2.71828 + *Day*) / *Rate, two*);

(f) **if** *Month* = *two* **then**
> > *Year* := *f*(*Hours, f*(*Rate, pi, two*), *Day*);

(g) while $f(Amount, 0, 0) < pi$ **do**
$\quad Amount := f(Amount, pi, 1);$

(h) repeat
$\quad Amount := f(Amount, 0, Code)$
until $Amount > 0;$

2. Write a function *Range* that calculates the range between two integers, that is, the larger integer minus the smaller integer.

3. Write a function *Wages* that calculates the wages for a given number of hours worked and a given hourly pay rate. Hours over 40 should be paid at 1.5 times the regular hourly rate.

4. Write a function that converts a temperature given in degrees Celsius to degrees Fahrenheit. (The conversion formula is $F = \dfrac{9}{5} C + 32$.)

5. Write a boolean-valued function *Digit* that determines whether a character is one of the digits 0 through 9.

6. Write a boolean-valued function *Vowel* that determines whether a character is one of the vowels A, E, I, O, or U.

7. Write a function *RoundOff* that accepts a real value *Amount* and an integer value *NumPlaces* and returns the value of *Amount* rounded to the specified number of places. For example, the function references *RoundOff*(10.536, 0), *RoundOff*(10.536, 1), and *RoundOff*(10.536, 2) should give the values 11.0, 10.5, and 10.54, respectively.

8. Write a function *GPA* that assigns the real values 4.0, 3.0, 2.0, 1.0, and 0.0 to the characters A, B, C, D, and F, respectively.

9. The number of bacteria in a culture can be estimated by

$$N \cdot e^{kt}$$

where N is the initial population, k is a rate constant, and t is time. Write a function to calculate the number of bacteria present at time t for given values of k and N; use it in a program that reads values for the initial population, the rate constant, and the time (e.g., 1000, 0.15, 100), and displays the number of bacteria at that time.

10. Write a program that uses the function *Power* given in the text to calculate a monthly loan payment given by

$$\frac{r \cdot A/n}{1 - \left(1 + \dfrac{r}{n}\right)^{-n \cdot y}}$$

where A is the amount borrowed, r is the interest rate (expressed as a decimal), y is the number of years, and n is the number of payments per year. Design the program to read values for the amount borrowed, the interest rate, the number of years, and the number of payments per year, and display the corresponding monthly payment.

11. Write a character-valued function *LetterGrade* that assigns a letter grade to an integer score using the following grading scale:

> 90–100: A
> 80–89: B
> 70–79: C
> 60–69: D
> Below 60: F

Use the function in a program that reads several scores and displays the corresponding letter grades.

12. Write two boolean-valued functions that have formal parameters p and q of boolean type and that compute the logical expressions

$$\sim p \wedge \sim q \quad (\text{not } p \text{ and not } q)$$

and

$$\sim(p \vee q) \quad (\text{not } (p \text{ or } q))$$

Write a program that uses these functions to print truth tables for these expressions.

13. A *prime number* is an integer $n > 1$ whose only positive divisors are 1 and n itself. Write a predicate (boolean-valued function) that determines whether n is a prime number. Use it in a program that reads several integers, uses the function to determine whether each is prime, and displays each number with the appropriate label "is prime" or "is not prime."

14. Write a program to approximate $f'(a)$, the value of the *derivative* of f at a, for a given function f and a given number a. The derivative of f at a is defined by

$$f'(a) = \lim_{h \to 0} \frac{f(a + h) - f(a)}{h}$$

Calculate values of this "difference quotient" for various values of h approaching 0, say for $h = 1/2^n$, then for $h = -1/2^n$, as n runs from 0 to 14.

15. It is often necessary to find a *zero* of a function f, that is, a value c where $f(c) = 0$. Geometrically, we are looking for a point c on the x axis at which the graph of $y = f(x)$ crosses the x axis. If f is a continuous function between $x = a$ and $x = b$, that is, if there is no break in the graph of $y = f(x)$ between these two

values, and $f(a)$ and $f(b)$ are of opposite signs, then f must have at least one zero between $x = a$ and $x = b$. One method for finding such a zero, or at least an approximation to it, is the *bisection method*. For this, bisect the interval $[a, b]$ and determine in which half f changes sign; then f must have a zero in that half of the interval. Now bisect this subinterval and determine in which half f changes sign. Repeating this process gives a sequence of smaller and smaller subintervals, each of which contains a zero of the function. The process can be terminated when a small subinterval, say of length less than 0.0001, is obtained or f has the value 0 at one of the endpoints.

Define a Pascal function to compute $x - \cos x$, and then write a program to find a zero of this function in the interval $\left[0, \frac{\pi}{2}\right]$.

16. Another method used to locate a zero of a function f is *Newton's method*. This method consists of taking an initial approximation x_1 and constructing a tangent line to the graph of f at that point. The point x_2 where this tangent line crosses the x axis is taken as the second approximation to the zero. Then another tangent line is constructed at x_2, and the point x_3 where this tangent line crosses the x axis is the next approximation. Figure 5.3 shows this process.

If x is an approximation to the zero of f, then the formula for obtaining the next approximation by Newton's method is

$$\text{new approximation} = x - \frac{f(x)}{f'(x)}$$

where f' is the derivative of f. Using Pascal functions to define a function f and its derivative f', write a program to locate a zero of f, using Newton's method. The process should terminate when a value of $f(x)$ is sufficiently small in absolute value or when the number of iterations exceeds some upper limit. Display the sequence of successive approximations.

Figure 5.3.

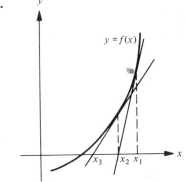

Procedures, like functions, are program units designed to perform a particular task. For example, the predefined procedures *readln* and *writeln* are designed to carry out input and output. In this section we discuss how to implement *user-defined procedures* in Pascal. These procedures, like user-defined functions, are defined in the subprogram section of the declaration part of a program.

User-Defined Procedures; Value Parameters and Variable Parameters

Although procedures and functions are similar in many ways, they differ in the following respects:

1. Functions usually return a single value to the program unit that references them. Procedures often return more than one value or they may return no value at all but simply perform some task such as an input/output operation.
2. A procedure name is not assigned a value, and thus no type is associated with a procedure name.
3. A function is referenced by using its name in an expression, whereas a procedure is referenced by a *procedure reference statement.*

Like a function definition, a procedure definition consists of a heading, a declaration part, and a statement part. Its syntax diagram is

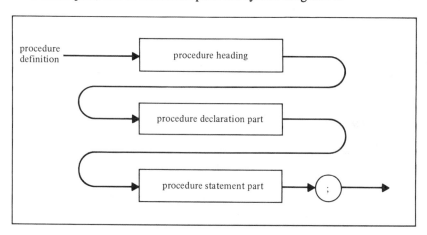

The procedure heading has the form

procedure *name* (*formal-parameter-list*);

where *name* is any legal Pascal identifier. The *formal-parameter-list* specifies the formal parameters of the procedure. These parameters are used to pass information to the procedure and/or to return information from the procedure to the program unit that references it. The formal parameter list has the form

ind-1 list-1 : *type-1*; *ind-2 list-2* : *type-2*; . . . ; *ind-k list-k* : *type-k*

where each *list-i* is a single identifier or a list of identifiers separated by commas, and *type-i* specifies their types; *ind-i* indicates how the identifiers in *list-i* are to be used. If this indicator is the reserved word **var,** then the identifiers in the list are *variable parameters* which may be used *both* to return information from the procedure to the program unit that references it *and* to pass information from that program unit to the procedure. If this indicator is omitted, then the identifiers in the list may be used *only* to pass information to this procedure and not to return information.

The following syntax diagrams summarize these forms for the procedure heading and the formal parameter list. (A more general form for the parameter list is given in Section 5.8.)

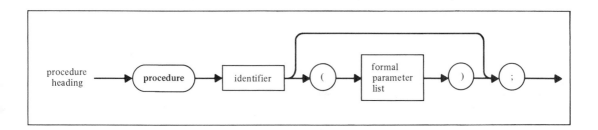

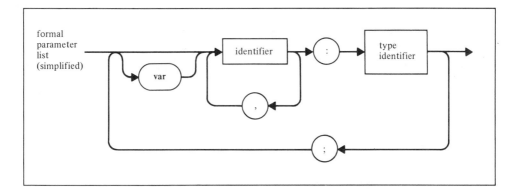

To illustrate, the following procedure accepts a month number, a day number, and a year number, and displays them in the form

$mm/dd/yy$

For example, the values 8, 18, and 1941 are displayed as

8/18/41

and the values 9, 3, and 1905 as

9/3/05

procedure *DisplayDate* (*Month, Day, Year* : *integer*);

    (∗ *Displays a date in the form mm/dd/yy.* ∗)

```
begin (* DisplayDate *)
    Year := Year mod 100;
    if Year < 10 then
        writeln (Month:1, '/', Day:1, '/0', Year:1)
    else
        writeln (Month:1, '/', Day:1, '/', Year:2)
end (* DisplayDate *);
```

Note that because *Month, Day,* and *Year* are used only to pass values to the procedure, they are not designated as variable parameters.

Such a procedure is called with a *procedure reference statement* of the form

> name *(actual-parameter-list)*

where *name* is the name of the procedure and *actual-parameter-list* is a list of actual parameters that are to be associated with the parameters in the formal parameter list of the procedure heading. For example, the procedure *DisplayDate* is called by the statement

> DisplayDate *(TheMonth, TheDay, TheYear)*

in the program of Figure 5.4. This statement causes the values of the actual parameters *TheMonth, TheDay,* and *TheYear* to be assigned to the formal parameters *Month, Day,* and *Year,* respectively, of the procedure *DisplayDate.*

```
PROGRAM Date (input, output);

(***************************************************************************

    Program using a procedure to display a given date in the form
                         mm/dd/yy

***************************************************************************)

VAR
    TheMonth, TheDay, TheYear : integer;    (* month, day, year *)

PROCEDURE DisplayDate (Month, Day, Year : integer);

    (***********************************************************************

            Displays a date in the form mm/dd/yy.

    ***********************************************************************)

    BEGIN (* DisplayDate *)
        Year := Year MOD 100;
        IF Year < 10 THEN
            writeln (Month:1, '/', Day:1, '/0', Year:1)
        ELSE
            writeln (Month:1, '/', Day:1, '/', Year:2)
    END (* DisplayDate *);
```

Figure 5.4.

Fig. 5.4. (cont.)

```
BEGIN (* main program *)
    writeln ('Enter 0''s for month, day, and year to stop.');
    writeln;
    writeln ('Enter month, day, and year:');
    readln (TheMonth, TheDay, TheYear);
    WHILE TheMonth <> 0 DO
        BEGIN
            DisplayDate (TheMonth, TheDay, TheYear);
            writeln;
            writeln ('Enter month, day, and year:');
            readln (TheMonth, TheDay, TheYear)
        END (* WHILE *)
END (* main program *).


Sample run:
==========

Enter 0's for month, day, and year to stop.

Enter month, day, and year:
8 14 1941
8/14/41

Enter month, day, and year:
9 3 1905
9/3/05

Enter month, day, and year:
0 0 0
```

In this example, the procedure *DisplayDate* does not return any values to the main program but only displays information that is passed to it. When the procedure is referenced, the formal parameters *Month, Day,* and *Year* are assigned the values of the corresponding actual parameters *TheMonth, TheDay,* and *TheYear,* but they are not used to return any values. Such formal parameters are called *value parameters.*

Before a *subprogram* (procedure or function) is referenced, its value parameters are undefined. At the time of reference, memory locations are associated with them, and the values of the corresponding actual parameters are copied into these locations. Thus, for the procedure *DisplayDate,* the formal parameters *Month, Day,* and *Year* are undefined until a procedure reference statement such as

DisplayDate (*TheMonth, TheDay, TheYear*)

is encountered. The values of the actual parameters *TheMonth, TheDay,* and *TheYear* are then assigned to *Month, Day,* and *Year,* respectively.

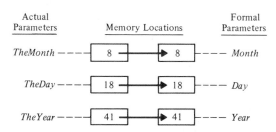

After execution of the procedure, these value parameters once again become undefined so that any values they had during execution of the procedure or function are lost.

We noted earlier that variable parameters may be used to return values from a procedure. A variable formal parameter and the corresponding actual parameter are associated with the same memory location, and thus a variable formal parameter is merely a temporary *alias* or *synonym* for the actual parameter it represents. Consequently, any modification of a variable formal parameter in a subprogram changes the value of the corresponding actual parameter. The actual parameter must therefore be a variable; constants and expressions are not allowed. Also, actual parameters must be of the same type as the corresponding formal parameters.

As a simple example of variable parameters, consider the problem of converting polar coordinates (r, θ) of a point P to rectangular coordinates (x, y). The first polar coordinate r is the distance from the origin to P, and the second polar coordinate θ is the angle from the positive x axis to the ray joining the origin with P.

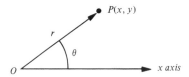

The formulas that relate the polar coordinates to the rectangular coordinates for a point are

$$x = r \cos \theta$$

$$y = r \sin \theta$$

The following procedure carries out this conversion:

```
procedure Convert (r, Theta : real; var x, y : real);

   (* Procedure to convert polar coordinates
      (r, Theta) to rectangular coordinates (x, y). *)

   begin (* Convert *)
      x := r * cos(Theta);
      y := r * sin(Theta)
   end (* Convert *);
```

Because the rectangular coordinates x and y are to be returned by the procedure, they must be declared to be variable parameters.

Figure 5.5 shows a complete program that reads the polar coordinates of a point, calls procedure *Convert* to find the rectangular coordinates of that point, and then displays these coordinates. In this program, the variable declarations

```
var
     rCoord, ThetaCoord,   (* polar coordinates *)
     xCoord, yCoord : real;   (* rectangular coordinates *)
```

```
PROGRAM Polar (input, output);

(*****************************************************************

   Program using a procedure to convert polar coordinates to
   rectangular coordinates.

   ***************************************************************)

VAR
   rCoord, ThetaCoord,        (* polar coordinates *)
   xCoord, yCoord : real;     (* rectangular coordinates *)
   Response : integer;        (* user response *)

PROCEDURE Convert (r, Theta: real; VAR x, y : real);

   (*****************************************************************

         Procedure to convert polar coordinates (r, Theta)
         to rectangular coordinates (x, y).

      ***********************************************************)

   BEGIN (* Convert *)
      x := r * cos(Theta);
      y := r * sin(Theta)
   END (* Convert *);

BEGIN (* main program *)
   REPEAT
      writeln ('Enter polar coordinates:');
      readln (rCoord, ThetaCoord);
      Convert (rCoord, ThetaCoord, xCoord, yCoord);
      writeln ('Rectangular coordinates are (',
               xCoord:4:2, ',', yCoord:4:2, ')');
      writeln;
      writeln ('More (0 = No, 1 = Yes)?');
      readln (Response)
   UNTIL Response <> 1
END (* main program *).


Sample run:
==========


Enter polar coordinates:
2.0 1.1
Rectangular coordinates are (0.91,1.78)

More (0 = No, 1 = Yes)?
1
Enter polar coordinates:
2.2 1.78
Rectangular coordinates are (-0.46,2.15)

More (0 = No, 1 = Yes)?
0
```

Figure 5.5.

associate memory locations with the four variables *rCoord, ThetaCoord, xCoord,* and *yCoord.*

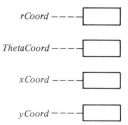

When the statement

Convert (*rCoord, ThetaCoord, xCoord, yCoord*)

is executed, new memory locations are associated with the value parameters *r* and *Theta,* and the values of *rCoord* and *ThetaCoord* are copied into these locations. No new memory locations are obtained for the variable parameters *x* and *y,* but instead these formal parameters are associated with the existing memory locations of the corresponding actual parameters *xCoord* and *yCoord.*

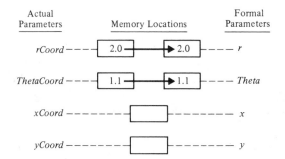

When the procedure *Convert* is executed, values are calculated for *x* and *y,* and because *x* and *y* are associated with the same memory locations as *xCoord* and *yCoord,* these calculated values are also the values of *xCoord* and *yCoord.*

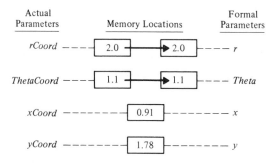

Because the memory locations associated with *r* and *Theta* are distinct from those for *rCoord* and *ThetaCoord,* changes to *r* and *Theta* in procedure *Convert* could not change the values of *rCoord* and *ThetaCoord.* When execution of the procedure is completed, the association of memory locations with *r, Theta, x,* and *y* is terminated, and these formal parameters become undefined.

The following rules summarize the relation between actual and formal parameters:

Rules for Parameter Association

---

1. There must be the same number of formal parameters as there are actual parameters.
2. The types of associated formal and actual parameters must agree; however, an actual parameter of integer type may be associated with a formal value parameter of real type.
3. An actual parameter associated with a variable formal parameter must be a variable; it may not be a constant or an expression.

Exercises

1. Consider the following program skeleton:

program *Demo* (*input, output*);

const
    pi = 3.14159;
    two = 2;

var
    Month, Day, Year, p, q : *integer*;
    Hours, Rate, Amount, u, v : *real*;
    Code, Class : *char*;

function *f(x, y* : *real*; *d* : *integer*) : *real*;
        ⋮

procedure *Calculate* (*a* : *real*; **var** *b* : *real*;
                    m : *integer*; **var** *k, n* : *integer*;
                    var *c* : *char*);
        ⋮

Determine whether each of the following statements can be used in the statement part of the program. If it cannot be used, explain why.

(a) *Calculate* (*u, v, two, p, q, Code*);

(b) *f(Hours, Rate, Month*);

(c) if *u* > 0 **then**
        Amount := *Calculate* (*u, v, two, p, q, Code*);

(d) *Calculate* (*pi, u, two, p, v, Class*);

(e) *Calculate* (*Hours, pi, two, Day, Year, Class*);

(f) while *u* > 0 **do**
        Calculate (*Rate, u, Day* + 2, *p, q,* 'M');

(g) if *Calculate* (0, *u*, 1, *p*, *Year*, *Class*) > 0 **then** *writeln* ('Okay');

(h) *Calculate* (0, *Hours*, (*p* + 1) / 2, *Day*, *Year*, *Code*);

(i) **repeat**

   Calculate (*two*, *Amount*, *Day*, *p* + *q*, *Day*, *Class*)
   until *Amount* > 0;

(j) *Calculate* (*f*(*u*, *v*, *Day*), *Rate*, 7, *p*, *q*, *Code*);

(k) *Amount* := *f*(*a*, *b*, *Day*);

(l) *Calculate* (*x*, *y*, *m*, *d*, *Day*, *Code*);

2. Write a procedure that has as parameters the amount of a purchase and an amount received in payment. Assume that both amounts are given in cents. The procedure should then calculate and display the change in dollars, half-dollars, quarters, dimes, nickels, and pennies. Write a program that reads the two amounts and then calls this procedure.

3. Write a procedure that interchanges the values of two variables. Thus, if *Switch* is the name of the procedure, *a* has value 3, and *b* has value 4, then the reference *Switch* (*a*, *b*) causes *a* to have the value 4 and *b* the value 3.

4. Write a procedure that calculates the amount of city income tax and the amount of federal income tax to be withheld from an employee's pay for one pay period. Assume that city income tax withheld is computed by taking 1.15 percent of gross pay on the first $15,000 earned per year and that federal income tax withheld is computed by taking the gross pay less $15 for each dependent claimed and multiplying by 20 percent.

   Use this procedure in a program that for each of several employees reads his or her employee number, number of dependents, hourly pay rate, city income tax withheld to date, federal income tax withheld to date, and hours worked for this pay period; and then calculates and prints the employee number, gross pay and net pay for this pay period, the amount of city income tax and amount of federal income tax withheld for this pay period, and the total amounts withheld through this pay period.

5. Write a program that reads a positive integer and then calls a procedure that displays its prime factorization, that is, a procedure that expresses a positive integer as a product of primes or indicates that it is a prime (see Exercise 13 in Section 5.2 for the definition of a prime number).

6. Write a program that reads two positive integers *n* and *b* and that then calls a procedure *ChangeBase* to calculate and display the base *b* representation of *n*. Assume that *b* is not greater than 10 (see Exercise 11 of Chapter 1 for one method for converting from base 10 to another base).

FUNCTIONS AND PROCEDURES

7. Write a program that reads a positive integer n and that then calls a procedure *Hexadecimal* to display the base 16 representation of n. The symbols A, B, C, D, E, and F should be displayed for 10, 11, 12, 13, 14, and 15, respectively (see Exercises 6 and 11 of Chapter 1 and the preceding exercise).

As we have seen, functions and procedures are program units whose structures **The Scope of** are similar to that of a Pascal program. Each consists of a heading followed **Identifiers** by a declaration part followed by a statement part. Consequently, in a program that contains functions and/or procedures, there may be several declaration parts. The portion of the program in which an identifier is accessible is called its *scope*. In this section we describe the rules that govern the scopes of identifiers.

There is one basic principle that prescribes the scope of an identifier. All of the other scope rules are consequences of this general principle.

> **Fundamental Scope Principle**
>
> The scope of an identifier is the program unit in which it is declared.

Recall that identifiers may be declared in either the heading of a program unit or its declaration part. Thus this scope principle applies both to formal parameters that appear in a heading and to constants, variables, function and procedure names (and user-defined types as discussed in Chapter 7) that appear in the declaration part of a program unit.

An immediate consequence of this principle is

> **Scope Rule 1**
>
> An identifier declared in a program unit is not accessible outside that unit.

To illustrate, consider the problem of calculating binomial coefficients $\binom{n}{k}$ for nonnegative integers n and k defined by

$$\binom{n}{k} = \frac{n!}{k!(n-k)!}$$

Here the expressions $n!$, $k!$, and $(n-k)!$ represent factorials defined in general by

$$m! = \begin{cases} 1 \text{ if } m = 0 \\ 1 \times 2 \times \cdots \times m \text{ if } m > 0 \end{cases}$$

The program in Figure 5.6 reads values for n and k and then displays the value of the binomial coefficient $\binom{n}{k}$, using the following function to calculate the necessary factorials:

> **function** *Factorial(m : integer) : integer*;
>
> > (* Function to calculate *m*! = the factorial of *m*. This is
> > defined to be 1 if *m* = 0, and 1 * 2 * $\cdots$ * *m* for *m* $>=$ 1. *)
> > **var**
> > > *k*,   (* index *)
> > > *Fac : integer*; (* partial factorial *)
> > **begin** (* *Factorial* *)
> > > *Fac* := 1;
> > > **for** *k* := 2 **to** *m* **do**
> > > > *Fac* := *Fac* * *k*;
> > > *Factorial* := *Fac*
> > **end** (* *Factorial* *);

According to the Fundamental Scope Principle, the scope of the formal parameter *m* and the variables *k* and *Fac* is the function *Factorial,* and by Scope Rule 1, they are not accessible outside this function. Such identifiers are

```
PROGRAM BinomialCoefficients (input, output);

(*******************************************************************
                                              n!
   Program to calculate binomial coefficients (n:k) = ---------
                                              k!*(n-k)!
   for various values of n and k.

 *****************************************************************)
VAR
   n, k,                        (* values entered *)
   BinomCoeff : integer;        (* binomial coefficient *)

FUNCTION Factorial (m : integer) : integer;

   (****************************************************************

      Function to calculate m! = the factorial of m.  This is
      defined to be 1 if m = 0, and 1 * 2 * ... * m for m >= 1.

    **************************************************************)
   VAR
      k,                        (* index *)
      Fac : integer;            (* partial factorial *)

   BEGIN (* Factorial *)
      Fac := 1;
      FOR k := 2 TO m DO
         Fac := Fac * k;
      Factorial := Fac
   END (* Factorial *);
```

Figure 5.6.

Fig. 5.6. (cont.)

```
BEGIN (* main program *)
    writeln ('Enter negative values for n and k to stop.');
    writeln;
    writeln ('Enter n and k:');
    readln (n,k);
    WHILE n >= 0 DO
        BEGIN
            BinomCoeff := Factorial(n) DIV (Factorial(k) * Factorial(n-k));
            writeln ('(', n:1, ':', k:1, ') = ', BinomCoeff:1);
            writeln;
            writeln ('Enter n and k:');
            readln (n, k)
        END (* WHILE *)
END (* main program *).


Sample run:
==========

Enter negative values for n and k to stop.

Enter n and k:
7 0
(7:0) = 1

Enter n and k:
8 3
(8:3) = 56

Enter n and k:
5 5
(5:5) = 1

Enter n and k:
10 4
(10:4) = 210

Enter n and k:
-1 -1
```

local to the function, and any attempt to use them outside the function is an error.

The Fundamental Scope Principle states that the scope of an identifier is the program unit in which it is declared. In particular, the "main program" is a program unit. The identifiers listed in the heading of the main program or declared in its declaration part are called *global variables* since they are accessible throughout the entire program except within program units in which they are declared locally.

Scope Rule 2

A global identifier is accessible in any program unit in which that identifier is not declared locally.

For example, in the program in Figure 5.6, the global variables n and *BinomCoeff* are accessible to both the main program and the function *Factorial*. The global variable k is not accessible to the function *Factorial*, however, since k is declared locally in *Factorial*. Reference to the variable k within the function *Factorial* yields the value of the local variable k, whereas a reference to k outside the function gives the value of the global variable k. Thus these k's represent two different variables which are associated with two different memory locations.

Although global variables can be used to share data between program units, it is usually unwise to do so since this practice destroys the independence of the various program units and thus makes modular programming more difficult. Changing the value of a global variable in one program unit has the side effect of changing the value of that variable in all of the other program units. Consequently, it is difficult to determine the value of that variable at any particular point in the program. The program in Figure 5.7 illustrates this. The value of the global variable y is modified in the procedure *Increment* and its value in the main program cannot be easily determined.

```
PROGRAM ValueChange (output);

(*****************************************************************

    Program demonstrating modification of a global variable by
    a subprogram.

*****************************************************************)
VAR
    x, y : integer;

PROCEDURE Increment (VAR Number : integer);

    BEGIN (* Increment *)
        y := Number DIV 2;
        Number := Number + y
    END (* Increment *);

BEGIN (* main program *)
    x := 2;
    y := 1;
    writeln ('x = ', x:1);
    writeln ('y = ', y:1);
    Increment (x);
    writeln ('x = ', x:1);
    Increment (y);
    writeln ('y = ', y:1)
END (* main program *).


Sample run:
==========


x = 2
y = 1
x = 3
y = 0
```

Figure 5.7

The second scope rule applies to identifiers in a main program and their accessibility in a subprogram. Recall that functions and procedures have declaration parts in which other functions and/or procedures may be defined. The third scope rule applies to such nested functions and procedures.

Scope Rule 3

An identifier declared in a subprogram can be accessed by any subprogram defined within it, provided that the identifier is not declared locally in the internal subprogram.

To illustrate this scope rule, we consider the problem of calculating binomial probabilities. Such probabilities arise in analyzing an experiment consisting of a sequence of trials, each of which has two possible outcomes, "success" and "failure." An example is a sequence of coin tosses in which the appearance of a head is considered a success and the appearance of a tail a failure. The probability of success on each trial of such an experiment is assumed to be some constant p, and the probability of failure is then $1 - p$. The probability of exactly k successes in n trials is given by

$$\binom{n}{k}p^k(1-p)^{n-k}$$

The program in Figure 5.8 reads values for n, k, and p. It uses the function *Binomial* to calculate the binomial coefficient $\binom{n}{k}$ and the function *Power* to calculate p^k and $(1-p)^{n-k}$. The function *Binomial* in turn references the function *Factorial* to calculate $n!$, $k!$, and $(n-k)!$. The relationship among these program units is indicated by the diagram in Figure 5.9, which shows clearly the nesting of the function *Factorial* within *Binomial*, and *Binomial* within the main program.

```
PROGRAM Probability (input, output);

(*********************************************************************

    Program to calculate binomial probabilities.  Functions Binomial,
    Factorial and Power are used.

*********************************************************************)

VAR
    n,                  (* number of trials *)
    k : integer;        (* number of successes *)
    p,                  (* probability of success *)
    Prob : real;        (* probability of k successes in n trials *)

FUNCTION Binomial (n, k : integer) : integer;

    (*******************************************************************

                                           n!
        Returns the binomial coefficient (n:k) = ---------
                                           k!*(n-k)!

    *******************************************************************)
```

Figure 5.8

Fig. 5.8 (cont.)

```
VAR
    Fact1, Fact2, Fact3 : integer;   (* Factorials *)

FUNCTION Factorial (m : integer) : integer;

    (******************************************************************

       Function to calculate m! = the factorial of m.  This is
       defined to be 1 if m = 0, and 1 * 2 * ... * m for m >= 1.

    ******************************************************************)

    VAR
       k,               (* index *)
       Fac : integer;   (* partial factorial *)

    BEGIN (* Factorial *)
       Fac := 1;
       FOR k := 2 TO m DO
          Fac := Fac * k;
       Factorial := Fac
    END (* Factorial *);

BEGIN (* Binomial *)
   Fact1 := Factorial(n);
   Fact2 := Factorial(k);
   Fact3 := Factorial(n - k);
   Binomial := Fact1 DIV (Fact2 * Fact3)
END (* Binomial *);

FUNCTION Power(x : real; n : integer) : real;

   (******************************************************************

      Function returns the n-th power of x for any real value x and
      any integer value n (positive, zero, or negative).

   ******************************************************************)

   VAR
      i : integer;     (* index *)
      Prod : real;     (* product of x's *)

   BEGIN (* Power *)
      IF x = 0 THEN
         Power := 0
      ELSE
         BEGIN
            Prod := 1;
            FOR i := 1 to abs(n) DO
               Prod := Prod * x;
            IF n >= 0 THEN
               Power := Prod
            ELSE
               Power := 1 / Prod
         END (* ELSE *)
   END (* Power *);
```

Fig. 5.8 (cont.)

```
BEGIN (* main program *)
    writeln ('Enter number of trials, number of successes desired,');
    writeln ('and probability of success (all 0''s to stop):');
    readln (n, k, p);
    WHILE n <> 0 DO
        BEGIN
            Prob := Binomial(n, k) * Power(p, k) * Power(1 - p, n - k);
            writeln ('Probability of ', k:1, ' successes in ', n:1,
                    ' trials is ', Prob:5:4);
            writeln;
            writeln ('# trials, # successes, probability of success?');
            readln (n, k, p)
        END (* WHILE *)
END (* main program *).


Sample run:
==========

Enter number of trials, number of successes desired,
and probability of success (all 0's to stop):
10 1 0.5
Probability of 1 successes in 10 trials is 0.0098

# trials, # successes, probability of success?
10 2 0.5
Probability of 2 successes in 10 trials is 0.0439

# trials, # successes, probability of success?
10 3 0.5
Probability of 3 successes in 10 trials is 0.1172

# trials, # successes, probability of success?
0 0 0
```

The third scope rule states that identifiers declared in a subprogram can be accessed in a subprogram contained within it, provided that they are not declared locally in the internal subprogram. Thus, in this example, the formal parameter n and the variables *Fact1*, *Fact2*, and *Fact3* of the function *Binomial* are accessible within it as well as within the function *Factorial*. The formal parameter k in *Binomial*, however, is not accessible to the function *Factorial*, because k is declared as a local variable within *Factorial*.

According to Scope Rule 2, the global variables p and *Prob* (as well as the files *input* and *output*) are accessible to both of the functions *Binomial* and *Factorial*. On the other hand, the global variables n and k are not accessible to the function *Binomial* and thus not to *Factorial*, since they are local variables in *Binomial*. Similarly, the global variables p, k and *Prob* are accessible to the function *Power*, whereas n is not.

It should be noted in this example that the function *Factorial* is not accessible to the main program or to the function *Power*, since it is defined within the function *Binomial*. This is undesirable if factorials need to be calculated in the main program, because the function *Factorial* is not available. This limitation can be removed by defining all of the functions *Power*, *Binomial*, and *Factorial* in the main program so that the program has the structure shown in Figure 5.10.

program *Probability*

parameters: *input, output*

var *n, k, p, Prob*

function *Binomial*

    parameters: *n, k*

    var *Fact1, Fact2, Fact3*

    function *Factorial*

        parameters: *m*

        var *k, F*

        begin (* *Factorial* *)
            ⋮
        end (* *Factorial* *);

    begin (* *Binomial* *)
        ⋮
      Fact1 := *Factorial* (*n*);
      Fact2 := *Factorial* (*k*);
      Fact3 := *Factorial* (*n* − *k*);
        ⋮
    end (* *Binomial* *);

function *Power*

    parameters: *x, n*

    var *i, Prod*

    begin (* *Power* *)
        ⋮
    end (* *Power* *);

begin (* main program *);
    ⋮
  Prob := *Binomial* (*n, k*) * *Power* (*p, k*) * *Power* (1 − *p, n* − *k*);
    ⋮
end (* main program *).

Figure 5.9.

Since the function *Factorial* is referenced by the function *Binomial*, it must be defined before *Binomial* is. In general, a function or procedure must be defined before it can be referenced by another function or procedure at the same level. This is the fourth scope rule.

Scope Rule 4

If *SubA* and *SubB* are subprograms defined in the same program unit and if *SubA* is referenced by *SubB*, then *SubA* must be defined before *SubB*.

According to this scope rule, the program in Figure 5.11 is an acceptable alternative to that in Figure 5.8 because the functions are arranged in the order *Factorial, Binomial, Power*. Other acceptable orderings of these functions are *Factorial, Power, Binomial* and *Power, Factorial, Binomial*. However, the ordering *Binomial, Factorial, Power* would not be valid since *Binomial* references *Factorial,* thus violating Scope Rule 4.

```
parameters: input, output
var n, k, p, Prob
function Factorial

    parameters: m
    var k, F
    begin (* Factorial *)
        ⋮
    end (* Factorial *);

function Binomial

    parameters: n, k
    var Fact1, Fact2, Fact3
    begin (* Binomial *)
        ⋮
        Fact1 := Factorial (n);
        Fact2 := Factorial (k);
        Fact3 := Factorial (n − k);
        ⋮
    end (* Binomial *);

function Power

    parameters: x, n
    var i, Prod
    begin (* Power *)
        ⋮
    end (* Power *);

begin (* main program *)
    ⋮
    Prob := Binomial (n, k) * Power (p, k) * Power (1 − p, n − k);
    ⋮
end (* main program *).
```

Figure 5.10

```
PROGRAM Probability (input, output);

(**********************************************************************

   Program to calculate binomial probabilities.  Functions Binomial,
   Factorial and Power are used.

**********************************************************************)

VAR
   n,              (* number of trials *)
   k : integer;    (* number of successes *)
   p,              (* probability of success *)
   Prob : real;    (* probability of k successes in n trials *)

FUNCTION Factorial (m : integer) : integer;

   (********************************************************************

       Function to calculate m! = the factorial of m.  This is
       defined to be 1 if m = 0, and 1 * 2 * ... * m for m >= 1.

   ********************************************************************)
```

Figure 5.11.

Fig. 5.11. (cont.)

```
VAR
    k,                   (* index *)
    Fac : integer;   (* partial factorial *)

BEGIN (* Factorial *)
    Fac := 1;
    FOR k := 2 TO m DO
        Fac := Fac * k;
    Factorial := Fac
END (* Factorial *);

FUNCTION Binomial (n, k : integer) : integer;

(*****************************************************************

                                n!
    Returns the binomial coefficient (n:k) = ---------
                                           k!*(n-k)!

*****************************************************************)

VAR
    Fact1, Fact2, Fact3 : integer;    (* Factorials *)

BEGIN (* Binomial *)
    Fact1 := Factorial(n);
    Fact2 := Factorial(k);
    Fact3 := Factorial(n - k);
    Binomial := Fact1 DIV (Fact2 * Fact3)
END (* Binomial *);

FUNCTION Power(x : real; n : integer) : real;

(*****************************************************************

    Function returns the n-th power of x for any real value x and
    any integer value n (positive, zero, or negative).

*****************************************************************)

VAR
    i : integer;      (* index *)
    Prod : real;      (* product of x's *)

BEGIN (* Power *)
    IF x = 0 THEN
        Power := 0
    ELSE
        BEGIN
            Prod := 1;
            FOR i := 1 to abs(n) DO
                Prod := Prod * x;
            IF n >= 0 THEN
                Power := Prod
            ELSE
                Power := 1 / Prod
        END (* ELSE *)
END (* Power *);
```

Fig. 5.11. (cont.)

```
BEGIN (* main program *)
   writeln ('Enter number of trials, number of successes desired,');
   writeln ('and probability of success (all 0''s to stop):');
   readln (n, k, p);
   WHILE n <> 0 DO
      BEGIN
         Prob := Binomial(n, k) * Power(p, k) * Power(1 - p, n - k);
         writeln ('Probability of ', k:1, ' successes in ', n:1,
               ' trials is ', Prob:5:4);
         writeln;
         writeln ('# trials, # successes, probability of success?');
         readln (n, k, p)
      END (* WHILE *)
END (* main program *).
```

5.5

Consider the problem of writing a program to simulate rolling a pair of ordinary dice, that is, to generate a "random" sequence of pairs of integers in the range 1 through 6. Such a program would use a *random number generator,* which is a function or procedure that produces a number selected "at random" from some fixed range in such a way that a sequence of these numbers tends to be uniformly distributed over the given range. Although it is not possible to develop an algorithm that produces truly random numbers, there are some methods that produce sequences of *pseudorandom numbers* that are adequate for most purposes.

An Example: Random Number Generation

Some computer systems provide a random number generator that produces random real numbers in the range 0 through 1. The numbers produced by such a generator can be used to generate a random sequence of pairs of integers from 1 through 6, as required by this problem. To demonstrate how this can be done, suppose that the random number generator is implemented as a function *Rand* having one integer argument. An expression of the form

$$1 + trunc(6 * Rand(n))$$

produces an integer randomly selected from the range 1 through 6. Thus the statements

$Die1 := 1 + trunc(6 * Rand(n));$
$Die2 := 1 + trunc(6 * Rand(n));$
$Pair := Die1 + Die2;$

simulate rolling two dice, and the value of *Pair* is the total number of spots showing.

If the random number generator is suitably constructed, the relative frequency of each value from 2 through 12 for *Pair* should correspond to the probability of that number occurring on one throw of a pair of dice. These probabilities (rounded to three decimal places) are given in the following table:

Outcome	Probability
2	0.028
3	0.056
4	0.083
5	0.111
6	0.139
7	0.167
8	0.139
9	0.111
10	0.083
11	0.056
12	0.028

The program in Figure 5.12 reads an integer indicating a possible outcome of a roll of two dice and an integer indicating the number of times the dice are to be tossed and displays the relative frequency of this outcome. In performing this simulation, the program uses the function *Rand* to generate random real numbers in the range 0 through 1. The random real number generated at each stage is calculated by using an integer *Seed* generated at the preceding stage, with the initial value of *Seed* entered by the user. Since local variables become undefined after the execution of a function, this variable *Seed* cannot be declared locally in the function *Rand*. The technique used in this program of making *Seed* a variable parameter instead of a value parameter of *Rand* ensures that its value is available during each execution of *Rand*.[1]

```
PROGRAM DiceRoll (input, output);

(*******************************************************************

    This program uses the random number generator Rand to simulate
    rolling a pair of dice, counting the number of times a specified
    number of spots occurs.

*******************************************************************)

VAR
    Spots,        (* # of spots to be counted *)
    Count,        (* number of times Spots occurred *)
    Rolls,        (* # of rolls of dice *)
    Seed,         (* seed for random number generator *)
    Die1, Die2,   (* # of spots on die #1, #2, respectively *)
    Pair,         (* sum of Die1 and Die2 = total # of spots on the dice *)
    i : integer;  (* index variable *)

FUNCTION Rand (VAR Seed : integer) : real;
```

Figure 5.12

---

[1] For details of this and other techniques of generating random numbers, see Donald Knuth, *The Art of Computer Programming: Seminumerical Algorithms,* vol. 2 (Reading, Mass.: Addison-Wesley, 1981).

Fig. 5.12 (cont.)

```
(*****************************************************************

    This function generates a random real number in the interval
    from 0 to 1.  The parameter Seed is initially the seed supplied
    by the user; thereafter, it is the random integer generated on
    the preceding reference to Rand.
    NOTE:  The constant 65536 used in this function is appropriate
    for a machine having 32-bit words.  For a machine having M-bit
    words, it should be replaced by the value of 2 to the power M/2.

 *****************************************************************)

    CONST Modulus = 65536;
          Multiplier = 25173;
          Increment = 13849;

    BEGIN (* Rand *)
       Seed := (Multiplier * Seed + Increment) MOD Modulus;
       Rand := Seed / Modulus
    END (* Rand *);


BEGIN (* main program *)
   writeln ('# of spots to count:');
   readln (Spots);
   writeln ('# of times to roll the dice:');
   readln (Rolls);
   writeln ('Seed for random # generator (an odd integer):');
   readln (Seed);
   Count := 0;
   FOR i := 1 TO Rolls DO
      BEGIN
         Die1 := 1 + trunc(6 * Rand(Seed));
         Die2 := 1 + trunc(6 * Rand(Seed));
         Pair := Die1 + Die2;
         IF Pair = Spots THEN
            Count := Count + 1
      END (* FOR *);
   writeln;
   writeln ('Relative frequency of ', Spots:1, ' was ', Count / Rolls:5:3)
END (* main program *).



Sample run:
=========

# of spots to count:
6
# of times to roll the dice:
500
Seed for random # generator (an odd integer):
13

Relative frequency of 6 was 0.138
```

Exercises

1. The *power series*

$$1 + x + \frac{x^2}{2!} + \frac{x^3}{3!} + \cdots = \sum_{n=0}^{\infty} \frac{x^n}{n!}$$

converges to e^x for all values of x. Write a function that uses this series to calculate values for e^x, using terms up to the first one that is less than 10^{-5} in absolute value, and that uses the functions *Factorial* and *Power* in the text. Use these functions in a program to calculate and print a table of values for the function

$$\cosh(x) = \frac{e^x + e^{-x}}{2}$$

for $x = -1$ to 1 in increments of 0.1.

2. A more efficient procedure for evaluating the power series in Exercise 1 is to observe that if

$$a_n = \frac{x^n}{n!}$$

and

$$a_{n+1} = \frac{x^{n+1}}{(n+1)!}$$

are two consecutive terms of the series, then

$$a_{n+1} = \frac{x}{n+1} a_n$$

Write a subprogram to calculate e^x using the series of Exercise 1 and this relationship between consecutive terms. Then use this subprogram in a program to print a table of values for the function

$$\sinh(x) = \frac{e^x - e^{-x}}{2}$$

for $x = -2$ to 2 in increments of 0.1.

3. The *greatest common divisor* of two integers a and b, GCD(a,b), not both of which are zero, is the largest positive integer that divides both a and b. The *Euclidean Algorithm* for finding this greatest common divisor of a and b is as follows: Divide a by b to obtain the integer quotient q and remainder r, so that $a = bq + r$ (if $b = 0$, interchange a and b). Then GCD(a,b) = GCD(b,r). Replace a with b and b with r and repeat this procedure. Since the remainders are decreasing, eventually a remainder of 0 results. The last nonzero remainder is GCD(a,b). For example:

$$
\begin{array}{ll}
1260 = 198 \cdot 6 + 72 & \mathrm{GCD}(1260\,,198) = \mathrm{GCD}(198\,,72) \\
198 = 72 \cdot 2 + 54 & \phantom{\mathrm{GCD}(1260\,,198)} = \mathrm{GCD}(72\,,54) \\
72 = 54 \cdot 1 + 18 & \phantom{\mathrm{GCD}(1260\,,198)} = \mathrm{GCD}(54\,,18) \\
54 = 18 \cdot 3 + 0 & \phantom{\mathrm{GCD}(1260\,,198)} = 18
\end{array}
$$

Note: If either a or b is negative, we replace them with their absolute values.
(a) Write a function or procedure that uses the Euclidean Algorithm to calculate the greatest common divisor of two integers.

(b) The *least common multiple* of integers a and b, LCM (a,b), is the smallest nonnegative integer that is a multiple of both a and b. It can be calculated using

$$\text{LCM}(a,b) = \frac{|a \cdot b|}{\text{GCD}(a,b)}$$

Write a function or procedure that uses the GCD subprogram of part (a) to calculate the least common multiple of two integers.

(c) Write a program that reads two integers and uses these two subprograms to calculate and display their greatest common divisor and least common multiple.

4. Write a program that uses the GCD subprogram in Exercise 3 to calculate and display the greatest common divisor of any finite set of integers, by using the following:

If $d = \text{GCD}(a_1, \ldots, a_n)$, then
$\text{GCD}(a_1, \ldots, a_n, a_{n+1}) = \text{GCD}(d, a_{n+1})$

For example:

$$\text{GCD}(1260, 198) = 18$$
$$\text{GCD}(1260, 198, 585) = \text{GCD}(18, 585) = 9$$
$$\text{GCD}(1260, 198, 585, 138) = \text{GCD}(9, 138) = 3$$

Simulation Exercises

5. A coin is tossed and a payoff of 2^n dollars is made, where n is the number of the toss on which the first head appears. For example, TTH pays \$8, TH pays \$4, and H pays \$2. Write a program to simulate playing this game 100 times, and print the average payoff for these games.

6. Suppose that a gambler places a wager of \$5.00 on the following game: A pair of dice is tossed, and if the result is odd, the gambler loses his wager. If the result is even, a card is drawn from a standard deck of fifty two playing cards. If the card drawn is an ace, 3, 5, 7, or 9, the gambler wins the value of the card; otherwise, he loses. What will be the average winnings for this game? Write a program to simulate the game.

7. Johann VanDerDoe, centerfielder for the Klavin Klodhoppers, has the following lifetime hitting percentages:

Out	63.4%
Walk	10.3%
Single	19%
Double	4.9%
Triple	1.1%
Home run	1.3%

Write a program to simulate 1000 times at bat for Johann, counting the number of outs, walks, singles, and so on, and calculating his batting average ((# of hits)/(1000 − # of walks)).

8. The classic *drunkard's walk problem* is as follows: Over an 8-block line, the home of an intoxicated chap is at block 8, and a pub is at block 1. Our poor friend starts at block n, $1 < n < 8$, and wanders at random, 1 block at a time, either toward or away from home. At any intersection, he moves toward the pub with a certain probability, say 2/3, and toward home with a certain probability, say 1/3. Having gotten either home or to the pub, he remains there. Write a program to simulate 500 trips in which he starts at block 2, another 500 in which he starts at block 3, and so forth up to block 7. For each starting point, calculate and print the percentage of the time he ends up at home and the average number of blocks he walked on each trip.

9. The famous *Buffon Needle Problem* is as follows: A board is ruled with equidistant parallel lines, and a needle of length equal to the distance between these lines is dropped at random on the board. Write a program to simulate this experiment and estimate the probability p that the needle crosses one of these lines. Display the values of p and $2/p$. (The value of $2/p$ should be approximately equal to a well-known constant. What constant is it?)

10. An unusual method for approximating the area under a curve is the following *Monte Carlo technique*. As illustrated in Figure 5.13, consider a rectangle with base $[a,b]$ and height m, where $f(x) \leq m$ for all x in $[a,b]$. Imagine throwing q darts at rectangle $ABCD$ and counting the total number p that hit the shaded region. For a large number of throws, we would expect

$$\frac{p}{q} \simeq \frac{\text{area of shaded region}}{\text{area of rectangle } ABCD}$$

Write a program to calculate areas using this Monte Carlo method. To simulate throwing a dart, generate two random numbers, X from $[a,b]$ and Y from $[0,m]$, and consider the point (X,Y) to be the point where the dart hits.

Figure 5.13.

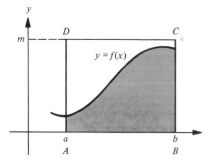

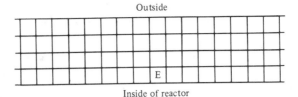

Outside

E

Inside of reactor

Figure 5.14.

11. Figure 5.14 shows a cross-section of the lead-shielding wall of a nuclear reactor. A neutron enters the wall at a point E and then follows a random path by moving forward, backward, right, or left, in jumps of one unit. A change of direction is interpreted as a collision with an atom of lead. After 10 such collisions suppose that the neutron's energy is dissipated and that it dies within the lead shielding, provided that it has not already passed back inside the reactor or outside the shielding (by moving forward a net distance of 4 units). Write a program to simulate 100 neutrons entering this shield, and calculate how many reach the outside of the reactor.

5.6 An Example: Top–Down Design and Modular Programming

As we noted in the introduction to this chapter, functions and procedures facilitate modular programming in which individual subprograms are designed to carry out particular tasks. To demonstrate this use of functions and procedures, we consider the following problem.

Suppose that the athletic department at a certain university wants a program for its secretarial staff that can be used to determine the academic eligibility of its athletes for the next academic year. This eligibility check is made at the end of each of the first three years of the student's academic career. Eligibility is determined by two criteria: the number of hours that the student has successfully completed and his or her cumulative grade point average. To maintain eligibility, the student must have completed at least 25 hours with a minimum grade point average (GPA) of 1.7 by the end of the first year. At the end of the second year, 50 hours must have been completed with a cumulative GPA of 1.85 or higher, and at the end of the third year, 85 hours must have been completed with a minimum cumulative GPA of 1.95.

The program should display the student's number, class, cumulative hours, GPA for the current year, and cumulative GPA, as well as an indication of his or her eligibility. At the end of this report, the program should also display the total number of students processed, the number who are eligible, and the average current GPA for all students. The information to be supplied to the program is the student's number, class level, hours accumulated, cumulative GPA, and hours and grades for courses taken during the current year.

Since this program will be used by personnel who are generally not regular users of a computer system, some instructions should be displayed each time the program is used. The first module in the program will be designed to carry out this task. The second task is to accept the given informa-

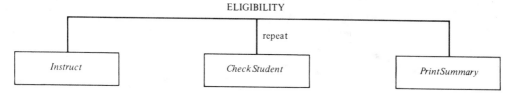

ELIGIBILITY

Figure 5.15.

tion for each student, calculate the relevant statistics, and determine eligibility. The final task is to generate and display the desired summary statistics after all the student information has been processed. The following outline along with the structure diagram in Figure 5.15 summarize this analysis:

Input data

student's number.
class level (1, 2, or 3).
cumulative hours.
cumulative GPA.
hours and grade for each course completed in the current year.

Output data

student's number.
current GPA.
updated cumulative hours and cumulative GPA.
indication of eligibility.
number of students processed.
number of students eligible.
average of all current GPAS.

Level-1 algorithm

1. Provide instructions to the user.
2. Repeat the following until the end-of-data flag is encountered:

   Read the given information for a student, calculate statistics, determine eligibility, and display report.

3. Calculate and display summary statistics.

The three tasks we have identified can be implemented as procedures: *Instruct, CheckStudent,* and *PrintSummary.* Since the procedure *Instruct* simply displays instructions to the user, it requires no information from other program units. The procedure *PrintSummary* requires the total number of students processed (*StudentCount*), the total number who are eligible to participate in athletics (*EligibleCount*), and the sum of all the current GPAs (*SumOfGpas*). These values must be calculated by the procedure *CheckStudent* and shared with *PrintSummary.* Thus, the entire program has the form

```
program Eligibility (input, output);

var
    StudentCount, EligibleCount : integer;
    SumOfGpas : real;
    Response : integer;

procedure Instruct;
        ⋮
procedure CheckStudent (var StudentCount, EligibleCount : integer;
                        var SumOfGpas : real);
        ⋮
procedure PrintSummary (Student, EligibleCount : integer;
                        SumOfGpas : real);
        ⋮
begin (* main program *)
    Instruct;
    StudentCount := 0;
    SumOfGpas := 0;
    repeat
        CheckStudent (StudentCount, EligibleCount, SumOfGpas);
        writeln ('More (0 = No, 1 = Yes)?');
        readln (Response)
    until Response <> 1;
    PrintSummary (StudentCount, EligibleCount, SumOfGpas)
end (* main program *).
```

Since *CheckStudent* is central to the entire program and is the most complex of the three procedures, we begin with its development. We can identify three main subtasks. The first is to read the information for a student and calculate the relevant statistics. The second subtask is to use these statistics to determine whether the student is eligible for athletics. The third subtask is to generate a report displaying some of these statistics and an indication of eligibility. Using the second-level procedures *ReadAndCalculate, CheckEligibility,* and *Report* to carry out these subtasks within the procedure *CheckStudent,* we obtain the structure diagram in Figure 5.16.

The procedure *ReadAndCalculate* reads a student's number (*Snumb*), class level (*Class*), cumulative hours (*CumHours*), and cumulative GPA

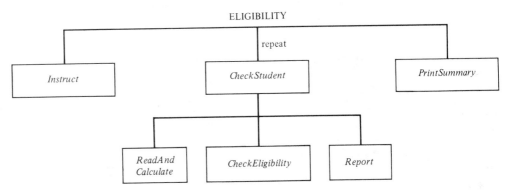

Figure 5.16.

(*CumGpa*). It then calculates the student's current GPA (*CurrGpa*) and updates the values of *CumHours, CumGpa, StudentCount, SumOfGpas.* Because each of these must be shared with other program units, they are variable parameters for this procedure, and so its heading is

> **procedure** *ReadAndCalculate* (**var** *Snumb, Class, StudentCount : integer;*
> **var** *CumHours, CumGpa, CurrGpa, SumOfGpas : real*);

The procedure *CheckEligibility* uses the values of *Class, CumHours,* and *CumGpa* to determine a student's eligibility. This eligibility status can be shared by using the boolean variable parameter *Eligible.* This procedure must also update the value of *EligibleCount.* These five variables are the parameters for *CheckEligibility,* and so its procedure heading is

> **procedure** *CheckEligibility* (*Class : integer; CumHours, CumGpa : real;*
> **var** *Eligible : boolean;*
> **var** *EligibleCount : integer*);

The procedure *Report* only displays the values of *Snumb, Class, CumHours, CurrGpa, CumGpa,* and the student's eligibility status (*Eligible*) in an appropriate format. These six values must be passed to this procedure, and so an appropriate heading is

> **procedure** *Report* (*Snumb, Class : integer;*
> *CumHours, CurrGpa, CumGpa : real;*
> *Eligible : boolean*);

The development of the procedure *ReadAndCalculate* and its implementation as a complete Pascal procedure are relatively straightforward. This procedure can be incorporated into the program and tested before the other procedures are developed. We insert a *writeln* statement in each of the unfinished procedures to signal a call to that procedure. For example,

```
procedure Instruct;
    begin (* Instruct *)
        writeln ('********** Instruct called **********')
    end (* Instruct *);
```

Thus we can verify the correctness of both *ReadAndCalculate* and the main program without being overly concerned with the details of the other procedures. In the program shown in Figure 5.17, the procedures *Instruct, PrintSummary,* and *CheckEligibility* contain *writeln* statements to signal their execution; *CheckEligibility* assigns a temporary value of *false* to *Eligible;* and *Report* produces a temporary printout to enable us to verify the correctness of *ReadAndCalculate.* The procedure *ReadAndCalculate* is in its final form, as are the statement parts of *CheckStudent* and the main program.

```
PROGRAM Eligibility (input, output);

(********************************************************************

   Program to determine academic eligibility of athletes according to
   two criteria:  cumulative hours and cumulative gpa.  It also
   counts the total # of students checked, the # found to be eligible
   and calculates the average current gpa for all students.

********************************************************************)

VAR
   StudentCount,                 (* count of all students processed *)
   EligibleCount : integer;      (* count of the # found to be eligible *)
   SumOfGpas : real;             (* sum of current gpas of all students *)
   Response : integer;           (* user response *)

PROCEDURE Instruct;

   BEGIN (* Instruct *)
      writeln ('********** Instruct called **********')
   END (* Instruct *);

PROCEDURE CheckStudent (VAR StudentCount, EligibleCount : integer;
                        VAR SumOfGpas : real);

   (*****************************************************************

      Accepts student information, determines eligibility,
      and maintains counts of # processed and # eligible,
      and a sum of the current gpa's.

   *****************************************************************)

   VAR
      Snumb,                  (* student number *)
      Class : integer;        (* student's class level -- 1, 2, or 3 *)
      CumHours,               (* cumulative hours *)
      CumGpa,                 (* cumulative grade point average *)
      CurrGpa : real;         (* current grade point average *)
      Eligible : boolean;     (* true if student eligible, else false *)

   PROCEDURE ReadAndCalculate ( VAR Snumb, Class, StudentCount : integer;
                        VAR CumHours, CumGpa, CurrGpa, SumOfGpas : real);

      (*****************************************************************

         Procedure to read a student's number, class, cumulative
         hours and cumulative gpa; then read hours and grades
         for courses taken during the current year, and calculate
         current gpa, update cumulative hours, cumulative gpa,
         and count of students processed.  Hours = 0 and grade = 0
         are used to signal the end of data for a student.

      *****************************************************************)

      VAR
         Hours,                  (* hours of credit for a course *)
         Grade,                  (* numeric grade for that course *)
         NewHours,               (* total hours earned during current year *)
         NewHonorPts,            (* honor points earned in current year *)
         OldHonorPts : real;     (* honor points earned in past years *)
```

Figure 5.17.

Fig. 5.17. (cont.)

```
BEGIN (* ReadAndCalculate *)
    writeln ('Enter student number, class, cum. hours, cum. gpa:');
    readln (Snumb, Class, CumHours, CumGpa);
    OldHonorPts := CumHours * CumGpa;
    NewHours := 0;
    NewHonorPts := 0;
    writeln ('Hours and grade?');
    readln (Hours, Grade);
    WHILE Hours > 0 DO
        BEGIN
            NewHours := NewHours + Hours;
            NewHonorPts := NewHonorPts + Hours * Grade;
            writeln ('Hours and grade?');
            readln (Hours, Grade);
        END (* WHILE *);
    IF NewHours = 0 THEN
        CurrGpa := 0
    ELSE
        CurrGpa := NewHonorPts / NewHours;
    SumOfGpas := SumOfGpas + CurrGpa;
    CumHours := CumHours + NewHours;
    CumGpa := (OldHonorPts + NewHonorPts) / CumHours;
    StudentCount := StudentCount + 1;
END (* ReadAndCalculate *);

PROCEDURE CheckEligibility (Class: integer; CumHours, CumGpa : real;
                            VAR Eligible : boolean;
                            VAR EligibleCount : integer);


BEGIN (* CheckEligibility *)
    writeln ('********* CheckEligibility called ***********');
    (***** Temporary assignment of false to Eligibility ******)
    Eligible := false
END (* CheckEligibility *);

PROCEDURE Report (Snumb, class : integer;
                  CumHours, CurrGpa, CumGpa : real;
                  Eligible : boolean);

BEGIN (* Report *)
    writeln ('********* Report called ***********');
    (***** Temporary printout *****)
    writeln ('Snumb:  ', Snumb:1);
    writeln ('Class:  ', Class:1);
    writeln ('Cum. hours:  ', CumHours:4:2);
    writeln ('Curr. gpa:  ', CurrGpa:4:2);
    writeln ('Cum. gpa:  ', CumGpa:4:2);
    writeln ('Eligible:  ', Eligible)
END (* Report *);

BEGIN (* CheckStudent *)
    ReadAndCalculate (Snumb, Class, StudentCount, CumHours, CumGpa,
                      CurrGpa, SumOfGpas);
    CheckEligibility (Class, CumHours, CumGpa, Eligible, EligibleCount);
    Report (Snumb, Class, CumHours, CurrGpa, CumGpa, Eligible)
END (* CheckStudent *);

PROCEDURE PrintSummary (StudentCount, EligibleCount : integer;
                        SumOfGpas : real);

BEGIN (* PrintSummary *)
    writeln ('********* PrintSummary called ***********')
END (* PrintSummary *);
```

Fig. 5.17. (cont.)

```
BEGIN (* main program *)
    Instruct;
    StudentCount := 0;
    EligibleCount := 0;
    SumOfGpas := 0;
    REPEAT
        Checkstudent (StudentCount, EligibleCount, SumOfGpas);
        writeln;
        writeln ('More (0 = No, 1 = Yes)?');
        readln (Response)
    UNTIL Response <> 1;
    PrintSummary (StudentCount, EligibleCount, SumOfGpas)
END (* main program *).
```

```
Sample run:
==========

********** Instruct called **********
Enter student number, class, cum. hours, cum. gpa:
12345 1 0 0
Hours and grade?
5 3.0
Hours and grade?
4 3.0
Hours and grade?
3.5 3.0
Hours and grade?
4 3.0
Hours and grade?
3 3.0
Hours and grade?
2 3.0
Hours and grade?
0 0
********** CheckEligibility called **********
********** Report called **********
Snumb:   12345
Class:   1
Cum. hours:   21.50
Curr. gpa:    3.00
Cum. gpa:     3.00
Eligible:  FALSE

More (0 = No, 1 = Yes)?
0
********** PrintSummary called **********
```

The sample run of this program indicates that the procedure *ReadAnd-Calculate* and the main program are correct. Therefore, we may now turn to developing the other procedures. A further analysis of the subtask of determining the student's eligibility reveals that there are two criteria used: an hours condition and a GPA condition. Figure 5.18 shows the two corresponding subtasks in a refined structure diagram. These can be conveniently implemented as boolean-valued functions *HoursCheck* and *GpaCheck* which return the value *true* or *false*, depending on whether the student satisfies the corresponding eligibility criterion. Replacing the temporary statements in *CheckEligibility* in the preceding program produces the refined program in Figure 5.19.

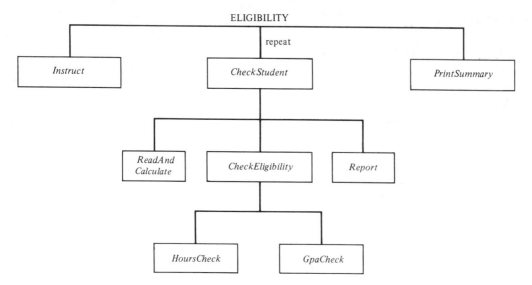

ELIGIBILITY

Figure 5.18.

```
PROGRAM Eligibility (input, output);

                .
                .
                .

    PROCEDURE CheckEligibility (Class: integer; CumHours, CumGpa : real;
                                VAR Eligible : boolean;
                                VAR EligibleCount : integer);

    (*******************************************************************

        Procedure to check eligibility.  Two criteria are used:
        cumulative hours, and cumulative gpa.  Functions HoursCheck
        GpaCheck implement these.

    ******************************************************************)

        FUNCTION HoursCheck(Class : integer; CumHours : real) : boolean;

        (*******************************************************************

                Check student's cumulative hours.

        ******************************************************************)

            CONST
                Freshman = 25;
                Sophomore = 50;
                Junior = 85;

            BEGIN (* HoursCheck *)
                CASE Class OF
                    1 : HoursCheck := CumHours >= Freshman;
                    2 : HoursCheck := CumHours >= Sophomore;
                    3 : HoursCheck := CumHours >= Junior
                END (* CASE *)
            END (* HoursCheck *);
```

Figure 5.19.

Fig. 5.19. (cont.)

```
FUNCTION GpaCheck(Class : integer; CumGpa : real) : boolean;

(********************************************************************

         Check student's cumulative gpa.

********************************************************************)

    CONST
        Gpa1 = 1.7;
        Gpa2 = 1.85;
        Gpa3 = 1.95;

    BEGIN (* GpaCheck *)
        CASE Class OF
            1 : GpaCheck := CumGpa >= Gpa1;
            2 : GpaCheck := CumGpa >= Gpa2;
            3 : GpaCheck := CumGpa >= Gpa3
        END (* CASE *)
    END (* GpaCheck *);

BEGIN (* CheckEligibility *)
    IF (Class < 1) OR (Class > 3) THEN
        BEGIN
            writeln ('*** Illegal class code ***');
            Eligible := false
        END (* IF *)
    ELSE
        Eligible := HoursCheck(Class, CumHours)
                    AND GpaCheck(Class, CumGpa);
    IF Eligible THEN
        EligibleCount := EligibleCount + 1
END (* CheckEligibility *);

                .
                .
                .
END (* main program *).



Sample run:
==========

*********** Instruct called ***********
Enter student number, class, cum. hours, cum. gpa:
12345 1 0 0
Hours and grade?
5 3.0
Hours and grade?
4 3.0
Hours and grade?
3.5 3.0
Hours and grade?
4 3.0
Hours and grade?
3 3.0
Hours and grade?
2 3.0
Hours and grade?
0 0
```

Fig. 5.19. (cont.)

```
********** Report called ***********
Snumb:  12345
Class:  1
Cum. hours:  21.50
Curr. gpa:    3.00
Cum. gpa:     3.00
Eligible:  FALSE

More (0 = No, 1 = Yes)?
1
Enter student number, class, cum. hours, cumgpa:
55555 5 0 0
Hours and grade?
3 3.0
Hours and grade?
0 0
********** Illegal class code **********
********** Report called ***********
Snumb:  55555
Class:  5
Cum. hours:  3.00
Curr. gpa:   3.00
Cum. gpa:    3.00
Eligible:  FALSE

More (0 = No, 1 = Yes)?
0
********** PrintSummary called ***********
```

We observe that the newly added procedure appears to be correct, and consequently, we proceed to develop the remaining procedures *Report, Instruct,* and *PrintSummary.* The final version of the complete program is shown in Figure 5.20.

```
PROGRAM Eligibility (input, output);

(*********************************************************************

  Program to determine academic eligibility of athletes according to
  two criteria:  cumulative hours and cumulative gpa.  It also
  counts the total # of students checked, the # found to be eligible
  and calculates the average current gpa for all students.

*********************************************************************)

VAR
   StudentCount,              (* count of all students processed *)
   EligibleCount : integer;   (* count of the # found to be eligible *)
   SumOfGpas : real;          (* sum of current gpas of all students *)
   Response : integer;        (* user response *)

PROCEDURE Instruct;

   (*************************************************************

           Print instructions to the user.

   *************************************************************)
```

Figure 5.20.

Fig. 5.20. (cont.)

```
BEGIN (* Instruct *)
    writeln ('You will first be asked to enter the student''s');
    writeln ('number, class, cumulative hours, and cumulative gpa.');
    writeln ('Enter these with at least one space separating them.');
    writeln;
    writeln ('You will then be asked to enter the number of hours and');
    writeln ('the numeric grade earned for each of the courses the');
    writeln ('student took during the current year.  Separate the');
    writeln ('number of hours from the grade by at least one space.');
    writeln ('Enter O for hours and O for grades when you are finished');
    writeln ('entering the information for each student.');
    writeln;
    writeln;
    writeln;
    writeln
END (* Instruct *);


PROCEDURE CheckStudent (VAR StudentCount, EligibleCount : integer;
                        VAR SumOfGpas : real);

(***************************************************************

    Accepts student information, determines eligibility,
    and maintains counts of # processed and # eligible,
    and a sum of the current gpa's.

***************************************************************)

VAR
    Snumb,                 (* student number *)
    Class : integer;       (* student's class level -- 1, 2, or 3 *)
    CumHours,              (* cumulative hours *)
    CumGpa,                (* cumulative grade point average *)
    CurrGpa : real;        (* current grade point average *)
    Eligible : boolean;    (* true if student eligible, else false *)

    PROCEDURE ReadAndcalculate ( VAR Snumb, Class, StudentCount : integer;
                                 VAR CumHours, CumGpa, CurrGpa, SumOfGpas : real);

    (***************************************************************

        Procedure to read a student's number, class, cumulative
        hours and cumulative gpa; then read hours and grades
        for courses taken during the current year, and calculate
        current gpa, update cumulative hours, cumulative gpa,
        and count of students processed.  Hours = 0 and grade = 0
        are used to signal the end of data for a student.

    ***************************************************************)

    VAR
        Hours,                 (* hours of credit for a course *)
        Grade,                 (* numeric grade for that course *)
        NewHours,              (* total hours earned during current year *)
        NewHonorPts,           (* honor points earned in current year *)
        OldHonorPts : real;    (* honor points earned in past years *)
```

Fig. 5.20. (cont.)

```
BEGIN (* ReadAndCalculate *)
    writeln ('Enter student number, class, cum. hours, cum. gpa:');
    readln (Snumb, Class, CumHours, CumGpa);
    OldHonorPts := CumHours * CumGpa;
    NewHours := 0;
    NewHonorPts := 0;
    writeln ('Hours and grade?');
    readln (Hours, Grade);
    WHILE Hours > 0 DO
        BEGIN
            NewHours := NewHours + Hours;
            NewHonorPts := NewHonorPts + Hours * Grade;
            writeln ('Hours and grade?');
            readln (Hours, Grade);
        END (* WHILE *);
    IF NewHours = 0 THEN
        CurrGpa := 0
    ELSE
        CurrGpa := NewHonorPts / NewHours;
    SumOfGpas := SumOfGpas + CurrGpa;
    CumHours := CumHours + NewHours;
    CumGpa := (OldHonorPts + NewHonorPts) / CumHours;
    StudentCount := StudentCount + 1;
END (* ReadAndCalculate *);

PROCEDURE CheckEligibility (Class: integer; CumHours, CumGpa : real;
                            VAR Eligible : boolean;
                            VAR EligibleCount : integer);

(*******************************************************************

    Procedure to check eligibility.  Two criteria are used:
    cumulative hours, and cumulative gpa.  Functions HoursCheck
    GpaCheck implement these.

*******************************************************************)

    FUNCTION HoursCheck(Class : integer; CumHours : real) : boolean;

    (*******************************************************************

            Check student's cumulative hours.

    *******************************************************************)

        CONST
            Freshman = 25;
            Sophomore = 50;
            Junior = 85;

        BEGIN (* HoursCheck *)
            CASE Class OF
                1 : HoursCheck := CumHours >= Freshman;
                2 : HoursCheck := CumHours >= Sophomore;
                3 : HoursCheck := CumHours >= Junior
            END (* CASE *)
        END (* HoursCheck *);

    FUNCTION GpaCheck(Class : integer; CumGpa : real) : boolean;
```

Fig. 5.20. (cont.)

```
(*******************************************************************

            Check student's cumulative gpa.

*******************************************************************)

      CONST
         Gpa1 = 1.7;
         Gpa2 = 1.85;
         Gpa3 = 1.95;

      BEGIN (* GpaCheck *)
         CASE Class OF
            1 : GpaCheck := CumGpa >= Gpa1;
            2 : GpaCheck := CumGpa >= Gpa2;
            3 : GpaCheck := CumGpa >= Gpa3
         END (* CASE *)
      END (* GpaCheck *);

   BEGIN (* CheckEligibility *)
      IF (Class < 1) OR (Class > 3) THEN
         BEGIN
            writeln ('*** Illegal class code ***');
            Eligible := false
         END (* IF *)
      ELSE
         Eligible := HoursCheck(Class, CumHours)
                     AND GpaCheck(Class, CumGpa);
      IF Eligible THEN
         EligibleCount := EligibleCount + 1
   END (* CheckEligibility *);

PROCEDURE Report (Snumb, Class : integer;
                  CumHours, CurrGpa, CumGpa : real;
                  Eligible : boolean);

(*******************************************************************

    Display the statistics for a given student.

*******************************************************************)

   BEGIN (* Report *)
      writeln;
      writeln ('***** Report for student ', Snumb:1, '  *****');
      writeln ('Class:              ', Class:1);
      writeln ('Cumulative hours:  ', CumHours:4:2);
      writeln ('Current gpa:       ', CurrGpa:4:2);
      writeln ('Cumulative gpa:    ', CumGpa:4:2);
      IF Eligible THEN
         writeln ('ELIGIBLE')
      ELSE
         writeln ('*** NOT ELIGIBLE ***');
      writeln ('**************************************');
      writeln
   END (* Report *);

BEGIN (* CheckStudent *)
   ReadAndCalculate (Snumb, Class, StudentCount, CumHours, CumGpa,
            CurrGpa, SumOfGpas);
   CheckEligibility (Class, CumHours, CumGpa, Eligible, EligibleCount);
   Report (Snumb, Class, CumHours, CurrGpa, CumGpa, Eligible)
END (* CheckStudent *);
```

Fig. 5.20. (cont.)

```
PROCEDURE PrintSummary (StudentCount, EligibleCount : integer;
                        SumOfGpas : real);

   (**********************************************************************

                 Print summary statistics.

    **********************************************************************)

   BEGIN (* PrintSummary *)
      writeln;
      writeln;
      writeln ('******************************************************');
      writeln ('*                 SUMMARY STATISTICS               *');
      writeln ('******************************************************');
      writeln;
      writeln ('NUMBER OF STUDENTS PROCESSED:      ', StudentCount:1);
      writeln ('AVERAGE CURRENT GPA OF STUDENTS:  ',
               SumOfGpas / StudentCount : 4:2);
      writeln ('NUMBER FOUND TO BE ELIGIBLE:      ', EligibleCount:1)
   END (* PrintSummary *);

   BEGIN (* main program *)
      Instruct;
      StudentCount := 0;
      EligibleCount := 0;
      SumOfGpas := 0;
      REPEAT
         Checkstudent (StudentCount, EligibleCount, SumOfGpas);
         writeln;
         writeln ('More (0 = No, 1 = Yes)?');
         readln (Response)
      UNTIL Response <> 1;
      PrintSummary (StudentCount, EligibleCount, SumOfGpas)
   END (* main program *).



   Sample run:
   ==========

   You will first be asked to enter the student's
   number, class, cumulative hours, and cumulative gpa.
   Enter these with at least one space separating them.

   You will then be asked to enter the number of hours and
   the numeric grade earned for each of the courses the
   student took during the current year.  Separate the
   number of hours from the grade by at least one space.
   Enter 0 for hours and 0 for grades when you are finished
   entering the information for each student.



   Enter student number, class, cum. hours, cum. gpa:
   12345 1 0 0
   Hours and grade?
   5 3.0
   Hours and grade?
   4 3.0
   Hours and grade?
   3.5 3.0
```

Fig. 5.20. (cont.)

```
Hours and grade?
4 3.0
Hours and grade?
3 3.0
Hours and grade?
2 3.0
Hours and grade?
0 0

***** Report for student 12345  *****
Class:              1
Cumulative hours:   21.50
Current gpa:        3.00
Cumulative gpa:     3.00
*** NOT ELIGIBLE ***
*************************************


More (0 = No, 1 = Yes)?
1
Enter student number, class, cum. hours, cum. gpa:
33333 2 30 3.3
Hours and grade?
5 3.3
Hours and grade?
5 4.0
Hours and grade?
5 2.7
Hours and grade?
5 3.0
Hours and grade?
3 3.7
Hours and grade?
0 0

***** Report for student 33333  *****
Class:              2
Cumulative hours:   53.00
Current gpa:        3.31
Cumulative gpa:     3.30
ELIGIBLE
*************************************


More (0 = No, 1 = Yes)?
1
Enter student number, class, cum. hours, cum. gpa:
44444 3 60 2.0
Hours and grade?
5 1.0
Hours and grade?
5 1.3
Hours and grade?
5 1.3
Hours and grade?
4 0.7
Hours and grade?
3 0.7
Hours and grade?
5 1.0
Hours and grade?
0 0
```

Fig. 5.20. (cont.)

```
***** Report for student 44444  *****
Class:               3
Cumulative hours:   87.00
Current gpa:         1.03
Cumulative gpa:      1.70
*** NOT ELIGIBLE ***
***************************************


More (0 = No, 1 = Yes)?
0


************************************************************
*                 SUMMARY STATISTICS                      *
************************************************************

NUMBER OF STUDENTS PROCESSED:      3
AVERAGE CURRENT GPA OF STUDENTS:   2.45
NUMBER FOUND TO BE ElIGIBLE:       1
```

5.7 Recursion

We have seen in previous sections that a function or procedure may reference other functions and/or procedures. A function or procedure may even reference itself, a phenomenon known as *recursion.*

Recursion is most useful when the quantity being defined or the problem being solved is described recursively. For example, a function definition is said to be *recursive* if it has two parts:

1. An *anchor* in which one or more values of the function are given.
2. An *inductive step* in which additional values of the function are defined in terms of previously defined values.

The factorial function defined in Section 5.4 by

$$m! = \begin{cases} 1 \text{ if } m = 0 \\ 1 \times 2 \times \cdots \times m \text{ if } m > 0 \end{cases}$$

can be defined recursively by

$$0! = 1 \qquad \text{(anchor)}$$
$$\text{If } m > 0, \, m! = m \times (m - 1)! \qquad \text{(inductive step)}$$

This recursive definition leads naturally to the following recursive function *Factorial:*

```
function Factorial(m : integer) : integer;
begin (* Factorial *)
   if m = 0 then
      Factorial := 1
   else
      Factorial := m * Factorial(m − 1)
end (* Factorial *);
```

The anchor in this definition should be obvious:

if $m = 0$ **then**
    $Factorial := 1$

and the inductive step is also clear:

else
    $Factorial := m * Factorial(m - 1)$

To demonstrate how this recursive version of *Factorial* calculates the value of *m*!, consider the case $m = 3$. The initial function reference is *Factorial*(3), which may be illustrated as follows:

Here the downward arrow labeled 3 represents the actual parameter for this function reference. Since *m* is not 0, the inductive step generates another function reference, with actual parameter 2:

Similarly, two additional function references are generated with actual parameters 1 and then 0.

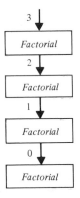

The function reference in which the actual parameter is 0 results in the assignment of the value 1 to *Factorial*. This fourth function reference is thus completed, and control returns to the preceding reference in which the actual parameter is 1. This is indicated by the upward arrow labeled with the function value 1 in the following diagram:

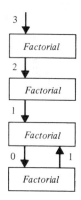

The third function reference is now completed by calculating the expression 1 * *Factorial*(0), and the resulting value 1 is returned to the next higher function reference.

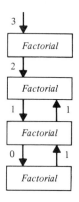

This process continues until 6 is returned as the value for the initial function reference *Factorial*(3).

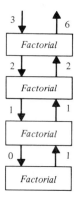

As a second example of a recursive function, consider the operation of exponentiation that can be defined recursively by

$$x^0 = 1 \quad \text{(anchor)}$$
$$\text{If } n > 0, x^n = x * x^{n-1} \text{ (inductive step)}$$

Like the factorial definition, this definition leads naturally to a recursive Pascal function:

```
function Power (x : real; n : integer) : real;
    begin (* Power *)
        if n = 0 then
            Power := 1
        else
            Power := x * Power(x, n − 1)
    end (* Power *);
```

The following diagram pictures the five levels of function references generated by the initial reference *Power*(2, 4):

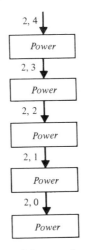

In the function reference with actual parameters 2 and 0, the value 1.0 is assigned to *Power*. This fifth function reference is thus completed, and control returns to the preceding reference in which the actual parameters are 2 and 1. This fourth reference is then completed by calculating the expression 2 * *Power*(2, 0) = 2 * 1.0 = 2.0, and this value is returned to the previous function reference. Eventually the expression 2 * *Power*(2, 3) = 2 * 8.0 = 16.0 is calculated in the first function reference, and 16.0 is returned as the value for the initial function reference *Power*(2, 4). The following diagram summarizes:

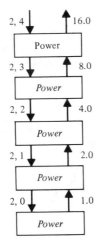

Procedures may also be recursive. To illustrate, consider the problem of printing the digits of a nonnegative integer in order from right to left. Although this problem can easily be solved without recursion (as the exercises ask you to do), it can also be solved by a recursive procedure.

procedure *Reverse* (*Number* : *integer*);

    (* Recursive procedure to display the digits of
      Number in order (from right to left). *)

var
      LeftDigits : *integer*;   (* the leftmost digits of Number *)

begin (* *Reverse* *)
    writeln (*Number* **mod** 10);
    LeftDigits := *Number* **div** 10;
    if *LeftDigits* <> 0 **then**
      Reverse (*LeftDigits*)
end (* *Reverse* *);

The following diagram illustrates the procedure references generated by the initial call *Reverse*(6285):

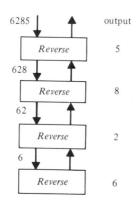

As an example of a problem that can be solved very easily by using recursion but for which a nonrecursive solution is quite difficult, consider the *Towers of Hanoi* problem. This problem is to solve the puzzle shown in Figure 5.21, in which one must move the disks from the left peg to the right peg according to the following rules:

1. When a disk is moved, it must be placed on one of the three pegs.
2. Only one disk may be moved at a time, and it must be the top disk on one of the pegs.
3. A larger disk may never be placed on top of a smaller one.

Legend has it that the priests in the Temple of Bramah were given a puzzle consisting of a golden platform with 3 golden needles on which were placed 64 golden disks. The world was to end when they had successfully finished moving the disks to another needle, following the rules given above. (Query: If the priests moved 1 disk per second and began their work in the year 0, when would the world come to an end?)

The Towers of Hanoi puzzle with only one disk is easy to solve: simply

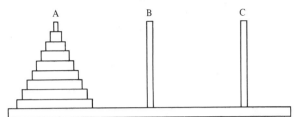

Figure 5.21.

move the disk from peg A to peg C. This obviously does not violate any of the three rules. A solution for the problem of moving $n > 1$ disks can easily be described recursively:

1. Move the topmost $n - 1$ disks from peg A to peg B, using C as an auxiliary peg.
2. Move the large disk remaining on peg A to peg C.
3. Move the $n - 1$ disks from peg B to peg C, using peg A as an auxiliary peg.

This scheme is implemented by the following recursive Pascal procedure:

```
procedure Move (n : integer; StartPeg, AuxPeg, EndPeg : char);

    (* Procedure to move n disks from StartPeg to
        EndPeg using AuxPeg as an auxiliary peg. *)

begin (* Move *)
    if n = 1 then
        writeln (' Move disk from ', StartPeg, ' to ', EndPeg)
    else
        begin
            (* Move n - 1 disks from StartPeg to AuxPeg using EndPeg *)

            Move (n - 1, StartPeg, EndPeg, AuxPeg);

            (* Move disk from StartPeg to EndPeg *)

            Move (1, StartPeg, ' ', EndPeg);

            (* Move n - 1 disks from AuxPeg to EndPeg using StartPeg *)

            Move (n - 1, AuxPeg, StartPeg, EndPeg)
        end (* else *)
end (* Move *);
```

Figure 5.22 shows a program that uses this procedure *Move* to solve the Towers of Hanoi problem and a sample run for four disks.

```
PROGRAM TowersOfHanoi (input, output);

(*************************************************************************

    Program using the recursive procedure Move to solve the
    Towers Of Hanoi puzzle.

*************************************************************************)
```

Figure 5.22.

Fig. 5.22. (cont.)

```
CONST
   Peg1 = 'A';
   Peg2 = 'B';
   Peg3 = 'C';

VAR
   NumDisks : integer;        (* number of disks *)

PROCEDURE Move (n : integer; StartPeg, AuxPeg, EndPeg : char);

   (************************************************************************

         Procedure to move n disks from StartPeg to EndPeg using
         AuxPeg as an auxiliary peg.

   ************************************************************************)

   BEGIN (* Move *)
      IF n = 1 THEN
         writeln ('Move disk from ', StartPeg, ' to ', EndPeg)
      ELSE
         BEGIN
            (* Move n-1 disks from StartPeg to AuxPeg using EndPeg *)

            Move (n - 1, StartPeg, EndPeg, AuxPeg);

            (* Move disk from StartPeg to EndPeg *)

            Move (1, StartPeg, ' ', EndPeg);

            (* Move n-1 disks from AuxPeg to EndPeg using StartPeg *)

            Move (n - 1, AuxPeg, StartPeg, EndPeg)
         END (* ELSE *)
   END (* Move *);


   BEGIN (* main program *)
      writeln ('# of disks:  ');
      readln (NumDisks);
      Move (NumDisks, Peg1, Peg2, Peg3);
   END (* main program *).


   Sample run:
   ==========

   # of disks:
   4
   Move disk from A to B
   Move disk from A to C
   Move disk from B to C
   Move disk from A to B
   Move disk from C to A
   Move disk from C to B
   Move disk from A to B
   Move disk from A to C
   Move disk from B to C
   Move disk from B to A
   Move disk from C to A
   Move disk from B to C
   Move disk from A to B
   Move disk from A to C
   Move disk from B to C
```

All our examples of recursion thus far have been of *simple* or *direct recursion*, in which a function or procedure references itself directly. Another kind of recursion occurs when one subprogram *A* references another subprogram *B* which then calls *A*. This kind of recursion is called *indirect* or *mutual recursion*.

The fourth scope rule in Section 5.4 states that if subprograms *A* and *B* are defined in the same program unit and *A* is referenced by *B*, then *A* must be defined before *B* in that program unit. This rule seems to preclude indirect recursion in Pascal, for if *A* references *B*, then *B* must be defined before *A*; but if *B* references *A*, then *A* must be defined before *B*.

To make indirect recursion possible, Pascal allows a *dummy definition* of a function or procedure in addition to its "actual" definition. A dummy definition consists of only a function heading of the form

function *name* (*formal-parameter-list*) : *result-type*; **forward**;

or

procedure *name* (*formal-parameter-list*); **forward**;

Here **forward** is a directive that indicates to the compiler that the actual definition of the function or procedure appears later in the subprogram section. In the heading of the corresponding actual definition, the formal parameter list and the result type for a function are omitted, and it thus has the form

function *name*;

or

procedure *name*;

To see that dummy definitions make indirect recursion possible, consider the situation of procedure *A* referencing procedure *B* and *B* referencing *A*. The following arrangement of dummy and actual procedure definitions makes possible this indirect recursion:

procedure *A* (...); **forward**; ---------- dummy definition of *A*
procedure *B* (...);
 ⋮
procedure *A*;   ---------------------- actual definition of *A*
 ⋮

According to Scope Rule 4, procedure *B* can reference *A* because *A* is defined before *B* (albeit in a dummy fashion). But *B* is also defined before any reference to it in the actual definition of *A*, which also is in accord with the fourth scope rule.

The directive **forward** is the only directive in standard Pascal, though many Pascal implementations also contain other directives, such as **external** which specifies that the actual definition of a subprogram is external to the program.

Many problems can be solved with equal ease using either a recursive algorithm or a nonrecursive one. For example, the factorial algorithm was implemented in this section as a recursive function and in Section 5.4 as a nonrecursive one. Nonrecursive functions and procedures may execute more rapidly and utilize memory more efficiently than corresponding recursive subprograms. Thus, if an algorithm can be described either recursively or nonrecursively with little difference in effort, it is usually appropriate to use the nonrecursive formulation.

For some problems, such as the Towers of Hanoi problem, recursion is the most natural and straightforward technique for solving the problem. Recursion is also appropriate when the problem's data are organized in a data structure that is defined recursively. (Such data structures are considered in Chapter 14.).

Functions and Procedures as Parameters

Up to now, the subprograms we have considered have involved two kinds of formal parameters: value parameters and variable parameters. In this section we consider two other kinds: *function parameters* and *procedure parameters*.

To illustrate the use of function parameters, consider a function *Integral* to approximate the area under the graph of a function $f(x)$ for $a \leqslant x \leqslant b$ (assuming that the graph of f does not go below the x axis in this interval). A simple technique for approximating this area is to subdivide the region into rectangles, as shown in Figure 5.23, and to sum the areas of these rectangles. These rectangles are constructed by subdividing the interval $[a, b]$ into n equal subintervals for some integer n and by forming rectangles with these subintervals as bases and with altitudes given by the values of f at the midpoints of the subintervals.

The function *Integral* must have the formal parameters a, b, and n, which are ordinary value parameters, and a function parameter f. When *Integral* is referenced, actual parameters of real type are associated with the formal parameters a and b, an actual parameter of integer type is associated with the formal parameter n, and an actual function will be associated with the formal parameter f.

Function parameters are designated as such by a function heading (with-

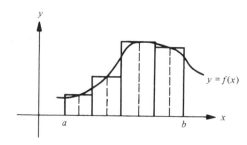

Figure 5.23.

out the closing semicolon) within the formal parameter list.[2] Thus an appropriate heading for the function *Integral* is

> **function** *Integral* (**function** $f(x : real) : real$;
> $a, b : real; n : integer) : real$;

Here **function** $f(x : real) : real$ specifies that f is a function parameter denoting a function whose formal parameter and value are of real type. The corresponding actual function parameter must be a function having a real formal parameter and a real value. For example, if *Integrand* is a real-valued function with a real parameter,

> $Area := Integral(Integrand, 0, 1.5, 20)$

is a valid function reference. Note that only the name of the actual function parameter is given; it is not accompanied by its own actual parameters.

Figure 5.24 shows a program that uses the function *Integral* to calculate the area under the graph of the function *Integrand* defined by $Integrand(x) = x^2 + 3x + 2$ for $0 \leq x \leq 4$.

---

[2] This is the standard form for specifying a function parameter and is different from that given by Wirth. In implementations of Pascal that use Wirth's form, the heading for the function *Integral* would be

> **function** *Integral* (**function** $f : real; a, b : real; n : integer) : real$;

```
PROGRAM AreaUnderCurve (input, output);

(***********************************************************************

   Program that uses the function Integral to calculate the area
   under the graph of the function Integrand.

**********************************************************************)

VAR
   Left, Right : real;        (* endpoints of intervals *)
   NumSubintervals : integer;  (* # of subintervals *)

FUNCTION Integrand (x : real) : real;

   (***********************************************************************

      The function for which area is being calculated.

   **********************************************************************)

   BEGIN (* Integrand *)
      Integrand := sqr(x) + 3 * x + 2;
   END (* Integrand *);
```

Figure 5.24.

Fig. 5.24. (cont.)

```
FUNCTION Integral (FUNCTION f(x : real): real;
                   a, b : real; n : integer) : real;

   (*********************************************************************

       Approximates definite integral of function f over the interval
       [a, b] using n subintervals.  The function is evaluated at the
       midpoints of the subintervals.

   ********************************************************************)

   VAR
       x,              (* midpoint of a subinterval *)
       Deltax,         (* size of subintervals *)
       Sum : real;     (* sum of areas of rectangles *)

   BEGIN (* Integral *)
       Deltax := (b - a) / n;
       Sum := 0;
       x := a + Deltax / 2;
       WHILE x <= b DO
           BEGIN
               Sum := Sum + f(x);
               x := x + Deltax
           END (* WHILE *);
       Integral := Sum * Deltax
   END (* Integral *);

BEGIN (* main program *)
   writeln ('Endpoints and # subintervals:');
   readln (Left, Right, NumSubintervals);
   writeln ('Approximate integral = ',
           Integral(Integrand, Left, Right, NumSubintervals):8:6)
END (* main program *).


Sample runs:
===========

Endpoints and # subintervals:
0 4 4
Approximate integral = 53.000000


Endpoints and # subintervals:
0 4 8
Approximate integral = 53.250000


Endpoints and # subintervals:
0 4 500
Approximate integral = 53.333312
```

Procedures may also be used as parameters in subprograms. In this case, a formal parameter is designated as a procedure parameter by including a procedure heading (without the closing semicolon) in the formal parameter list.

The syntax diagram for the general form of the formal parameter list of a function or procedure heading is shown in Figure 5.25. If F is a formal function or procedure parameter and A is the corresponding actual parameter then the following rules apply:

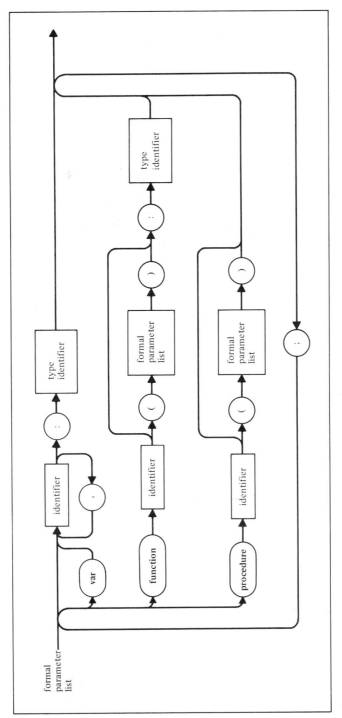

Figure 5.25.

1. *A* must be defined within the program; it may not be a predefined function or procedure.
2. If *F* denotes a function whose value is of type *T,* then *A* must also denote a function whose value is of type *T.*
3. If

   > *Flist-1* : *type-1*; *Flist-2* : *type-2*; . . . ; *Flist-n* : *type-n*

   is the formal parameter list of *F,* then the formal parameter list of *A* must have the form

   > *Alist-1* : *type-1*; *Alist-2* : *type-2*; . . . ; *Alist-n* : *type-n*

   where each *Flist-i* and *Alist-i* contain the same number of parameters, and all of these parameters are value parameters, all are variable parameters, all are function parameters, or all are procedure parameters. (In the case of function or procedure parameters, they must also satisfy these same rules.)

To illustrate Rule 2, consider the following procedure heading:

procedure *Demo* (**procedure** *F*(*x, y* : *integer*; **var** *V* : *real*));

The heading of the procedure defining the actual procedure *A* corresponding to *F* could be

procedure *A* (*Num1, Num2* : *integer*; **var** *Alpha* : *real*);

but it could not be any of the following:

procedure *A* (*Num1, Num2* : *integer*; **var** *Num3* : *integer*);

procedure *A* (*Num1* : *integer*; **var** *Alpha* : *real*);

procedure *A* (*Num1, Num2* : *integer*; *Alpha* : *real*);

procedure *A* (*Num1* : *integer*; *Num2* : *integer*; **var** *Alpha* : *real*);

Programming Pointers

Program Design

1. *Programs for solving complex problems should be designed in a modular fashion.*

   - *The problem should be divided into simpler subproblems so that a function or procedure can be written to solve each of these subproblems.*
   - *Local identifiers should be used whenever possible to avoid conflict with identifiers in other program units and to make the program as modular as possible.*
   - *Formal parameters in subprograms should be declared as value parameters whenever possible so that subprograms cannot unexpectedly change the values of the actual parameters.*

2. *Recursive functions and procedures may be used when the problem's data are organized in a data structure that is defined recursively. They may also be used for problems for which a simple recursive algorithm can be given. If a nonrecursive algorithm can be given that is no more complex than the recursive one, it is usually best to use the nonrecursive version.*

Potential Problems

1. *When a function or procedure is referenced, the number of actual parameters must be the same as the number of formal parameters in the function or procedure heading, and the type of each actual parameter must be compatible with the type of the corresponding actual parameter.* For example, consider the function with the heading

   function *Maximum(Number1, Number2 : integer) : integer;*

   The statements

   Larger1 := *Maximum(k, m, n);*

   and

   Larger2 := *Maximum(Number, 3.75);*

   are incorrect. In the first case, the number of actual parameters does not agree with the number of formal parameters, and in the second, the real value 3.75 cannot be assigned to the integer parameter *Number2*.

2. *Parameters that are to return values from a procedure must be declared as variable parameters using the indicator* **var.** *The actual parameters that correspond to variable formal parameters must be variables; they may not be constants or expressions.* For example, the procedure whose heading is

   procedure *Taxes (Income : real;* **var** *NetIncome, Tax : real);*

   can return only values of *NetIncome* and *Tax* to the calling program unit, and it cannot be called by the statement

   Taxes (Salary, 3525.67, IncomeTax)

   because the constant 3525.67 cannot be associated with the variable parameter *NetIncome.*

3. *Formal parameters in functions and procedures are defined only during execution of that function or procedure; they are undefined both before and after execution.* Any attempt to use these parameters outside the function or procedure is an error.

4. *The scope of any identifier is the program unit in which it is declared.* For example, for the procedure

```pascal
procedure Calculate (x : integer; y : real);

    var
        a, b : integer;
            ⋮
```

the local variables *x, y, a,* and *b* cannot be accessed outside the procedure *Calculate.*

5. *Using global variables to share information between different program units should usually be avoided, since changing the value of such a variable in one program unit changes its value in all program units.* This may make it difficult to determine the value of such a variable at any point in the program because its value may have been changed by any of the program units.

6. *A function or procedure must be defined before it is referenced.* For example, if the procedure *Taxes* references the procedure *Calculate,* then *Calculate* must be defined before *Taxes.*

```pascal
procedure Calculate . . . ;

        ⋮

procedure Taxes . . . ;

        ⋮
```

7. *Functions and procedures that have formal parameters cannot be referenced without corresponding actual parameters.* An error commonly made by beginning programmers is illustrated by the following attempt to define the function *Factorial:*

```pascal
function Factorial(m : integer) : integer;

    var
        k : integer;
    begin (* Factorial *)
        Factorial := 1;
        for k := 1 to m do
            Factorial := Factorial * k
    end (* Factorial *);
```

In this example, the statement

```pascal
Factorial := Factorial * k
```

is not valid since the right side of this assignment statement contains a reference to the function *Factorial* with no actual parameters.

Program Style

1. *Functions and procedures should be documented in the same way that programs are.* The documentation should include a brief description of the processing carried out by the function or procedure, the values passed to it, and the values returned by it.

2. *Procedures and functions are separate program units, and the program format should reflect this.* In this text we:

    (a) Insert a blank line before and after each function and procedure definition to separate it from other program units.

    (b) Indent the declarations and statement within each subprogram.

    (c) Follow the stylistic standards described in earlier chapters when writing subprograms.

Exercises

1. A *complex number* is a number of the form $a + bi$, where a and b are real numbers and $i^2 = -1$. Using a top–down approach, develop a menu-driven program that reads two complex numbers (where $a + bi$ is entered simply as the pair of real numbers a and b) and allows the user to select one of the operations of addition, subtraction, multiplication, or division to be performed. The program should then call an appropriate procedure to perform the specified arithmetic operation and display the result in the form $a + bi$. These four operations are defined as follows:

$$(a + bi) + (c + di) = (a + c) + (b + d)i$$
$$(a + bi) - (c + di) = (a - c) + (b - d)i$$
$$(a + bi) * (c + di) = (ac - bd) + (ad + bc)i$$
$$(a + bi) / (c + di) = \left(\frac{ac + bd}{c^2 + d^2}\right) + \left(\frac{bc - ad}{c^2 + d^2}\right)i$$

provided c and d are not both zero in the case of division.

2. Many everyday situations involve *queues* (waiting lines): at supermarket checkout lanes, at ticket counters, at bank windows, at gas stations, and so on. Consider the following example: An airport has one runway. Each airplane takes 3 minutes to land and 2 minutes to take off. On the average, in 1 hour, 8 planes land and 8 take off. Assume that the planes arrive at random instants of time. (Delays make the assumption of randomness quite reasonable.) There are two types of queues: airplanes waiting to land and airplanes waiting to take off. Because it is more expensive to keep a plane airborne than to have one waiting on the ground, we assume that an airplane waiting to land has priority over one waiting to take off.

    Write a computer simulation of this airport's operation. To simulate landing arrivals, generate a random number corresponding to a 1-minute interval: if it is less than 8/60, then a "landing arrival" occurs and joins the queue of planes waiting to land. Generate another random number to determine if a "take-off arrival" occurs; if so, it joins the take-off queue. Next check to determine if the runway is free. If so, first check the landing queue, and if planes are waiting, allow the first airplane in the landing queue to land;

otherwise, consider the queue of planes waiting to take off. Have the program calculate the average queue lengths and the average time an airplane spends in a queue. For this, you might simulate a 24-hour day. You might also investigate the effect of varying arrival and departure rates to simulate prime and slack times of day, or what happens if the amount of time it takes to land or take off is increased or decreased.

3. Write a nonrecursive version of the recursive procedure *Reverse* in the text.

4. The *Euclidean Algorithm* for calculating the greatest common divisor $GCD(a,b)$ of two integers a and b is described in Exercise 3 of Section 5.5. Write a recursive function or procedure to calculate $GCD(a,b)$. Also, draw a diagram like those in the text to show the references generated by the initial reference $GCD(1260,198)$.

5. The sequence of *Fibonacci numbers* 1, 1, 2, 3, 5, 8, 13, 21, . . . (see Exercise 10 of Section 4.5) can be defined recursively by

$$\left.\begin{array}{l} f_1 = 1 \\ f_2 = 1 \end{array}\right\} \text{(anchor)}$$
$$\text{For } n > 2, f_n = f_{n-1} + f_{n-2} \text{ (inductive step)}$$

where f_k denotes the kth Fibonacci number.
   (a) Write a recursive function *Fibonacci* to calculate the kth Fibonacci number for a positive integer k.
   (b) Draw a diagram like those in the text showing the function references generated by the initial reference *Fibonacci*(5). Since there will be two function references at each stage after the first reference, the diagram has a treelike structure.
   (c) Write a nonrecursive function to calculate the kth Fibonacci number.
   (d) Which of the two subprograms in (a) and (c) is the more efficient?

6. A *palindrome* is a numeral that has the same value whether it is read from left to right or from right to left. For example, 121, 35653, and 1 are palindromes. Write a recursive function or procedure to determine whether a given number is a palindrome. Write a program to read an integer, call the subprogram to determine whether it is a palindrome, and display an appropriate message.

7. Binomial coefficients can be defined recursively as follows:

$$\left.\begin{array}{r}\binom{n}{0}=1\\[4pt]\binom{n}{n}=1\end{array}\right\} \quad \text{(anchor)}$$

For $0<k<n$, $\binom{n}{k}=\binom{n-1}{k-1}+\binom{n-1}{k}$ (inductive step)

Write a recursive function or procedure to calculate binomial coefficients. Use it in a program that reads values for n and k and displays the value of $\binom{n}{k}$, using the subprogram to obtain this value.

8. Write a subprogram to accept as arguments a function and the endpoints of an interval known to contain a zero of the function, and uses the bisection method to find this zero (see Exercise 15 of Section 5.2). Use the subprogram to find a zero of the function $x^5 - 3.7x^4 + 7.4x^3 - 10.8x^2 + 10.8x - 6.8$ in the interval $[1, 2]$.

9. Write a program like that in the text to approximate the area under a curve, but use trapezoids instead of rectangles, as shown in Figure 5.26. Using trapezoids generally produces better results than using rectangles.

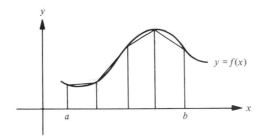

Figure 5.26.

6

Input/Output

When I read some of the rules for speaking and writing the English language correctly
. . . I think
>*Any fool can make a rule*
>*And every fool will mind it.*

Henry Thoreau

An average English word is four letters and a half. By hard, honest labor I've dug
all the large words out of my vocabulary and shaved it down till the average is three
and a half. . . .

Mark Twain

As we noted in the last chapter, all useful programs involve the input and
output of information, and therefore, these operations deserve special consid-
eration. Up to this point we have used the standard procedures *readln* and
writeln for this purpose and have restricted our attention primarily to numeric
input/output. We noted that the procedures *read* and *write* are also provided
in Pascal and that the boolean-valued functions *eof* and *eoln* may be used
in conjunction with input. In this chapter we discuss these procedures and
functions in more detail and we also consider the input and output of character
data.

In our introduction to input/output in Chapter 3, we observed that
these operations are carried out using *files*. We have thus far used only the
standard system files *input* and *output* which are associated with the standard
system input and output devices. In this chapter we introduce text files because
interactive input is cumbersome for large data sets and may be quite difficult
with some Pascal compilers.

6.1

Input/Output Procedures

In Section 3.4 we considered the predefined Pascal procedures *readln* and
writeln that are used for the input and output of information. We also noted

that there are two other input/output procedures, *read* and *write*. In this section we review the *readln* and *writeln* procedures and describe the *read* and *write* procedures. We also consider in detail the input of numeric and character data.

We begin by reviewing the *writeln* procedure. This procedure is called with a statement of the form

> *writeln* (*output-list*)

where *output-list* is an expression or a list of expressions separated by commas. Execution of such a statement displays the values of the expressions on a single line and then advances to a new line. For example, if the value of the integer variable *Number* is 27, the statements

> *writeln* ('Square of ', *Number*, ' is ', *sqr*(*Number*));
> *writeln* ('and its square root is ', *sqrt*(*Number*))

produce output like the following:

> Square of   27 is   729
> and its square root is   5.196152423E+00

The actual spacing within each line and the form in which real values are displayed are system dependent and may not be exactly as shown.

Recall that the format of the output can be specified by appending a format descriptor of the form :*w* or :*w*:*d* to the items in the output list. For example, the statements

> *writeln* ('Square of ', *Number*:2, ' is ', *sqr*(*Number*):4);
> *writeln* ('and its square root is ', *sqrt*(*Number*):8:3)

produce as output

> Square of 27 is   729
> and its square root is   5.196

The *writeln* procedure may also be called with no input list

> *writeln*

and in this case the parentheses are also omitted. This statement serves simply to advance to the next line.

The *write* procedure is called with a statement of the form

> *write* (*output-list*)

where the output list has the same form as the output list for the *writeln* procedure; format descriptors may be used as just described. When this statement is executed, the values are displayed on the current line, but *there is no advance to a new line.*[1] Consequently, any subsequent output will be displayed on this same line. For example, the statements

    write ('A');
    write ('B');
    write ('C');
    writeln;
    writeln ('DEF');
    writeln;
    writeln ('GHI')

produce as output

    ABC
    DEF

    GHI

and the statements

    write ('The first 5 squares are:');
    for $i := 1$ **to** 5 **do**
        write $(sqr(i){:}3)$;
    writeln (' *****');
    writeln ('*****')

produce

    The first 5 squares are: 1   4   9   16   25 *****
    *****

    Up to now, values have been read by using the *readln* procedure, which is called with a statement of the form

    readln (*input-list*)

where *input-list* is a variable or a list of variables separated by commas. When this statement is executed, values are read from the standard system file *input* and assigned to the variables in the input list. In a batch mode of operation, these values are typically obtained from data cards that accompany the deck of program cards. In an interactive mode, execution of the program is suspended while the user enters values for the variables. In this text the examples illustrate interactive input.

    When the statements

    writeln ('Enter employee number, hours worked, and hourly rate:');
    readln (*EmpNumber, Hours, Rate*)

---

[1] In some implementations of Pascal, *write* may not produce immediate output but rather "buffer" it (store it temporarily) for output at a later time. In fact, this may also be true for *writeln*. In this text we assume that both *write* and *writeln* produce immediate output.

are executed, the prompt

Enter employee number, hours worked, and hourly rate:

is displayed and execution of the program is interrupted. The user must enter values for the three variables before execution of the program can resume. To assign the values 31523, 38.5, and 7.50 to *EmpNumber, Hours,* and *Rate,* respectively, where *EmpNumber* is of integer type and *Hours* and *Rate* are of real type, the appropriate input is

31523 38.5 7.50

The values that are read are actually obtained from the standard system file *input.* Values are copied into this file sequentially as they are entered, and each time the end of a line of input is encountered, an *end-of-line mark* is placed in the file. Thus, if the user enters the values

31523 38.5 7.50
31564 40.0 8.75

the contents of the file *input* are

| 3 | 1 | 5 | 2 | 3 | | 3 | 8 | . | 5 | | 7 | . | 5 | 0 | ● | 3 | 1 | 5 | 6 | 4 | | 4 | 0 | . | 0 | | 8 | . | 7 | 5 | ● |

where we have used ● to indicate an end-of-line mark.

As values are read from this file by a *readln* statement, a data pointer, which is initially positioned at the beginning of the file, advances through the file. If we indicate the data pointer by ↑, then the initial status of the file *input* is

| 3 | 1 | 5 | 2 | 3 | | 3 | 8 | . | 5 | | 7 | . | 5 | 0 | ● | 3 | 1 | 5 | 6 | 4 | | 4 | 0 | . | 0 | | 8 | . | 7 | 5 | ● |
↑

When a value for the integer variable *EmpNumber* is read from this file, the longest sequence of characters that forms an integer is read. That value is assigned to *EmpNumber,* and the data pointer advances to the first character that is not a digit. Thus, for the statement

readln (*EmpNumber, Hours, Rate*)

the value read for *EmpNumber* is 31523, and the data pointer is advanced to the blank that follows the last digit of this number.

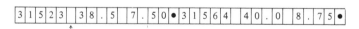

A value must now be read for the real variable *Hours.* The longest sequence of characters that represents a value that can be assigned to a real variable is read, with leading blanks ignored. Thus the value read for *Hours* is 38.5, and the data pointer advances to the blank following the last digit of this number.

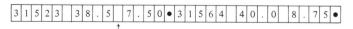

Similarly, the value 7.50 is read for *Rate,* and the data pointer is advanced to the end-of-line mark.

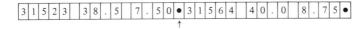

The *readln* procedure then advances the data pointer past this end-of-line mark

so that the values read for variables in subsequent *readln* statements begin at this point.

For the statement

    readln (EmpNumber, Hours, Rate)

the values might be entered one per line:

    31523
    38.5
    7.50
    31564
    40.0
    8.75

In this case, the contents of the file *input* are

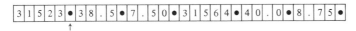

The value read for *EmpNumber* is 31523, and the data pointer advances to the end-of-line mark following the last digit of this number.

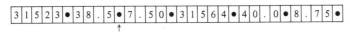

Next a value must be read for *Hours;* the end-of-line mark is ignored so that the value 38.5 is read and assigned to *Hours* and the data pointer is advanced.

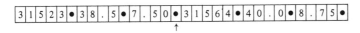

Similarly, the value 7.50 is read and assigned to *Rate,* and the data pointer is advanced.

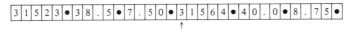

Because values have been read and assigned to each variable in the input list, the *readln* procedure now advances the data pointer past this end-of-line mark.

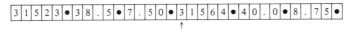

Suppose that the preceding data values are entered as

31523 38.5 7.50 31564
40.0   8.75

so that the contents of the file *input* are

```
|3|1|5|2|3| |3|8|.|5| |7|.|5|0| |3|1|5|6|4|●|4|0|.|0| |8|.|7|5|●|
 ↑
```

When the statement

  readln (*EmpNumber, Hours, Rate*)

is executed, the values 31523, 38.5, and 7.50 are read and assigned to *Emp-Number, Hours,* and *Rate,* respectively, as before. Because values have been read for each of the variables in the input list, the *readln* procedure now causes the data pointer to advance past the next end-of-line mark

```
|3|1|5|2|3| |3|8|.|5| |7|.|5|0| |3|1|5|6|4|●|4|0|.|0| |8|.|7|5|●|
                                          ↑
```

so that the value 31564 is not read. Subsequent input continues from this point. If the statement

  readln (*EmpNumber, Hours, Rate*)

is executed again, the value read for *EmpNumber* is 40, since this is the longest sequence of characters that represents an integer; the data pointer advances to the decimal point following this integer.

```
|3|1|5|2|3| |3|8|.|5| |7|.|5|0| |3|1|5|6|4|●|4|0|.|0| |8|.|7|5|●|
                                             ↑
```

Next a value must be read for the real variable *Hours.* An error occurs and execution terminates, however, since a real number may not begin with a decimal point. The error message displayed might be

  *** I/O ERROR at character 3 of line 2;
    '.' found where '+', '−', or digit expected.

  The *read* procedure can also be used for input. It is called with a statement of the form

  read (*input-list*)

where *input-list* is a variable or a list of variables separated by commas. The *read* procedure is similar to the *readln* procedure except that the *read* procedure does *not* advance the data pointer past an end-of-line mark after values have been read for the variables in the input list. To illustrate, consider the statement

  read (*EmpNumber, Hours, Rate*)

and suppose that the data are entered as described above:

31523 38.5 7.50 31564
40.0   8.75

As in the case of the *readln* statement, the values read for *EmpNumber,* *Hours,* and *Rate* are 31523, 38.5, and 7.50, respectively. For the *read* statement, however, the data pointer is not advanced past the end-of-line mark.

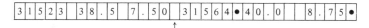

| 3 | 1 | 5 | 2 | 3 | | 3 | 8 | . | 5 | | 7 | . | 5 | 0 | | 3 | 1 | 5 | 6 | 4 | ● | 4 | 0 | . | 0 | | | 8 | . | 7 | 5 | ● |

Thus if the statement

 read (EmpNumber, Hours, Rate)

is executed again, the value 31564 is read for *EmpNumber,* 40.0 for *Hours* (the end-of-line mark preceding this number is ignored), and 8.75 for *Rate,* and the data pointer is advanced to the end-of-line mark following this last value.

| 3 | 1 | 5 | 2 | 3 | | 3 | 8 | . | 5 | | 7 | . | 5 | 0 | | 3 | 1 | 5 | 6 | 4 | ● | 4 | 0 | . | 0 | | | 8 | . | 7 | 5 | ● |

 A second distinction between the *read* and *readln* procedures is that *readln* but not *read* may be called with no input list:

 readln

Note that in this case the parentheses are also omitted. Execution of this statement advances the data pointer past the next end-of-line mark so that subsequent input begins with a new line. It may thus be used to skip a line of input or to skip over values that remain in the current line.

 When a value is read for a numeric variable, the longest sequence of characters that can be interpreted as a value for that variable is read, and the data pointer is advanced to the nondigit character that follows that value. The value of a character variable, however, is only a single character. Thus, when a value is read for a character variable, the next character is read and assigned to the variable, and the data pointer is advanced one position. Since blanks are legitimate characters, they are not ignored but, rather, are read and assigned as values for character variables. Similarly, end-of-line marks are not ignored but are read and interpreted as blanks when reading values for character variables.

 To illustrate, consider the statement

 read (Ch1, Ch2, Ch3, Ch4)

where *Ch1, Ch2, Ch3,* and *Ch4* are of character type. Suppose that the following data are entered:

 AB CD

so that the file *input* has the contents

When this statement is executed, the characters A and B are read and assigned to *Ch1* and *Ch2*, respectively; a blank is read and assigned to *Ch3*; C is read and assigned to *Ch4*; and the data pointer is advanced to the next character.

If characters are entered one per line

A
B
C
D

the contents of the file *input* are

When the preceding *read* statement is executed, the value read for *Ch1* is A. The next character read is an end-of-line mark; it is interpreted as a blank and assigned to *Ch2*. Similarly, the letter B is read and assigned to *Ch3*; an end-of-line mark is read, interpreted as a blank, and assigned to *Ch4*; and the data pointer is advanced to the next character.

A•B•C•D•

      If we wish to assign A, B, C, and D to the character variables *Ch1*, *Ch2*, *Ch3*, and *Ch4*, respectively, by using the statement

    read (*Ch1, Ch2, Ch3, Ch4*)

the data should be entered on a single line with no intervening blanks:

    ABCD

When this statement is executed, the data pointer advances to the end-of-line mark following the D.

A B C D•

Subsequent reading of values begins at this point. Thus if a value is read for a character variable, this end-of-line mark is read and a blank is assigned to this variable.

    It is important to remember how numeric and character values are read when variables of different types appear in the same input list. Suppose that *Num1* and *Num2* are integer variables and that *Ch1* and *Ch2* are character variables, and consider the statement

    readln (*Num1, Ch1, Num2, Ch2*)

If the following data are entered on a single line

23A45B

then the values read and assigned are

$Num1 \leftarrow 23$
$Ch1 \leftarrow A$
$Num2 \leftarrow 45$
$Ch2 \leftarrow B$

If we enter the values on separate lines, however,

23
A
45
B

then the value 23 is read and assigned to *Num1* and an end-of-line mark is read and a blank is assigned to *Ch1*. But an error now occurs in reading a value for the integer variable *Num2* because the next character A is not a digit. The same error occurs if the data are entered as

23 A 45 B

with blanks separating the values.
    If the data are entered as

23A 45B

then the values read and assigned are

$Num1 \leftarrow 23$
$Ch1 \leftarrow A$
$Num2 \leftarrow 45$
$Ch2 \leftarrow B$

No error occurs, since the blank separating A and 45 is ignored when reading a value for *Num2*. These same values are read and assigned if the data is entered as

23A
45B

since in this case the end-of-line mark separating A and 45 is ignored when reading a value for *Num2*.

Exercises

1. Suppose that *Num1, Num2, Num3,* and *Num4* are integer variables and that for each of the following *read* and *readln* statements, these data are entered:

```
1  −2  3
4−5  6
7       −8       9
```

What values will be assigned to these variables when each of the following statements is executed?

(a) *read (Num1, Num2, Num3, Num4);*

(b) *readln (Num1, Num2, Num3, Num4);*

(c) *read (Num1, Num2);*
   read (Num3);
   read (Num4);

(d) *readln (Num1, Num2);*
   readln (Num3, Num4);

(e) *readln;*
   readln (Num1, Num2, Num3, Num4);

2. Assume the following declarations:
     var
       N1, N2, N3 : integer;
       R1, R2, R3 : real;
       C1, C2, C3 : char;
and that for each of the following *read* and *readln* statements, the following data are entered:

    123   45.6
    X78 −909.8 7
    −65$ 432.10

List the values that are assigned to each of the variables in the input list, or explain why an error occurs:

(a) *readln (N1, R1);*
   read (C1, N2);
   readln (R2);
   read (C2, N3, C3);

(b) *readln (N1);*
   read (C1, C2, R1, R2);
   read (N2, N3, C3);
   read (R3);

(c) *read (N1, R1);*
   readln (C1, C2, R2, N2, C3, R3);
   readln (N3);

(d) *readln;*
   read (C1, N1, C2, R1, R2);
   read (N2, C3, R3);

(e) *read (N1, R1, C1);*
   read (C2, N2, R2);
   readln (N3, C3, R3);

(f) *readln (N1, R1, C1, C2, N2, R2, N3, R3, C3);*

(g) *read (N1, R1);*
readln (C1, N2, R2, N3);
readln (R3, C3);

(h) *readln (N1, R1);*
readln (C1, N2, N3, R2);
readln (R3, C3);

3. Assume the following declarations:

var
    N1, N2, N3 : integer;
    R1, R2, R3 : real;
    C1, C2, C3 : char;

and that the contents of the file *input* are

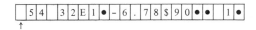

List the values that are assigned to each of the variables in the input list for each of the following statements, or explain why an error occurs. Also show the position of the data pointer after each of the sequences of statements is executed:

(a) *read (N1, N2, C1, C2, R1, C3, N3);*

(b) *read (N1, R1, R2, C1, C2, C3, N2);*

(c) *readln (N1, N2);*
readln (C1, R1, C2, R2);

(d) *read (N1);*
read (N2);
read (C1);
read (C2);
read (R1);
read (C3);
read (N3);

(e) *readln (N1);*
readln (N2);
readln (N3);

(f) *read (C1, C2, C3, N1);*
readln;
readln (N2);

(g) *readln (R1, R2);*
readln (C1, N1, C2, N2, C3, N3);

(h) *read (R1, C1, N1, C2);*
readln (N2, C3, R2);

Up to this point, we have assumed that the data for the sample programs were entered from a terminal during program execution. In this interactive mode, the data values are copied into the standard system file *input*, and values are obtained from this file by the *read* or *readln* procedures. In general, **Introduction to Text Files; the *eof* and *eoln* Functions** any collection of data items that are input to or output by a program is called a *file*. It is possible to create a file before a program is executed and then to read values from this file during execution. There are several reasons that this may be desirable. It may be inconvenient for the user to enter the data each time the program is executed, especially if the volume of data is large; and, as we have noted, interactive input may be somewhat difficult with some systems. These problems can be avoided by preparing a data file in advance and designing the program to read the values from this file. In this section we introduce a simple kind of file called a *text file* and describe how input and output using such files are carried out.

Files are usually stored on magnetic tape or magnetic disks or some other form of external (secondary) memory. Magnetic tape is coated with a substance that can be magnetized. Such a tape stores information for computer processing in somewhat the same way that an audio tape stores "sound information." Information can be written onto or read from a tape using a device called a *tape drive*. A standard tape drive can record 1,600 bytes per inch of tape. This means that a 2,400-foot reel of tape can store approximately 46 million characters. A magnetic disk is also coated with a substance that can be magnetized. Information is stored on such disks in tracks arranged in concentric circles and is written onto or read from a disk using a *disk drive*. This device transfers information by means of a movable read/write head which is positioned over one of the tracks of the rotating disks. Some disk packs consisting of several such disks can store more than a billion characters.

To illustrate how text files are declared and processed in a Pascal program, consider once again the problem in Section 4.6 of calculating wages for each of a number of employees. Some employee information such as the employee number and hourly pay rate is "permanent" information that usually does not change from one pay period to the next, and we wish to avoid having to enter this information each time the payroll program is executed. The number of hours that an employee works is usually not the same for all pay periods, however, and must be entered each time the program is run. Consequently, to solve this problem, we must

1. Create a file containing the permanent employee information.
2. Design a program to use this file and the hours information that is entered during execution to calculate the wages for each employee.

The employee information file might contain data such as the following:

31523   7.50
31564   8.75
31585   9.35
32012 10.50
35559   6.35
  ⋮
48813 11.60

This file might be created using a text editor and stored in secondary memory, or it might be produced by some other program. Here the information for each employee appears on a separate line, and one or more blanks separate the items in that line. A text file, like the standard system file *input*, is a sequence of characters and thus this file should be viewed as having the form

where ● denotes an end-of-line mark and ▼ denotes an *end-of-file mark*.

The standard system files are referenced in a program by using the predefined Pascal identifiers *input* and *output*. User-defined files are referenced by using identifiers called *file variables*. The type of a variable whose value is a text file can be declared by using the predefined type identifier *text*. Thus, to process the text file containing the permanent employee information, we might use the file variable *EmpFile* declared by

> **var**
>   *EmpFile* : *text*;

Files that exist before and/or after execution of a program are called *permanent* (or *external*) files. Names of all permanent files used in a program, including the standard files *input* and *output*, must appear in the file list of the program heading. In our example, *EmpFile* is a permanent file and must, therefore, be listed in the program heading:

> **program** *Payroll* (*input*, *output*, *EmpFile*);

Before the contents of a file can be read, the file must be *opened for input*, that is, a data pointer must be positioned at the beginning of the file. Files are opened for input by using the predefined Pascal procedure *reset*. This procedure is called with a statement of the form

> *reset* (*file-name*)

The data pointer is advanced sequentially through the file as the items are read, in the same manner as described for the file *input* in the preceding section. Thus, for our example, the statement

> *reset* (*EmpFile*)

opens the employee information file for input, positioning the data pointer at the beginning of the file.[2]

[2] In some implementations of Pascal, the procedure *reset* is also used to associate the file name used in the program with the name of the actual data file stored in secondary memory, by allowing a second parameter:

> *reset* (*file-name, actual-file-name*)

This is not standard, however, and the way that this association is made is system dependent and must be determined by consulting the system reference manuals.

The values in a text file are read by using the standard input procedures *readln* and *read*. In this case the input statements have the form

    readln (*file-name*, *input-list*)

or

    read (*file-name*, *input-list*)

where *file-name* is the name of the text file from which the values are to be read. If *file-name* is omitted, the standard file *input* is assumed; thus the statements

    readln (*input-list*)   and   *read* (*input-list*)

are equivalent to

    readln (*input*, *input-list*)   and   *read* (*input*, *input-list*)

respectively.

When an input statement is executed, values are read from the specified file and assigned to the variables in the input list. After each value is read, the data pointer is advanced in the same manner as described earlier for the standard file *input*. Thus, for the employee information file *EmpFile*, the statement

    readln (*EmpFile*, *EmpNumber*, *Rate*)

reads values for the integer variable *EmpNumber* and the real variable *Rate* from *EmpFile*. The data pointer is then advanced so that it is positioned after the next end-of-line mark. The first execution of this statement therefore assigns the value 31523 to *EmpNumber* and the value 7.50 to *Rate* and then advances the data pointer past the first end-of-line mark.

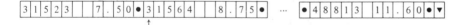

The end of a file can be detected by using the boolean-valued function *eof*. This function is referenced by an expression of the form

    eof (*file-name*)

and has the value true if the data pointer is positioned at the end-of-file mark; otherwise, it has the value false. It can thus be used in a boolean expression to control repetition of an input loop, for example,

```
    while not eof(EmpFile) do
        begin
            readln (EmpFile, EmpNumber, Rate);
                ⋮
        end (* while *)
```

If the file name and the parentheses are omitted, the standard system file *input* is assumed. Thus

  eof

is equivalent to

  eof (*input*)

Figure 6.1 shows the complete program *Payroll*, a listing of the employee file used in the sample run, and the output produced. After the last values 48813 and 11.60 are read and assigned to *EmpNumber* and *Rate,* respectively, the *readln* procedure advances the data pointer past the last end-of-line mark so that it is positioned at the end-of-file mark. The *eof* function now returns the value true, and execution of the **while** loop is terminated.

```
PROGRAM Payroll (input, output, EmpFile);

(*********************************************************************

    Program to calculate wages for several employees whose employee
    numbers and hourly rates are read from the file EmpFile.  For each
    employee, the number of hours worked is entered by the user during
    execution.  Hours above HoursLimit are paid at OvertimeFactor times
    the hourly rate.  Total wages for this payroll are also calculated.

*********************************************************************)

CONST
    OvertimeFactor = 1.5;      (* overtime multiplication factor *)
    HoursLimit = 40.0;         (* overtime hours limit *)

VAR
    EmpFile : text;            (* the permanent employee file *)
    EmpNumber : integer;       (* employee number *)
    Hours,                     (* hours worked *)
    Rate,                      (* hourly pay rate *)
    RegWages,                  (* regular wages *)
    OverWages,                 (* overtime pay *)
    Wages,                     (* total wages for employee *)
    TotalPayroll : real;       (* total wages for this payroll *)

FUNCTION RoundCents (Amount : real) : real;

    (*********************************************************************

            Returns Amount rounded to the nearest cent.

    *********************************************************************)

    BEGIN (* RoundCents *)
       RoundCents := round(100 * Amount) / 100
    END (* RoundCents *);
```

Figure 6.1.

Fig. 6.1. (cont.)

```
BEGIN (* main program *)
   reset (EmpFile);
   TotalPayroll := O;
   WHILE NOT eof (EmpFile) DO
      BEGIN
         readln (EmpFile, EmpNumber, Rate);
         write ('Hours worked for ', EmpNumber:1, ':  ');
         readln (Hours);
         IF Hours > HoursLimit THEN
            BEGIN (* Overtime *)
               RegWages := RoundCents(Rate * HoursLimit);
               OverWages :=
                  RoundCents(OvertimeFactor * Rate * (Hours - HoursLimit))
            END (* Overtime *)
         ELSE
            BEGIN (* No overtime *)
               RegWages := RoundCents(Rate * Hours);
               OverWages := O
            END (* No overtime *);
         Wages := RegWages + OverWages;
         TotalPayroll := TotalPayroll + Wages;
         writeln ('Hourly rate:   $', Rate:4:2);
         writeln ('Wages:  $', Wages:4:2);
         writeln;
      END (* WHILE *);
   writeln;
   writeln ('Total wages = $', TotalPayroll:4:2)
END (* main program *).


Listing of EmpFile:
===================


31523   7.50
31564   8.75
31585   9.35
32102  10.50
35559   6.35
36800  10.85
40013   7.15
44009   9.15
47123   8.75
48813  11.60


Sample run:
==========


Hours worked for 31523:   40
Hourly rate:   $7.50
Wages: $300.00

Hours worked for 31564:   35.5
Hourly rate:   $8.75
Wages:  $310.63

Hours worked for 31585:   43.5
Hourly rate:   $9.35
Wages:  $423.09
```

Fig. 6.1. (cont.)

```
Hours worked for 32102:   45
Hourly rate:    $10.50
Wages:  $498.75

Hours worked for 35559:   29.5
Hourly rate:    $6.35
Wages:  $187.32

Hours worked for 36800:   39
Hourly rate:    $10.85
Wages:  $423.15

Hours worked for 40013:   38
Hourly rate:    $7.15
Wages:  $271.70

Hours worked for 44009:   44
Hourly rate:    $9.15
Wages:  $420.90

Hours worked for 47123:   40
Hourly rate:    $8.75
Wages:  $350.00

Hours worked for 48813:   40.5
Hourly rate:    $11.60
Wages:  $472.70


Total wages = $3658.24
```

Care must be taken to avoid attempting to read beyond the end of the file. To illustrate, if the *readln* statement in this program is replaced with

> read (*EmpFile*, *EmpNumber*, *Rate*);

an error results. After the last data values 48813 and 11.60 are read, the data pointer is positioned at the end-of-line mark following these values.

Since *eof*(*EmpFile*) has the value false, the *read* statement is executed again. Attempting to read a value for *EmpNumber* results in an attempt to read beyond the end of the file. Execution of the program is terminated and an error message such as the following is displayed:

> ***I/O ERROR while reading EMPFILE,
> trying to read past end of file.

In the program in Figure 6.1, the wages for each employee are written to the standard system file *output* so that they are displayed using the standard output device. It is also possible to write the output to a user-defined text file so that it can be stored for additional processing. For example, the wages calculated in the program *Payroll* might be written to a text file *WageFile* to be processed later by a program that prints paychecks. In this case, the file *WageFile* must be listed in the program heading and declared to be of type *text:*

program *Payroll* (*input, output, EmpFile, WageFile*);
> ⋮

var
> *EmpFile,*
> *WageFile* : *text*;

Before data can be written to a text file it must be opened for output by using the predefined procedure *rewrite*. A reference to this procedure has the form

> *rewrite* (*file-name*)

This statement creates an empty file with the specified name, destroying any previous contents of the file.[3] In our example we would thus include in the program the statement

> *rewrite* (*WageFile*)

Output may be directed to a text file by using statements of the form

> *writeln* (*file-name, output-list*)

or

> *write* (*file-name, output-list*)

If *file-name* is omitted, the output is directed to the system file *output* and thus is displayed using the standard system output device. The statements

> *writeln* (*output-list*)   and   *write* (*output-list*)

are thus equivalent to

> *writeln* (*input, output-list*)   and   *write* (*input, output-list*)

---

[3] As in the case of the procedure *reset*, some implementations of Pascal also use the procedure *rewrite* to associate the file name used in the program with the name of the actual data file to be stored in secondary memory, by allowing a second parameter:

> *rewrite* (*file-name, actual-file-name*);

This again is system dependent, and details must be obtained from the system manuals.

respectively. In our example, the statement

writeln (*WageFile*, *EmpNumber*:6, *Hours*:8:2, *Rate*:8:2, *Wages*:10:2)

writes the values of *EmpNumber, Hours, Rate,* and *Wages* followed by an end-of-line mark to the text file *WageFile*.

The program in Figure 6.2 reads the permanent employee information from the text file *EmpFile* whose contents are as shown, reads the current number of hours worked from the standard system input device, writes the employee number, hours worked, hourly rate, and wages to the text file *WageFile,* and displays the total wages on the standard system output device. The contents of *EmpFile* and *WageFile* are also shown.

```
PROGRAM Payroll (input, output, EmpFile, WageFile);

(***********************************************************************

    Program to calculate wages for several employees whose employee
    numbers and hourly rates are read from the file EmpFile.  For each
    employee, the number of hours worked is entered by the user during
    execution.  Hours above HoursLimit are paid at OvertimeFactor times
    the hourly rate.  The employee numbers, hours, rate, and wages are
    written to the file WageFile in a format that could be read by
    some other program.  Total wages for this payroll are also
    calculated and displayed.

***********************************************************************)

CONST
    OvertimeFactor = 1.5;      (* overtime multiplication factor *)
    HoursLimit = 40.0;         (* overtime hours limit *)

VAR
    EmpFile,                   (* the permanent employee file *)
    WageFile : text;           (* the output file produced *)
    EmpNumber : integer;       (* employee number *)
    Hours,                     (* hours worked *)
    Rate,                      (* hourly pay rate *)
    RegWages,                  (* regular wages *)
    OverWages,                 (* overtime pay *)
    Wages,                     (* total wages for employee *)
    TotalPayroll : real;       (* total wages for this payroll *)

FUNCTION RoundCents (Amount : real) : real;

    (*******************************************************************

            Returns Amount rounded to the nearest cent.

    *******************************************************************)

    BEGIN (* RoundCents *)
       RoundCents := round(100 * Amount) / 100
    END (* RoundCents *);
```

Figure 6.2.

Fig. 6.2. (cont.)

```
BEGIN (* main program *)
   reset (EmpFile);
   rewrite (WageFile);
   TotalPayroll := 0;
   WHILE NOT eof (EmpFile) DO
      BEGIN
         readln (EmpFile, EmpNumber, Rate);
         write ('Hours worked for ', EmpNumber:1, ':  ');
         readln (Hours);
         IF Hours > HoursLimit THEN
            BEGIN (* Overtime *)
               RegWages := RoundCents(Rate * HoursLimit);
               OverWages :=
                  RoundCents(OvertimeFactor * Rate * (Hours - HoursLimit))
            END (* Overtime *)
         ELSE
            BEGIN (* No overtime *)
               RegWages := RoundCents(Rate * Hours);
               OverWages := 0
            END (* No overtime *);
         Wages := RegWages + OverWages;
         TotalPayroll := TotalPayroll + Wages;
         writeln (WageFile, EmpNumber:6, Hours:8:2, Rate:8:2, Wages:10:2)
      END (* WHILE *);
   writeln;
   writeln ('Total wages = $', TotalPayroll:4:2)
END (* main program *).
```

```
Listing of EmpFile:
===================


31523   7.50
31564   8.75
31585   9.35
32102  10.50
35559   6.35
36800  10.85
40013   7.15
44009   9.15
47123   8.75
48813  11.60




Sample run:
==========


Hours worked for 31523:   40
Hours worked for 31564:   35.5
Hours worked for 31585:   43.5
Hours worked for 32102:   45
Hours worked for 35559:   29.5
Hours worked for 36800:   39
Hours worked for 40013:   38
Hours worked for 44009:   44
Hours worked for 47123:   40
Hours worked for 48813:   40.5

Total wages = $3658.24
```

Fig. 6.2. (cont.)

```
Listing of WageFile:
====================

   31523    40.00     7.50     300.00
   31564    35.50     8.75     310.63
   31585    43.50     9.35     423.09
   32102    45.00    10.50     498.75
   35559    29.50     6.35     187.32
   36800    39.00    10.85     423.15
   40013    38.00     7.15     271.70
   44009    44.00     9.15     420.90
   47123    40.00     8.75     350.00
   48813    40.50    11.60     472.70
```

A *writeln* statement of the form

> *writeln* (*file-name*)

in which the output list is omitted produces an advance to a new line in the specified text file. Such a statement can thus be used to write blank lines to this file. (The predefined procedure *page* can also be used with text files; it is described in Appendix F.)

The preceding example uses the boolean-valued function *eof* to detect the end-of-file mark. End-of-line marks can be detected by using the boolean-valued function *eoln*. This function is referenced by an expression of the form

> *eoln* (*file-name*)

and has the value true if the data pointer is positioned at an end-of-line mark; otherwise, it has the value false. As with the *eof* function, if the file name and the parentheses are omitted, the standard system file *input* is assumed; thus

> *eoln*

is equivalent to

> *eoln* (*input*)

To illustrate the use of the *eoln* function, consider the problem of reading a text file and replacing multiple blanks with a single blank. Each line of the input file *InFile* is read character by character and copied to the output file *OutFile*, except that multiple blanks are not written.

To read each character in a line of *InFile*, we use an input loop whose repetition is controlled by the boolean expression **not** *eoln*(*InFile*):

INTRODUCTION TO TEXT FILES; THE *EOF* AND *EOLN* FUNCTIONS

```
    while not eoln(InFile) do
        begin
            read (InFile, Character);
                ⋮
        end (* while not edn *);
```

A character is written to *OutFile* if it is not a blank or if the preceding character is not a blank; otherwise, it is not written. The following statements, where *PreviousNotBlank* and *CurrentNotBlank* are boolean variables, accomplish this:

```
    PreviousNotBlank := true;
    while not eoln(InFile) do
        begin
            read (InFile, Character);
            CurrentNotBlank := Character <> Blank;
            if CurrentNotBlank or PreviousNotBlank then
                write (InFile, Character);
            PreviousNotBlank := CurrentNotBlank
        end (* while not eoln *);
    writeln (OutFile);
    readln (InFile)
```

When an end-of-line mark is reached, the function *eoln* returns the value true, and no more characters are read from that line. The data pointer in *InFile* must be advanced past this end-of-line mark by using a *readln* statement with no input list:

```
    readln (InFile)
```

An end-of-line mark must be written to *OutFile* by using the statement

```
    writeln (OutFile)
```

containing no output list.

This processing can be repeated for each line of *InFile* by placing these statements within a **while** statement controlled by the boolean expression **not** *eof(InFile)*. The complete program together with listings of *InFile* and *OutFile* are shown in Figure 6.3.

```
PROGRAM BlankStripper (InFile, OutFile);

(*******************************************************************

    Program to read the file InFile character by character and
    copy each line to OutFile but with multiple blanks replaced
    by single blanks.

********************************************************************)
```

Figure 6.3.

INPUT/OUTPUT

Fig. 6.3. (cont.)

```
CONST
   Blank = ' ';

VAR
   InFile,                     (* the input file *)
   OutFile : text;             (* the output file *)
   Character : char;           (* character read from InFile *)
   PreviousNotBlank,           (* previous character was not a blank *)
   CurrentNotBlank : boolean;  (* current character is not a blank *)

BEGIN
   reset (InFile);
   rewrite (OutFile);
   WHILE NOT eof (InFile) DO
      BEGIN
         PreviousNotBlank := true;
         WHILE NOT eoln(InFile) DO
            BEGIN
               read (InFile, Character);
               CurrentNotBlank := Character <> Blank;
               IF CurrentNotBlank OR PreviousNotBlank THEN
                  write (OutFile, Character);
               PreviousNotBlank := CurrentNotBlank
            END (* WHILE NOT eoln *);
         writeln (OutFile);
         readln (InFile)
      END (* WHILE NOT eof *)
END.
```

```
Listing of InFile:
==================


Fourscore and    seven    years ago,
our   fathers  brought
forth
on            this continent    a       new         nation
conceived           in                           liberty
and dedicated to the proposition
that
all         men
are       created         equal.
```

```
Listing of OutFile:
==================


Fourscore and seven years ago,
our fathers brought
forth
on this continent a new nation
conceived in liberty
and dedicated to the proposition
that
all men
are created equal.
```

Programming Pointers

In this chapter we described the input/output operations in Pascal programs and noted several features and rules that must be remembered. The major points are the following:

1. *After values have been read for each variable in the input list, the readln procedure advances the data pointer past the next end-of-line mark.* Thus, if there are more values in a line of input data than there are variables in the input list, some data values are not read. For example, suppose that *Number* is an integer variable, *xCoord* is a real variable, and the file *input* from which values are to be read contains

Then the statement

    readln (*Number*, *xCoord*)

reads the value 137 for *Number* and 8.24 for *xCoord* and advances the data pointer past the end-of-line mark.

Consequently, the value 145 is skipped. Moreover, if this statement is executed again, the value 13 is read for *Number,* but an error then occurs, since a real value cannot begin with a decimal point.

2. *After values have been obtained for each variable in the input list, the read procedure advances the data pointer so that it is positioned immediately after the last character read.* Thus, if the preceding *readln* statement is replaced with

    read (*Number*, *xCoord*)

the value 137 will be read for *Number,* 8.24 for *xCoord,* and the data pointer positioned at the blank following the character 4.

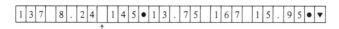

If the statement is executed again, the value 145 is read and assigned to *Number,* the end-of-line mark is ignored, and the value 13.75 is read for *xCoord.* The data pointer is then positioned at the blank following the character 5.

A potential problem in using the *read* statement is that an attempt to read beyond the end of the file may be made. For example, consider the following input loop:

```
while not eof(input) do
    begin
        read (Number, xCoord);
        ⋮
    end (* while *)
```

where the file *input* contains

↑

The values read and assigned to *Number* and *xCoord* are

Number	xCoord
137	8.24
145	13.75
167	15.95

After the last pair of values is obtained, the data pointer is positioned at the last end-of-line mark.

| 1 | 3 | 7 | | 8 | . | 2 | 4 | ● | 1 | 4 | 5 | | 1 | 3 | . | 7 | 5 | ● | 1 | 6 | 7 | | 1 | 5 | . | 9 | 5 | ● | ▼ |
↑

Because the data pointer is not positioned at the end-of-file mark, *eof(input)* is false, and so the *read* statement is executed again. This results in an attempt to read past the end of the file, which is an error. Note that the error does not occur if a *readln* statement is used, since after the last values 167 and 15.95 are read, the data pointer is advanced past the last end-of-line mark to the end-of-file mark. The boolean expression *eof(input)* is then true, and so execution of the **while** loop is terminated.

The way that the end-of-file mark is actually placed at the end of the file is system dependent. Usually in a batch mode of operation, this end-of-file mark is automatically placed at the end of the file after the last data card has been read. In an interactive mode, the user must usually enter some special control character from the keyboard to signal the end of the file.

3. *Leading blanks and end-of-line marks are ignored when reading numeric values but not when reading values for character variables.* One consequence of this is that consecutive numeric values may be entered on separate lines. For example, if the data

    123
    456

are entered, the file *input* contains

↑

The statement

readln (Num1, Num2)

where *Num1* and *Num2* are integer variables, reads the value 123
for *Num1,* and advances the data pointer to the first end-of-line
mark. This end-of-line mark is ignored when reading a value for
Num2 so that the value 456 is read. The *readln* procedure then
advances the data pointer past the next end-of-line mark.

In contrast, if *Ch1* and *Ch2* are character variables and the
data

A
B

are entered so that the file *input* contains

the statement

    readln (Ch1, Ch2)

reads and assigns the letter A to *Ch1* and advances the data pointer
to the first end-of-line mark. This end-of-line mark is then read,
and a blank is assigned to *Ch2*. The data pointer is then advanced
past the next end-of-line mark, and thus, the character B is not
read.

4. *The data pointer in an input file always points to the next character
to be read.* This "look ahead" property of the data pointer is a
common source of difficulty for beginning programmers. This is especially true for interactive input. To illustrate, consider the following
statements:

    Sum := 0;
    while not *eof(input)* **do**
        begin
            writeln ('Enter number:');
            readln (Number);
            Sum := *Sum* + *Number*
        end (* **while** *)

On most systems, when the **while** statement is encountered, the boolean expression *eof(input)* cannot be evaluated since the system file
input is empty because no values have yet been copied into it from
the terminal. Before execution can proceed, the user must enter some
value. As soon as the first character is entered, *eof(input)* can be
evaluated and the statements within the loop executed. For example,
if the user attempts to enter 123 as the first value for *Number,* the
following may occur: As soon as the first character 1 is entered,
the boolean expression *eof(input)* becomes false (since the data
pointer is pointing at 1), and the *writeln* statement is executed:

    1Enter number:

The remaining digits can then be entered and the return key de-
pressed:

1Enter number:
23

The value 123 is then read for *Number* by the *readln* statement, the data pointer is advanced past the end-of-line mark, and the value 123 is added to *Sum*.

Since there is no character following this end-of-line mark, once again the boolean expression *eof(input)* cannot be evaluated, and the process is repeated. Thus, entering 456 as the second value for *Number* may result in

4Enter number:
56

One way to avoid this difficulty is to enter a blank as the first character to be read for *Number* so that the expression *eof(input)* can be evaluated and execution can proceed; this leading blank will be ignored in reading the value for *Number:*

ƀEnter number:
123

Of course, if a value for a character variable was being read, this leading blank would be read and assigned.

In summary, interactive input can be rather difficult with some systems, especially when the next character in the file *input* must be known so that some expression such as *eof(input)* can be evaluated. In the preceding example, perhaps the best solution is to use a data flag

```
Sum := 0;
writeln ('Enter number (−999 to stop):');
readln (Number);
while Number <> −999 do
    begin
        Sum := Sum + Number;
        writeln ('Enter number:');
        readln (Number)
    end (* while *)
```

or to ask if there are more data values:

```
Sum := 0;
repeat
    writeln ('Enter number:');
    readln (Number);
    Sum := Sum + Number;
    writeln ('More (Y or N)?');
    readln (Response)
until Response <> 'Y'
```

5. *Each file variable that names a permanent text file must appear in the file list of the program heading and must be declared in the variable section of the program to be of type text.*

6. *Before any data can be read from a user-defined text file, that file must be opened for input by using the procedure reset. Similarly, before any data can be written to a user-defined text file, it must be opened for output by using the procedure rewrite.* Remember the following, however:

   - Each call to *reset* positions the data pointer at the beginning of the file.
   - Each call to *rewrite* creates an empty file and any previous contents of the file are destroyed.

Exercises

For descriptions of the files *UserFile, InventoryFile,* and *LeastSquares-File* see Appendix E.

1. Suppose that *InFile* contains the following:

   > I think that I shall never see
   > A poem lovely as a tree
   >
   > —JOYCE KILMER (1914)

   and that a program begins with

   program *Echo* (*InFile, output*);

   var
       Character : *char*;
       Infile : *text*;

   What output will be produced by each of the following statement parts?

   (a) begin
       reset (*InFile*);
       while not *eof*(*InFile*) **do**
         begin
           while not *eoln*(*InFile*) **do**
             begin
               read (*InFile, Character*);
               write (*Character*)
             end (* **while not** *eoln* *);
           readln (*InFile*);
           writeln
         end (* **while not** *eof* *)
     end.

(b) **begin**
  reset (*InFile*);
  while not *eof*(*InFile*) **do**
    begin
      while not *eoln*(*InFile*) **do**
        begin
          read (*InFile*, *Character*);
          write (*Character*)
        end (* **while not** *eoln* *);
      readln (*InFile*)
    end (* **while not** *eof* *)
  end.

(c) **begin**
  reset (*InFile*);
  while not *eof*(*InFile*) **do**
    begin
      while not *eoln*(*InFile*) **do**
        begin
          read (*InFile*, *Character*);
          write (*Character*)
        end (* **while not** *eoln* *);
      writeln
    end (* **while not** *eof* *)
  end.

2. Write a program to read a text file and copy it into another text file in which the lines are numbered 1, 2, 3, . . . with a number at the left of each line.

3. Write a program that reads a text file and counts the vowels in the file.

4. Write a program that reads a text file and counts the occurrences in the file of specified characters entered during execution of the program.

5. People from three different income levels A, B, and C rated each of two different products with a number from 0 through 10. Construct a text file in which each line contains the income level and product rankings for one respondent. Then write a program that reads this information and calculates

   (a) For each income bracket, the average rating for Product 1.
   (b) The number of persons in Income Bracket B who rated both products with a score of 5 or higher.
   (c) The average rating for Product 2 by persons who rated Product 1 lower than 3.

   Label all output and design the program so that it automatically counts the number of respondents.

6. Write a program that reads identification numbers and resources used to date from *UsersFile* to find and display the resources used to date for specified users whose identification numbers are entered during execution of the program.

7. Write a program to search *InventoryFile* to find an item with a specified item number. If a match is found, display the item number and the number currently in stock; otherwise, display a message indicating that it was not found.

8. At the end of each month, a report is produced that shows the status of the account of each user in *UsersFile*. Write a program to accept the current date and produce a report of the following form:

USER ACCOUNTS—09/30/83

USER-ID	RESOURCE LIMIT	RESOURCES USED
100101	$750	$380
100102	$650	$598***
⋮	⋮	⋮

where the three asterisks (***) indicate that the user has already used 90 percent or more of the resources available to him or her.

9. Suppose that a collection of data indicates that the relation between two quantities x and y is roughly linear; that is, if we plot the points (x, y), they tend to fall along a straight line. In this case, one may ask for the linear equation

$$y = mx + b$$

which "best fits" these observed points. This *regression equation* could then be used to predict the value of y by evaluating the equation for a given value of x. A standard method for finding the *regression coefficients* m and b is the *method of least squares,* so named because it produces the line $y = mx + b$, for which the sum of the squares of the deviations of the observed y values from the predicted y values (using the equation) is as small as possible. This least squares line has the equation $y = mx + b$, where

$$\text{slope} = m = \frac{(\Sigma xy) - (\Sigma x)\bar{y}}{(\Sigma x^2) - (\Sigma x)\bar{x}}$$

$$y \text{ intercept} = b = \bar{y} - m\bar{x}$$

where

Σx is the sum of x values.

Σx^2 is the sum of the squares of the x values.

Σxy is the sum of the products xy of corresponding x and y values.

$\bar{x}$ and $\bar{y}$ are the means of the x and y values, respectively.

Write a program to calculate the regression coefficients m and b for your own test data and then use the data in *LeastSquaresFile.* Design the program to count the number of values so that it can be used for any collection of data.

10. Related to Exercise 9 is the problem of determining whether there is a linear relationship between the two quantities x and y. One statistical measure used for this purpose is the *correlation coefficient.* It is equal to 1 if there is a perfect positive linear relationship between x and y, that is, if y increases linearly as x increases. If there is a perfect negative linear relationship between x and y, that is, if y decreases linearly as x increases, then the correlation coefficent has the value -1. A value of zero for the correlation coefficient indicates that there is no linear relationship between x and y, and nonzero values between -1 and 1 indicate a partial linear relationship between the two quantities. The correlation coefficient for a set of n pairs of x and y values is calculated by

$$\frac{n(\Sigma xy) - (\Sigma x)(\Sigma y)}{\sqrt{(n\Sigma x^2 - (\Sigma x)^2)(n\Sigma y^2 - (\Sigma y)^2)}}$$

where

Σx is the sum of the x values.
Σy is the sum of the y values.
Σx^2 is the sum of the squares of the x values.
Σy^2 is the sum of the squares of the y values.
Σxy is the sum of the products of corresponding x and y values.

Write a program to calculate the correlation coefficient for the x and y values in *LeastSquaresFile.*

11. Write a program that reads a text file and counts the number of characters in each line. The program should display the line number and the length of the shortest and of the longest line in the file as well as the average number of characters per line.

12. Write a program that reads a text file and writes it to another text file but with leading blanks and blank lines removed. Run this program using the last two Pascal programs you have written as input files, and comment on whether you think indenting Pascal programs makes them more readable.

13. Write a file pagination program that reads a text file and prints it in blocks of 20 lines. If after printing a block of lines there still are lines in the file, then the program should allow the user to indicate whether more output is desired; if so, the next block should be printed; otherwise, execution of the program should terminate.

14. Write a program that reads a text file, counts the nonblank characters, the nonblank lines, the words, and the sentences, and that calculates the average number of characters per word and the average number of words per sentence. You may assume the following: the file contains only letters, blanks, commas, periods, semicolons, and colons; a word is any sequence of letters that begins a line or is preceded by one or more blanks and that is terminated by a blank, comma, semicolon, colon, period, or the end of a line; a sentence is terminated by a period.

Ordinal Data Types: Enumerated and Subrange

God created the integers; all the rest is the work of man.

LEOPOLD KRONECKER

The old order changeth, yielding place to new.

ALFRED LORD TENNYSON

In Chapter 3 we introduced the four predefined Pascal data types:

> *integer*
> *boolean*
> *char*
> *real*

These data types are called *simple* because a datum of one of these types is atomic, that is, it consists of a single entity that cannot be subdivided. In addition to these simple data types, Pascal provides *structured* data types in which a datum consists of a collection of entities, and a *pointer* type used for data that are memory addresses. These are discussed in later chapters.

A simple data type is said to be an *ordinal* type if the values of that type are ordered so that each value except the first has an immediate predecessor, and each value except the last has an immediate successor. The type *integer* is an ordinal type since integer values are ordered by the natural ordering $-maxint, \ldots, -2, -1, 0, 1, 2, \ldots, maxint$. The type *boolean* is an ordinal type with the ordering *false, true*. The type *char* is also an ordinal type in which the ordering is that established by the collating sequence for the Pascal character set (see Section 4.3). The type *real* is not an ordinal type, however, because a given real number does not have an immediate predecessor or an immediate successor.

In addition to the predefined data types, Pascal allows user-defined data types. In this chapter we consider user-defined ordinal types.

The declaration part of a program consists of five sections arranged in the **The Type** following order: **Section**

> label section
> constant section
> type section
> variable section
> subprogram section

We previously described the constant, variable, and subprogram sections, and we now consider the type section. (The label section is described in Appendix F.)

The type section is used to declare new data types or to rename previously defined types. It has the form

> **type**
> $name$-1 = $type$-1;
> $name$-2 = $type$-2;
> $\vdots$
> $name$-n = $type$-n;

where each $name$-i is a legal identifier which names the data type given by $type$-i. Each $type$-i is a predefined Pascal data type or a user-defined type. For example, the type section

> **type**
> $Symbol$ = $char$;
> $Logical$ = $boolean$;

declares $Symbol$ and $Logical$ to be synonyms for $char$ and $boolean$, respectively. In the variable section we can then declare variables to be of type $Symbol$ or $Logical$:

> **var**
> $Code$, $Class$: $Symbol$;
> p, q, r : $Logical$;

Of course, the standard identifiers $char$ and $boolean$ may still be used in place of or in addition to the names $Symbol$ and $Logical$, respectively.

Because the names of user-defined data types are Pascal identifiers, the scope rules for identifiers given in Section 5.4 apply to type identifiers as well. Recall that the first scope rule states that an identifier declared in a program unit is not accessible outside that unit. Thus, the data type *Floating-Point* declared in the function *Power* by

function *Power*(*x* : *real*; *n* : *integer*) : *real*;

    type
        FloatingPoint = *real*;

    var
        Prod : *FloatingPoint*;
        ⋮

may be used only to declare the types of local variables such as *Prod* within the function *Power*. It is not accessible outside this function and thus cannot be used to declare the type of *Power* itself or any identifiers outside this function.

Scope Rule 2 states that a global identifier is accessible within any subprogram in which that identifier is not declared locally. Thus any type declared in the type section of the main program is accessible within any subprogram that does not declare that identifier locally. For example, suppose that the type section

    type
        Symbol = *char*;
        Logical = *boolean*;

appears in the declaration part of the main program, and consider the following procedure skeleton:

    procedure *Gamma* (*x*, *y* : *Logical*; **var** *c* : *char*);

        const
            Symbol = 'A';

        type
            Bit = *Logical*;
            ⋮

Since the global identifier *Logical* is not declared locally within procedure *Gamma,* it is accessible within *Gamma*. Thus parameters *x* and *y* may be declared of type *Logical,* and *Bit* may be declared as a synonym for *Logical* (and hence also *boolean*). The identifier *Symbol* is declared locally as the name of a constant in procedure *Gamma;* hence the global type identifier *Symbol* is not accessible within *Gamma*. Thus the type of the parameter *c* cannot be specified as *Symbol.*

The third scope rule asserts that identifiers declared in a subprogram can be accessed by any subprogram contained within it, provided that the identifier is not declared locally in the internal subprogram. Like the other scope rules, this rule also applies to type identifiers.

User-defined ordinal types can be divided into two classes: *enumerated* and **Enumerated**
subrange. Enumerated data types are considered in this section and subrange **Data Types**
types in the next.

Enumerated data types are defined simply by listing the values of that
data type, separated by commas and enclosed in parentheses. These values
must be legal identifiers, and no identifier may be listed in two different
enumerated type definitions. For example,

(*Sunday, Monday, Tuesday, Wednesday, Thursday, Friday, Saturday*)

defines an enumerated data type whose values are the identifers *Sunday,
Monday, Tuesday, Wednesday, Thursday, Friday,* and *Saturday.*

The values of an enumerated data type are ordered by the listing of
the values in the definition of that type. Thus, in this example, the predecessor
of *Wednesday* is *Tuesday,* and *Thursday* is the successor of *Wednesday;
Sunday* has no predecessor, and *Saturday* has no successor.

The listing of values that defines an enumerated data type may appear
in the variable section to declare the type of a variable:

var
    Day : (*Sunday, Monday, Tuesday, Wednesday, Thursday,*
       Friday, Saturday);

It is usually preferable, however, to associate a type identifier with this listing
in the type section

type
    DaysOfWeek = (*Sunday, Monday, Tuesday, Wednesday, Thursday,*
       Friday, Saturday);

and then use this identifier to specify the types of variables, formal parameters,
and function values:

var
    Day : *DaysOfWeek*;
    ⋮

function *Convert*(*x, y* : *integer*) : *DaysOfWeek*;
    ⋮

procedure *Schedule* (*Day* : *DaysOfWeek*; **var** *NumberOfDay* : *integer*);
    ⋮

Note that the type identifier *DaysOfWeek* must be used in the function and
procedure headings because the types of formal parameters and function
values must be specified by type identifiers; listing the values of an enumerated
data type in a subprogram heading is *not* allowed.

As we noted, the values of an enumerated data type are ordered. One
consequence of this is that elements of the same enumerated type may be

compared by using the relational operators $<$, $>$,=, $<=$, $>=$, and $<>$. For example, each of

$$Tuesday < Friday$$
$$Thursday > Monday$$

is a valid boolean expression with the value *true,* as is

$$Day <= Saturday$$

for each value of the variable *Day* of type *DaysOfWeek*.

The predefined Pascal functions *pred* and *succ* may be used to find the predecessor and successor, respectively, of any value of ordinal type. The following table gives several examples:

Function Reference	Value
pred(*Monday*)	*Sunday*
succ(*Friday*)	*Saturday*
succ(3)	4
pred(17)	16
pred('G')	'F'
succ('W')	'X'
succ(*false*)	*true*
pred(*true*)	*false*
pred(*Sunday*)	undefined
succ(*Saturday*)	undefined

Note that the function *pred* is undefined if its parameter is the first element of the ordinal type being considered, as is *succ* if its parameter is the last element.

Another predefined function used for processing ordinal data is *ord*. This function returns the *ordinal number* of an element; that is, it's value is the number of the position of that element in the ordering for that type. Thus, for the data type *DaysOfWeek*,

$$ord(Sunday)$$

has the value 0, and

$$ord(Tuesday)$$

has the value 2. For the enumerated data type *FaceCard* defined by

type
    FaceCard = (*Jack, Queen, King*);

$ord(Jack) = 0$, $ord(Queen) = 1$, and $ord(King) = 2$.

For an integer n, $ord(n)$ has the value n. Thus

$ord(7) = 7$

$ord(-3) = -3$

For boolean type, $ord(false)$ has the value 0, and $ord(true)$ has the value 1. For character data, the ordinal number of a character is the number of its position in the collating sequence and is thus compiler dependent. If ASCII code is used, $ord('A') = 65$, $ord('Z') = 90$, and $ord('2') = 50$, whereas for EBCDIC, $ord('A') = 193$, $ord('Z') = 233$, and $ord('2') = 242$ (see the tables of ASCII and EBCDIC codes in Appendix A).

For character data, the function chr is the inverse of ord. This function has an integer parameter and its value is the character whose ordinal number is that integer, provided that there is such a character. Thus $chr(65) = 'A'$ and $chr(50) = '2'$ if ASCII is used, whereas $chr(193) = 'A'$ and $chr(242) = '2'$ for EBCDIC. Note that for any element c of character type

$chr(ord(c)) = c$

and if n is the ordinal number of some character, then

$ord(chr(n)) = n$

Because variables of an ordinal data type have values that are ordered, they may be used as index variables in **for** statements or as labels in a **case** statement. For example, if the variable *Day* is of type *DaysOfWeek* described earlier, the statement

```
case Day of
     Sunday    : writeln ('Sunday');
     Monday    : writeln ('Monday');
     Tuesday   : writeln ('Tuesday');
     Wednesday : writeln ('Wednesday');
     Thursday  : writeln ('Thursday');
     Friday    : writeln ('Friday');
     Saturday  : writeln ('Saturday')
end (* case *)
```

can be used to display the day corresponding to the value of *Day*. The simple program in Figure 7.1 uses the variable *Day* of type *DaysOfWeek* in a **for** statement containing a similar **case** statement to display the names of the weekdays:

```
for Day := Monday to Friday do
     case Day of
          Monday    : writeln ('Monday');
          Tuesday   : writeln ('Tuesday');
          Wednesday : writeln ('Wednesday');
          Thursday  : writeln ('Thursday');
          Friday    : writeln ('Friday')
     end (* case *)
```

```
PROGRAM DisplayWeekdays (input, output);

(********************************************************************

    Program illustrating use of the enumerated data type DaysOfWeek.

 ********************************************************************)

TYPE
    DaysOfWeek = (Sunday, Monday, Tuesday, Wednesday, Thursday,
                    Friday, Saturday);

VAR
    Day : DaysOfWeek;

BEGIN
    FOR Day := Monday to Friday DO
        CASE Day OF
            Monday    : writeln ('Monday');
            Tuesday   : writeln ('Tuesday');
            Wednesday : writeln ('Wednesday');
            Thursday  : writeln ('Thursday');
            Friday    : writeln ('Friday');
        END (* CASE *)
END.




Sample run:
==========


Monday
Tuesday
Wednesday
Thursday
Friday
```

Figure 7.1.

A **while** statement can also be used in place of the **for** statement in this program. In this case, the function *succ* is used to "increment" the value of *Day*:

```
Day := Monday;
while Day <= Friday do
    begin
        case Day of
            Monday    : writeln ('Monday');
            Tuesday   : writeln ('Tuesday');
            Wednesday : writeln ('Wednesday');
            Thursday  : writeln ('Thursday');
            Friday    : writeln ('Friday')
        end (* case *);
        Day := succ(Day)
    end (* while *)
```

If we attempt to print the names of all the days of the week by modifying this **while** statement as

```
Day := Sunday;
while Day <= Saturday do
    begin
        case Day of
            Sunday    : writeln ('Sunday');
            Monday    : writeln ('Monday');
            Tuesday   : writeln ('Tuesday');
            Wednesday : writeln ('Wednesday');
            Thursday  : writeln ('Thursday');
            Friday    : writeln ('Friday');
            Saturday  : writeln ('Saturday')
        end (* case *);
        Day := succ(Day)
    end (* while *)
```

an error results. When the value of *Day* is *Saturday,* the value of *succ(Day)* is undefined.

Values of enumerated data types cannot be read from or written to text files, including the standard system files *input* and *output.* Nevertheless, it is sometimes convenient to use them to improve program readability by using a meaningful identifier rather than a cryptic code to represent an item. For example, using the values *Sunday, Monday, Tuesday, . . .* in place of the codes 0, 1, 2, . . . for the days of the week in a program obviously makes the program easier to read and understand. In such programs it may be necessary to use **case** statements like those described earlier to carry out the necessary conversion between the values of an enumerated data type and the numeric codes that can be input or character strings that can be displayed. The program in Figure 7.2 illustrates. It is a modification of the program in Figure 6.1 to read an employee number and an hourly rate from a permanent text file and calculate wages. During execution, the user enters the number of hours worked for each day from Sunday through Saturday. The following procedure *PrintDay* is used to display the character string corresponding to the value of *Day*:

```
procedure PrintDay (Day : DaysOfWeek);

    (* Procedure to print the name of the day corresponding
       to the value of Day of enumerated type DaysOfWeek *)

begin (* PrintDay *)
    case Day of
        Sunday    : write ('Sunday:     ');
        Monday    : write ('Monday:     ');
        Tuesday   : write ('Tuesday:    ');
        Wednesday : write ('Wednesday: ');
        Thursday  : write ('Thursday:   ');
        Friday    : write ('Friday:     ');
        Saturday  : write ('Saturday:   ')
    end (* case *)
end (* PrintDay *);
```

```
PROGRAM Payroll (input, output, EmpFile);

(*****************************************************************************

   Program to calculate wages for several employees whose employee
   number and hourly rate are read from the text file EmpFile.
   For each employee, the number of hours worked for each day from
   Sunday through Saturday is entered by the user during execution.
   Hours above HoursLimit are paid at OvertimeFactor times the
   hourly rate.  Total wages for this payroll are also calculated.

*****************************************************************************)

CONST
   OvertimeFactor = 1.5;      (* overtime multiplication factor *)
   HoursLimit = 40.0;         (* overtime hours limit *)

TYPE
   DaysOfWeek = (Sunday, Monday, Tuesday, Wednesday, Thursday,
                 Friday, Saturday);

VAR
   EmpFile : text;            (* the permanent employee file *)
   EmpNumber : integer;       (* employee number *)
   DayHours,                  (* hours worked for a given day *)
   WeekHours,                 (* hours worked for the week *)
   Rate,                      (* hourly pay rate *)
   RegWages,                  (* regular wages *)
   OverWages,                 (* overtime pay *)
   Wages,                     (* total wages for employee *)
   TotalPayroll : real;       (* total wages for this payroll *)
   Day : DaysOfWeek;          (* day of the week *)

FUNCTION RoundCents (Amount : real) : real;

   (**************************************************************************

          Returns Amount rounded to the nearest cent.

   **************************************************************************)

   BEGIN (* RoundCents *)
      RoundCents := round(100 * Amount) / 100
   END (* RoundCents *);

PROCEDURE PrintDay (Day : DaysOfWeek);

   (**************************************************************************

          Procedure to print the name of the day corresponding to
          the value of Day of enumerated type DaysOfWeek.

   **************************************************************************)

   BEGIN (* PrintDay *)
      CASE Day OF
         Sunday    : write ('Sunday:      ');
         Monday    : write ('Monday:      ');
         Tuesday   : write ('Tuesday:     ');
         Wednesday : write ('Wednesday:   ');
         Thursday  : write ('Thursday:    ');
         Friday    : write ('Friday:      ');
         Saturday  : write ('Saturday:    ');
      END (* CASE *)
   END (* PrintDay *);
```

Figure 7.2.

Fig. 7.2. (cont.)

```
BEGIN (* main program *)
   reset (EmpFile);
   TotalPayroll := 0;
   WHILE NOT eof (EmpFile) DO
      BEGIN
         readln (EmpFile, EmpNumber, Rate);
         writeln ('Hours worked by ', EmpNumber:1, ' on ');
         WeekHours := 0;
         FOR Day := Sunday TO Saturday DO
            BEGIN
               PrintDay (Day);
               readln (DayHours);
               WeekHours := WeekHours + DayHours
            END (* FOR *);
         IF WeekHours > HoursLimit THEN
            BEGIN (* Overtime *)
               RegWages := RoundCents(Rate * HoursLimit);
               OverWages := RoundCents(OvertimeFactor
                                       * Rate * (WeekHours - HoursLimit))
            END (* Overtime *)
         ELSE
            BEGIN (* No overtime *)
               RegWages := RoundCents(Rate * WeekHours);
               OverWages := 0
            END (* No overtime *);
         Wages := RegWages + OverWages;
         TotalPayroll := TotalPayroll + Wages;
         writeln ('Hours worked:  ', WeekHours:4:2);
         writeln ('Hourly rate:   $', Rate:4:2);
         writeln ('Wages:  $', Wages:4:2);
         writeln;
      END (* WHILE *);
   writeln;
   writeln ('Total wages = $', TotalPayroll:4:2)
END (* main program *).
```

```
Listing of EmpFile:
=======================


31523   7.50
31564   8.75
31585   9.35
32102  10.50


Sample run:
==========


Hours worked by 31523 on
Sunday:     0
Monday:     8
Tuesday:    8
Wednesday:  8
Thursday:   8
Friday:     8
Saturday:   0
Hours worked:  40.00
Hourly rate:   $7.50
Wages:  $300.00
```

Fig. 7.2. (cont.)

```
Hours worked by 31564 on
Sunday:     0
Monday:     7.5
Tuesday:    9.25
Wednesday:  8
Thursday:   8
Friday:     10
Saturday:   0
Hours worked:  42.75
Hourly rate:   $8.75
Wages:  $386.09

Hours worked by 31585 on
Sunday:     0
Monday:     8
Tuesday:    8
Wednesday:  9
Thursday:   8.5
Friday:     6
Saturday:   4
Hours worked:  43.50
Hourly rate:   $9.35
Wages:  $423.09

Hours worked by 32102 on
Sunday:     0
Monday:     0
Tuesday:    0
Wednesday:  0
Thursday:   8
Friday:     8
Saturday:   0
Hours worked:  16.00
Hourly rate:   $10.50
Wages:  $168.00


Total wages = $1277.18
```

7.3
Subrange Data Types

In the preceding section we considered the predefined ordinal data types *integer*, *boolean*, and *char*, and enumerated types. The set of values of each of these types is an ordered set. In some cases it may be convenient to use a data type that is a *subrange* of such a set. Subrange types are defined by specifying the first and last elements in the subrange in a declaration of the form

first-value .. *last-value*

where *first-value* and *last-value* are values of some ordinal type called the *base type* and *first-value* ≤ *last-value*. A value of this subrange type may be any value *x* of the associated base type such that

first-value ≤ *x* ≤ *last-value*

Subrange definitions may be used in the variable section of a program unit to declare the type of a variable, or they may be associated with a type identifier in the type section. To illustrate, consider the following:

type
> *DaysOfWeek* = (*Sunday, Monday, Tuesday, Wednesday, Thursday,*
>   *Friday, Saturday*);
> *Weekdays* = *Monday .. Friday*;
> *WholeNumber* = 0 .. *maxint*;
> *Digit* = '0' .. '9';

var
> *SchoolDay* : *Weekdays*;
> *n* : *WholeNumber*;
> *DaysInMonth* : 28..31;
> *Cents* : 0..99;

function *Factorial*(*n* : *WholeNumber*) : *WholeNumber*;
> ⋮

procedure *WorkSchedule* (*Day* : *Weekdays*; **var** *Code* : *Digit*);
> ⋮

Note that although the same value may not be listed in two different enumerated type definitions, it is permissible to use a value in two different subrange definitions.

A value to be assigned to a variable or function of a subrange type is checked to determine whether this value is in the specified range. If such *range checking* indicates that a value is out of range, an error message to that effect is displayed and execution is usually terminated. Thus, in the preceding example, if the value to be assigned to *n* is negative, then this value is out of range, and an out-of-range error occurs.

The rules that govern the use of an ordinal type also apply to any subrange of that type. For example, because an integer value may be assigned to a real variable, it is also permissible to assign a value of type *WholeNumber* to a real variable in the preceding example. In general, two simple data types are said to be *compatible* if they are the same type, one is a subrange of the other, or both are subranges of the same base type. If *A* and *B* are two compatible data types, then wherever *A* may be used, *B* may also be used. Thus, in the preceding example, the function reference

> *Cents* := *Factorial*(*DaysInMonth*)

is valid, since the types of *Cents, Factorial,* and *DaysInMonth* are 0..99, *WholeNumber,* and 28..31, respectively, all of which are subranges of type *integer* and hence are compatible. Similarly, the statement

> *writeln* ('Number of cents = ', *Cents*:1)

is valid, since *Cents* is of type 0..99 which is compatible with type *integer*. It must be realized, of course, that range checking is performed. Thus, if the value of *Factorial* in this reference is 100 or larger, range checking of the value to be assigned to *Cents* indicates an error.

Programming Pointers

In this chapter we discussed user-defined ordinal types. The following are some of the major points to remember when using them:

1. *Type identifiers must be used to declare formal parameters in a subprogram and the type of a function.* One may not list the values of an ordinal type in a function or procedure heading to specify the type of a parameter or the type of a function value. For example, the heading

   function *CardValue(Card* : (*Jack, Queen, King*)) : 11..13;

   is not valid. The enumerated type (*Jack, Queen, King*) and the subrange type 11..13 must be associated with type identifiers such as

   type
      FaceCard = (*Jack, Queen, King*);
      FaceValue = 11..13;

   in a program unit that contains this function definition, and these type identifiers used in the heading:

   function *CardValue* (*Card* : *FaceCard*) : *FaceValue*;

2. *The scope rules given in Chapter 5 apply to type identifiers.*

   (a) A type identifier declared in a function or procedure is not accessible outside that function or procedure.

   (b) A global type identifier is accessible in any function or procedure in which that identifier is not declared locally.

   (c) Type identifiers declared in a subprogram are accessible to any subprogram contained within it, provided that they are not declared locally in the internal subprogram.

3. *Values listed in an enumerated type definition must be legal identifiers and may not appear in any other enumerated type definition within that program unit.* For example, the declaration

   type
      Assortment = (123A, 579, P-123, ABC-DE, 'Monday', 'A');

   is not allowed, nor is

   type
      Weekdays = (*Monday, Tuesday, Wednesday, Thursday, Friday*);
      VacationDays = (*Friday, Saturday, Sunday, Monday*);

4. *The function* pred(*x*) *is undefined if* x *is the first value of an ordinal type;* succ(*x*) *is undefined if* x *is the last value.*

5. *Values of an enumerated data type cannot be input from or output to text files, including the standard files input and output.*

6. *If a variable or function is declared to be of some subrange type, an error results if one attempts to assign it a value that is not in this subrange.* For example, if *x* and *y* are declared by

> **var**
>> *x, y* : 1..10;

the statement

> **for** *x* := 1 **to** 10 **do**
>> **begin**
>>> *y* := *x* * *x*;
>>> *writeln* (*y*)
>> **end**

results in an error when *x* reaches the value 4 because the value of *x* * *x* is then outside the range 1..10.

Output:

> 1
> 4
> 9
> *** Value (16) out of range, must be <= 10

Exercises

1. (a) Write a type section that defines the enumerated type *MonthAbbrev* whose values are abbreviations of the months of the year and consist of the first three letters of the months' names; also define the subrange type *MonthNumber* consisting of the values 1, 2, 3, . . . , 12.

   (b) Write a function whose parameter is the number of a month and whose value is the corresponding value of type *MonthAbbrev.*

2. (a) Write a type section that defines type *Numeral* to be the subrange of character type consisting of the characters '0', '1'. '2', . . . , '9' and the type *Number* to be the subrange of integers consisting of the values 0, 1, 2, . . . , 9.

   (b) Write a function whose parameter is a variable of type *Numeral* and whose value is the corresponding numeric value. (*Hint:* Use the function *ord.*)

   (c) Write another function whose parameter is an integer in the range 0 through 9 and whose value is the corresponding numeral. (*Hint:* Use the functions *ord* and *chr.*)

3. For the enumerated type *MonthAbbrev* of Exercise 1, find the values of the following expressions:

(a) *Jan < Aug*   (b) *Sep <= Sep*   (c) *succ(Sep)*

(d) *pred(Apr)*   (e) *succ(succ(Aug))*   (f) *pred(pred(Aug))*

(g) *succ(pred(Mar))*   (h) *succ(pred(Jan))*   (i) *ord(Jun)*

(j) *ord(Sep) − ord(Jan)*   (k) *ord(succ(May)) − ord(May)*

(l) *chr(ord(Sep) + ord('0'))*

4. Write a function or procedure whose parameters are a nonnegative integer *n* and a month abbreviation *Abbrev* like that in Exercise 1 and that finds the "*n*th successor" of *Abbrev*. The 0th successor of *Abbrev* is *Abbrev* itself; for *n > 0*, the *n*th successor of *Abbrev* is the *n*th month following *Abbrev*. For example, the fourth successor of *Aug* is *Dec,* and the sixth successor of *Aug* is *Feb.*

5. Repeat Exercise 4 but define the function or procedure recursively.

6. Using the enumerated type *DaysOfWeek* in the text, write a program to read a customer's account number and current balance; then for each weekday (Monday through Friday) read a series of transactions by that customer of the form D (deposit) or W (withdrawal) followed by an amount, and update the balance with this amount. Display the new balance after all transactions for the week have been processed.

7. (a) Write a function whose parameters are a month of type *MonthAbbrev* (see Exercise 1) and a year in the range from 1538 through 1999 and whose value is the number of days in the month. Remember that February has 28 days, except in a leap year, when it has 29. A leap year is one in which the year number is divisible by 4, except for centesimal years (those ending in 00); these centesimal years are not leap years unless the year number is divisible by 400. Thus 1950 and 1900 are not leap years, but 1960 and 1600 are.)

(b) Use the function of part (a) in a program to read two dates in the form *mm dd yyyy* (such as 7 4 1776 and 1 1 1984), and calculate the number of days that have elapsed between the two dates.

One-Dimensional Arrays and String Processing

With silver bells, and cockle shells,
And pretty maids all in a row.

MOTHER GOOSE

I've got a little list, I've got a little list.

GILBERT AND SULLIVAN, *The Mikado*

The simple data types we have considered thus far represent single values. In many situations, however, it is necessary to process a collection of values that are related in some way, for example, a list of test scores, a collection of measurements resulting from some experiment, or a sales-tax table. Processing such collections using only simple data types can be extremely cumbersome, and for this reason, most high-level languages include special features for structuring such data. In this chapter we consider the *data structure* known as an *array* and its implementation in Pascal.

8.1

In Chapter 6 we introduced files, which are collections of related data items used in input/output operations. In standard Pascal, these data items can be retrieved only sequentially; that is, an item can be accessed only by searching from the beginning of the file. This property of files, together with the fact that they are usually stored in secondary memory, means that data retrieval from files is a rather slow operation and is thus not practical in many applications.

In some cases, it is better to store the data items in a sequence of

Introduction to Arrays and Subscripted Variables

main memory locations, each of which can be accessed directly. Such a data structure is called an *array*. In Pascal, we can refer to the entire array by an *array name* and to each individual item or component in the array by a *subscripted variable,* formed by affixing to the array name a *subscript* or *index* enclosed in brackets.

For example, if the test scores for fifteen students are to be processed in a program, we might use an array to store these scores. The computer must first be instructed to reserve a sequence of fifteen memory locations for the scores. The declarations

type
    ListOfScores = **array**[1..15] **of** *integer*;

var
    Score : *ListOfScores*;

instruct the compiler to establish an array with name *Score* consisting of fifteen memory locations in which integer values will be stored and to associate the subscripted variables *Score*[1], *Score*[2], *Score*[3], . . . , *Score*[15] with these locations.

Memory

Score[1] ⟷	
Score[2] ⟷	
Score[3] ⟷	
Score[4] ⟷	
Score[5] ⟷	
Score[6] ⟷	
Score[7] ⟷	
Score[8] ⟷	
Score[9] ⟷	
Score[10] ⟷	
Score[11] ⟷	
Score[12] ⟷	
Score[13] ⟷	
Score[14] ⟷	
Score[15] ⟷	

Each subscripted variable names an individual memory location and hence can be used in much the same way as an ordinary variable can. For example, the assignment statement

    Score[4] := 83

stores the value 83 in the fourth location of the array *Score;* and the output statement

    writeln (*Score*[10])

displays the value stored in the tenth location of the array *Score*. As these examples illustrate, each item of an array is directly accessible. This is one of the major advantages of using an array to store a collection of data.

An important feature of the notation used for arrays is that the subscript attached to the array name may be a variable or an expression. For example, the statement

> **if** *Score*[*n*] > 90 **then**
>   *writeln* (*Score*[*n*]:3, ' = A')

retrieves the *n*th item of the array *Score,* compares it with 90, and prints it with a letter grade of A if it exceeds 90. The statement

> **if** *Score*[*i*] > *Score*[*i* + 1] **then**
>   **begin**
>   *Temp* := *Score*[*i*];
>   *Score*[*i*] := *Score*[*i* + 1];
>   *Score*[*i* + 1] := *Temp*
>   **end**

interchanges the contents of *Score*[*i*] and *Score*[*i* + 1] if the first is greater than the second.

Using an array reference in which the subscript is a variable or an expression within a loop that changes the value of the subscript on each pass through the loop is a convenient way to process each item in the array. Thus

> **for** *i* := 1 **to** 15 **do**
>   **if** *Score*[*i*] > 90 **then**
>   *writeln* (*Score*[*i*], ' = A')

retrieves each item of the array *Score* in sequence, beginning with *Score*[1], compares it with 90, and prints it with a letter grade of A if it exceeds 90. Figure 8.1 illustrates.

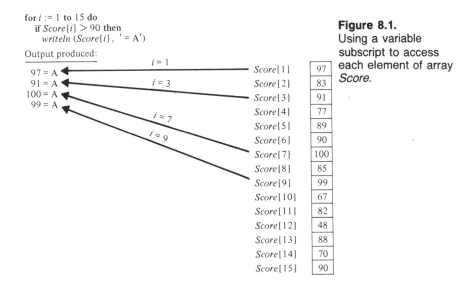

Figure 8.1.
Using a variable subscript to access each element of array *Score.*

Arrays such as *Score* involve only a single subscript and are commonly called *one-dimensional arrays*. Pascal programs, however, may process arrays of more than one dimension, in which case, each element of the array is designated by attaching the appropriate number of subscripts to the array name. In this chapter we consider only one-dimensional arrays; multidimensional arrays are considered in the next chapter.

The name of a one-dimensional array, the type of its components, and the type of its subscript are declared by means of an *array declaration* of the form

array[*index-type*] **of** *component-type*

where *index-type* may be any ordinal type except *integer;* it specifies the type of values for the subscript; *component-type* specifies the type of the array elements, or components, and may be any type. For example, the array declaration

array[1..10] **of** *real*

specifies that the subscript may be any of the values 1, 2, 3, . . . , 10 and that the type of each array element is *real*. The array declaration

array['A'..'Z'] **of** *integer*

specifies a one-dimensional array whose subscript may be any of the characters A, B, . . . , Z, and whose components are of integer type.

Such array declarations may appear in the variable section of the declaration part of a program to declare the type of an array, as in

var
      Coordinate : **array**[1..15] **of** *real*;
      Number : **array**[0..100] **of** 1..999;
      CharCount : **array**['A'..'Z'] **of** *integer*;
      TextLine : **array**[1..80] **of** *char*;

but it is preferable to associate them with type identifiers, as in

type
      Letter = 'A'..'Z';
      RealArray = **array**[1..15] **of** *real*;
      ArrayOfNumbers = **array**[0..100] **of** 1..999;
      FrequencyArray = **array**[*Letter*] **of** *integer*;
      Line = **array**[1..80] **of** *char*;

and then use these type identifiers to declare the types of arrays:

var
      Coordinate : *RealArray*;
      Number : *ArrayOfNumbers*;
      CharCount : *FrequencyArray*;
      TextLine : *Line*;

The syntax diagram for declarations of one-dimensional arrays is shown in the following display. Note that an array declaration may include the specification **packed.** This directs the compiler to store the data internally in a special compact format. Packed arrays are considered in more detail in Section 8.4.

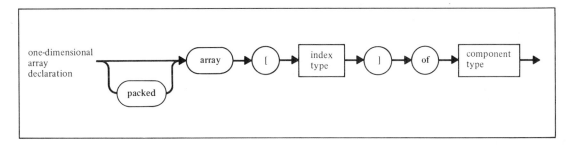

In the preceding section we used the one-dimensional array *Score* to store a list of numbers. This allowed us to access any one of these numbers by using a subscripted variable consisting of the array name *Score* followed by the index or subscript that indicated the position of that number in the list. In this section we consider various techniques for processing lists using one-dimensional arrays. (An alternative method using linked lists is described in Chapter 13.)

List Processing Using One-Dimensional Arrays

An input or output statement may be used within a repetition structure to read or display the components of an array. For example, suppose that *Score* is declared by

> **type**
>> *ListOfScores* = **array**[1..15] **of** *integer*;
>
> **var**
>> *Score* : *ListOfScores*;

and we wish to read fifteen integer values into this one-dimensional array. This can be accomplished by using the **for** statement

> **for** $i := 1$ **to** 15 **do**
>> *readln* (*Score*[i])

where the type of the index variable i is compatible with the subrange type 1..15 specified for the subscripts in the array declaration.

Because each execution of a *readln* statement causes the data pointer to advance to the next line, values to be read must appear on fifteen different lines, one per line. If a *read* statement is used in place of the *readln* statement

> **for** $i := 1$ **to** 15 **do**
>> *read* (*Score*[i])

the values need not be on separate lines. All of the entries may be on one line, or nine entries may be on the first line with six on the next, or three entries may be on each of five lines, and so on.

Input or output of arrays can also be accomplished by using a **while** or a **repeat** statment. For example, the values read by the statement

```
for i := 1 to 15 do
    read (Score[i])
```

can also be read by

```
i := 1;
while i <= 15 do
    begin
        read (Score[i]);
        i := i + 1
    end
```

or

```
i := 1;
repeat
    read (Score[i]);
    i := i + 1
until i > 15
```

If we wish to declare a larger array

```
const
    ScoresLimit = 100;

type
    ListOfScores = array[1..ScoresLimit] of integer;

var
    Score : ListOfScores;
    NumScores : integer;
```

and use only part of it, the statements

```
readln (NumScores);
if NumScores > ScoresLimit then
    writeln ('At most ', ScoresLimit:1, ' scores can be processed')
else
    for i := 1 to NumScores do
        read (Score[i])
```

might be used. Note that after a value is read for *NumScores*, a check is made to ensure that this value is not too large, since an error results if an attempt is made to use a subscript that is out of range. If the value 15 is read for *NumScores*, the *read* statement is executed fifteen times, and values are assigned to the first fifteen positions *Score*[1], *Score*[2], . . . , *Score*[15] of the array. The rest of the array, *Score*[16], . . . , *Score*[100], is unchanged;

these array elements are undefined unless values have previously been assigned to them.

The elements of an array can be displayed by placing an output statement within a repetition structure. For example, the statement

```
for i := 1 to NumScores do
    writeln (Score[i]:3)
```

displays the first *NumScores* on entries of the list *Score* on separate lines, one per line. The statement

```
for i := 1 to NumScores do
    write (Score[i]:3)
```

displays these entries on the same line. Note that subsequent output will also appear on this same line. This can be avoided by following the **for** statement with a *writeln* statement having no output list:

```
for i := 1 to NumScores do
    write (Score[i]:3);
writeln
```

Other kinds of list processing are also easy using repetition structures. For example, we can read *NumScores* components of the array *Score* and calculate the mean of the scores *MeanScore* (declared to be of real type) as follows:

```
writeln ('Enter the number of scores:');
readln (NumScores);
if NumScores > ScoresLimit then
    writeln ('At most ', ScoresLimit:1, ' scores can be processed')
else
    begin
        Sum := 0;
        writeln ('Enter the scores, as many per line as desired:');
        for i := 1 to NumScores do
            begin
                read (Score[i]);
                Sum := Sum + Score[i]
            end (* for *);
        MeanScore := Sum / NumScores;
        writeln ('Mean of the scores is: ', MeanScore:3:1)
    end (* else *);
```

To display the scores that are greater than the mean, we can use the statement

```
for i := 1 to NumScores do
    if Score[i] > MeanScore then
        writeln (Score[i]:3)
```

The program in Figure 8.2 uses these statements to read a list of up to one hundred scores, calculate their mean, and display a list of scores greater than the mean.

```
PROGRAM TestScores (input, output);

(*****************************************************************

   Program to read a list of test scores, calculate their mean,
   and print a list of scores greater than the mean.

*****************************************************************)

CONST
    ScoresLimit = 100;   (* maximum number of scores *)

TYPE
    ListOfScores = ARRAY[1..ScoresLimit] OF integer;

VAR
    Score : ListOfScores;   (* list of scores *)
    NumScores,              (* number of scores *)
    i : integer;            (* index *)
    Sum,                    (* sum of the scores *)
    MeanScore : real;       (* mean of the scores *)

BEGIN
    writeln ('Enter number of scores:');
    readln (NumScores);
    IF NumScores > ScoresLimit THEN
        writeln ('At most ', ScoresLimit:1, ' scores can be processed')
    ELSE
        BEGIN
            Sum := 0;
            writeln ('Enter the scores, as many per line as desired.');
            FOR i := 1 TO NumScores DO
                BEGIN
                    read (Score[i]);
                    Sum := Sum + Score[i]
                END (* FOR *);
            MeanScore := Sum / NumScores;
            writeln ('Mean of the scores is ', MeanScore:3:1);
            writeln;
            writeln ('List of scores greater than the mean:');
            FOR i := 1 TO NumScores DO
                IF Score[i] > MeanScore THEN
                    writeln (Score[i]:3)
        END (* ELSE *)
END.




Sample run:
==========

Enter number of scores:
15
Enter the scores, as many per line as desired.
88 77 56 89 100 99 55 35 78 65
69 83 71 38 95
Mean of the scores is 73.2
```

Figure 8.2

Fig. 8.2 (cont.)

```
List of scores greater than the mean:
  88
  77
  89
 100
  99
  78
  83
  95
```

In most of our examples of arrays, the subscripts have been positive-valued integers, ranging from 1 up through some upper limit. This is probably the most common subscript type, but as stated in the preceding section, the type of the subscript may be any ordinal type except *integer*. For example, the declarations

> **type**
> > *DaysOfWeek* = (*Sunday, Monday, Tuesday, Wednesday, Thursday,*
> > > *Friday, Saturday*);
> > *DaysArray* = **array**[*DaysOfWeek*] **of** *integer*;
>
> **var**
> > *DayCount* : *DaysArray*;

establish a one-dimensional array *DayCount* with seven locations, each of which can store an integer:

Values can be read into these seven locations by the statement

> **for** *Day* := *Sunday* **to** *Saturday* **do**
> > *read* (*DayCount*[*Day*])

where the index *Day* is assumed to be of type *DaysOfWeek,* and the values read into the array are of integer type (or some subrange of it). In general, the type of the subscript in any array reference must be compatible with that specified in the array declaration, and the type of values stored in the array must be compatible with the component type. Recall that two types are compatible if they are the same, one is a subrange of the other, or both are subranges of the same underlying type.

To illustrate further the use of nonnumeric subscripts to access array elements, consider the problem of reading a line of upper-case text and counting the number of occurrences of each of the letters A, B, . . . , Z. The program in Figure 8.3 solves this problem by using the array *Frequency* declared by

> **type**
>   *Letter* ='A'..'Z';
>   *CharCountArray* = **array**[*Letter*] **of** *integer*;
>
> **var**
>   *Frequency* : *CharCountArray*;

The array *Frequency* is used to count the occurrences of each of the letters so that *Frequency*['A'] is the number of occurrences of A in the line of text, *Frequency*['B'] is the number of occurrences of B, and so on.

```
PROGRAM LetterCount (input, output);

(*******************************************************************

   Program to count the occurrences of each of the upper-case letters
   A, B, ..., Z in a line of text.  The array Frequency indexed by
   the subrange 'A'..'Z' is used for this.  If Character is any one
   of these 26 letters, Frequency[Character] is the number of
   occurrences of Character in the text line.

********************************************************************)

TYPE
   Letter = 'A'..'Z';
   CharCountArray = ARRAY[Letter] OF integer;

VAR
   Frequency : CharCountArray;   (* frequencies of letters *)
   Character : char;             (* character from text line *)

BEGIN

   (* First initialize all frequencies to 0 *)

   FOR Character := 'A' TO 'Z' DO
      Frequency[Character] := 0;

   (* Read the line of text and count occurrences of letters *)

   writeln ('Enter the line of text:');
   WHILE NOT eoln DO
      BEGIN
         read (Character);
         IF ('A' <= Character) AND (Character <= 'Z') THEN
            Frequency[Character] := Frequency[Character] + 1
      END (* WHILE *);

   (* Print the frequencies *)

   writeln;
   FOR Character := 'A' TO 'Z' DO
      writeln ('Frequency of ', Character, ':   ', Frequency[Character]:2)
END.
```

Figure 8.3

Fig. 8.3 (cont.)

```
Sample run:
==========


Enter the line of text:
THE QUICK BROWN FOX JUMPED OVER THE LAZY DOGS AND RAN AWAY.

Frequency of A:    5
Frequency of B:    1
Frequency of C:    1
Frequency of D:    3
Frequency of E:    4
Frequency of F:    1
Frequency of G:    1
Frequency of H:    2
Frequency of I:    1
Frequency of J:    1
Frequency of K:    1
Frequency of L:    1
Frequency of M:    1
Frequency of N:    3
Frequency of O:    4
Frequency of P:    1
Frequency of Q:    1
Frequency of R:    3
Frequency of S:    1
Frequency of T:    2
Frequency of U:    2
Frequency of V:    1
Frequency of W:    2
Frequency of X:    1
Frequency of Y:    2
Frequency of Z:    1
```

Sometimes it is necessary to copy the elements of one array into a second array. Suppose, for example, that arrays *Alpha* and *Beta* are declared by

> **type**
>   *RealList* = **array**[1..5] **of** *real*;
>
> **var**
>   *Alpha*, *Beta* : *RealList*;

If values have been assigned to the array *Alpha,* these values can be copied to the array *Beta* by the statement

> **for** $i := 1$ **to** 5 **do**
>   *Beta*[i] := *Alpha*[i]

This assignment of the elements of the array *Alpha* to array *Beta* can be done more simply by the assignment statement

> *Beta* := *Alpha*

In general, one array may be assigned to another array only when they have the *same type*. This means that they must be declared by the same type identifier or by *equivalent* type identifiers. Two type identifiers are equivalent if their definitions can be traced back to a common *type identifier*. For example, consider the following type definitions:

type
    Aarray = **array**[1..5] **of** *real*;
    Barray = *Aarray*;
    Carray = *Aarray*;
    Darray = *Barray*;
    Earray = **array**[1..5] **of** *real*;

Type identifiers *Barray, Carray,* and *Darray* are equivalent since they are all synonyms for the type identifier *Aarray*. It is important to note, however, that *Barray* is not equivalent to *Aarray* because these type identifiers are not defined with a common type *identifier*. Similarly, *Carray* and *Darray* are not equivalent to *Aarray*. Note also that even though the definitions of types *Aarray* and *Earray* are identical, these type identifiers are not equivalent because they are not defined using a common type *identifier*. Thus, if arrays *A, B, C, D,* and *E* are declared by

var
    A : *Aarray*;
    B : *Barray*;
    C : *Carray*;
    D : *Darray*;
    E : *Earray*;

the array assignment statements

    B := *C*;
    B := *D*;
    C := *D*;

are all valid because arrays *B, C,* and *D* all have the same type, but the assignment statements

    A := *B*;
    A := *E*;

are not valid.[1]

Arrays may also be used as parameters for functions and procedures, but the value of a function may not be an array. To illustrate, consider the function *Max*, which finds the largest value in an integer array *Number* having *NumElements* components for *NumElements* ≤ 100. If the array

---

[1] In some versions of Pascal, the definition of "same type" may not be quite so strict; arrays *A, B, C, D,* and *E* might all be considered to have the same type.

type *NumList* has been declared in a program unit containing the declaration of the function *Max* by

> **type**
>   *ListOfNumbers* = **array**[1..100] **of** *integer*;

then an appropriate definition of *Max* is

> **function** *Max*(*Number* : *ListOfNumbers*; *NumElements* : *integer*) : *integer*;
>   (* Function to find the largest value in the array
>   *Number* having *NumElements* elements. *)
>
>   **var**
>   *i, Temp* : *integer*;
>
>   **begin** (* *Max* *)
>   *Temp* := *Number*[1];
>   **for** *i* := 2 **to** *NumElements* **do**
>   **if** *Number*[*i*] > *Temp* **then** *Temp* := *Number*[*i*];
>   *Max* := *Temp*
>   **end** (* *Max* *);

Because the types of formal parameters must be specified by *type identifiers,* the array declaration **array**[1..100] **of** *integer* could not be used to specify the type of the formal parameter *Number.*

When this function is referenced, the types of those actual parameters which are arrays must be the same as the types of the corresponding formal parameters. Thus, if array *Score* and variable *NumScores* have been declared by

> **var**
>   *Score* : *ListOfNumbers*;
>   *NumScores* : *integer*;

in the main program, then the function reference in the statement

> *writeln* (*Max*(*Score, NumScores*))

is valid.

In this example, the array *Number* is a value parameter, and consequently the values of the actual array *Score* are copied into *Number*. This produces two copies of the same list of values and is therefore not an efficient use of memory. Moreover, the process of copying the elements of one array into another is time-consuming. These difficulties may be overcome by specifying that the array *Number* is a variable parameter:

> **function** *Max*(**var** *Number* : *ListOfNumbers*; *NumElements* : *integer*) : *integer*;

An array must be a variable parameter when the subprogram is to return the array to the program unit that calls it. For example, a procedure to read an array *Number,* to count the number of elements that were read, and to return both this array and the count to the main program must declare both the array and the count as variable parameters:

> **procedure** *ReadArray* (**var** *Number* : *ListOfNumbers*; **var** *Count* : *integer*);

Example 1: Class Averages. Consider the problem of calculating the average score received on a test by students in each of the four classes freshman, sophomore, junior, and senior. For each student, a score is to be read together with a class code of 1, 2, 3, or 4, representing the class to which the student belongs. For each class we must calculate the average score received by the students in that class. To do this, we must find the number of students in each class and the sum of the scores for all of the students in that class. To illustrate the use of arrays having an enumerated data type for indices, we use the following one-dimensional arrays:

Number: *Number*[*Class*] is the number of students in the class specified by the index *Class* where the value of *Class* is *Freshman, Sophomore, Junior,* or *Senior.*

SumOfScores: *SumOfScores*[*Class*] is the sum of the scores for all students in the class specified by the value of *Class.*

The program in Figure 8.4 solves this problem by using three procedures, *Initialize, ReadTheData,* and *Calculate,* and the function *ConvertCode.* The first procedure is used to initialize the arrays *Number* and *SumOfScores* to zero; this is necessary because otherwise these arrays would be undefined. The procedure *ReadTheData* is then called repeatedly until an end-of-data flag is encountered. This procedure reads the pairs of class codes and scores, calls the function *ConvertCode* to convert the numeric class codes 1, 2, 3, 4 to *Freshman, Sophomore, Junior, Senior,* respectively, increases the appropriate counter *Number*[*Class*] by 1, and adds the test score to the appropriate sum *SumOfScores*[*Class*]. When the end-of-data flag is read, the procedure *Calculate* is called to find and display the class averages.

```
PROGRAM ClassAverages (input, output);

(*********************************************************************

   Program to calculate the average score received on a test by
   students in each of four classes:  Freshman (1), Sophomore (2),
   Junior (3) and Senior (4).

*********************************************************************)

TYPE
   ClassName = (Freshman, Sophomore, Junior, Senior);
   ClassList = ARRAY[ClassName] OF integer;
```

Figure 8.4

Fig. 8.4 (cont.)

```
VAR
   Number,                      (* Number[Class] = # of students in Class *)
   SumOfScores : ClassList;     (* SumOfScores[Class] = sum of scores for
                                   students in Class *)
   Class : ClassName;           (* index *)

PROCEDURE Initialize (VAR Number, SumOfScores : ClassList);

   (************************************************************************

      Procedure to initialize the arrays Number and SumOfScores to zero.

   ************************************************************************)

   VAR
      Class : ClassName;

   BEGIN (* Initialize *)
      FOR Class := Freshman TO Senior DO
         BEGIN
            Number[Class] := O;
            SumOfScores[Class] := O
         END (* FOR *)
   END (* Initialize *);

PROCEDURE ReadTheData (VAR Number, SumOfScores : ClassList);

   (*************************************************************************

      Procedure to read each pair of class codes and scores, increase
      the appropriate counter Number[Class] by 1, and add the test
      score to SumOfScores[Class], the sum  of scores for this class.

   *************************************************************************)

   TYPE
      ClassNumber = 1..4;

   VAR
      ClassCode : integer;   (* class code *)
      Class : ClassName;     (* class name corresponding to class code *)
      Score : integer;       (* student's test score *)

   FUNCTION ConvertCode(ClassCode : ClassNumber) : ClassName;

      (**********************************************************************

         Function to convert class code (1, 2, 3, 4) to the
         corresponding value of enumerated type ClassName.

      **********************************************************************)

      BEGIN (* ConvertCode *)
         CASE ClassCode OF
            1 : ConvertCode := Freshman;
            2 : ConvertCode := Sophomore;
            3 : ConvertCode := Junior;
            4 : ConvertCode := Senior
         END (* CASE *)
      END (* ConvertCode *);
```

Fig. 8.4 (cont.)

```
   BEGIN (* ReadTheData *)
      writeln ('Enter the class codes and the test scores in pairs,');
      writeln ('as many per line as desired.  Enter 0''s to signal');
      writeln ('the end of data.');
      writeln;
      read (ClassCode, Score);
      WHILE ClassCode <> 0 DO
         BEGIN
            IF (ClassCode < 1) OR (ClassCode > 4) THEN
               writeln ('** Illegal class code **')
            ELSE
               BEGIN
                  Class := ConvertCode(ClassCode);
                  Number[Class] := Number[Class] + 1;
                  SumOfScores[Class] := SumOfScores[Class] + Score
               END (* ELSE *);
            read (ClassCode, Score)
         END (* WHILE *)
   END (* ReadTheData *);

PROCEDURE Calculate (VAR Number, SumOfScores : ClassList);

   (*******************************************************************

      Procedure to calculate and display the average score for each
      of the four classes.

   *******************************************************************)

   VAR
      Class : ClassName;    (* index *)

   BEGIN (* Calculate *)
      writeln;
      writeln ('CLASS #  AVE. SCORE');
      writeln ('=======  ==========');
      FOR Class := Freshman TO Senior DO
         BEGIN
            write (1 + ord(Class):4);
            IF Number[Class] = 0 THEN
               writeln ('      No scores')
            ELSE
               writeln (SumOfScores[Class] / Number[Class]:11:1)
         END (* FOR *)
   END (* Calculate *);

BEGIN (* main program *)
   Initialize (Number, SumOfScores);
   ReadTheData (Number, SumOfScores);
   Calculate (Number, SumOfScores)
END (* main program *).
```

```
Sample run:
==========


Enter the class codes and the test scores in pairs,
as many per line as desired.  Enter 0's to signal
the end of data.
```

Fig. 8.4 (cont.)

```
1 95    1 88    3 77    4 100   4 67    1 58    3 62    3 99
3 87    4 72    4 58    1 66    4 89
0 0
```

```
CLASS #    AVE. SCORE
=======    ==========
   1         76.8
   2        No scores
   3         81.3
   4         77.2
```

Example 2: Sorting.   A common data-processing problem is *sorting* a list of items, that is, arranging these items so that they are in either ascending or descending order. There are many sorting methods, most of which use arrays to store the items to be sorted. In this section we describe the sorting method known as *bubble sort.*

Suppose that the items to be sorted have been read and assigned to *Item*[1], *Item*[2], . . . , *Item*[*NumItems*]. We scan the array, comparing *Item*[1] and *Item*[2] and interchanging them if they are in the wrong order. Then we compare *Item*[2] with *Item*[3], interchanging them if they are in the wrong order. This process of comparing and interchanging continues throughout the entire array. This constitutes one complete pass through the array. For example, suppose that the following list is to be sorted into increasing order:

77
30
89
54
62

We first compare 77 and 30 and interchange them, giving

30
77
89
54
62

Now we compare 77 and 89 but do not interchange them, as they already are in the correct order. Next 89 and 54 are compared and interchanged, giving

30
77
54
89
62

Finally, 89 and 62 are compared and interchanged, giving

30
77
54
62
89

This completes one pass through the list.

Note that the largest item in the list "sinks" to the bottom of the list and that some of the smaller items have "bubbled up" toward the top. We scan the list again, comparing consecutive items and interchanging them when they are out of order, but this time we leave the last item out of the pass, as it is already in its proper position. This pass produces

30
54
62
77

the second largest number sinks to its proper position, and more small numbers bubble up toward the top into their positions.

For this short list, we can easily see that the sorting is now complete, but for a long list, this is not so easy to determine. One method for determining when the sorting is complete is simply to record whether any interchanges took place during each pass through the list. When we eventually scan the list and find that no interchanges have taken place, we know that the list is sorted, and so we can terminate the procedure.

Algorithm

(*Algorithm to bubble sort a list of items $X_1, X_2, \ldots, X_N$ so that they are in ascending order. *)

1. Set *NumPairs* equal to $N - 1$; this is the number of pairs that must be examined in the current pass through the list.
2. Repeat the following until the boolean variable *Done* is true:
   a. Set *Done* to true. The value of *Done* will remain true if a pass through the list is made with no interchanges taking place, thus indicating that the items are in order; it will be set to false if interchanges are made.
   b. For each value of the subscript i from 1 through *NumPairs*, compare X_i with X_{i+1}. If $X_i > X_{i+1}$, then interchange them and set *Done* to false; otherwise proceed to the next pair of items.
   c. Decrease *NumPairs* by 1. At the end of each pass through the list, the largest item will have sunk into place and thus need not be examined on the next pass.

This algorithm sorts the items into ascending order. To sort them into descending order, one need only change $>$ to $<$ in the comparison of X_i with X_{i+1} in Step 2-b.

The program in Figure 8.5 implements this algorithm as the procedure *BubbleSort.* It reads a list of up to one hundred items, sorts them using *BubbleSort,* and then displays the sorted list.

```
PROGRAM Sort (input, output);

(*********************************************************************

   Program to read and count a list of items
         Item[1], Item[2], ..., Item[NumItems],
   sort them in ascending order, and then display the sorted list.

 *********************************************************************)

CONST
   ListLimit = 100;  (* maximum # of items in the list *)

TYPE
   ItemType = integer;
   List = ARRAY[1..ListLimit] of ItemType;

VAR
   NumItems,       (* number of items *)
   i: integer;     (* index *)
   Item : List;    (* list of items to be sorted *)

PROCEDURE ReadItems (VAR Item : List; VAR Count : integer);

   (*********************************************************************

      Procedure to read values into the array Item and count them.

    *********************************************************************)

   VAR
      Response : char;  (* user response *)

   BEGIN (* ReadItems *)
      NumItems := 0;
      writeln ('Enter the list of items, as many per line as desired.');
      writeln;
      REPEAT
         write ('Items:  ');
         WHILE NOT eoln DO
            BEGIN
               Count := Count + 1;
               read (Item[Count])
            END (* WHILE *);
         readln;
         writeln;
         write ('More (Y or N)?  ');
         readln (Response)
      UNTIL Response <> 'Y'
   END (* ReadItems *);
```

Figure 8.5

Fig. 8.5 (cont.)

```
PROCEDURE BubbleSort (VAR Item : List; N : integer);

   (************************************************************

      Procedure to sort Item[1], ..., Item[N] into ascending order
      using the bubble sort algorithm.  For descending order,
      change > to < in the boolean expression Item[i] > Item[i+1].

   ************************************************************)

   VAR
      i,                     (* index *)
      NumPairs : integer;    (* # of pairs examined in current scan *)
      Temporary : ItemType;  (* used to interchange two items *)
      Done : boolean;        (* indicates if sorting completed *)

   BEGIN (* BubbleSort *)
      NumPairs := N - 1;

      (* Scan the list comparing consecutive items *)

      REPEAT
         Done := true;
         FOR i := 1 TO NumPairs DO
            IF Item[i] > Item[i+1] THEN
               BEGIN
                  Temporary := Item[i];
                  Item[i] := Item[i+1];
                  Item[i+1] := Temporary;
                  Done := false  (* interchange occurred, so scan again *)
               END (* IF *);

         (* Largest item has sunk into place, so eliminate
            it from the next scan *)

         NumPairs := NumPairs - 1
      UNTIL Done
   END (* BubbleSort *);

PROCEDURE PrintItems (VAR Item : List; NumItems : integer);

   (************************************************************

         Procedure to print the list of items.

   ************************************************************)

   VAR
      i : integer;      (* index *)

   BEGIN (* PrintItems *)
      writeln;
      writeln ('Sorted list of ', Numitems:1, ' items:');
      writeln;
      FOR i := 1 TO NumItems DO
         writeln (Item[i])
   END (* PrintItems *);

BEGIN (* main program *)
   ReadItems (Item, NumItems);
   BubbleSort (Item, NumItems);
   PrintItems (Item, NumItems)
END (* main *).
```

Fig. 8.5 (cont.)

```
Sample run:
==========


Enter the list of items, as many per line as desired.

Items:   55 88 34 85 21

More (Y or N)?   Y
Items:   99 5 83 71

More (Y or N)?   N

Sorted list of 9 items:

    5
   21
   34
   55
   71
   83
   85
   88
   99
```

Example 3: Searching.   Another important problem in data processing is *searching* a collection of data for a specified item and retrieving some information associated with that item. For example, one searches a telephone directory for a specific name in order to retrieve the phone number listed with that name. In a *linear search,* one begins with the first item in a list and searches sequentially until either the desired item is found or the end of the list is reached. Although this might be an adequate method for small data sets, a more efficient technique is needed for large collections.

If the data to be searched have been previously sorted, then the *binary search* procedure can be used. With this method, we first examine the middle item in the list; if this is the desired entry, then the search is successful. Otherwise, we determine whether the item being sought is in the first half or the second half of the list and then repeat this process, using the middle entry of that sublist.

To illustrate, suppose that the list to be searched is

```
1331
1373
1555
1824
1882
1898
1983
2002
2335
2665
3103
```

and that we are looking for 1983. We first examine the middle number 1898 in the sixth position. Because 1983 is greater than 1898, we can disregard the first half of the list and concentrate on the second half

1983
2002
2335
2665
3103

The middle number in this sublist is 2335, and the desired item 1983 is less than 2335, so we discard the second half of this sublist and concentrate on the first half

1983
2002

Because there is no middle number in this half, we take the number immediately preceding the "middle position," that is, the number 1983. In this case, we have located the desired entry with three comparisons, as compared with seven, as would be required by a linear search.

Algorithm
(* Algorithm to perform a binary search on a list of items X_1, X_2, . . . , X_N previously sorted into ascending order. *)

1. Set *First* equal to 1 and *Last* equal to N. These represent the positions of the first and last items in the list or sublist being searched.
2. Set the boolean variable *Found* to false.
3. While *First* $\leq$ *Last* and *Found* is false do the following:
   a. Find the middle position in the list by setting *Middle* equal to the integer quotient of (*First* + *Last*) divided by 2.
   b. Compare the *Item* being searched for with X_{Middle}. There are three possibilities:
      (i) *Item* = X_{Middle}: *Item* has been found; set *Found* to true so that the search terminates.
      (ii) *Item* > X_{Middle}: *Item* is in the last half of the sublist; set *First* equal to *Middle* + 1.
      (iii) *Item* < X_{Middle}: *Item* is in the first half of the sublist; set *Last* equal to *Middle* − 1.
4. If *Found* is true, *Item* has been found at position *Middle* in the list; otherwise in which case *Item* is not in the list.

In the program of Figure 8.6, this algorithm is implemented as the procedure *BinarySearch*. This program reads student numbers, class codes, and test scores from a text file and stores these values so that subsequently the user can input a student's number and retrieve his or her class code and test score. Three arrays are used:

 Snumb: *Snumb*[i] is the ith student number.
  Class: *Class*[i] is the class code for the ith student.
 TestScore: *TestScore*[i] is the test score for the ith student.

In this program, the procedure *ReadAndStore* reads the three data items for each student and stores each in the appropriate array. The procedure *Sort* uses the bubble sort algorithm to arrange these three arrays so that the student numbers are in ascending order. Note that when items in the array *Snumb* are interchanged, the corresponding items in the arrays *Class* and *TestScore* must also be interchanged so that the correspondence between the items in the three arrays is maintained. This makes it possible to search the list of student numbers more efficiently, by using the binary search method, and to retrieve the class and test information for a given student.

```
PROGRAM TestProcessing (input, output,TestFile);

(*******************************************************************

   This program reads in a list of student numbers, class codes,
   and test scores from TestFile and then sorts them so the student
   numbers are in ascending order.  A student number can then be
   input, the list searched using a binary search, and the
   corresponding class code and test score displayed.

   *******************************************************************)

CONST
   ListLimit = 100;   (* maximum # of items in the list *)

TYPE
   DataType = integer;
   List = ARRAY[1..ListLimit] OF DataType;

VAR
   Snumb,                  (* Snumb[i] = i-th student number *)
   Class,                  (* Class[i] = class code for i-th student *)
   TestScore: List;        (* TestScore[i] = test score for i-th student *)
   NumScores : integer;    (* number of test scores *)
   TestFile : text;        (* file from which student data is read *)

PROCEDURE ReadAndStore (VAR Snumb, Class, TestScore : List;
                        VAR Count : integer);

   (*******************************************************************

      Procedure to read the items from TestFile and store them in
      the arrays Snumb, Class, and TestScore.

      *******************************************************************)

   BEGIN (* ReadAndStore *)
      reset (TestFile);
      Count := 0;
      WHILE NOT eof(TestFile) DO
         BEGIN
            Count := Count + 1;
            readln (TestFile, Snumb[Count], Class[Count], TestScore[Count])
         END (* WHILE *)
   END (* ReadAndStore *);
```

Figure 8.6

Fig. 8.6 (cont.)

```
PROCEDURE Sort (VAR ItemA, ItemB, ItemC : List; NumItems : integer);

    (*********************************************************************

        Procedure to sort the lists itemA, itemB, itemC using the
        bubblesort algorithm so that ItemA[1], ..., ItemA[NumItems]
        are in ascending order.  For descending order, change > to <
        in the boolean expression ItemA[i] > ItemA[i+1].

    *********************************************************************)

    VAR
        NumPairs,          (* # of pairs examined in current pass *)
        i : integer;       (* index *)
        Done : boolean;    (* indicates if sorting completed *)

    PROCEDURE Interchange (VAR X, Y : DataType);

        (*****************************************************************

            Procedure to interchange two items X and Y.

        *****************************************************************)

        VAR
            Temporary : DataType;   (* used to interchange items *)

        BEGIN (* Interchange *)
            Temporary := X;
            X := Y;
            Y := Temporary
        END (* Interchange *);

    BEGIN (* Sort *)
        NumPairs := NumItems - 1;

        (* Scan the list comparing consecutive items *)

        REPEAT
            Done := true;
            FOR i := 1 TO NumPairs DO
                IF ItemA[i] > ItemA[i+1] THEN
                    BEGIN
                        Interchange (ItemA[i], ItemA[i+1]);
                        Interchange (ItemB[i], ItemB[i+1]);
                        Interchange (ItemC[i], ItemC[i+1]);
                        Done := false  (* interchange occurred, so scan again *)
                    END (* IF *);

            (* Largest item has sunk into place, so eliminate
               it from the next scan *)
            NumPairs := NumPairs - 1
        UNTIL Done
    END (* Sort *);

PROCEDURE RetrieveInfo (VAR Snumb, Class, TestScore : List;
                        NumItems : integer);

    (*********************************************************************

        Procedure to accept a student number and then search the list
        Snumb for it.  If it is found, the class code and test score
        for that student are displayed.

    *********************************************************************)
```

Fig. 8.6 (cont.)

```
VAR
    SnumbDesired : DataType;    (* student # to search for *)
    Found : boolean;           (* indicates if search was successful *)
    Location : integer;        (* location of number in the list *)

PROCEDURE BinarySearch (VAR Item : List; NumItems : integer;
                        ItemSought : DataType; VAR Found : boolean;
                        VAR Location : integer);

    (***************************************************************

    Procedure to search the list Item for ItemSought using the
    binary search algorithm.  If ItemSought is found in the list,
    a value of true is returned for Found and the Location of the
    item is returned; otherwise, false is returned for Found and
    0 for Location.

    ***************************************************************)

    VAR
        First,              (* first item in sublist being searched *)
        Last,               (* last item in sublist *)
        Middle : integer;   (* middle item in sublist *)

    BEGIN (* BinarySearch *)
        First := 1;
        Last := NumItems;
        Found := false;
        WHILE (First <= Last) AND (NOT Found) DO
            BEGIN
                Middle := (First + Last) DIV 2;
                IF ItemSought = Item[Middle] THEN
                    BEGIN
                        Found := true;
                        Location := Middle
                    END (* IF *)
                ELSE IF ItemSought > Item[Middle] THEN
                    First := Middle + 1  (* item in last half of sublist *)
                ELSE
                    Last := Middle - 1   (* item in first half of sublist *)
            END (* WHILE *)
    END (* BinarySearch*);

BEGIN (* RetrieveInfo *)
    writeln ('To stop searching, enter student number of 0.');
    write ('Student number?  ');
    readln (SnumbDesired);
    WHILE SnumbDesired <> 0 DO
        BEGIN
            BinarySearch (Snumb, NumScores, SnumbDesired, Found, Location);
            IF Found THEN
                BEGIN
                    writeln ('Student ', SnumbDesired:1, ' is in class ',
                            Class[Location]:1);
                    writeln ('His/her test score was ', TestScore[Location]:1)
                END (* IF Found *)
            ELSE
                writeln ('Student ', SnumbDesired:1, ' not found');
            writeln;
            write ('Student number?  ');
            readln (SnumbDesired)
        END (* WHILE *)
END (* RetrieveInfo *);
```

Fig. 8.6 (cont.)

```
BEGIN (* main program *)
    ReadAndStore (Snumb, Class, TestScore, NumScores);
    Sort (Snumb, Class, TestScore, NumScores);
    RetrieveInfo (Snumb, Class, TestScore, NumScores)
END (* main program *).



Listing of TestFile:
====================


11111 1  99
22222 2 100
33333 3  77
44444 1  55
55555 2  87
66666 1  63
77777 3  93


Sample run:
==========

To stop searching, enter student number of 0.
Student number?  11111
Student 11111 is in class 1
His/her test score was 99

Student number?  55555
Student 55555 is in class 2
His/her test score was 87

Student number?  88888
Student 88888 not found

Student number?  33333
Student 33333 is in class 3
His/her test score was 77

Student number?  0
```

Exercises

1. Assume that the following declarations have been made:

> **type**
>> *Color* = (*red, yellow, blue, green, white, black*);
>> *ColorArray* = **array**[*Color*] **of** *real*;
>> *LittleArray* = **array**[1..10] **of** *integer*;
>> *CharCountArray* = **array**['A'..'F'] **of** *integer*;
>
> **var**
>> *Price* : *ColorArray*;
>> *Number* : *LittleArray*;
>> *LetterCount* : *CharCountArray*;
>> *i* : *integer*;
>> *Ch* : *char*;
>> *Col* : *Color*;

For each of the following, tell what value (if any) will be assigned to each array element, or explain why an error occurs.

(a) for $i := 1$ to 10 do
      $Number[i] := i$ **div** 2

(b) for $i := 1$ to 6 do
      $Number[i] := i * i;$
   for $i := 7$ to 10 do
      $Number[i] := Number[i - 5]$

(c) $i := 0;$
   while $i <> 10$ do
      begin
         if $(i$ **mod** $3) = 0$ then
            $Number[i] := 0$
         else
            $Number[i] := i;$
         $i := i + 1$
      end

(d) $Number[1] := 1;$
   $i := 2;$
   repeat
      $Number[i] := 2 * Number[i - 1];$
      $i := i + 1$
   until $i = 10$

(e) for $Ch :=$ 'A' to 'F' do
      if $Ch =$ 'A' then
         $LetterCount[Ch] := 1$
      else
         $LetterCount[Ch] := LetterCount[pred(Ch)] + 1$

(f) for $Col := yellow$ to $white$ do
   $Price[Col] := 13.95$

(g) for $Col := red$ to $black$ do
   case Col of
      $red, blue :$ $Price[Col] := 19.95;$
      $yellow :$ $Price[Col] := 12.75;$
      $green, black :$ $Price[Col] := 14.50;$
      $white :$
   end (* **case** *)

2. For each of the following, write appropriate declarations and statements to create the specified array:

(a) An array whose subscripts are the integers from 0 through 5 and in which each element is the same as the subscript.

(b) An array whose subscripts are the integers from -5 through 5 and for which the elements are the subscripts in reverse order.

(c) An array whose subscripts are the upper-case letters and in which each element is the same as the subscript.

(d) An array whose subscripts are the integers from 1 through 20 and for which an array element has the value true if the corresponding subscript is even, and false otherwise.

(e) An array whose subscripts are the upper-case letters and for which each element is the letter preceding the subscript, except that the array element corresponding to A is Z.

(f) An array whose subscripts are the upper-case letters and in which each array element is the number of the position of the corresponding subscript in the sequence A, B, C, . . . , Z.

(g) An array whose subscripts are the lower-case letters and in which an array element has the value true if the subscript is a vowel, and false otherwise.

(h) An array whose subscripts are the names of the five subjects mathematics, chemistry, speech, history, and economics and in which the array elements are the letter grades received: A in mathematics and speech, B in chemistry, F in history, and C in economics.

3. Write a program to read two lists of real numbers and then find and display the intersection of the lists, that is, the collection of items common to both lists. The lists are not required to contain the same number of elements.

4. Repeat Exercise 3 but find and display the union of the two lists, that is, the collection of items that are elements of at least one of the lists.

5. Write a program to read a list of integers and then locate and display the smallest and largest numbers in the list and their positions in the list. Also find the range of the numbers, that is, the difference between the largest number and the smallest.

6. A *mode* of a list of numbers is a value that appears most often. A list may have more than one mode; for example, the list 3, 5, 3, 7, 8, 5, 4, 9 has modes 3 and 5. Write a program to read a list of integers and find all modes.

7. If $\bar{x}$ denotes the mean of the numbers $x_1, x_2, \ldots, x_n$, then the *variance* is the average of the squares of the deviations of the numbers from the mean

$$\text{variance} = \frac{1}{n} \sum_{i=1}^{n} (x_i - \bar{x})^2$$

and the *standard deviation* is the square root of the variance. Write a program that reads a list of real numbers, counts them, and then calculates their mean, variance, and standard deviation. Print with appropriate labels how many numbers there are, their mean, variance, and standard deviation. Use functions or procedures to calculate the mean, variance, and standard deviation.

8. Letter grades are sometimes assigned to numeric scores by using the grading scheme commonly called "grading on the curve." In this scheme, a letter grade is assigned to a numeric score, according to the following table:

x = Numeric Score	Letter Grade
$x < m - \dfrac{3}{2}\sigma$	F
$m - \dfrac{3}{2}\sigma \le x < m - \dfrac{1}{2}\sigma$	D
$m - \dfrac{1}{2}\sigma \le x < m + \dfrac{1}{2}\sigma$	C
$m + \dfrac{1}{2}\sigma \le x < m + \dfrac{3}{2}\sigma$	B
$m + \dfrac{3}{2}\sigma \le x$	A

where m is the mean score and σ is the standard deviation. Extend the program of Exercise 7 to read a list of real numbers representing numeric scores, and then calculate their mean and standard deviation, and find and display the letter grade corresponding to each numeric score.

9. The *skewness*, or the tendency of data values to pile up more at one end of a distribution than at the other end or the middle, can be measured by

$$\text{index of skewness} = \frac{\sum\limits_{i=1}^{n}(x_i - \bar{x})^3}{n \cdot \sigma^3}$$

where $\bar{x}$ is the mean of $x_1, x_2, \ldots, x_n$, and σ is the standard deviation. (See Exercise 7.) Write a program to read and count a set of real numbers and calculate the index of skewness.

10. A very simple, but not very efficient, method of sorting a list of items $x_1, x_2, \ldots, x_n$ into ascending order is the following:

Step 1: Locate the smallest item in the list x_1 through x_n; exchange it with x_1.

Step 2: Locate the smallest item in the list x_2 through x_n; exchange it with x_2.

Step 3: Locate the smallest item in the list x_3 through x_n; exchange it with x_3.

$\vdots$

At the last step, the last two items are compared and exchanged if necessary, and sorting is complete. Write a program to sort a list of items, using this method.

11. One problem with bubble sort is that while larger values move rapidly toward their proper positions, smaller values move slowly in the other direction. "Shell sort" (named after Donald Shell) attempts to improve this. A series of compare-interchange scans are made, but consecutive items are not compared on each scan. Instead, there is a fixed "gap" between the items that are compared. When no more interchanges can be made for a given gap, the gap is cut in half, and the compare-interchange scans continue. The initial gap is commonly taken to be $n/2$, for a list of n items. For example, for the list

    6,1,5,2,3,4,0

the following sequence of gaps and scans would be used:

Scan #	Gap	Rearranged List	Interchanges
1	3	2,1,4,0,3,5,6	(6,2), (5,4), (6,0)
2	3	0,1,4,2,3,5,6	(2,0)
3	3	0,1,4,2,3,5,6	none
4	1	0,1,2,3,4,5,6	(4,2), (4,3)
5	1	0,1,2,3,4,5,6	none

Write a program to sort a list of items, using the Shell sort method.

12. "Insertion" sort is an efficient sorting method for small data sets. It begins with the first item x_1, then inserts x_2 into this one-item list in the correct position to form a sorted two-element list, then inserts x_3 into this two-element list in the correct position, and so on. For example, to sort the list 7, 1, 5, 2, 3, 4, 6, 0, the steps are as follows (the element being inserted is underlined):

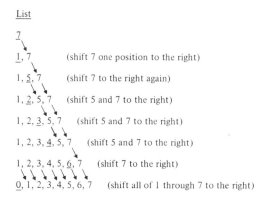

Write a program to sort a list of items, using this insertion sort method.

     ONE-DIMENSIONAL ARRAYS AND STRING PROCESSING

13. Suppose that we begin with a special deck of cards numbered from 1 through 150, with all the numbers face up. Beginning with card 2, we turn every even-numbered card face down. Next, beginning with card 3, we turn every third card over, that is, turn it face up if it is face down, and turn it face down if it is face up. We repeat this procedure with every fourth card, then every fifth card, and so on. Write a program to determine which cards will be face up when this process is completed.

14. A *prime number* is an integer greater than 1 whose only positive divisors are 1 and the integer itself. One method for finding all the prime numbers in the range from 1 through n is known as the *Sieve of Eratosthenes*. Consider the list of numbers from 2 through n. Two is the first prime number, but the multiples of 2 (4, 6, 8, . . .) are not, and so they are "crossed out" in the list. The first number after 2 that was not crossed out is 3, the next prime. We then cross out from the list all higher multiples of 3 (6, 9, 12, . . .). The next number not crossed out is 5, the next prime, and so we cross out all higher multiples of 5 (10, 15, 20, . . .). We repeat this procedure until we reach the first number in the list that has not been crossed out and whose square is greater than n. Then all the numbers that remain in the list will be the primes from 2 through n. Write a program that uses this sieve method to find all the prime numbers from 2 through n. Run it for $n = 50$ and for $n = 500$.

15. Write a program to add two large integers of length up to three hundred digits. One approach is to treat each number as a list, each of whose elements is a block of digits of the number. For example, the integer 179,534,672,198 might be stored with $Block[1] = 198$, $Block[2] = 672$, $Block[3] = 534$, $Block[4] = 179$. Then add the two integers (lists) element by element, carrying from one element to the next when necessary.

16. Proceeding as in Exercise 15, write a program to multiply two large integers of length up to three hundred digits.

17. Write a recursive procedure to carry out the binary search method described in this section.

18. A data structure that is sometimes implemented as an array is a *stack*. A stack is a list in which elements may be inserted or deleted at only one end of the list, called the *top* of the stack. Because the last element added to a stack will be the first one removed, a stack is a Last-In-First-Out (LIFO) structure. A stack can be implemented as an array *Stack* whose subscript type is 1..*StackLimit*. The array element *Stack*[1] is the element at the bottom of the stack, and *Stack*[*Top*] is the element at the top. Write procedures *Push* and *Pop* to implement the insertion and deletion operations for a stack. Use these procedures in a program that reads a command

I (Insert) or D (Delete); for I, an integer is then read and inserted into ("pushed onto") the stack; for D, an integer is deleted ("popped") from the stack and displayed.

19. Another data structure that can be implemented as an array is a *queue*. A queue is a list in which elements may be inserted at one end of the list, called the *rear,* and removed at the other end, called the *front.* Because the first element added is the first to be removed, a queue is a First-In-First-Out (FIFO) structure. Write procedures to implement insertion and deletion operations for a queue. Use these procedures in a program like that in Exercise 18 to insert integers into or delete integers from a queue. (Note: The most efficient representation of a queue as an array is obtained by thinking of the array as being circular, with the first array element immediately following the last array element.)

String Processing

The word *compute* usually suggests arithmetic operations performed on numeric data; thus, computers are sometimes thought to be mere "number-crunchers," devices whose only function is to process numeric information. In Chapter 1, we considered coding schemes used to represent character information in a computer, and in subsequent chapters, we introduced some of the character-processing capabilities of Pascal. In this section we extend our study to data that consist of strings of characters and to the processing of such strings by using arrays.

In Chapter 3 we introduced the data type *char* and defined a *character* to be any of the symbols in the Pascal character set. A *character constant* was defined to be any character enclosed in single quotes. A finite sequence of characters is commonly called a *string,* and a *string constant* consists of a string enclosed in single quotes. In many of our sample programs we used such string constants in the output list of a *write* or *writeln* statement to label the output or to prompt the user to enter appropriate data.

A variable of type *char* can be used to store a single character. Such a value may be assigned by means of an assignment statement or an input statement. For example, if *Letter* is declared by

var
    Letter : *char*;

then the character A can be assigned to *Letter* by the statement

    Letter := 'A'

This same value could also be assigned to *Letter* by means of an input statement such as

    read (*Letter*)

In this case the input datum is a character rather than a character constant; that is, it is a single character, but it is not enclosed within quotes.

In situations where it is necessary to process a string of characters, such as a name or an address, rather than a single character, arrays of character type are used. In this case, each array element is a single character in the string. For example, a one-dimensional array *Name* having five components of character type might be used to store the string SMITH; *Name*[1] would have the value S, *Name*[2] the value M, and so on.

In our discussion in Section 1.3 of the internal representation of data, we noted that the commonly used coding schemes ASCII and EBCDIC require only 8 bits (or 1 byte) to store a single character. In many computers, the length of each memory word is more than 8 bits and thus can store more than one character. Some Pascal compilers, however, allocate an entire memory word for each variable, in particular for variables of character type. Because the values assigned to such variables require only 8 bits for storage, this is an inefficient use of memory. For example, in a 32-bit word machine, only 8 bits of a 32-bit word are used to store a character, and thus three fourths of each such word is wasted. Memory utilization in such machines can be improved by using *packed arrays* in which several array elements or characters are stored in a single word.

To illustrate the difference between unpacked and packed arrays, suppose that arrays *U* and *P* are declared by

type
    UnpackedCharArray = **array**[1..8] **of** *char*;
    PackedCharArray = **packed array**[1..8] **of** *char*;

var
    U : *UnpackedCharArray*;
    P : *PackedCharArray*;

For some computers, the array *U* would be allocated eight memory words:

$U[1] \longleftrightarrow$
$U[2] \longleftrightarrow$
$U[3] \longleftrightarrow$
$U[4] \longleftrightarrow$
$U[5] \longleftrightarrow$
$U[6] \longleftrightarrow$
$U[7] \longleftrightarrow$
$U[8] \longleftrightarrow$

For a 32-bit machine, however, the packed array need be allocated only two memory words, since each word can store four characters:

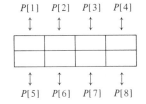

Memory is obviously used more efficiently in the second case than in the first.

The usual operations that may be performed on arrays can also be applied to packed arrays. (One exception is that a component of a packed array may not be an actual parameter that corresponds to a variable formal parameter.) For example, packed arrays of the same type may appear in an assignment statement of the form

$$array1 := array2$$

This assignment statement would not be valid, however, if either of *array1* or *array2* was not packed.

Although arrays of any type may be specified as packed arrays, the most important use of packed arrays is to process strings. Thus we restrict our attention to packed arrays of characters in this chapter. (Packed arrays of other types are considered in Appendix F.)

A packed array of type <u>char</u> whose subscript type is a subrange of the form <u>$1..n$ for some integer $n \geq 1$ is called</u> a <u>string type.</u>[2] For example, consider the following type definitions:

type
      A = **packed array**[1..10] **of** *char*;
      B = **array**[1..10] **of** *char*;
      C = **packed array**[0..9] **of** *char*;
      D = **packed array**[1..10] **of** 'A'..'Z';
      E = **packed array**[1..1] **of** *char*;

Only type A is of string type. B, C, D, and E are not string types because arrays of type B are not packed, the subscript type for C does not begin with 1, the component type for D is not *char*, and the subscript type for E does not have two or more values.

A string constant may be used to assign a value to an array of string type provided that its length (number of characters) is the same as the number of array elements. For example, if the string type *NameString* is defined by

type
      NameString = **packed array**[1..10] **of** *char*;

and the array *Name* is declared by

var
      Name : *NameString*;

then the assignment statement

      Name := 'John Smith'

---

[2] Some versions of Pascal include a predefined type *alfa* which is equivalent to **packed array**[1..*L*] **of** *char* for some system-dependent constant L (such as 8 or 10).

is valid. The string J. Doe cannot be assigned to *Name* since it has only six characters. If four blanks are appended to this string, however, the resulting string may be assigned to *Name:*

Name := 'J. Doe   '

Similarly, the string constant 'Johann VanderDoe' cannot be assigned to *Name* because it has more than ten characters.

Two values of string type may be compared with the relational operators $<, >, =, <=, >=$, and $<>$, provided they have the same length. Thus,

'cat' $<$ 'dog'

is a valid boolean expression and is evaluated by comparing, character by character, the strings cat and dog, using the collating sequence described in Section 4.3. Thus this boolean expression is true because c precedes d in the collating sequence. Similarly, the boolean expression

'cat' $>$ 'car'

is true because t follows r in the collating sequence. Note, however, that the string constants 'apples' and 'oranges' cannot be compared because they have different lengths; that is, they do not have the same number of characters. The boolean expression

'apples ' $<$ 'oranges'

is valid, however, and is true. Similarly, if each of *Name1* and *Name2* is of type *NameString*, then the following are valid boolean expressions:

Name1 $<$ 'John Smith'

Name2 $<>$ 'apples   '

Name1 $>=$ *Name2*

Values of string type may also appear in the output list of a *write* or *writeln* statement. We have already used this feature when string constants appeared in an output statement such as

writeln ('Mean =', *Mean*);

The name of an array of string type also may appear in the output list. Thus if *Name* and *EmpNumber* are declared by

type
    String12 = **packed array**[1..12] **of** *char*;

var
    Name : *String12;*
    EmpNumber : *integer*;

and have values JohnbDoebbbb and 13520, respectively, then the statement

>   writeln (Name, EmpNumber:6)

produces the output

>   John Doe   13520

Many Pascal compilers do not allow the name of an array of string type to appear in the input list of a *read* or *readln* statement. Thus, a statement such as

>   readln (Name)

would not be allowed.[3] Instead, the array elements must be read individually:

>   **for** i := 1 **to** 12 **do**
>   read (Name[i])

If the string

>   JohnbDoebbbb

is entered, then the value assigned to *Name* is the string JohnbDoebbbb. The value of *Name*[1] is the character J, the value of *Name*[2] is o, and so on.[4]

In this example, twelve characters must be read. Although we may prefer to enter only the name John Doe, we are forced to enter also characters for the other four elements of the array. Thus we entered four trailing blanks to be assigned to *Name*[9], . . . , *Name*[12].

Entering blanks or some other characters to fill up the positions of a character array is rather tedious. We prefer to enter only the characters in which we are interested and have the program assign blanks to the remaining positions.

In Section 6.2 we noted that *eoln* has the value true if the end of the current input line has been reached; otherwise, it has the value false. Assuming declarations of the form

>   **const**
>   StringLimit = ...   (* limit on the length of a string *);
>
>   **type**
>   CharacterArray = **packed array**[1..StringLimit] **of** char;

---

[3] Versions of Pascal that allow an array of string type in an input list also frequently allow a second parameter, for example,

>   readln (Name : Length)

Length will be assigned the number of characters that are read.

[4] Some compilers do not allow reading the elements of a packed array. In this case, values must be read into an unpacked array, and these elements then must be copied into the packed array.

var
      CharArray : *CharacterArray*;
      i : *integer*;

we can use the following statements to read values into the first positions of the character array *CharArray* and fill any remaining positions with blanks:

    for *i* := 1 **to** *StringLimit* **do**
      if not *eoln* **then**
          read (*CharArray*[*i*])
      else
          CharArray[*i*] := ' '

Suppose, for example, that *StringLimit* is 12. If the string

    John Doe

is entered, the eight characters J, o, h, n, b, D, o, and e are read and assigned to *CharArray*[1], *CharArray*[2], . . . , *CharArray*[8]. Because the end of the input line is now encountered, the value of *eoln* is true. No more characters are read, and blanks are assigned to *CharArray*[9], . . . , *CharArray*[12].

In our discussion of input in Chapter 6, we observed that values for the variables in the input list of an input statement are obtained from the standard system file *input*. When this file is loaded from data cards or data is entered from the terminal, a data pointer is positioned at the beginning of the file and advances through the file as the values are read. When the end of an input line is reached, an *end-of-line mark* is entered into the input file. For example, the two lines of input

    John Doe
    Mary Smith

produce the following contents in the file *input*

where, as before, • denotes an end-of-line mark and ↑ represents the data pointer. When the statement

    for *i* := 1 **to** *StringLimit* **do**
      if not *eoln* **then**
          read (*CharArray*[*i*])
      else
          CharArray[*i*] := ' '

is executed, the reading of characters from the input file terminates, and blank filling begins when the data pointer advances to the first end-of-line mark:

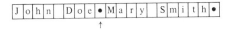

Care must be exercised when using the *eoln* function for the input of character data. To illustrate, consider this same input file with the data pointer reset to the beginning of the file, and consider the following attempt to read and display the two names in this file:

```
for j := 1 to 2 do
    begin
        for i := 1 to StringLimit do
            if not eoln then
                read (CharArray[i])
            else
                CharArray[i] := '*';
        writeln (CharArray)
    end (* for *)
```

The first pass through the outer **for** loop with *j* equal to 1 reads the characters J, o, h, n, ♭, D, o, and e for the first eight elements of the array *CharArray,* advancing the data pointer to the first end-of-line mark:

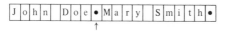

and then pads the rest of *CharArray* with asterisks and displays

J o h n   D o e * * * *

The outer **for** loop is then repeated with *j* equal to 2. When the inner **for** loop is executed, however, the value of *eoln* is true, because the data pointer is positioned at the end-of-line mark. Consequently, no characters are read, and the entire array *CharArray* is filled with asterisks. The resulting output is

* * * * * * * * * * * *

To eliminate this difficulty, the data pointer must be advanced beyond the end-of-line mark so that *eoln* becomes false before the outer **for** loop is executed for the second time. Insertion of a *readln* statement to be executed before the outer **for** loop is repeated is what is needed:

```
for j := 1 to 2 do
    begin
        for i := 1 to StringLimit do
            if not eoln then
                read (CharArray[i])
            else
                CharArray[i] := '*';
        writeln (CharArray);
        readln
    end (* for *)
```

In many text-processing problems, the number of characters read into a character array must be determined during execution. This can be done by initializing a counter to 0 and then incrementing it by 1 each time a character is read:

```
NumChars := 0;
for i := 1 to StringLimit do
    if not eoln then
        begin
            read (CharArray[i]);
            NumChars := NumChars + 1
        end
    else
        CharArray[i] := ' '
```

In some situations it may not be necessary to blank fill a character array, as we have been doing in these examples. Values may be read into the first positions of a character array, and only those positions are processed. In the example above, *NumChars* is the number of positions of the array *CharArray* into which values have been read, and if we confine all subsequent processing to positions 1, 2, . . . , *NumChars,* no values previously assigned to the array positions *NumChars* + 1, . . . , *StringLimit* will be used.

To read values for only the first part of an array without blank filling the remaining positions, we could simply remove the **else** clause in the preceding set of statements. However, the resulting sequence of statements is not very efficient because the **for** loop is executed *StringLimit* times in every case. An alternate set of statements in which the repetition structure is executed only *NumChars* times is the following:

```
NumChars := 0;
while (not eoln) and (NumChars < StringLimit) do
    begin
        NumChars := NumChars + 1;
        read (CharArray[NumChars])
    end (* while *)
```

A **repeat** statement could also be used:

```
NumChars := 0;
repeat
    NumChars := NumChars + 1;
    read (CharArray[NumChars])
until eoln or (NumChars = StringLength)
```

As noted in Chapter 6, an attempt to read the end-of-line character does not result in an error. Rather, the end-of-line character is read as a blank. For example, if the preceding set of statements is executed twice and the file *input* has the contents

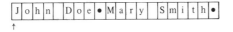

the first execution assigns the characters J, o, h, n, ♭, D, o, and e to the array elements *CharArray*[1], *CharArray*[2], . . . , *CharArray*[8] and advances the data pointer to the first end-of-line mark. The second execution of these statements then assigns the characters ♭, M, a, r, y, ♭, S, m, i, and t to *CharArray*[1], *CharArray*[2], . . . , *CharArray*[10]. The source of the extra leading blank is the end-of-line mark that is read as a blank for *CharArray*[1]. Once again, the problem is solved by using a *readln* statement to advance the data pointer past the end-of-line mark before reading another string.

The program in Figure 8.7 uses the techniques described in this section for reading values into a character array. It reads a line of text into the string array *TextLine,* converts each upper-case letter to lower case, and then displays the new line.

Because access to elements of a packed array may be more time-consuming than that of an unpacked array, the method used to input the elements of the packed array *TextLine* in the program of Figure 8.7 may be inefficient and, as we have noted, may not be allowed with some compilers. This difficulty

```
PROGRAM ConvertToLowerCase (input, output);

(********************************************************************

   Program to read a line of text and then convert all upper case
   letters to lower case.  The resulting text is then displayed.

********************************************************************)

CONST
   StringLimit = 70;    (* maximum string length *)

TYPE
   String = PACKED ARRAY[1..StringLimit] OF char;

VAR
   TextLine : String;    (* a line of text *)
   NumChars : integer;   (* # of characters in TextLine *)
   Response : char;      (* user response *)

PROCEDURE UpperToLower (VAR TextLine : String; NumChars : integer);

   (********************************************************************

       Procedure to convert upper case letters to lower case.

   ********************************************************************)

   VAR
      Shift,          (* shift in code of character *)
      i : integer;    (* index *)

   BEGIN (* UpperToLower *)
      Shift := ord('a') - ord('A');
      FOR i := 1 TO NumChars DO
         IF ('A' <= TextLine[i]) AND (TextLine[i] <= 'Z') THEN
            TextLine[i] := chr(ord(TextLine[i]) + Shift)
   END (* UpperToLower *);
```

Figure 8.7

Fig. 8.7. (cont.)

```
BEGIN (* main program *)
   REPEAT
      writeln ('Enter text:');
      NumChars := 0;
      WHILE NOT eoln DO
         BEGIN
            NumChars := NumChars + 1;
            read (TextLine[NumChars])
         END (* WHILE NOT eoln *);
      readln;
      UpperToLower (TextLine, NumChars);
      writeln (TextLine:NumChars);
      writeln;
      write ('More (Y or N)?  ');
      readln (Response)
   UNTIL Response <> 'Y'
END (* main program *).



Sample run:
==========

Enter text:
FOURSCORE AND SEVEN YEARS AGO, OUR FATHERS
fourscore and seven years ago, our fathers

More (Y or N)?  Y
Enter text:
BROUGHT FORTH ON THIS CONTINENT A NEW NATION ...
brought forth on this continent a new nation ...

More (Y or N)?  Y
Enter text:
A. LINCOLN -- 16th president.
a. lincoln -- 16th president.

More (Y or N)?  N
```

can be avoided by reading each character into a temporary character variable and then assigning it to the appropriate array element. For example, the program of Figure 8.7 could be modified to declare the character variable

TempChar : *char*;

and replace the **while** statement with

while (**not** *eoln*) **and** (*NumChars* < *StringLimit*) **do**
   begin
      read (*TempChar*);
      NumChars := *NumChars* + 1;
      TextLine[*NumChars*] := *TempChar*
   end (* **while** *);

Alternatively, we could use the predefined Pascal procedures *pack* and *unpack* to transfer elements between an unpacked array and a packed array. These procedures are described in Appendix F.

The preparation of textual material such as letters, books, and computer **Application:** programs often involves the insertion, deletion, and replacement of parts of **Text Editing** the text. The software of most computer systems includes an *editing* package which makes it easy to carry out these operations. To illustrate how these text-editing functions can be implemented in Pascal, we consider the problem of replacing a specified substring with another string in a given line of text. A solution to this problem is given in the program in Figure 8.8. The sample run shows that in addition to string replacements, the program can be used to make insertions and deletions. For example, changing the substring

A N

in the line of text

A NATION CONCEIVED IN LIBERTY AND AND DEDICATED

to

A NEW N

yields the edited line

A NEW NATION CONCEIVED IN LIBERTY AND AND DEDICATED

Entering the edit change

AND //

changes the substring

AND♭

(where ♭ denotes a blank) in the line of text to an empty string containing no characters, and so the edited result is

A NEW NATION CONCEIVED IN LIBERTY AND DEDICATED

```
PROGRAM TextEditor (input, output, TextFile, NewTextFile);

(*****************************************************************************

    Program to perform some basic text-editing functions on lines of
    text.  The basic operation is that of replacing a substring of
    the text by another string.  This replacement is accomplished
    by a command of the form
                         OldString/NewString/
    where OldString specifies the substring in the text to be replaced
    by the specified string NewString; NewString may be an empty
    string which then causes the substring OldString (if found) to be
    deleted.  The text lines are read from TextFile, and after editing
    has been completed, the edited lines are written to NewTextFile.

*****************************************************************************)
```

Figure 8.8

Fig. 8.8 (cont.)

```
CONST
   StringLimit = 80;   (* maximum length of lines of text *)

TYPE
   String = PACKED ARRAY[1..StringLimit] OF char;

VAR
   TextFile,                 (* file of original text *)
   NewTextFile : text;       (* file of edited text *)
   TextLine : String;        (* line of text to be edited *)
   LineLength : integer;     (* length of TextLine *)

PROCEDURE GetTextLine (VAR TextLine : String; VAR CharCount : integer);

   (*********************************************************************

      Procedure to read a line of text from TextFile and count the
      number of characters in it.

   *********************************************************************)

   VAR
      i : integer;  (* index *)

   BEGIN (* GetTextLine *)
      CharCount := 0;
      FOR i := 1 TO StringLimit DO
         IF NOT eoln(TextFile) THEN
            BEGIN
               CharCount := CharCount + 1;
               read (TextFile, TextLine[CharCount])
            END (* IF *)
         ELSE
            TextLine[i] := ' ';
      readln (TextFile);
      writeln;
      writeln (TextLine: CharCount)
   END (* GetTextLine *);

PROCEDURE Edit (TextLine : String; LineLength : integer);

   (*********************************************************************

      Procedure to carry out the editing operations on TextLine.
      After editing is completed, edited line is written to
      NewTextFile.

   *********************************************************************)

   VAR
      OldString,                (* old string in edit change *)
      NewString : String;       (* new string in edit change *)
      OldLength,                (* length of oldstring *)
      NewLength,                (* length of newstring *)
      Location : integer;       (* location of OldString in TextLine *)
      Response : char;          (* user response *)
```

Fig. 8.8 (cont.)

```
PROCEDURE GetEditChange (VAR OldString, NewString : String;
                         VAR OldLength, NewLength : integer);

   (*****************************************************************

      Procedure to read the edit change of the form
                OldString/NewString/
      It returns OldString, NewString, and their lengths.

      ****************************************************************)

   VAR
      Symbol : char;        (* a symbol in edit change *)
      EndOfOld,             (* indicates end of OldString *)
      EndOfNew : boolean;   (* indicates end of NewString *)

   BEGIN (* GetEditChange *)
      writeln ('Edit change:  ');
      OldLength := 0;
      EndOfOld := false;
      WHILE NOT EndOfOld DO
         BEGIN
            read (Symbol);
            IF Symbol = '/' THEN
               EndOfOld := true
            ELSE
               BEGIN
                  OldLength := OldLength + 1;
                  OldString[OldLength] := Symbol
               END (* ELSE *)
         END (* WHILE *);
      NewLength := 0;
      EndOfNew := false;
      WHILE NOT EndOfNew DO
         BEGIN
            read (Symbol);
            IF Symbol = '/' THEN
               EndOfNew := true
            ELSE
               BEGIN
                  NewLength := NewLength + 1;
                  NewString[NewLength] := Symbol
               END (* ELSE *)
         END (* WHILE *);
      readln
   END (* GetEditChange *);

FUNCTION Index (TextLine, SubString : String;
                LineLength, SubLength : integer) : integer;

   (*****************************************************************

      Function to determine the first occurrence of SubString in the
      specified line of text.  The value of Index is the position in
      TextLine of the first character of the first occurrence of
      SubString, or 0 if SubString does not appear in TextLine.
      Textlength and SubLength are the number of characters in
      TextLine and SubString, respectively.

      ****************************************************************)
```

Fig. 8.8 (cont.)

```
    VAR
        TextPos,                (* position in TextLine *)
        SubPos : integer;       (* position in SubString *)
        Found : boolean;        (* indicates if SubString found *)

    BEGIN (* Index *)
        TextPos := 1;
        Found := false;
        WHILE (TextPos <= LineLength) AND (NOT Found) DO
            BEGIN
                Index := TextPos;
                SubPos := 1;
                WHILE (SubString[SubPos] = TextLine[TextPos]) AND
                      (SubPos <= SubLength) AND (TextPos <= LineLength) DO
                    BEGIN
                        TextPos := TextPos + 1;
                        SubPos := SubPos + 1
                    END (* WHILE *);
                IF SubPos > SubLength THEN
                    Found := true;
                TextPos := TextPos + 1
            END (* WHILE *);
        IF NOT Found THEN
            Index := 0
    END (* Index *);

PROCEDURE Replace (VAR TextLine: String; VAR LineLength : integer;
                   NewString : String; OldLength, NewLength,
                   Start : integer);

    (************************************************************

    Procedure to replace a substring of length OldLength beginning
    at position Start of TextLine with NewString of length
    NewLength; LineLength will be the length of the modified string.

    ************************************************************)

    VAR
        Shift,           (* amount to shift end of TextLine *)
        i : integer;     (* index *)

    BEGIN (* Replace *)
        Shift := NewLength - OldLength;
        IF (Shift + LineLength) > StringLimit THEN
            writeln ('*** Change makes line of text too long ***')
        ELSE
            BEGIN
                IF Shift > 0 THEN  (* shift last part to the right *)
                    FOR i := LineLength DOWNTO Start + OldLength DO
                        TextLine[i + Shift] := TextLine[i];
                        IF Shift < 0 THEN  (* shift last part to the left *)
                            FOR i := Start + OldLength TO LineLength DO
                                TextLine[i + Shift] := TextLine[i];

                        (* Now insert the new string *)
                        FOR i := 1 TO NewLength DO
                            TextLine[Start + i - 1] := NewString[i];
                        LineLength := LineLength + Shift;
                    END (* ELSE *);
                writeln (TextLine:LineLength);
            END (* Replace *);
```

Fig. 8.8 (cont.)

```
      BEGIN (* Edit *)
         writeln ('Edit this line?  ');
         readln (Response);
         WHILE Response = 'Y' DO
            BEGIN
               GetEditChange (OldString, NewString, OldLength, NewLength);
               Location := Index (TextLine, OldString, LineLength, OldLength);
               IF Location = O THEN
                  writeln (OldString:OldLength, ' not found')
               ELSE
                  Replace (TextLine, LineLength, NewString, OldLength,
                           NewLength, Location);
               writeln ('More editing (Y or N)?  ');
               readln (Response)
            END (* WHILE *);
         writeln (NewTextFile, TextLine:LineLength)
      END (* Edit *);

   BEGIN (* main program *)
      reset (TextFile);
      rewrite (NewTextFile);
      WHILE NOT eof (TextFile) DO
         BEGIN
            GetTextLine (TextLine, LineLength);
            Edit (TextLine, LineLength)
         END (* WHILE *)
   END (* main program *).



Listing of TextFile:
====================



FOURSCORE AND FIVE YEARS AGO, OUR MOTHERS
BROUGHT FORTH ON CONTINENT
A NATION CONCEIVED IN LIBERTY AND AND DEDICATED
TO THE PREPOSITION THAT ALL MEN
ARE CREATED EQUAL.


Sample run:
==========



FOURSCORE AND FIVE YEARS AGO, OUR MOTHERS
Edit this line?
Y
Edit change:
FIVE/SEVEN/
FOURSCORE AND SEVEN YEARS AGO, OUR MOTHERS
More editing (Y or N)?
Y
Edit change:
MOTHERS/FATHERS/
FOURSCORE AND SEVEN YEARS AGO, OUR FATHERS
More editing (Y or N)?
N
```

Fig. 8.8 (cont.)

```
BROUGHT FORTH ON CONTINENT
Edit this line?
Y
Edit change:
ON C/ON THIS C/
BROUGHT FORTH ON THIS CONTINENT
More editing (Y or N)?
N

A NATION CONCEIVED IN LIBERTY AND AND DEDICATED
Edit this line?
Y
Edit change:
A N/A NEW N/
A NEW NATION CONCEIVED IN LIBERTY AND AND DEDICATED
More editing (Y or N)?
Y
Edit change:
AND //
A NEW NATION CONCEIVED IN LIBERTY AND DEDICATED
More editing (Y or N)?
N

TO THE PREPOSITION THAT ALL MEN
Edit this line?
Y
Edit change:
PRE/PRO/
TO THE PROPOSITION THAT ALL MEN
More editing (Y or N)?
N

ARE CREATED EQUAL.
Edit this line?
N


Listing of NewTextFile:
=======================

FOURSCORE AND SEVEN YEARS AGO, OUR FATHERS
BROUGHT FORTH ON THIS CONTINENT
A NEW NATION CONCEIVED IN LIBERTY AND DEDICATED
TO THE PROPOSITION THAT ALL MEN
ARE CREATED EQUAL.
```

Programming Pointers

In this chapter we discussed one-dimensional arrays. It is quite common for beginning programmers to have some difficulty when using arrays. The following are some of the major points to remember.

1. *The types of the components of an array may be any predefined or user-defined type. The types of the subscripts may be any ordinal type except integer.*

2. *When processing array elements, the subscript must be compatible with the type specified in the array declaration.* The most common

error is that of a subscript getting "out of range." For example, suppose that the array *Number* is declared by

type
> *ListOfNumbers* = **array**[1..10] **of** *integer*;

var
> *Number* : *ListOfNumbers*;

and consider the following statements designed to read and to count the elements of this array, where *i* is assumed to be of integer type, *Temp* is of integer type, and −999 is an end-of-data flag:

```
i := 0;
repeat
    i := i + 1;
    read (Temp);
    if Temp <> −999 then
    Number[i] := Temp
until Temp = −999
```

These statements correctly read values for the entries of *Number*, provided that there are no more than ten values preceding the end-of-data flag. But if there are more than ten values, an error results when the value of *i* reaches 11, because an attempt is made to read a value for *Number*[11], and an error message such as the following may be displayed:

*** Value 11 out of range, must be <= 10 ***

As this example demonstrates, it is important to check *boundary conditions* when processing the elements of arrays, that is, to check to make sure that the subscript is not out of range. Thus, the preceding set of statements could better be written as

```
i := 0;
repeat
    i := i + 1;
    read (Temp);
    if Temp <> −999 then
    Number[i] := temp
until (Temp = −999) or (i = 10);
if Temp <> −999 then
    writeln ('End-of-data flag not encountered')
```

3. When *reading the elements of an array of characters, remember that end-of-line marks are read as blanks.*

4. *Assignment of one array to another requires that the arrays have the same type.*

5. *Values of string type may be compared with the standard relational operators, provided they have the same length. They may also be output using the write and writeln procedures.* This is not the case, however, for unpacked arrays. Also, the elements of arrays cannot usually be read by including the array name in the input list of a

read or *readln* statement. This must be accomplished by reading the individual elements of the arrays, and in some versions of Pascal, these may not be elements of a packed array.

6. *To utilize memory efficiently, it is usually advisable to specify as variable parameters the formal parameters of functions and procedures that represent arrays (especially if they are large).* If value parameters are used for arrays, two copies of the array are stored in memory; also, the elements of the actual array must be copied to that of the subprogram, and this is quite time-consuming for large arrays.

Exercises

1. Assume that the following declarations have been made:

type
     Color = (*red, yellow, blue, green, white, black*);
     ColorCodeArray = **packed array**[*Color*] **of** *char*;
     ArrayOfCharacters = **array**[1..10] **of** *char*;
     String = **packed array**[1..10] **of** *char*;

var
     ColorCode : *ColorCodeArray*;
     CharArray : *ArrayOfCharacters*;
     TextLine : *String*;
     Col : *Color*;
     i, j : *integer*;

Assume also that the following data are entered:

ABCDEFG
HI$

For each of the following, tell what value (if any) will be assigned to each array element, or explain why an error occurs.

(a) **for** *i* := 1 **to** 7 **do**
          read (*TextLine*[*i*]);
     readln;
     for *i* := 8 **to** 10 **do**
          read (*TextLine*[*i*])

(b) **for** *Col* := *black* **downto** *red* **do**
          read (*ColorCode*[*Col*])

(c) **for** *i* := 1 **to** 10 **do**
          read (*TextLine*[*i*])

(d) **for** *i* := 10 **downto** 1 **do**
          read (*TextLine*[*i*])

(e) for *Col* := *red* to *black* do
    read (*ColorCode*[*Col*]);
for *Col* := *red* to *black* do
    TextLine[ord(*Col*) + 1] := *ColorCode*[*Col*];
for *i* := 7 to 10 do
    read (*TextLine*[*i*])

(f) for *Col* := *red* to *black* do
    read (*ColorCode*[*Col*]);
TextLine := *ColorCode*

(g) for *i* := 1 to 10 do
    read (*CharArray*[*i*]);
TextLine := *CharArray*;

(h) for *i* := 1 to 10 do
    read (*CharArray*[*i*]);
write (*CharArray*)

(i) for *i* := 1 to 10 do
    if not *eoln* then
        read (*TextLine*[*i*])
    else
        TextLine[*i*] := '¢'

(j) for *i* := 1 to 10 do
    if not *eoln* then
        read (*TextLine*[*i*])
    else
        readln

(k) for *i* := 1 to 5 do
    if not *eoln* then
        read (*CharArray*[*i*], *CharArray*[*i* + 5])
    else
        begin
            CharArray[*i*] := '$';
            CharArray[*i* + 5] := '¢'
        end

(l) *i* := 0;
for *j* := 1 to 2 do
    begin
        while not *eoln* do
            begin
                i := *i* + 1;
                read (*TextLine*[*i*])
            end (* while *);
        readln
    end (* for *)

(m) $i := 0;$
repeat
    while not *eoln* **do**
        begin
            $i := i + 1;$
            read (*TextLine*[*i*])
        end (* **while** *);
    readln
until *TextLine*[*i*] = '$'

2. Write a program to determine whether a specified string occurs in a given string, and if so, print an asterisk (*) under the first position of each occurrence.

3. Write a program to count the number of occurrences of each of the articles a, an, and the in several lines of text.

4. Write a program to count the number of occurrences of a specified string in several lines of text.

5. Write a program to find all double-letter occurrences in a given line of text.

6. Develop a procedure to concatenate two strings. Then use this procedure in a program that reads two strings, calls the procedure to concatenate them, and then displays the resulting string.

7. Write a program that permits the input of a name consisting of a first name, a middle name or initial, and a last name, in that order, and that then prints the last name, followed by a comma, and then the first and middle initials, each followed by a period. For example, the input John H. Doe should produce Doe, J. H.

8. Write a program that accepts a message and an integer and that then scrambles the message by converting each character of the message to its numeric code, adding the specified integer to this code, and then converting the resulting number back to a character. For example, on an ASCII machine, the message THE RED-COATS ARE COMING and the integer 5 should produce YMJ%WJIHTFYX%FWJ%HTRNSL#.

9. The encoding scheme used in Exercise 8 to produce a *cryptogram* consists simply of adding a specified integer to the code of each character of the message. This is a special case of the technique known as *keyword* encoding, in which a sequence of integers corresponding to the characters of a specified keyword is added in order to the codes of the message characters. To illustrate, if the keyword is ABC and the message is MEETATNOON, the codes for A, B, and C are added to the codes for M, E, and E, respectively, and then added to the codes for T, A, and T, respectively, and so forth, producing the cryptogram NGHUCWOQRO (assuming this is an ASCII machine). Write a program to implement this keyword method of encoding.

10. Another method of encoding uses substitutions, for example:

letter: A B C D E F G H I J K L M N O P Q R S T U V W X Y Z
substitute: T F H X Q J E M U P I D C K V B A O L R Z W G N S Y

Each letter of the input message is then replaced with its substitute, for example:

message: T H E R E D C O A T S A R E C O M I N G
crytogram: R M Q O Q X H V T R L T O Q H V C U K E

Write a program that permits the input of either a message or a cryptogram and then encodes or decodes it by using substitutions.

11. Write a program to print a "personalized" contest letter like those frequently received in the mail. It might have a format like that of the following sample, with the underlined locations filled in with appropriate data:

Mr. Paul Revere
31416 Belltower Road
Concord, New Hampshire 99999

Dear Mr. Revere:

How would you like to see a brand new palomino pony tied to the hitching post in front of 31416 Belltower Road in Concord, New Hampshire? Impossible, you say? No, it isn't, Mr. Revere. You are one of the few chosen to enter our REDCOAT SWEEPSTAKES!!! Just send the enclosed ticket with 10 labels from REDCOAT Chewing Tobacco and a $10.00 entry fee for shipping and handling. That's all there is to it, Paul. You may be a winner!!!

12. There are 3 teaspoons in a tablespoon, 4 tablespoons in a quarter of a cup, 2 cups in a pint, and 2 pints in a quart. Write a program to convert units in cooking. The program should call for the input of the amount, the units used, and the new units desired. For example, the input 0.5, CUPS, TEASPOONS asks for the conversion of one-half cup to teaspoons.

13. Write a program to convert ordinary Hindu-Arabic numerals into Roman numerals and vice versa. (I = 1, V = 5, X = 10, L = 50, C = 100, D = 500, and M = 1000.)

14. Frequency counts like those in Exercises 3 and 4 can be graphically displayed by using a *histogram*. For example, if the frequency counts of a, an, and the in Exercise 3 were 15, 6, and 20, respectively, these could be displayed by the following histogram:

a : XXXXXXXXXXXXXXX
an : XXXXXX
the : XXXXXXXXXXXXXXXXXXXX

Write a program to read several pairs of strings and frequencies and to plot a histogram displaying the information.

15. A string is said to be a *palindrome* if it does not change when the order of characters in the string is reversed. For example,

MADAM

463364

ABLE WAS I ERE I SAW ELBA

are palindromes. Write a program to read a string and then determine whether it is a palindrome.

16. Graphs of equations can also be plotted by using the computer. For example, Figure 8.9 shows computer-generated plots of

$$Y = X^2 \text{ for } -3 \leq X \leq 3$$

and

$$Y = X^3 \text{ for } -2 \leq X \leq 2$$

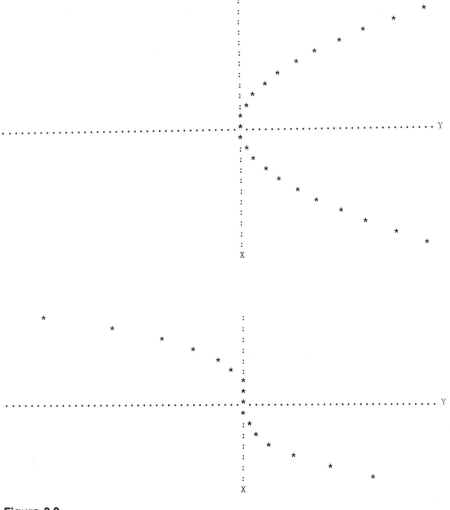

Figure 8.9.
Plots of $Y = X^2$ and $Y = X^3$.

using an X increment of 0.25 in each case. Note that for convenience, the X axis has been printed vertically and the Y axis horizontally. Write a program to produce a similar plot of a given equation using a packed character array with the number of array elements equal to the width of the page. For each X value, set all of the array elements equal to blanks, or equal to the marks comprising the Y axis if $X = 0$; then set one array element equal to the X axis mark and another equal to the plotting character; the position of this latter array element should correspond to the Y coordinate of the point on the graph for that X value.

17. Write a program that uses the Sieve Method of Eratosthenes to find all prime numbers from 2 through some integer n. (See Exercise 14 of Section 8.3.) Use a packed array *Sieve* of boolean type in which *Sieve*$[i]$ is true if i is in the list, false if i has been crossed out.

18. Repeat Exercise 15 but this time use a recursive procedure to determine whether a string is a palindrome.

19. Write a program that accepts two strings and that determines whether one string is an *anagram* of the other, that is, whether one string is a permutation of the characters in the other string. For example, "dear" is an anagram of "read," as is "dare."

9

Multidimensional Arrays

Everyone knows how laborious the usual Method is of attaining to Arts and Sciences; whereas by his Contrivance, the most ignorant Person at a reasonable Charge, and with a little bodily Labour, may write Books in Philosophy, Poetry, Politicks, Law, Mathematicks, and Theology, without the least Assistance from Genius or Study. He then led me to the Frame, about the sides whereof all his Pupils stood in Ranks. It was Twenty Foot square . . . linked by slender Wires. These Bits . . . were covered on every Square with Paper pasted upon them; and on These Papers were written all the Words of their Language . . . .

The Professor then desired me to observe, for he was going to set his Engine at work. The Pupils at this Command took each of them hold of an Iron Handle, whereof there were Forty fixed round the Edges of the Frame; and giving them a sudden Turn, the whole Disposition of the Words was entirely changed . . . .

JONATHAN SWIFT, *Gulliver's Travels*

In the preceding chapter we considered one-dimensional arrays and used them to process lists of data. We also observed that Pascal allows arrays of more than one dimension, and that two-dimensional arrays are useful when the data being processed can be arranged in rows and columns. Similarly, a three-dimensional array is appropriate when the data can be arranged in rows, columns, and ranks. When there are several characteristics associated with the data, still higher dimensions may be appropriate, with each dimension corresponding to one of these characteristics. In this chapter we consider how such multidimensional arrays are processed in Pascal programs.

9.1

There are many problems in which the data being processed can be naturally organized as a table. For example, if for each of twenty-five different students, four test scores are to be processed in a program, the data can be arranged in a table having twenty-five rows and four columns:

Introduction to Multidimensional Arrays; Multiply Subscripted Variables

Student		Test Number		
Number	1	2	3	4
1	79.5	80.0	64.5	91.0
2	99.5	90.0	92.0	97.5
⋮	⋮	⋮	⋮	⋮
25	100.0	62.5	73.5	88.0

In this table, the four scores of student 1 are in the first row, the four scores of student 2 are in the second row, and so on.

These one hundred data items can be conveniently stored in a two-dimensional array. The declaration

type
    ArrayOfGrades = **array**[1..25, 1..4] **of** *real*;

var
    Grades : *ArrayOfGrades*;

reserves one hundred memory locations for these data items. The subscripted variable

Grades[2,3]

refers to the entry in the second row and third column of the table, that is, to the score 92.0 earned by student 2 on test 3. In general,

Grades[i,j]

refers to the entry in the ith row and jth column, that is, to the score earned by student i on test j.

To illustrate the use of an array with more than two dimensions, suppose that a retailer maintains an inventory of jeans. He carries several different brands of jeans and for each brand stocks a variety of colors, waist sizes, and inseam lengths. A four-dimensional array can be used to record the inventory, with each element of the array being the number of jeans of a particular brand, color, waist size, and inseam length currently in stock. The first subscript represents the brand; thus it might be of type

Brand = (*Levi*, *Wrangler*, *CalvinKlein*, *Lee*, *BigYank*);

The second subscript represents color and is of type

Color = (*lightblue*, *khaki*, *blue*, *white*, *yellow*, *green*);

The third and fourth subscripts represent waist size and inseam length, respectively. Their types might be given by

Waist = 28..40;

Inseam = 28..36;

MULTIDIMENSIONAL ARRAYS

In a Pascal program for maintaining this inventory, the following type section is thus appropriate:

```
type
    Brand = (Levi, Wrangler, CalvinKlein, Lee, BigYank);
    Color = (lightblue, khaki, blue, white, yellow, green);
    Waist = 28..40;
    Inseam = 28..36;
    JeansArray = array[Brand, Color, Waist, Inseam] of integer;
```

The four-dimensional array *JeansInStock* having subscripts of the types just described can then be declared by

```
var
    JeansInStock : JeansArray;
```

The value of the quadruply subscripted variable

$$JeansInStock[Levi, blue, 32, 31]$$

is the number of Levi blue 32×31 jeans in stock. The statement

$$JeansInStock[b, c, w, i] := JeansInStock[b, c, w, i] - 1$$

records the sale of one pair of jeans of brand *b*, color *c*, waist size *w*, and inseam length *i*.

The Pascal standard places no limit on the number of dimensions of an array, but the type of each subscript must be declared. The general form of the declaration of an *n-dimensional array* is

array[*index-type-1, index-type-2, ..., index-type-n*] **of** *component-type*

where *index-type-i* specifies the type of the *i*th subscript and may be any ordinal type except *integer*. The syntax diagram for array declarations is

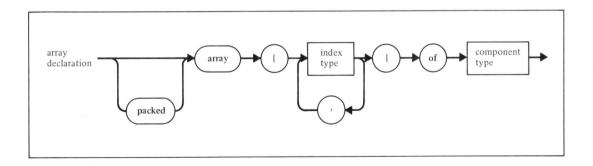

An equivalent method of declaring a multidimensional array is as an *array of arrays,* that is, an array whose elements are other arrays. To illustrate, reconsider the table of test scores given earlier:

Student	Test Number			
Number	1	2	3	4
1	79.5	80.0	64.5	91.0
2	99.5	99.0	92.0	97.5
:	:	:	:	:
25	100.0	62.5	73.5	88.0

For each student there is an array of test scores corresponding to one row of the table. The entire table might then be viewed as an array of of these test score arrays, one for each student. Thus, if we define the type *TestScores* by

type
> *TestScores* = **array**[1..4] **of** *real*;
> *ArrayOfScores* = **array**[1..25] **of** *TestScores*;

then the declaration

var
> *Table* : *ArrayOfScores*;

establishes one hundred memory locations for these data items. The subscripted variable

> *Table*[2]

refers to the second row of the table, that is, to the array of test scores for the second student. The subscripted variable

> *Table*[2][3]

as well as *Table*[2,3], then refers to the third score in this row, that is, the score 92.0 earned by the second student on the third test. In general, either

> *Table*[*i*][*j*]

or

> *Table*[*i,j*]

refers to the *j*th score in the *i*th row of the table of test scores, that is, to the score earned by the *i*th student on the *j*th test.

Another problem in which it might be natural to structure the data as an array of arrays is in processing several pages of text. A book can be thought of as an array of pages and each page as an array of lines of text; thus a book can be viewed as an array of arrays of lines. Similarly, a line is an array of characters; consequently, a page is an array of arrays of characters, and a book is an array of arrays of arrays of characters.

MULTIDIMENSIONAL ARRAYS

To illustrate, if the types *Line, Page,* and *Book* are defined by

type
    Line = **packed array**[1..70] **of** *char*;
    Page = **packed array**[1..45] **of** *Line*;
    Book = **packed array**[1..30] **of** *Page*;

and the array name *PascalText* is declared as

var
    PascalText : *Book*;

then

    PascalText[30]

denotes the thirtieth page;

    PascalText[30][5]

or

    PascalText[30,5]

denotes the fifth line on that page; and

    PascalText[30][5][10]

or

    PascalText [30,5,10]

denotes the tenth character on that line. This character could also be denoted
by

    PascalText[30,5][10]

or

    PascalText[30][5,10]

but these notations are seldom used.

9.2

Processing Multidimensional Arrays

In the preceding section we gave several examples of multidimensional arrays
and showed how such arrays are declared in a Pascal program. We also
noted that any element of the array can be accessed directly by using a

multiply subscripted variable consisting of the array name followed by the subscripts that indicate that item's location in the array. In this section we consider the processing of multidimensional arrays, including the input and output of arrays or parts of arrays, copying the elements of one array into another array, and using multidimensional arrays as parameters in subprograms.

As we observed in the preceding chapter, the most natural order for processing the elements of a one-dimensional array is the usual sequential order, from first item to last. For multidimensional arrays there are several different orders in which the subscripts may be varied when processing the array elements.

Two-dimensional arrays are often used when the data can be organized as a table consisting of rows and columns. This leads to two natural orders for processing the entries of a two-dimensional array, *rowwise* and *columnwise*. Rowwise processing means that the array elements in the first row are processed first, then those in the second row, and so on, as shown in Figure 9.1(a) for the 3×4 array A having three rows and four columns. In columnwise processing, the entries in the first column are processed first, then those in the second column, and so on, as illustrated in Figure 9.1(b).

In the list of array elements shown in Figure 9.1(b), we observe that in the columnwise processing of a two-dimensional array, it is the first subscript that varies first and the second subscript second; that is, the first subscript must vary over its entire set of values before the second subscript changes. For arrays of three or more dimensions, the same pattern of processing is commonly used; that is, the first subscript varies first, followed by the second subscript, and then by the third, and so on. This is illustrated

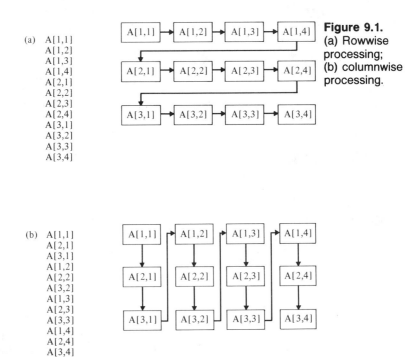

Figure 9.1.
(a) Rowwise processing;
(b) columnwise processing.

B[1,1,1]
B[2,1,1]
B[1,2,1]
B[2,2,1]
B[1,3,1]
B[2,3,1]
B[1,4,1]
B[2,4,1]
B[1,1,2]
B[2,1,2]
B[1,2,2]
B[2,2,2]
B[1,3,2]
B[2,3,2]
B[1,4,2]
B[2,4,2]
B[1,1,3]
B[2,1,3]
B[1,2,3]
B[2,2,3]
B[1,3,3]
B[2,3,3]
B[1,4,3]
B[2,4,3]

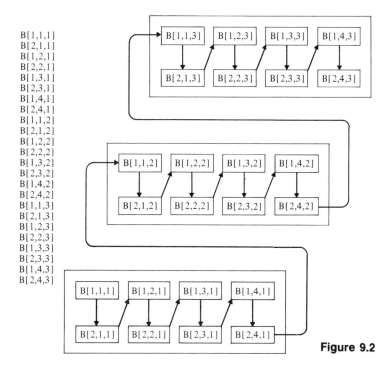

Figure 9.2

in Figure 9.2 for the $2 \times 4 \times 3$ array B having two rows, four columns, and three ranks.

The elements of a multidimensional array can be processed by using nested repetition structures. For example, the nested **for** statements

> **for** *row* := 1 **to** 3 **do**
>   **for** *column* := 1 **to** 4 **do**
>   *readln* ($A[row,column]$)

read values for the twelve entries of the 3×4 array A in rowwise order. The data values to be assigned must be entered one per line so that twelve separate lines of data are required. Thus, to store the table

$$\begin{bmatrix} 22 & 37 & 0 & 0 \\ 0 & 1 & 17 & 32 \\ 6 & 18 & 4 & 12 \end{bmatrix}$$

the values would be entered as follows:

22
37
0
0
0
1

17
32
6
18
4
12

To read the entries of this table in columnwise order, we could use the nested **for** statements

```
for column := 1 to 4 do
    for row := 1 to 3 do
        readln (A[row,column])
```

and enter the values as

22
0
6
37
1
18
0
17
4
0
32
12

If a *read* statement is used in place of a *readln* statement to read the entries in rowwise order,

```
for row := 1 to 3 do
    for column := 1 to 4 do
        read (A[row,column])
```

then all the values can be read from the same line

22 37 0 0 0 1 17 32 6 18 4 12

or from three lines each containing four values

22 37 0 0
0 1 17 32
6 18 4 12

or from as many lines as desired.

It should be noted that some care must be taken when reading values for a character array. For example, consider the 3×3 table

　　　　　　　　　　　　　　　　　　　MULTIDIMENSIONAL ARRAYS

$$\begin{bmatrix} A & B & C \\ D & E & F \\ G & H & I \end{bmatrix}$$

To read these nine characters into the 3×3 character array *CharArray* in rowwise order, we could use the statement

for *row* := 1 **to** 3 **do**
    for *column* := 1 **to** 3 **do**
        readln (*CharArray*[*row*,*column*])

with the data entered one character per line:

A
B
C
D
E
F
G
H
I

If a *read* statement is used in place of the *readln* statement:

for *row* := 1 **to** 3 **do**
    for *column* := 1 **to** 3 **do**
        read (*CharArray*[*row*,*column*])

we enter all the data on one line

    ABCDEFGHI

But the data cannot be entered on separate lines because an end-of-line character is read and stored as a blank. Thus, if the data are entered as

    ABC
    DEF
    GHI

then the table actually stored in the array *CharArray* is

$$\begin{bmatrix} A & B & C \\ b & D & E \\ F & b & G \end{bmatrix}$$

because the end-of-line character is read for *CharArray*[2,1] and *CharArray*[3,2] and stored as a blank (b) in these locations. If the preceding nested **for** statements are changed to

```
for row := 1 to 3 do
    begin
        for column := 1 to 3 do
            read (CharArray[row,column]);
        readln
    end
```

the data can be entered as

```
ABC
DEF
GHI
```

because in this case the *readln* statement with no input list advances the data pointer to the next line.

Nested **while** statements may be used instead of **for** statements in these input loops. For example, the 3 × 4 table

$$\begin{bmatrix} 22 & 37 & 0 & 0 \\ 0 & 1 & 17 & 32 \\ 6 & 18 & 4 & 12 \end{bmatrix}$$

considered earlier can be read in rowwise order into the 3 × 4 integer array *A* using the statements

```
row := 1;
while row <= 3 do
    begin
        column := 1;
        while column <= 4 do
            begin
                read (A[row,column]);
                column := column + 1
            end;
        row := row + 1
    end
```

Nested **repeat** statements can also be used, but neither of these methods seems as natural as the nested **for** statements.

The elements of an array can be displayed by using repetition structures similar to those used for input. For example, the statement

```
for row := 1 to 3 do
    begin
        for column := 1 to 4 do
            write (A[row,column]:4);
        writeln
    end
```

where *A* is the integer array just considered produces as output

```
22  37   0   0
 0   1  17  32
 6  18   4  12
```

Note that the *write* statement displays the values in each row on the same line and that a *writeln* statement is used to begin a new line.

These same input/output techniques can be applied to higher-dimensional arrays. For example, values could be read into the 2 × 4 × 3 array *B* in the order indicated in Figure 9.2 by the nested **for** statements

```
for rank := 1 to 3 do
    for column := 1 to 4 do
        for row := 1 to 2 do
            readln (B[row,column,rank])
```

Here the values must be entered one per line on twenty-four separate lines. Using a *read* statement in place of *readln* allows other arrangements of the data.

Other types of array processing can also be carried out using nested repetition structures. To illustrate, consider the 25 × 4 array *Grades* used in Section 9.1 to store the following table of test scores:

| Student | Test Number | | | |
Number	1	2	3	4
1	79.5	80.0	64.5	91.0
2	99.5	99.0	92.0	97.5
⋮	⋮	⋮	⋮	⋮
25	100.0	62.5	73.5	88.0

To calculate the average grade on the four tests for each of the twenty-five students, it is necessary to calculate the sum of the entries in each row and to divide each of these sums by 4. The following program segment can be used to carry out this computation and to display the average grade for each student:

```
for Student := 1 to 25 do
    begin
        Sum := 0;
        for Test := 1 to 4 do
            Sum := Sum + Grades[Student, Test];
        Average := Sum / 4;
        writeln ('Ave. grade for student ', Student:1, ' is ', Average:3:1)
    end
```

Nested repetition structures can also be used to copy the entries of one array into another array. For example, if *A* and *B* are 5 × 10 arrays, the nested **for** statements

```
for row := 1 to 5 do
    for column := 1 to 10 do
        B[row,column] := A[row,column]
```

will copy the entries of *A* into the corresponding locations of array *B*, assuming, of course, that the component type of *A* is compatible with the component type of *B*. If A and B have the *same type* (see Section 8.2), this can be done more simply with the array assignment statement

$$B := A$$

Multidimensional arrays may also be used as parameters for functions and procedures. The rules governing the use of arrays as parameters, which were described in detail in Section 8.2 for one-dimensional arrays, also apply to multidimensional arrays. These rules are summarized as follows:

1. The types of formal parameters in a function or procedure heading must be specified by type identifiers. Thus, for example, the array declaration *Grades* : **array**[1..25, 1..4] **of** *real* may not be used to declare the type of a formal parameter in a procedure or function heading. It may be given in the form *Grades : Table* where *Table* is a type identifier associated with **array**[1..25, 1..4] **of** *real*.
2. The types of arrays used as actual parameters must be the same as the types of the corresponding arrays used as formal parameters.
3. The type of a function value may not be an array.

9.3 Application to String Processing

In Section 8.4 we examined in detail the use of packed arrays to process strings. A collection of such strings can be processed using an array of strings. To illustrate, suppose that a list of names, each consisting of a first name followed by a blank followed by a last name, is to be sorted so that the last names are in alphabetical order. The names in this sorted list are then to be displayed in the form last name, first name.

Each name to be processed can be stored in an array of string type. Thus we might define the type identifier *NameString* by

```
const
    NameLength = 30;
    ListLimit = 100;
type
    NameString = packed array[1..NameLength] of char;
```

where *NameLength* is a constant specifying the number of characters (including trailing blanks) in each name. If the type identifier *List* is then defined by

```
    List = array[1..ListLimit] of NameString;
```

it may be used to declare arrays that store the list of names, for example,

> *Name : List*;

The singly subscripted variable *Name*[*i*] then refers to the *i*th name in the list. The *j*th character of the *i*th name can be accessed by the doubly subscripted variable *Name*[*i,j*] or *Name*[*i*][*j*].

The following algorithm solves this problem and the program in Figure 9.3 implements the algorithm.

Algorithm

1. Repeat the following until all the names have been read.
   a. Read a name and store it in the temporary one-dimensional array *Buffer*.
   b. Search *Buffer* to find the first name and last name in this string and interchange them.
   c. Store this reversed name in the array *Name*.
2. Alphabetize the array *Name* using the bubble sort method.
3. Display the sorted list of names in the desired format.

```
PROGRAM NameSort (input, output);

(*****************************************************************************

   Program to read in a list of first and last names, sort them
   so last names are in alphabetical order, and display them
   in the form:    Last-name, First-name.

*****************************************************************************)

CONST
    NameLength = 30;    (* maximum length of names *)
    ListLimit = 100;    (* limit on length of list *)

TYPE
    NameString = PACKED ARRAY[1..NameLength] of char;
    List = ARRAY[1..ListLimit] of NameString;

VAR
    Name : List;         (* list of names *)
    i,                   (* index *)
    NumNames : integer;  (* number of names in list *)

PROCEDURE ReadAndReverseNames (VAR Name : List; VAR Count : integer);

    (*************************************************************************

        Procedure to read and count the names, reverse them so they have
        the form
                        Last-Name, First-Name
        and store these reversed names in the array Name.

    *************************************************************************)

    VAR
        Buffer : NameString;  (* temporary array for name *)
        i : integer;          (* index *)
```

Figure 9.3

Fig. 9.3 (cont.)

```pascal
    PROCEDURE Reverse (VAR Buffer : NameString);

    (***************************************************************

       Procedure to reverse the order of the first and last names in
       each name, and insert a comma so each has the form
                    Last-name, First-name

    ***************************************************************)

    VAR
       BlankPos,              (* position of first blank in name *)
       i,                     (* index *)
       First,                 (* index to scan first name *)
       Last : integer;        (* index to scan last name *)
       FirstName : NameString;  (* first name *)

    BEGIN (* Reverse *)

       (* Locate position of first blank and store first name *)

       BlankPos := 0;
       REPEAT
          BlankPos := BlankPos + 1;
          FirstName[BlankPos] := Buffer[BlankPos]
       UNTIL Buffer[BlankPos] = ' ';

       (* Move last name to beginning of Buffer *)

       First := 0;
       REPEAT
          First := First + 1;
          Last := First + BlankPos;
          Buffer[First] := Buffer[Last]
       UNTIL (Buffer[Last] = ' ') OR (Last = NameLength);

       (* Insert comma and copy first name to end of Buffer *)

       Buffer[First] := ',';
       First := First + 1;
       Buffer[First] := ' ';
       FOR i := 1 TO BlankPos - 1 DO
          Buffer[i + First] := FirstName[i]
    END (* Reverse *);

BEGIN (* ReadAndReverseNames *)
    writeln ('Enter the names, 1 per line.  Enter * to stop.');
    writeln;
    Count := 0;
    REPEAT
       FOR i := 1 TO NameLength DO
          IF NOT eoln THEN
             read (Buffer[i])
          ELSE
             Buffer[i] := ' ';
       readln;
       IF Buffer[1] <> '*' THEN      (* not the end-of-data flag *)
          BEGIN
             Reverse (Buffer);
             IF Count < ListLimit THEN
                BEGIN
                   Count := Count + 1;
                   Name[Count] := Buffer
                END (* IF *)
```

MULTIDIMENSIONAL ARRAYS

Fig. 9.3 (cont.)

```
                   ELSE
                      BEGIN
                         writeln ('*** Too many names -- processing first ',
                                  ListLimit:1, ' names ***');
                         Buffer[1] := '*'    (* force end of data *)
                      END (* ELSE *)
               END (* IF *)
        UNTIL Buffer[1] = '*';
     END (* ReadAndReverseNames *);

  PROCEDURE BubbleSort (VAR Item : List; N : integer);

     (*************************************************************************

        Procedure to sort Item[1], ..., Item[N] into ascending order
        using the bubble sort algorithm.  For descending order,
        change > to < in the boolean expression Item[i] > Item[i+1].

        *************************************************************************)

     VAR
        i,                         (* index *)
        NumPairs : integer;        (* # of pairs examined in current scan *)
        Temporary : NameString;    (* used to interchange two items *)
        Done : boolean;            (* indicates if sorting completed *)

     BEGIN (* BubbleSort *)
        NumPairs := N - 1;

        (* Scan the list comparing consecutive items *)

     REPEAT
        Done := true;
        FOR i := 1 TO NumPairs DO
           IF Item[i] > Item[i+1] THEN
              BEGIN
                 Temporary := Item[i];
                 Item[i] := Item[i+1];
                 Item[i+1] := Temporary;
                 Done := false  (* interchange occurred, so scan again *)
              END (* IF *);

        (* Largest Item has sunk into place, so eliminate
           it from the next scan *)

        NumPairs := NumPairs - 1
     UNTIL Done
  END (* BubbleSort *);

BEGIN (* main program *)
   ReadAndReverseNames (Name, NumNames);
   BubbleSort (Name, NumNames);
   FOR i := 1 TO NumNames DO
      writeln (Name[i])
END (* main program *).




Sample run:
==========

Enter the names, 1 per line.  Enter * to stop.
```

Fig. 9.3 (cont.)

```
John Doe
Mary Smith
Johann VanderVan
Fred Jones
Jesse James
Merry Christmas
*
Christmas, Merry
Doe, John
James, Jesse
Jones, Fred
Smith, Mary
VanderVan, Johann
```

9.4

Example 1: Automobile Sales. Suppose that a certain automobile dealership sells fifteen different models of automobiles and employs ten salesmen. A record of sales for each month can be represented by a table, the first row of which contains the number of sales of each model by salesman 1, the second row contains the number of sales of each model by salesman 2, and so. For example, suppose that the sales table for a certain month is the following:

Numeric Applications: Automobile Sales, Matrix Multiplication

```
0 0 2 0 5 6 3 0 10 0 3 2 5 7  5
5 1 9 0 0 2 3 2  1 1 3 1 5 3  0
0 0 0 1 0 0 0 0  0 0 2 0 8 2  3
1 1 1 0 2 2 2 1  1 0 2 0 3 0 12
5 3 2 0 0 2 5 5  7 0 0 2 0 0  2
2 2 1 0 1 1 0 0  6 8 0 0 0 2  0
3 2 5 0 1 2 0 4  8 0 0 2 2 2  1
3 0 7 1 3 5 2 4  4 3 5 1 7 2  4
0 2 6 1 0 5 2 1  4 3 0 0 4 0  5
4 0 2 0 3 2 1 0  9 0 1 4 5 4  8
```

A program is to be written to produce a monthly sales report, displaying the monthly sales table in the form

								MODEL								
SALESMAN:		1	2	3	4	5	6	7	8	9	10	11	12	13	14	15
1	:	0	0	2	0	5	6	3	0	10	0	3	2	5	7	5
2	:	5	1	9	0	0	2	3	2	1	1	3	1	5	3	0
3	:	0	0	0	1	0	0	0	0	0	0	2	0	8	2	3
4	:	1	1	1	0	2	2	2	1	1	0	2	0	3	0	12
5	:	5	3	2	0	0	2	5	5	7	0	0	2	0	0	2
6	:	2	2	1	0	1	1	0	0	6	8	0	0	0	2	0
7	:	3	2	5	0	1	2	0	4	8	0	0	2	2	2	1
8	:	3	0	7	1	3	5	2	4	4	3	5	1	7	2	4
9	:	0	2	6	1	0	5	2	1	4	3	0	0	4	0	5
10	:	4	0	2	0	3	2	1	0	9	0	1	4	5	4	8

and which also displays the total number of automobiles sold by each salesman and the total number of each model sold by all salesmen.

The input to the program is to be a sales table, as just described, and the output is to be a report of the indicated form. The required processing is given by the following algorithm:

Algorithm
1. Read the sales table into a 10 × 15 array *Sales* so that each of the ten rows contains the sales information for one of the ten salesmen, and each of the fifteen columns contains the information for one of the fifteen models.
2. Print the array *Sales* with appropriate headings.
3. Calculate and print the totals of the entries in each of the rows. These totals are the sales totals for each of the ten salesmen.
4. Calculate and print the totals of the entries in each of the columns. These totals are the total sales for each of the fifteen models.

The program in Figure 9.4 implements this algorithm.

```
PROGRAM AutomobileSales (input, output, SalesFile);

(*********************************************************************

   Program to read in a sales table and calculate total sales for
   each salesman and total sales of each model of automobile.

*********************************************************************)

CONST
   RowLimit = 25;       (* limit on # of rows in table *)
   ColumnLimit = 25;    (* limit on # of columns in table *)

TYPE
   Table = ARRAY[1..RowLimit, 1..ColumnLimit] OF integer;

VAR
   Rows,               (* # of rows (salesmen) in sales table *)
   Columns : integer;  (* # of columns (models) in sales table *)
   Sales : Table;      (* sales table *)
   SalesFile : text;   (* file containing the sales data *)

PROCEDURE ReadTable (VAR Sales : Table; VAR Rows, Columns : integer);

   (*********************************************************************

      Procedure to read the number of rows and columns in the sales
      table and then read the table.  The data is read from the
      text file SalesFile.

   *********************************************************************)

   VAR
      Man,               (* row index -- salesman # *)
      Model : integer;   (* column index -- model # *)
```

Figure 9.4

Fig. 9.4 (cont.)

```
      BEGIN (* ReadTable *)
         reset (SalesFile);
         readln (SalesFile, Rows, Columns);
         FOR Man := 1 TO Rows DO
            FOR Model := 1 TO Columns DO
               read (SalesFile, Sales[Man, Model])
      END (* ReadTable *);

   PROCEDURE PrintSalesTable (VAR Sales : Table; Rows, Columns : integer);

      (********************************************************************

         Procedure to print the sales table in the desired format.

       ********************************************************************)

      VAR
         Man,                (* salesman number *)
         Model : integer;   (* model number *)

      BEGIN (* PrintSalesTable *)
         writeln ('MODEL' : 2*Columns + 9);
         write ('SALESMAN:');
         FOR Model := 1 TO Columns DO
            write (Model:4);
         writeln;
         FOR Model := 1 TO 4*Columns + 9 DO
            write('-');
         writeln;
         FOR Man := 1 TO Rows DO
            BEGIN
               write (Man:5, '   :');
               FOR Model := 1 TO Columns DO
                  write (Sales[Man, Model]:4);
               writeln
            END (* FOR *)
      END (* PrintSalesTable *);

   PROCEDURE FindSalesmanTotals (VAR Sales : Table; Rows, Columns : integer);

      (********************************************************************

         Procedure to find and display sum of each row of sales table.

       ********************************************************************)

      VAR
         Man,                   (* row index -- salesman # *)
         Model,                 (* column index -- model # *)
         RowTotal : integer;   (* row total *)

      BEGIN (* FindSalesmanTotals *)
         writeln;
         FOR Man := 1 TO Rows DO
            BEGIN
               RowTotal := O;
               FOR Model := 1 TO Columns DO
                  RowTotal := RowTotal + Sales[Man, Model];
               writeln ('Sales of salesman', Man:3, ':', RowTotal:4)
            END (* FOR *);
      END (* FindSalesmanTotals *);
```

MULTIDIMENSIONAL ARRAYS

Fig. 9.4 (cont.)

```
PROCEDURE FindModelTotals (VAR Sales : Table; Rows, Columns : integer);

   (*****************************************************************

      Procedure to find and display sum of each column of sales table.

    *****************************************************************)

   VAR
      Man,                    (* row index -- salesman # *)
      Model,                  (* column index -- model # *)
      ColTotal : integer;   (* column total *)

   BEGIN (* FindModelTotals *)
      writeln;
      FOR Model := 1 TO Columns DO
         BEGIN
            ColTotal := 0;
            FOR Man := 1 TO Rows DO
               ColTotal := ColTotal + Sales[Man, Model];
            writeln ('Sales of model   ', Model:3, ':', ColTotal:4)
         END (* FOR *)
   END (* FindModelTotals *);

BEGIN (* main program *)
   ReadTable (Sales, Rows, Columns);
   PrintSalesTable (Sales, Rows, Columns);
   FindSalesmanTotals (Sales, Rows, Columns);
   FindModelTotals (Sales, Rows, Columns)
END (* main program *).
```

```
Sample run:
==========

                                        MODEL
SALESMAN:   1   2   3   4   5   6   7   8   9  10  11  12  13  14  15
        --------------------------------------------------------------
      1 :   0   0   2   0   5   6   3   0  10   0   3   2   5   7   5
      2 :   5   1   9   0   0   2   3   2   1   1   3   1   5   3   0
      3 :   0   0   0   1   0   0   0   0   0   0   2   0   8   2   3
      4 :   1   1   1   0   2   2   2   1   1   0   2   0   3   0  12
      5 :   5   3   2   0   0   2   5   5   7   0   0   2   0   0   2
      6 :   2   2   1   0   1   1   0   0   6   8   0   0   0   2   0
      7 :   3   2   5   0   1   2   0   4   8   0   0   2   2   2   1
      8 :   3   0   7   1   3   5   2   4   4   3   5   1   7   2   4
      9 :   0   2   6   1   0   5   2   1   4   3   0   0   4   0   5
     10 :   4   0   2   0   3   2   1   0   9   0   1   4   5   4   8

Sales of salesman  1:   48
Sales of salesman  2:   36
Sales of salesman  3:   16
Sales of salesman  4:   28
Sales of salesman  5:   33
Sales of salesman  6:   23
Sales of salesman  7:   32
Sales of salesman  8:   51
Sales of salesman  9:   33
Sales of salesman 10:   43
```

Fig. 9.4 (cont.)

```
Sales of model      1:   23
Sales of model      2:   11
Sales of model      3:   35
Sales of model      4:    3
Sales of model      5:   15
Sales of model      6:   27
Sales of model      7:   18
Sales of model      8:   17
Sales of model      9:   50
Sales of model     10:   15
Sales of model     11:   16
Sales of model     12:   12
Sales of model     13:   39
Sales of model     14:   22
Sales of model     15:   40
```

Example 2: Matrix Multiplication. A two-dimensional array having m rows and n columns is called an $m \times n$ *matrix*. An important operation of matrix algebra is matrix multiplication, defined as follows: Suppose that *Mat1* is an $m \times n$ matrix and *Mat2* is an $n \times p$ matrix. Note that the number of columns (n) in *Mat1* is equal to the number of rows in *Mat2*, which must be the case for the product of *Mat1* with *Mat2* to be defined. The product *Prod* of *Mat1* with *Mat2* will then be an $m \times p$ matrix with the entry *Prod*[i,j], which appears in the ith row and the jth column given by

$$Prod[i,j] = \text{the sum of the products of the entries in row } i \text{ of } Mat1$$
$$\text{with the entries of column } j \text{ of } Mat2$$
$$= Mat1[i,1]*Mat2[1,j] + Mat1[i,2]*Mat2[2,j] + \cdots + Mat1[i,n]*Mat2[n,j]$$

For example, suppose that *Mat1* is the 2×3 matrix

$$\begin{bmatrix} 1 & 0 & 2 \\ 3 & 0 & 4 \end{bmatrix}$$

and that *Mat2* is the 3×4 matrix

$$\begin{bmatrix} 4 & 2 & 5 & 3 \\ 6 & 4 & 1 & 8 \\ 9 & 0 & 0 & 2 \end{bmatrix}$$

Because the number of columns (3) in *Mat1* equals the number of rows in *Mat2*, the product matrix *Prod* is defined. The entry in the first row and first column, *Prod*[1,1], is

$$1*4 + 0*6 + 2*9 = 22$$

Similarly, the entry *Prod*[1,2] in the first row and second column is

$$1*2 + 0*4 + 2*0 = 2$$

The complete product matrix *Prod* is the 2×4 matrix given by

$$\begin{bmatrix} 22 & 2 & 5 & 7 \\ 48 & 6 & 15 & 17 \end{bmatrix}$$

Algorithm

(* Algorithm for multiplying a *Rows1* $\times$ *Cols1* matrix *A* with *Rows2* $\times$ *Cols2* matrix *B*. *)

1. If *Cols1* $\neq$ *Rows2*, then the number of columns in *Mat1* is not equal to the number of rows in *Mat2*, and the product *Prod* = *Mat1* * *Mat2* is not defined; terminate the algorithm. Otherwise proceed with the following steps:
2. For an index *i* ranging from 1 to the number of rows *Rows1* of *Mat1* do the following:
   a. For an index *j* ranging from 1 to the number of columns *Cols2* of *Mat2* do the following:
      (i) Set *Sum* equal to 0.
      (ii) For an index *k* ranging from 1 to the number of columns *Cols1* of *Mat1* (which is equal to the number of rows *Rows2* of *Mat2*), add *Mat1*[*i,k*] * *Mat2*[*k,j*] to *Sum*.
      (iii) Set *Prod*[*i,j*] equal to *Sum*.

```
PROGRAM MatrixMultiplication (input, output);

(*********************************************************************

   Program to read two matrices and calculate their product.

 *********************************************************************)

CONST
   RowLimit = 20;      (* limit on # of rows in a matrix *)
   ColumnLimit = 20;   (* limit on # of columns in a matrix *)

TYPE
   Matrix = ARRAY[1..RowLimit, 1..ColumnLimit] OF integer;

VAR
   Mat1, Mat2,                (* matrices being multiplied *)
   Prod : Matrix;             (* product of Mat1 with Mat2 *)
   Rows1, Cols1,              (* dimensions of Mat1 *)
   Rows2, Cols2 : integer;    (* dimensions of Mat2 *)
   ProductDefined : boolean;  (* true if Cols1 = Rows2, else false *)

PROCEDURE ReadMatrix (VAR Mat : Matrix; VAR Rows, Columns : integer);

   (********************************************************************

      Procedure to read # of rows and columns in a matrix and then
      read a matrix of those dimensions.

    ********************************************************************)
```

Figure 9.5

Fig. 9.5 (cont.)

```
    VAR
       i, j : integer;    (* row, column indices *)

    BEGIN (* ReadMatrix *)
       write ('Enter # of rows & columns:  ');
       readln (Rows, Columns);
       writeln ('Enter the matrix rowwise:');
       FOR i := 1 TO Rows DO
          FOR j := 1 to Columns DO
             read (Mat[i,j]);
       readln
    END (* ReadMatrix *);

PROCEDURE PrintMatrix (VAR Mat : Matrix; Rows, Columns : integer);

    (************************************************************************

       Procedure to display an integer Rows X Columns matrix.

    ************************************************************************)

    CONST
       FieldWidth = 5;   (* width of field used to display an entry *)

    VAR
       i, j : integer;    (* row, column indices *)

    BEGIN (* PrintMatrix *)
       writeln;
       FOR i := 1 TO Rows DO
          BEGIN
             FOR j := 1 TO Columns DO
                write (Mat[i,j]:FieldWidth);
             writeln;
             writeln
          END (* FOR *)
    END (* PrintMatrix *);

PROCEDURE MatMultiply (VAR Mat1, Mat2, Prod : Matrix;
                           Rows1, Cols1, Rows2, Cols2 : integer;
                           VAR ProductDefined : boolean);

    (************************************************************************

       Procedure to multiply the Rows1 X Cols1 matrix Mat1 and the
       Rows2 X Cols2 matrix Mat2; Cols1 must equal Rows2 for the
       product Prod to be defined.

    ************************************************************************)

    VAR
       i, j, k,         (* indices *)
       Sum : integer;   (* used to calculate product matrix *)

    BEGIN (* MatMultiply *)
       IF Cols1 <> Rows2 THEN
          ProductDefined := false
       ELSE
          BEGIN
             ProductDefined := true;
             FOR i := 1 TO Rows1 DO
                FOR j := 1 to Cols2 DO
```

Fig. 9.5 (cont.)

```
                        BEGIN
                           Sum := O;
                           FOR k := 1 to Cols1 DO
                              Sum := Sum + Mat1[i,k] * Mat2[k,j];
                           Prod[i,j] := Sum
                        END (* FOR j *)
            END (* ELSE *)
      END (* MatMultiply *);

BEGIN (* main program *)
   ReadMatrix (Mat1, Rows1, Cols1);
   writeln ('First Matrix:');
   PrintMatrix (Mat1, Rows1, Cols1);
   ReadMatrix (Mat2, Rows2, Cols2);
   writeln ('Second Matrix:');
   PrintMatrix (Mat2, Rows2, Cols2);
   MatMultiply (Mat1, Mat2, Prod, Rows1, Cols1, Rows2, Cols2,
                ProductDefined);
   IF ProductDefined THEN
      BEGIN
         writeln ('Product:');
         PrintMatrix (Prod, Rows1, Cols2)
      END (* IF *)
   ELSE
      BEGIN
         writeln ('Product undefined -- # of columns ', Cols1:1,
                  ' in first matrix');
         writeln (' is not equal to # of rows ', Rows2:1,
                  ' in second matrix')
      END (* ELSE *)
END (* main program *).


Sample run:
==========
Enter # of rows & columns:  2 3
Enter the matrix rowwise:
1 2 3
4 0 1
First Matrix:

    1    2    3

    4    0    1

Enter # of rows & columns:  3 4
Enter the matrix rowwise
1 0 0 1
2 1 1 2
3 0 1 1
Second Matrix:

    1    0    0    1

    2    1    1    2

    3    0    1    1

Product:

   14    2    5    8

    7    0    1    5
```

Programming Pointers

The difficulties encountered when using multidimensional arrays are similar to those for one-dimensional arrays, considered in the preceding chapter. The first five of the programming pointers that follow are simply restatements of some of the programming pointers in Chapter 8, and the reader should refer to those for an expanded discussion.

1. *The types of the components of an array may be any predefined or user-defined data type, and the type of each subscript may be any ordinal type except integer.*

2. *When processing the elements of a multidimensional array, each subscript must be compatible with the type specified for that subscript in the array declaration.*

3. *When reading the elements of an array of characters, remember that end-of-line marks are read as blanks.*

4. *Assignment of one array to another requires that the arrays have the same type.*

5. *Multidimensional arrays that are parameters of procedures or functions should be variable parameters so that memory is utilized more efficiently.*

6. *The amount of memory required to store a multidimensional array may be quite large, even though each subscript is restricted to a small range of values.* For example, the three-dimensional array *ThreeD* declared by

   type
       ThreeDimArray = **array**[1..20, 1..20, 1..20] **of** *integer*;
   var
       ThreeD : *ThreeDimArray*;

   requires $20 \times 20 \times 20 = 8{,}000$ memory locations. This allocation of 8K of memory may be much too large for small computer systems.

7. *When processing the elements of a multidimensional array by using nested repetition structures, these structures must be arranged so that the subscripts vary in the intended order.* To illustrate, suppose that the two-dimensional array *Table* is declared by

   type
       Array3X4 = **array**[1..3, 1..4] **of** *integer*;
   var
       Table : *Array3X4*;

   and the following data are to be read into the array:

   11   22   27   35   39   40   48   51   57   66   67   92

If these values are to be read and assigned in a rowwise manner so that the value of *Table* is the matrix

$$\begin{bmatrix} 11 & 22 & 27 & 35 \\ 39 & 40 & 48 & 51 \\ 57 & 66 & 67 & 92 \end{bmatrix}$$

then the following nested **for** statements are appropriate:

    for *row* := 1 **to** 3 **do**
        for *col* := 1 **to** 4 **do**
            read (*Table*[*row*,*col*])

If the values are to read and assigned in a columnwise manner so that *Table* is

$$\begin{bmatrix} 11 & 35 & 48 & 66 \\ 22 & 39 & 51 & 67 \\ 27 & 40 & 57 & 92 \end{bmatrix}$$

then the statements should be

    for *col* := 1 **to** 4 **do**
        for *row* := 1 **to** 3 **do**
            read (*Table*[*row*,*col*])

Exercises

1. Consider the following type declarations:

    type
        Color = (*red*, *yellow*, *blue*, *green*, *white*, *black*);
        BigTable = **array**[1..50, 1..100] **of** *integer*;
        PointTable = **array**[−10..10, −10..10] **of** *real*;
        CharTable = **packed array**['A'..'Z', 'A'..'Z'] **of** *char*;
        BooleanTable = **array**[*boolean*, *boolean*] **of** *boolean*;
        BitArray = **array**[0..1, 0..1, 0..1, 0..1] **of** 0..1;
        Shirt = **array** [*Color*, 14..18, 32..36] **of** *integer*;
        MixedArray = **array** [*Color*, 'A'..'F', 0..10, *boolean*] **of** *real*;

How many elements can be stored in an array of each of the following types?

(a) *BigTable*

(b) *PointTable*

(c) *CharTable*

(d) *BooleanTable*

(e) *BitArray*

(f) *Shirt*

(g) *MixedArray*

2. Assume that the following declarations have been made:

```
type
    String = packed array[1..6] of char;
    Array3X3 = array[1..3, 1..3] of integer;
    ArrayOfStrings = array[1..2] of String;
var
    TextLine : ArrayOfStrings;
    Matrix : Array3X3;
    i, j : integer;
```

and that the following data are entered for those of the following statements that involve input:

```
ABCD
EFGH
IJKL
MNOP
QRST
UVWX
```

For each of the following, tell what value (if any) is assigned to each array element, or explain why an error results.

```
(a) for i := 1 to 3 do
        for j := 1 to 3 do
            Matrix[i,j] := i + j
(b) for i := 1 to 2 do
        begin
            for j := 1 to 6 do
                read (TextLine[i,j]);
            readln
        end
```

```
(c) for i := 1 to 2 do
        begin
            for j := 1 to 6 do
                read (TextLine[i][j]);
            readln
        end
```

```
(d) for i := 1 to 2 do
        for j := 1 to 6 do
            read (TextLine[i,j])
(e) for j := 1 to 6 do
        begin
            for i := 1 to 2 do
                read (TextLine[i,j]);
            readln
        end
```

(f) for $j := 1$ **to** 6 **do**
    begin
        for $i := 1$ **to** 2 **do**
            read (*TextLine*[j,i]);
        readln
    end

(g) for $i := 1$ **to** 2 **do**
    for $j := 6$ **downto** 1 **do**
        if not *eoln* **then**
            read (*TextLine*[i,j])
        else
            readln

(h) for $i := 1$ **to** 3 **do**
    for $j := 3$ **downto** 1 **do**
        if $i = j$ **then**
            Matrix[i,j] $:= 0$
        else
            Matrix[i,j] $:= 1$

(i) for $i := 1$ **to** 3 **do**
    for $j := 1$ **to** 3 **do**
        if $i < j$ **then**
            Matrix[i,j] $:= -1$
        else if $i = j$ **then**
            Matrix[i,j] $:= 0$
        else
            Matrix[i,j] $:= 1$

(j) for $i := 1$ **to** 3 **do**
    begin
        for $j := 1$ **to** i **do**
            Matrix[i,j] $:= 0$;
        for $j := i + 1$ **to** 3 **do**
            Matrix[i,j] $:= 2$
    end

3. Modify the program segment on page 323 so that it calculates and displays the average score for each of the four tests.

4. If A and B are two $m \times n$ matrices, their *sum* is defined as follows: If A_{ij} and B_{ij} are the entries in the ith row and jth column of A and B, respectively, then $A_{ij} + B_{ij}$ is the entry in the ith row and jth column of their sum, which will also be an $m \times n$ matrix. Write a program using procedures to read two $m \times n$ matrices, display them, and calculate and display their sum.

5. Write a program that reads the dimensions of a matrix, reads and displays the matrix, and then finds the largest and the smallest entries of the matrix and their locations.

6. A certain company has a product line that includes five items that sell for $100.00, $75.00, $120.00, $150.00, and $35.00. There are four salespersons working for this company, and the following table gives the sales report for a typical week:

Salesperson Number	Item Number				
	1	2	3	4	5
1	10	4	5	6	7
2	7	0	12	1	3
3	4	9	5	0	8
4	3	2	1	5	6

Write a program to

(a) Compute the total dollar sales for each salesperson.

(b) If the sales commission is 10 percent, compute the total commission for each salesperson.

(c) If each salesperson receives a fixed salary of $200 per week in addition to commission payments, find the total income for each salesperson for the week.

7. Write a program to calculate and display the first ten rows of *Pascal's triangle*. The first part of the triangle has the form

```
        1
      1   1
    1   2   1
  1   3   3   1
1   4   6   4   1
```

where each row begins and ends with 1's, and each of the other entries in a row is the sum of the two entries just above it. If this form for the output seems too challenging, you might display the triangle as

```
1
1  1
1  2  1
1  3  3  1
1  4  6  4  1
```

8. The *Morse Code* is a standard encoding scheme that uses substitutions similar to those in the scheme described in Exercise 10 of Section 8.5. The substitutions used in this case are shown in the following table. Write a program to read a message either in plain text or in Morse Code and then encode or decode the message.

A · —	M — —	Y — · — —
B — · · ·	N — ·	Z — — · ·
C — · — ·	O — — —	1 · — — — —
D — · ·	P · — — ·	2 · · — — —
E ·	Q — — · —	3 · · · — —
F · · — ·	R · — ·	4 · · · · —
G — — ·	S · · ·	5 · · · · ·
H · · · ·	T —	6 — · · · ·
I · ·	U · · —	7 — — · · ·
J · — — —	V · · · —	8 — — — · ·
K — · —	W · — —	9 — — — — ·
L · — · ·	X — · · —	0 — — — — —

9. The Reverend Mr. Zeller developed a formula for computing the day of the week on which a given date fell or will fall. Suppose that we let a, b, c, and d be integers defined as follows:

$a =$ the month of the year, with March $= 1$, April $= 2$, and so on, with January and February being counted as months 11 and 12 of the preceding year.

$b =$ the day of the month.

$c =$ the year of the century.

$d =$ the century.

For example, for July 31, 1929, $a = 5$, $b = 31$, $c = 29$, and $d = 19$; for January 3, 1983, $a = 11$, $b = 3$, $c = 82$, and $d = 19$. Now calculate the following integer quantities:

$w =$ the integer quotient $(13a - 1) \div 5$.

$x =$ the integer quotient $c \div 4$.

$y =$ the integer quotient $d \div 4$.

$z = w + x + y + b + c - 2d$.

$r = z$ reduced modulo 7; that is, r is the remainder of z divided by 7; $r = 0$ represents Sunday, $r = 1$ represents Monday, and so on.

Write a program to read a date in the form month-name, day, year as input and then calculate on what day of the week that date fell or will fall. Use your program to verify that December 12, 1960, fell on a Monday and that January 1, 1981, fell on a Thursday. Also determine on what day of the week each of the following dates fell: January 25, 1963; June 2, 1964; July 4, 1776; your birthday.

10. Suppose that the prices for the fifteen automobile models in the first example of Section 9.4 are as follows:

Model #	Model Price
1	$ 7,450
2	$ 9,995
3	$26,500
4	$ 5,999
5	$10,400
6	$ 8,885
7	$11,700
8	$14,440
9	$17,900
10	$ 9,550
11	$10,500
12	$ 8,050
13	$ 7,990
14	$12,300
15	$ 6,999

Write a program to read this list of prices and the sales table given in Section 9.4 and calculate the total dollar sales for each salesman and the total dollar sales for all salesmen.

11. The famous mathematician G. H. Hardy once mentioned to the brilliant young Indian mathematician Ramanujan that he had just ridden in a taxi whose number he considered to be a very dull number. Ramanujan promptly replied that on the contrary, the number was very interesting because it was the smallest positive integer that could be written as the sum of two cubes (that is, written in the form $x^3 + y^3$, with x and y integers) in two different ways. Write a program to find the number of Hardy's taxi.

12. A *magic square* is an $n \times n$ matrix in which each of the integers 1, 2, 3, . . . , n^2 appears exactly once and all column sums, row sums, and diagonal sums are equal. For example, the following is a 5 × 5 magic square in which all the rows, columns, and diagonals add up to 65:

17	24	1	8	15
23	5	7	14	16
4	6	13	20	22
10	12	19	21	3
11	18	25	2	9

The following is a procedure for constructing an $n \times n$ magic square for any odd integer n. Place 1 in the middle of the top row. Then after integer k has been placed, move up one row and one column to the right to place the next integer $k + 1$, unless one of the following occurs:

(i) If a move takes you above the top row in the jth column, move to the bottom of the jth column and place the integer there.

(ii) If a move takes you outside to the right of the square in the ith row, place the integer in the ith row at the left side.

(iii) If a move takes you to an already filled square or if you move out of the square at the upper-right-hand corner, place $k + 1$ immediately below k.

Write a program to construct an $n \times n$ magic square for any odd value of n.

13. A *directed graph* or *digraph* consists of a set of *vertices* and a set of *directed arcs* joining certain of these vertices. For example, the following diagram pictures a directed graph having five vertices numbered 1, 2, 3, 4, and 5, and seven directed arcs joining vertices 1 to 2, 1 to 4, 1 to 5, 3 to 1, 3 to itself, 4 to 3, and 5 to 1:

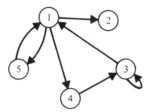

A directed graph having n vertices can be represented by its *adjacency matrix*, which is an $n \times n$ matrix, with the entry in the ith row and jth column a 1 if vertex i is joined to vertex j, 0 otherwise. The adjacency matrix for the above graph is

$$\begin{bmatrix} 0 & 1 & 0 & 1 & 1 \\ 0 & 0 & 0 & 0 & 0 \\ 1 & 0 & 1 & 0 & 0 \\ 0 & 0 & 1 & 0 & 0 \\ 1 & 0 & 0 & 0 & 0 \end{bmatrix}$$

If A is the adjacency matrix for a directed graph, then the entry in the ith row and jth column of A^k gives the number of ways that vertex j can be reached from vertex i by following k edges. Write a program to read the number of vertices in a directed graph and a collection of ordered pairs of vertices representing directed arcs; construct the adjacency matrix; and then find the number of ways that each vertex can be reached from every other vertex by following k edges for some value of k.

14. The game of *Life*, invented by the mathematician John H. Conway, is intended to model life in a society of organisms. Consider a rectangular array of cells, each of which may contain an organism. If the array is considered to extend indefinitely in both directions, then each cell has eight neighbors, the eight cells surrounding it. Births and deaths occur according to the following rules:

(i) An organism is born in any empty cell having exactly three neighbors.

(ii) An organism dies from isolation if it has less than two neighbors.

(iii) An organism dies from overcrowding if it has more than three neighbors.

(iv) All other organisms survive to the next generation.

To illustrate, the following shows the first five generations of a particular configuration of organisms:

```
                           o
           o     ooo       o     ooo
    ooo   ooo            o o    o o
     o    ooo   o o       o     ooo
                 o        o
```

Write a program to play the game of Life and investigate the patterns produced by various initial configurations. Some configurations die off rather rapidly; others repeat after a certain number of generations; others change shape and size and may move across the array; and still others may produce "gliders" that detach themselves from the society and sail off into space.

15. The game of Nim is played by two players. There are usually three piles of objects, and on his or her turn, each player is allowed to take any number (at least one) of objects from one pile. The player taking the last object loses. Write a program that allows the user to play Nim against the computer. You might have the computer play a perfect game, or you might design the program to "teach" the computer. One way for the computer to "learn" is to assign a value to every possible move, based on experience gained from playing games. The value of each possible move is stored in some array; initially, each value is 0. The value of each move in a winning sequence of moves is increased by 1, and those in a losing sequence are decreased by 1. At each stage, the computer selects the best possible move (that having the highest value).

16. The game of Hangman is played by two persons. One person selects a word and the other person tries to guess the word by guessing individual letters. Design a program to play Hangman. You might store a list of words in an array or file and have the program randomly select a word for the user to guess. (See Section 5.5 for a technique to generate random numbers.)

17. Write a program that allows the user to play Tic-Tac-Toe against the computer.

18. The eight-squares puzzle consists of eight numbered tiles in a square frame having room for nine tiles. One of the positions is empty, and so the tiles may be slid from one position to another, but they may not be removed from the frame. The object of the puzzle

is to rearrange the tiles from some scrambled configuration such as

2	6	5
1		8
4	3	7

into some predetermined configuration such as

1	2	3
4	5	6
7	8	

Write a program to solve the eight-square puzzle for a given initial configuration.

19. On a chessboard, the queen can attack any chess piece that is on the same row, column, or diagonal as the queen. The n queens problem is to position n queens on an $n \times n$ chessboard so that no queen can attack any other. Write a program to solve this problem for a given value of n.

20. A knight on a chessboard is permitted to make L-shaped moves, two squares vertically followed by one square horizontally or two squares horizontally followed by one square vertically. The knight's tour problem is to start the knight at some specified square on an $n \times n$ chessboard and to move around the board, visiting each square exactly one time. Write a program to solve this problem on an $n \times n$ chessboard for some given value of n, specifying the knight's initial position.

10

Sets

No one shall expel us from the paradise which
Cantor has created for us.

DAVID HILBERT

In mathematics and computer science the term *set* denotes an unordered collection of objects called the *elements* or *members* of the set. For example, the set of digits contains the elements 0, 1, 2, 3, 4, 5, 6, 7, 8, and 9; the set of upper-case letters consists of the letters A, B, C, . . . , Z; the set of even prime numbers contains the single element 2; and the set of even prime numbers greater than 3 is the empty set, that is, the set containing no elements.

Sets differ from arrays in that the elements of an array are ordered in a certain sequence, but the elements of a set are unordered. Thus we can speak of the first, second, third, . . . elements of an array, but it does not make sense to refer to the first, second, third, . . . elements of a set. For example, the set whose elements are the even digits 0, 2, 4, 6, and 8 is the same as the set whose elements are 4, 8, 0, 2, and 6 or the set whose elements are 8, 0, 6, 4, and 2. The ordering of array elements makes it possible to access an element directly by specifying its location in the array. Because sets are unordered, no such direct access to the elements of a set is possible.

In this chapter we discuss how sets are implemented in Pascal using the data type **set** and how they are processed using the operations of set assignment, union, intersection and difference, the **in** relation, and the set relations of subset and equality.

In a problem involving sets, the elements are selected from some given set called the *universal set* for that problem. For example, if the set of vowels or the set whose elements are X, Y, and Z are being considered, the universal set might be the set of all letters. If the universal set is the set of names of months of the year, then one might use the set of summer months: June, July, August; the set of months whose names do not contain the letter r: May, June, July, August; or the set of all months having fewer than thirty days: February.

In a Pascal program, all of the elements of a set must be of the same type, called the *base type* of the set. This base type must be an ordinal type; thus sets of real elements or sets of arrays are not allowed. A *set declaration* has the form

> **set of** *base-type*

For example, if the ordinal types *Digits* and *Months* are defined by

> **type**
>   *Digits* = 0..9;
>   *Months* = (*January, February, March, April, May, June, July, August, September, October, November, December*);

then

> **set of** *Digits*
> **set of** *Months*
> **set of** *char*

are valid set declarations for most Pascal compilers.

Many Pascal compilers, however, impose certain restrictions on sets. The most common restriction is a limit on the number of elements that a set may have. This limit usually excludes *integer* as a base type and, for some compilers, also excludes *char*. In these cases, subranges of integers and/or subranges of characters must be used.

Set declarations may be used in the variable section of the declaration part of a Pascal program to specify the types of variables. They may also be assigned to type identifiers. To illustrate, consider the declarations

> **type**
>   *Digits* = 0..9;
>   *Months* = (*January, February, March, April, May, June, July, August, September, October, November, December*);
>   *DigitSet* = **set of** *Digits*;
>   *MonthSet* = **set of** *Months*;
>   *CapLetterSet* = **set of** 'A'..'Z';
>   *MonthArray* = **array**[1..4] **of** *MonthSet*;

var
      Dig1, Dig2 : Digits;
      Numbers, Evens, Odds : DigitSet;
      Winter : MonthSet;
      Vowels, Consonants : CapLetterSet;
      Season : MonthArray;

The variables *Numbers, Evens,* and *Odds* may have as values any sets of elements chosen from 0, 1, 2, . . . , 9; the value of *Winter* may be any set of elements selected from *January, February, . . . , December;* the variables *Vowels* and *Consonants* have values that are sets of capital letters. The array *Season* has four components, each of which is a set of months.

A *set constant* in Pascal has the form

    [*element-list*]

where *element-list* is a list (possibly empty) of constants, variables, or expressions separated by commas and enclosed in brackets [and]. The elements in this list must be of the same type (which must be an ordinal type), and consecutive values may be indicated by subrange notation. Thus, for the base types just defined,

    [0, 2, 4, 6, 8]

is a valid set constant which might be the value of *Evens.* This same set constant could also be denoted by

    [4, 0, 8, 2, 6]

or

    [8, 6, 4, 2, 0]

or by using any other arrangement of the elements. If *Dig1* has the value 0 and *Dig2* has the value 4, then

    [*Dig1, Dig1* + 2, *Dig1* + 4, *Dig1* + 6, *Dig1* + 8]

is another representation of this same set constant, as is

    [*Dig1, Dig2* **div** 2, *Dig2, Dig2* + 2, 2 * *Dig2*]

The set constant

    [0, 1, 2, 3, 4]

can be expressed by using subrange notation as

    [0..4]

or

[*Dig1..Dig2*]

and the set constant

[0, 1, 2, 5, 7, 8, 9]

can be expressed in any of the following ways:

[0..2, 5, 7..9]
[0..2, *Dig2* + 1, 7..9]
[*Dig1*..2, 5, (*Dig2* + 3) .. (2 * *Dig2* + 1)]

The value of the set variable *Winter* might be the set constant

[*December, January .. March*]

but it could not be

['D', 'J', 'F', 'M']

because the base type of this set constant is not compatible with the base type of *Winter*. The array element *Season*[1] could have the value

[*December, January, February*]

but it could not have ['D', 1, *February*] as a value because this is not a valid set constant (the types of the elements are not the same).

The empty set is denoted in Pascal by the set constant

[ ]

and may be assigned to a set variable of any base type. Thus [ ] could be the value of both *Numbers* and *Winter*, even though these set variables have different base types.

To assign a value to a variable of set type, an assignment statement of the form

set-variable := *set-value*

may be used where *set-value* may be a set constant, a set variable, or a set expression (as described in the next section). The base type of *set-value* must be compatible with the base type of *set-variable*. Thus, for the base types defined earlier, the statement

Evens := [0, 2, 4, 6, 8]

is a valid assignment statement and assigns the set constant [0, 2, 4, 6, 8] to the set variable *Evens*. Similarly, the statements

Winter := [*December, January .. March*];

Season[1] := [*December, January, February*];

Vowels := [ ];

Consonants := *Vowels*;

Numbers := [*Dig1*]

are valid assignment statements.

Because sets are collections of elements, it is important to be able to determine **Set Operations** whether a particular element belongs to a given set. This test for set member- **and Relations** ship is implemented in Pascal by the relational operator **in.** Boolean expressions used to test set membership have the form

element **in** *set*

where *set* is a set constant, set variable, or set expression, and the type of *element* and the base type of *set* are compatible. For example, if set variables *Vowels, Evens, Numbers,* and *Bits* are declared by

type
    DigitSet = **set of** 0..9;
    BinarySet = **set of** 0..1;
    SetOfCharacters = **set of** *char*;

var
    Evens, Numbers : *DigitSet*;
    Bits : *BinarySet*;
    Vowels : *SetOfCharacters*;
    Num : *integer*;

and have been assigned values by

    Evens := [0, 2, 4, 6, 8];
    Bits := [0, 1];
    Numbers := [0..2, 6..9];
    Vowels := ['A', 'E', 'I', 'O', 'U'];

then

2 **in** *Evens*

3 **in** *Numbers*

'I' **in** *Vowels*

are valid boolean expressions and have the values *true, false,* and *true,* respectively. Similarly, if *Num* has the value 3,

Num **in** *Evens*

'B' **in** [ ]

Num + 3 **in** *Numbers*

are valid boolean expressions which have the values *false, false,* and *true,* respectively. The expressions

5 **in** *Vowels*

'B' **in** *Numbers*

are not valid boolean expressions because of type incompatibility.

The relational operator **in** is used to determine whether a single element is a member of a given set, but sometimes it is necessary to determine whether all of the elements of some set *set1* are also members of another set *set2*, that is, to determine whether *set1* is a *subset* of *set2*. This can be done in Pascal by using the relational operators <= and >= to construct boolean expressions of the form

set1 <= *set2*

or equivalently

set2 >= *set1*

where *set1* and *set2* are set constants, variables, or expressions with compatible base types. These expressions are true if *set1* is a subset of *set2* and are false otherwise. The following table shows some valid boolean expressions and their values, given that the variables have the values previously assigned:

Boolean Expression	Value
[0,1,4] <= [0,1,2,3,4]	*true*
[2,4] <= *Evens*	*true*
Bits >= *Evens*	*false*
Vowels <= *Vowels*	*true*
Numbers <= *Bits*	*false*
['A', 'B'] >= ['A', 'C']	*false*
[ ] <= *Numbers*	*true*

Two sets are said to be *equal* if they contain exactly the same elements. Set equality can be checked in Pascal with a boolean expression of the form

(*set1* <= *set2*) **and** (*set2* <= *set1*)

or simply

set1 = *set2*

where again *set1* and *set2* must have compatible base types. The relational operator <> may also be used,

> *set1* <> *set2*

and is equivalent to the boolean expression

> **not** (*set1* = *set2*)

For example,

> *Bits* = [0, 1]
>
> *Bits* <> *Evens*

are valid boolean expressions, and both have the value *true*.

In addition to the relational operators **in,** <=, >=, =, and <>, there are three binary set operations that may be used to combine two sets to form another set. These are the operations of union, intersection, and difference which are denoted in Pascal by +, *, and −, respectively. The *union* of two sets *set1* and *set2* is the set of elements that are in *set1* or *set2* or both and is denoted by a set expression of the form

> *set1* + *set2*

The *intersection* of *set1* and *set2* is the set of elements that are in both sets and is denoted by

> *set1* * *set2*

The set *difference*

> *set1* − *set2*

is the set of elements that are in *set1* but are not in *set2*. For each of these set expressions, the base types of *set1* and *set2* must be compatible. The following table illustrates these set operations:

Set Expression	Value
[1,2,3] + [4,5,6]	[1,2,3,4,5,6]
[1,2,3,4] + [2,4,6]	[1,2,3,4,6]
[1,2,3] + [ ]	[1,2,3]
[1,2,3,4] * [2,4,6]	[2,4]
[1,2,3] * [4,5,6]	[ ]
[1,2,3] * [ ]	[ ]
[1,2,3,4] − [2,4]	[1,3]
[1,2,3,4] − [2,4,6]	[1,3]
[1,2,3] − [4,5,6]	[1,2,3]
[1,2,3] − [1,2,3,4]	[ ]
[1,2,3] − [ ]	[1,2,3]

When a set expression contains two or more of these operators, it is evaluated according to the following priorities:

```
*        ------------   high priority
+, −     ------------   low priority
```

Thus in the expression

[2,3,5] + [2,4,7] * [2,4,6,8]

the intersection operation is performed first, giving the set [2,4], and

[2,3,5] + [2,4]

is then evaluated, yielding

[2,3,4,5]

Operations having the same priority are evaluated in the order in which they appear in the expression, from left to right. For example, in the expression

[1,2,3,4] − [1,3] + [1,2,5]

the subexpression

[1,2,3,4] − [1,3]

is evaluated first, giving [2,4] and

[2,4] + [1,2,5]

is then evaluated, yielding

[1,2,4,5]

Parentheses may be used in the usual way to alter the standard order of evaluation. Thus in the expression

([2,3,5] + [2,4,7]) * [2,4,6,8]

the subexpression

[2,3,5] + [2,4,7]

is evaluated first, giving [2,3,4,5,7], and the expression

[2,3,4,5,7] * [2,4,6,8]

then gives

[2,4]

We have examined five relational operators and three binary set operations which are the standard relations and operations in Pascal used for processing sets. Some versions of Pascal may allow additional relational operators (e.g., $<$ for proper subset) or set operations (e.g., $-S$ for the complement of set S).

Compound boolean expressions that are formed using the boolean operators **not, and,** and **or** with relational operators and operations for sets and other data types are evaluated using the following precedence levels:

Operator	Priority
not	1 (highest)
$*$, /, **div, mod, and**	2
$+$, $-$, **or**	3
$<$, $<=$, $>$, $>=$, $=$, $<>$, **in**	4 (lowest)

Here $+$, $-$, and $*$ may refer to either arithmetic operations or set operations, and the relational operators may be used with numeric, character, ordinal, string, or set data (except that $<$ and $>$ may not be used with sets).

The expression

0 **in** *Evens* **and** 0 **in** *Bits*

is not a valid boolean expression because **and** has higher priority than **in;** consequently, the first operation attempted is evaluation of *Evens* **and** 0, which results in an error because *Evens* and 0 are not of boolean type. Parentheses may be used in the usual way to modify the standard order of evaluation. Thus, if *Evens* has the value [0,2,4,6,8] and *Bits* has the value [0,1],

(0 **in** *Evens*) **and** (0 **in** *Bits*)

is a valid boolean expression and has the value *true*.

Set relations and operations may be used to avoid complex boolean expressions. For example, the boolean expression

(*ch* $=$ 'A') **or** (*ch* $=$ 'L') **or** (*ch* $=$ 'M') **or** (*ch* $=$ 'N')

can be expressed more compactly as

ch **in** ['A', 'L'..'N']

The boolean expression

((*ch* $>=$ 'a') **and** (*ch* $<=$ 'z')) **or** ((*ch* $>=$ 'A') **and** (*ch* $<=$ 'Z'))

to determine whenever the value of *ch* is a lower-case or upper-case letter (assuming ASCII representation) can be expressed equivalently as

$$ch \text{ in } ['a'..'z', 'A'..'Z']$$

or

$$ch \text{ in } Lower + Upper$$

where *Lower* and *Upper* are set variables whose values are ['a'..'z'] and ['A'..'Z'], respectively.

One situation in which such boolean expressions are useful is in checking the value of a selector in a **case** statement to ensure that it is in the correct range. For example, consider the **case** statement

```
case Num of
    5, 10, 15 : writeln ('Multiple of 5');
    7, 14     : writeln ('Multiple of 7');
    11        : writeln ('Multiple of 11')
end (* case *)
```

If the value of *Num* is not one of the integers listed as case labels, execution of the **case** statement results in an error. The following statement avoids this error:

```
if Num in [5,7,10,11,14,15] then
    case Num of
        5, 10, 15 : writeln ('Multiple of 5');
        7, 14     : writeln ('Multiple of 7');
        11        : writeln ('Multiple of 11')
    end (* case *)
```

10.3 Processing Sets

In the preceding section we used the assignment statement to assign a value to a set variable. In this section we show how to construct a set by reading its elements, how to display the elements of a set, and how to use sets as parameters for subprograms.

To construct a set S, we first initialize S to the empty set

$$S := [\ ]$$

and then read each element x of the set and add it to the set S, using the union (+) operation:

$$S := S + [x]$$

For example, to read the set of primes less than 30 and to assign this set to *PrimeSet*, declare *PrimeSet* by

```
type
    Element = 1..30;
    NumberSet = set of Element;
```

var
    PrimeSet, TempSet : NumberSet;
    Prime : integer;

and then use the following statements to read the elements of *PrimeSet:*

```
PrimeSet := [ ];
read (Prime);
while Prime <> 0 do      (* 0 is an end-of-data flag *)
    begin
        PrimeSet := PrimeSet + [Prime];
        read (Prime)
    end
```

If the data

2 3 5 7 11 13 17 19 23 29 0

are entered, *PrimeSet* has the value

[2, 3, 5, 7, 11, 13, 17, 19, 23, 29]

To display the elements of a set *S,* we can use the following algorithm:

Algorithm
1. Copy the elements of *S* into a set *TempSet* having a base type compatible with that of *S*.
2. Let *x* be a variable of the base type of *TempSet* and initialize *x* to the first element of this base type.
3. While *TempSet* is nonempty, do the following:
    (i) If *x* is in *TempSet*, then display *x* and remove it from *TempSet*
    (ii) Replace *x* with its successor.

The following program segment uses this algorithm to display the elements of set *PrimeSet* (note that in this example *succ(Prime)* could be replaced with *Prime + 1*):

```
TempSet := PrimeSet;
Prime := 1;
while TempSet <> [ ] do
    begin
        if Prime in TempSet then
            begin
                write (Prime:3);
                TempSet := TempSet − [Prime]
            end (* if *);
        Prime := succ(Prime)
    end (* while *);
writeln
```

It should be noted that the set *TempSet* is reduced to the empty set during the output of its elements. It is for this reason that it, rather than *PrimeSet,* was used for the output processing. If a set is not needed after its elements are displayed, then it is not necessary to use a temporary set. Step 1 of the algorithm may be omitted and *TempSet* replaced with *S* in Steps 2 and 3.

Sets may also be used as parameters of functions and procedures. The type of a function must be a simple data type, however, and hence may not be of set type. The following procedure *ReadSet* illustrates the use of sets as parameters:

procedure *ReadSet* (**var** *S* : *TypeOfSet*);

(* Procedure to read the elements of a set *S* of type *TypeOfSet*; the base type of the elements of *S* is *ElementType* which is *char* or a subrange of character or integer type. *)

```
    var
        x : ElementType;

    begin (* ReadSet *)
        S := [ ];
        while not eof do
            begin
                read (x);
                S := S + [x]
            end (* while *)
    end (* ReadSet *);
```

A similar procedure to display the elements of a set is left as an exercise.

In the preceding sections we discussed the basic techniques for constructing, combining, and comparing sets, as well as some common techniques for processing sets. In this section we illustrate these ideas with two examples.

Example 1: Sieve of Eratosthenes. A *prime number* is defined to be an integer *n* greater than 1 whose only divisors are 1 and *n* itself. Thus, 2, 3, 5, 7, 11, 13, 17, and 19 are prime numbers, whereas 4, 6, 8, and 9 are not primes because 2 divides 4, 6, and 8, and 3 divides 9. The Greek mathematician Eratosthenes developed an algorithm for finding all prime numbers less than or equal to a given number *n,* that is, all primes in the range 2 . . . *n*. This algorithm was described in Exercise 14 of Section 8.3 and can be rephrased using sets, as follows:

Algorithm

1. Initialize the set *Sieve* to contain the integers from 2 through *n*.
2. Select the smallest element *Prime* in *Sieve*.
3. While $Prime^2 \leq n$ do the following:
   a. Remove from *Sieve* all elements of the form *Prime* * *k* for $k > 1$.

b. Replace *Prime* with the smallest element in *Sieve* that is greater than *Prime*.

The elements remaining in *Sieve* when this algorithm terminates are the primes in the range 2 through *n*.

To illustrate Eratosthenes' algorithm, consider the problem of finding all primes in the range from 2 through 30. The following diagram shows the processing of the set *Sieve* using this algorithm:

Sieve

[2,3,4,5,6,7,8,9,10,11,12,13,14,15,16,17,18,19,20,21,22,23,24,25,26,27,28,29,30]

Step 2 (*Prime* = 2)

[2,3,5,7,9,11,13,15,17,19,21,23,25,27,29]

Step 2 (*Prime* = 3)

[2,3,5,7,11,13,17,19,23,25,29]

Step 2 (*Prime* = 5)

[2,3,5,7,11,13,17,19,23,29]

Terminate since $Prime^2 > 30$ for $Prime = 7$

The program in Figure 10.1 implements this algorithm. It uses the set *Sieve* which is declared to have elements in the subrange 1..*LargestNumber*. Because most Pascal compilers limit the size of sets, this program is restricted to small values of *LargestNumber*. For large values, the algorithm can be modified to use an array of sets; this modification is left as an exercise.

```
PROGRAM SieveofEratosthenes (input, output);

(*******************************************************************

    Program to find all prime numbers in the range from 2 through n
    using the Sieve Method of Eratosthenes.

 *******************************************************************)

CONST
    LargestNumber = 100;   (* limit on largest value of n *)

TYPE
    NumberSet = SET OF 1..LargestNumber;

VAR
    Sieve : NumberSet;   (* set of numbers used in the algorithm *)
    n : integer;         (* 2, 3, 4, ..., n are numbers considered *)

PROCEDURE FillTheSieve (VAR Sieve : NumberSet; n : integer );

    (*******************************************************************

        Procedure to initialize the set Sieve to be [2, 3, 4, ..., n].

     *******************************************************************)
```

Figure 10.1

Fig. 10.1. (cont.)

```
    VAR
       Number : integer;  (* number added to Sieve *)

    BEGIN (* FillTheSieve *)
       Sieve := [];
       FOR Number := 2 TO n DO
          Sieve := Sieve + [Number]
    END (* FillTheSieve *);

PROCEDURE Eratosthenize (VAR Sieve : NumberSet; n : integer);

    (*****************************************************************

       Apply the sieve method of Eratosthenes to remove all nonprimes
       from Sieve.

    *****************************************************************)

    VAR
       Prime,          (* prime whose multiples are removed *)
       k : integer;   (* used to form multiples  prime*k  *)

    BEGIN (* Eratosthenize *)
       Prime := 2;
       WHILE sqr(Prime) <= n DO
          BEGIN
             FOR k := 2 TO n DIV Prime DO
                Sieve := Sieve - [Prime * k];
             REPEAT
                Prime := Prime + 1
             UNTIL Prime IN Sieve
          END (* WHILE *)
    END (* Eratosthenize *);

PROCEDURE PrintPrimes (Sieve: NumberSet; n  : integer);

    (*****************************************************************

       All numbers remaining in Sieve are primes; print them.

    *****************************************************************)

    VAR
       Number: integer;  (* number to be checked as an element of Sieve *)

    BEGIN (* PrintPrimes *)
       writeln ('Primes <= ', n:1, ' are:');
       Number := 2;
       WHILE Sieve <> [] DO
          BEGIN
             WHILE NOT (Number IN Sieve) DO
                Number := Number + 1;
             Sieve := Sieve - [Number];
             writeln (Number)
          END (* WHILE *)
    END (* PrintPrimes *);

BEGIN (* main program *)
   writeln ('To find primes in range 2 through n, enter n:');
   readln (n);
   FillTheSieve (Sieve, n);
   Eratosthenize (Sieve, n);
   PrintPrimes (Sieve, n)
END (* main program *).
```

Fig. 10.1. (cont.)

```
Sample run:
==========

To find primes in range 2 through n, enter n:
30
Primes <= 30 are:
        2
        3
        5
        7
       11
       13
       17
       19
       23
       29
```

Example 2: Simple Lexical Analyzer.   In our discussion of system software in Chapter 1, we mentioned *compilers,* which are programs whose function is to translate a source program written in some high-level language, such as Pascal, into an object program in machine code. This object program is then executed by the computer.

The input to a compiler is a stream of characters which comprise the source program. Before the translation can actually be carried out, this stream of characters must be broken up into meaningful groups, such as identifiers, reserved words, constants, and operators. For example, the assignment statement

$$\text{alpha} := 200*\text{beta} + 5$$

is input as the string of characters

$$\text{alpha}\flat := \flat 200*\text{beta}\flat + \flat 5$$

and must be broken down into the following units:

alpha	----------	identifier
:=	----------	operator
200	----------	integer constant
*	----------	operator
beta	----------	identifier
+	----------	operator
5	----------	integer constant

These units are called *tokens,* and the section of the compiler that recognizes these tokens is called the *lexical analyzer.*

The program in Figure 10.2 implements a simple lexical analyzer which processes Pascal assignment statements involving only identifiers, integer constants, and the operators +, −, *, /, and :=, and ; which marks the end of the statement. Blanks may be used as separators in these assignment statements.

```
PROGRAM LexicalAnalyzer (input, output);

(*****************************************************************************

   This program implements a simple lexical analyzer for Pascal
   assignment statements involving only identifiers, integer
   constants, and operators +, -, *, /, :=, and ; (which marks
   the end of the statement).

*****************************************************************************)

CONST
   EndOfStatementMark = ';';   (* marks end of assignment statement *)
   MaxLength = 80;             (* maximum length of statement *)

TYPE
   CharacterSet = SET OF char;
   TextLine = PACKED ARRAY[1..MaxLength] OF char;
   String = PACKED ARRAY[1..21] OF char;

VAR
   Statement : TextLine;        (* assignment statement being processed *)
   LetterSet,                   (* set of letters *)
   DigitSet,                    (* set of digits *)
   ArithmeticOperators,         (* set of arithmetic operators *)
   Delimiters : CharacterSet;   (* set of delimiters *)
   i : integer;                 (* index *)
   Response : char;             (* user response *)

PROCEDURE ReadStatement (VAR Statement : TextLine;
                         EndOfStatementMark : char);

   (*****************************************************************************

         Read characters in Statement until EndOfStatementMark.

   *****************************************************************************)

   VAR
      i : integer;  (* index *)

   BEGIN (* ReadStatement *)
      writeln ('Enter assignment statement:');
      i := 0;
      REPEAT
         i := i + 1;
         read (Statement[i])
      UNTIL (Statement[i] = EndOfStatementMark) OR (i = MaxLength);
      readln;
   END (* ReadStatement *);

PROCEDURE IllegalCharacter (VAR Statement : TextLine; VAR i : integer;
                            Delimiters : CharacterSet);

   (*****************************************************************************

      Procedure to handle processing when i-th character in Statement
      is not a legal character.  All characters up to the next
      delimiter will be skipped.

   *****************************************************************************)
```

Figure 10.2

Fig. 10.2. (cont.)

```
    BEGIN (* IllegalCharacter *)
        write (Statement[i]);
        writeln ('   <** Illegal character:  ', Statement[i], ' **>');
        WHILE NOT (Statement[i] IN Delimiters) DO
            i := i + 1;
    END (* IllegalCharacter *);

PROCEDURE Process (Statement : TextLine; VAR i : integer; TokenSet,
                   Delimiters : CharacterSet; TokenType : String);

    (****************************************************************

        Process characters until not in the specified TokenSet; then
        check if next character (i-th) is a delimiter, and if so
        recognize the specified TokenType, else an illegal character.

    ****************************************************************)

    BEGIN (* Process *)
        REPEAT
            write (Statement[i]);
            i := i + 1
        UNTIL NOT (Statement[i] IN TokenSet);
        IF Statement[i] IN Delimiters THEN
            writeln ('      ', TokenType)
        ELSE
            IllegalCharacter (Statement, i, Delimiters)
    END (* Process *);

PROCEDURE CheckForOperator (Statement : TextLine; VAR i : integer;
                            Delimiters : CharacterSet; NextSymbol : char;
                            TokenType : String);

    (****************************************************************

        Check for arithmetic operator or assignment operator and
        advance to next character (i-th) in Statement.

    ****************************************************************)

    VAR
        LegalOperator : boolean;    (* indicates if a legal operator *)

    BEGIN (* CheckForOperator *)
        write (Statement[i]);
        i := i + 1;
        LegalOperator := true;
        IF NextSymbol = '=' THEN
            IF Statement[i] <> '=' THEN
                BEGIN
                    LegalOperator := false;
                    IllegalCharacter (Statement, i, Delimiters)
                END (* IF *)
            ELSE
                BEGIN
                    write (Statement[i]);
                    i := i + 1
                END (* ELSE *);
        IF LegalOperator THEN
            writeln ('      ', TokenType)
    END (* CheckForOperator *);
```

Fig. 10.2. (cont.)

```
BEGIN (* main program *)
   LetterSet := ['a'..'z', 'A'..'Z'];
   DigitSet := ['0'..'9'];
   ArithmeticOperators := ['+', '-', '*', '/'];
   Delimiters := ArithmeticOperators + [EndOfStatementMark]
                 + [' '] + [':'];
   REPEAT
      ReadStatement (Statement, EndOfStatementMark);

      (* Now process the statement *)

      writeln;
      i := 1;
      WHILE Statement[i] <> EndOfStatementMark DO
         BEGIN
            (* skip blanks *)
            WHILE Statement[i] = ' ' DO
               i := i + 1;

            (* check for identifier *)
            IF Statement[i] IN LetterSet THEN
               Process (Statement, i, LetterSet + DigitSet, Delimiters,
                        '<identifier>          ')

            (* check for integer constant *)
            ELSE IF statement[i] IN DigitSet THEN
               Process (Statement, i, DigitSet, Delimiters,
                        '<integer constant>   ')

            (* check for arithmetic operator *)
            ELSE IF Statement[i] IN ArithmeticOperators THEN
               CheckForOperator (Statement, i, Delimiters, ' ',
                        '<arithmetic operator>')

            (* check for assignment operator *)
            ELSE IF Statement[i] = ':' THEN
               CheckForOperator (Statement, i, Delimiters, '=',
                        '<assignment operator>')

            (* check for illegal character *)
            ELSE IF Statement[i] <> EndOfStatementMark THEN
               IllegalCharacter (Statement, i, Delimiters)
         END (* WHILE *);
      writeln;
      write ('More statements (Y or N)?  ');
      readln (Response)
   UNTIL NOT (Response IN ['Y', 'y'])
END (* main program *).
```

Sample run:
==========


```
Enter assignment statement:
alpha := 37*BETA - gamma/delta      -3;

alpha      <identifier>
:=     <assignment operator>
37     <integer constant>
*      <arithmetic operator>
```

Fig. 10.2. (cont.)

```
BETA      <identifier>
-         <arithmetic operator>
gamma        <identifier>
/         <arithmetic operator>
delta        <identifier>
-         <arithmetic operator>
3         <integer constant>

More statements (Y or N)?   Y
Enter assignment statement:
X123 : z456*456ZETA - 8&9;

X123         <identifier>
:    <** Illegal character:    **>
z456         <identifier>
*         <arithmetic operator>
456Z    <** Illegal character:   Z **>
-         <arithmetic operator>
8&    <** Illegal character:  & **>

More statements (Y or N)?   N
```

Programming Pointers

In this chapter we considered sets and their implementation in Pascal with the set data type. Some of the key points to remember when using this structured data type are

1. *All of the elements of a set must be of the same type, called the base type for that set. This base type must be an ordinal type.*

2. *Most versions of Pascal limit the size of sets, that is, the number of elements a set may have.* In particular, the declaration

   set of *integer*

   is usually not allowed, and in some versions,

   set of *char*

   is also not allowed. In such cases, to use sets whose elements are integers or characters, a subrange must be specified for these elements, for example,

   set of 1..100
   set of 'A'..'Z'

3. *The only standard set operations are* + *(union)*, * *(intersection), and* − *(difference).* Some versions of Pascal may also allow a unary minus to denote the complement of a set.

4. *The only standard relational operators that may be used to compare sets are* <= *(subset),* >= *(superset),* = *(equal),* <> *(not equal).* Some versions of Pascal may also allow the relational operators < (proper subset) and > (proper superset).

5. *The* **in** *relation for set membership can be used to simplify complex boolean expressions and to determine whether the value of the selector in a* **case** *statement is one of the case labels.* The examples at the end of Section 10.2 illustrate.

6. *A set value cannot be read by including the name of the set in the input list of a read or readln statement.* Instead, each element x of the set must be read, and the union operation can then be used in a statement of the form

$$S := S + [x]$$

to add this element to the set.

7. *A set value cannot be displayed by including the name of the set in the output list of a write or writeln statement.* Instead, each element must be removed and displayed. The algorithm on page 357 indicates how this can be done.

Exercises

1. Given that A, B, C, and D are set variables assigned values as follows: $A := [3, 5..9, 11]$; $B := [1..5, 11, 12]$; $C := [2, 4, 6, 8]$; $D := [6..10]$; calculate the following:

(a) $A * B$ (b) $A + B$ (c) $A - B$

(d) $B - A$ (e) $A + D$ (f) $A - D$

(g) $A * D$ (h) $D - A$ (i) $C + C$

(j) $C * C$ (k) $C - C$ (l) $C - [\ ]$

(m) $A + B + C + D$ (n) $(A - B) - C$ (o) $A - (B - C)$

(p) $A * B * C * D$ (q) $A + B * C$ (r) $A * B + C$

(s) $A * B - C * D$ (t) $(A - (B + C)) * D$ (u) $A * B - (A + B)$

(v) $A - B - C - D$ (w) $B - B - C$ (x) $B - (B - C)$

2. Write appropriate declarations for the following set type identifiers:

(a) *SmallIntegers:* set of integers from 1 through 99.

(b) *FirstLetters:* set of letters in the first half of the alphabet.

(c) *AlternateLetters:* set of alternate letters of the alphabet, starting with A.

(d) *Days:* the set of names of days of the week.

(e) *Suit:* set of thirteen cards in a suit.

3. Write appropriate variable declarations for the following set variables, and write statements to assign to each the specified value.

(a) *Evens:* the set of all even integers from 1 through 99; and *Odd:* the set of all odd integers in the range from 1 though 99.

(b) *OneModThree:* the set of all numbers of the form $3k + 1$ in the range from 1 through 99 with k as an integer.

(c) *Null:* the empty set.

(d) *LargeFactors:* the set of all numbers in the range 1 through 99 that are not divisible by 2, 3, 5, or 7.

(e) *Divisors:* the set of all divisors of 184800.

(f) *Vowels:* the set of all vowels; and *Consonants:* the set of all consonants.

(g) *WeekDays:* the set of all weekdays.

(h) *FaceCards:* the set of all face cards in a suit; and *NumberCards:* the set of all number cards in a suit.

4. Write a procedure to print any set of characters or integers by using the usual mathematical notation in which the elements are enclosed in braces { and } and are separated by commas. For example, the set of numbers 2, 5, and 7 should be displayed as {2, 5, 7}, the set whose element is 4 as {4}, and the empty set as { }.

5. Write a function to calculate the *cardinal number* of a set, that is, the number of elements in the set.

6. Write a program to find the set of all vowels and the set of all consonants that appear in a given line of text.

7. Write a program to read two lines of text, and find all characters that appear in both lines.

8. Write a program to find all letters that are not present in a given line of text and display them in alphabetical order.

9. Write a program to read several lines of text, and find all words having three or more distinct vowels.

10. Write a program to deal two ten-card hands from a standard deck of fifty-two cards. Use a random number generator (see Section 5.5), and use sets to ensure that the same card is not dealt twice.

11. A real number in Pascal has one of the forms $m.n$, $+m.n$, or $-m.n$, where m and n are nonnegative integers; or it may be expressed in exponential form $x\mathrm{E}e$, $x\mathrm{E}+e$, $x\mathrm{E}-e$, where x is an integer or a real number not in exponential form and e is a nonnegative integer. Write a program that accepts a string of characters and then checks to see if it represents a valid real constant.

12. Write a program for a lexical analyzer to recognize assignment statements of the form *identifier* : = *string-constant*.

13. Write a program for a lexical analyzer that processes assignment statements of the form *set-variable* : = *set-value*. Have it recognize the following tokens:

    identifier

    set constant

    set operation $(+, *, -)$

    set assignment $(: =)$

14. Write a program that uses the Sieve Method of Eratosthenes to find all primes in the range 2 through n for large values of n. (Hint: Use an array *Sieve* of sets, *Sieve*[0], *Sieve*[1], *Sieve*[2], . . . , whose elements are integers in the range 0 through 99. Each element of *Sieve*[1] must be interpreted as 100 plus its value, each element of *Sieve*[2] as 200 plus its value, and so on.)

11

Records

Yea, from the table of my memory
I'll wipe away all trivial fond records.

WILLIAM SHAKESPEARE, *Hamlet*

In Chapters 8, 9, and 10, we introduced two of Pascal's structured data types: arrays and sets. All the elements of an array must be of the same type, and each element can be accessed directly by attaching a subscript to the array name to specify its position in the array. Similarly, all the elements of a set must be of the same type, but these elements are not directly accessible.

In many situations we need to process items that are related in some way but that are not all of the same type. For example, a date consists of a month name (array of characters), a day (of type 1..31), and a year (of type 1900..2000 perhaps); an employee record might contain, among other items, an employee name (array of characters), age (integer), number of dependents (integer), and an hourly pay rate (real). Such related data items of different types can be processed in Pascal by using the structured data type **record.** In this chapter we consider how records are declared and processed in a Pascal program.

11.1

Introduction to Records and Fields

A *record* is a collection of related data items that may be of different data types. These items are called the *fields* of the record. Thus, an employee record might contain a name field, an age field, a dependents field, and an hourly pay rate field. The declaration of this structured data type in a Pascal program specifies the name of the record and the name and type of each of its fields. This declaration has the form

> **record**
> > *field-list*
>
> **end**;

where *field-list* is of the form

> *list-1* : *type-1*;
> *list-2* : *type-2*;
> > :
>
> *list-k* : *type-k*

Each *list-i* is a single identifier or a list of identifiers that name the fields of the record, and *type-i* specifies the type of each of these fields. This is summarized in the following syntax diagrams:

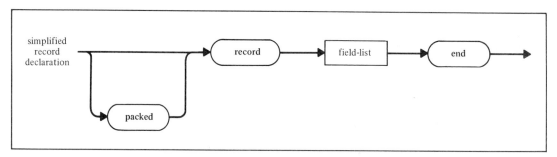

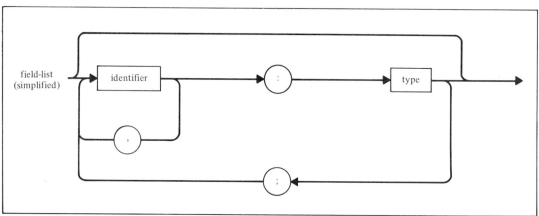

To illustrate, an employee record, as we have described it, could be declared by

> **record**
> > *Name* : **packed array**[1..20] **of** *char*;
> > *Age, Dependents* : *integer*;
> > *HourlyRate* : *real*
>
> **end**;

Such declarations of records, like those of other data types, may be used in the variable section of the declaration part of a program to specify the types of variables. But as with other structured types, it is preferable to assign them to type identifiers in the type section and use these identifiers to declare record variables. For example, consider

```
type
     NameString = packed array[1..20] of char;
     NameOfMonth = packed array[1..8] of char;
     EmployeeRecord = record
                          Name : NameString;
                          Age, Dependents : integer;
                          HourlyRate : real
                      end;
     BirthRecord = record
                          Month : NameOfMonth;
                          Day : 1..31;
                          Year : 1900..2000
                      end;

var
     Employee : EmployeeRecord;
     Birth : BirthRecord;
```

The variable *Employee* may have as a value any record of type *Employee-Record*. The first field of the record is of type *NameString* and is named with the field identifier *Name;* the second and third fields are of type *integer* and have the names *Age* and *Dependents;* and the fourth field is of type *real* and is named *HourlyRate*. The variable *Birth* may have as a value any record of type *BirthRecord*. The first field of the record is of type *NameOf-Month* and is named *Month;* the second field is of type 1..31 and is named *Day;* and the third field is of type 1900..2000 and is named *Year*. Typical values for *Employee* and *Birth* might be pictured as follows:

Name	Age	Dependents	HourlyRate
John Q. Doe	43	4	12.25

Month	Day	Year
January	15	1941

We have seen that each element of an array can be accessed directly by attaching a subscript enclosed in brackets to the array name. In a similar manner, one can access each field of a record directly by using a *field designator* of the form

> *record-name.field-name*

in which the field name preceded by a period is attached as a suffix to the record name. Thus *Employee.Name* specifies the first field of the value of record variable *Employee*. For the record displayed here, the value of *Employee.Name* would be the string JohnƀQ.ƀDoeƀƀƀƀƀƀƀƀƀ (where ƀ denotes a blank). Similarly, *Employee.Age*, *Employee.Dependents,* and *Employee.Hour-*

lyRate refer to the second, third, and fourth fields and would have the values 43, 4, and 12.25, respectively. If the second record is the value of the record variable *Birth,* then *Birth.Month* has the value January6, *Birth.Day* has the value 15, and *Birth.Year* has the value 1941.

The scope of a field identifier is the record in which that identifier is declared. This means that the same identifier may not be used to specify two different fields within the same record but an identifier that names a field may be used elsewhere in the program for some other purpose. It also means that the value in a field cannot be accessed by simply giving the field identifier; a complete field designator of the form

record-name.field-name

must be used whenever the field is referenced.

The fields that comprise a record may be of any data type; in particular, they may be other records. For example, the declarations

type
    NameString = **packed array**[1..20] **of** *char*;
    NameOfMonth = **packed array**[1..8] **of** *char*;
    Date = **record**
          Month : *NameOfMonth*;
          Day : 1..31;
          Year : 1900..2000
      end;
    PersonnelRecord = **record**
          Name : *NameString*;
          Birth : *Date*;
          Age, Dependents : *integer*;
          HourlyRate : *real*
      end;

var
    Employee : *PersonnelRecord*;

specify that variable *Employee* may have as values any record of type *PersonnelRecord,* each of which consists of five fields: the first field is of type *NameString* and is identified by *Name;* the second field is of type *Date* and is itself a record having three fields (*Month, Day,* and *Year*); the third and fourth fields are named *Age* and *Dependents* and are of type *integer;* and the fifth field is of type *real* and is named *HourlyRate.* A typical value for *Employee* might be pictured as follows:

	Birth					
Name	Month	Day	Year	Age	Dependents	HourlyRate
John Q. Doe	January	15	1941	43	4	12.25

The fields within such a *nested record* or *hierarchical record* may be accessed by simply affixing a second field identifier to the name of the larger record. Thus, *Employee.Birth.Month* refers to the first field in the inner record of type *Date;* for this record, its value would be the string January16. Similarly, the values of *Employee.Birth.Day* and *Employee.Birth.Year* would be 15 and 1941, respectively.

The records considered in this section all consist of a fixed number of fields, each of which has a fixed type. It is also possible to declare records in which some of the fields are fixed but the number and types of other fields may vary. Thus, the number and types of fields in a value of a variable of this record type may change during program execution. Such *variant records* are discussed in Section 11.4.

11.2

In the previous section we saw that records may be used to store several related data items that may be of different types and that each item or field in a record can be accessed with a field designator of the form

Processing Records; the with Statement

record-name.field-name

In this section we discuss how values can be assigned to the fields within a record, how these values can be read and displayed, and how the value of one record variable can be copied into another.

Because field designators and subscripted variables both serve to specify a particular item in a structure, the rules governing their use are much the same. To illustrate, consider the record type *ClassRecord* and record variable *Student* declared by

```
const
    NameLength = 15;
    NumScores = 5;
    MaxScore = 100;

type
    NameString = packed array[1..NameLength] of char;
    ListOfScores = array[1..NumScores] of 0..MaxScore;
    ClassRecord = record
                    Snumb : integer;
                    Name : NameString;
                    Sex : char;
                    TestScore : ListOfScores;
                    Eligible : boolean
                  end;

var
    Student : ClassRecord;
```

Because the field designator *Student.Snumb* is of integer type, it may be assigned an integer value in an assignment statement

Student.Snumb := 12345

or by an input statement

> *readln (Student.Snumb)*

and its value can be displayed by using an output statement

> *writeln* ('Student number: ', *Student.Snumb*)

Similarly, the field designator *Student.Eligible* is of boolean type and thus may be used to form boolean expressions, as in the statement

> **if** (*Student.Snumb* < 4000) **and** *Student.Eligible* **then**
>   *writeln* (*Student.Name*)

Because the field designator *Student.TestScore* is an array, the subscripted variable *Student.TestScore*[1] may be used to reference the first test score for this particular student.

Because records are structured data types, the value of a record variable can be neither read as a unit from the system file *input* (or any other text file) nor written as a unit to the system file *output* (or any other text file). Instead, input or output of records is done by reading or displaying the value of each field in the record by using the appropriate field designator. For example, to read a value for the record variable *Student* from the file *input,* the following statements might be used:

> *readln (Student.Snumb)*;
> **for** *i* : = 1 **to** *NameLength* **do**
>   *read (Student.Name*[*i*]);
> *readln*;
> *readln (Student.Sex)*;
> **for** *i* : = 1 **to** *NumScores* **do**
>   *read (Student.TestScore*[*i*]);
> *readln*;
> *readln (EligCode)*;
> **case** *EligCode* **of**
>   'T' : *Student.Eligible* : = *true*;
>   'F' : *Student.Eligible* : = *false*
> **end** (* **case** *)

Note that it is not possible to read values for *Student.Eligible* because this field is of boolean type and boolean values cannot be read from the file *input.*

The statements

> *Sum* : = 0;
> **for** *i* : = 1 **to** *NumScores* **do**
>   *Sum* : = *Sum* + *Student.TestScore*[*i*];
> *AveScore* : = *Sum* / *NumScores*

could then be used to calculate the average of the test scores.

The program in Figure 11.1 uses similar statements to read several records of type *ClassRecord,* by reading values from the text file *StudentInfoFile* for the individual fields. For each record, it calculates the average test score and then displays the student's number, name, sex, average test score, and eligibility status.

```
PROGRAM StudentAverages (input, output, StudentInfoFile);

(*******************************************************************

    Program to read student records each of which includes a student's
    number, name, sex, 5 test scores, and eligibility status; calculate
    the average of the test scores; display this average together
    with the student's number, name, sex, and eligibility status.
    The student records are read from the text file StudentInfoFile.

*******************************************************************)

CONST
    NameLength = 15;
    NumScores = 5;
    MaxScore = 100;

TYPE
    NameString = PACKED ARRAY[1..NameLength] OF char;
    ListOfScores = ARRAY[1..NumScores] OF 0..MaxScore;
    ClassRecord = RECORD
                    Snumb : integer;
                    Name : NameString;
                    Sex : char;
                    TestScore : ListOfScores;
                    Eligible : boolean
                END;

VAR
    StudentInfoFile : text;   (* file containing student records *)
    Student : ClassRecord;    (* record for current student *)
    EligCode : char;          (* eligibility code read (Y or N) *)
    i,                        (* index *)
    Sum : integer;            (* sum of test scores *)
    AveScore : real;          (* average test score *)

BEGIN
    reset (StudentInfoFile);

    (* Print headings *)

    writeln ('Student                    Test');
    writeln ('Number      Name      Sex Average  Eligible?');
    writeln ('======      ====      === =======  =========');

    WHILE NOT eof(StudentInfoFile) DO
        BEGIN

            (* Read student's record *)

    readln (StudentInfoFile, Student.Snumb);
    FOR i := 1 TO NameLength DO
        IF NOT eoln(StudentInfoFile) THEN
            read (StudentInfoFile, Student.Name[i])
        ELSE
            Student.Name[i] := ' ';
```

Figure 11.1

Fig. 11.1. (cont.)

```
            readln (StudentInfoFile);
            readln (StudentInfoFile, Student.Sex);
            FOR i := 1 TO NumScores DO
                read (StudentInfoFile, Student.TestScore[i]);
            readln (StudentInfoFile);
            readln (StudentInfoFile, EligCode);
            CASE EligCode OF
                'Y' : Student.Eligible := true;
                'N' : Student.Eligible := false
            END (* CASE *);

            (* Calculate average test score *)

            Sum := 0;
            FOR i := 1 TO NumScores DO
                Sum := Sum + Student.TestScore[i];
            AveScore := Sum / NumScores;

            (* Display desired information *)

            write (Student.Snumb:5, Student.Name:17, Student.Sex:2,
                    AveScore:8:1);
            IF Student.Eligible THEN
                writeln ('Yes':9)
            ELSE
                writeln ('No ':9)
    END (* WHILE *)
END.



Listing of StudentInfoFile:
===========================



12345
John Doe
M
44 55 78 83 72
Y
15651
Mary Smith
F
94 85 62 66 83
Y
22001
Pete Vandervan
M
34 44 29 51 47
N

Sample run:
==========
```

```
Student                        Test
Number         Name      Sex  Average  Eligible?
======        ====      ===  =======  =========
12345   John Doe         M     66.4     Yes
15651   Mary Smith       F     78.0     Yes
22001   Pete Vandervan   M     41.0     No
```

As another example, consider the record type *PersonnelRecord* of the preceding section:

type
    NameString = **packed array**[1..20] **of** *char*;
    NameOfMonth = **packed array**[1..8] **of** *char*;
    Date = **record**
                Month : *NameOfMonth*;
                Day : 1..31;
                Year : 1900..2000
        end;
    Personnel Record = **record**
                      Name : *NameString*;
                      Birth : *Date*;
                      Age, Dependents : *integer*;
                      HourlyRate : *real*
                end;

var
    Employee : *PersonnelRecord*;

To display the value of *Employee,* we must display the value of each of its fields:

    writeln (*Employee.Name*);
    writeln ('Birthday: ', *Employee.Birth.Month*,
            Employee.Birth.Day:3, ',', *Employee.Birth.Year*:5,
            ' Age = ', *Employee.Age*:1);
    writeln ('# of dependents: ', *Employee.Dependents*:1);
    writeln ('Hourly pay rate: $', *Employee.HourlyRate*:4:2)

These examples clearly show that specifying the field designators for each of a record's fields may be quite cumbersome. For this reason, Pascal provides an option in which it is not necessary to specify the record name each time that a field within that record is referenced. This is accomplished by using the **with** statement of the form

    with *record-name* **do**
        statement

The record name is automatically combined with each field identifier in the specified statement to form a complete field designator. Thus the statement.

    with *Student* **do**
        write (*Snumb*:5, *Name*:17, *Sex*:2)

attaches the record name *Student* to the field identifiers *Snumb, Name,* and *Sex* to form the field designators *Student.Snumb, Student.Name,* and *Student.Sex.* It is thus equivalent to the statement

    write (*Student.Snumb*:5, *Student.Name*:17, *Student.Sex*:2)

Identifiers in a **with** statement that are not field identifiers are not combined with the record name but rather are treated in the usual way. Thus, in the statement

> **with** *Student* **do**
> write (*Snumb*:5, *Name*:17, *Sex*:2, *AveScore*:8:1);

the identifier *AveScore* is not a field identifier and hence is not modified by the **with** statement. This statement is equivalent, therefore, to

> write (*Student.Snumb*:5, *Student.Name*:17, *Student.Sex*:2, *AveScore*:8:1)

The program in Figure 11.2 uses **with** statements to simplify the program in Figure 11.1.

```
PROGRAM StudentAverages (input, output, StudentInfoFile);

(*********************************************************************

    Program to read student records each of which includes a student's
    number, name, sex, 5 test scores, and eligibility status; calculate
    the average of the test scores; display this average together
    with the student's number, name, sex, and eligibility status.
    The student records are read from the text file StudentInfoFile.

*********************************************************************)

CONST
    NameLength = 15;
    NumScores = 5;
    MaxScore = 100;

TYPE
    NameString = PACKED ARRAY[1..NameLength] OF char;
    ListOfScores = ARRAY[1..NumScores] OF 0..MaxScore;
    ClassRecord = RECORD
                      Snumb : integer;
                      Name : NameString;
                      Sex : char;
                      TestScore : ListOfScores;
                      Eligible : boolean
                  END;

VAR
    StudentInfoFile : text;    (* file containing student records *)
    Student : ClassRecord;     (* record for current student *)
    EligCode : char;           (* eligibility code read (Y or N) *)
    i,                         (* index *)
    Sum : integer;             (* sum of test scores *)
    AveScore : real;           (* average test score *)

BEGIN
    reset (StudentInfoFile);

    (* Print headings *)

    writeln ('Student                     Test');
    writeln ('Number      Name        Sex Average  Eligible?');
    writeln ('======      ====        === =======  =========');
```

Figure 11.2

Fig. 11.2. (cont.)

```
WHILE NOT eof(StudentInfoFile) DO
    BEGIN

        (* Read student's record *)

        WITH Student DO
            BEGIN
                readln (StudentInfoFile, Snumb);
                FOR i := 1 TO NameLength DO
                    IF NOT eoln(StudentInfoFile) THEN
                        read (StudentInfoFile, Name[i])
                    ELSE
                        Name[i] := ' ';
                readln (StudentInfoFile);
                readln (StudentInfoFile, Sex);
                FOR i := 1 TO NumScores DO
                    read (StudentInfoFile, TestScore[i]);
                readln (StudentInfoFile);
                readln (StudentInfoFile, EligCode);
                CASE EligCode OF
                    'Y' : Eligible := true;
                    'N' : Eligible := false
                END (* CASE *);
            END (* WITH *);

        (* Calculate average test score *)

        Sum := 0;
        FOR i := 1 TO NumScores DO
            Sum := Sum + Student.TestScore[i];
        AveScore := Sum / NumScores;

        (* Display desired information *)

        WITH Student DO
            BEGIN
                write (Snumb:5, Name:17, Sex:2, AveScore:8:1);
                IF Eligible THEN
                    writeln ('Yes':9)
                ELSE
                    writeln ('No ':9)
            END (* WITH *)
    END (* WHILE *)
END.
```

With statements may also be *nested;* that is, one **with** statement may appear within another **with** statement. To illustrate, consider the statements used to display the value of the record variable *Employee:*

writeln (*Employee.Name*);
writeln ('Birthday: ', *Employee.Birth.Month*,
        Employee.Birth.Day:3, ',', *Employee.Birth.Year*:5,
        ' Age = ', *Employee.Age*:1);
writeln ('# of dependents: ', *Employee.Dependents*:1);
writeln ('Hourly pay rate: $', *Employee.HourlyRate*:4:2)

These statements could be replaced by the **with** statement

```
with Employee do
    begin
        writeln (Name);
        writeln ('Birthday: ', Birth.Month, Birth.Day:3, ', ',
                    Birth.Year:5, ' Age = ', Age:1);
        writeln ('# of dependents: ', Dependents:1);
        writeln ('Hourly pay rate: $', HourlyRate:4:2)
    end
```

or nested **with** statements might be used:

```
with Employee do
    begin
        writeln (Name);
        with Birth do
            writeln ('Birthday: ', Month, Day:3, ', ', Year:5,
                        'Age = ', Age:1);
        writeln ('# of dependents: ', Dependents:1);
        writeln ('Hourly pay rate: $', HourlyRate:4:2)
    end
```

In this case, the inner **with** statement first attaches the record name *Birth* to the field identifiers *Month, Day,* and *Year* to form the field designators *Birth.Month, Birth.Day,* and *Birth.Year;* but it does not attach *Birth* to the identifier *Age,* because this is not a field identifier within the record *Birth.* The outer **with** statement then attaches the record name *Employee* to form the field designators *Employee.Name, Employee.Birth.Month, Employee. Birth.Day, Employee.Birth.Year,* and *Employee.Age.*

An extended form of the **with** statement allows several record names to be listed:

```
with record-name-1, record-name-2, . . . , record-name-n do
    statement
```

This form is equivalent to

```
with record-name-1 do
    with record-name-2 do
            .
            .
            .
            with record-name-n do
                statement
```

For example, the nested **with** statement above could also be written

```
with Employee, Birth do
    begin
        writeln (Name);
        writeln ('Birthday: ', Month, Day:3, ', ', Year:5, ' Age = ', Age:1);
```

```
        writeln ('# of dependents: ', Dependents:1);
        writeln ('Hourly pay rate: $', HourlyRate:4:2)
    end
```

Sometimes it is necessary to copy the fields of one record into another record. This can be done with a series of assignment statements containing the field designators of the two records, but it can be done more conveniently with a single assignment statement of the form

record-variable-1 := *record-variable-2*

In this case the two record variables must have the same type, which means that they must be declared using the same or equivalent type identifiers (see Section 8.2).

Recall that the value of a function may not be a structured type; in particular, it may not be a record. Records may, however, be used as parameters of functions and procedures, and in this case, the corresponding records must have the same type.

To illustrate the use of records as parameters for subprograms, consider the problem of finding the length of the segment joining two points in a plane and finding the equation of the line that passes through these points. The length of the segment joining point P_1 with coordinates (x_1, y_1) and point P_2 with coordinates (x_2, y_2) is given by

$$\sqrt{(x_2 - x_1)^2 + (y_2 - y_1)^2}$$

The *slope-intercept* form of the equation of the line through P_1 and P_2 is

$$y = mx + b$$

where m is the *slope* of the line and is calculated by

$$m = \frac{y_2 - y_1}{x_2 - x_1}$$

(provided that $x_1 \neq x_2$); and b is the *y-intercept* of the line, that is, $(0, b)$ is the point where the line crosses the y axis. Using the slope m, we can calculate b as

$$b = y_1 - mx_1$$

In case $x_1 = x_2$, there is no *y-intercept* and the slope is not defined; the line through P_1 and P_2 is the vertical line having the equation

$$x = x_1$$

The Program in Figure 11.3 uses the function *Length* to calculate the length of the segment joining points *P1* and *P2* and calls the procedure *FindLine* to find the equation of the line passing through *P1* and *P2*. Points are represented as records having two fields of real type named x and y, which represent the x and y coordinates, respectively:

```
    Point = record
            x, y : real
        end;
```

```
PROGRAM PointsAndLines (input, output);

(*****************************************************************

   Program to read two points represented as records, calculate
   the length of the line segment joining them, and find the
   slope-intercept equation of the line passing through them.

*****************************************************************)

TYPE
   Point = RECORD
                x, y : real
            END;

VAR
   P1, P2 : Point;   (* 2 points being processed *)
   Response : char;  (* user response *)

FUNCTION Length (P1, P2 : Point) : real;

   (*****************************************************************

      Function to calculate the length of the line segment joining
      the two points P1 and P2.

   *****************************************************************)

   BEGIN (* Length *)
      Length := sqrt(sqr(P2.x - P1.x) + sqr(P2.y - P1.y))
   END (* Length *);

PROCEDURE FindLine (P1, P2 : Point);

   (*****************************************************************

      Procedure to find the slope-intercept equation  y = mx + b
      of the line passing though points P1 and P2.

   *****************************************************************)

   VAR
      m,           (* slope of line *)
      b : real;    (* y intercept of line *)

   BEGIN (* FindLine *)
      IF P1.x = P2.x THEN
         writeln ('Line is vertical line  x = ', P1.x:4:2)
      ELSE
         BEGIN
            m := (P2.y - P1.y) / (P2.x - P1.x);
            b := P1.y - m * P1.x;
            writeln ('Equation of line is y = ', m:4:2, 'x + ', b:4:2)
         END (* ELSE *)
   END (* FindLine *);

BEGIN (* main program *)
   REPEAT
      writeln ('Enter coordinates of points P1 and P2:  ');
      readln (P1.x, P1.y, P2.x, P2.y);
      writeln ('For points (', P1.x:4:2, ',', P1.y:4:2, ') and (',
               P2.x:4:2, ',', P2.y:4:2, '):');
      writeln ('Length of segment joining P1 & P2 is ',
               Length(P1,P2):4:2);
```

Figure 11.3

Fig. 11.3. (cont.)

```
      FindLine (P1, P2);
      writeln;
      write ('More (Y or N)?  ');
      readln (Response)
   UNTIL Response <> 'Y'
END (* main program *).
```

```
Sample run:
==========


Enter coordinates of points P1 and P2:
0 0  1 1
For points (0.00,0.00) and (1.00,1.00):
Length of segment joining P1 & P2 is 1.41
Equation of line is y = 1.00x + 0.00

More (Y or N)?  Y
Enter coordinates of points P1 and P2:
1 1  1 5
For points (1.00,1.00) and (1.00,5.00):
Length of segment joining P1 & P2 is 4.00
Line is vertical line  x = 1.00

More (Y or N)?  Y
Enter coordinates of points P1 and P2:
3.1 4.2  -5.3 7.2
For points (3.10,4.20) and (-5.30,7.20):
Length of segment joining P1 & P2 is 8.92
Equation of line is y = -0.36x + 5.31

More (Y or N)?  N
```

11.3 Application of Records: Sorting

In Section 8.3 we considered the problem of sorting a collection of items and then searching this sorted collection for a specified item. The specific example given there used three different items: a student's number, class code, and a test score, and these items were stored in three separate arrays. Because these items are related but are not all of the same type, it would be more natural to store them using an array of records.

Consider the problem of assigning letter grades to students by using the grading scheme commonly called "grading on the curve." In this scheme, a letter grade is assigned to a numerical grade according to the following table:

x = Numeric Score	Letter Grade
$x < m - \dfrac{3}{2}\sigma$	F
$m - \dfrac{3}{2}\sigma \le x < m - \dfrac{1}{2}\sigma$	D
$m - \dfrac{1}{2}\sigma \le x < m + \dfrac{1}{2}\sigma$	C
$m + \dfrac{1}{2}\sigma \le x < m + \dfrac{3}{2}\sigma$	B
$m + \dfrac{3}{2}\sigma \le x$	A

where m is the mean numeric score and σ is the standard deviation (see Exercises 7 and 8 of Section 8.3).

For each student we have the following information: student number and name and three numeric scores, one for homework, another for tests, and the third for the final examination. The final numeric grade is a weighted average of these scores and is to be calculated by

$$.2 \times (\text{homework score}) + .5 \times (\text{tests score}) + .3 \times (\text{exam score})$$

The output is to be a list of student numbers, final numeric scores, and final letter grades, arranged so that the scores are in descending order.

In the program in Figure 11.4, the given information, together with the calculated numeric score and letter grade for each student, is stored in a record having the following structure:

```
StudentRecord = record
                    Snumb : integer;
                    Name : NameString;
                    Scores : record
                                HomeWork, Tests, Exam : real
                             end;
                    FinalNumScore : real;
                    LetterGrade : char
                end;
```

There is one record for each student, and the array *Student* is used to store these records so that *Student*[i] refers to the record of the ith student.

The program first reads the student's number, name, and three scores, storing these in the array *Student*. It then passes each record in this array to the procedure *CalculateNumScore*, which calculates the final numeric score for each student and inserts it in the field *FinalNumScore* of his or her record. The entire array of records is then passed to the procedure *Assign-Grades*, which inserts the final letter grade in the field *LetterGrade* of each record. The procedure *AssignGrades* uses the procedure *CalculateStats* to calculate the mean and standard deviation of the final scores needed by the function *GradeOnTheCurve*, which calculates the final letter grade. Finally, the program calls the procedure *BubbleSort* to arrange the records so that final numeric grades are in descending order and then displays the desired information. The procedure *BubbleSort* uses the bubble sort algorithm described in Section 8.3 with the modification that entire records are interchanged when necessary.

```
PROGRAM GradeAssignment (input, output, ScoresFile);

(***********************************************************************

    Program to read students' records, each of which contains a
    student's number, name, and three numeric scores, one for
    homework, another for tests, and a third for the final exam.
    It calculates the final numeric grade as a weighted average of
    these scores using the weighting constants HomeworkWeight,
    TestWeight, and ExamWeight.  A letter grade is then calculated by
    "grading on the curve."  A list of student numbers with final
    numeric and letter grades is then displayed with numeric grades
    in descending order.  The student information is read from the
    text file ScoresFile.

***********************************************************************)

CONST
    NameLength = 15;
    ListLimit = 100;

TYPE
    NameString = PACKED ARRAY[1..NameLength] OF char;
    StudentRecord = RECORD
        Snumb : integer;
        Name : NameString;
        Scores : RECORD
            Homework, Tests, Exam : real
            END;
        FinalNumScore : real;
        LetterGrade : char
        END;
    StudentRecordList = ARRAY[1..ListLimit] of StudentRecord;

VAR
    ScoresFile : text;                (* file of student scores *)
    Student : StudentRecordList;      (* list of student records *)
    NumStudents,                      (* number of students *)
    i : integer;                      (* index *)

PROCEDURE ReadRecords (VAR Student : StudentRecordList;
                       VAR Count : integer);

    (***********************************************************

        Procedure to read and count the list Student[1], Student[2], ...
        Student[NumStudents] of student records.

    ***********************************************************)

    VAR
        i : integer;  (* index *)

    BEGIN (* ReadRecords *)
        reset (ScoresFile);
        Count := 0;
        WHILE NOT eof(ScoresFile) DO
```

Figure 11.4

Fig. 11.4. (cont.)

```
        BEGIN
            Count := Count + 1;
            WITH Student[Count], Scores DO
                BEGIN
                    readln(ScoresFile, Snumb);
                    FOR i := 1 TO NameLength DO
                        IF NOT eoln(ScoresFile) THEN
                            read (ScoresFile, Name[i])
                        ELSE
                            Name[i] := ' ';
                    readln (ScoresFile);
                    readln (ScoresFile, Homework, Tests, Exam)
                END (* WITH *)
        END (* WHILE *)
    END (* ReadRecords *);

PROCEDURE CalculateNumScore (VAR StuRec : StudentRecord);

    (*****************************************************************

        Procedure to calculate student's final numeric grade as a
        weighted average and insert it into his/her record.

    *****************************************************************)


    CONST
        HomeWorkWeight = 0.2;
        TestWeight = 0.5;
        ExamWeight = 0.3;

    BEGIN (* CalculateNumScore *)
        WITH StuRec, Scores DO
            FinalNumScore := HomeWorkWeight * Homework + TestWeight * Tests
                            + ExamWeight * Exam
        END (* CalculateNumScore *);

PROCEDURE AssignGrades (VAR Student : StudentRecordList;
                        NumStudents : integer);

    (*****************************************************************

        Procedure to insert letter grades in the students' records.

    *****************************************************************)

    VAR
        i : integer;                    (* index *)
        Mean,                           (* mean of final numeric scores *)
        StandardDeviation : real;   (* standard deviation of final scores *)

    PROCEDURE CalculateStats (VAR Student : StudentRecordList;
                              NumStudents : integer;
                              VAR Mean, StandardDeviation : real);

        (*****************************************************************

            Procedure to find the mean and standard deviation of the
            students' final numeric grades.

        *****************************************************************)
```

Fig. 11.4. (cont.)

```
    VAR
        i : integer;        (* index *)
        Sum,                (* used to calculate necessary totals *)
        Variance : real;    (* variance of the scores *)

    BEGIN (* CalculateStats *)

        (* Find the mean *)

        Sum := 0;
        FOR i := 1 TO NumStudents DO
            Sum := Sum + Student[i].FinalNumScore;
        Mean := Sum / NumStudents;

        (* Find the variance and standard deviation *)

        Sum := 0;
        FOR i := 1 TO NumStudents DO
            Sum := Sum + sqr(Student[i].FinalNumScore - Mean);
        Variance := Sum / NumStudents;
        StandardDeviation := sqrt(Variance)
    END (* CalculateStats *);

FUNCTION GradeOnTheCurve (Score, m, Sigma : real) : char;

    (****************************************************************

        Function using 'grading on the curve' to assign letter grade
        to numeric score; m is the mean score, Sigma is the standard
        deviation.

    ****************************************************************)

    BEGIN (* GradeOnTheCurve *)
        IF Score < (m - 1.5 * Sigma) THEN
            GradeOnTheCurve := 'F'
        ELSE IF Score < (m - 0.5 * Sigma) THEN
            GradeOnTheCurve := 'D'
        ELSE IF Score < ( m + 0.5 * Sigma) THEN
            GradeOnTheCurve := 'C'
        ELSE IF Score < ( m + 1.5 * Sigma) THEN
            GradeOnTheCurve := 'B'
        ELSE
            GradeOnTheCurve := 'A'
    END (* GradeOnTheCurve *);

BEGIN (* AssignGrades *)
    CalculateStats (Student, NumStudents, Mean, StandardDeviation);
    FOR i := 1 TO NumStudents DO
        WITH Student[i] DO
            LetterGrade :=
                GradeOnTheCurve (FinalNumScore, Mean, StandardDeviation)
END (* AssignGrades *);

PROCEDURE BubbleSort (VAR Student : StudentRecordList;
                      NumStudents : integer);

    (****************************************************************

        Procedure to sort Student[1], ..., Student[NumStudents] using
        the bubble sort algorithm so that key fields FinalNumScore
        are in descending order.

    ****************************************************************)
```

Fig. 11.4. (cont.)

```
    VAR
        NumPairs : integer;           (* # of pairs examined in current scan *)
        Temporary : StudentRecord;    (* used to interchange two records *)
        i : integer;                  (* index *)
        Done : boolean;               (* indicates if sorting completed *)

    BEGIN (* BubbleSort *)
        NumPairs := NumStudents - 1;

        (* Scan the list comparing consecutive keys *)

        REPEAT
            Done := true;
            FOR i := 1 TO NumPairs DO
                IF Student[i].FinalNumScore > Student[i+1].FinalNumScore THEN
                    BEGIN
                        Temporary := Student[i];
                        Student[i] := Student[i+1];
                        Student[i+1] := Temporary;
                        Done := false  (* interchange occurred, so scan again *)
                    END (* IF *);

            (* Record with largest key has sunk into place, so
               eliminate it from the next scan *)

            NumPairs := NumPairs - 1
        UNTIL Done
    END (* BubbleSort *);

PROCEDURE PrintTheRecords (VAR Student : StudentRecordList;
                               NumStudents : integer);

    (***********************************************************************

        Procedure to print the final grades for all students.

    ***********************************************************************)

    VAR
        i : integer;    (* index *)

    BEGIN (* PrintTheRecords *)
        writeln ('Student    Final      Final');
        writeln ('Number     Score      Grade');
        writeln ('=======    =====      =====');
        FOR i := 1 TO NumStudents DO
            WITH Student[i] DO
                writeln (Snumb:5, FinalNumScore:11:2, LetterGrade:8)
    END (* PrintTheRecords *);

BEGIN (* main program *)
    ReadRecords (Student, NumStudents);
    FOR i := 1 TO NumStudents DO
        CalculateNumScore (Student[i]);
    AssignGrades (Student, NumStudents);
    BubbleSort (Student, NumStudents);
    PrintTheRecords (Student, NumStudents)
END (* main program *).
```

Fig. 11.4. (cont.)

```
Listing of ScoresFile:
======================


1234
John Doe
50 53 57
1441
Mary Smith
62 59 65
1531
Fred Jones
72 65 70
1554
Pete Vander
100 100 100
1638
Jane Doe
22 15 19
1734
Al Johnson
62 58 55


Sample run:
===========
```

Student Number	Final Score	Final Grade
=======	=====	=====
1638	17.60	F
1234	53.60	C
1734	57.90	C
1441	61.40	C
1531	67.90	C
1554	100.00	A

*11.4

Variant Records

As we noted in Section 11.2, records may have a *variant part* in addition to a *fixed part*. The number and types of the fields in the fixed part of a value assigned to a record variable do not change during program execution, but those in the variant part may change in number and/or in type. In this section we discuss such *variant records*.

To illustrate variant records, consider the employee record described by

> *EmployeeRecord1* = **record**
> > *Name* : *NameString*;
> > *Age, Dependents* : *integer*;
> > *DeptCode* : *char*;
> > *HourlyRate* : *real*
> >
> > **end**;

where *NameString* is a user-defined type such as **packed array**[1..20] **of** *char*. Such records are appropriate for factory employees who are paid on an hourly basis. For office employees, the records might have the following structure:

EmployeeRecord2 = **record**
               Name : *NameString*;
               Age, Dependents : *integer*;
               Salary : *real*
        end;

and for salespersons, an appropriate record structure might be

EmployeeRecord3 = **record**
               Name : *NameString*;
               Age, Dependents : *integer*;
               MileageAllowance : *integer*;
               BasePay, CommissionRate : *real*
        end;

All of these record structures can be incorporated into a single record by using a record with a variant part:

EmployeeRecord = **record**
               Name : *NameString*;
               Age, Dependents : *integer*;
               case *EmpCode* : *char* **of**
                  'F' : (*DeptCode* : *char*;
                      HourlyRate : *real*);
                  'O' : (*Salary* : *real*);
                  'S' : (*MileageAllowance* : *integer*;
                      BasePay, CommissionRate : *real*)
        end;

This record has a fixed part which is the same for all values of type *EmployeeRecord*, and this fixed part consists of the fields *Name, Age,* and *Dependents*. In addition to these three fields, some values have *DeptCode* and *HourlyRate* fields; others have only a *Salary* field; and still others have *MileageAllowance, BasePay,* and *CommissionRate* fields. If *EmpCode* has the value F, then the fields *DeptCode* and *HourlyRate* are in effect; if *EmpCode* has the value O, then the field *Salary* is in effect; and if the value of *Empcode* is S, then the *MileageAllowance, BasePay,* and *CommissionRate* fields are in effect.

    The field *EmpCode* is called the *tag field* in this record. The values it may have are used to label the variant fields of the record and to determine the structure of a particular value of type *EmployeeRecord*. Thus, if the value of *EmpCode* is F, which labels the variant fields for a factory employee, the structure of the record is the same as one of type *EmployeeRecord1*. If the value of *EmpCode* is O, which labels the variant field for an office employee, the structure of the record is that of type *EmployeeRecord2*. Finally, if the value of *EmpCode* is S, which labels the variant fields for a salesperson, the structure is the same as that of type *EmployeeRecord3*. Note that the variant part of a record follows the fixed part and that each variant field list is enclosed in parentheses.

In a variant record, several tag field values may label the same variant field list. It is also permissible for tag field values to label empty variant field lists. To illustrate, suppose that the following type declarations have been made:

```
type
    NameString = packed array[1..20] of char;
    TransactionType = (Deposit, Withdrawal, LoanPayment, Transfer, Void);
    Date = record
                Month, Day, Year : integer
            end;
```

and consider the following definition of a record to store certain items of information related to banking transactions:

```
    Transaction = record
                        CustomerName : NameString;
                        Number : integer;
                        TransDate : Date;
                        case TransType : TransactionType of
                            Deposit, Withdrawal : (Amount : real);
                            LoanPayment         : (LoanNumber : integer;
                                                   Payment, Interest,
                                                   NewBalance : real);
                            Transfer            : (TransferAccount : integer;
                                                   AmountOfTransfer : real;
                                                   Code : char);
                            Void                : ()
            end;
```

Note that the tag field *TransType* may have any of the five values specified by the enumerated type *TransactionType*. If the value of *TransType* is either *Deposit* or *Withdrawal*, the field in effect is the single real field *Amount*. If the value of *TransType* is *LoanPayment*, then four fields are in effect: one integer field *LoanNumber* and three real fields, *Payment*, *Interest*, and *New-Balance*. For the value *Transfer* of *TransType*, there are three effective fields: *TransferAccount* of integer type, *AmountOfTransfer* of real type, and *Code* of character type (which indicates whether the transfer is to or from *Transfer-Account*). Finally, the value of *TransType* may be *Void*, in which case no information is required and thus no field is in effect.

Now suppose that the following variables have been declared:

```
var
    Account : Transaction;
    TransactionCode : char;
```

To read information into the record variable *Account*, one typically first reads values for the fixed field identifiers:

```
with Account do
    begin
        for i := 1 to 20 do
            read (CustomerName[i]);
        readln;
        readln (Number);
        with TransDate do
            readln (Month, Day, Year)
    end (* with *);
```

Next a value is read for *TransactionCode* which indicates whether the transaction is a deposit (D), withdrawal (W), loan payment (L), transfer (T), or void (V). This value can then be used to set the corresponding value of the tag field *TransType*. These codes of type *char*, rather than the actual values of *TransType*, are read, because values of the enumerated type *Transaction-Type* cannot be read from the system file *input* (or from any other text file). A **case** statement within a **with** statement might be used to set the tag field and read the values for items in the corresponding field list:

```
with Account do
    case TransactionCode of
        'D' : begin
                TransType := Deposit;
                readln (Amount)
              end;
        'W'   begin
                TransType := Withdrawal;
                readln (Amount)
              end;
        'L' : begin
                TransType := LoanPayment;
                readln (LoanNumber, Payment)
              end;
        'T' : begin
                TransType := Transfer
                readln (TransferAccount, AmountOfTransfer, Code)
              end;
        'V' : TransType := Void
    end (* case *)
```

As this example illustrates, a record structure may be quite complex, as there may be records nested within records (e.g., *TransDate* of record type *Date* nested within *Account* of record type *Transaction*); and although our example does not illustrate it, these nested records may themselves have variant parts.

The general form of a record structure is

```
record
    fixed-field-list-1;
    fixed-field-list-2;
        ⋮
        ⋮
```

> *fixed-field-list-m*;
>   **case** *tag-field-identifier* : *tag-type-identifier* **of**
>   *tag-value-list-1* : (*variant-field-list-1*);
>   *tag-value-list-2* : (*variant-field-list-2*);
>   ⋮
>   *tag-value-list-n* : (*variant-field-list-n*)
> **end** (* **record** *);

where each *field-list-i* (either *fixed* or *variant*) is an empty list or has one of the forms

    field-name : *field-type*

or

    field-name-1, *field-name-2*, . . . , *field-name-k* : *field-type*

or is a list of such field specifications separated by semicolons. The type of the tag field may be any ordinal type, and each of the possible values of the tag field must appear in exactly one of the tag value lists. This general form of a record is displayed in the syntax diagrams on page 394.

Note that a record may have both a fixed part and a variant part, only a fixed part, or only a variant part. It might also be noted that the tag field identifier, but not its type identifier, may be omitted. In this case, access to the items in a variant field list is still possible; but because no tag field identifier is used, the tag field itself cannot be accessed. Such records might be used when it is possible to determine by some other means which variant field list is in effect, for example, when the first fifty records in an array of one hundred records all use the same variant field list and the remaining fifty records involve some other variant field list. Omitting the tag field identifier, however, can easily lead to subtle errors and should be avoided. Finally, as the syntax diagram indicates, records may be packed so as to permit the compiler to minimize the amount of storage required for a record.

Programming Pointers

A record is a collection of related data items called fields which may be of different types. In some situations, such as in assignment statements and subprogram references, records may be processed as single units. In other situations it is necessary to process the fields of a record separately by using field designators. The following are some of the important points to remember when using records:

1. *The reserved word* **end** *must be used to mark the end of each record declaration.*

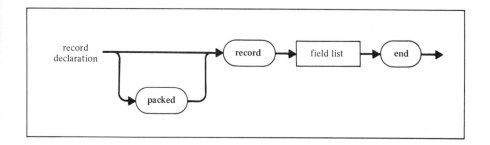

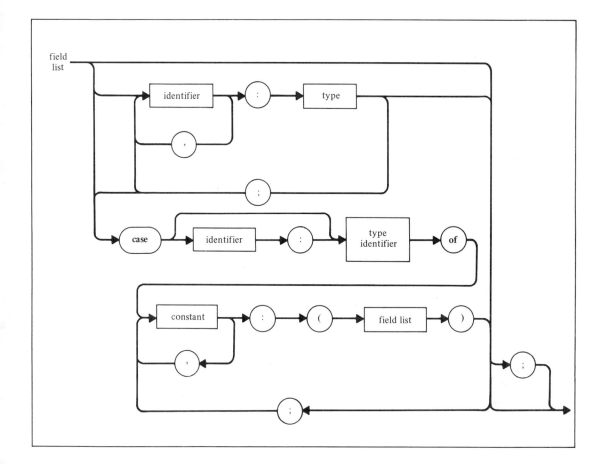

2. *The scope of each field identifier is the record in which it appears.*
This scope rule has the following consequences:

- *The same identifier may not be used to name two different fields within the same record.*
- *An identifier that names a field within a record may be used for some other purpose outside that record (but see Programming Pointer 4).*
- *A field cannot be accessed by simply giving the field identifier; instead, a field designator of the form record-name.field-name must be used.*

3. *Records cannot be read or written as units to or from text files; instead individual fields must be read or written.* For example, if *InfoRec* is a record of type *InformationRecord* defined by

type
    String20 = **packed array** [1..20] **of** *char*;
    String12 = **packed array** [1..12] **of** *char*;
    AddressRecord = **record**
                    StreetAddress : *String20*;
                    City, State : *String12*;
                    ZipCode : *integer*
            end;
    InformationRecord = **record**
                    Name : *String20*;
                    Address : *AddressRecord*;
                    Age : *integer*;
                    MaritalStatus : *char*
            end;

its fields can be displayed as follows:

writeln (*InfoRec.Name*);
writeln (*InfoRec.Address.StreetAddress*);
writeln (*InfoRec.Address.City*, ', ', *InfoRec.Address.State*,
    InfoRec.Address.ZipCode);
writeln ('Age: ', *InfoRec.Age*);
writeln ('Marital Status: ', *InfoRec.MaritalStatus*)

4. *The* **with** *statement attaches a given record name(s) to each identifier within the statement that names a field within the specified record(s).* For example, the output statements in Programming Pointer 3 could be replaced with

with *InfoRec* **do**
  begin
    writeln (*Name*);
    writeln (*Address.StreetAddress*);
    writeln (*Address.City*, ', ', *Address.State*, *Address.ZipCode*);
    writeln ('Age: ', *Age*);
    writeln ('Martial Status: ', *MaritalStatus*)
  end (* **with** *)

The **with** statement attaches a record name to *every* identifier appearing in the **with** statement that names a field within the specified record. Consequently, if one of these identifiers is used for some other purpose outside the record, the **with** statement attaches the record name to this identifier so that the field within the record is processed and not the value of the identifier outside the record.

A **with** statement of the form

with *record-name-1, record-name-2* **do**
  statement

is equivalent to

> **with** *record-name-1* **do**
>   **with** *record-name-2* **do**
>   *statement*

(and similarly for **with** statements with more than two record names). This means that *record-name-2* will first be attached to all identifiers that name fields within it before *record-name-1* is attached. Thus, the preceding **with** statement to display the fields within *InfoRec* could also be written

> **with** *InfoRec, Address* **do**
>   **begin**
>   *writeln* (*Name*);
>   *writeln* (*StreetAddress*);
>   *writeln* (*City*, ', ', *State, ZipCode*);
>   *writeln* ('Age: ', *Age*);
>   *writeln* ('Marital Status: ', *MaritalStatus*)
>   **end** (* **with** *)

One result of this order of attachment is that if an identifier names a field in *record-name-1* and a field in *record-name-2*, then *record-name-2* will be attached to this field identifier.

5. *The value of a record may be copied into another record by using an assignment statement, provided that the two records have the same type, which means that they must be declared by the same or equivalent type identifiers* (see Section 8.2). Thus, if the type *PersonRecord* is defined by

> *PersonRecord* = *InformationRecord*;

where *InformationRecord* is as described in Programming Pointer 3, then the record variables *RecA* and *RecB* declared by

> **var**
>   *RecA* : *InformationRecord*;
>   *RecB* : *PersonRecord*;

are not usually considered to have the same types because they are not declared by equivalent type identifiers.

6. *Records may be used as parameters in functions or procedures; but each actual parameter must have the same type as the corresponding formal parameter. The value of a function may not be a record.*

7. *When variant records are used, sufficient memory is usually allocated to store the variant that requires the most memory, and all other variants of that record are stored using this same portion of memory.* To illustrate, consider declarations of the form

```
type
    EmployeeRecord = record
                        ⋮          (* fixed part of record *)
                    case EmpCode : char of
                         'F': (DeptCode : char;
                               HourlyRate : real);
                         'O': (Salary : real)
        end;
```

Because the first variant is the larger, sufficient memory is allocated to store it, but the same memory locations are used for the second variant:

If values such as M and 11.25 are assigned to the fields of the first variant, then a subsequent reference to this same record with the second variant is improper. An error or a "garbage" value for *Salary* may result, because an attempt is made to interpret the internal representation of the character M as part of a real value for *Salary*.

8. *The tag field in a variant record must be of ordinal type; each possible value of the tag field must appear in exactly one tag value list; the value of the tag field may not be passed to a variable formal parameter.*

Exercises

1. For each of the following, develop an appropriate record structure for the given information, and then write type declarations for the records:

   (a) Cards in a deck of playing cards.

   (b) Time measured in hours, minutes, and seconds.

   (c) Length measured in yards, feet, and inches.

   (d) Listings in a telephone directory.

   (e) Description of an automobile (make, model, style, color, and the like).

   (f) Description of a book in a library's card catalogue (author, publisher, and the like).

   (g) Teams in a baseball league (name, won-lost record, and the like).

   (h) Position of a checker on a checker board.

2. The data files *StudentFile, InventoryFile,* and *UsersFile* are described in Appendix E. Write appropriate record declarations to describe the information in these files.

3. For each of the following, develop a record structure using variant records for the given information, and then write type declarations for the records:

   (a) Information about a person: name; birthday; age; sex; social security number; height; weight; hair color; eye color; marital status, and if married, number of children.

   (b) Statistics about a baseball player: name; age; birth date; position (pitcher, catcher, infielder, outfielder); for a pitcher: won-lost record, earned-run average, number of strikeouts, number of walks; if a starting pitcher, number of complete games; and if a relief pitcher, number of innings pitched and number of saves; for the other positions: batting average; slugging average; bats right, left, or is a switch hitter; fielding percentage; also, for an infielder, the positions he can play; for a catcher, whether he can catch a knuckleball.

   (c) Weather statistics: date; city and state, province, or country; time of day; temperature; barometric pressure; weather conditions (clear skies, partly cloudy, cloudy, stormy); if cloudy conditions prevail, cloud level and type of clouds; for partly cloudy, percentage of cloud cover; for stormy conditions, snow depth if it is snowing; amount of rainfall if it is rainy; size of hail if it is hailing.

4. Extend the program in Figure 11.3 to find

   (a) The midpoint of the line segment joining two points.

   (b) The equation of the perpendicular bisector of this line segment.

5. The *point-slope* equation of a line having slope m and passing through the point P with coordinates (x_1, y_1) is

$$y - y_1 = m(x - x_1)$$

   (a) Write a record description for a line given its slope and a point on the line.

   (b) Write a program that reads the slope of a line and the coordinates of a point on the line and that then

   (i) Finds the point-slope equation of the line.

   (ii) Finds the slope-intercept equation of the line.

   (c) Write a program to read the point and slope information of two lines and determine whether they intersect or are parallel. If they intersect, find the point of intersection and also determine whether they are perpendicular.

6. The (x, y) coordinates of a point P used in the example in Section 11.2 are known as the *rectangular coordinates* of P. P can also be assigned *polar coordinates* (r, θ) where r is the distance from the origin to P and θ is the measure of the angle from the positive x axis to the directed line segment from the origin to P:

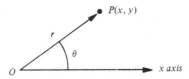

Polar coordinates can be converted to rectangular coordinates using the equations

$$x = r \cos \theta$$
$$y = r \sin \theta$$

and one set of polar coordinates for a point P can be obtained from the rectangular coordinates of P with the equations

$$r = \sqrt{x^2 + y^2} \text{ if } x \geq 0, \; r = -\sqrt{x^2 + y^2} \text{ if } x < 0$$
$$\theta = arctan(y/x) \text{ (provided } x \neq 0).$$

Write procedures to convert from rectangular to polar coordinates and from polar to rectangular coordinates. Use these in a program that reads in a letter R (rectangular) or P (polar) and two real numbers representing the coordinates of a point and then calls the appropriate procedure to find the point's coordinates in the other representation.

7. Write a program that accepts a time of day in military format and finds the corresponding usual representation in hours, minutes and A.M./P.M. or accepts the time in the usual format and finds the corresponding military representation. For example, the input 0100 should produce 1:00 A.M. as output, and the input 3:45 P.M. should give 1545.

8. Write a record declaration for cards in a standard deck having fifty-two cards and two jokers. Then write a program to deal two ten-card hands from such a deck. (See Section 5.5 regarding a random number generator.) Be sure that the same card is not dealt more than once.

9. Write a declaration of a record having only a variant part for four geometric figures: circle, square, rectangle, and triangle. For a circle, the record should store its radius; for a square, the length of a side; for a rectangle, the length of two adjacent sides; and for a triangle, the lengths of the three sides. Then write a program that reads one of the letters C (circle), S (square), R (rectangle), T (triangle) and the appropriate numeric quantity or quantities for a figure of that type and then calculates its area. For example, the input R 7.2 3.5 represents a rectangle with length 7.2 and width 3.5, and T 3 4 6.1 represents a triangle having sides of lengths 3, 4, and 6.1. (For a triangle, the area can be found by using *Hero's formula*: area = $\sqrt{s(s-a)(s-b)(s-c)}$, where a, b, and c are the lengths of the sides and s is one half of the perimeter.

10. A *complex number* has the form $a + bi$, where a and b are real numbers and $i^2 = -1$. The four basic arithmetic operations for complex numbers are defined as follows:

    addition: $(a + bi) + (c + di) = (a + c) + (b + d)i.$
    subtraction: $(a + bi) - (c + di) = (a - c) + (b - d)i.$
    multiplication: $(a + bi) * (c + di) = (ac - bd) + (ad + bc)i$
    division: $\dfrac{a + bi}{c + di} = \dfrac{ac + bd}{c^2 + d^2} + \dfrac{bc - ad}{c^2 + d^2} i$ provided $c^2 + d^2 \neq 0.$

    Write a program to read two complex numbers and a symbol for one of these operations and to perform the indicated operation. Use a record to represent complex numbers, and use procedures to implement the operations.

11. A *rational number* is of the form a/b where a and b are integers with $b \neq 0$. Write a program to do rational number arithmetic, representing each rational number as a record with a numerator field and a denominator field. The program should read and display all rational numbers in the format a/b, or simply a if the denominator is 1. The following examples illustrate the menu of commands that the user should be allowed to enter:

Input	Output	Comments
3/8 + 1/6	13/24	$a/b + c/d = (ad + bc)/bd$ reduced to lowest terms.
3/8 − 1/6	5/24	$a/b - c/d = (ad - bc)/bd$ reduced to lowest terms.
3/8 * 1/6	1/16	$a/b * c/d = ac/bd$ reduced to lowest terms.
3/8 / 1/16	9/4	$a/b / c/d = ad/bc$ reduced to lowest terms.
3/8 I	8/3	Invert a/b.
8/3 M	2 + 2/3	Write a/b as a mixed fraction.
6/8 R	3/4	Reduce a/b to lowest terms.
6/8 G	2	Greatest common divisor of numerator and denominator.
1/6 L 3/8	12	Lowest common denominator of a/b and c/d.
1/6 < 3/8	true	$a/b < c/d$?
1/6 <= 3/8	true	$a/b \leq c/d$?
1/6 > 3/8	false	$a/b > c/d$?
1/6 >= 3/8	false	$a/b \geq c/d$?
3/8 = 9/24	true	$a/b = c/d$?
2/3 X + 2 = 4/5	X = −9/5	Solution of linear equation $(a/b)X + c/d = e/f$.

12

Files

It became increasingly apparent to me that, over the years, Federal agencies have amassed vast amounts of information about virtually every American citizen. This fact, coupled with technological advances in data-collecting and dissemination, raised the possibility that information about individuals conceivably could be used for other than legitimate purposes and without the prior knowledge or consent of the individuals involved.

PRESIDENT GERALD R. FORD

The right of the people to be secure in their persons, houses, papers, and effects, against unreasonable searches and seizures, shall not be violated . . . .

FOURTH AMENDMENT OF THE U.S. CONSTITUTION

The programs that we have written up to this point have involved relatively small amounts of input/output data. In most of our examples, we have assumed that the input data were read from the standard system file *input,* which refers to an input device such as a terminal or card reader. For the most part, output has been directed to the standard system file *output,* referring to a system output device such as a terminal or printer. However, many applications involve large data sets, and these may be processed more conveniently if stored on magnetic tape or a magnetic disk or some other *secondary* (*auxiliary*) memory. Once data have been stored on such media, they may be used as often as desired without being reentered from a terminal or from a set of data cards. Also, several different data sets can be processed by a program, and the output produced by one program can be stored and used as input to another program.

Data stored in secondary memory can be processed in a Pascal program by using the structured data type called **file.** Files may be the predefined Pascal files *input* and *output,* or they may be user-defined files. The programmer usually need not be concerned with the details of the actual external medium on which the data are stored because these details are handled by the operating system. Instead, the programmer deals with the logical structure of the file, that is, with the relationship among the items stored in the file, and with the algorithms needed to process these items. In this chapter we discuss how the file data structure is implemented in Pascal and illustrate some common file-processing techniques.

A *file* is a collection of related data items (usually stored on some external **Review of Text** medium) for input to or output by a program. In contrast to arrays and **Files** records, the size of this collection is not fixed and is limited only by the amount of secondary memory available. Consequently, files are commonly used when there is too much data to store in main memory.

In standard Pascal, files are ordered collections of data that must be processed *sequentially.* This means that the data items in a file cannot be accessed directly but only in the order in which they are stored.[1]

The items in a file may be of any data type, simple or structured, except that they may not be of file type. The simplest files are those in which all the items are of type *char.* Such files are called *text files.* The standard Pascal files *input* and *output* are text files, and we considered user-defined text files in Chapter 6. Much of that discussion also applies to the other types of files that are considered in this chapter.

The principal rules governing the use of text files in Pascal programs as discussed in Chapter 6 may be summarized as follows:

1. *Program heading:* Pascal permits the use of *temporary* (*internal*) files and *permanent* (*external*) files. Temporary files exist only during the execution of a program, whereas permanent files exist before and/or after program execution as well. The names of all permanent files used in a program (including the standard text files *input* and *output*) must appear in the file list of the program heading.
2. *Declaration:* All user-defined files must be declared in the declaration part of the program. For text files, this is most easily accomplished by using the predefined type identifier *text* to specify the types of file variables.
3. *Opening files for input:* Each file from which data are to be read must be opened for input by using the predefined procedure *reset* in a statement of the form

    reset (*filename*)

    Each such procedure call resets the data pointer to the beginning of the specified file. (The standard system file *input* need not be opened for input).
4. *Opening files for output:* Each file to which data are to be written must be opened for output with the predefined procedure *rewrite,* using a statement of the form

    rewrite (*filename*)

---

[1] In many applications it is convenient to have direct access to the items in a file, and so some extensions of Pascal provide direct access (random access) files for such applications.

Each such procedure call empties the specified file, and so any previous contents of the file are destroyed. (The standard system file *output* need not be opened for output.)

5. *File input:* Information can be read from a text file by using the predefined procedures *read* and *readln* in the forms

> read (*filename, input-list*)
> readln (*filename, input-list*)

If *filename* is omitted, values are read from the standard system file *input.*

6. *File output:* Output can be directed to a text file by using the predefined procedures *write* and *writeln* in the forms

> write (*filename, output-list*)
> writeln (*filename, output-list*)

If *filename* is omitted, output is directed to the standard file *output.*

12.2

Files of Other Types

The files reviewed in the preceding section were text files, that is, files whose elements were of type *char.* The elements of a file, called the *file components,* may, however, be of any predefined or user-defined data type, except another file type.

The general file declaration has the form

file of *component-type*

where *component-type* specifies the type of the components of the file. Such file declarations may appear in the variable section of the declaration part of a program to specify the types of file variables, as in

var
> *NumberFile* : **file of** *integer*;

but as with other structured types, it is preferable to assign these to type identifiers in the type section; for example,

type
> *FileOfNumbers* = **file of** *integer*;

The predefined file type *text* is simply a standard type identifier associated with the declaration **file of** *char:*

type
> *text* = **file of** *char*;

The following illustrate some file declarations:

type
> *DaysOfWeek* = (*Sunday, Monday, Tuesday, Wednesday, Thursday, Friday, Saturday*);

```
String = packed array[1..20] of char;
List = array[1..100] of integer;
FileOfNumbers = file of integer;
EmployeeRecord = record
                        Name : String;
                        Number, Dependents : integer;
                        HourlyRate : real
                    end;
EmployeeFile = file of EmployeeRecord;
LongStringsFile = file of packed array[1..80] of char;
FileOfLists = file of List;
FileOfDays = file of DaysOfWeek;

var
    NumberFile : FileOfNumbers;
    EmpFile : EmployeeFile;
    ListFile : FileOfLists;
    AddressFile : LongStringsFile;
    CharacterSetFile : text;
    DayFile : FileOfDays;
```

Files of type other than *char* usually can be created only with a program, and their components can be accessed only within a program. Attempting to list the contents of such a file by using the system text editor or some other system command usually causes "garbage" or some error message to be displayed. The characters that comprise a text file are stored using a standard coding scheme such as ASCII and EBCDIC, and when a text file is listed, these codes are automatically converted to the corresponding characters by the terminal, printer, or other output device. On the other hand, the components of other types of files are stored using the internal representation scheme for the particular computer being used, and this representation usually cannot be correctly displayed in character form by the output device.

There are, however, some advantages in using files other than text files. The primary advantage is that values of structured data types, such as arrays and records, and values of enumerated data types can be read from or written to nontext files. Another advantage is that the information in such files can be transferred more rapidly, as it is already in a form that requires no decoding or encoding. A third advantage is that data are usually stored more compactly if they are stored using their internal representation rather than their external representation in one of the standard coding schemes.

Recall that the name of each permanent file used in the program must be included in the file list of the program heading. Also, each file from which values are to be read (except *input*) must be opened by using the procedure *reset* before any of its components may be accessed. The statement

reset (filename)

calls this procedure and opens the specified file for input.[2] Because this procedure has a single argument, a separate procedure call is required for each file being opened for input. Similarly, each file to be used for output (except *output*) must be opened by using a *rewrite* procedure reference of the form

    rewrite (filename)

Because in most computer systems, files other than text files must be created by a Pascal program, we first consider the *write* and *put* procedures that are used for this purpose. Values can be written into a file by using an output statement of the form

    write (filename, output-list)

where *output-list* is an expression (constant, variable, or formula) or a list of expressions separated by commas, each of which must be compatible with the type of the components of *filename*. Note that the procedure *writeln* may *not* be used for files that are not text files.

As a simple illustration, consider the problem of creating a file of data points (x,y), where x and y are real numbers. This file can be created by a program that reads from the terminal pairs of real values representing points and then writes each pair into the file *PointsFile* whose components are of type

    DataPoint = **record**
                x, y : *real*;
        end;

Because this file is to be a permanent file, we must list it in the program heading

    program *CreatePointsFile (input, output, PointsFile)*;

The type definitions and variable declarations required to declare the file *PointsFile* with components of type *DataPoint* are

    type
        DataPoint = **record**
                 x, y : *real*;
            end;
        FileOfDataPoints = **file of** *DataPoint*;

---

[2] As was noted in Chapter 6, some versions of Pascal allow modified forms of the procedure calls for *reset* and *rewrite* to associate the file name with the name of an actual data file in secondary memory. One form that these procedure references may take is

    reset (filename, actual-file-name)

or

    rewrite (filename, actual-file-name)

```
         var
              Point : DataPoint;
              PointsFile : FileOfDataPoints;
```

The program in Figure 12.1 creates the desired file. It first opens file
PointsFile for output and then reads pairs of real numbers representing points,
writing each pair to *PointsFile*.

```
PROGRAM CreatePointsFile (input, output, PointsFile);

(**********************************************************************

   Program to create the nontext file PointsFile having components
   of type DataPoint.  Coordinates of points are input by the
   user during execution.

**********************************************************************)

TYPE
   DataPoint = RECORD
                   x, y : real
               END;
   FileOfDataPoints = FILE OF DataPoint;

VAR
   Point : DataPoint;                 (* coordinates of a point *)
   PointsFile : FileOfDataPoints;     (* file of data points created *)
   Response : char;                   (* user response *)

BEGIN
   rewrite (PointsFile);
   writeln;
   REPEAT
      write ('Enter coordinates of a point:  ');
      readln (Point.x, Point.y);
      write (PointsFile, Point);
      writeln;
      write ('More (Y or N)?  ');
      readln (Response)
   UNTIL NOT (Response IN ['Y', 'y']);
   writeln;
   writeln ('Creation of PointsFile completed')
END.


Sample run:
==========

Enter coordinates of a point:   1.1  5.6

More (Y or N)?  Y
Enter coordinates of a point:  -2.3  7.5

More (Y or N)?  Y
Enter coordinates of a point:  -4.7 -3.8

More (Y or N)?  Y
Enter coordinates of a point:   -1   0

More (Y or N)?  Y
Enter coordinates of a point:    0   0
```

Figure 12.1

Fig. 12.1. (cont.)

```
More (Y or N)?   Y
Enter coordinates of a point:      O    4

More (Y or N)?   Y
Enter coordinates of a point:    4.2  -6.8

More (Y or N)?   Y
Enter coordinates of a point:    7.1   6.5

More (Y or N)?   Y
Enter coordinates of a point:   -8.2   9.7

More (Y or N)?   Y
Enter coordinates of a point:   -3.3  -1.8

More (Y or N)?   N

Creation of PointsFile completed
```

Declaration of a file creates a *file buffer variable,* also known as the *file window,* which has the same type as the file components. If *filename* represents the name of the file, then this buffer variable is denoted by

> *filename*↑

or

> *filename*^

In our example, therefore, the variable

> *PointsFile*↑

is the buffer variable associated with the file *PointsFile.* This buffer variable is of type *DataPoint* since this is the type of the components in the file *PointsFile,* and it may be used in the same manner as any other variable of type *DataPoint.* For example, the assignment statement

> *PointsFile*↑ $:=$ *Point*

assigns the value of the record variable *Point* to *PointsFile*↑. The input statement

> *readln* (*PointsFile*↑*.x,* *PointsFile*↑*.y*)

or

> **with** *PointsFile*↑ **do**
>   *readln* (*x, y*)

reads values for the two fields in *PointsFile*↑.

    Assignment of a value to a file buffer variable does not write this value into the associated file; it merely copies the value into the memory location assigned to this buffer variable. The predefined procedure *put* can be used to transfer the contents of the buffer variable to the file. This procedure is called with a statement of the form

   put (*filename*)

This statement transfers the value of the buffer variable *filename*↑ to the associated file *filename*. This value is actually *transferred* rather than copied, and consequently, after execution of this statement, *filename*↑ is undefined.

   As an illustration, the program in Figure 12.2 is a modification of

```
PROGRAM CreatePointsFile (input, output, PointsFile);

(*******************************************************************

    Program to create the nontext file PointsFile having components
    of type DataPoint.  Coordinates of points are input by the
    user during execution.

*******************************************************************)

TYPE
    DataPoint = RECORD
                     x, y : real
                END;
    FileOfDataPoints = FILE OF DataPoint;

VAR
    Point : DataPoint;                 (* coordinates of a point *)
    PointsFile : FileOfDataPoints;     (* file of data points created *)
    Response : char;                   (* user response *)

BEGIN
    rewrite (PointsFile);
    REPEAT
       write ('Enter coordinates of a point:  ');
       readln (PointsFile^.x, PointsFile^.y);
       put (PointsFile);
       writeln;
       write ('More (Y or N)?  ');
       readln (Response)
    UNTIL NOT (Response IN ['Y', 'y']);
    writeln;
    writeln ('Creation of PointsFile completed')
END.



Sample run:
==========


Enter coordinates of a point:   1.1  5.6

More (Y or N)?  Y
Enter coordinates of a point:  -2.3  7.5

More (Y or N)?  Y
Enter coordinates of a point:  -4.7 -3.8
```

Figure 12.2

Fig. 12.2. (cont.)

```
More (Y or N)?   Y
Enter coordinates of a point:    -1   0

More (Y or N)?   Y
Enter coordinates of a point:    0    0

More (Y or N)?   Y
Enter coordinates of a point:    0    4

More (Y or N)?   Y
Enter coordinates of a point:    4.2 -6.8

More (Y or N)?   Y
Enter coordinates of a point:    7.1   6.5

More (Y or N)?   Y
Enter coordinates of a point:    -8.2   9.7

More (Y or N)?   Y
Enter coordinates of a point:    -3.3 -1.8

More (Y or N)?   N

Creation of PointsFile completed
```

the program in Figure 12.1 for creating a file of data points. Each pair of real numbers representing a point is read directly into the fields of the buffer variable with the statement

$$readln \ (PointsFile\uparrow.x, \ PointsFile\uparrow.y)$$

and the statement

$$put \ (PointsFile)$$

then transfers this point from the buffer variable $PointsFile\uparrow$ to the file. As these examples indicate, an output statement of the form

$$write \ (filename, \ item\text{-}1, \ item\text{-}2, \ ..., \ item\text{-}n)$$

is equivalent to the set of statements

$$filename\uparrow := item\text{-}1;$$
$$put \ (filename);$$
$$filename\uparrow := item\text{-}2;$$
$$put \ (filename);$$
$$\vdots$$
$$filename\uparrow := item\text{-}n;$$
$$put \ (filename)$$

Once a file has been created, it can be opened for input with the procedure *reset,* as described earlier. A component of this file can then be read by using an input statement of the form

$$read \ (filename, \ input\text{-}list)$$

where *input-list* is a single variable or a list of variables separated by commas. The type of each variable for which a value is to be read and the type of the file components must be compatible. Note that the procedure *readln* may *not* be used for files that are not text files.

As an illustration of input from files, suppose that we wish to examine the contents of the file *PointsFile* created by the program in Figure 12.1 or Figure 12.2. This file must first be opened for input by using the statement

    reset (PointsFile)

Each component of the file can then be read and assigned to the variable *Point* of record type *DataPoint* by using the procedure *read:*

    read (PointsFile, Point)

and the values of the two fields of *Point* can then be displayed with the statement

    writeln (Point.x:5:1, Point.y:7:1)

In the program in Figure 12.3, these two statements are repeated until the end-of-file mark in *PointsFile* is encountered. This end-of-file mark is automatically placed at the end of each file created by a Pascal program.

```
PROGRAM ReadPointsFile (input, output, PointsFile);

(*********************************************************************

    Program to read and display the contents of the permanent file
    PointsFile created by the program of Figure 12.1 or 12.2.

**********************************************************************)

TYPE
    DataPoint = RECORD
                    x, y : real
                END;
    FileOfDataPoints = FILE OF DataPoint;

VAR
    Point : DataPoint;                 (* coordinates of a point *)
    PointsFile : FileOfDataPoints;   (* file of data points created *)

BEGIN
    reset (PointsFile);
    writeln ('Contents of PointsFile:');
    WHILE NOT eof(PointsFile) DO
        BEGIN
            read (PointsFile, Point);
            writeln (Point.x:5:1, Point.y:7:1)
        END (* WHILE *)
END.
```

Figure 12.3

Fig. 12.3. (cont.)

```
Sample run:
==========


Contents of PointsFile:
   1.1     5.6
  -2.3     7.5
  -4.7    -3.8
  -1.0     0.0
   0.0     0.0
   0.0     4.0
   4.2    -6.8
   7.1     6.5
  -8.2     9.7
  -3.3    -1.8
```

In the examples of this section, we used one program to create the file *PointsFile* and a separate program to read the file. In the first program, *PointsFile* was opened for output by using the procedure *rewrite*. After the file was created, this same program could have opened the file for input by using the procedure *reset* and then read and displayed the contents. The program in Figure 12.4 does precisely this and thus combines the functions of the programs in Figures 12.1 and 12.3 into a single program. Recall that opening a file for input and reading its contents does not alter the contents of the file but that opening a file for output does destroy any previous contents of the file.

```
PROGRAM CreateAndVerifyPointsFile (input, output, PointsFile);

(*****************************************************************

    Program to create the nontext file PointsFile having components
    of type DataPoint.  Coordinates of points are input by the user
    during execution.  The contents of the file are then verified
    by opening it for input, reading the contents, and displaying
    each point.

*****************************************************************)

TYPE
    DataPoint = RECORD
                    x, y : real
                END;
    FileOfDataPoints = FILE OF DataPoint;

VAR
    Point : DataPoint;                  (* coordinates of a point *)
    PointsFile : FileOfDataPoints;      (* file of data points created *)
    Response : char;                    (* user response *)

BEGIN

    (* Create PointsFile *)
```

Figure 12.4

Fig. 12.4. (cont.)

```
   rewrite (PointsFile);
   writeln;
   REPEAT
      write ('Enter coordinates of a point:  ');
      readln (Point.x, Point.y);
      write (PointsFile, Point);
      writeln;
      write ('More (Y or N)?  ');
      readln (Response)
   UNTIL NOT (Response IN ['Y', 'y']);


   (* Verify the contents of PointsFile *)


   reset (PointsFile);
   writeln;
   writeln ('Contents of PointsFile:');
   WHILE NOT eof(PointsFile) DO
      BEGIN
         read (PointsFile, Point);
         writeln (Point.x:5:1, Point.y:7:1)
      END (* WHILE *)
END.



Sample run:
==========



Enter coordinates of a point:   1.1   5.6

More (Y or N)?   Y
Enter coordinates of a point:  -2.3   7.5

More (Y or N)?   Y
Enter coordinates of a point:  -4.7  -3.8

More (Y or N)?   Y
Enter coordinates of a point:   -1    0

More (Y or N)?   Y
Enter coordinates of a point:    0    0

More (Y or N)?   Y
Enter coordinates of a point:    0    4

More (Y or N)?   Y
Enter coordinates of a point:   4.2  -6.8

More (Y or N)?   Y
Enter coordinates of a point:   7.1   6.5

More (Y or N)?   Y
Enter coordinates of a point:  -8.2   9.7

More (Y or N)?   Y
Enter coordinates of a point:  -3.3  -1.8

More (Y or N)?   N
```

Fig. 12.4. (cont.)

```
Contents of PointsFile:
   1.1     5.6
  -2.3     7.5
  -4.7    -3.8
  -1.0     0.0
   0.0     0.0
   0.0     4.0
   4.2    -6.8
   7.1     6.5
  -8.2     9.7
  -3.3    -1.8
```

The file buffer variable or file window can be used together with the predefined procedure *get* to access the components of a file. When a file is opened for input with the procedure *reset,* the corresponding file buffer variable is created. This buffer variable always contains a copy of the next component of the associated file, thus providing a "window" through which the next file component may be accessed.

The procedure *get* is called with a statement of the form

> *get* (*filename*)

This statement advances the data pointer to the next file component and copies it into the associated buffer variable *filename*↑. An input statement of the form

> *read* (*filename, variable-1, variable-2, . . . , variable-n*)

is equivalent, therefore, to the set of statements

> *variable-1* := *filename*↑;
> *get* (*filename*);
> *variable-2* := *filename*↑;
> *get* (*filename*);
>   ⋮
> *variable-n* := *filename*↑;
> *get* (*filename*)

The program in Figure 12.5 is a modification of the program in Figure 12.4 for creating and reading the file *PointsFile.* It uses the procedures *get* and *put* in place of *read* and *write.*

As we have seen, the procedures *read* and *get* advance the data pointer to the next file component and copy that component into the file window. If the data pointer is advanced to the end-of-file mark, the value of

> *eof* (*filename*)

is true (it is false otherwise), and the file buffer variable is undefined. Any subsequent calls to the procedures *read* or *get* result in an error, as an attempt is made to advance the data pointer beyond the end of the file.

FILES OF OTHER TYPES

```
PROGRAM CreateAndVerifyPointsFile (input, output, PointsFile);

(*********************************************************************

    Program to create the nontext file PointsFile having components
    of type DataPoint.  Coordinates of points are input by the user
    during execution.  The contents of the file are then verified
    by opening it for input, reading the contents, and displaying
    each point.

*********************************************************************)

TYPE
    DataPoint = RECORD
                    x, y : real
                END;
    FileOfDataPoints = FILE OF DataPoint;

VAR
    Point : DataPoint;                (* coordinates of a point *)
    PointsFile : FileOfDataPoints;    (* file of data points created *)
    Response : char;                  (* user response *)

BEGIN

    (* Create PointsFile *)

    rewrite (PointsFile);
    writeln;
    REPEAT
        write ('Enter coordinates of a point:   ');
        readln (PointsFile^.x, PointsFile^.y);
        put (PointsFile);
        writeln;
        write ('More (Y or N)?   ');
        readln (Response)
    UNTIL NOT (Response IN ['Y', 'y']);

    (* Verify the contents of PointsFile *)

    reset (PointsFile);
    writeln;
    writeln ('Contents of PointsFile:');
    WHILE NOT eof(PointsFile) DO
        BEGIN
            Point := PointsFile^;
            writeln (Point.x:5:1, Point.y:7:1);
            get (PointsFile)
        END (* WHILE *)
END.
```

Figure 12.5

The procedures *get* and *put* may be used with files of any type, including text files. Because text files are files of type *char,* the corresponding file buffer variables store single characters.

When the data pointer advances to an end-of-line mark in a text file, the value of

   eoln (*filename*)

becomes true (it is false otherwise), and a blank is placed in the file window. It is this blank that is read as the next file component, unless the data pointer is first advanced past the end-of-line mark. This can be done by using a statement of the form

> get (*filename*)

A statement of the form

> readln (*filename*)

may also be used to advance the data pointer past an end-of-line mark, as it is equivalent to

> **while not** *eoln* (*filename*) **do**
>   get (*filename*);
> get (*filename*)

Note that the file window *filename*↑ then contains the first character of the next line.

Our examples in this section have thus far dealt only with permanent (external) files, which exist before and/or after as well as during program execution. The comments in this section regarding files also apply to temporary (internal) files, that is, to files that exist only during execution of the program. One exception, however, is that names of temporary files are not listed in the program heading

A data-processing problem in which it is convenient to use temporary files is that of appending data to an existing permanent file. Because opening a file for output erases its previous contents, it is not possible to add the data by simply writing to the existing file. Instead, we must first copy the permanent file to a temporary work file, then add the additional data to this file, and finally, copy the resulting work file back to the permanent file. Because the work file is needed only during program execution, it may be a temporary file. The program in Figure 12.6 uses the temporary file *WorkFile* to append data entered from the terminal to the file *PointsFile* created earlier. Note that although *WorkFile* is not listed in the program heading, it is declared and opened in the usual manner.

In this example, it is necessary to move the contents of the original file into another file, and this is accomplished with the following statements:

```
while not eof(PointsFile) do
    begin
        WorkFile↑ : = PointsFile↑;
        put (WorkFile);
        get (PointsFile)
    end (* while *)
```

These statements copy one record at a time from the file *PointsFile* into *WorkFile*. This is necessary because the contents of a file can be accessed only one item at a time; it is *not* possible to copy one file into another file by using an assignment statement of the form *file-1* : = *file-2*.

Because it is frequently necessary to copy the contents of one file into

```
PROGRAM AppendToPointsFile (input, output, PointsFile);

(***********************************************************************

    Program to read coordinates of points entered by the user and
    add these points to the end of the previously created PointsFile.
    The contents of PointsFile are first copied into the temporary
    file WorkFile, the new points are appended to WorkFile, and
    the contents of WorkFile are then copied back to PointsFile.
    The contents of PointsFile are then verified by reading and
    displaying each point in it.

***********************************************************************)

TYPE
    DataPoint = RECORD
                    x, y : real
                END;
    FileOfDataPoints = FILE OF DataPoint;

VAR
    Point : DataPoint;                 (* coordinates of a point *)
    WorkFile,                          (* temporary file of data points *)
    PointsFile : FileOfDataPoints;     (* file of data points created *)
    Response : char;                   (* user response *)

BEGIN

    (* Copy contents of PointsFile to WorkFile *)

    reset (PointsFile);
    rewrite (WorkFile);
    WHILE NOT eof (PointsFile) DO
        BEGIN
            WorkFile^ := PointsFile^;
            put (WorkFile);
            get (PointsFile)
        END (* WHILE *);

    (* Append new points to the end of WorkFile *)

    writeln;
    REPEAT
        write ('Enter coordinates of a point:  ');
        readln (Point.x, Point.y);
        write (WorkFile, Point);
        writeln;
        write ('More (Y or N)?  ');
        readln (Response)
    UNTIL NOT (Response IN ['Y', 'y']);

    (* Now copy the contents of WorkFile to PointsFile *)

    reset (WorkFile);
    rewrite (PointsFile);
    WHILE NOT eof(WorkFile) DO
        BEGIN
            PointsFile^ := WorkFile^;
            put (PointsFile);
            get (WorkFile)
        END (* WHILE *);

    (* Finally, verify the contents of PointsFile *)
```

Figure 12.6

Fig. 12.6. (cont.)

```
    reset (PointsFile);
    writeln;
    writeln ('Contents of PointsFile:');
    WHILE NOT eof(PointsFile) DO
        BEGIN
            read (PointsFile, Point);
            writeln (Point.x:5:1, Point.y:7:1)
        END (* WHILE *)
END.
```

```
Sample run:
==========


Enter coordinates of a point:    6.6 -1.4

More (Y or N)?   Y
Enter coordinates of a point:    7.9  0

More (Y or N)?   Y
Enter coordinates of a point:   -1.7 -1.7

More (Y or N)?   Y
Enter coordinates of a point:   -6.7  0.5

More (Y or N)?   Y
Enter coordinates of a point:    0.9  10.1

More (Y or N)?   Y
Enter coordinates of a point:    9.7  10.3

More (Y or N)?   N

Contents of PointsFile:
   1.1     5.6
  -2.3     7.5
  -4.7    -3.8
  -1.0     0.0
   0.0     0.0
   0.0     4.0
   4.2    -6.8
   7.1     6.5
  -8.2     9.7
  -3.3    -1.8
   6.6    -1.4
   7.9     0.0
  -1.7    -1.7
  -6.7     0.5
   0.9    10.1
   9.7    10.3
```

another file, it is natural to develop a procedure to carry this out. The parameters of such a procedure are files, and they *must be declared as variable parameters.* Corresponding actual file parameters and formal file parameters must have the *same type,* and as for other structured data types, this means that they must be declared by the same or equivalent type identifiers (see Section 8.2). Using value parameters for files is *not* allowed, because this would require copying the entire actual file into the corresponding formal file parameter. The program in Figure 12.7 is a modification of the program

FILES OF OTHER TYPES

417

```
PROGRAM AppendToPointsFile (input, output, PointsFile);

(*********************************************************************

   Program to read coordinates of points entered by the user and
   add these points to the end of the previously created PointsFile.
   The contents of PointsFile are first copied into the temporary
   file WorkFile, the new points are appended to WorkFile, and
   the contents of WorkFile are then copied back to PointsFile.
   The contents of PointsFile are then verified by reading and
   displaying each point in it.

   *********************************************************************)

TYPE
   DataPoint = RECORD
                   x, y : real
               END;
   FileOfDataPoints = FILE OF DataPoint;

VAR
   Point : DataPoint;                 (* coordinates of a point *)
   WorkFile,                          (* temporary file of data points *)
   PointsFile : FileOfDataPoints;     (* file of data points created *)
   Response : char;                   (* user response *)

PROCEDURE CopyFile (VAR FromFile, ToFile : FileOfDataPoints);

   (*********************************************************************

      Procedure to copy the contents of FromFile into ToFile.

      *********************************************************************)

   BEGIN (* CopyFile *)
      reset (FromFile);
      rewrite (ToFile);
      WHILE NOT eof(FromFile) DO
         BEGIN
            ToFile^^ := FromFile^^;
            put (ToFile);
            get (FromFile)
         END (* WHILE *)
   END (* CopyFile *);

BEGIN (* main program *)

   (* Copy contents of PointsFile to WorkFile *)

   CopyFile (PointsFile, WorkFile);

   (* Append new points to the end of WorkFile *)

   REPEAT
      write ('Enter coordinates of a point:  ');
      readln (Point.x, Point.y);
      write (WorkFile, Point);
      writeln;
      write ('More (Y or N)?  ');
      readln (Response)
   UNTIL NOT (Response IN ['Y', 'y']);
   writeln;

   (* Now copy the contents of WorkFile to PointsFile *)
```

Figure 12.7

Fig. 12.7. (cont.)

```
    CopyFile (WorkFile, PointsFile);

    (* Finally, verify the contents of PointsFile *)

    reset (PointsFile);
    writeln;
    writeln ('Contents of PointsFile:');
    WHILE NOT eof(PointsFile) DO
        BEGIN
            read (PointsFile, Point);
            writeln (Point.x:5:1, Point.y:7:1)
        END (* WHILE *)
END (* main program *).
```

in Figure 12.6 that uses the procedure *CopyFile* to copy the contents of the original file *PointsFile* into the temporary work file and then to copy the updated work file back into the permanent file.

12.3

To illustrate the file-processing techniques discussed in this chapter, we consider the important problem of updating a master file with the contents of a transaction file. For example, the master file may be an inventory file that is to be updated with a transaction file containing the day's sales; or the master file might be a file of students' records and the transaction file a file containing the students' grades for the semester just concluded.

Application: Updating a File

In this section we consider the particular problem of updating a master file containing information regarding the users of a university's computing system. Suppose that components of the master file *UsersFile* are records containing the following information about each system user: identification number, name, password, limit on resources, and resources used to date. A daily log of the system's activity is also maintained. Among other items of information, this log contains a list of user identification numbers and resources used for each job entered into the system. This list is maintained in the transaction file *UpdateFile*. At the end of each day, the master file *UsersFile* must be updated with the contents of *UpdateFile* so as to incorporate the activities of that day. We assume that both *UsersFile* and *UpdateFile* have been sorted so that the identification numbers are in ascending order. An algorithm for performing the file update is as follows:

Algorithm.
1. Read the first record from *UsersFile* and assign it to *UserRec*.
2. Read the first record from *UpdateFile* and assign it to *UpdateRec*.
3. Set a boolean variable *EndOfUpdate* to *false*.
4. While *EndOfUpdate* is false, do the following updating:
   Compare the identification number in *UserRec* with that in *UpdateRec*. If they match, do the following:
   a. Update *UserRec* by adding the value of *ResourcesUsed* from *UpdateRec* to *UsedToDate* in *UserRec*.

b. If the end of *UpdateFile* has been reached,
    set *EndOfUpdate* to *true;*
otherwise,
    read the next value for *UpdateRec* from *UpdateFile.*
If the identification numbers do not match, do the following:
a. Write *UserRec* to *NewMasterFile.*
b. Read a new value for *UserRec* from *UsersFile.*
5. Because the last updated user record has not been written, write *UserRec* to *NewMasterFile.*
6. Copy any remaining records in *UsersFile* into *NewMasterFile.*

The program in Figure 12.8 implements this algorithm. Also shown are the contents of two small files used in a test run and the output file produced. These listings were obtained by executing a program that reads each record from a nontext file and then displays each field of the record by using a program segment of the form

```
reset (NonTextFile);
while not eof(NonTextFile) do
    begin
        with NonTextFile↑ do
            writeln (field-1, field-2, ... );
        get (NonTextFile)
    end
```

```
PROGRAM UserFileUpdate (UsersFile, UpdateFile, NewMasterFile);

(*****************************************************************

    Program to update the entries in the master file UsersFile with
    the entries in the transactions file UpdateFile.  The records
    in UsersFile contain the id-number, name, password, resource
    limit, and resources used to date for each system user;
    UpdateFile represents the log of a day's activities; each
    record contains a user's id-number and resources used for a
    job entered into the system.  Both files are sorted so that
    id-numbers are in ascending order.  The updated records are
    written to the output file NewMasterFile.

*****************************************************************)

CONST
    NameLength = 20;
    PasswordLength = 4;

TYPE
    NameString = PACKED ARRAY[1..NameLength] OF char;
    PasswordString = PACKED ARRAY[1..PasswordLength] OF char;
    UserRecord = RECORD
                    IdNumber : integer;
                    Name : NameString;
                    Password : PasswordString;
                    ResourceLimit,
                    UsedToDate : integer
                 END;
```

Figure 12.8

Fig. 12.8. (cont.)

```
      UserUpdateRecord = RECORD
                           UpdateNumber,
                           ResourcesUsed : integer
                        END;
      MasterFile = FILE OF UserRecord;
      TransactionFile = FILE OF UserUpdateRecord;

   VAR
      UserRec : UserRecord;                  (* record from UsersFile *)
      UpdateRec : UserUpdateRecord;          (* record from UpdateFile *)
      UsersFile,                             (* file containing user information *)
      NewMasterFile : MasterFile;            (* udpated user file *)
      UpdateFile : TransactionFile;          (* file to update UsersFile *)
      EndOfUpdate : boolean;                 (* signals end of UpdateFile *)

   BEGIN
      reset (UsersFile);
      reset (UpdateFile);
      rewrite (NewMasterFile);

   (* Read first record from each file *)

   read (UsersFile, UserRec);
   read (UpdateFile, UpdateRec);

   (* Update records of UsersFile with records of UpdateFile *)

   EndOfUpdate := false;
   WHILE NOT EndOfUpdate DO
      BEGIN
         WITH UserRec, UpdateRec DO
            IF IdNumber = UpdateNumber THEN       (* id-numbers match *)
               BEGIN
                  UsedToDate := UsedToDate + ResourcesUsed;
                  IF eof(UpdateFile) THEN
                     EndOfUpdate := true
                  ELSE
                     read (UpdateFile, UpdateRec)
               END (* IF *)
            ELSE                                  (* no match *)
               BEGIN
                  write (NewMasterFile, UserRec);
                  read (UsersFile, UserRec)
               END (* ELSE *)
      END (* WHILE *);

   (* Write UserRec to NewMasterFile; then copy any
      remaining records from UsersFile *)

   write (NewMasterFile, UserRec);
   WHILE NOT eof (UsersFile) DO
      BEGIN
         read (UsersFile, UserRec);
         write (NewMasterFile, UserRec)
      END (* WHILE *)
END.


Contents of UsersFile:
=======================

12300JOHN DOE              GERM 200 125
12310MARY SMITH            SNOW 200  75
```

Fig. 12.8. (cont.)

```
13320PETE VANDERVAN       RAIN 300 228
13400FRED JONES           FROM 100   0
13450JANE TARZAN          JUST 200  63
13490JACK JACKSON         DATE 300 128
14000ALBERT ALBERTS       LIST 400 255
14010JESSE JAMES          GUNS 100  38
14040DIRTY GERTIE         MESS 100  17
14100PRINCE ALBERT        CANS 300 185
```

```
Contents of UpdateFile:
=======================
```

```
12300 10
12300 24
12310 17
12310 3
12310 5
12310 10
13400 28
13450 25
13450 3
13450 1
13450 13
14010 22
14010 5
14010 12
14010 7
```

```
Contents of NewMasterFile:
==========================
```

```
12300JOHN DOE             GERM 200 159
12310MARY SMITH           SNOW 200 110
13320PETE VANDERVAN       RAIN 300 228
13400FRED JONES           FROM 100  28
13450JANE TARZAN          JUST 200 105
13490JACK JACKSON         DATE 300 128
14000ALBERT ALBERTS       LIST 400 255
14010JESSE JAMES          GUNS 100  84
14040DIRTY GERTIE         MESS 100  17
14100PRINCE ALBERT        CANS 300 185
```

Programming Pointers

In this chapter we reviewed text files and introduced files of other types. Many of the programming pointers at the end of Chapter 6 regarding text files apply to files in general. These are summarized here; for additional details, see the Programming Pointers of Chapter 6.

1. *Each file variable that names a permanent file must appear in the file list of the program heading and must be declared to be of file type in the variable section of the program.*

2. *Before any input operation can be attempted from a file, that file must be opened for input by using the procedure reset. Similarly, before any output to a file is attempted, the file must be opened for output by using the procedure rewrite.*

3. *Each call of the procedure reset positions the data pointer at the first component of the file and loads the file window with this first component.*

4. *Each call of the procedure rewrite empties the file, and any previous contents the file may have had are destroyed.*

5. *After values have been obtained for each variable in the input list, the procedure read advances the data pointer so that it is positioned immediately after the last file component read.*

6. *Nontext files have no line structure, and thus the procedures readln and writeln and the function eoln cannot be used with nontext files.*

7. *The data pointer in an input file always points to the next file component, and the file window contains that component.* For text files, the file components are characters. Consequently, if *Number* is a numeric variable, an assignment statement of the form

    Number $:=$ *TextFile*↑

    is an error, because it attempts to assign a character to *Number*.

8. *The procedure get advances the data pointer in the specified file before it copies a file component into the file window.* Thus, *get* should not be referenced before the processing of the file component currently in the file window has been completed.

9. *The procedure put transfers (does not copy) the component currently in the file window to the specified file.* Thus, *put* should not be called until the processing of the file component currently in the file window has been completed. After the procedure *put* has been executed, the file window is undefined.

Exercises

In these exercises, the files *UsersFile, InventoryFile, StudentFile, InventoryUpdate,* and *StudentUpdate* should be processed as files of records. For descriptions of these files, see Appendix E.

1. Each of the following program segments is intended to read a text file *InFile* in which each line contains an integer and to find the sum of all the integers in the file. Explain why each fails to do so.

(a) reset (*InFile*);
    Sum := 0;
    while not *eof(InFile)* **do**
        begin
            read (*InFile, Number*);
            Sum := *Sum* + *Number*
        end (* **while** *)

(b) reset (*InFile*);
    Sum := 0;
    readln (*InFile, Number*);
    while not *eof(InFile)* **do**
        begin
            Sum := *Sum* + *Number*;
            readln (*InFile, Number*)
        end (* **while** *)

(c) reset (*InFile*);
    Sum := 0;
    repeat
        get (*InFile*);
        Sum := *Sum* + *InFile*↑
    until *eof(InFile)*

2. Each of the following program segments is intended to display all nonblank characters in the text file *InFile,* with no error resulting. For each, describe a text file for which it fails.

(a) reset (*InFile*);
    read (*Infile, Ch*);
    repeat
        if *InFile*↑ = ' ' **then**
            get (*InFile*)
        else
            begin
                writeln (*InFile*↑);
                get (*InFile*)
            end (* **else** *)
    until *eof(InFile)*

(b) reset (*InFile*);
    read (*InFile, Ch*);
    while not *eof(InFile)* **do**
        begin
            while *Ch* = ' ' **do**
                read (*InFile, Ch*);
            writeln (*Ch*);
            read (*InFile, Ch*)
        end (* **while** *)

(c) reset (*InFile*);
    read (*InFile, Ch*);
    while not *eof(InFile)* **do**
        begin
            if *Ch* <> ' ' **then**
                writeln (*Ch*);
            read (*InFile, Ch*)
        end (* **while** *)

3. Modify Exercise 11 of Section 8.5 to print "personalized" junk-mail letters in which certain blanks in a form letter are filled in with personal information obtained from a file containing that information.

4. Write a program to read *UsersFile* to find and display the password for a specified user's identification number.

5. Write a program to read *StudentFile* and produce a report for all freshmen with GPAs below 2.0. This report should include the

student's first name, middle initial, last name, major, and cumulative GPA, with appropriate headings.

6. Write a program to search *InventoryFile* to find an item with a specified stock number. If a match is found, display the item name and number currently in stock; otherwise, display a message indicating that it was not found.

7. At the end of each month, a report is produced that shows the status of the account of each user in *UsersFile*. Write a program to read the current date and produce a report of the following form:

USER ACCOUNTS—09/30/83

USER NAME	USER-ID	RESOURCE LIMIT	RESOURCES USED
Joseph Miltgen	100101	$750	$380
Isaac Small	100102	$650	$598***
⋮	⋮	⋮	⋮

where the three asterisks (***) indicate that the user has already used 90 percent or more of the resources available to him or her.

8. Write a procedure to concatenate two files of identical type.

9. Write a procedure *Merge* to merge two files of type *integer* (or some other type) in which the integers are in ascending order. The integers in the resulting file should also be in ascending order. Use *Merge* in a program to demonstrate that it works correctly.

10. Write a program to update *InventoryFile* with *InventoryUpdate* to produce a new inventory file. Each record in *InventoryFile* for which there is no record in *InventoryUpdate* with a matching item number should remain unchanged. Each record with one or more corresponding records in *InventoryUpdate* should be updated with the entries in the update file. For transaction code R, the number of items returned should be added to the number in stock. For transaction code S, the number of items sold should be subtracted from the number currently in stock; if more items are sold than are in stock, display a message showing the order number, stock number, item name, and how many should be back-ordered (that is, the difference between the number ordered and the number in stock) and set the number currently in stock to zero.

11. Write a program to read the files *StudentFile* and *StudentUpdate* and produce an updated grade report. This grade report should show

(a) the current date.

(b) the student's name and student number.

(c) a list of the names, grade, and credits for each of the current courses under the headings COURSE, GRADE, and CRED-ITS.

(d) current GPA (multiply credits by numeric grade—A = 4.0, A– = 3.7. B+ = 3.3, B = 3.0, . . . , D– = 0.7, F = 0.0—for each course to find honor points earned for that course, sum these to find total new honor points, and then divide total new honor points by total new credits to give the current GPA, rounded to two decimal places).

(e) total credits taken (old credits from *StudentFile* plus total new credits).

(f) new cumulative GPA (first calculate old honor points = old credits times old cumulative GPA and then new cumulative GPA = sum of old honor points and new honor points divided by updated total credits).

12. Write a simple *text-formatting* program that reads a text file and produces another text file in which no lines are longer than some given length. Put as many words as possible on the same line. You will have to break some lines of the given file, but do not break any words or put punctuation marks at the beginning of a new line.

13. Extend the text-formatting program of Exercise 12 to right-justify each line in the new text file by adding evenly distributed blanks in lines where necessary. Also, preserve all indentation of lines in the given text file that begin a new paragraph.

14. Most system text formatters also allow command lines to be placed within the unformatted text. These command lines might have forms like the following:

.P *m n* Insert *m* blank lines before each paragraph and indent each paragraph *n* spaces.
.W *n*   Width of page (line length) is *n*.
.L *n*   Page length (number of lines per page) is *n*.
.I *n*   Indent all lines following this command line *n* spaces.
.U   Undent all following lines and reset to previous left margin.

Extend the program of Exercises 12 and 13 to implement command lines.

15. Modify and extend the *text-editor* program of Section 8.5 so that edit operations can be performed on the lines in a text file. Include commands of the following forms in the menu of options:

F *n*	Find and display the *n*th line of the file.
P *n*	Print *n* consecutive lines beginning with the current line.
M *n*	Move ahead *n* lines from the current line.
T	Move to the top line of the file.
C/*string1*/*string2*/	Change the current line by replacing *string1* with *string2*.
L *string*	Search the file starting from the current line to find a line containing *string*.
D *n*	Delete *n* consecutive lines beginning with the current line.
I *line*	Insert the given *line* after the current line.

16. Write a program to implement a computer dating service. It should accept a person's name, sex, and interests (sports, music preference, religion, and the like) and then search a file containing records having these items of information to find the person(s) of the opposite sex who has the most interests in common with the given individual.

17. A *pretty-printer* is a special kind of text formatter that reads a text file containing a program and then prints it in a "pretty" format. For example, a pretty-printer for Pascal programs might insert blank lines between procedures and indent and align statements within other statements, such as **if** statements, compound statements, type declarations, variable declarations, and the like to produce a format similar to that used in the sample programs of this text. Write a pretty-print program for Pascal programs to indent and align statements in a pleasing format.

18. Write a *menu-driven* program that uses *StudentFile* and *StudentUpdate* and allows (some of) the following options. For each option, write a separate procedure so that options and corresponding procedures can be easily added or removed.

   1. Locate a student's permanent record when given his or her student number and print it in a nicer format than that in which it is stored.

   2. Same as Option 1, but locate the record when given his or her name.

   3. Print a list of all student names and numbers in a given class (1, 2, 3, 4, 5).

   4. Same as Option 3, but for a given major.

   5. Same as Option 3, but for a given range of cumulative GPAs.

   6. Find the average cumulative GPAs for all
      (a) females   (b) males   (c) student with a specified

major   (d) all students. (These are suboptions of Menu Option 6.)

7. Produce updated grade reports having the following format:

GRADE REPORT—SEMESTER 1 12/23/83

DISPATCH UNIVERSITY

10103   James L. Johnson

	GRADE	CREDITS
ENGL 176	C	4
EDUC 268	B	4
EDUC 330	B+	3
P E 281	C	3
ENGR 317	D	4

Cumulative Credits: 33
Current GPA: 2.22
Cumulative GPA: 2.64

(See Exercise 11 for descriptions of these last items.)

8. Same as Option 7, but instead of producing grade reports, produce a new permanent file containing the updated total credits and new cumulative GPAs.

9. Produce an updated file when a student (a) drops or (b) adds a course.

10. Produce an updated file when a student (a) transfers into or (b) withdraws from the college.

13

Pointers and Dynamic Data Structures

Algorithms + Data Structures = Programs

NIKLAUS WIRTH

[Pointers] are like jumps, leaping wildly from one part of a data structure to another. Their introduction into high-level languages has been a step backward from which we may never recover.

C. A. R. HOARE

Variables are symbolic addresses of memory locations. This relationship between variable names and memory locations is a static relationship that is established by the declaration of the variables in a program unit and that exists throughout the execution of that unit. Although the contents of a memory location associated with a variable may change during execution, that is, the value of the variable may change, variables themselves can be neither created nor destroyed during execution. Consequently, the variables we have considered thus far are called *static variables*.

In some situations, however, we do not know in advance how much memory will be required by a program. In such cases it is convenient to have a method for acquiring additional memory locations as needed during program execution and to release them when they are no longer needed. Variables that are created and disposed of during execution are called *dynamic variables*. Pascal provides for such dynamic memory allocation and de-allocation by using *pointers* and the predefined procedures *new* and *dispose*.

Dynamic variables can be used to create *dynamic data structures* that can expand or contract as required during program execution. A dynamic data structure is a collection of elements called the *nodes* of the structure—usually of record type—that are linked together. This linking is established by associating with each node a pointer that points to the next node in the structure. One of the simplest linked structures is a *linked list* that might be pictured as follows:

| Data | Link | Data | Link | Data | Link | Data | Link |

Dynamic data structures are especially useful in storing and processing data sets that change frequently, for example, the collection of jobs that have been entered into a computer system and are awaiting execution or the collection of passenger names and seat assignments on a given airplane flight. In this chapter we consider pointers and the procedures *new* and *dispose* and how they can be used to construct and process dynamic data structures.

13.1.

Pointers; the Procedures *new* and *dispose*

As noted in the introduction, construction of a dynamic data structure requires the ability to allocate memory locations as needed. Because the number of locations is not known in advance, they cannot be allocated in the usual manner using variable declarations. Instead the procedure *new* is used for this purpose. When it is called, it returns the address of a memory location in which a node of the data structure can be stored. To reference this memory location so that data may be stored in it or retrieved from it, a special kind of variable called a *pointer variable,* or simply a *pointer,* is used. The value of a pointer is thus the address of some memory location.

The nodes of a dynamic data structure may be of any type but are most often of some record type. The type of a pointer that is used to reference the memory location storing one of these nodes must be specified by

↑ *type-indentifier*

or

^*type-identifier*

where *type-identifier* specifies the type of the nodes. The pointer is said to be *bound* to this type, as it may not be used for nodes of any other type. For example, if the nodes are records defined by

type
    Employeerecord = **record**
                Number : *integer*;
                HourlyRate : *real*
          end;

then the type of a pointer *EmployeePointer* for such nodes is

↑ *EmployeeRecord*

Such a pointer type declaration may be used in the variable section to declare that a variable is a pointer of this type

>**var**
>   *EmployeePointer* : ↑*EmployeeRecord*;

but it is usually preferable to assign it to a type identifier which is then used to specify the pointer type:

>**type**
>   *EmployeeRecord* = **record**
>   *Number* : *integer*;
>   *HourlyRate* : *real*
>   **end**;
>   *PointerToEmployeeRecord* = ↑*EmployeeRecord*;
>
>**var**
>   *EmployeePointer* : *PointerToEmployeeRecord*;

In either case, *EmployeePointer* is bound to the type *EmployeeRecord* and may be used only for nodes of this type.

The procedure *new* may then be used during program execution to acquire a memory location in which an employee record may be stored. This procedure is called with a statement of the form

>*new* (*pointer*)

which assigns the address of a memory location to *pointer*. Thus the statement

>*new* (*EmployeePointer*)

assigns to *EmployeePointer* a memory location in which an employee record can be stored. The diagram

indicates that *EmployeePointer* "points" to such a memory location. The boxes representing fields of an employee record contain question marks indicating that these fields are initially undefined.[1]

Each call of the procedure *new* acquires a new memory location and assigns its address to the specified pointer. Thus, if *TempPointer* is also a pointer of type *PointerToEmployeeRecord*, the statement

>*new* (*TempPointer*)

acquires a memory location pointed to by *TempPointer*.

----

[1] An alternative form of reference to the procedure *new* may be used for variant records which allows the system to allocate memory locations more efficiently. This form is described in Appendix F.

	Number	HourlyRate
EmployeePointer →	?	?

	Number	HourlyRate
TempPointer →	?	?

The value of a pointer is the address of a memory location. The value stored in this memory location is denoted by

pointer↑

or

*pointer^*

For the pointer *EmployeePointer* of type *PointerToEmployeeRecord,* the value of *EmployeePointer↑* is therefore the employee record pointed to by *EmployeePointer.* Thus, *EmployeePointer↑* is a variable of type *EmployeeRecord* and may be used in the same manner as is any other record variable of this type. For example, values can be assigned to the fields of this record by the input statement

readln (EmployeePointer↑.Number, EmployeePointer↑.HourlyRate)

or

with *EmployeePointer↑* **do**
    readln (Number, HourlyRate)

If the values

35331 7.50

are read, we then have

	Number	HourlyRate
EmployeePointer →	35331	7.50

The statement

TempPointer↑ := EmployeePointer↑

is a valid assignment statement, as both *EmployeePointer* and *TempPointer* are bound to the type *EmployeeRecord,* and so *EmployeePointer↑* and *TempPointer↑* are of the same type. It copies the contents of the record pointed to by *EmployeePointer* into the location pointed to by *TempPointer:*

	Number	HourlyRate
EmployeePointer →	35331	7.50

	Number	HourlyRate
TempPointer →	35331	7.50

Similarly, if *NewEmpRecord* is a static variable of type *EmployeeRecord*, the statement

$$NewEmpRecord := EmployeePointer\uparrow$$

is valid.

Because the values of pointers are addresses of memory locations, the operations that may be performed on them are limited: only assignment and comparison using the relational operators = and <> are allowed. If *pointer1* and *pointer2* are bound to the same type, an assignment statement of the form

$$pointer1 := pointer2$$

assigns the value of *pointer2* to *pointer1* so that both point to the same memory location. The previous location (if any) pointed to by *pointer1* can no longer be accessed unless pointed to by some other pointer. The following diagrams illustrate:

Before assignment:

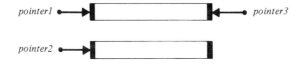

After assignment:

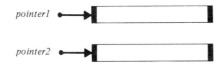

Before assignment:

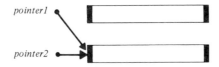

After assignment:

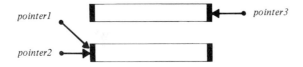

Because inaccessible nodes cannot be reused by the system, the situation pictured in the second diagram should be avoided.

As an illustration, suppose that *TempPointer* and *EmployeePointer* are pointers of type *PointerToEmployeeRecord*, pointing to the following employee records:

	Number	HourlyRate
TempPointer ●──▶	35331	7.50

	Number	HourlyRate
EmployeePointer ●──▶	44622	9.25

The assignment statement

$$TempPointer := EmployeePointer$$

causes *TempPointer* to point to the same employee record as does *Employee-Pointer,* and so the first employee record can no longer be accessed (unless pointed to by some other pointer of type *PointerToEmployeeRecord*):

	Number	HourlyRate
TempPointer ●	35331	7.50

	Number	HourlyRate
EmployeePointer ●──▶	44622	9.25

Note that this result is very different from that produced by the assignment statement

$$TempPointer\uparrow := EmployeePointer\uparrow$$

which copies the employee record pointed to by *EmployeePointer* into the memory location pointed to by *TempPointer:*

	Number	HourlyRate
TempPointer ●──▶	44622	9.25

	Number	HourlyRate
EmployeePointer ●──▶	44622	9.25

In some situations it may be necessary to indicate that a pointer does not point to any memory location. This can be done by using the reserved word **nil** in an assignment statement of the form

$$pointer := \textbf{nil}$$

The value **nil** may be assigned to a pointer of any type. We picture a nil pointer as simply a dot with no arrow emanating from it:

$$pointer \ \bullet$$

The relational operators = and <> can be used to determine whether two pointers *bound to the same type* point to the same memory location. Thus the boolean expression

$$TempPointer = EmployeePointer$$

is true only if *TempPointer* and *EmployeePointer* point to the same memory location

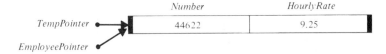

	Number	Hourly Rate
	44622	9.25

TempPointer

EmployeePointer

Note that this is *not* equivalent to the boolean expression

$$TempPointer\uparrow = EmployeePointer\uparrow$$

as this is an attempt to compare the record pointed to by *TempPointer* with the record pointed to by *EmployeePointer,* and records cannot be compared with relational operators; thus this is *not* a valid boolean expression. Obviously, if *TempPointer = EmployeePointer* is true, then the records pointed to by *TempPointer* and *EmployeePointer,* that is, the values of *TempPointer*↑ and *EmployeePointer*↑, are identical. The converse is not true, however. These two records may be identical, that is, *TempPointer*↑ and *EmployeePointer*↑ may have the same value, but *TempPointer = EmployeePointer* may be false.

The relational operators = and <> can also be used to determine whether the value of a pointer is **nil.** A boolean expression of the form

$$pointer = \textbf{nil}$$

is true if *pointer* has the value **nil** and is false if *pointer* points to some memory location. It should be noted that *pointer* having the value **nil** is *not* the same as *pointer* being undefined, as the boolean expression *pointer* = **nil** is valid in the first case but not in the second.

If the memory location pointed to by a pointer is no longer needed, it may be released and made available for later allocation by calling the procedure *dispose* with a statement of the form

$$dispose\ (pointer)$$

This procedure frees the memory location pointed to by *pointer* and leaves *pointer* undefined.[2]

Pointers may also be used as parameters in user-defined functions and procedures. These parameters may be either value or variable parameters, but corresponding pointer parameters must be bound to the same type. The value of a function may also be a pointer.[3] Pointers are used as parameters in several examples of the next section.

In the introduction to this chapter we noted that pointers are especially useful in constructing dynamic structures such as *linked lists.* Such linked structures are most appropriate when modeling a data set that changes fre-

Linked Lists, Stacks, Queues

---

[2] An alternative form of reference to the procedure *dispose* may be used for variant records; see Appendix F.

[3] If *f* is a pointer-valued function, a function reference of the form *f(actual-parameters)*↑ is not permitted. The value of the function must be assigned to a pointer variable, and this variable used to access the contents of the memory location to which it points.

quently because of deletion of items or insertion of new items. These operations of insertion and deletion can be carried out quite easily with linked structures. In this section we show how to construct linked lists and how to carry out the insertion and deletion operations in two special cases: stacks and queues. A *stack* is a list in which elements may be inserted or deleted at only one end of the list, called the *top* of the stack. A *queue* is a list in which elements may be deleted at only one end of the list, called the *front* or *head* of the queue, and inserted only at the other end, called the *back* or *rear* of the queue.

The nodes in a linked list contain two different kinds of information: (1) the actual data being stored and (2) a *link* or pointer to the next node in the list. A linked list might thus be pictured as

In this diagram, the dot in the last node having no arrow emanating from it represents a nil pointer and indicates that there is no next node in the list.

The nodes in a linked list are represented in Pascal as records having two kinds of fields, *data fields* and *link fields*. The data fields have types that are appropriate for storing the necessary information, and the link fields are of pointer type. To illustrate, suppose that we wish to store a list of integers in a linked list. The records that represent the nodes in this list may be declared by

```
type
     ListPointer  = ↑IntegerNode;
     IntegerNode = record
                          Number : integer;
                          Next : ListPointer
                   end;
```

Each node in this list is a record of type *IntegerNode* consisting of two fields. The first field *Number* is of integer type and is used to store the data. The second field *Next* is a pointer of type *ListPointer* and points to the next node in the list. Note that the definition of the pointer type *ListPointer*

```
     ListPointer = ↑IntegerNode;
```

precedes the definition of the record type *IntegerNode*. This is the only situation in which it is permissible to use an identifier (*IntegerNode*) before it is defined.

A linked list consists of a collection of nodes linked together by pointers, together with a pointer to the first element in the list. As a simple example, suppose that we wish to construct a linked list containing the three integers 95, 47, and 83. In the construction, we use two pointers: *FirstPointer* to point to the first node in the list and *TempPointer* as a temporary pointer.

```
     var
          FirstPointer, TempPointer : ListPointer;
```

To begin the construction, we first acquire a node in which to store the integer 83:

> *new* (*FirstPointer*);

The integer 83 is stored in the data field of this record

> *FirstPointer↑.Number* := 83;

and the link field is set to **nil:**

> *FirstPointer↑.Next* := **nil;**

To insert the value 47 at the beginning of this list, we acquire a new node temporarily pointed to by *TempPointer,*

> *new* (*TempPointer*);

and assign a value to its data field:

> *TempPointer↑.Number* := 47;

This node must then be joined to the list by setting its link field so that it points to the first node:

> *TempPointer↑.Next* := *FirstPointer*;

The pointer *FirstPointer* is then updated to point to this node

> *FirstPointer* := *TempPointer*;

so that our linked list now contains two nodes:

Another node is then created and attached to this linked list in a similar manner

> *new* (*TempPointer*);
> *TempPointer↑.Number* := 95;
> *TempPointer↑.Next* := *FirstPointer*;
> *FirstPointer* := *TempPointer*

giving the desired linked list:

In practice, such linked lists are usually constructed by reading the data values rather than assigning them by means of assignment statements. In this example, the linked list could be constructed by using the following program segment:

```
(* Initially the list is empty *)
FirstPointer := nil;

(* Read the data values and construct the list *)
while not eof do
    begin
        new (TempPointer);
        readln (TempPointer↑.Number);
        TempPointer↑.Next := FirstPointer;
        FirstPointer := TempPointer
    end (* while *)
```

To process the items in a linked list in the order in which they are stored, we begin at the first node and move through the list using the links until we reach the end of the list as indicated by a nil value for the link field. This is done by using an auxiliary pointer *CurrPointer* which initially points to the first node in the list and which is "moved" from one node to the next by assigning to *CurrPointer* the value of the link field of the current node:

```
CurrPointer := CurrPointer↑.Next
```

The integers in the linked list of our example can thus be displayed using the following program segment:

```
CurrPointer := FirstPointer;
while CurrPointer <> nil do
    begin
        writeln (CurrPointer↑.Number);
        CurrPointer := CurrPointer↑.Next
    end (* while *)
```

One simple but important data structure that is commonly implemented by a linked list is a *stack*. As noted earlier, a stack is a list in which elements may be inserted or deleted at only one end of the list, called the *top* of the stack. Such a data structure is a *Last-In-First-Out* (LIFO) structure, because the last item added to the stack will be the first one removed. This structure is called a stack because it functions in the same manner as does a spring-loaded stack of plates or trays used in a cafeteria. Plates are added to the stack by pushing them onto the top of the stack. When a plate is removed from the top of the stack, the spring causes the next plate to pop up. For this reason, the insertion and deletion operations for a stack are commonly called *push* and *pop*, respectively.

Stacks were introduced in Exercise 18 of Section 8.4 in connection with arrays. An array may be used to implement a stack only if the maximum size of the stack is known in advance. If this size is not known, the stack can better be implemented as a linked list.

In our earlier example in which we constructed the linked list of integers 95, 47, and 83, the elements were added at the beginning of the list. The technique used there is thus essentially the push operation for a stack. Assuming type declarations of the form

```
type
    DataType = . . . ; (* type of data part of nodes *)
    StackPointer = ↑StackNode;
    StackNode = record
                    Data : DataType;
                    Next : StackPointer
                end;
```

we can use the following procedure *Push* to carry out this operation:

procedure *Push* (**var** *TopPointer* : *StackPointer*; *Element* : *DataType*);
    (* Procedure to push *Element* onto the stack pointed to by *Top-Pointer*. The new pointer to the top of the stack is returned. *)

var
    TempPointer : *StackPointer*;

begin (* *Push* *)
    new (*TempPointer*);
    TempPointer↑.*Data* := *Element*;
    TempPointer↑.*Next* := *TopPointer*;
    TopPointer := *TempPointer*
end (* *Push* *);

To pop an element from a stack implemented as a linked list, we must remove the first node of this linked list. This can be done very easily by simply changing some pointers. For example, to delete the first node of the linked list

we need only change the value of *FirstPointer* so that it points to the second node:

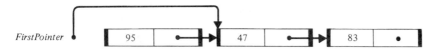

The statement

    FirstPointer := *FirstPointer*↑.*Next*

accomplishes this. However, to make this deleted node available for future allocation, we should also dispose of it. For this, we must maintain access to it by means of a temporary pointer so that the procedure *dispose* can be called to release this node. The following sequence of steps is the correct one to use:

TempPointer := *FirstPointer*;
FirstPointer := *FirstPointer*↑.*Next*;
dispose (*TempPointer*)

The following procedure *Pop* uses this sequence of statements. It returns the new value of the pointer to the top of the stack, the value *true* or *false* for the boolean variable *StackEmpty* to indicate whether the stack is empty, and the element popped from the stack (provided that the stack is not empty).

procedure *Pop* (**var** *TopPointer* : *StackPointer*; **var** *StackEmpty* : *boolean*;
             var *Element* : *DataType*);

    (* Procedure to pop and return the top *Element* from the stack
    pointed to by *TopPointer*. If the stack is empty, true is returned
    for *StackEmpty*; otherwise false is returned as well as the new
    pointer to the top of the stack. *)

var
    TempPointer : *StackPointer*;

begin (* *Pop* *)
    if *TopPointer* = **nil then**
        StackEmpty := *true*
    else
        begin
            StackEmpty := *false*;
            Element := *TopPointer*↑.*Data*;
            TempPointer := *TopPointer*;
            TopPointer := *TopPointer*↑.*Next*;
            dispose (*TempPointer*)
        end (* *else* *)
    end (* *Pop* *);

As a simple illustration of the push and pop stack operations, consider the problem of reversing the characters in a string. The program in Figure 13.1 reads a sequence of characters and pushes each character onto a stack. When the special symbol $ is read, the stack is emptied by popping individual characters from the stack and displaying them. Because a stack is a last-in-first-out structure, the characters are displayed in reverse order.

A second data structure that is often implemented as a linked list is a *queue*. Recall that a queue is a list in which deletions are made at one end of the list, called its *front* or *head,* and insertions are made at the other end, called the *back* or *rear* of the queue. This data structure is thus a *First-In-First-Out* (FIFO) structure, as the items are removed from the list in the same order as they are entered.

For stacks, insertions and deletions are made at only one end of the stack; consequently, only one pointer to the top of the stack is needed. For

```
PROGRAM ReverseAString (input, output);

(*****************************************************************

   Program to reverse a string by pushing the characters onto a
   stack until the end-of-string mark ($) is read, then popping and
   displaying the characters on the stack.  The stack is
   implemented as a linked list.

*****************************************************************)

TYPE
   DataType = char;
   StackPointer = ^StackNode;
   StackNode = RECORD
                  Data : DataType;
                  Next : StackPointer
               END;

VAR
   TopPointer : StackPointer;        (* pointer to top of stack *)
   Symbol : char;                    (* current character from string or stack *)
   EndOfString,                      (* signals end of string mark $ *)
   StackEmpty : boolean;             (* signals empty stack *)

PROCEDURE Push (VAR TopPointer : StackPointer; Element : DataType);

   (*****************************************************************

      Procedure to push Element onto the stack pointed to by TopPointer.
      The new pointer to the top of the stack is returned.

   *****************************************************************)

   VAR
      TempPointer: StackPointer;  (* temporary pointer *)

   BEGIN (* Push *)
      new (TempPointer);
      TempPointer^.Data := Element;
      TempPointer^.Next := TopPointer;
      TopPointer := TempPointer
   END (* Push *);

PROCEDURE Pop (VAR TopPointer: StackPointer; VAR Element : DataType;
               VAR StackEmpty : boolean);

   (*****************************************************************

      Procedure to pop and return the top Element from the stack
      pointed to by TopPointer.  If the stack is empty, true is
      returned for StackEmpty; otherwise false is returned as well
      as the new pointer to the top of the stack.

   *****************************************************************)

   VAR
      TempPointer: StackPointer;  (* temporary pointer *)
```

Figure 13.1

Fig. 13.1 (cont.)

```
    BEGIN (* Pop *)
       IF TopPointer = NIL THEN
          StackEmpty := true
       ELSE
          BEGIN
             StackEmpty := false;
             Element := TopPointer^.Data;
             TempPointer := TopPointer;
             TopPointer := TempPointer^.Next;
             dispose (TempPointer)
          END (* ELSE *)
    END (* Pop *);

BEGIN (* main program *)

   (* Initialize stack as empty *)

   TopPointer := NIL;

   (* Read the string, pushing each character onto stack *)

   writeln ('Enter the string to be reversed:');
   EndOfString := false;
   WHILE NOT EndOfString DO
      BEGIN
         read (Symbol);
         IF Symbol = '$' THEN
            EndOfString := true
         ELSE
            Push (TopPointer, Symbol)
      END (* WHILE *);
   readln;

   (* Now pop and display elements from the stack *)

   writeln;
   writeln ('Reversed string:');
   Pop (TopPointer, Symbol, StackEmpty);
   WHILE NOT StackEmpty DO
      BEGIN
         write (Symbol);
         Pop (TopPointer, Symbol, StackEmpty)
      END (* WHILE *);
   writeln
END (* main program *).


Sample runs:
===========

Enter the string to be reversed:
Kelloggs Cornflakes$

Reversed string:
sekalfnroC sggolleK



Enter the string to be reversed:
able was I ere I saw elba$

Reversed string:
able was I ere I saw elba
```

a queue, however, deletions are made at one end and insertions at the other, and thus we use two pointers *FrontPointer* and *RearPointer*.

A procedure for deleting an element from a queue is similar to the procedure for popping an element from a stack, as we need only change the value of *FrontPointer* so that it points to the second node in the queue. Assuming type declarations of the form

```
type
    DataType = . . . ; (* Type of data part of nodes *)
    QueuePointer = ↑QueueNode;
    QueueNode = record
                    Data : DataType;
                    Next : QueuePointer
                end;
```

we can use the following procedure to carry out this operation:

```
procedure QueueDelete (var FrontPointer : QueuePointer;
                       var QueueEmpty : boolean; var Element : DataType);

    (* Procedure to delete and return Element from the front of the
       linked queue pointed to by FrontPointer. If the queue is empty
       (FrontPointer = nil), true is returned for QueueEmpty; otherwise,
       false is returned as well as the new front pointer. *)

    var
        TempPointer : QueuePointer;

    begin (* QueueDelete *)
        if FrontPointer = nil then
            QueueEmpty := true
        else
            begin
                QueueEmpty := false;
                Element := FrontPointer↑.Data;
                TempPointer := FrontPointer;
                FrontPointer := FrontPointer↑.Next;
                dispose (TempPointer)
            end (* else *)
    end (* QueueDelete *);
```

Inserting an element at the end of a queue requires the following steps:

1. Obtain a node to store the element.
2. Load the data into this node and set its link field to **nil.**
3. If the queue is empty (as indicated by *FrontPointer* having the value **nil**), set *FrontPointer* to point to this node; otherwise, join this node to the queue by setting the link field of the last node to point to this node.
4. Set *RearPointer* to point to this new node.

To illustrate, consider the following queue:

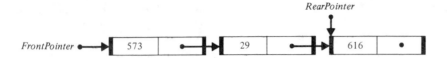

Inserting the number 127 produces the following queue:

The following procedure *QueueInsert* uses these steps to add an element to a queue:

```
procedure QueueInsert (var FrontPointer, RearPointer : QueuePointer;
                            Element : DataType);

   (* Procedure to add Element to the rear of the linked queue pointed
      to by RearPointer. New pointers for the queue are returned. *)

var
      TempPointer : QueuePointer;

begin (* QueueInsert *)
      new (TempPointer);
      TempPointer↑.Data := Element;
      TempPointer↑.Next := nil;
      if FrontPointer = nil then (* queue empty *)
         FrontPointer := TempPointer
      else
            RearPointer↑.Next := TempPointer;
      RearPointer := TempPointer
end (* QueueInsert *);
```

13.3

General Linked Lists, Ordered Lists

In the previous section we used linked lists to implement the stack and queue data structures. In the case of a stack, we were concerned with the element at one end of the list, as insertions and deletions were carried out at only one end. In the case of queues, we were concerned with the elements at each end of the list, as insertions were carried out at one end of the list and deletions at the other end. In general, however, we do not restrict our attention to the elements at the ends of the list but rather are interested in inserting or deleting at any point in the list. In this section we develop such general insertion and deletion procedures and apply them to both unordered and ordered lists.

We begin by considering the problem of searching a linked list to find the location of a particular item in the list or to ascertain that it is not in the list. For example, consider a linked list of employee records in which each node is a record containing an employee number and an hourly rate as data fields and a pointer to the next employee record. Suppose that the following declarations have been made:

type
  EmployeePointer = ↑*EmployeeRecord*;
  EmployeeRecord = **record**
        Number : *integer*;
        HourlyRate : *real*;
        Next : *EmployeePointer*
      end;

var
  FirstPointer, *CurrPointer* : *EmployeePointer*;
  EmpNumber : *integer*;
  NewRate : *real*;
  Found : *boolean*;

Access to this list of records is by means of the pointer *FirstPointer* which points to the first employee record:

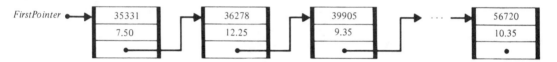

   To locate a record for a particular employee, we use an auxiliary pointer *CurrPointer* that begins at the first node

  CurrPointer := *FirstPointer*

and moves through the list via the link fields

  CurrPointer := *CurrPointer*↑.*Next*

until the desired node is found. If we are searching for the record of the employee whose number is *EmpNumber*, the following statements may be used:

  Found := *false*;
  CurrPointer := *FirstPointer*;
  while (*CurrPointer* <> **nil**) **and** (**not** *Found*) **do**
   if *CurrPointer*↑.*Number* = *EmpNumber* **then**
    Found := *true*
   else
    CurrPointer := *CurrPointer*↑.*Next*

   The above **while** loop is terminated when the desired record is found, in which case *CurrPointer* points to that record, or the end of the list is reached and the record is not found; in this last case, *CurrPointer* has the value **nil.** If the record is found, then the information in this record can be displayed

```
    if CurrPointer <> nil then
        writeln ('Hourly rate for employee ', EmpNumber:1, ' is ',
                CurrPointer↑.HourlyRate:4:2)
    else
        writeln ('Employee ', EmpNumber:1, ' not found')
```

or perhaps modified, for example, by changing the hourly rate

```
    if CurrPointer <> nil then
        CurrPointer↑.HourlyRate := NewRate
    else
        writeln ('Employee ', EmpNumber:1, ' not found)
```

or processed in some other way.

We can use a similar technique to *traverse* a linked list, examining each of the nodes in this list. For example, the statements

```
CurrPointer := FirstPointer;
while CurrPointer <> nil do
    begin
        with CurrPointer↑ do
            writeln ('Number: ', EmpNumber:1,
                    ' Rate: $', HourlyRate:4:2);
        CurrPointer := CurrPointer↑.Next
    end (* while *)
```

display the employee number and hourly rate for each employee in the list of employee records.

As with stacks and queues, insertion and deletion are the two basic operations performed on general linked lists. There are two cases to consider for insertion: (1) inserting an item at the beginning of the list; (2) inserting an item after some specified item in the list. The first case is simply the push operation for stacks and consists of the following steps:

1. Obtain a new node.
2. Load the data into its data field.
3. Set the link field of this node to point to the first node in the list.
4. Reset the pointer *FirstPointer* to point to this new node.

For the second case, suppose that the node pointed to by *NewNode-Pointer* is to be inserted between the nodes pointed to by *PredPointer* and *CurrPointer*:

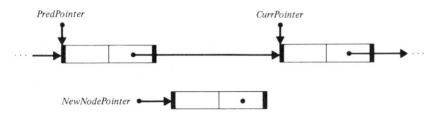

Insertion is accomplished by setting the pointer in the link field of the new node to point to the node pointed to by *CurrPointer*

$$NewNodePointer\uparrow.Next := CurrPointer$$

and then resetting the pointer in the link field of the node pointed to by *PredPointer* to point to the new node

$$PredPointer\uparrow.Next := NewNodePointer$$

The following diagram illustrates:

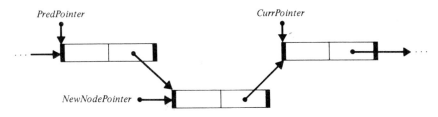

Assuming type declarations of the form

type
    DataType = . . . ; (* type of data part of nodes *)
    ListPointer = ↑*ListNode*;
    ListNode = **record**
                Data : *DataType*;
                Next : *ListPointer*
        end;

we can incorporate the preceding techniques for inserting an element into a general linked list as follows:

    procedure *Insert* (**var** *FirstPointer* : *ListPointer*;
                   PredPointer, *CurrPointer* : *ListPointer*; *Element* : *DataType*);

      (* Procedure to insert *Element* into the list having first node pointed
      to by *FirstPointer*. This element is to be inserted between the
      nodes pointed to by *PredPointer* and *CurrPointer*. A **nil** value
      for *PredPointer* indicates insertion at the beginning of the list. *)

    var
        NewNodePointer : *ListPointer*;

    begin (* *Insert* *)
       new (*NewNodePointer*);
       NewNodePointer↑.*Data* := *Element*;
       if *PredPointer* = **nil then**
          begin
             NewNodePointer↑.*Next* := *FirstPointer*;
             FirstPointer := *NewNodePointer*
          end (* **if** *)

            else
                begin
                    NewNodePointer↑.Next := *CurrPointer*;
                    PredPointer↑.Next := *NewNodePointer*
                end (* *else* *)
        end (* *Insert* *);

As with insertion, there are two cases to consider for the deletion operation: (1) deleting the first element in the list, and (2) deleting an element that has a predecessor. The first case is simply the pop operation for stacks and consists of the following steps, assuming that *CurrPointer* points to the node to be deleted.

1. Set *FirstPointer* to point to the second node in the list.
2. Dispose of the node pointed to by *CurrPointer*.

For the second case, suppose that the predecessor of the node to be deleted is pointed to by *PredPointer:*

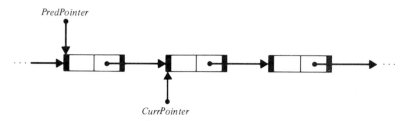

Deletion is accomplished by setting the link field of the node pointed to by *PredPointer* so that it points to the successor of the node to be deleted:

   PredPointer↑.Next := *CurrPointer↑.Next*

The following diagram illustrates:

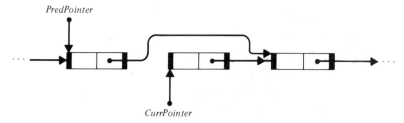

The procedure *Delete* implementing these techniques is as follows:

   procedure *Delete* (**var** *FirstPointer* : *ListPointer*;
                    PredPointer, *CurrPointer* : *ListPointer*;
                    var *Element* : *DataType*);

   (* Procedure to delete an element from the list whose first node is
      pointed to by *FirstPointer* and return *Element*. *CurrPointer* points
      to the node to be deleted; *PredPointer* points to its predecessor
      or is **nil** if there is none. *)

```
begin (* Delete *)
    if PredPointer = nil then (* first node to be deleted *)
        FirstPointer := FirstPointer↑.Next
    else                      (* node has a predecessor *)
        PredPointer↑.Next := CurrPointer↑.Next;
    Element := CurrPointer↑.Data;
    dispose (CurrPointer)
end (* Delete *);
```

One of the important data-processing problems we have considered on several occasions is that of sorting a list of items. In each of our examples, these items were stored in an array, as direct access to each element of the array was required to use the sorting techniques we considered. However, when the problem also involves insertions and deletions of items, an array is not the best data structure to use. For if an item is inserted into a sorted array, all the array elements following it must be moved to make room for it; and when an item is deleted from a sorted array, all items following it must be moved forward, or a "hole" results. Maintaining an ordered list whose contents change frequently because of insertions and deletions is done most efficiently by using an ordered linked list.

An *ordered linked list* is a linked list in which the nodes are linked in such a way that the items stored in the nodes occur in ascending (or descending) order as the list is traversed. If the data part of a node consists of more than one field, then one of these fields is designated as the *key field,* and the ordering is based on the values that appear in this field.

The procedures *Insert* and *Delete* use the two pointers *PredPointer* and *CurrPointer.* For *Insert,* the item is to be inserted between the nodes pointed to by *PredPointer* and *CurrPointer;* and for *Delete, CurrPointer* points to the node to be deleted and *PredPointer* to its predecessor. To use these procedures, a search procedure is needed to position these pointers. The following procedure *Search* advances *CurrPointer* through an ordered linked list until either it reaches the first node containing a value in its key field that is greater than or equal to the item sought, or it reaches the end of the list, in which case a **nil** value is returned for *CurrPointer.* The pointer *PredPointer* points to the predecessor of the node pointed to by *CurrPointer* or has the value **nil** if *CurrPointer* points to the first node in the list.

```
procedure Search (FirstPointer : ListPointer; Item : KeyType;
                  var PredPointer, CurrPointer : ListPointer);
```

(* Procedure to search an ordered linked list having first node pointed to by *FirstPointer* for a node containing *Item* in its key field or for a position to insert a new node. *CurrPointer* points to the first node containing key value > = *Item* or is **nil** if *Item* follows all keys in the list. *PredPointer* points to its predecessor or is **nil** if *Item* precedes all keys in the list. This procedure assumes the key fields are in ascending order; for descending order, change > = to < = in the **if** statement. *)

```
var
    Found : boolean;
```

```
begin (* Search *)
    CurrPointer := FirstPointer;
    PredPointer := nil;
    Found := false;
    while (not Found) and (CurrPointer <> nil) do
        if CurrPointer↑.Data.Key > = Item then
            Found := true
        else
            begin
                PredPointer := CurrPointer;
                CurrPointer := CurrPointer↑.Next
            end (* else *)
end (* Search *);
```

This procedure is appropriate for ordered linked lists in which the nodes are records in which *Key* is a field identifier of type *KeyType,* and the list is ordered so that the values stored in the field *Key* are in ascending order.

The insertion and deletion operations for ordered linked lists are now easy. We need only find the location of the item to be deleted or the position where it is to be inserted by using the procedure *Search* and then call the appropriate procedure *Insert* or *Delete.* The program in Figure 13.2 uses these procedures to maintain an ordered linked list of employee records, each of which contains an employee's name, age, number of dependents, and hourly rate. This list is ordered so that employee names are in alphabetical order. Because the following declarations are made

```
type
    NameString = packed array[1..NameLength] of char;
    EmployeeRecord = record
                        Name : NameString;
                        Age, Dependents : integer;
                        HourlyRate : real
                    end;
    ListPointer = ↑ListNode;
    ListNode = record
                    Data : EmployeeRecord;
                    Next : ListPointer
                end;
```

the procedures *Search, Insert,* and *Delete* given in this section have been implemented with *Key* replaced with *Name, KeyType* with *NameString,* and *DataType* with *EmployeeRecord.* In this program, the list of operations that may be performed on the list is displayed, and the user selects options from this list or menu:

1. Print the list of options.
2. Terminate processing.
3. Build the list by reading the records from a file.
4. Retrieve an employee's record and display it.
5. Insert the record for a new employee into the list.
6. Delete the record of an employee from the list.
7. List the names of all employees in the list.
8. Copy the updated list to the permanent file of employee records.

```
PROGRAM LinkedEmployeeRecords (input, output, EmpFile);

(*********************************************************************

    Program to process employee records.  Options are displayed
    by procedure PrintMenu.  The records are stored in an ordered
    linked list; employee names are in alphabetical order.

*********************************************************************)


CONST
    NameLength = 20;
    NumberOfOptions = 8;


TYPE
    NameString = PACKED ARRAY[1..NameLength] OF char;
    EmployeeRecord = RECORD
                        Name : NameString;
                        Age, Dependents : integer;
                        HourlyRate : real
                     END;
    EmployeeFile = FILE of EmployeeRecord;
    ListPointer = ^ListNode;
    ListNode = RECORD
                  Data : EmployeeRecord;
                  Next : ListPointer
               END;


VAR
    FirstPointer : ListPointer;    (* pointer to first employee record *)
    Option : integer;              (* option selected by user *)
    EmpRecord : EmployeeRecord;    (* record for an employee *)
    EmpFile : EmployeeFile;        (* permanent file of employee records *)

PROCEDURE ReadName (VAR EmpName : NameString; VAR More : boolean);

    (*********************************************************************

       Procedure to read an employee name, padding with blanks where
       necessary; More is false if the string  Q*  is read.

    *********************************************************************)


    VAR
       i : integer;   (* index *)

    BEGIN (* ReadName *)
       More := true;
       FOR i := 1 TO NameLength DO
          IF NOT eoln THEN
             read (EmpName[i])
          ELSE
             EmpName[i] := ' ';
       readln;
       IF (EmpName[1] = 'Q') AND (EmpName[2] = '*') THEN
          More := false
    END (* ReadName *);

PROCEDURE Search (FirstPointer : ListPointer; Item : NameString;
                  VAR PredPointer, CurrPointer : ListPointer);
```

Figure 13.2

Fig. 13.2 (cont.)

```
(*********************************************************************

    Procedure to search an ordered linked list having first node
    pointed to by FirstPointer for a node containing Item in its
    Name field or for a position to insert a new node.
    CurrPointer points to first node containing Name >= Item
    or is NIL if none is found; PredPointer points to its
    predecessor or is NIL if Item precedes all names in the list.
    This procedure assumes the Name fields are in ascending order;
    for descending order, change >= to <= in the IF statement.

*********************************************************************)

VAR
    Found : boolean;      (* indicates when position for item found *)

BEGIN (* Search *)
    CurrPointer := FirstPointer;
    PredPointer := NIL;
    Found := false;
    WHILE (NOT Found) AND (CurrPointer <> NIL) DO
        IF CurrPointer^.Data.Name >= Item THEN
            Found := true
        ELSE
            BEGIN
                PredPointer := CurrPointer;
                CurrPointer := CurrPointer^.Next
            END (* ELSE *)
END (* Search *);

PROCEDURE Insert (VAR FirstPointer : ListPointer; PredPointer,
                CurrPointer : ListPointer; Element : EmployeeRecord);

(*********************************************************************

    Procedure to insert Element into list having first node
    pointed to by FirstPointer.  This element is to be inserted
    between the nodes pointed to by PredPointer and CurrPointer.
    A NIL value for PredPointer indicates insertion at the
    beginning of the list.  Currpointer = NIL indicates
    insertion at the end of the list.

*********************************************************************)

VAR
    NewNodePointer: ListPointer;  (* new node in which to store item *)

BEGIN (* Insert *)
    new (NewNodePointer);
    NewNodePointer^.Data := Element;
    IF PredPointer = NIL THEN
        BEGIN
            NewNodePointer^.Next := FirstPointer;
            FirstPointer := NewNodePointer
        END (* IF *)
    ELSE
        BEGIN
            NewNodePointer^.Next := CurrPointer;
            PredPointer^.Next := NewNodePointer
        END (* ELSE *)
END (* Insert *);
```

Fig. 13.2 (cont.)

```
PROCEDURE PrintMenu;                                          (* OPTION 1 *)

   (*******************************************************************

        Procedure to print the list of options.

   *******************************************************************)

   BEGIN (* PrintMenu *)
      writeln ('The following options are available:');
      writeln ('(1)  Print this list of options');
      writeln ('(2)  Stop');
      writeln ('(3)  Get list of employee records from file');
      writeln ('(4)  Retrieve an employee''s record');
      writeln ('(5)  Insert the record for a new employee');
      writeln ('(6)  Delete the record of an employee');
      writeln ('(7)  List names of all employees');
      writeln ('(8)  Copy updated list to the permanent file')
   END (* PrintMenu *);

PROCEDURE AddToList (VAR FirstPointer : ListPointer;    (* OPTIONS 3 & 5 *)
                     EmpRecord : EmployeeRecord; Code : char);

   (*******************************************************************

       Procedure for adding to a linked list (possibly empty) of
       employee records by repeated calls to the Insert procedure;
       code = 'F' for input from a file, else 'T'.

   *******************************************************************)

   VAR
      More : boolean;          (* indicates if more records *)
      CurrPointer,             (* points to place to insert *)
      PredPointer: ListPointer; (* points to predecessor *)

   BEGIN (* AddToList *)
      More := true;
      IF Code = 'T' THEN
         writeln ('To stop, enter  Q*  for employee name.');
      WHILE More DO
         BEGIN
            WITH EmpRecord DO
               IF Code = 'T' THEN
                  BEGIN
                     write ('Name:  ');
                     ReadName (Name, More);
                     IF More THEN
                        BEGIN
                           write ('Age:  ');
                           readln (Age);
                           write ('Dependents:  ');
                           readln (Dependents);
                           write ('Hourly rate:  ');
                           readln (HourlyRate)
                        END (* IF *)
                  END (* IF *);
            IF More THEN
               BEGIN
                  Search (FirstPointer, EmpRecord.Name, PredPointer,
                        CurrPointer);
                  Insert (FirstPointer, PredPointer, CurrPointer, EmpRecord)
               END (* IF *);
```

Fig. 13.2 (cont.)

```
                IF Code = 'F' THEN
                    More := false
            END (* WHILE *)
    END (* AddToList *);

PROCEDURE CreateList (VAR EmpFile : EmployeeFile;
                      VAR FirstPointer : ListPointer);   (* OPTION 3 *)

    (*****************************************************************

        Procedure to read employee records from EmpFile and construct
        linked list of these records with first record pointed to by
        FirstPointer.

    *****************************************************************)

    BEGIN (* CreateList *)
        reset (EmpFile);
        WHILE NOT eof(EmpFile) DO
            BEGIN
                AddToList (FirstPointer, EmpFile^, 'F');
                get (EmpFile)
            END (* WHILE *)
    END (* CreateList *);

PROCEDURE RetrieveRecords (FirstPointer : ListPointer);  (* OPTION 4 *)

    (*****************************************************************

        Procedure to read employee names, retrieve their records from
        the linked list of employee records with first record pointed
        to by FirstPointer, and display them.

    *****************************************************************)

    VAR
        EmpName : NameString;       (* name of employee *)
        i : integer;                (* index *)
        CurrPointer,                (* pointer to record *)
        PredPointer: ListPointer;   (* pointer to predecessor *)
        More : boolean;             (* indicates if more records *)

    BEGIN (* RetrieveRecords *)
        writeln ('To stop, enter  Q*  for employee name.');
        More := true;
        WHILE More DO
            BEGIN
                write ('Name of employee:  ');
                ReadName (EmpName, More);
                IF More THEN
                    BEGIN
                        Search (FirstPointer, EmpName, PredPointer, CurrPointer);
                        WITH CurrPointer^ , Data DO
                            IF (CurrPointer = NIL) OR (Name <> EmpName) THEN
                                writeln (EmpName, ' not Found')
                            ELSE
                                BEGIN
                                    writeln ('Employee name:  ', Name);
                                    writeln ('Age:  ', Age:2);
                                    writeln ('# dependents:  ', Dependents:1);
                                    writeln ('Hourly rate:  $', HourlyRate:6:2)
                                END (* ELSE *)
                    END (* IF *);
```

Fig. 13.2 (cont.)

```
                        writeln
                   END (* WHILE *)
          END (* RetrieveRecords *);

      PROCEDURE DeleteEmployees (VAR FirstPointer: ListPointer);   (* OPTION 6 *)

          (*****************************************************************

              Procedure to remove employee records from the list having
              first node pointed to by FirstPointer.

          ****************************************************************)

          VAR
              EmpName : NameString;           (* name of employee *)
              EmpRecord :  EmployeeRecord;    (* an employee record *)
              CurrPointer,                    (* pointer to node to be deleted *)
              PredPointer : ListPointer;      (* pointer to predecessor *)
              More,                           (* indicates if more records *)
              ListEmpty : boolean;            (* indicates if list is empty *)

          PROCEDURE Delete (VAR FirstPointer : ListPointer; PredPointer,
                            CurrPointer: ListPointer; VAR Element: EmployeeRecord);

              (*****************************************************************

                  Procedure to delete an element from a list whose first node
                  is pointed to by FirstPointer and return Element; CurrPointer
                  points to the node to be deleted; PredPointer points to its
                  predecessor or is NIL if there is none.

              ****************************************************************)

              BEGIN (* Delete *)
                  IF PredPointer = NIL THEN     (* first node to be deleted *)
                      FirstPointer := FirstPointer^.Next
                  ELSE                          (* node has a predecessor *)
                      PredPointer^.Next := CurrPointer^.Next;
                  Element := CurrPointer^.Data;
                  dispose (CurrPointer)
              END (* Delete *);

          BEGIN (* DeleteEmployees *)
              writeln ('To stop, enter  Q*  for employee name.');
              More := true;
              WHILE More DO
                  BEGIN
                      write ('Name of employee:  ');
                      ReadName (EmpName, More);
                      IF More THEN
                          BEGIN
                              Search (FirstPointer, EmpName, PredPointer, CurrPointer);
                              IF (CurrPointer = NIL) THEN
                                  writeln (EmpName, ' not Found')
                              ELSE IF (CurrPointer^.Data.Name <> EmpName) THEN
                                  writeln (EmpName, ' not Found')
                              ELSE
                                  Delete (FirstPointer, PredPointer, CurrPointer,
                                          ListEmpty, CurrPointer^.Data);
                          END (* IF *)
                  END (* WHILE *)
          END (* DeleteEmployees *);
```

Fig. 13.2 (cont.)

```
PROCEDURE PrintAllEmployees (FirstPointer : ListPointer);(* OPTION 7 *)

   (*****************************************************************

      Procedure to print names of all employees in the linked list
      with first record pointed to by FirstPointer.

   *****************************************************************)

   VAR
      CurrPointer : ListPointer;      (* pointer to current node *)

   BEGIN (* PrintAllEmployees *)
      CurrPointer := FirstPointer;
      WHILE CurrPointer <> NIL DO
         BEGIN
            writeln (CurrPointer^.Data.Name);
            CurrPointer := CurrPointer^.Next
         END (* WHILE *)
   END (* PrintAllEmployees *);

PROCEDURE CopyListToFile (FirstPointer: ListPointer;      (* OPTION 8 *)
                          VAR EmpFile : EmployeeFile);

   (*****************************************************************

      Procedure to write the list pointed to by FirstPointer to
      EmpFile.

   *****************************************************************)

   VAR
      CurrPointer: ListPointer;    (* pointer to current node *)

   BEGIN (* CopyListToFile *)
      rewrite (EmpFile);
      CurrPointer := FirstPointer;
      WHILE CurrPointer <> NIL DO
         BEGIN
            write (EmpFile, CurrPointer^.Data);
            CurrPointer := CurrPointer^.Next
         END (* WHILE *)
   END (* CopyListToFile *);

BEGIN (* main program *)
   FirstPointer := NIL;
   PrintMenu;
   writeln;
   write ('Option?  ');
   readln (Option);
   WHILE Option <> 2 DO
      BEGIN
         IF Option IN [1..NumberOfOptions] THEN
            CASE Option OF
               1 : PrintMenu;
               2 : (* Stop *);
               3 : CreateList (EmpFile, FirstPointer);
               4 : RetrieveRecords (FirstPointer);
               5 : AddToList (FirstPointer, EmpRecord, 'T');
               6 : DeleteEmployees (FirstPointer);
               7 : PrintAllEmployees (FirstPointer);
               8 : CopyListToFile (FirstPointer, EmpFile)
            END (* CASE *)
```

Fig. 13.2 (cont.)

```
        ELSE
            writeln ('Illegal Option');
        writeln;
        write ('Option?  ');
        readln (Option)
    END (* WHILE *)
END (* main program *).
```

```
Sample run:
==========


The following options are available:
(1)  Print this list of options
(2)  Stop
(3)  Get list of employee records from file
(4)  Retrieve an employee's record
(5)  Insert the record for a new employee
(6)  Delete the record of an employee
(7)  List names of all employees
(8)  Copy updated list to the permanent file

Option?  3

Option?  7
Adams, John
Doe, John
Jones, Fred
Smith, Mary
Vander, Peter
Zzcyk, Stan

Option?  4
To stop, enter  Q*  for employee name.
Name of employee:  Smith, Mary
Employee name:  Smith, Mary
Age:  21
# dependents:  0
Hourly rate:  $  7.85

Name of employee:  James, Jese
James, Jese          not Found

Name of employee:  Q*


Option?  6
To stop, enter  Q*  for employee name.
Name of employee:  Smith, Mary
Name of employee:  Q*

Option?  1
The following options are available:
(1)  Print this list of options
(2)  Stop
(3)  Get list of employee records from file
(4)  Retrieve an employee's record
(5)  Insert the record for a new employee
(6)  Delete the record of an employee
(7)  List names of all employees
(8)  Copy updated list to the permanent file
```

Fig. 13.2 (cont.)

```
Option?  5
To stop, enter  Q*  for employee name.
Name:  James, Jesse
Age:  36
Dependents:  0
Hourly rate:  6.36
Name:  Q*

Option?  7
Adams, John
Doe, John
James, Jesse
Jones, Fred
Vander, Peter
Zzcyk, Stan

Option?  8

Option?  2
```

Programming Pointers

The variables that we have considered in previous chapters have as values specific data items such as integers, real numbers, characters, strings, sets, and records. Pointer variables, however, have memory addresses as values. Consequently, the manner in which pointer variables are used is quite different from that in which other kinds of variables are manipulated, and thus, pointers can cause special difficulties for both beginning and experienced programmers. Pointers are used to create dynamic data structures, such as linked lists, which are processed in a way quite different from that in which static data structures, such as sets and arrays, are processed. The following are some of the main features to remember when using pointer variables and dynamic structures in Pascal programs.

1. *Each pointer variable is bound to a certain type; a pointer is the address of a memory location in which only a value of that type can be stored.* For example, if P and Q are pointer variables declared by

   type
       String = **packed array**[1..20] **of** *char*;

   var
       P : ↑*integer*;
       Q : ↑*String*;

   then P is bound to the type *integer* and Q to the specified type *String*. Memory locations pointed to by P can store only integers, whereas those to which Q points can store only strings of length 20.

2. *Because pointers have memory addresses as values, the operations that can be performed on them are limited.* Some of these limitations are:

- *The only values that may be assigned to a pointer variable using an assignment statement are the value **nil** or the value of another pointer variable bound to the same type.* Other values are assigned to pointers by using the procedure *new* which obtains a memory location in which a value of the type to which the pointer is bound can be stored and assigns the address of this location to the pointer.
- *Arithmetic operations cannot be performed on pointers.* For example, the values (memory addresses) of two pointer variables cannot be added, nor can a numeric value be added to the value of a pointer variable.
- *Pointer values cannot be compared with the relational operators <, <=, >, and >=.* Only the relational operators = and <> are allowed, and then only to determine whether two pointers bound to the same type point to the same memory location or to determine whether a pointer is nil.
- *Pointer values cannot be read or displayed.*
- *Pointers may be used as parameters in functions and procedures, but corresponding actual and formal parameters cannot be bound to different types.* Also, because the types of formal parameters must be specified using type identifiers, if pointer variable *P* of type ↑*integer* is used as a formal parameter of a function or procedure, it cannot be declared in the subprogram heading using

     . . . *P* : ↑*integer*; . . .

A type identifier must be associated with the pointer type ↑*integer*

type
     IntegerPointer = ↑*integer*;

and this type identifier used to specify the type of *P*:

     . . . *P* : *IntegerPointer*; . . .

Similarly, the value of a function may be a pointer, but it must also be specified by a type identifier.

3. *The value of a pointer P is the address of a memory location, whereas the value of P↑ is the data item stored in that location.* For example, suppose that the pointer variable *P* is declared by

     var
          P : ↑*integer*;

The statement *writeln* (*P*) is not allowed, because the value (memory address) of a pointer cannot be output. The statement *writeln* (*P*↑) is valid, however, provided that *P* has been assigned to a memory location and a value has been stored in that location. This statement displays the integer stored in the location pointed to by *P*. Similarly, the statement *P* := *P* + 1 is not valid, but *P*↑ := *P*↑+ 1 is valid, assuming again that *P* has been assigned some memory location.

4. *An undefined pointer is not the same as a nil pointer.* A pointer becomes defined when it is assigned the address of a memory location or the value **nil.** Assigning a pointer the value **nil** is analogous to "blanking out" a character (or string) variable or "zeroing out" a numeric variable.

5. *If P is a pointer that is undefined or nil, then an attempt to use P↑ is an error.*

6. *Memory locations that were once associated with a pointer variable and that are no longer needed should be returned to the "storage pool" of available locations by using the procedure dispose.* Special care is required so that inaccessible memory locations are avoided. For example, if *P* and *Q* are pointer variables bound to the same type, the assignment statement

   $P := Q$

   causes *P* to point to the same memory location as that pointed to by *Q*. Any memory location previously pointed to by *P* becomes inaccessible and cannot be disposed of properly unless it is pointed to by some other pointer. One should always use temporary pointers when necessary to maintain access, as in the following statements:

   TempPointer := *P*;
   P := *Q*;
   dispose (*TempPointer*)

7. *Processing linked structures requires attention to special cases and to the problem of losing access to nodes.* Some errors commonly made when using linked lists include the following:

   • *Attempting to process data items beyond the end of a linked list.* For example, consider the following attempt to search a nonempty linked list for a given item:

   CurrPointer := *FirstPointer*;
   while *CurrPointer*↑.*Data* <> *ItemSought* **do**
       CurrPointer := *CurrPointer*↑.*Next*

   If the item is not present in any node of the linked list, *CurrPointer* eventually reaches the last node in the list. *CurrPointer* then becomes nil, and an attempt is made to examine the *Data* field of a nonexistent node, resulting in an error message such as

   *** Attempted access via NIL pointer ***

   An attempted solution to the problem might be the following:

   CurrPointer := *FirstPointer*;
   while (*CurrPointer* <> **nil**) **and** (*CurrPointer*↑.*Data* <> *ItemSought*) **do**
       CurrPointer := *CurrPointer*↑.*Next*

In most versions of Pascal this also results in an error if the item is not in the list. The reason for this is that boolean expressions are usually evaluated in their entirety. Thus, when the end of the list is reached and *CurrPointer* becomes nil, the second part of the boolean expression is evaluated, and an error results when an attempt is made to access the *Data* field of a nonexistent node.

Another attempt to avoid running past the end of a nonempty list might be the following:

```
Found := false;
CurrPointer := FirstPointer;
while CurrPointer↑.Next <> nil do
    if CurrPointer↑.Data = ItemSought then
        Found := true
    else
        CurrPointer := CurrPointer↑.Next
```

Although this avoids the problem of moving beyond the end of the list, it fails to locate the desired item (that is, set *Found* to *true*) if this item is the last one in the list. When *CurrPointer* reaches the last node, the value of *CurrPointer↑.Next* is nil, and repetition is terminated without examining the *Data* field of this last node. Another problem is that if the item is found in the list, the remaining nodes (except the last) are also examined.

One solution is to use a boolean variable together with an end-of-list check to control the repetition:

```
Found := false;
CurrPointer := FirstPointer;
while (CurrPointer <> nil) and (not Found) do
    if CurrPointer↑.Data = ItemSought then
        Found := true
    else
        CurrPointer := CurrPointer↑.Next
```

If the item is found in the list, then *Found* is set to *true* and repetition is terminated. If it is not in the list, then *CurrPointer* eventually becomes nil and repetition terminates.

- *Attempting to access items in an empty list.* An example of this is the set of statements

```
CurrPointer := FirstPointer;
while CurrPointer↑.Data <> ItemSought do
    CurrPointer := CurrPointer↑.Next
```

An error results if the list is empty—that is, if *FirstPointer* is nil—because the first value of *CurrPointer* is then nil and an attempt is made to examine a field in a nonexistent node. This is also the case with the following example:

```
Found := false;
CurrPointer := FirstPointer;
while CurrPointer↑.Next <> nil do
```

if *CurrPointer↑.Data* = *ItemSought* **then**
  Found := *true*
else
  CurrPointer := *CurrPointer↑.Next*

For an empty list, *CurrPointer* is initially nil, and the *Next* field of a nonexistent node cannot be examined.

- *"Burning bridges before they are crossed,"* more precisely, changing some link in a list before certain other links have been reset. As an example, suppose that a node pointed to by *NewNodePointer* is to be pushed onto a stack with top node pointed to by *TopPointer*. The statements

TopPointer := *NewNodePointer*;
NewNodePointer↑.Next := *TopPointer*

are not used in the correct order. As soon as *TopPointer* is set to *NewNodePointer*, access to the remaining nodes in the stack (those previously pointed to by *TopPointer*) is lost. The second statement then simply sets the *Next* field of the node pointed to by *NewNodePointer* (and by *TopPointer*) to point to the node itself. The new node must first be linked into the stack before *TopPointer* is reset:

NewNodePointer↑.Next := *TopPointer*;
TopPointer := *NewNodePointer*

Exercises

In these exercises, the files *InventoryFile*, *StudentFile*, and *UsersFile* should be processed as files of records. For descriptions of these files, see Appendix E.

1. Assume the following declarations:

   var
     X : integer;
     P1, P2 : ↑integer;
     Q1, Q2 : ↑real;

   What (if anything) is wrong with each of the following statements?

   (a) *writeln* (*P1*);

   (b) *readln* (*P1↑*);

   (c) *P1* := *Q1*;

   (d) *new* (*X*);

   (e) **if** *P1↑* = **nil then**
       Q1 := *Q2*;

2. Write type declarations needed to construct a linked list of records from
   (a) *InventoryFile*   (b) *StudentFile*   (c) *UsersFile*

3. Write a function to count the nodes in a linked list.

4. Write a boolean-valued function that determines whether the data items in a linked list are arranged in ascending order.

5. Write a function that returns a pointer to the last node in a linked list having first node pointed to by *FirstPointer*.

6. Write a procedure to reverse a linked list; that is, the last node becomes the first node and all links between nodes are reversed.

7. Modify procedures *Insert* and *Delete* so that they require only the pointer *PredPointer* to the predecessor of the item to be inserted or deleted rather than the two pointers *PredPointer* and *CurrPointer*. Also write a function *Predecessor* that searches the linked list and returns this pointer.

8. The procedures *Insert* and *Delete* given in the text require checking to see whether the item to be inserted or deleted has a predecessor in the list. These procedures can be shortened if we require every linked list to have a dummy node, called a *head node,* at the beginning of the list so that the first node that stores the actual data has the head node as a predecessor. Modify the procedures *Insert* and *Delete* for linked lists having head nodes.

9. A *deque* (double-ended queue) is a list in which insertion and deletion are allowed at either end. Write procedures to insert and delete items in a linked list representing a deque.

10. The method of successive division for converting a base-10 number to base *b* described in Exercise 11 of Section 1.3 produces the digits of the base-*b* representation in reverse order. Write a program implementing this algorithm to convert a base-10 integer to base *b;* use a stack to print the digits in the usual left-to-right order.

11. Write a program that reads a question from a file, displays it, and accepts an answer from the user. If the answer is correct, go on to the next question. If it is not correct, put the question into a linked queue. Then when the file of questions is exhausted, the questions that were missed are displayed again. Keep a count of the number of correct answers and display the final count. Also, display the correct answer when necessary in the second round of questioning.

12. Suppose that jobs entering a computer system are assigned a job number and a priority from 0 through 9. Numbers of jobs awaiting execution by the system are kept in a *priority queue.* A job entered into this queue is placed ahead of all jobs of lower priority but after all those of equal or higher priority. Write a program to read one of the letters R (remove), A (add), or L (list). For R, remove the first item in the queue; for A, read a job number and priority and then add it to the priority queue in the manner just described; for L, list all the job numbers in the queue. Maintain the priority queue as a linked list.

13. Write a program to read the records from *StudentFile* and construct five linked lists of records containing a student's name, number, and cumulative GPA, one list for each class. Each list is to be an ordered linked list in which the names are in alphabetical order. After the lists have been constructed, print each of them with appropriate headings.

14. A *polynomial of degree n* has the form

$$a_n x^n + a_{n-1} x^{n-1} + \ldots + a_1 x + a_0$$

where $a_0, a_1, \ldots, a_n$ are numeric constants called the *coefficients* of the polynomial and $a_n \neq 0$. For example,

$$5x^4 - 7x^3 + 3x + 1$$

is a polynomial of degree 4 with integer coefficients.

(a) Develop an ordered linked list that can represent any such polynomial. Let each node store a nonzero coefficient and the corresponding exponent.

(b) Write a program to read the nonzero coefficients and exponents of a polynomial, construct its linked representation, and then print it using the usual mathematical format with x^n written as $x \uparrow n$.

(c) Then read values for x and evaluate the polynomial for each of these values.

15. The *derivative* of the nth degree polynomial

$$a_n x^n + a_{n-1} x^{n-1} + \ldots + a_1 x + a_0$$

where the a_i are real numbers with $a_n \neq 0$, is the following polynomial of degree $n - 1$:

$$n a_n x^{n-1} + (n-1) a_{n-1} x^{n-2} + \ldots + a_1$$

For example, the derivative of

$$5x^4 - 7x^3 + 3x + 1$$

is

$$20x^3 - 21x^2 + 3$$

Extend the program of Exercise 14 to calculate the derivative of the polynomial, representing it as a linked list, then display it and also evaluate it for given values of x.

16. Write a program that reads the nonzero coefficients and exponents of two polynomials of possibly different degrees, stores them in

linked lists (as described in Exercise 14), and then calculates and displays their sum and product.

17. The number of elements in an ordered list may grow so large that searching the list, always beginning with the first node, is not efficient. One way to improve efficiency is to maintain several smaller linked lists with an array of pointers to the first nodes of these lists. Write a program to read several lines of upper-case text and to produce a *text concordance* which is a list of all distinct words in the text. Store distinct words beginning with A alphabetically ordered in one linked list, those beginning with B in another, and so on. Use an array with subscripts of type 'A'..'Z', with each array element being a pointer to the first node in the list of words that begin with the corresponding subscript. After all the text lines have been read, print a listing of all these words in alphabetical order.

18. Modify the program of Exercise 17 so that the concordance also includes the frequency with which each word occurs in the text.

19. *Directed graphs* and their representations using adjacency matrices were described in Exercise 13 of Section 9.4.

(a) Imitating the construction in Exercise 17, develop a representation of a directed graph by using an array of pointers (one for each vertex) to linked lists containing the vertices that can be reached directly (following a single directed arc) from the vertex corresponding to the subscript.

(b) Draw a diagram showing the linked representation for the following directed graph:

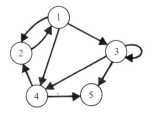

(c) Write a program to read the numbers (or names) of the vertices of a directed graph and ordered pairs of vertices representing the directed arcs, construct the linked representation for the digraph, and then use it to display the adjacency matrix.

20. In Chapter 9 we represented matrices by two-dimensional arrays. For a *sparse matrix*, that is, one with few nonzero entries, this is not an efficient representation.

(a) Imitating the construction in Exercise 17, develop a representation for a sparse matrix by using one ordered linked list for each row and an array of pointers to the first nodes in these lists. Do not store zero entries of the matrix. (*Hint:* Store a matrix entry and the number of the column in which it appears.)

(b) Write a program to read the nonzero entries of a sparse matrix and their locations in the matrix and construct its linked representation. Then print the matrix in the usual table format with all entries (including 0's) displayed.

21. Extend the program of Exercise 20 to read two sparse matrices and calculate their sum and product. (see Section 9.4).

Advanced Applications

I think that I shall never see
A poem lovely as a tree.

JOYCE KILMER

So she went on, wondering more and more at every step, as everything turned into a
tree the moment she came up to it.

LEWIS CARROLL, *Through the Looking Glass*

There is nothing more difficult to take in hand, more perilous to conduct, or more
uncertain in its success, than to take the lead in the introduction of a new order of
things.

NICCOLÒ MACHIAVELLI, *The Prince*

We have now considered most of the Pascal statements, data types, procedures
and functions and have illustrated these with numerous examples and programs. Most of these examples have been designed to show as simply as
possible the various features of the Pascal language. In this chapter we do
not introduce any new features of Pascal but instead consider several advanced
applications. In the first section we apply the stack data structure introduced
in Chapter 13 to transform an arithmetic expression from the ordinary *infix*
notation to *reverse Polish notation.* The second section introduces a new
data structure, a *tree,* which is implemented as a linked structure. We examine
recursive algorithms for searching and traversing trees and describe a sorting
algorithm that uses a tree to store the data items. The third section discusses
the elegant and efficient sorting technique known as *quicksort* and implements
it by a recursive algorithm. Finally, the last section considers the problem
of sorting data sets that may be too large to fit in main memory and describes
the *external* sorting method known as *mergesort* that is commonly used in
such situations.

Arithmetic expressions are ordinarily written in *infix* notation in which the **Application of** symbol for each binary operation is placed between the operands. Thus the **Stacks: Reverse** sum of integers 2 and 3 is written in infix notation as **Polish Notation**

$$2 + 3$$

We might, however, also express this sum in *prefix* notation

$$+ \ 2 \ 3$$

in which the symbol for a binary operation precedes the operands, or we might use *postfix* notation

$$2 \ 3 \ +$$

in which the operation symbol follows the operands.

When infix notation is used for arithmetic expressions containing two or more operators, parentheses may be needed to indicate the order in which these operations are to be carried out. For example, parentheses are placed in the expression

$$2 * (3 + 5)$$

to indicate that the addition is to be performed before the multiplication. If the parentheses were omitted,

$$2 * 3 + 5$$

the standard priority rules would dictate that the multiplication is to be performed before the addition.

In the early 1950s, the Polish logician Jan Lukasiewicz observed that parentheses are not necessary in prefix or postfix notation for arithmetic expressions. For example, the expression

$$2 * (3 + 5)$$

can be expressed without parentheses in prefix notation as

$$* \ 2 + 3 \ 5$$

or in postfix notation as

$$2 \ 3 \ 5 + *$$

In this section we confine our attention to postfix notation, also known as *reverse Polish notation* (RPN), and develop an algorithm for converting arithmetic expressions from infix notation to postfix notation. Development of a similar algorithm for conversion from infix notation to prefix notation is left as an exercise.

Many compilers convert arithmetic expressions into reverse Polish notation and then generate the machine instructions required to evaluate this expression. Likewise, calculators commonly evaluate arithmetic expressions using reverse Polish notation. This is because the conversion from infix notation to RPN and the evaluation of the RPN expression both are straightforward.

To illustrate evaluation of an arithmetic expression given in RPN, consider

$$2 \; 3 \; 5 + *$$

This expression can be evaluated by scanning it from left to right until an operator is encountered. At that point, the two preceding operands are combined using this operation. For our example, the first operator encountered in a left-to-right scan is +, and its operands are 3 and 5, as indicated by the underline in the following:

$$2 \; \underline{3 \; 5 +} \; *$$

Replacing this subexpression with its value 8 yields the reduced RPN expression

$$2 \; 8 \; *$$

Resuming our left-to-right scan, we next encounter the * operator and determine its two operands:

$$\underline{2 \; 8 \; *}$$

Evaluating this expression gives 16. Because the end of the string has been reached, evaluation of the original RPN expression is complete. The following diagram summarizes the evaluation by placing a line under each operator and its two operands:

$$2 \; 3 \; 5 + *$$

As another example, consider the RPN expression

$$2 \; 5 + 8 \; 4 \; 1 + - *$$

which corresponds to the infix expression $(2 + 5) * (8 - (4 + 1))$. Using the underlining technique, we have

$$\underline{2 \; 5 +} \; 8 \; \underline{4 \; 1 +} - *$$

The following sequence of steps evaluates this expression:

$$2 \; 5 + 8 \; 4 \; 1 + - *$$
$$\downarrow$$
$$7 \; 8 \; 4 \; 1 + - *$$
$$\downarrow$$
$$7 \; 8 \; 5 - *$$
$$\downarrow$$
$$7 \; 3 \; *$$
$$\downarrow$$
$$21$$

Before developing an algorithm to evaluate RPN expressions, we must first decide on an appropriate data structure. In the examples, we scanned the expression from left to right until an operator was found; we then had to "backtrack" to find its two operands, the last two numbers preceding it. A last-in-first-out structure, that is, a stack, is therefore the appropriate data structure to store operands. Each time we encounter a numeric value, we push it onto the stack. Then when an operator is encountered, we pop the top two values from the stack, perform the operation, and push the result back onto the stack. The following algorithm summarizes this procedure:

Algorithm

1. Initialize an empty stack.

2. Repeat the following until the end of the expression is encountered:

   a. Get the next token (constant, variable, arithmetic operator) in the RPN expression.
   b. If the token is an operand, push it onto the stack. If it is an operator, then do the following:
      (i) Pop the top two values from the stack. (If the stack does not contain two items, an error due to a malformed RPN expression has occurred and evaluation is terminated.)
      (ii) Apply the operator to these two values.
      (iii) Push the resulting value back onto the stack.

3. When the end of the expression is encountered, its value is on top of the stack (and in fact must be the only value in the stack).

Figure 14.1 illustrates this algorithm for the RPN expression

$$2\,4 * 9\,5 + -$$

The up-arrow ($\uparrow$) indicates the current token being considered.

A stack can also be used to convert an infix expression to RPN. An algorithm for this conversion is:

Algorithm

1. Initialize an empty stack.
2. Repeat the following until the end of the infix expression is reached.

   a. Get the next input token (constant, variable, arithmetic operator, left parenthesis, right parenthesis) in the infix expression.
   b. If this token is
      (i) a left parenthesis: Push it onto the stack.
      (ii) an operand: Display it.
      (iii) an operator: If the stack is empty or the operator has higher priority than the top stack element, push the operator onto the stack. Otherwise, display the operator and pop an operator from the stack; then repeat the comparison of this operator with the top stack item. Note: a left parenthesis in the stack is assumed to have a lower priority than that of operators.

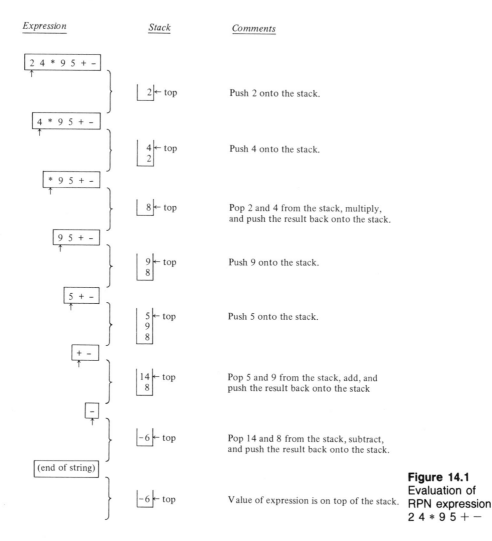

Expression	Stack	Comments

Figure 14.1
Evaluation of
RPN expression
2 4 * 9 5 + −

(iv) a right parenthesis: Pop and display stack elements until a left parenthesis is on top of the stack. Pop it also, but do not display it.

3. When the end of the infix expression is reached, pop and display stack items until the stack is empty.

Figure 14.2 illustrates this algorithm for the infix expression

$$7 * 8 - (2 + 3)$$

An up-arrow (↑) has been used to indicate the current input symbol and the symbol displayed by the algorithm. The program in Figure 14.3 implements this algorithm.

Expression	Stack	Output	Comments

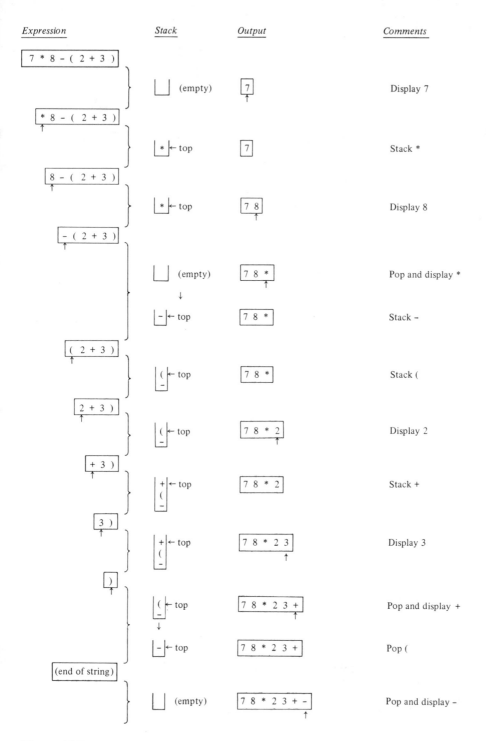

Figure 14.2
Converting infix expression 7 * 8 − (2 + 3) to RPN

```
PROGRAM InfixToRPN (input, output);

(*****************************************************************************

    Program to convert an infix expression to Reverse Polish Notation.

******************************************************************************)

CONST
   MaxExpression = 80;    (* limit on expression length *)
   StackLimit = 50;       (* limit on stack size *)

TYPE
   Expression = PACKED ARRAY[1..MaxExpression] OF char;
   StackArray = PACKED ARRAY[0..StackLimit] OF char;
   CharacterSet = SET OF char;

VAR
   Exp : Expression;                (* infix expression *)
   Length : integer;                (* length of infix expression *)
   OperatorSet : CharacterSet;      (* set of arithmetic operators *)
   Response : char;                 (* user response *)

PROCEDURE ConvertToRPN (Exp : Expression; Length : integer;
                        OperatorSet : CharacterSet);

   (*****************************************************************

       Procedure to convert infix expression Exp to RPN.

   ******************************************************************)

   VAR
      Stack : StackArray;      (* stack represented by an array *)
      i,                       (* index *)
      Top : integer;           (* Stack[Top] is the top of the stack *)
      Symbol,                  (* a character in the expression *)
      TempSymbol : char;       (* temporary symbol *)

   FUNCTION Priority (Operator : char) : integer;

      (*****************************************************************

          Function to find the priority of an arithmetic operator or (.

      ******************************************************************)

      BEGIN  (* Priority *)
         CASE Operator OF
            '(' :       Priority := 0;
            '+', '-' : Priority := 1;
            '*', '/' : Priority := 2
         END (* CASE *)
      END (* Priority *);

   PROCEDURE Pop (VAR Stack : StackArray; VAR Top : integer;
                  VAR Element : char);

      (*****************************************************************

          Procedure to pop and return Element = Stack[Top] from a stack
          represented as an array.  The new value for Top is also
          returned.

      ******************************************************************)
```

Figure 14.3

Fig. 14.3 (cont.)

```
    BEGIN (* Pop *)
       IF Top = O THEN
          writeln ('Stack empty')
       ELSE
          BEGIN
             Element := Stack[Top];
             Top := Top - 1
          END (* ELSE *)
    END (* Pop *);

PROCEDURE Push (VAR Stack : StackArray; VAR Top : integer;
                Element : char);

    (***************************************************************

       Procedure to push Element onto the stack represented as an
       array with Stack[Top] the top item.  The new value for Top
       and the modified array Stack are returned.

    ***************************************************************)

    BEGIN (* Push *)
       IF Top >= StackLimit THEN
          writeln ('Stack full')
       ELSE
          BEGIN
             Top := Top + 1;
             Stack[Top] := Element
          END (* ELSE *)
    END (* Push *);

BEGIN (* ConvertToRPN *)

    (* Initialize an empty stack *)
    Top := O;

    FOR i := 1 TO Length DO
       BEGIN
          Symbol := Exp[i];
          IF Symbol <> ' ' THEN                    (* We skip blanks *)
             IF Symbol = '(' THEN                   (* left parenthesis *)
                Push (Stack, Top, Symbol)
             ELSE IF Symbol = ')' THEN              (* right parenthesis *)
                BEGIN
                   WHILE Stack[Top] <> '(' DO
                      BEGIN
                         Pop (Stack, Top, Symbol);
                         write (Symbol:2)
                      END (* WHILE *);
                   Pop (Stack, Top, Symbol)
                END (* ELSE IF *)
             ELSE IF Symbol IN OperatorSet THEN     (* arithmetic operator *)
                BEGIN
                   WHILE (Top <> O) AND
                         (Priority(Symbol) <= Priority(Stack[Top])) DO
                      BEGIN
                         Pop (Stack, Top, TempSymbol);
                         write (TempSymbol:2)
                      END (* WHILE *);
                   Push (Stack, Top, Symbol)
                END (* ELSE IF *)
             ELSE                                   (* operand *)
                write (Symbol:2)
       END (* FOR *);
```

Fig. 14.3 (cont.)

```
      WHILE Top <> O DO
         BEGIN
            Pop (Stack, Top, Symbol);
            write (Symbol:2)
         END (* WHILE *);
      writeln
   END (* ConvertToRPN *);

BEGIN (* main program *)

   (* Initialize set of arithmetic operators *)

   Operatorset := ['+', '-', '*', '/'];

   REPEAT
     (* read infix expression *)
     write ('Enter infix expression: ');
     Length := 0;
     WHILE NOT eoln DO
        BEGIN
           Length := Length + 1;
           read (Exp[Length])
        END;
     readln;

     (* convert to RPN *)

     writeln;
     write ('RPN Expression:          ');
     ConvertToRPN (Exp, Length, OperatorSet);
     writeln;
     write ('More (Y or N)?  ');
     readln (Response)
   UNTIL NOT (Response IN ['Y', 'y'])
END (* main program *).
```

```
Sample run:
==========


Enter infix expression: A + B

RPN Expression:         A B +

More (Y or N)?  Y
Enter infix expression: A - B - C

RPN Expression:         A B - C -

More (Y or N)?  Y
Enter infix expression: A - (B - C)

RPN Expression:         A B C - -

More (Y or N)?  Y
Enter infix expression: ((A + 5)/B - 2)*C

RPN Expression:         A 5 + B / 2 - C *

More (Y or N)?  N
```

Exercises

1. Suppose that $A = 7.0$, $B = 4.0$, $C = 3.0$, $D = -2.0$. Evaluate the following RPN expressions:

   (a) $A\ B + C\ /\ D\ *$ (b) $A\ B\ C + /\ D\ *$

   (c) $A\ B\ C\ D + /\ *$ (d) $A\ B + C + D +$

   (e) $A\ B + C\ D + +$ (f) $A\ B\ C + + D +$

   (g) $A\ B\ C\ D + + +$ (h) $A\ B - C - D -$

   (i) $A\ B - C\ D - -$ (j) $A\ B\ C - - D -$

   (k) $A\ B\ C\ D - - -$

2. Convert the following infix expressions to RPN:

   (a) $A * B + C - D$ (b) $A + B\ /\ C + D$

   (c) $(A + B)\ /\ C + D$ (d) $A + B\ /\ (C + D)$

   (e) $(A + B)\ /\ (C + D)$ (f) $(A - B) * (C - (D + E))$

   (g) $(((A - B) - C) - D) - E$ (h) $A - (B - (C - (D - E)))$

3. Convert the following RPN expressions to infix notation:

   (a) $A\ B\ C + - D\ *$ (b) $A\ B + C\ D - *$

   (c) $A\ B\ C\ D + - *$ (d) $A\ B + C - D\ E\ *\ /$

   (e) $A\ B\ /\ C\ /\ D\ /$ (f) $A\ B\ /\ C\ D\ /\ /$

   (g) $A\ B\ C\ /\ D\ /\ /$ (h) $A\ B\ C\ D\ /\ /\ /$

4. Suppose that $A = 7.0$, $B = 4.0$, $C = 3.0$, and $D = -2.0$. Evaluate the following prefix expressions:

   (a) $*\ A\ /\ + B\ C\ D$ (b) $*\ /\ + A\ B\ C\ D$

   (c) $- A - B - C\ D$ (d) $- - A\ B - C\ D$

   (e) $- A - - B\ C\ D$ (f) $- - - A\ B\ C\ D$

   (g) $+ A\ B * - C\ D$ (h) $+ * A\ B - C\ D$

   (i) $+ * - A\ B\ C\ D$

5. Convert each of the infix expressions in Exercise 2 to prefix notation.

6. Convert the following prefix expressions to infix notation:

   (a) $+ A\ B * - C\ D$ (b) $+ * A\ B - C\ D$

   (c) $- - A\ B - C\ D$ (d) $- - A - B\ C\ D$

   (e) $- - - A\ B\ C\ D$ (f) $/ + * A\ B - C\ D\ E$

   (g) $/ + * A\ B\ C - D\ E$ (h) $/ + A * B\ C - D\ E$

7. The symbol $-$ cannot be used for the unary minus operation in prefix or postfix notation. For example, 5 3 $-$ $-$ could be interpreted as either $5 - (-3) = 8$ or $-(5 - 3) = -2$. Suppose that $\sim$ is used for unary minus.

   (a) Evaluate the following RPN expressions if $A = 7$, $B = 5$, $C = 3$:

       (i) $A \sim B\ C + -$ **(ii)** $A\ B \sim C + -$

       (iii) $A\ B\ C \sim + -$ **(iv)** $A\ B\ C + \sim -$

       (v) $A\ B\ C + - \sim$ **(vi)** $A\ B\ C - - \sim \sim \sim$

   (b) Convert the following infix expressions to RPN:

       (i) $A * (B + \sim C)$ **(ii)** $\sim(A + B / (C - D))$

       (iii) $(\sim A) * (\sim B)$ **(iv)** $\sim(A - (\sim B * (C + \sim D)))$

   (c) Convert the infix expressions in (b) to prefix notation.

8. Convert the following boolean expressions to RPN:

   (a) A **and** B **or** C

   (b) A **and** $(B$ **or not** $C)$

   (c) **not** $(A$ **and** $B)$

   (d) $(A$ **or** $B)$ **and** $(C$ **or** $(D$ **and not** $E))$

   (e) $(A = B)$ **or** $(C = D)$

   (f) $((A < 3)$ **and** $(A > 9))$ **or not** $(A > 0)$

   (g) $((B * B - 4 * A * C) >= 0)$ **and** $((A > 0)$ **or** $(A < 0))$

9. Convert each of the boolean expressions in Exercise 8 to prefix notation.

10. Write a procedure to implement the algorithm for evaluating RPN expressions that involve only one-digit integers and the binary operators $+$, $-$, and $*$.

11. Write a procedure to convert infix expressions to prefix.

12. Write a procedure to evaluate prefix expressions containing only one-digit integers and the binary operators $+$, $-$, and $*$.

13. Write a program that reads an RPN expression and determines whether it is well formed, that is, whether each binary operator has two operands and the unary operator $\sim$ has one (see Exercise 7).

14. Write a program that converts an integer expression involving the operators $+$, $-$, $*$, **div, mod,** and integer constants to RPN.

Linked structures were introduced in Chapter 13. We confined our attention there to linked lists and considered in detail linked representations of stacks, queues, and ordered lists. In each of these linked representations each node contained a single link field pointing to the successor of that node, but it is also possible to have linked lists in which the nodes have more than one link field. For example, to traverse a linked list in either direction, it is convenient to use two link fields, one containing a pointer to the predecessor of a node and the other containing a pointer to its successor. Such a *doubly linked list* might be pictured as follows:

Multiply Linked Structures: Trees

This is a special kind of *multiply linked list,* that is, a list in which each node has two or more links. In this chapter we consider the important data structure known as a *tree* and its representation as a multiply linked list. Other applications of multiply linked lists are explored in the exercises.

A tree is a special case of a more general structure called a *directed graph*. A directed graph consists of a finite set of elements called *vertices* or *nodes* and a finite set of *directed arcs* which connect pairs of vertices. For example, a directed graph having five vertices numbered 1, 2, 3, 4, 5, and seven directed arcs joining vertices 1 to 2, 1 to 4, 1 to 5, 2 to 3, 2 to 4, 3 to itself, 4 to 2, and 4 to 3 might be pictured as

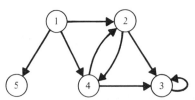

A *tree* is a directed graph in which one of the nodes, called the *root*, has no incoming arcs but from which each node in the tree can be reached by following a unique sequence of consecutive arcs. Thus the preceding directed graph is not a tree. The only vertex having no incoming arcs is vertex 1, and hence it is the only possibility for a root. However, because there are many different paths from vertex 1 to vertex 3 $(1 \rightarrow 2 \rightarrow 3, 1 \rightarrow 4 \rightarrow 3, 1 \rightarrow 4 \rightarrow 2 \rightarrow 3, 1 \rightarrow 4 \rightarrow 2 \rightarrow 4 \rightarrow 3, 1 \rightarrow 2 \rightarrow 3 \rightarrow 3 \rightarrow 3$, and so on), this graph is not a tree.

Trees are so named because they have a treelike appearance except that they are usually drawn upside down with the root at the top. For example,

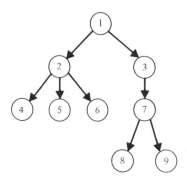

shows a tree having nine vertices in which vertex 1 is the root. Vertices having no outgoing arcs are called *leaves;* in this example, vertices 4, 5, 6, 8, and 9 are the leaves of the tree. Nodes that can be reached directly from a given node—that is, by using only one directed arc—are called the *children* of that node, and a node is said to be the *parent* of each of its children. For example, in the tree just shown, vertex 2 is the parent of vertices 4, 5, and 6, and these vertices are the children of vertex 2.

Trees in which each node has at most two children are called *binary trees,* and we confine our attention to these. (This is not a serious limitation, however, because any tree can be represented as a binary tree. See Exercise 5 at the end of this section.)

Binary trees can be represented as multiply linked lists in which each node has two link fields, one of which is a pointer to the left child of that node and the other is a pointer to the right child. Such nodes can be represented in Pascal by records whose declarations have the form

> *TreePointer* = ↑ *TreeNode*;
> *TreeNode* = **record**
> > *Data* : *DataType*;
> > *LChild, RChild* : *TreePointer*
> > **end**;

The two link fields *LChild* and *RChild* are pointers to nodes representing the left and right children, respectively,

or are nil if the node does not have a left or right child. A leaf node is characterized, therefore, by having nil values for both *LChild* and *RChild.*

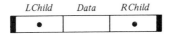

The binary tree

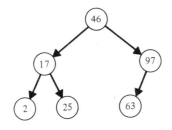

can thus be represented as the following linked tree of records:

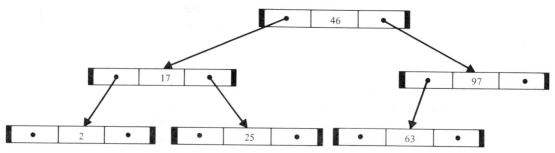

This tree has directed arcs from the root node containing 46 to the nodes containing 17 and 97. Each of these nodes is itself the root of a *subtree;*

In the same way, there are arcs from the node containing 17 to the nodes containing 2 and 25. Each of these may be thought of as the root of a subtree consisting of a single node:

This leads to the following *recursive definition for a binary tree:*

A binary tree is either
(a) empty, or
(b) it consists of a node called the *root* which has pointers to two disjoint subtrees called the *left subtree* and the *right subtree.*

This recursive definition suggests that recursive algorithms can be developed for manipulating binary trees. In this section we consider recursive algorithms for traversing binary trees and algorithms for searching and creating sorted binary trees. Other operations on binary trees are examined in the exercises.

The first operation for binary trees that we discuss is *traversing* the tree, that is, visiting each node in the binary tree exactly once. There are three basic steps in traversing a binary tree recursively: (1) visit a node, (2) traverse the left subtree, and (3) traverse the right subtree. These three steps can be performed in any order. If we denote these steps by

N: visit a node
L: traverse the left subtree
R: traverse the right subtree

then the six different orders are

NLR
LNR
LRN
NRL
RNL
RLN

We can reduce this list to the first three orders if we agree to always traverse the left subtree before the right subtree. The traversals that result from these three orders are given special names:

NLR: *preorder traversal*
LNR: *inorder traversal*
LRN: *postorder traversal*

To illustrate these traversals, consider the following binary tree:

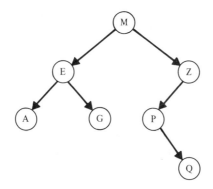

The three types of traversals visit the nodes in the following sequences:

preorder: M E A G Z P Q
inorder: A E G M P Q Z
postorder: A G E Q P Z M

The postorder traversal is obtained as follows: We begin at the root M, but before we list it, we must traverse its left and right subtrees. These subtrees are the shaded regions in the following diagram:

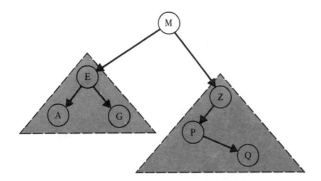

The left subtree has root E, but before listing it, we must traverse its left and right subtrees.

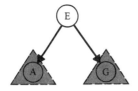

The left subtree has root A, but again we must first traverse its left and right subtrees before listing it.

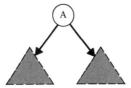

Because these subtrees are empty, A may now be listed. The right subtree of E has root G, which also has empty left and right subtrees,

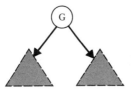

and thus G may be listed. Because both the left and right subtrees of E have been traversed, E may now be listed. The sequence of nodes visited thus far is

A G E

Because the left subtree of M has been traversed, we consider its right subtree having root Z. Before listing Z, we must traverse its left and right subtrees.

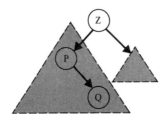

The left subtree has root P, and before listing P, we must traverse its left and right subtrees.

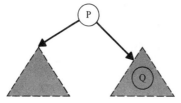

The left subtree is empty, and the right subtree has root Q.

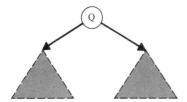

Because the left and right subtrees of Q are empty, Q may now be listed:

    A G E Q

The left and right subtrees of P have now been traversed, and so P is listed:

    A G E Q P

The left subtree of Z has now been traversed, and because its right subtree is empty, Z may now be listed:

    A G E Q P Z

Finally, we may list the vertex M, as both its left and right subtrees have been traversed:

    A G E Q P Z M

The reader should derive the preorder and inorder traversals in a similar manner.

    The names preorder, inorder, and postorder for traversals of a binary tree are appropriate because they correspond to the prefix, infix, and postfix forms for an arithmetic expression. To illustrate, consider the arithmetic expression

    A − B ∗ C + D

This can be represented as a binary tree by representing each operand as a child of a node that represents the corresponding operator:

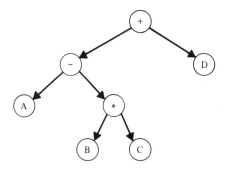

An inorder traversal of this binary tree produces the infix expression

    A − B ∗ C + D

a preorder traversal yields the prefix expression

    + − A ∗ B C D

and a postorder traversal gives the postfix (RPN) expression

    A B C ∗ − D +

    The method we have used for traversing a binary tree is a recursive one, as traversing a tree (or subtree) requires traversing each of the subtrees pointed to by its root. Thus it is natural to use recursive procedures to traverse a binary tree. To illustrate, if the following type declarations have been made

type
   DataType = . . . ; (* type of data part of nodes *)
   TreePointer = ↑ *TreeNode*;
   TreeNode = **record**
                     Data : *DataType*;
                     LChild, RChild : *TreePointer*
                end;

then a recursive procedure for inorder traversal is

procedure *InOrder* (*RootPointer* : *TreePointer*);

   (* Procedure for inorder traversal of a binary tree *)

   begin (* *InOrder* *)
       if *RootPointer* <> **nil then**   (* tree is not empty *)
           begin
               InOrder (*RootPointer*↑.*LChild*);   (* L operation *)
               Visit (*RootPointer*);   (* N operation *)
               InOrder (*RootPointer*↑.*RChild*)   (* R operation *)
           end (* **if** *)
   end (* *InOrder* *);

Here *Visit* is a procedure to process the data field *RootPointer*↑.*Data* of the node pointed to by *RootPointer*.

To demonstrate how this procedure operates, suppose that the procedure *Visit* simply displays the data stored in a node, and consider the following binary tree:

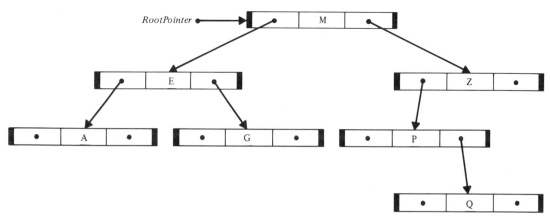

The statement

   InOrder (*RootPointer*)

calls the procedure *InOrder* to perform an inorder traversal of this tree. The action of this procedure while traversing the tree is indicated by the following table:

Contents of Current Node	Level in the Tree	Action	Output
M	1	Call *InOrder* with pointer to root (E) of left subtree.	
E	2	Call *InOrder* with pointer to root (A) of left subtree.	
A	3	Call *InOrder* with pointer (nil) to root of left subtree.	
none	4	None; return to parent node.	
A	3	Display contents of node.	A
A	3	Call *InOrder* with pointer (nil) to root of right subtree	
none	4	None; return to parent node.	
A	3	Return to parent node.	
E	2	Display contents of node.	E
E	2	Call *InOrder* with pointer to root (G) of right subtree.	
G	3	Call *InOrder* with pointer (nil) to root of left subtree.	
none	4	None; return to parent node.	
G	3	Display contents of node.	G
G	3	Call *InOrder* with pointer (nil) to root of right subtree.	
none	4	None; return to parent node.	
G	3	Return to parent node.	
E	2	Return to parent node.	
M	1	Display contents of node.	M
M	1	Call *InOrder* with pointer to root (Z) of right subtree.	
Z	2	Call *InOrder* with pointer to root (P) of left subtree.	
P	3	Call *InOrder* with pointer (nil) to root of left subtree.	
none	4	None; return to parent node.	
P	3	Display contents of node.	P
P	3	Call *InOrder* with pointer to root (Q) of right subtree.	
Q	4	Call *InOrder* with pointer (nil) to root of left subtree.	
none	5	None; return to parent node.	
Q	4	Display contents of node.	Q
Q	4	Call *InOrder* with pointer (nil) to root of right subtree.	

Contents of Current Node	Level in the Tree	Action	Output
none	5	None; return to parent node.	
Q	4	Return to parent node.	
P	3	Return to parent node.	
Z	2	Display contents of node.	Z
Z	2	Call *InOrder* with pointer (nil) to root of right subtree.	
none	3	None; return to parent node.	
Z	2	Return to parent node.	
M	1	Terminate procedure; traversal complete.	

Procedures for the preorder and postorder traversals are obtained by simply changing the order of the statments representing the L, N, and R operations in *InOrder*.

procedure *PreOrder* (*RootPointer* : *TreePointer*);

    (∗ Procedure for preorder traversal of binary tree ∗)

    begin (∗ *PreOrder* ∗)
      if *RootPointer* <> **nil then**   (∗ tree is not empty ∗)
        begin
          Visit (*RootPointer*);   (∗ N operation ∗)
          PreOrder (*RootPointer*↑.*LChild*);   (∗ L operation ∗)
          PreOrder (*RootPointer*↑.*RChild*)   (∗ R operation ∗)
       end (∗ **if** ∗)
    end (∗ *PreOrder* ∗);

procedure *PostOrder* (*RootPointer* : *TreePointer*);

    (∗ Procedure for postorder traversal of binary tree ∗)

    begin (∗ *PostOrder* ∗)
      if *RootPointer* <> **nil then**   (∗ tree is not empty ∗)
        begin
          PostOrder (*RootPointer*↑.*LChild*);   (∗ L operation ∗)
          PostOrder (*RootPointer*↑.*RChild*);   (∗ R operation ∗)
          Visit (*RootPointer*)   (∗ N operation ∗)
       end (∗ **if** ∗)
    end (∗ *PostOrder* ∗);

In the preceding example, the output produced by *InOrder* was

A E G M P Q Z

Note that the letters are in alphabetical order. This is because these letters were stored in a *sorted binary tree* in which the items stored in the left subtree of a node are less than the item in the given node which in turn is less than all the items in the right subtree. Such trees can be created by repeated insertion of items into a sorted binary tree that is initially empty; thus we now develop an algorithm for this insertion operation.

To find the position at which an item is to be inserted in a sorted binary tree, we begin by comparing that item with the item stored in the root. If the item is less than the root item, it must be placed in the left subtree; otherwise it must be placed in the right subtree. A comparison is then made of the item with the root of this subtree to determine in which of its subtrees the item should be placed. We repeat this until an empty subtree is found in which the item is to be inserted. The following recursive procedure *TreeInsert* carries out this insertion operation:

```
procedure TreeInsert (var RootPointer : TreePointer; Item : DataType);

    (* Procedure to insert node containing Item
       into a sorted binary tree *)

    begin (* TreeInsert *)
        if RootPointer = nil then                    (* insert in empty tree *)
            begin
                new (RootPointer);
                with RootPointer↑ do
                    begin
                        Data := Item;
                        LChild := nil;
                        RChild := nil
                    end (* with *)
            end (* if *)
        else if Item < RootPointer↑.Data then        (* insert in left subtree *)
            TreeInsert (RootPointer↑.LChild, Item)
        else                                         (* insert in right subtree *)
            TreeInsert (RootPointer↑.RChild, Item)
    end (* TreeInsert *);
```

While a sorted binary tree is being created or after it has been created, it is often necessary to search the tree to determine whether a given item is in some node. An algorithm to perform such a search is quite similar to that for insertion. The following recursive function *Search* returns a pointer to a node containing a specified item or a nil pointer if the item is not in the tree:

```
function Search (RootPointer : TreePointer; Item : DataType) : TreePointer;

    (*Function to return a pointer to a node in a sorted binary tree
       that contains Item, or nil if Item is not in the tree *)

    begin (* Search *)
        if RootPointer = nil then                    (* empty tree *)
            Search := nil
```

```
                else
             with RootPointer↑ do
                 if Item = Data then                 (* item found *)
                     Search := RootPointer
                 else if Item < Data then             (* search left subtree *)
                     Search := Search(LChild, Item)
                 else                                 (* search right subtree *)
                     Search := Search(RChild, Item)
        end (* Search *);
```

Deleting a leaf node in a binary tree is easy to do, but deleting an interior node (a node having at least one child) is more complex. The exercises explore the operation of deletion in more detail.

```
PROGRAM SortedBinaryTree (input, output);

(*******************************************************************

    Program to construct a sorted binary tree.  Tree may be traversed
    at any time using preorder, inorder, or postorder.

*******************************************************************)

TYPE
    DataType = char;
    TreePointer = ^TreeNode;
    TreeNode = RECORD
                   Data : DataType;
                   LChild, RChild : TreePointer
               END;

VAR
    RootPointer : TreePointer;   (* pointer to root of tree *)
    Char1,                       (* 1st character of command *)
    Char2 : char;                (* 2nd character of command *)
    Item : DataType;             (* item to insert in tree *)

FUNCTION Search (RootPointer : TreePointer; Item : DataType) : TreePointer;

    (*******************************************************************

        Function to return a pointer to the node in a sorted binary
        tree that contains Item, or NIL if Item is not in the tree.

    *******************************************************************)

    BEGIN (* Search *)
        IF RootPointer = NIL THEN                (* empty tree *)
            Search := NIL
        ELSE
            WITH RootPointer^ DO
                IF Item = Data THEN              (* item found *)
                    Search := RootPointer
                ELSE IF Item < Data THEN         (* search left subtree *)
                    Search := Search (LChild, Item)
                ELSE                             (* search right subtree *)
                    Search := Search (RChild, Item)
    END (* Search *);
```

Figure 14.4

ADVANCED APPLICATIONS

Fig. 14.4 (cont.)

```
PROCEDURE TreeInsert (VAR RootPointer : TreePointer; Item : DataType);

    (***************************************************************

       Procedure to insert Item into sorted binary tree.   The new
       of RootPointer is returned.

    ***************************************************************)

    BEGIN (* TreeInsert *)
       IF RootPointer = NIL THEN                    (* empty tree *)
          BEGIN
             new (RootPointer);
             WITH RootPointer^ DO
                BEGIN
                   Data := Item;
                   LChild := NIL;
                   RChild := NIL
                END (* WITH *)
          END (* IF *)
       ELSE IF Item < RootPointer^.Data THEN   (* insert in left subtree *)
          TreeInsert (RootPointer^.LChild, Item)
       ELSE                                     (* insert in right subtree *)
          TreeInsert (RootPointer^.RChild, Item)
    END (* TreeInsert *);


PROCEDURE InOrder (RootPointer : TreePointer);

    (***************************************************************

       Procedure for inorder traversal of binary tree.

    ***************************************************************)

    BEGIN (* InOrder *)
       IF RootPointer <> NIL THEN                   (* tree not empty *)
          WITH RootPointer^ DO
             BEGIN
                InOrder (LChild);                    (* L operation *)
                write (Data);                        (* N operation *)
                InOrder (RChild)                     (* R operation *)
             END (* WITH *)
    END (* InOrder *);


PROCEDURE PreOrder (RootPointer : TreePointer);

    (***************************************************************

       Procedure for preorder traversal of binary tree.

    ***************************************************************)

    BEGIN (* PreOrder *)
       IF RootPointer <> NIL THEN                   (* tree not empty *)
          WITH RootPointer^ DO
             BEGIN
                write (Data);                        (* N operation *)
                PreOrder (LChild);                   (* L operation *)
                PreOrder (RChild)                    (* R operation *)
             END (* WITH *)
    END (* PreOrder *);
```

Fig. 14.4 (cont.)

```pascal
PROCEDURE PostOrder (RootPointer : TreePointer);

   (**********************************************************************

      Procedure for postorder traversal of binary tree.

   *********************************************************************)

   BEGIN (* PostOrder *)
      IF RootPointer <> NIL THEN                    (* tree not empty *)
         WITH RootPointer^ DO
            BEGIN
               PostOrder (LChild);                  (* L operation *)
               PostOrder (RChild);                  (* R operation *)
               write (Data)                         (* N operation *)
            END (* WITH *)
   END (* PostOrder *);

BEGIN (* main program *)
   writeln ('Commands:');
   writeln ('   I followed by a character  -- to insert that character');
   writeln ('   S followed by a character -- to search for that character');
   writeln ('   TI -- for inorder traversal');
   writeln ('   TP -- for preorder traversal');
   writeln ('   TR -- for postorder traversal');
   writeln ('   QU -- to quit');
   writeln;
   RootPointer := NIL;                          (* initialize empty tree *)
   REPEAT
      write ('Command:  ');
      readln (Char1, Char2);
      IF Char1 IN ['S', 'I','T', 'Q'] THEN
         CASE Char1 OF
            'S' :  IF Search(RootPointer, Char2) <> NIL THEN
                      writeln (Char2, ' is in the tree')
                   ELSE
                      writeln (Char2, ' not in the tree');
            'I' :  TreeInsert (RootPointer, Char2);
            'T' :  BEGIN
                      IF Char2 IN ['I', 'P', 'R'] THEN
                         CASE Char2 OF
                            'I' :  InOrder (RootPointer);
                            'P' :  PreOrder (RootPointer);
                            'R' :  PostOrder (RootPointer)
                         END (* CASE *)
                      ELSE
                         write ('Illegal traversal');
                      writeln
                   END;
            'Q' :  (* Quit *)
         END (* CASE *)
      ELSE
         writeln ('Illegal command')
   UNTIL Char1 = 'Q'
END (* main program *).
```

Sample run:

Commands:
    I followed by a character -- to insert that character
    S followed by a character -- to search for that character

Fig. 14.4 (cont.)

```
    TI -- for inorder traversal
    TP -- for preorder traversal
    TR -- for postorder traversal
    QU -- to quit

Command:   IM
Command:   IE
Command:   IZ
Command:   IP
Command:   IA
Command:   IG
Command:   SP
P is in the tree
Command:   SQ
Q not in the tree
Command:   IQ
Command:   TI
AEGMPQZ
Command:   TR
MEAGZPQ
Command:   TR
AGEQPZM
Command:   IB
Command:   IC
Command:   ID
Command:   IF
Command:   TI
ABCDEFGMPQZ
Command:   TP
MEABCDGFZPQ
Command:   TR
DCBAFGEQPZM
Command:   QU
```

The program in Figure 14.4 uses the procedures developed in this section to process a sorted binary tree whose nodes contain characters. The user may select from the following menu of options:

I followed by a character: To insert a character
S followed by a character: To search for a character
TI: for inorder traversal
TP: for preorder traversal
TR: for postorder traversal
QU: to quit

Exercises

1. For each of the following lists of letters,

(a) Draw the sorted binary tree that is constructed when the letters are inserted in the order given.

(b) Perform inorder, preorder, and postorder traversals of the tree and show the sequence of letters that results in each case.

    (i) M, I, T, E, R   **(ii)** T, I, M, E, R

    (iii) R, E, M, I, T   **(iv)** C, O, R, N, F, L, A, K, E, S

2. For the trees in Exercise 1, traverse each tree using the following orders:

(a) NRL   **(b)** RNL   **(c)** RLN

3. For each of the following arithmetic expressions, draw a binary tree that represents the expression, and then use tree traversals to find the equivalent prefix and postfix (RPN) expressions:

(a) $A + B + C / D$ **(b)** $(A + B) / C - D$

(c) $(A + B) * ((C + D) / (E + F))$

(d) $A - (B - (C - (D - E)))$

4. (a) Preorder traversal of a certain binary tree produced

     A D F G H K L P Q R W Z

and inorder traversal produced

     G F H K D L A W R Q P Z

Draw the binary tree.

(b) Postorder traversal of a certain binary tree produced

     F G H D A L P Q R Z W K

and inorder traversal gave the same result as in (a). Draw the binary tree.

(c) Show by example that knowing the results of a preorder traversal and a postorder traversal does not uniquely determine the binary tree; that is, give an example of two different binary trees for which a preorder traversal of each gives the same result and so does a postorder traversal.

5. As noted in the text, every tree can be represented as a binary tree. This can be done by letting node x be a left child of node y in the binary tree if x is the leftmost child of y in the given tree, and by letting x be the right child of y if x and y are siblings (have the same parent) in the original tree. For example, the tree

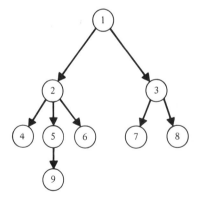

can be represented as the binary tree

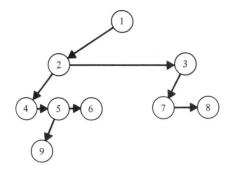

Represent each of the following as binary trees:

(a)

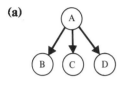

(b)

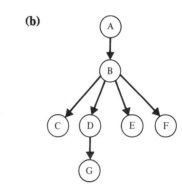

(c)

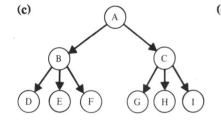

(d)

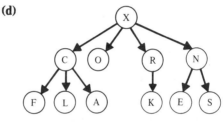

6. Write a recursive function to count the number of leaves in a binary tree. (Hint: How is the number of leaves in the entire tree related to the number of leaves in the left and right subtrees of the root?)

7. Write a recursive function to find the level in a binary tree at which a given item is located. The root is at level 0 and its children at level 1.

8. Write a recursive function to find the depth of a binary tree. The depth of an empty tree is 0, and for a nonempty tree it is one more than the larger of the depths of the left and right subtrees of the root.

9. If we use the notation $x(y,z)$ to mean that x is a node of a binary tree with left child y and right child z, then the binary tree

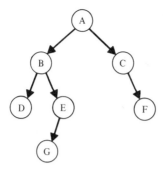

can be represented as

A(B(D, E(G, −)), C(−, F))

where − denotes an empty subtree. Write a program to read a string of this form representing a binary tree and

(a) Construct its linked representation.

(b) Traverse the tree in some specified order.

(c) Display the tree in some graphical format resembling the usual one.

10. For a *doubly linked list* as described in the text:

   (a) Write the necessary type declarations for constructing such a doubly linked list.

   (b) Write a procedure for traversing the list from left to right.

   (c) Write a procedure for traversing the list from right to left.

   (d) Write a procedure for inserting an item (1) after or (2) before some other given item in a doubly linked list.

   (e) Write a procedure to delete an item from a doubly linked list.

11. A *doubly linked ring* or *doubly linked circular list* is a doubly linked list in which the nil right pointer in the last node is replaced with a pointer to the first node, and the nil left pointer in the first node is replaced with a pointer to the last node.

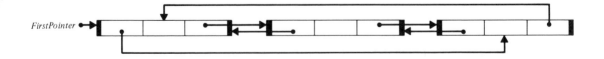

Assuming that *FirstPointer* points to the first node, write procedures to

(a) Traverse the list from left to right.

(b) Traverse the list from right to left.

(c) Insert an item (1) after or (2) before a given item in the list.

(d) Delete an item from the list.

12. One application of multiply linked lists is to maintain a list sorted in two different ways. For example, consider the following multiply linked lists having two links per node:

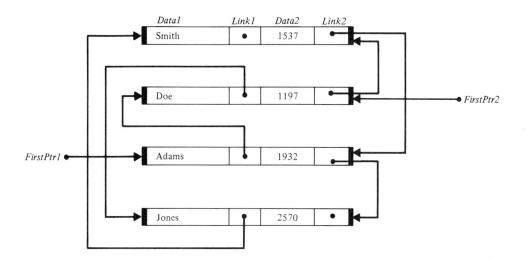

If this list is traversed and the data fields displayed by using *FirstPtr1* to point to the first node and following the pointers in the field *Link1,* the names are in alphabetical order:

Adams	1932
Doe	1197
Jones	2570
Smith	1537

A traversal using *FirstPtr2* to point to the first node and following pointers in the field *Link2* gives the id numbers in ascending order:

Doe	1197
Smith	1537
Adams	1932
Jones	2570

This list is logically ordered, therefore, in two different ways. Write a program to read the first ten records from *UsersFile* (see Appendix E), and store them in a multiply linked list that is logically sorted so that the user id numbers are in ascending order and the resources used to date are in descending order. Traverse the list and display the records so that the id numbers are in ascending order. Then traverse the list and display the records so that the resources used to date are in descending order.

13. In Exercise 14 of Chapter 13, a linked list representation for a polynomial in x,

$$P(x) = a_n x^n + a_{n-1} x^{n-1} + \cdots + a_1 x + a_0$$

was described. A *polynomial in two variables* x and y can be viewed as a polynomial in one variable y with coefficients that are polynomials in x; that is, it has the form

$$P(x,y) = A_m(x) y^m + A_{m-1}(x) y^{m-1} + \cdots + A_1(x) y + A_0(x)$$

where each $A_i(x)$ is a polynomial in x. For example,

$$7x^5 y^3 + 5x^2 y^3 + 4x^5 y^2 - 3xy^2 + y^2 + 7x + 1$$

can be rewritten as

$$(7x^5 + 5x^2) y^3 + (4x^5 - 3x + 1) y^2 + (7x + 1)$$

A multiply linked representation for such polynomials is obtained by representing each term of the form $A_k(x) y^k$ by a node that stores the exponent of y and two links, one containing a pointer to a linked list representing the polynomial $A_k(x)$ and the other a pointer to the next term. For example, the first term in the above example can be represented as

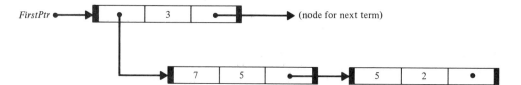

(a) Draw a multiply linked representation for

$$P(x,y) = 3x^9 y^5 + 5x^7 y^5 - 7x^5 y^5 + 6x^2 y^4 + xy^4 + 2xy$$
$$+ 9y + x^2 + 4x + 1$$

(b) Write a program to read triples of the form

(coefficient, x-exponent, y-exponent)

for a polynomial in x and y and construct its linked representation. Then read values for x and y and find the value of the polynomial.

(c) Modify the program in part (b) so that the exponents of x and the exponents of y need not be read in decreasing order.

14. To delete a node x from a sorted binary tree, three cases must be considered:

(a) *x* is a leaf.

(b) *x* has only one subtree.

(c) *x* has two subtrees.

Case a is easily handled. For Case b, simply replace *x* by the root of its subtree by linking the parent of *x* to this root. For Case c, *x* must be replaced by its inorder successor (or predecessor). The following diagram illustrates this case:

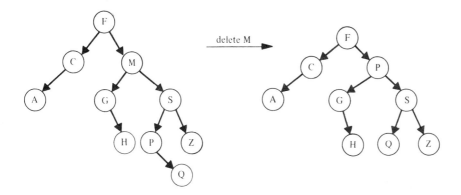

Write a procedure to delete an item from a sorted binary tree. A procedure like *Search* in the text can be used to find the location of the item in the tree and its parent.

15. For a certain company, the method by which the pay for each employee is computed depends on whether that employee is classified as an *Office* employee, a *Factory* employee, or a *Salesman*. Suppose that a file of employee records is maintained in which each record is a variant record containing the following information for each employee:

> name (20 characters)
> social security number (integer)
> age (integer)
> number of dependents (integer)
> employee code (character O, F, S representing *Office, Factory, Salesman,* respectively)
> hourly rate if employee is *Factory*
> annual salary if employee is *Office*
> a base pay (real) and a commission percentage (real) if employee is *Salesman*

Write a menu-driven program that allows at least the following options to be selected by the user of the program:

> GET : Gets the records from the employee file and stores them in a sorted binary tree, sorted so that the names are in alphabetical order.

INS : Insert the record for a new employee into the binary tree.

UPD : Update the record of an employee already in the tree. (Allow a change of name, social security number, and so on)

RET : Retrieve and display the record for a specified employee (by name or by social security number)

LIS : List the records (or perhaps selected items in the records) in order. This option should allow suboptions

ALL -- to list for all employees
OFF -- to list for only *Office* employees
FAC -- " " " " *Factory* "
SAL -- " " " " *Salesman* "

SAV : To copy the records from the binary tree into a permanent file.

DEL : To delete the record of an employee from the binary tree.

14.3 Quicksort

On several occasions we considered the important data-processing problem of sorting a list of items. In several examples we used the *bubble sort* algorithm, and the exercises in Section 8.3 described other sorting schemes such as *Shell sort* and *insertion sort*. A *tree sort* method was described in the preceding section, and in this section we describe the *quicksort* method. This scheme is one of the fastest methods of sorting and is most often implemented by a recursive algorithm. In our description of this method, we assume for the sake of simplicity that the items being sorted are simple items. If they are records, then the sorting is carried out using a key field in the records.

The basic idea of quicksort for sorting a list of items into ascending order is to select one item from the list and then rearrange the list so that this selected item is in its proper position; that is, all list elements that precede it are less than this item, and all those that follow are greater than the item. This divides the original list into two sublists, each of which may then be sorted independently in the *same* way. As might be expected, this leads naturally to a recursive algorithm for quicksort.

To illustrate this splitting of a list into two sublists, consider the following list of integers:

50, 30, 20, 80, 90, 70, 95, 85, 10, 15, 75, 25

If we select the first number as the item to be properly positioned, we must rearrange the list so that 30, 20, 10, 15, and 25 are placed before 50, and 80, 90, 70, 95, 85, and 75 are placed after it. To carry out this rearrangement, we search from the right end of the list for an item less than 50 and from the left end for an item greater than 50.

This locates the two numbers 25 and 80 which we now interchange to obtain

We then resume the search from the right for a number less than 50 and from the left for a number greater than 50:

This locates the numbers 15 and 90 which are then interchanged:

50 , 30 , 20 , 25 , 15 , 70 , 95 , 85 , 10 , 90 , 75 , 80

A continuation of the searches locates 10 and 70

Interchanging these gives

50 , 30 , 20 , 25 , 15 , 10 , 95 , 85 , 70 , 90 , 75 , 80

When we resume our search from the right for a number less than 50, we locate the value 10 that was found on the previous left-to-right search. This signals the end of the two searches, and we interchange 50 and 10, thus giving

10 , 30 , 20 , 25 , 15 , 50 , 95 , 85 , 70 , 90 , 75 , 80

The two underlined sublists now have the required properties: all items in the first sublist are less than 50, and all those in the right sublist are greater than 50. Consequently, 50 has been properly positioned.

Both the sublist

10, 30, 20, 25, 15

consisting of the numbers in positions 1 through 5 and the sublist

95, 85, 70, 90, 75, 80

of numbers in positions 7 through 12 can now be sorted independently. For this, a procedure is needed to split a list of items in the array positions given by two parameters *Low* and *High* denoting the beginning and end positions of the sublist, respectively. If we assume declarations of the form

const
     ListLimit = . . . ; (∗ limit on length of list ∗)

type
     DataType = . . . ; (∗ type of elements in the list ∗)
     List = **array**[1..*ListLimit*] **of** *DataType*;

then the following procedure carries out the desired splitting of the (sub)list *X*[*Low*], . . . , *X*[*High*].

procedure *Split* (**var** *X* : *List*; *Low*, *High* : *integer*; **var** *Mid* : *integer*);

(∗ Procedure to rearrange *X*[*Low*], . . . , *X*[*High*] so that one item is properly positioned; it returns the rearranged list and the final position *Mid* of that item. ∗)

     var
     Left,   (∗ index for searching from the left ∗)
     Right : *integer*;   (∗ index for searching from the right ∗)
     TempItem : *DataType*; (∗ temporary item used for interchanging ∗)
begin (∗ *Split* ∗)
     (∗ Initialize indices for left and right searches ∗)
     Left := *Low*;
     Right := *High*;

     (∗ Carry out the searches ∗)
     while *Left* < *Right* **do**   (∗ While searches haven't met ∗)
        begin
           (∗ Search from the right ∗)
           while *X*[*Right*] > *X*[*Low*] **do**
             Right := *Right* − 1;

           (∗ Search from the left ∗)
           while (*Left* < *Right*) **and** (*X*[*Left*] <= *X*[*Low*]) **do**
             Left := *Left* + 1;

           (∗ Interchange items if searches have not met ∗)
           if *Left* < *Right* **then**

```
            begin
                TempItem := X[Left];
                X[Left] := X[Right];
                x[Right] := TempItem
            end (* if *)
        end (* while *);

    (* End of searches; place selected item in proper position *)
    Mid := Right;
    TempItem := X[Mid];
    X[Mid] := X[Low];
    X[Low] := TempItem
end (* Split *);
```

A recursive procedure to sort a list is now easy to write:

```
        procedure QuickSort (var X : List; Low, High : integer);
            (* Procedure to quicksort X[Low], . . . , X[High] *)

            var
                Mid : integer;        (* final position of selected item *)

            begin (* QuickSort *)
(*1*)           if Low < High then      (* list has more than one item *)
                    begin
(*2*)                   Split (X, Low, High, Mid);           (* split into two sublists *)
(*3*)                   QuickSort (X, Low, Mid − 1);         (* sort first sublist *)
(*4*)                   QuickSort (X, Mid + 1, High)         (* sort second sublist *)
                    end (* if *)
(*5*)       end (* QuickSort *);
```

(Some of the statements have been numbered for later reference.) This procedure is called with a statement of the form

$$QuickSort\ (Item,\ 1,\ NumItems)$$

where *NumItems* is the number of elements in the given list *Item* to be sorted.

To demonstrate this procedure, suppose that the following list of integers is to be sorted:

8, 2, 13, 5, 14, 3, 7

We use a tree to display the action of *QuickSort*. In this tree, a circular node indicates an item placed in its proper position, with a shaded circular node indicating the item being properly positioned at this step. Rectangular nodes represent sublists to be sorted, and a shaded rectangle indicates the next sublist to be sorted. In the list of comments, a label such as II.3 indicates the level (II) in the tree of the sublist being processed and the statement (3) in *QuickSort* currently being executed.

Tree	Comments

Tree   **Comments**

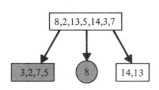

First call to *QuickSort* (*Low* = 1, *High* = 7).

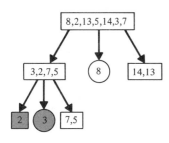

I.1: 1 < 7 so
I.2: Split the list and position 8.
I.3: Call *QuickSort* on left sublist
(*Low* = 1, *High* = 4).

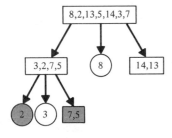

II.1: 1 < 4 so
II.2: Split the sublist and position 3.
II.3: Call *QuickSort* on left sublist
(*Low* = 1, *High* = 1)

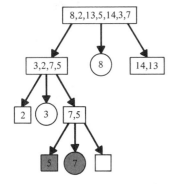

III.1: 1 ≮ 1 (one-element sublist) so
III.5: Return to previous level.

II.4: Call *QuickSort* on right sublist
(*Low* = 3, *High* = 4).

III.1: 3 < 4 so
III.2: Split the sublist and position 7.
III.3: Call *QuickSort* on left sublist
(*Low* = 3, *High* = 3).

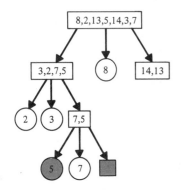

IV.1: 3 ≮ 3 (one-element sublist) so
IV.5: Return to previous level.

III.4: Call *QuickSort* on right sublist
(*Low* = 5, *High* = 4).

Tree	Comments

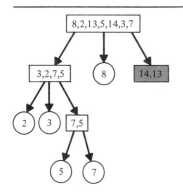

IV.1: $5 \nless 4$ (empty sublist) so
IV.5: Return to previous level.

III.5: Return to previous level.

II.5: Return to previous level.

I.4: Call *QuickSort* on right sublist
(*Low* = 6, *High* = 7).

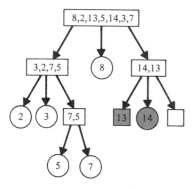

II.1: $6 < 7$, so
II.2: Split the sublist and position 14.
II.3: Call *QuickSort* on left sublist
(*Low* = 6, *High* = 6)

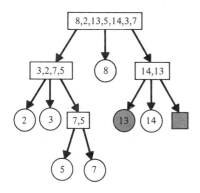

III.1: $6 \nless 6$ (one-element sublist) so
III.5: Return to previous level.

II.4: Call *QuickSort* on right sublist
(*Low* = 8, *High* = 7).

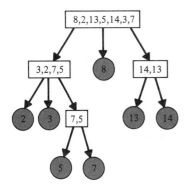

III.1: $8 \nless 7$ (empty sublist) so
III.5: Return to previous level.

II.5: Return to previous level.

I.5: Return to main program; sorting
is completed.

The program in Figure 14.5 reads a list of numbers, calls the procedures *Split* and *QuickSort* to sort the numbers into ascending order, and then displays the sorted list.

```
PROGRAM SortWithQuickSort (input, output);

(***********************************************************************

   Program to read and count a list of items, sort them using the
   quicksort algorithm, and then display the sorted list.

***********************************************************************)

CONST
   ListLimit = 100;

TYPE
   DataType = integer;
   List = ARRAY[1..ListLimit] OF DataType;

VAR
   Item : List;          (* list of items to be sorted *)
   Temp : DataType;      (* temporary item read *)
   NumItems,             (* number of items *)
   i : integer;          (* index *)

PROCEDURE Split (VAR X : List; Low, High : integer; VAR Mid : integer);

   (***********************************************************************

      Procedure to rearrange X[Low], ..., X[High] so that one item
      (originally in position Low) is properly positioned; it returns
      rearranged list and the final position Mid of that item.

   ***********************************************************************)

   VAR
      Left,               (* index for searching from the left *)
      Right : integer;    (* index for searching from the right *)
      TempItem : DataType;  (* temporary item used for interchanging *)

   BEGIN (* Split *)

      (* Initialize indices for left and right searches *)

      Left := Low;
      Right := High;

      (* Continue searches until they meet *)

      WHILE Left < Right DO
         BEGIN
            (* search from the right *)

            WHILE X[Right] > X[Low] DO
               Right := Right - 1;

            (* search from the left *)

            WHILE (Left < Right) AND (X[Left] <= X[Low]) DO
               Left := Left + 1;

            (* interchange items if searches haven't met *)
```

Figure 14.5

ADVANCED APPLICATIONS

Fig. 14.5 (cont.)

```
            IF Left < Right THEN
                BEGIN
                    TempItem := X[Left];
                    X[Left] := X[Right];
                    X[Right] := TempItem
                END (* IF *)
            END (* WHILE *);

    (* End of search; place selected item in proper position *)

    Mid := Right;
    TempItem := X[Mid];
    X[Mid] := X[Low];
    X[Low] := TempItem
  END (* Split *);

PROCEDURE QuickSort (VAR X : List; Low, High : integer);

    (***************************************************************

            Procedure to QuickSort X[Low], ..., X[High]

    ***************************************************************)

    VAR
        Mid : integer;   (* final position of selected item *)

    BEGIN (* QuickSort *)
        IF Low < High THEN                     (* list has more than one item *)
            BEGIN
                Split (X, Low, High, Mid);        (* split into two sublists *)
                QuickSort (X, Low, Mid - 1);      (* sort first sublist *)
                QuickSort (X, Mid + 1, High)      (* sort second sublist *)
            END (* IF *)
    END (* QuickSort *);

    BEGIN (* main program *)
        NumItems := 0;
        writeln ('Enter the items (-9999 to signal the end of data).');
        read (Temp);
        WHILE (Temp <> -9999) AND (NumItems < ListLimit) DO
            BEGIN
                NumItems := NumItems + 1;
                Item[NumItems] := Temp;
                read (Temp)
            END (* WHILE *);
        QuickSort (Item, 1, NumItems);
        writeln ('Sorted list:');
        FOR i := 1 TO NumItems DO
            writeln (Item[i])
    END (* main program *).

Sample run:
==========

Enter the items (-9999 to signal the end of data).
54 67 34 99 27 5 62 45 83
-9999
Sorted list:
        5
        27
        34
        45
        54
        62
        67
        83
        99
```

Exercises

1. Draw a sequence of trees like those in the text to illustrate the actions of *Split* and *QuickSort* while sorting the following lists:

   (a) 5, 1, 6, 4, 3, 2   (b) 1, 2, 3, 6, 5, 4

   (c) 6, 5, 4, 3, 2, 1   (d) 1, 2, 3, 4, 5, 6

2. One of the lists in Exercise 1 shows why the condition *Left* < *Right* is needed to control the search from the left in procedure *Split*. Which list is it? What would happen if this condition were omitted?

3. Modify the procedures *Split* and *QuickSort* to sort a list of records so that the values in a key field are in ascending order. Use these procedures in a program to read the student names and student numbers and addresses from *StudentFile* and then quicksort them so the students' last names are in alphabetical order. (See Appendix E for a description of *StudentFile*.)

4. The procedure *QuickSort* always sorts the left sublist before the right. Its performance improves if the shorter of the two sublists is the first to be sorted. Modify *QuickSort* to do this.

5. Another improvement of the quicksort method is to use some other sorting algorithm to sort small sublists. For example, insertion sort is usually better than quicksort when the list has fewer than twenty items. Modify the quicksort scheme to use insertion sort (see Exercise 12 of Section 8.3) if the sublist has fewer than *LBound* items for some constant *LBound* and otherwise uses quicksort.

6. The procedure *Split* always selects the first element of the sublist to position. Another common practice is to use the "median-of-three" rule in which the median of the three numbers $X[Low]$, $X[Middle]$, and $X[High]$ is selected, where $Middle = (Low + High)$ **div** 2. (The median of three numbers a, b, and c, arranged in ascending order, is the middle number b.) Modify *Split* to use this median-of-three rule.

7. Suppose that we sort a list of records in which some of the values in the key field may be the same. A sorting scheme is said to be *stable* if it does not change the order of such records. For example, consider a list of records containing a person's name and age which is to be sorted so that the ages are in ascending order. Suppose that

| Doe | 39 |

comes before

| Smith | 39 |

in the original list (with possibly several records between them). For a stable sorting scheme, Doe's record still comes before Smith's after the sorting is carried out. Determine whether quicksort is a stable method.

All of the sorting algorithms we have considered thus far are *internal* sorting **External Sorting:** schemes; that is, the entire collection of items to be sorted must be stored **Mergesort** in main memory. In many data-processing problems, however, the data sets are too large to store in main memory and must be stored in external memory. To sort such collections of data, an *external* sorting algorithm is required. One popular and efficient external sorting method is the *mergesort* technique, a variation of which, called *natural mergesort,* is examined in this section.

As the name mergesort suggests, the basic operation in this sorting scheme is merging data files. The merge operation combines two files that have previously been sorted so that the resulting file is also sorted. To illustrate, suppose that *File1* has been sorted and contains the integers

File1 : 2 4 5 7 9 15 16 20

and *File2* contains

File2 : 1 6 8 10 12

To merge these files to produce *File3*, we read one element from each file, say X from *File1* and Y from *File2*.

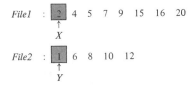

We write the smaller of these values, in this case Y, into *File3:*

File3 : 1

and then read another value for Y from *File2:*

File2 : [2] 4 5 7 9 15 16 20
          ↑
          X

File2 : 1 [6] 8 10 12
             ↑
             Y

Now X is smaller than Y, and so it is written to *File3*, and a new value for X is read from *File1:*

```
File1  :   2  [4]  5   7   9   15  16  20
              ↑
              X
File2  :   1  [6]  8   10  12
              ↑
              Y
File3  :   1   2
```

Again X is less than Y, and so X is written to *File3*, and a new X value is read from *File1*:

```
File1  :   2   4  [5]  7   9   15  16  20
                  ↑
                  X
File2  :   1  [6]  8   10  12
              ↑
              Y
File3  :   1   2   4
```

Continuing in this manner, we eventually reach the value 15 for X and the value 12 for Y :

```
File1  :   2   4   5   7   9  [15]  16  20
                              ↑
                              X
File2  :   1   6   8  10  [12]
                          ↑
                          Y
File3  :   1   2   4   5   6   7   8   9   10
```

Because Y is smaller than X, we write Y to *File3* :

```
File3  :   1   2   4   5   6   7   8   9   10  12
```

Because the end of *File2* has been reached, we simply copy the remaining values in *File1* to *File3* to obtain the final sorted file *File3* :

```
File3  :   1   2   4   5   6   7   8   9   10  12  15  16  20
```

The general algorithm to merge two sorted files *File1* and *File2* is:

Algorithm

1. Open *File1* and *File2* for input, *File3* for output.
2. Read the first element X from *File1* and the first element Y from *File2*.
3. Repeat the following until the end of either *File1* or *File2* is reached:
   If $X < Y$, then
      (i) write X to *File3*.
      (ii) read a new X value from *File1*.
   otherwise:
      (i) write Y to *File3*.
      (ii) read a new Y value from *File2*.
4. If the end of *File1* was encountered, copy any remaining elements from *File2* into *File3*. If the end of *File2* was encountered, copy the rest of *File1* into *File3*.

In this algorithm, we have assumed that the file components are simple components. If the files contain records that are sorted on the basis of some key field, then the key field of X is compared with the key field of Y in Step 3.

To see how the merge operation is used in sorting a file, consider the following file F containing fifteen integers:

F : 75 55 15 20 80 30 35 10 70 40 50 25 45 60 65

Notice that several segments of F contain elements that are already in order:

F : | 75 | 55 | 15 20 80 | 30 35 | 10 70 | 40 50 | 25 45 60 65 |

These segments, enclosed by the vertical bars, are called *subfiles* or *runs* in F and subdivide F in a natural way.

We begin by reading these subfiles of F and alternately writing them to two other files $F1$ and $F2$

$F1$: | 75 | 15 20 80 | 10 70 | 25 45 60 65 |
$F2$: | 55 | 30 35 | 40 50 |

and then identifying the sorted subfiles in $F1$ and $F2$.

$F1$: | 75 | 15 20 80 | 10 70 | 25 45 60 65 |
$F2$: | 55 | 30 35 40 50 |

Note that although the subfiles of $F1$ are the same as those copied from F, two of the original subfiles written into $F2$ have combined to form a larger subfile.

We now merge the first subfile of $F1$ with the first subfile of $F2$, storing the elements back in F.

F : | 55 75 |

Next the second subfile of $F1$ is merged with the second subfile of $F2$ and written to F.

F : | 55 75 | 15 20 30 35 40 50 80 |

This merging of corresponding subfiles continues until the end of either or both of the files $F1$ and $F2$ is reached. If either file still contains subfiles, these are simply copied into F. Thus, in our example, because the end of $F2$ has been reached, the remaining subfiles of $F1$ are copied back into F.

F : | 55 75 | 15 20 30 35 40 50 80 | 10 70 | 25 45 60 65 |

Now, file F is again split into files $F1$ and $F2$ by copying its subfiles alternately into $F1$ and $F2$.

$F1$: | 55 75 | 10 70 |
$F2$: | 15 20 30 35 40 50 80 | 25 45 60 65 |

Identifying the sorted subfiles in each of these files, we see that for this splitting, none of the original subfiles written into either *F1* or *F2* combine to form larger ones. Once again we merge corresponding subfiles of *F1* and *F2* back into *F*.

F : | 15 20 30 35 40 50 55 75 80 | 10 25 45 60 65 70 |

When we now split *F* into *F1* and *F2*, each of the files *F1* and *F2* contains a single sorted subfile, and each is, therefore, completely sorted.

F1 : | 15 20 30 35 40 50 55 75 80 |
F2 : | 10 25 45 60 65 70 |

Thus when we merge *F1* and *F2* back into *F*, *F* will also contain only one sorted subfile and hence will be sorted.

F : | 10 15 20 25 30 35 40 45 50 55 60 65 70 75 80 |

From this example we see that the mergesort method has two steps: (1) splitting the file *F* into two other files *F1* and *F2* and (2) merging corresponding subfiles in these two files. These steps are repeated until each of the the smaller files contains a single sorted subfile, and when these are merged, the resulting file is completely sorted.

The splitting operation is carried out by the following algorithm:

Algorithm

1. Open the file *F* for input and the files *F1* and *F2* for output.
2. While the end of *F* has not been reached, do the following:
   a. Copy a sorted subfile of *F* into *F1* as follows: Repeatedly read an element of *F* and write it into *F1* until the next element in *F* is smaller than this copied item or the end of *F* is reached.
   b. If the end of *F* has not been reached, copy the next sorted subfile of *F* into *F2* in a similar manner.

In this algorithm we have assumed that the elements of the file *F* are simple. If they are records, then the key field on which the sorting is based is used in comparing file elements.

The following algorithm implements the merge operation illustrated in the example.

Algorithm

1. Open files *F1* and *F2* for input; open *F* for output.
2. While neither the end of *F1* nor the end of *F2* has been reached, do the following:
   a. While the end of no subfile in *F1* nor in *F2* has been reached, do the following:
      If the next element in *F1* is less than the next element in *F2*, then copy the next element from *F1* into *F*; otherwise, copy the next element from *F2* into *F*.
   b. If the end of a subfile in *F1* has been reached, then copy the rest of the corresponding subfile in *F2* to *F*; otherwise, copy the rest of the corresponding subfile in *F1* to *F*.

3. Copy any remaining subfiles remaining in *F1* or *F2* to *F*.

In this algorithm, the copying of a subfile from *F1* into *F* can be done by using the technique described in the splitting algorithm, if the roles of *F* and *F1* are interchanged. A similar modification can be used to copy a subfile from F2 into F.

The program in Figure 14.6 reads a file of names from *NameFile* and copies these into file *F*. It displays the names in their original order and then calls the procedures *SplitFile* and *Merge* to sort the file of names using the mergesort algorithm and finally displays the contents of the sorted file. The procedures *SplitFile* and *Merge* use the procedures *CopyOneItem* to copy one item from a file to another file and *CopySubfile* to copy a sorted subfile from one file to another.

```
PROGRAM MergeSort (input, output, NameFile);

(*********************************************************************

    Program to sort the external file NameFile using the natural
    mergesort algorithm.

*********************************************************************)

CONST
    MaxString = 30;

TYPE
    String = PACKED ARRAY[1..MaxString] OF char;
    FileType = String;
    DataFile = FILE OF FileType;

VAR
    NumSubFiles : integer;     (* number of subfiles merged at each stage *)
    F1, F2, F,                 (* files to be used in mergesort *)
    NameFile : DataFile;       (* external file to be sorted *)

PROCEDURE CopyOneItem (VAR FileA, FileB : DataFile;
                       VAR NextItemSmaller : boolean);

    (********************************************************************

        Procedure to copy one item from FileA to FileB and to check
        if the next item in FileA is smaller than the one just copied
        (indicating the end of a subfile in FileA).

    ********************************************************************)

    BEGIN (* CopyOneItem *)
       IF NOT eof(FileA) THEN
          BEGIN
             read (FileA, FileB^);
             IF eof(FileA) THEN
                NextItemSmaller := true
             ELSE
                NextItemSmaller := (FileA^ < FileB^);
             put (FileB)
          END (* IF *)
    END (* CopyOneItem *);

PROCEDURE CopySubFile (VAR FileA, FileB: DataFile; VAR EndSubfile : boolean);
```

Figure 14.6

Fig. 14.6 (cont.)

```
(**********************************************************************

    Procedure to copy a sorted subfile from FileA to FileB.

***********************************************************************)

BEGIN (* CopySubFile *)
   EndSubfile := false;
   WHILE NOT EndSubfile DO
      CopyOneItem (FileA, FileB, EndSubfile)
END (* CopySubFile *);

PROCEDURE SplitFile (VAR F, F1, F2 : DataFile);

(**********************************************************************

    Procedure to read sorted subfiles from file F and write them
    alternately to files F1 and F2.

***********************************************************************)

VAR
   FileNum : 1..2;            (* # of file being written to *)
   EndSubfile : boolean;      (* indicates end of subfile *)

BEGIN (* SplitFile *)

   (* Open the files *)

   reset (F);
   rewrite (F1);
   rewrite (F2);

   (* Split the file *)

   FileNum := 1;
   WHILE NOT eof(F) DO
      BEGIN
         CASE FileNum OF
                  1 : CopySubFile (F, F1, EndSubfile);
                  2 : CopySubFile (F, F2, EndSubfile)
         END (* CASE *);

         (* Switch to other file *)

         FileNum := 3 - FileNum
      END (* WHILE *)
END (* SplitFile *);

PROCEDURE Merge (VAR F, F1, F2 : DataFile; VAR NumSubFiles : integer);

(**********************************************************************

    Procedure to merge sorted subfiles in F1 and F2 and write these
    to file F; NumSubFiles is the number of subfiles written to F.

***********************************************************************)

VAR
   FileNum :    1..2;              (* # of file being used *)
   EndSubfile : ARRAY[1..2] OF boolean;
                                   (* indicate end of subfiles in F1 and F2 *)
```

ADVANCED APPLICATIONS

Fig. 14.6 (cont.)

```
BEGIN (* Merge *)

    (* Open the files *)

    reset (F1);
    reset (F2);
    rewrite (F);

    (* Now merge subfiles of F1 & F2 into F *)

    NumSubFiles := 0;
    WHILE NOT (eof(F1) OR eof(F2)) DO
        BEGIN

            (* set end-of-subfile indicators *)

            EndSubfile[1] := false;
            EndSubfile[2] := false;

            (* merge two subfiles *)

            WHILE NOT (eof(F1) OR eof(F2) OR
                        EndSubfile[1] OR EndSubfile[2]) DO
                IF F1^ < F2^ THEN
                    CopyOneItem (F1, F, EndSubfile[1])
                ELSE
                    CopyOneItem (F2, F, EndSubfile[2]);

            (* copy rest of other subfile *)

            IF EndSubfile[1] THEN
                CopySubFile (F2, F, EndSubfile[2])
            ELSE
                CopySubFile (F1, F, EndSubfile[1]);
            NumSubFiles := NumSubFiles + 1
        END (* WHILE *);

    (* Now copy any remaining subfiles in F1 or F2 to F *)

    WHILE NOT eof(F1) DO
        BEGIN
            CopySubFile (F1, F, EndSubfile[1]);
            NumSubFiles := NumSubFiles + 1
        END (* WHILE *);
    WHILE NOT eof(F2) DO
        BEGIN
            CopySubFile (F2, F, EndSubfile[2]);
            NumSubFiles := NumSubFiles + 1
        END (* WHILE *);
END (* Merge *);

PROCEDURE ReadNames (VAR F, NameFile : DataFile);

    (*************************************************************

    Procedure to read the names from NameFile and copy them
    to file F.

    *************************************************************)

    BEGIN (* ReadNames *)
        reset (NameFile);
        rewrite (F);
```

Fig. 14.6 (cont.)

```
      writeln ('Contents of original file:');
      writeln;
      WHILE NOT eof(NameFile) DO
         BEGIN
             read (NameFile, F^);
             writeln (F^);
             put (F);
         END (* WHILE *);
      writeln
   END (* ReadNames *);

PROCEDURE PrintFile (VAR F : DataFile);

   (********************************************************************

             Procedure to print the contents of file F.

   *******************************************************************)

      BEGIN (* PrintFile *)
         reset (F);
         WHILE NOT eof(F) DO
             BEGIN
                 writeln (F^);
                 get (F)
             END (* WHILE *)
      END (* PrintFile *);

   BEGIN (* main program *)
      ReadNames (F, NameFile);

      (* Now split and merge subfiles until number of sorted subfiles is 1 *)

      REPEAT
         SplitFile (F, F1, F2);
         Merge (F, F1, F2, NumSubFiles)
      UNTIL NumSubFiles = 1;

      (* Display sorted file *)

      writeln ('Contents of sorted file:');
      writeln;
      PrintFile (F)
   END (* main program *).


   Sample run:


   Contents of original file:

   Doe, John Q.
   Smith, Mary J.
   Jones, Frederick N.
   Vandervan, Peter F.
   Adams, John Q.
   Zzcyk, Stanislaw S.
   Gertie, Dirty
   James, Jesse
   Terrific, Tom T.
   Jackson, R.
```

Fig. 14.6 (cont.)

```
Contents of sorted file:

Adams, John Q.
Doe, John Q.
Gertie, Dirty
Jackson, R.
James, Jesse
Jones, Frederick N.
Smith, Mary J.
Terrific, Tom T.
Vandervan, Peter F.
Zzcyk, Stanislaw S.
```

Exercises

1. Following the example of the text, show the various splitting–merging stages of mergesort for the following lists of numbers:

   (a) 1, 5, 3, 8, 7, 2, 6, 4

   (b) 1, 8, 2, 7, 3, 6, 5, 4

   (c) 1, 2, 3, 4, 5, 6, 7, 8

   (d) 8, 7, 6, 5, 4, 3, 2, 1

2. Modify mergesort to sort a file of records so that the values in a key field are in order. Then write a program to read records from *UsersFile* (described in Appendix E) and sort them so that the resources used to date are in increasing order.

3. One variation of the mergesort method is obtained by modifying the splitting operation as follows: copy some fixed number of elements into main memory, sort them using an internal sorting method such as quicksort, and write this sorted list to *F1;* then read the same number of elements from *F* into main memory, sort them internally, and write this sorted list to *F2,* and so on, alternating between *F1* and *F2.* Write procedures for this modified mergesort scheme, using quicksort to sort internally the sublists containing *Size* elements for some constant *Size.*

4. *Stable* sorting algorithms were described in Exercise 7 of Section 14.3. Determine whether mergesort is a stable sorting scheme.

5. Write a program to read titles of books or magazine articles and prepare a KWIC (Key Word In Context) index. Each word in a title except for such simple words as AND, OF, THE, A, and the like is considered to be a key word. The program should read the titles and construct a file containing the key words together with the corresponding title, sort the file using the mergesort method, and then display the KWIC index. For example, the titles

FUNDAMENTALS OF PROGRAMMING

PROGRAMMING FUNDAMENTALS FOR DATA STRUC-
TURES

would produce the following KWIC index:

DATA	PROGRAMMING FUNDAMEN-TALS FOR DATA STRUCTURES
FUNDAMENTALS	FUNDAMENTALS OF PRO-GRAMMING
	PROGRAMMING FUNDAMEN-TALS FOR DATA STRUCTURES
PROGRAMMING	FUNDAMENTALS OF PRO-GRAMMING
	PROGRAMMING FUNDAMEN-TALS FOR DATA STRUCTURES
STRUCTURES	PROGRAMMING FUNDAMEN-TALS FOR DATA STRUCTURES

ASCII and EBCDIC

Decimal	Binary	Octal	Hexa-decimal	ASCII	EBCDIC
0	00000000	0	0	NUL	NUL
.	.	.	.	.	.
.	.	.	.	.	.
.	.	.	.	.	
32	00100000	40	20	space	
33	00100001	41	21	!	
34	00100010	42	22	"	
35	00100011	43	23	#	
36	00100100	44	24	$	
37	00100101	45	25	%	
38	00100110	46	26	&	
39	00100111	47	27	'	
40	00101000	50	28	(	
41	00101001	51	29	)	
42	00101010	52	2A	*	
43	00101011	53	2B	+	
44	00101100	54	2C	,	
45	00101101	55	2B	—	
46	00101110	56	2E	.	
47	00101111	57	2F	/	

Decimal	Binary	Octal	Hexa-decimal	ASCII	EBCDIC
48	00110000	60	30	0	
49	00110001	61	31	1	
50	00110010	62	32	2	
51	00110011	63	33	3	
52	00110100	64	34	4	
53	00110101	65	35	5	
54	00110110	66	36	6	
55	00110111	67	37	7	
56	00111000	70	38	8	
57	00111001	71	39	9	
58	00111010	72	3A	:	
59	00111011	73	3B	;	
60	00111100	74	3C	<	
61	00111101	75	3D	=	
62	00111110	76	3E	>	
63	00111111	77	3F	?	
64	01000000	100	40	@	blank
65	01000001	101	41	A	
66	01000010	102	42	B	
67	01000011	103	43	C	
68	01000100	104	44	D	
69	01000101	105	45	E	
70	01000110	106	46	F	
71	01000111	107	47	G	
72	01001000	110	48	H	
73	01001001	111	49	I	
74	01001010	112	4A	J	¢
75	01001011	113	4B	K	.
76	01001100	114	4C	L	<
77	01001101	115	4D	M	(
78	01001110	116	4E	N	+
79	01001111	117	4F	O		
80	01010000	120	50	P	&
81	01010001	121	51	Q	
82	01010010	122	52	R	
83	01010011	123	53	S	
84	01010100	124	54	T	
85	01010101	125	55	U	
86	01010110	126	56	V	
87	01010111	127	57	W	
88	01011000	130	58	X	
89	01011001	131	59	Y	
90	01011010	132	5A	Z	!
91	01011011	133	5B	[	$
92	01011100	134	5C	\	*
93	01011101	135	5D	]	)
94	01011110	136	5E	∧ (or ↑)	;
95	01011111	137	5F	__(or ←)	¬
96	01100000	140	60	`	—
97	01100001	141	61	a	/
98	01100010	142	62	b	
99	01100011	143	63	c	
100	01100100	144	64	d	
101	01100101	145	65	e	
102	01100110	146	66	f	

Decimal	Binary	Octal	Hexa-decimal	ASCII	EBCDIC
103	01100111	147	67	g	
104	01101000	150	68	h	
105	01101001	151	69	i	
106	01101010	152	6A	j	
107	01101011	153	6B	k	,
108	01101100	154	6C	l	%
109	01101101	155	6D	m	—
110	01101110	156	6E	n	>
111	01101111	157	6F	o	?
112	01110000	160	70	p	
113	01110001	161	71	q	
114	01110010	162	72	r	
115	01110011	163	73	s	
116	01110100	164	74	t	
117	01110101	165	75	u	
118	01110110	166	76	v	
119	01110111	167	77	w	
120	01111000	170	78	x	
121	01111001	171	79	y	
122	01111010	172	7A	z	:
123	01111011	173	7B	{	#
124	01111100	174	7C			@
125	01111101	175	7D	}	'
126	01111110	176	7E	~	=
127	01111111	177	7F	DEL	"
128	10000000	200	80		
129	10000001	201	81		a
130	10000010	202	82		b
131	10000011	203	83		c
132	10000100	204	84		d
133	10000101	205	85		e
134	10000110	206	86		f
135	10000111	207	87		g
136	10001000	210	88		h
137	10001001	211	89		i
.	.	.	.		.
.	.	.	.		.
.	.	.	.		.
145	10010001	221	91		j
146	10010010	222	92		k
147	10010011	223	93		l
148	10010100	224	94		m
149	10010101	225	95		n
150	10010110	226	96		o
151	10010111	227	97		p
152	10011000	230	98		q
153	10011001	231	99		r
.	.	.	.		.
.	.	.	.		.
162	10100010	242	A2		s
163	10100011	243	A3		t
164	10100100	244	A4		u
165	10100101	245	A5		v
166	10100110	246	A6		w

Decimal	Binary	Octal	Hexa-decimal	ASCII	EBCDIC
167	10100111	247	A7		x
168	10101000	250	A8		y
169	10101001	251	A9		z
.	.	.	.		.
.	.	.	.		.
.	.	.	.		.
192	11000000	300	C0		}
193	11000001	301	C1		A
194	11000010	302	C2		B
195	11000011	303	C3		C
196	11000100	304	C4		D
197	11000101	305	C5		E
198	11000110	306	C6		F
199	11000111	307	C7		G
200	11001000	310	C8		H
201	11001001	311	C9		I
.	.	.	.		.
.	.	.	.		.
.	.	.	.		.
208	11010000	320	D0		}
209	11010001	321	D1		J
210	11010010	322	D2		K
211	11010011	323	D3		L
212	11010100	324	D4		M
213	11010101	325	D5		N
214	11010110	326	D6		O
215	11010111	327	D7		P
216	11011000	330	D8		Q
217	11011001	331	D9		R
.	.	.	.		.
.	.	.	.		.
.	.	.	.		.
224	11100000	340	E0		\
225	11100001	341	E1		
226	11100010	342	E2		S
227	11100011	343	E3		T
228	11100100	344	E4		U
229	11100101	345	E5		V
230	11100110	346	E6		W
231	11100111	347	E7		X
232	11101000	350	E8		Y
233	11101001	351	E9		Z
.	.	.	.		.
.	.	.	.		.
.	.	.	.		.
240	11110000	360	F0		0
241	11110001	361	F1		1
242	11110010	362	F2		2
243	11110011	363	F3		3
244	11110100	364	F4		4
245	11110101	365	F5		5
246	11110110	366	F6		6
247	11110111	367	F7		7
248	11111000	370	F8		8
249	11111001	371	F9		9

Decimal	Binary	Octal	Hexa-decimal	ASCII	EBCDIC
.	.	.	.		
.	.	.	.		
.	.	.			
255	11111111	377	FF		

Note: Entries for which there is no character shown indicate that these codes have not been assigned or are used for control.

B

Reserved Words, Standard Identifiers, and Operators

and	end	mod	repeat
array	file	nil	set
begin	for	not	then
case	forward	of	to
const	function	or	type
div	goto	packed	until
do	if	procedure	var
downto	in	program	while
else	label	record	with

Standard Identifiers

Standard Constants

false   *true*   *maxint*

Standard Types

boolean   *char*   *integer*   *real*   *text*

Standard Files

input   *output*

Standard Functions

abs	*exp*	*sin*
arctan	*ln*	*sqr*
chr	*odd*	*sqrt*
cos	*ord*	*succ*
eof	*pred*	*trunc*
eoln	*round*	

Standard Procedures

dispose	*put*	*unpack*
get	*read*	*write*
new	*readln*	*writeln*
pack	*reset*	
page	*rewrite*	

Operators

Unary Arithmetic Operators

Operator	Operation	Type of Operand	Type of Result
+	unary plus	integer real	integer real
−	unary minus	integer real	integer real

Binary Arithmetic Operators

Operator	Operation	Type of Operands	Type of Result
+	addition	integer or real	integer if both operands are integer, otherwise real
−	subtraction	integer or real	integer if both operands are integer, otherwise real
*	multiplication	integer or real	integer if both operands are integer, otherwise real
/	division	integer or real	real
div	integer division	integer	integer
mod	modulo	integer	integer

Relational Operators

Operator	Operation	Type of Operands	Type of Result
=	equality	simple, string, set, or pointer	boolean
<>	inequality	simple, string set, or pointer	boolean
<	less than	simple or string	boolean
>	greater than	simple or string	boolean
<=	less than or equal to, or subset	simple, string, or set	boolean
>=	greater than or equal to, or superset	simple, string, or set	boolean
in	set membership	first operand: ordinal type second operand: set type	boolean

Boolean Operators

Operator	Operation	Type of Operands	Type of Result
and	conjunction	boolean	boolean
not	negation	boolean	boolean
or	disjunction	boolean	boolean

Set Operators

Operator	Operation	Type of Operands	Type or Result
+	set union	set type	same as operands
−	set difference	set type	same as operands
*	set intersection	set type	same as operands

Assignment Operator

Operator	Operation	Type of Operands
:=	assignment	any type except file types

C
Syntax Diagrams

program ⟶ [program heading]

[declaration part]

[statement part] ⟶ (.) ⟶

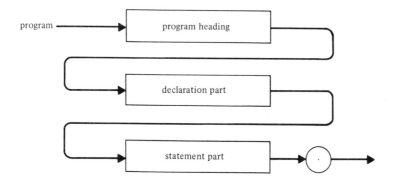

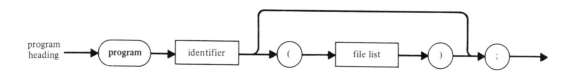

identifier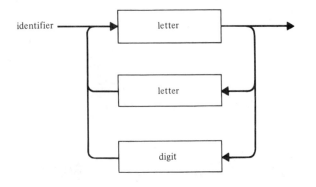

file list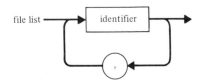

declaration part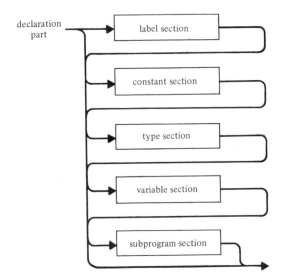

label section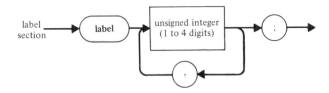

unsigned integer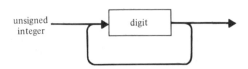

SYNTAX DIAGRAMS

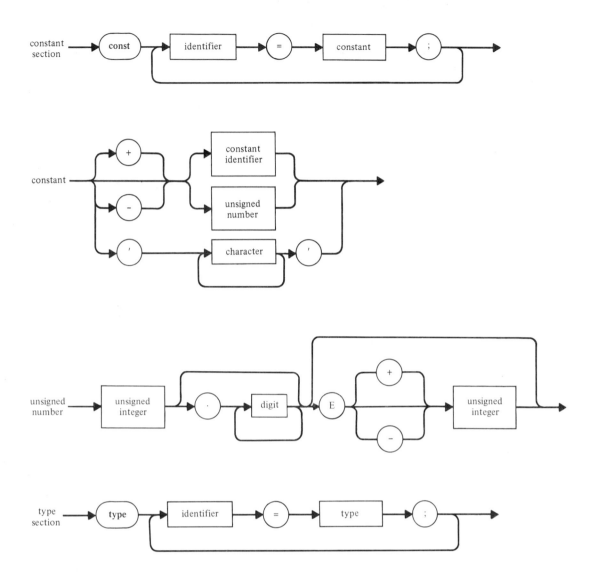

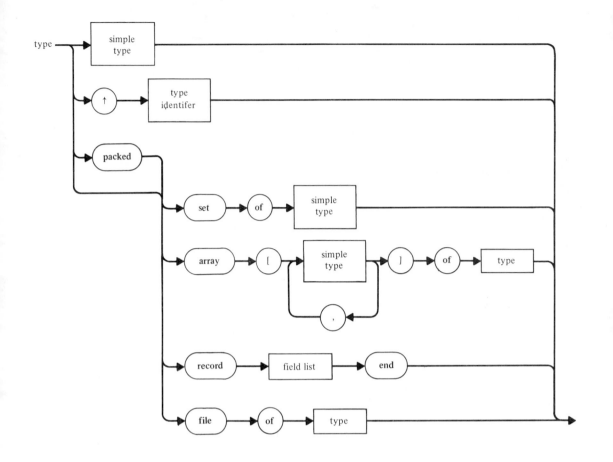

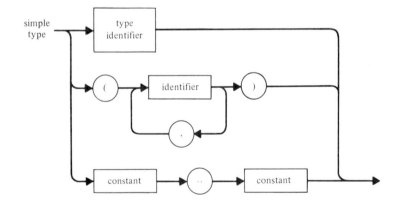

SYNTAX DIAGRAMS

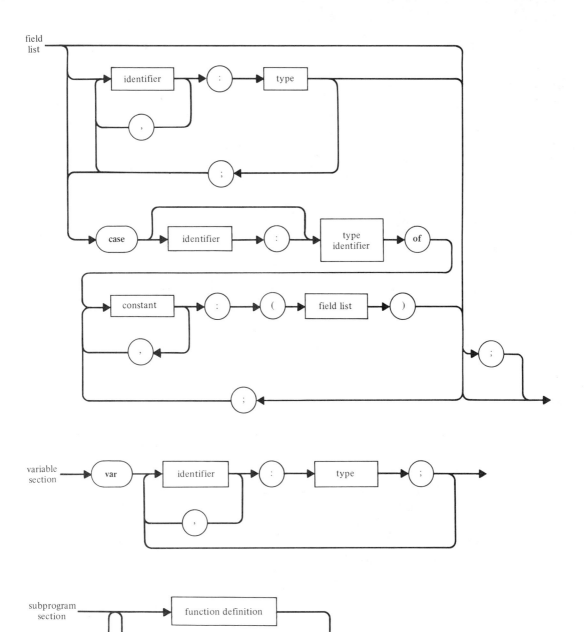

field
list

case

constant : (field list)

variable
section → var → identifier : type ;

subprogram
section → function definition

procedure definition

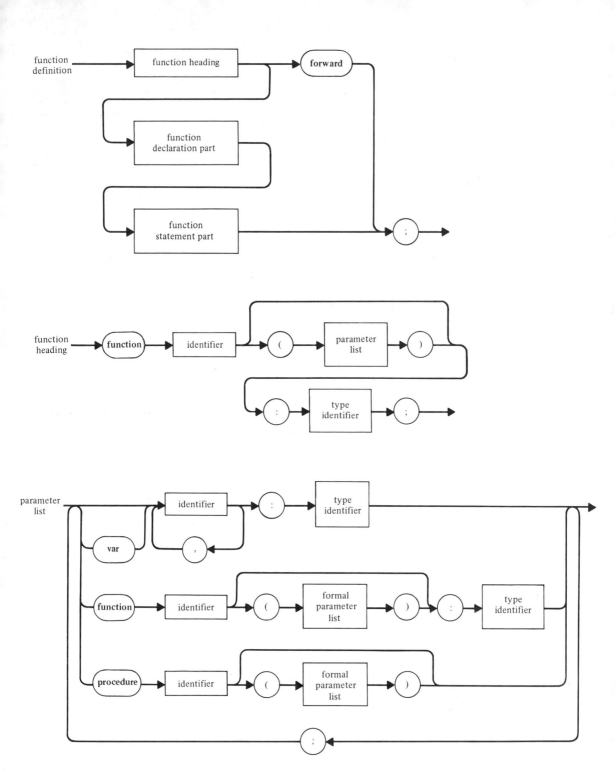

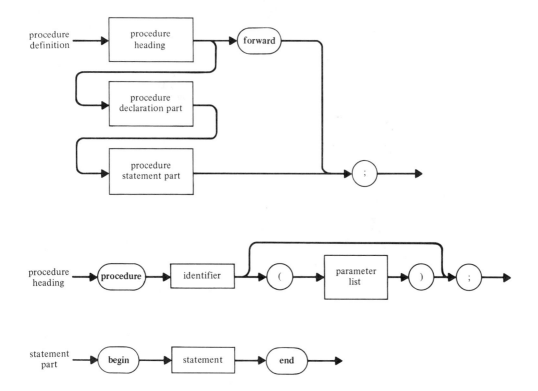

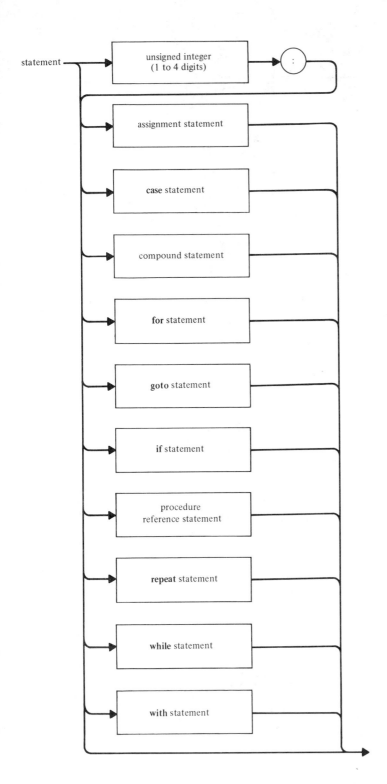

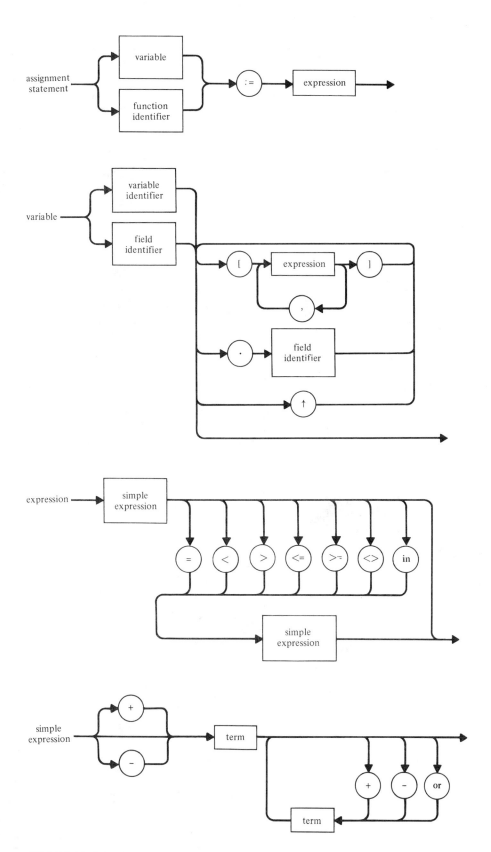

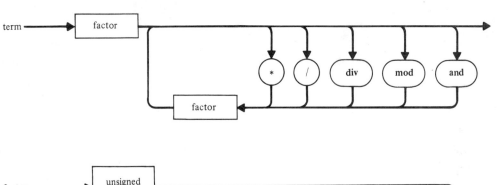

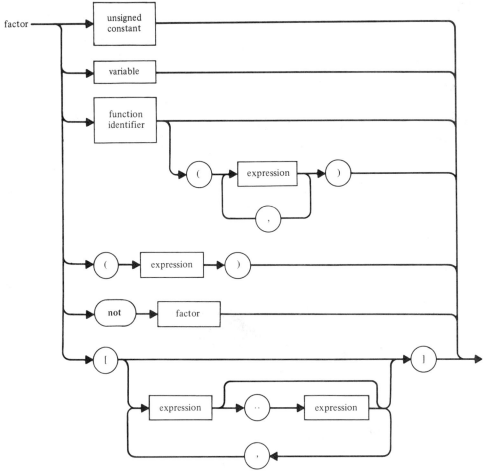

SYNTAX DIAGRAMS

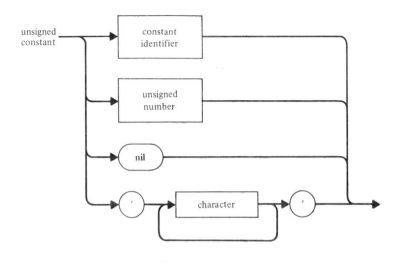

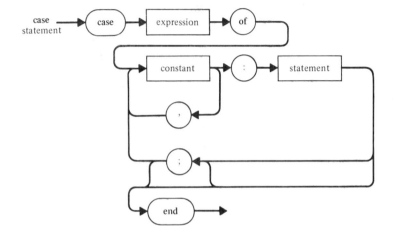

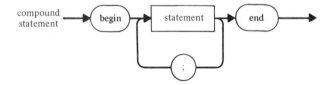

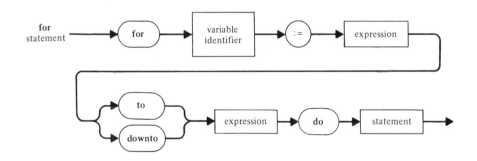

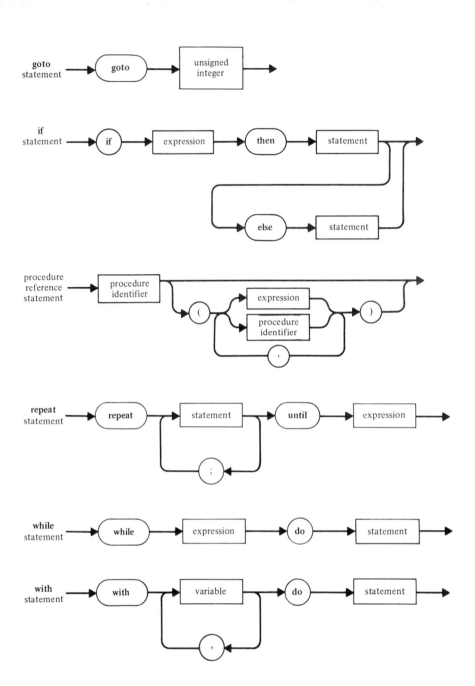

D

Predefined Functions and Procedures

Predefined Functions

Function	Description	Type of Argument	Type of Value
abs(x)	Absolute value of x	Integer or real	Same as arguments
arctan(x)	Inverse tangent of x (value in radians)	Integer or real	Real
cos(x)	Cosine of x (in radians)	Integer or real	Real
exp(x)	Exponential function e^x	Integer or real	Real
ln(x)	Natural logarithm of x	Integer or real	Real
round(x)	x rounded to nearest integer	Real	Integer
sin(x)	Sine of x (in radians)	Integer or real	Real
sqr(x)	x^2	Integer or real	Same as argument
sqrt(x)	Square root of x	Integer or real	Real
trunc(x)	x truncated to its integer part	Real	Integer

Predefined Procedures

Procedure	Description
dispose (P) *dispose* (P, *tag-value-list*)	Releases the memory location pointed to by pointer variable P, leaving P undefined. The second form may be used for variant records.
get (F)	Advances the data pointer in file F to the next component and assigns this component to the file buffer variable F↑.
new (P) *new* (P, *tag-value-list*)	Acquires a memory location and assigns its address to pointer variable P. The second form may be used for variant records.
pack (U, *First*, P)	Copies the elements of unpacked array U beginning at position *First* to the packed array P.
page (F)	Causes a system-dependent effect on the text file F such that subsequent text written to F will be on a new page if F is printed on a suitable output device.
put (F)	Transfers the contents of the buffer variable F↑ to the file F.
read (F, *input-list*)	Reads values from the file F and assigns these to the variables in the input list. If F is not specified, the standard file *input* is assumed.
readln (F, *input-list*)	Reads values from the text file F, assigns these to the variables in the input list, and then advances the data pointer in F past the next end-of-line mark. If F is not specified, the standard file *input* is assumed.
reset (F)	Opens the file F for input, positions the data pointer in F at the first file component, and assigns this component to the file buffer variable F↑.
rewrite (F)	Creates the empty file F and opens it for output. Any previous contents of F are destroyed.
unpack (P, U, *First*)	Copies the elements of the packed array P beginning at position *First* to the unpacked array U.
write (F, *output-list*)	Writes the values of the items in the output list to file F. If F is not specified, the standard file *output* is assumed.
writeln (F, *output-list*)	Writes the values of the items in the output list to text file F followed by an end-of-line mark. If F is not specified, the standard file *output* is assumed.

Sample Data Files

Several exercises in the text use the files *InventoryFile, InventoryUpdate, Least-SquaresFile, StudentFile, StudentUpdate,* and *UsersFile*. This appendix describes the contents of these files and gives a sample listing for each.

InventoryFile
Item number: a six-digit integer
Number currently in stock: an integer in the range 0 through 999
Unit price: a real value
Minimum inventory level: an integer in the range 0 through 999
Item name: a 25-character string

File is sorted so that item numbers are in increasing order.

```
Sample InventoryFile:
======================

101001   20   54.95   15  TELEPHOTO POCKET CAMERA
101002   12   24.95   15  MINI POCKET CAMERA
102001   20   49.95   10  POL. ONE-STEP CAMERA
102002   13  189.95   12  SONAR 1-STEP CAMERA
102003   15   74.95    5  PRONTO CAMERA
103001    9  279.99   10  8MM ZOOM MOVIE CAMERA
103002   15  310.55   10  SOUND/ZOOM 8MM CAMERA
104001   10  389.00   12  35MM SLR XG-7 MINO. CAM.
104002   11  349.95   12  35MM SLR AE-1 PENT. CAM.
104003   20  319.90   12  35MM SLR ME CAN. CAM.
104101   13  119.95   12  35MM HI-MATIC CAMERA
104102   20   89.99   12  35MM COMPACT CAMERA
151001    7  129.95    5  ZOOM MOVIE PROJECTOR
151002    9  239.99    5  ZOOM-SOUND PROJECTOR
152001   10  219.99    5  AUTO CAROUSEL PROJECTOR
152002    4  114.95    5  CAR. SLIDE PROJECTOR
201001    4   14.95    5  POCKET STROBE
201002   12   48.55   10  STROBE SX-10
201003   10   28.99   15  ELEC.FLASH SX-10
301001   13   32.99   15  TELE CONVERTER
301002   14   97.99   15  28MM WIDE-ANGLE LENS
301003   13   87.95   15  135MM TELEPHOTO LENS
301004    8  267.95    5  35-105 MM ZOOM LENS
301005    7  257.95    5  80-200 MM ZOOM LENS
311001    4   67.50    5  HEAVY-DUTY TRIPOD
311002   10   19.95    5  LIGHTWEIGHT TRIPOD
351001   10  159.99    5  35MM ENLARGER KIT
401001    4   35.98    5  40X40 DELUXE SCREEN
401002   10   44.98    5  50X50 DELUXE SCREEN
501001   17    4.29   25  120-SLIDE TRAY
501002   33    2.95   25  100-SLIDE TRAY
502001   12    6.25   15  SLIDE VIEWER
503001   12   55.95   10  MOVIE EDITOR
601001   10   59.95    5  CONDENSER MICROPHONE
611001   80    0.89  100  AA ALKALINE BATTERY
701001   19   19.79   20  GADGET BAG
801001   45    1.49   50  135-24 COLOR FILM
802001   60    0.99   50  110-12 COLOR FILM
802002   42    1.45   50  110-24 COLOR FILM
802003   37    0.59   25  110-12 B/W FILM
802004   43    0.95   25  110-24 B/W FILM
803001   44    0.89   50  126-12 COLOR FILM
803002   27    0.59   25  126-12 B/W FILM
804001   39    6.89   50  8MM FILM CASSETTE
```

Figure E.1

InventoryUpdate
Order number: three letters followed by four digits
Item number: a six-digit integer (same as those in *InventoryFile*)
Transaction code: a character (S = sold, R = returned)
Number of items sold or returned: an integer in the range 0 through 999

File is sorted so that item numbers are in increasing order. (Some items in *InventoryFile* may not have update records; others may have more than one.)

```
CCI7543 101002S  2          BTP5396 301003S  1
LTB3429 101002S  7          GFL4913 301003S  8
DJS6762 102001S  9          EHQ7510 301003S  7
NQT1850 102002S  1          QQL6472 301003S  5
WYP6425 102003S  4          SVC6511 301004S  4
YOK2210 102003R  2          XJQ9391 301004S  4
QGM3144 102003S  1          ONO5251 311001S  3
NPQ8685 103001S  5          CXC7780 311001S  1
MAP8102 103001S 13          VGT8169 311002S  8
JRJ6335 103001S  1          IMK5861 351001S  2
UWR9386 103002S  3          QHR1944 351001S  1
TJY1913 103002S 11          ZPK6211 401001S  2
YHA9464 104001S  5          VDZ2970 401002S  6
SYT7493 104001S  3          BOJ9069 501001S  6
FHJ1657 104002S  7          MNL7029 501001S  9
OJQ2215 104003S  8          MRG8703 502001S 10
UOX7714 104003S  2          DEM9289 502001S  1
ERZ2147 104003S  7          BXL1651 503001S  2
MYW2540 104101S  1          VAF8733 611001S 65
UKS3587 104102S  2          UYI0368 701001S  2
AAN3759 104102S  2          VIZ6879 801001S 16
WZT4171 104102S 12          GXX9093 801001S 19
TYR9475 151001S  1          HHO5605 802001S 41
FRQ4184 151001S  1          BOL2324 802001S 49
TAV3604 151002S  2          PAG9289 802003S 15
DCW9363 152002S  1          MDF5557 802003S 17
EXN3964 152002R  1          IQK3388 802004S 12
OIN5524 152002S  1          OTB1341 802004S 28
EOJ8218 152002S  1          SVF5674 803001S 24
YFK0683 201001S  2          ZDP9484 803001S 15
PPX4743 201002S  4          OSY8177 803002S 15
DBR1709 201003S  4          GJQ0185 803002S  8
JOM5408 201003S  3          VHW0189 804001S 20
PKN0671 201003S  1          WEU9225 804001S  6
LBD8391 301001S  9          YJO3755 804001S  8
DNL6326 301002S  9
```

Figure E.2

LeastSquaresFile

This is a text file in which each line contains a pair of real numbers
representing the x coordinate and the y coordinate of a point.

Sample LeastSquaresFile: **Figure E.3**
=========================

```
2.18  1.06                  7.39  12.17
7.46  12.04                 1.88  0.58
5.75  8.68                  6.31  10.09
3.62  4.18                  2.53  2.04
3.59  3.87                  5.44  8.25
7.5   12.32                 1.21  -0.76
7.49  11.74                 9.07  15.5
7.62  12.07                 3.95  5.0
```

9.63	17.01	4.82	6.91
9.75	16.91	9.68	16.24
9.99	16.67	1.21	-0.22
3.61	4.69	4.54	5.64
9.06	15.0	1.48	0.3
5.03	6.62	6.58	9.8
4.45	6.12	3.05	3.56
4.54	5.89	6.19	9.62
0.92	-1.02	6.47	9.83
0.82	-1.5	8.13	10.75
2.62	2.1	7.31	11.73
5.66	8.53	0.33	-1.93
8.05	13.05	5.12	7.41
8.99	14.85	5.23	7.73
5.12	7.03	7.14	11.02
3.85	4.43	1.27	-0.21
6.08	9.21	2.51	1.59
1.42	0	5.26	7.86
2.58	2.38	4.74	6.19
5.99	9.42	2.1	2.12
0.63	-1.63	5.27	7.73
9.98	17.25	2.85	2.63
5.63	8.58	1.99	1.09
8.94	15.27	8.91	15.03
7.34	11.48	2.19	1.21
6.55	9.92	1.6	-0.05
4.89	7.07	8.93	15.12
9.59	15.82	3.19	3.56
1.81	0.45	3.37	3.64
0.99	-0.71		

StudentFile

Student number: a six-digit integer
Student's last name: a 15-character string
Student's first name: a 10-character string
Student's middle initial: a character
Hometown: 25-character string
Phone number: a seven-digit integer
Sex: a character (M or F)
Class level: a one-digit integer (1, 2, 3, 4, or 5 for special)
Major: a four-character string
Total credits earned to date: an integer
Cumulative GPA: a real value

File is arranged so that student numbers are in increasing order.

```
Sample StudentFile:                              Figure E.4
====================


010103JOHNSON          JAMES     L
WAUPUN, WISCONSIN           7345229M1ENGR 15 3.15
010104ANDREWS          PETER     J
GRAND RAPIDS, MICHIGAN   9493301M2CPSC 42 2.78
010110PETERSON         SAMUEL    L
```

```
LYNDEN, WASHINGTON          3239550M5ART  63 2.05
010113VANDEN KLOP      MARILYN    K
FREMONT, MICHIGAN           5509237F4HIST110 3.74
010126BROOKS           SUSAN      R
CHINO, CALIFORNIA           3330861F3PHIL 78 3.10
010144LUCKETT          FREDERICK M
GRANDVILLE, MICHIGAN        7745424M5HIST 66 2.29
010179DE VRIES         NANCY      L
THREE RIVERS, MICHIGAN  6290017F1MATH 15 3.83
010191NAKAMURA         BENJAMIN   C
CHICAGO, ILLINOIS           4249665M1SOCI 12 1.95
010226MORRIS           REBECCA    J
LYNDEN, WASHINGTON          8340115F1PSYC 15 1.85
010272JEFFERSON        GREGORY    W
GRAND RAPIDS, MICHIGAN  2410744M5ENGL102 2.95
010274JACKOWSKI        MICHELLE   M
BYRON CENTER, MICHIGAN  8845115F3MUSC 79 2.75
010284ORANGE           WILLIAM    B
GRAAFSCHAAP, MICHIGAN   3141660M2ENGR 42 2.98
010297KING             RODNEY     L
DENVER, COLORADO            4470338M4HIST117 3.25
010298BLAINE           DAWN       J
DE MOTTE, INDIANA           5384609F4PSYC120 2.99
010301ELDER            KENNETH    L
GALLUP, NEW MEXICO          6632997M1EDUC 14 1.95
010302PATRICK          ELIZABETH A
SHEBOYGAN, WISCONSIN        5154997F2CHEM 40 3.85
010304OLSON            KATHLEEN   E
SPARTA, MICHIGAN            8861201F5GERM 14 3.05
010307ANDREWS          STEVEN     J
PEORIA, ILLINOIS            2410744M3MUSC 76 2.87
010310ISMOND           SIDNEY     O
LAKEWOOD, CALIFORNIA        7172339M2CPSC 46 3.83
010319HOPKINS          GREGORY    L
YORKTOWN, PENNSYLVANIA  3385494M2MATH 41 3.00
010323HOLMES           JILL       D
TRAVERSE CITY, MICHIGAN 6763991F3MATH 77 2.75
010330JACOBSON         MARSHA     A
SILVER SPRINGS, MD          4847932F5HIST 25 2.98
010339NOOYER           ROCHELLE   J
SALT LAKE CITY, UTAH        6841129F2EDUC 41 3.83
010348BRINK            ALBERT     J
SAGINAW, MICHIGAN           6634401M4CPSC115 3.25
010355ZYLSTRA          CATHERINE  E
DOWNS, KANSAS               7514008F1ENGL 16 1.95
010377WORKMAN          RONALD     K
COLUMBUS, OHIO              4841771M2SOCI 44 2.78
010389YOUNG            GLORIA     L
CHEYENNE, WYOMING           7712399F4EDUC115 2.99
010395MENDELSOHN       DOUGLAS    M
WHITINSVILLE, MA            9294401M3ENGR 80 3.10
010406KRAMER           CHERYL     L
SEATTLE, WASHINGTON         5582911F1CPSC 15 2.99
010415ANDERSON         DANIEL     R
GRANDVILLE, MICHIGAN        5325912M2ENGR 43 2.79
010422BROUWER          DAVID      J
WHEATON, ILLINOIS           6631212M2PSYC 42 2.48
010431VAN DER PLOEG    THOMAS     K
CAWKER CITY, KANSAS         6349971M1CPSC 15 4.00
010448SMITTER          DEBORAH    S
SIOUX CENTER, IOWA          2408113F1ART  77 2.20
```

```
010458LOTTERMAN        ALICE     H
REDLANDS, CALIFORNIA       9193001F1POLS 15 3.15
010467HUITING          THEODORE  A
HAWTHORNE, NEW JERSEY      5513915M3ECON 78 2.75
010470PARKS            SANDRA    L
TROY, MICHIGAN             8134001F4MUSC118 3.25
010482NYENBERG         WILLIAM   K
ROCHESTER, NEW YORK        7175118M1ENGL 15 3.15
010490CHAPMAN          ROBERT    J
CHINO, CALIFORNIA          3132446M2P E  43 2.78
010501COOPER           REBECCA   J
WINDOW ROCK, ARIZONA       4245170F1BIOL 16 3.10
010519HOUSEMAN         JANICE    A
BOZEMAN, MONTANA           8183226F3SPEE 77 3.40
010511RIDDERING        ELIZABETH L
NEW ERA, MICHIGAN          6461125F4E SC114 3.37
010515ALLENHOUSE       GERALD    T
BOISE, IDAHO               5132771M5EDUC 87 1.99
010523VOS              ROGER     D
FARMINGTON, MICHIGAN       9421753M1BIOL 13 1.77
010530VERMEER          SHARLENE  M
OKLAHOMA CITY, OK          3714377F5ENGL 95 2.66
010538ROSSMAN          STEVEN    G
ST LOUIS, MISSOURI         8354112M3ENGR 74 2.75
010547PATTERSON        SHIRLEY   A
PETOSKEY, MICHIGAN         4543116F5CPSC 55 2.95
010553SMITH            GERRIT    C
BURKE, VIRGINIA            2351881M1HIST 15 1.77
010560VELDERMAN        MARILYN   K
FT LAUDERDALE, FLORIDA     4421885F1SOCI 13 1.95
010582JEMISON          JONATHAN  B
RUDYARD, MICHIGAN          3451220M3MATH 76 2.99
010590STRONG           ELLEN     M
SPRINGFIELD, ILLINOIS      6142449F1CPSC 14 1.88
010597QUIST            MICHAEL   J
PORTLAND, OREGON           4631744M4P E 116 1.98
010610BLACK            CALVIN    R
SPRING LAKE, MICHIGAN      9491221M5E SC135 2.95
010623ENGELSMA         CAROL     J
CINCINATTI, OHIO           3701228F4GREE119 3.25
010629COOPER           FREDERICK A
BOULDER, COLORADO          5140228M1MATH 13 1.95
010633BROWN            CAROLYN   J
RIPON, CALIFORNIA          4341883F5GEOG 89 2.29
010648PETERSON         PAMELA    J
ALBANY, NEW YORK           7145513F1EDUC 14 1.75
010652JACKSON          FREDERICK R
RAPID CITY, SD             3335910M3LATI 77 2.87
010657WILSON           STEVEN    L
DETROIT, MICHIGAN          4841962M4PHIL115 2.99
010663LONG             ALIDA     C
LINCOLN, NEBRASKA          7120111F5EDUC100 2.70
010668FREDRICKSON      ALBERT    M
NEWARK, NEW JERSEY         3710225M2ENGR 41 2.78
010675GREGORY          ROBERT    L
NASHVILLE, TENNESSEE       4921107M4MATH115 3.25
010682HEERES           STEPHANIE M
AUSTIN, TEXAS              5132201F4ART 117 3.74
010688STONE            DANIEL    E
BROOKLYN, NEW YORK         7412993M1CPSC 15 1.98
```

StudentUpDate

Student number: a six-digit integer (same as those used in *StudentFile*)

For each of five courses:

   Course name: a seven-character string (e.g., CPSC131)
   Letter grade: a two-character string (e.g., A−, B+, C♭
   Course credit: an integer

The file is sorted so that student numbers are in increasing order. There is one update record for each student in *StudentFile*.

```
Sample StudentUpdate:                                          Figure E.5
=====================
```

```
010103ENGL176C 4EDUC268B 4EDUC330B+3P E 281C 3ENGR317D 4
010104CPSC271D+4E SC208D-3PHIL340B+2CPSC146D+4ENGL432D+4
010110ART 520D 3E SC259F 1ENGL151D+4MUSC257B 4PSYC486C 4
010113HIST498F 3P E 317C+4MUSC139B-3PHIL165D 3GEOG222C 3
010126PHIL367C-4EDUC420C-3EDUC473C 3EDUC224D-3GERM257F 4
010144HIST559C+3MATH357D 3CPSC323C-2P E 246D-4MUSC379D+4
010179MATH169C-4CHEM163C+4MUSC436A-3MATH366D-2BIOL213A-4
010191SOCI177F 4POLS106A 4EDUC495A-3ENGR418B+2ENGR355A 4
010226PSYC116B 3GERM323B-4ART 350A 4HIST269B+4EDUC214C+3
010272ENGL558A-4EDUC169D+3PSYC483B+4ENGR335B+2BIOL228B 4
010274MUSC351B 4PSYC209C-4ENGR400F 1E SC392A 4SOCI394B-3
010284ENGR292D 4PSYC172C 4EDUC140B 4MATH274F 4MUSC101D+4
010297HIST464F 1HIST205F 1ENGR444F 1MATH269F 1EDUC163F 1
010298PSYC452B 3MATH170C+4EDUC344C-2GREE138C-2SPEE303A-3
010301EDUC197A 4P E 372B 3ENGR218D 4MATH309C 4E SC405C-4
010302CHEM283F 1P E 440A 2MATH399A-3HIST455C-4MATH387C-3
010304GERM526C-2CHEM243C 4POLS331B-4EDUC398A 3ENGR479D+4
010307MUSC323B+3MATH485C 4HIST232B+4EDUC180A 3ENGL130B+4
010310CPSC264B 2POLS227D+3ENGR467D-3MATH494D-4ART 420C+4
010319MATH276B 2E SC434A 3HIST197B-4GERM489B-2ART 137C-3
010323MATH377D-4EDUC210D 4MATH385D-4ENGR433C 2HIST338A-4
010330HIST546C+3E SC440B+3GREE472C+3BIOL186B 4GEOG434C+2
010339EDUC283B 3CPSC150B 3ENGR120D 4CPSC122F 4ART 216B 4
010348CPSC411C-3HIST480C+4PSYC459B 4BIOL299B+4ECON276B+3
010355ENGL130C-3CPSC282C+4CPSC181A-4CPSC146C-4SOCI113F 1
010377SOCI213D+3PSYC158D 4MUSC188C 3PSYC281D+4ENGR339B+4
010389EDUC414B+4PSYC115C+2PSYC152C-4ART 366A-3ENGR366B+4
010395ENGR396B 4HIST102F 3ENGL111A 4PSYC210D-2GREE128A 4
010406CPSC160C+4CPSC233C 1LATI494C+3ENGL115C-3MATH181A 3
010415ENGR287C 4EDUC166B-4EDUC106A-3P E 190F 3MATH171B-3
010422PSYC275A-4MATH497A 4EDUC340F 1GERM403C-4MATH245D+4
010431CPSC187D-4CPSC426F 4ENGR476B-4BIOL148B+3CPSC220F 3
010448ART 171D-4CPSC239C-3SOCI499B-4HIST113D+3PSYC116C 4
010458POLS171F 1CPSC187C+4CHEM150B 2PHIL438D-4PHIL254D 4
010467ECON335D-3E SC471B+4MATH457C+3MATH207C 2BIOL429D 4
010470MUSC415C+3POLS177C 3CPSC480A 4PSYC437B 3SOCI276D 4
010482ENGL158D-4EDUC475B 3HIST172B-2P E 316F 4ENGR294A-3
010490P E 239F 4ENGL348F 3LATI246F 4CPSC350F 4MATH114F 1
010501BIOL125F 4CPSC412F 3E SC279F 4ENGR153F 2ART 293F 1
010519SPEE386B+4HIST479C 4PSYC249B-2GREE204B-4P E 421A 1
010511E SC416B 3MATH316D-4MATH287C 2MATH499A-4E SC288D 3
010515EDUC563D+3PHIL373D-3ART 318B 4HIST451F 1ART 476C+3
010523BIOL183D-2HIST296D+4HIST380B+4ENGR216C 4MATH412B-2
010530ENGL559F 1EDUC457D+4CPSC306A 3ENGR171B+1CPSC380A 4
010538ENGR328A-4ENGR336C 3EDUC418D+3PHIL437B+4CPSC475D 4
010547CPSC537A-4ART 386D 4HIST292D-4ENGR467A-4P E 464B+4
```

```
010553HIST170A-4SOCI496D-3PHIL136B+4CPSC371D-4CPSC160A-1
010560SOCI153D+3MATH438D+4CPSC378C 4BIOL266F 3EDUC278D+3
010582MATH388A-3P E 311B 3ECON143D 4MATH304C+3P E 428C+4
010590CPSC134B-3E SC114B+3CPSC492C 4ENGL121C 4ENGR403A-4
010597P E 423A-3BIOL189D+3PHIL122D-4ENGL194C-4SOCI113D+3
010610E SC594C-3PHIL344F 4CPSC189B+2ENGR411D-3MATH241A 4
010623GREE412B-4ENGL415D-3ENGL234D-4MATH275F 1SOCI124B+3
010629MATH137D 2MATH481F 3E SC445F 1MATH339D 4ART 219B+4
010633GEOG573B 4ENGL149C+4EDUC113B+4ENGR458C-2HIST446D+4
010648EDUC132D+4MUSC103D-4ENGL263C 4ENGL134B+4E SC392A 3
010652LATI363F 3BIOL425F 1CPSC267C 4EDUC127C+3MATH338B 4
010657PHIL429F 1ART 412D-4MUSC473B-4SOCI447C-4MATH237D+2
010663EDUC580B-4ENGR351B+4SOCI283D 4ART 340C 4PSYC133D+3
010668ENGR274B+4SOCI438C 1P E 327C 4BIOL158A 4EDUC457A-4
010675MATH457A 4ENGR114C 4CPSC218C 3E SC433C-3PSYC243C+1
010682ART 483D+3GERM432C 3ENGL103B+4MUSC169C-3SOCI381C-2
010688CPSC182F 1HIST371C+4PSYC408F 1MUSC214B+4MATH151C 3
```

UsersFile

Identification number: a six-digit integer
User's name: A 30-character string in the form Last Name, First Name
Password: a 5-character string
Resource limit (in dollars): an integer of up to four digits
Resources used to date: a real value

This file is arranged so that identification numbers are in increasing order.

```
Sample UsersFile:                                    Figure E.6
==================


100101MILTGEN, JOSEPH                    MOE
 750 380.81
100102SMALL, ISAAC                       LARGE
 650 598.84
100103SNYDER, LAWRENCE                   R2-D2
 250 193.74
100104EDMUNDSEN, RONALD                  ABCDE
 250 177.93
100105BRAUNSCHNEIDER, CHRISTOPHER        BROWN
 850 191.91
100106PIZZULA, NORMA                     PIZZA
 350 223.95
100107VANDERPOL, HENRY                   VAN
 750 168.59
100108VANZWALENBERG, FLORENCE            VANZ
 450  76.61
100109ALEXANDER, ALVIN                   AL
 650 405.04
100110COSTEMAN, MICHAEL                  MICKY
  50  42.57
100111WYZOREK, GEORGE                    ZIGGY
 350  73.50
100112NAWSADIS, BARBARA                  HAPPY
 850  33.28
```

```
100113SINKE, LAUREL                 SWIM
 750 327.53
100114VELTEMA, DONALD               DONV
 550 382.03
100115KENIEWSKI, KEN                KEKEN
 550  28.82
100116BEECHEM, WILLIAM              BOAT
 950 256.18
100117DOYLE, YVONNE                 CONAN
 450 337.01
100118ZWIER, ALEXANDER              GREAT
 350 249.48
100119JESTER, MICHELLE              JOKER
 450 281.16
100120MCCONNEL, STEPHEN             STEVE
 250  35.00
100121WITCZAK, ROGER                WITTY
 650  38.36
100122VRIESMAN, BENJAMIN            DUTCH
 850  37.32
100123JAGER, JEFFREY                TIGER
 250 246.73
100124TRAVIS, DANIEL                XXXXX
 150 100.19
100125BRYANT, MARY                  CUTIE
 250   0.03
100126BRINK, MARILEE                LEE
 750  67.35
100127ARMSTRONG, KENNETH            JACK
 550 392.00
100128ENGELS, BARBARA               HOUSE
 150  16.39
100129DYKSEN, DIRK                  HUMOM
 950  89.57
100130FELTON, GEORGE                JAWGE
 850 466.95
100131ZEILSTRA, LAWRENCE            LARRY
 750 332.12
100132SMITH, ALEXANDER              RADIO
 850 337.43
200101VITO, ANTHONY                 TONY
  50  32.81
200102VENEMA, VERNON                VEVE
 250 109.34
200103STOB, SIMON                   SLIM
 350 269.93
200104KUIPERS, JESSAMINE            JESSE
 950 183.93
200105BROWN, CALVIN                 GREEN
 350 128.69
200106RHODES, LAWRENCE              HIWAY
 150 100.31
200107NYHOFF, JOEL                  NIGHT
 350  63.63
200108LEESTMA, SAM                  SANDY
 850 202.24
200109MULLER, CHRISTOPHER           KRIS
 550 168.49
200110JOHNSON, JANET                JJ
 550 333.47
200111STEVENS, JEFFREY              CONNY
 950  37.02
```

```
200112BOONSTRA, ALFRED            BOON
 750 337.74
200113HARRISON, BENJAMIN          BEN
 550 262.97
200114JAMES, JESSE                GUNS
 250  58.81
200115SCOTT, FRANCINE             FLAG
 350 168.11
200116PHILLIPS, JAMES             GAS66
 650 322.22
200117BROOKS, ANN-MARIE           WATER
 350  26.34
200118SANDERS, PETER              BEACH
 350  22.86
200119LEWIS, GEORGE               LULU
 950 460.30
200120NEWMANN, ALFRED             MAD
 450 116.00
200121VAN, GEORGE                 VAN
 550 486.05
200122PETERSON, STEVEN            PETE
 250  35.31
200124JANSMA, BENJAMIN            SMOKE
 150 127.70
```

F

Miscellany

In the main part of this text we mentioned some special features of the Pascal language that, because they are used only infrequently, were not described in detail. These include

1. Statement labels and the **goto** statement.
2. The procedure *page.*
3. Alternate forms of procedures *new* and *dispose.*
4. The procedures *pack* and *unpack.*

Statement Labels and the goto Statement

All programs can be written using the three control structures we considered in Chapter 4: sequence, selection, and repetition. For some problems, however, it may be awkward or inefficient to use only these structures. A typical example is a program for which the input data may contain errors, and in this case, provision should be made for detecting these errors. When such an error occurs, control might be passed to some other part of the program for error handling, or execution of the program may be terminated. The processing of these abnormal situations can be handled by using statement labels and the **goto** statement. For example, if all of the data processed by a program should be no greater than 100, the following **if** statement might be used:

read (Data);
if *Data > 100* **then**
    goto 50
        .
        .
        .

50: *writeln* ('*** Input data error ***');
    .
    .
    .

In this example, 50 is a *statement label*. Such labels must be declared in the label section in the declaration part of the program. This section has the form

label
    label-1, label-2, . . . label-n;

and must be the first section in the declaration part. Each *label-i* must be a positive integer of up to four digits and can be used to label only one statement. Control can then be transferred to that statement by using a **goto** statement of the form

    goto *label-i*

The grading program in Figure F.1 is a modification of that in Figure 4.16 that incorporates input-data error checking. If a score greater than 100 or a student number greater than 40000 is read, the statement

if (*Score > MaxScore*) **or** (*Snumb > MaxSnumb*) **then**
    begin
        writeln ('*** Input data error ***');
        goto 50
    end

displays an error message and then transfers control to the statement with label 50. This statement with label 50 is an empty statement preceding the reserved word **end** that marks the end of the program and thus serves to terminate execution.

The positive integers declared in a label section and used to label statements need not be distinct from the labels that appear in a **case** statement. Thus in the program of Figure F.1, the label 10 could be used instead of 50, although the program is more readable if distinct labels are used.

The scope rules considered in Section 5.4 dealt only with identifiers and did not mention statement labels. The scope rules for labels may be obtained by simply replacing the word "identifier" with "statement label"

```
PROGRAM Grader (input, output);

(*********************************************************************

    Program to assign letter grades to numeric test scores, count # of
    A's and # of F's, and calculate class average.

*********************************************************************)

LABEL 50;

CONST
    MaxSnumb = 40000;    (* maximum student number *)
    MaxScore = 100;      (* maximum score *)

VAR
    Grade : char;        (* letter grade *)
    Snumb,               (* student number *)
    Score,               (* test score *)
    Acount,              (* count of A's *)
    Fcount,              (* count of F's *)
    TotalCount,          (* count of all scores *)
    Sum : integer;       (* sum of scores *)

BEGIN
    writeln ('*** Enter 0 for student # and any value for the score');
    writeln ('*** to signal the end of data.');
    writeln;
    Acount := 0;
    Fcount := 0;
    TotalCount := 0;
    Sum := 0;
    writeln ('Student # and score:');
    readln (Snumb, Score);
    WHILE Snumb <> 0 DO
        BEGIN
            IF (Score > MaxScore) OR (Snumb > MaxSnumb) THEN
                BEGIN
                    writeln ('*** Input data error ***');
                    GOTO 50      (* Terminate processing *)
                END (* IF *)
            ELSE
                BEGIN
                    CASE Score DIV 10 OF
                                9, 10 : BEGIN
                                            Grade := 'A';
                                            Acount := Acount + 1
                                        END;
                                    8 : Grade := 'B';
                                    7 : Grade := 'C';
                                    6 : Grade := 'D';
                        0, 1, 2, 3, 4, 5 : BEGIN
                                            Grade := 'F';
                                            Fcount := Fcount + 1
                                        END
                    END (* CASE *);
                    TotalCount := TotalCount + 1;
                    Sum := Sum + Score;
                    writeln ('Grade = ', Grade);
                    writeln
                END (* ELSE *);
            writeln ('Student # and score:');
            readln (Snumb, Score)
        END (* WHILE *);
```

Figure F.1

```
    writeln;
    writeln ('Number of A''s:  ', Acount:1);
    writeln ('Number of F''s:  ', Fcount:1);
    writeln ('Class average:  ', Sum / TotalCount:3:1);
50:
END.



Sample runs:
===========


*** Enter 0 for student # and any value for the score
*** to signal the end of data.

Student # and score:
12345 99
Grade = A

Student # and score:
16688 110
*** Input data error ***




*** Enter 0 for student # and any value for the score
*** to signal the end of data.

Student # and score:
35580 55
Grade = F

Student # and score:
49333 88
*** Input data error ***
```

in the fundamental scope principle and in the first three scope rules. Thus the *fundamental scope principle for labels* is

> The scope of a statement label is the program unit in which it is declared.

and the three *scope rules for labels* are

1. A statement label declared in a program unit is not accessible outside that unit.
2. A global statement label is accessible in any subprogram in which that label is not declared locally.
3. Statement labels declared in a subprogram can be accessed by any subprogram defined within it, provided that the label is not declared locally in the internal subprogram.

To illustrate these scope rules for labels, consider the following program skeleton:

```
program P . . . ;
    label 10, 99;
        .
        .
        .
    procedure A . . . ;
        label 10, 20;
            .
            .
            .
        begin (* A *)
            .
            .
            .
        10: x := 0;
            .
            .
            .
        20: read (Num);
            .
            .
            .
        end (* A *);
    begin (* main program *)
        .
        .
        .
    10: writeln (Alpha, Beta, Gamma);
        .
        .
        .
    99:
    end (* main program *).
```

Applying the first scope rule, we see that statement labels 10 and 20 declared in procedure *A* are not accessible outside *A*. Thus control cannot be transferred to the statements

10: *x* := 0

or

20: *read* (*Num*)

from anywhere outside *A*. A statement

goto 10

in the main program transfers control to the statement

     10: *writeln* (*Alpha, Beta, Gamma*);

in the main program.

According to the second scope rule, the global statement labels 10 and 99 are accessible throughout the program except in subprograms in which they are declared locally as labels. Thus a statement

     goto 10

in procedure *A* transfers control to the statement

     10: *x* := 0

also in *A*. A statement

     goto 99

in *A* or in the main program transfers control to the empty statement preceding the end of the main program. Such a transfer of control from within a subprogram to the end of the main program serves to terminate execution of the program. This may be desirable if some serious error has occurred during the execution of the subprogram. For example, if procedure *A* is designed to process nonnegative values for the variable *n*, then the statement

     if *n* < 0 **then**
        goto 99

serves to abort the program if the value of *n* is negative.

The third scope rule states that the statement labels declared in a subprogram are accessible to the subprograms internal to it, provided that they are not declared locally within the internal subprograms. Thus, if procedure *A* contains another procedure *B* that does not declare 20 as a local label, then a statement

     goto 20

in *B* will transfer control to the statement

     20: *read* (*Num*)

in procedure *A*.

The procedure *page* is designed to insert page breaks into the output produced by a program. This procedure is called with a statement of the form

The Procedure
page

page (*file-name*)

or

page

In the second form, the standard file *output* is assumed. The effect of a call to procedure *page* is system dependent, and the details must be determined by consulting the system reference manuals. The Pascal standard states only that

> *Page*(*f*) shall cause an implementation-defined effect on the textfile *f*, such that subsequent output to *f* will be on a new page if the textfile is printed on a suitable device and shall perform an implicit *writeln*. . . .

Alternate forms of reference to the procedures *new* and *dispose* may be used for variant records. The procedure *new* may be called with a statement of the form

Alternate Forms of Procedures *new* and *dispose*

    new (*pointer, tag-value-1, tag-value-2, . . . , tag-value-n*)

Here *tag-value-1, tag-value-2, . . . , tag-value-n* represent values of tag fields in increasingly nested variant parts of the record; that is, this procedure reference may be used to allocate a memory location for a record having the structure

record
    fixed-part-1;
    case *tag-field-1* : *tag-type-1* **of**

              .

              .

              .

       tag-value-1 : (*fixed-part-2*;
                case *tag-field-2* : *tag-type-2* **of**

                    .

                    .

                    .

             tag-value-2 : (*fixed-part-3*;
                      case *tag-field-3* : *tag-type-3* **of**

                            .

                            .

                            .

                        tag-value-3 : (. . .

                  .

                    .

                    .

  end;

When a memory location is allocated for a variant record with a procedure call of the form

new (*pointer*)

it is sufficiently large to store the largest variant in that record. If it is known that a record with a particular variant is being processed, the alternative form of the procedure call may be used. This allows the system to allocate a location whose size is appropriate for that variant. To illustrate, consider the following declarations:

```
type
    NameString = packed array[1..20] of char;
    EmployeeRecord = record
                        Name : NameString;
                        Age, Dependents : integer;
                        case EmpCode : char of
                            'F' : (DeptCode : char;          (* Factory employee *)
                                   HourlyRate : real);
                            'O' : (Salary : real);           (* Office employee *)
                            'S' : (MileageAllowance : integer;  (* Salesperson *)
                                   BasePay,
                                   CommissionRate : real)
                    end;
```

If it is known that a location is needed to store the record of an office employee (*EmpCode* is O) and *P* is to point to this location, the procedure reference

new (*P*, 'O')

may be used.

When a memory location is allocated in this manner, however, it may then be used only for a record with this particular structure, that is, to store a record for an office employee. Also, to dispose of this memory location, an alternate form of reference to the procedure *dispose* is required. For this example, it would be

dispose (*P*, 'O')

The form for *dispose* that corresponds to the general form of the procedure reference for *new* is

dispose (*pointer, tag-value-1, tag-value-2, . . . , tag-value-n*)

The alternate forms of procedure references to *new* and *dispose* allow the system (but do not require it) to allocate memory more efficiently for variant records. When each of the variant parts is about the same size, however, there is no real advantage in using these alternate forms.

The procedures *pack* and *unpack* transfer elements between unpacked arrays

and packed arrays. The procedure *pack* is called with a statement of the form

 pack (*unpackedarray*, *first*, *packedarray*)

where *unpackedarray* is the unpacked array and *first* is the position of the first element of *unpackedarray* to be transferred to the packed array *packedarray*. To illustrate, the program of Figure 8.7 could be modified to declare the unpacked array *Buffer* by

 Buffer : **array**[1..*StringLimit*] **of** *char*;

and replace the **while** statement with

 while (**not** *eoln*) **and** (*NumChars* < *StringLimit*) **do**
  begin
    NumChars := *NumChars* + 1;
    read (*Buffer*[*NumChars*])
  end (* while *);
  pack (*Buffer*, 1, *TextLine*);

The procedure *unpack* transfers the elements from a packed array to an unpacked array. This procedure is called with a statement of the form

 unpack (*packedarray*, *unpackedarray*, *first*)

where *packedarray* is the packed array whose elements are to be transferred to the unpacked array *unpackedarray; first* denotes the position in *unpackedarray* where the first element of *packedarray* is to be placed.

For both of the procedures *pack* and *unpack,* the component-type of the two arrays must be the same, but the indices may be of different ordinal types. The number of array elements transferred is the number of elements in the packed array. Consequently, the segment of the unpacked array to which or from which values are being transferred must be at least as large as the number of elements in the packed array.

Arrays of any type may be packed. In particular, packing may be useful in processing boolean arrays since the boolean constants *false* and *true* are normally represented internally as 0 and 1, each of which may be stored in a single bit. A 32-bit memory word can, therefore, store 32 boolean constants. The declaration

 type
    Barray = **packed array**[1..100] **of** *boolean*;

causes, therefore, memory to be allocated more efficiently than

 type
    Barray = **array**[1..100] **of** *boolean*;

The beginning programmer should not be overly concerned with the details of how data is stored internally but instead should expect the computer to utilize the memory as efficiently as possible. Consequently, the procedures *pack* and *unpack* and the packed array specification are seldom used except for character arrays.

Answers to Selected Exercises

Section 1.3 (P. 17)

4. (a) 9   **(c)** 64   **(e)** 1.5

5. (a) 83   **(c)** 4096   **(e)** 7.25

6. (a) 18   **(c)** 2748   **(e)** 8.75

7. (a) 1010011   **(c)** 1000000000000   **(e)** 111.01

8. (a) 10010   **(c)** 101010111100   **(e)** 1000.11

9. (a) 11   **(c)** 100   **(e)** 1.4

10. (a) 9   **(c)** 40   **(e)** 1.8

11. (a) (i) $(11011)_2$ **(ii)** $(33)_8$ **(iii)** $(1B)_{16}$

     (c) (i) $(100111010)_2$ **(ii)** $(472)_8$ **(iii)** $(13A)_{16}$

12. (a) (i) $(0.1)_2$ **(ii)** $(0.4)_8$ **(iii)** $(0.8)_{16}$

     (d) (i) $(10000.0001)_2$ **(ii)** $(20.04)_8$ **(iii)** $(10.1)_{16}$

13. (a) (i) $(0.0\overline{1001})_2$ **(ii)** $(0.2\overline{3146})_8$ **(iii)** $(0.4\overline{C})_{16}$

     (c) (i) $(0.000\overline{011})_2$ **(ii)** $(0.03\overline{146})_8$ **(iii)** $(0.0\overline{C})_{16}$

14. (a) (i)

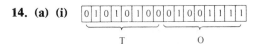

$$\underbrace{\quad}_{T} \quad \underbrace{\quad}_{O}$$

(ii)

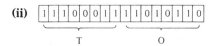

$$\underbrace{\quad}_{T} \quad \underbrace{\quad}_{O}$$

(d) (i)

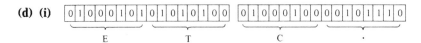

$$\underbrace{\quad}_{E} \quad \underbrace{\quad}_{T} \quad \underbrace{\quad}_{C} \quad \underbrace{\quad}_{.}$$

(ii)

$$\underbrace{\quad}_{E} \quad \underbrace{\quad}_{T} \quad \underbrace{\quad}_{C} \quad \underbrace{\quad}_{.}$$

Section 2.4 (P. 41)

2. Given information: Two temperature scales. Celsius and Fahrenheit, with 0° Celsius corresponding to 32° Fahrenheit, 100° Celsius corresponding to 212° Fahrenheit, and that a linear relationship of the form $F = aC + b$ holds in general. Also given some temperature C on the Celsius scale.

To find: The corresponding number F of degrees on the Fahrenheit scale.

We first must find the specific linear relationship between the two scales. In general, C° Celsius corresponds to F° Fahrenheit, where $F = aC + b$ for some constants a and b. Because 0° Celsius corresponds to 32° Fahrenheit, we must have

$$32 = a \cdot 0 + b,$$

so that $b = 32$. This means, then, that

$$F = aC + 32.$$

Because 100° Celsius corresponds to 212° Fahrenheit, we must have

$$212 = a \cdot 100 + 32$$

which gives $a = 9/5$, so that our equation becomes

$$F = \frac{9}{5}C + 32$$

The algorithm for solving the problem is now straightforward;

(* This algorithm converts a temperature of *DegreesC* on the Celsius scale to the corresponding *DegreeF* on the Fahrenheit scale. *)
  1. Enter *DegreesC*.
  2. Calculate
     DegreesF = (9 * *DegreesC*) / 5 + 32.
  3. Display *DegreesF*.

5. Given information: A list of scores in the range 50 through 100 and a method for assigning letter grades: A if score $\geq$ 90, B if $75 \leq$ score < 90, and C if $50 \leq$ score < 75.

To find: The corresponding letter grades for the scores in the list. An algorithm for solving this problem is the following:

(∗ Algorithm to assign letter grades to numeric scores. A negative score is used to signal the end of data. ∗)

1. Initialize *ALine, BLine,* and *CLine* to 90, 75, and 50, respectively.
2. Enter first value for *Score.*
3. While *Score* $\geq$ 0 do the following:
   a. If *Score* $\geq$ *ALine,* display 'A'; else if *Score* $\geq$ *BLine,* display 'B'; else if *Score* $\geq$ *CLine,* display 'C'; else display 'Erroneous score'.
   b. Enter next value for *Score.*

12. **program** *CelsiusToFahrenheit* (input, output);

(∗ Program to convert a temperature on the Celsius scale to the corresponding temperature on the Fahrenheit scale. ∗)

var
    DegreesC,   (∗ degrees Celsius ∗)
    DegreesF : *real*; (∗ degrees Fahrenheit ∗)

begin
    writeln ('Enter temperature in degrees Celsius:');
    readln (*DegreesC*);
    DegreesF := (9 ∗ *DegreesC*) / 5 − 32;
    writeln ('Corresponding temperature in degrees Fahrenheit is ',
        DegreesF:8:2)

end.

Section 3.1 (P. 50)

2. (a) 12 is an integer constant.

   (b) 12. is not a valid constant (real constants may not end in a period).

   (c) 12.0 is a real constant.

3. (a) 'X' is legal.

   (b) IS' is not legal (missing first quote)

   (c) 'DO' 'ESNT' is legal.

4. (c) **var**
      Mileage : *real*;
      Cost, Distance : *integer*;

5. (c) const
        Year = 1984;
        Female = 'F';
        Blank = ' ';

Section 3.2 (P. 54)

1. (a) 1

   (d) Not a valid expression. 9 / 2 is a real value, and **div** requires integer operands.

   (g) 2

   (j) 2

   (m) 0

   (p) 18.0

   (s) 3.25

   (v) 4.0

2. (a) 8.0   **(c)** $2.\overline{6}$ **(e)** 5.1   **(g)** 6.25

3. (a) $10 + 5 * B - 4 * A * C$

   (c) $sqrt(a + 3 * sqr(b))$

Section 3.3 (P. 60)

1. (a) Valid

   (d) Valid

   (g) Not valid; variable must be to the left of an assignment operator.

   (j) Valid

   (m) Not valid; character constant may not be assigned to a boolean variable.

2. (a) 15.0

   (d) 6

   (g) Not valid; an integer value may not be assigned to a character variable.

   (j) Not valid; a real value may not be assigned to a character variable.

   (m) Not valid; a character value may not be assigned to a real variable.

   (p) 2

3. **(a)** *Distance* := *Rate* * *Time*

   (d) *Area* := (*b* * *h*) / 2

4. **(a)** For *a* = 2, *b* = 4, *c* = 8, *a* * (*b* **div** *c*) = 0,
   a * *b* **div** *c* = 1.

Section 3.4 (P. 70)

1. **(a)** `___-567.4__436_____`
   `Tolerance:_0.00040`

2. **(a)** `__New_balance_=_2559.50`
   `____C____8.02_____`

3. **(a)** *writeln* (*R1*:9:4, *C*:4, *N1*:5);
   writeln (*N2*:5, 'PDQ', *R2*:8:5)

Section 3.7 (P. 84)

4. **program** *RightTriangle* (*input, output*);

   > (* Program to read the lengths of two legs of a right triangle
   > and calculate the area of the triangle and the length of the
   > hypotenuse. *)

   var
   > *Leg1*, *Leg2*,
   > *Area*,
   > *Hypotenuse* : *real*;

   begin
   > *writeln* ('Enter the lengths of the two legs of right triangle:');
   > *readln* (*Leg1*, *Leg2*);
   > *Area* := (*Leg1* + *Leg2*)/2;
   > *Hypotenuse* := *sqrt*(*sqr*(*Leg1*) + *sqr*(*Leg2*));
   > *writeln* ('Area = ', *Area*:4:2);
   > *writeln* ('Hypotenuse = ', *Hypotenuse*:4:2)
   end.

Section 4.5 (P. 106)

1. **(b)** 6
   4
   5
   6
   7

2. (a) **while** $x > 0$ **do**
    begin
        writeln ('x = ', x);
        $x := x - 0.5$
    end (* **while** *)

(d) **for** *Number* $:= 1$ **to** 100 **do**
    writeln (*sqr*(*Number*))

Section 4.7 (P. 132)

1. (a) **if** *Code* $= 1$ **then**
    begin
        readln (*X, Y*);
        Sum $:= X + Y$;
        writeln ('X = ', *X*, 'Y = ', *Y*, 'Sum = ', *Sum*)
    end (* **if** *)

(d) **if** (*Distance* $>= 0$) **and** (*Distance* $<= 100$) **then**
        Cost $:= 5.00$
    else if *Distance* $<= 500$ **then**
        Cost $:= 8.00$
    else if *Distance* < 1000 **then**
        Cost $:= 10.00$
    else
        Cost $:= 12.00$

Section 5.2 (P. 148)

1. (a) Can be used

(d) Cannot be used; incorrect number of parameters.

(g) Can be used

3. **function** *Wages*(*HoursWorked, HourlyRate* : *real*) : *real*;

    (* Function to calculate wages; hours above 40 are paid at 1.5
    times the hourly rate. *)

var
    RegularWages, OvertimeWages : *real*;

begin (* *Wages* *)
    if *HoursWorked* > 40 **then**
        begin
            RegularWages $:= 40 * HourlyRate$;
            OvertimeWages $:= 1.5 * (HoursWorked - 40) *$
                                HourlyRate
        end (* **if** *)
    else
        begin
            RegularWages $:= HoursWorked * HourlyRate$;
            OvertimeWages $:= 0$

        end (* **else** *);
        Wages := *RegularWages* + *OvertimeWages*
    end (* *Wages* *);

5. function *IsADigit*(*Character* : *char*) : *boolean*;

    (* Function to determine if *Character* is a digit. *)

    begin (* *IsADigit* *)
      if (*Character* >= '0') **and** (*Character* <= '9') **then**
        IsADigit := *true*
      else
        IsADigit := *false*
    end (* *IsADigit* *);

Section 5.3 (P. 159)

1. (a) Can be used

   (d) Cannot be used; *v* and *n* must have the same type.

   (g) Cannot be used; invalid boolean expression

   (j) Can be used

3. procedure *Switch* (**var** *VarA, VarB* : *integer*);
    (* Procedure to interchange the values of *VarA* and *VarB*. *)

    var
      TempVar : *integer*;

    begin (* *Switch* *)
      TempVar := *VarA*;
      VarA := *VarB*;
      VarB := *TempVar*
    end (* *Switch* *);

Section 6.1 (P. 219)

1. (a) The values assigned to *Num1, Num2, Num3,* and *Num4* will be 1, −2, 3, and 4, respectively.

   (d) The values assigned to *Num1, Num2, Num3,* and *Num4* will be 1, −2, 4, and −5, respectively.

2. (a) $N1 \leftarrow 123$ (d) $C1 \leftarrow$ X
     $R1 \leftarrow 45.6$ $N1 \leftarrow 78$
     $C1 \leftarrow$ X $C2 \leftarrow$ ♭ (blank)
     $N2 \leftarrow 78$ $R1 \leftarrow -909.8$
     $R2 \leftarrow -909.8$ $R2 \leftarrow 7.0$
     $C2 \leftarrow -$ $N2 \leftarrow -65$
     $N3 \leftarrow 65$ $C3 \leftarrow \$$
     $C3 \leftarrow \$$ $R3 \leftarrow 432.10$

(g) 123 is read and assigned to *N1;* 45.6 is read and assigned to *R1;* the end-of-line mark is read, and a blank is assigned to *C1;* then an error occurs because X is nonnumeric and thus cannot be read for *N2.*

3. (a) $N1 \leftarrow 54$
$N2 \leftarrow 32$
$C1 \leftarrow E$
$C2 \leftarrow 1$
$R1 \leftarrow -6.78$
$C3 \leftarrow \$$
$N3 \leftarrow 90$

5	4		3	2	E	1	●	-	6	.	7	8	$	9	0	●	●		1	●

(d) Same as (a).

(g) $R1 \leftarrow 54.0$
$R2 \leftarrow 32E1$
$C1 \leftarrow -$
$N1 \leftarrow 6$
$C2 \leftarrow .$
$N2 \leftarrow 78$
$C3 \leftarrow \$$
$N3 \leftarrow 90$

5	4		3	2	E	1	●	-	6	.	7	8	$	9	0	●	●		1	●

Section 7.3 (P. 256)

1. (a) type
    MonthAbbrev = (*Jan, Feb, Mar, Apr, May, Jun, Jul, Aug,*
                    Sep, Oct, Nov, Dec);
    MonthNumber = 1..12;

3. (a) *true*   **(d)** *Mar*   **(g)** *Mar*   **(j)** 8

Section 8.3 (P. 284)

1. (a) *Number*[1] ← 0   **(d)** *Number*[1] ← 1
    Number[2] ← 1   *Number*[2] ← 2
    Number[3] ← 1   *Number*[3] ← 4
    Number[4] ← 2   *Number*[4] ← 8
    Number[5] ← 2   *Number*[5] ← 16
    Number[6] ← 3   *Number*[6] ← 32
    Number[7] ← 3   *Number*[7] ← 64
    Number[8] ← 4   *Number*[8] ← 128
    Number[9] ← 4   *Number*[9] ← 256
    Number[10] ← 5   *Number*[10] no value assigned

(g) *Price*[*red*] ← 19.95
    Price[*yellow*] ← 12.75
    Price[*blue*] ← 19.95

$Price[green] \leftarrow 14.50$
$Price[white]$ no value assigned
$Price[black] \leftarrow 14.50$

2. **(a)** Declarations:

> **type**
>> $SmallNumberArray = $ **array**$[0..5]$ **of** $[0..5];$
>
> **var**
>> $Number : SmallNumberArray;$
>> $i : integer;$

> Statement:

>> **for** $i := 0$ **to** 5 **do**
>>> $Number[i] := i$

(d) Declarations:

> **type**
>> $BooleanArray = $ **array**$[1..20]$ **of** $boolean;$
>
> **var**
>> $TFQuestion : BooleanArray;$
>> $Num : integer;$

> Statement:

>> **for** $Num := 1$ **to** 20 **do**
>>> **if** $odd(Num)$ **then**
>>>> $TFQuestion[Num] := false$
>>> **else**
>>>> $TFQuestion[Num] := true$

Section 8.5 (P. 307)

1. **(a)**

$TextLine[1] \leftarrow A$	**(d)** $TextLine[1] \leftarrow I$
$TextLine[2] \leftarrow B$	$TextLine[2] \leftarrow H$
$TextLine[3] \leftarrow C$	$TextLine[3] \leftarrow ♭$
$TextLine[4] \leftarrow D$	$TextLine[4] \leftarrow G$
$TextLine[5] \leftarrow E$	$TextLine[5] \leftarrow F$
$TextLine[6] \leftarrow F$	$TextLine[6] \leftarrow E$
$TextLine[7] \leftarrow G$	$TextLine[7] \leftarrow D$
$TextLine[8] \leftarrow H$	$TextLine[8] \leftarrow C$
$TextLine[9] \leftarrow I$	$TextLine[9] \leftarrow B$
$TextLine[10] \leftarrow \$$	$TextLine[10] \leftarrow A$

(g) $CharArray[1]$ and $TextLine[1] \leftarrow A$
$CharArray[2]$ and $TextLine[2] \leftarrow B$
$CharArray[3]$ and $TextLine[3] \leftarrow C$
$CharArray[4]$ and $TextLine[4] \leftarrow D$
$CharArray[5]$ and $TextLine[5] \leftarrow E$
$CharArray[6]$ and $TextLine[6] \leftarrow F$
$CharArray[7]$ and $TextLine[7] \leftarrow G$

$CharArray[8]$ and $TextLine[8] \leftarrow \flat$
$CharArray[9]$ and $TextLine[9] \leftarrow H$
$CharArray[10]$ and $TextLine[10] \leftarrow I$

(j) Same as (a).   **(m)** Same as (a).

Section 9.4 (P. 337)

1. (a) 5000   **(d)** 4   **(g)** 792

2. (a) $\begin{bmatrix} 2\ 3\ 4 \\ 3\ 4\ 5 \\ 4\ 5\ 6 \end{bmatrix}$ **(d)** $\begin{bmatrix} A\ B\ C\ D\ \flat\ E \\ F\ G\ H\ \flat\ I\ J \end{bmatrix}$

(g) $\begin{bmatrix} E\ ?\ D\ C\ B\ A \\ J\ I\ ?\ H\ G\ F \end{bmatrix}$ **(j)** $\begin{bmatrix} 0\ 2\ 2 \\ 0\ 0\ 2 \\ 0\ 0\ 0 \end{bmatrix}$

(? = undefined)

Section 10.4 (P. 366)

1. (a) [3, 5, 11]   **(d)** [1, 2, 4, 12]   **(g)** [6..9]

(j) [2, 4, 6, 8]   **(m)** [1..12]   **(p)** [ ]

(s) [3, 5, 11]   **(v)** [ ]

2. (a) type
    $SmallIntegers$ = **set of** 1..99;

(d) type
    $DaysOfWeek$ = ($Sunday,\ Monday,\ Tuesday,\ Wednesday,$
                $Thursday,\ Friday,\ Saturday$);
    $Days$ = **set of** $DaysOfWeek$;

3. (a) Declarations:

type
    $SetOfNumbers$ = **set of** 1..99;

var
    $Even,\ Odd$: $SetOfNumbers$;
    $Number$: $integer$;
Statements:
    $Even$:= [ ];
    for $Number$:= 1 **to** 49 **do**
        $Even$:= $Even$ + [2 * $Number$];
    Odd := [1..99] − $Even$

(f) Declarations:

type
    $LetterSet$ = **set of** $char$;

var
      Vowels, Consonants : LetterSet;

Statements:
    Vowels := ['A', 'E', 'I', 'O', 'U', 'a', 'e', 'i', 'o', 'u'];
    Consonants := ['A'..'Z', 'a'..'z'] — *Vowels*

(g) Declarations:
  type
      DaysOfWeek = (*Sunday, Monday, Tuesday,*
                           Wednesday, Thursday, Friday,
                           Saturday);

      SetOfDays = **set of** *DaysOfWeek*;

  var
      WeekDays : SetOfDays;

Statements:
    WeekDays := [*Monday..Friday*]

Section 11.3 (P. 397)

1. **(a) type**
    CardSuit = (*Hearts, Diamonds, Spades, Clubs*);
    PlayingCard = **record**
                  Suit : CardSuit;
                  CardValue : 1..13
          end;

  (d) type
    String7 = **packed array**[1..7] **of** *char*;
    String20 = **packed array**[1..20] **of** *char*;
    Listing = **record**
               Name, Address : String20;
               PhoneNumber : String7
        end;

3. **(a) type**
    NameString = **packed array**[1..20] **of** *char*;
    NumberString = **packed array**[1..11] **of** *char*;
    Color = (*blue, brown, green, other*);
    MaritalStatus = (*Married, Single*);
    Date = **record**
            Month : 1..12;
            Day : 1..31;
            Year : 1900..2000
        end;

$PersonalInfo$ = **record**
$\quad\quad Name$: $NameString$;
$\quad\quad BirthDay$: $Date$;
$\quad\quad Age$: $integer$;
$\quad\quad Sex$: $char$;
$\quad\quad SocSecNumber$: $NumberString$;
$\quad\quad Height, Weight$: $integer$;
$\quad\quad EyeColor$: $Color$;
$\quad\quad$ **case** $MarStat$: $MaritalStatus$ **of**
$\quad\quad\quad Married$: ($NumChildren$: $integer$);
$\quad\quad\quad Single$: ()
$\quad$ **end**;

Section 12.3 (P. 423)

1. **(a)** Attempts to read beyond the end of the file when the data pointer is positioned at the end-of-line mark.

2. **(a)** Fails for all text files whose first character is not a blank.

Section 13.3 (P. 462)

1. **(a)** Values of pointer variables cannot be displayed.

(d) The procedure *new* is used only to assign a value to a pointer variable.

3. **function** $CountNodes(FirstPointer$: $ListPointer)$: $integer$;

(* Function to count the nodes in a linked list with first node pointed to by $FirstPointer$. *)

var
$\quad TempPointer$: $ListPointer$;
$\quad Count$: $integer$;

begin (* $CountNodes$ *)
$\quad Count$:= 0;
$\quad TempPointer$:= $FirstPointer$;
$\quad$ **while** $TempPointer$ <> **nil do**
$\quad\quad$ **begin**
$\quad\quad\quad Count$:= $Count$ + 1;
$\quad\quad\quad TempPointer$:= $TempPointer\uparrow.Next$
$\quad\quad$ **end** (* while *);
$\quad CountNodes$:= $Count$
end (* $CountNodes$ *);

Section 14.1 (P. 476)

1. (a) $-7.\overline{3}$ (d) 12.0   (g) 12.0   (j) 8.0

2. (a) $A\ B\ *\ C + D -$ (d) $A\ B\ C\ D + / +$

    (g) $A\ B - C - D - E -$

3. (a) $(A - (B + C)) * D$ (d) $((A + B) - C) / (D * E)$

    (g) $A\ /\ ((B\ /\ C)\ /\ D)$

4. (a) -24.5 (d) -2.0 (g) 55.0

5. (a) $-\ +\ *\ A\ B\ C\ D$ (d) $+\ A\ /\ B + C\ D$

    (g) $-\ -\ -\ -\ A\ B\ C\ D\ E$

6. (a) $(A + B) * (C - D)$ (d) $A - (B - C) - D$

    (g) $(A * B + C) / (D - E)$

7. (a) (i) -15 (iv) 15

    (b) (i) $A\ B\ C\ \sim\ +\ *$ (iii) $A \sim B \sim *$

    (c) (i) $*\ A + B \sim C$ (iii) $* \sim A \sim B$

8. (a) $A\ B$ **and** C **or**   (e) $A\ B = C\ D =$ **or**

9. (a) **or and** $A\ B\ C$ (e) **or** $= A\ B = C\ D$

Section 14.2 (P. 491)

1. (a)

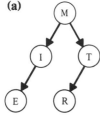

    (b) (i) Inorder: E I M R T
             Preorder: M I E T R
             PostOrder: E I R T M

2. (a) (i) M T R I E

    (b) (i) T R M I E

    (c) (i) R T E I M

3. (a)

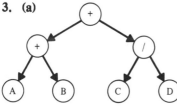

    Prefix: $+\ +\ A\ B\ /\ C\ D$
    Postfix: $A\ B + C\ D\ /\ +$

5. (a)

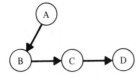

6. function *LeafCount*(*RootPointer* : *TreePointer*) : *integer*);

(∗ Function to count the number of leaves in a binary tree with root note pointed to by *RootPointer*. ∗)

> **begin** (∗ *LeafCount* ∗)
>   **if** *RootPointer* = **nil then**
>   *LeafCount* := 0
>   **else if** (*RootPointer*↑.*Left* = **nil**) **and**
>   (*RootPointer*↑.*Right* = **nil**) **then**
>   *LeafCount* := 1
>   **else**
>   *LeafCount* := *LeafCount*(*RootPointer*↑.*Left*)
>   + *LeafCount*(*RootPointer*↑.*Right*)
>
> **end** (∗ *LeafCount* ∗);

Section 14.3 (P. 506)

1. (a)

5, 1, 6, 4, 3, 2

First call to *QuickSort*
($Low = 1$, $High = 6$)

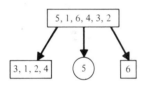

I.1: $1 < 6$ so
I.2: Split the list and position 5.
I.3: Call *QuickSort* on left sublist
    ($Low = 1$, $High = 4$).

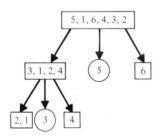

II.1: $1 < 4$ so
II.2: Split sublist and position 3.
II.3: Call *QuickSort* on left sublist
    ($Low = 1$, $High = 2$).

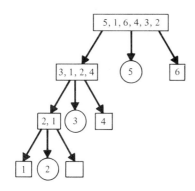

III.1: $1 < 2$ so

III.2: Split sublist and position 2.

III.3: Call *QuickSort* on left sublist
($Low = 1$, $High = 1$).

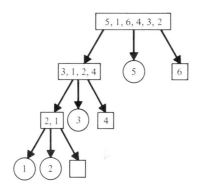

IV.1: $1 \not< 1$ (one-element sublist) so

IV.5: Return to previous level.

III.4: Call *QuickSort* on right sublist
($Low = 4$, $High = 3$).

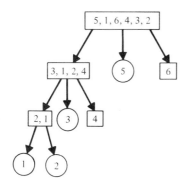

IV.1: $4 \not< 3$ (empty sublist) so

IV.5: Return to previous level.

III.5: Return to previous level.

II.4: Call *QuickSort* on right sublist
($Low = 4$, $High = 4$).

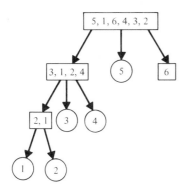

III.1: $4 \not< 4$ (one-element sublist) so

III.5: Return to previous level.

II.5: Return to previous level.

I.4: Call *QuickSort* on right sublist
($Low = 6$, $High = 6$).

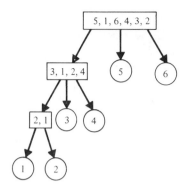

II.1: $6 \nless 6$ (one-element sublist) so
II.5: Return to previous level.

I.5: Return to main program;
sorting is completed.

Section 14.4 (P. 515)

1. **(a)** F: |1   5|3   8|7|2   6|4|

F1: |1   5   7|4 |
F2: |3   8|2   6|

F:
|1   3   5   7   8|2   4   6|

F1: |1   3   5   7   8|
F2: |2   4   6|

F:
|1   2   3   4   5   6   7   8|

INDEX

A

abacus, 1
abs function, 54, 140, A23
abundant number, 135
actual parameter, 142 ff, 154 ff
Ada Augusta, 7
addition, 51
address, 15
adjacency matrix, 343
ALGOL, 11
alfa type, 292
algorithm, 22
alias, 156
Analytical Engine, 7
anchor, 192
and, 96
ANSII/IEEE Pascal standard, 45
arctan function, 54, 140, A23
arithmetic expression, 52–53
arithmetic functions, 51, 53, 54, 140
arithmetic operations, 51–53, A8
arithmetic-logic unit, 12
array, 262, 315
arrays
  of arrays, 315
  assignment, 269–270
  columns of, 313
  columnwise processing of, 318 ff
  components of, 262
  declaration of, 262–263, 315
  multidimensional, 313–345
  n-dimensional, 315
  one-dimensional, 260–312
  packed, 291 ff
  as parameters, 270–272
  ranks of, 313
  rows of, 313
  rowwise processing of, 318 ff
  three-dimensional, 313
  two-dimensional, 313
ASCII, 16, 291, A1–A5

assignment
  operator, 55, A9
  statement, 55–59, 269–270, 324, 350, 381, 433, A19

B

Babbage, Charles, 7
Backus, John, 11
base type
  of a set, 348
  of a subrange, 253
batch mode, 12
begin, 72
binary number system, 14
binary point, 15
binary search, 279–280
binary trees, 479–491
  inorder traversal of, 481–491
  postorder traversal of, 481–491
  preorder traversal of, 481–491
  sorted, 486–491
  traversing, 480–491
binomial coefficients, 161, 207
bisection method, 151
bit, 14
boolean, 46
boolean constant, 47, 95
boolean expression, 95–98
boolean operators, 96–97, A9
  and, 96, A9
  or, 96, A9
  not, 96, A9
bubble sort, 275–279, 385
Buffon Needle Problem, 176
byte, 16

C

cardinal number, 367
case statement, 122–125, A21

central processing unit (cpu), 12
char, 46
character, 47, 290
character constant, 47, 290
children of a node, 478
chr function, 248
collating sequence, 98
columns of an array, 313
columnwise processing of arrays, 318 ff
comments, 31, 73
compatible types, 254, 267
compile-time errors, 38
compiler, 11, 361
complex number, 207, 399
components
  of an array, 262
  of a file, 403
compound **if** statement, 119
compound statement, 88–89, A21
conjunction, 96
const, 49, 72
constant, 46, A13
  boolean, 47, 95
  character, 47, 290
  integer, 46
  named, 49
  predefined, 50
  real, 46
  set, 349–350
constant section, 49, 72, 244, A13
continued fraction, 110
control cards, 33
control unit, 12
correlation coefficient, 240
cos function, 54, 140, A23
cryptogram, 309

D

data field, 436
data pointer, 214 ff
data structure, 259
  dynamic, 429
data types (*see* type)
decimal number system, 14
decimal representation, 46
declaration part, 48, 71, 141, 152, 244, A12
  constant section, 49, 72, 244, 529
  function, 141, 145
  label section, 72, 244, A12, A36
  procedure, 152
  subprogram section, 72, 141, 244, A15

type section, 244–245, A13
  variable section, 49, 72, 244, A15
deficient number, 135
deque, 463
derivative of a function, 150
Difference Engine, 7
digraph, 343
direct recursion, 199
directed arcs, 478
directed graph, 343, 478, 465
disjunction, 96
disk drive, 222
dispose procedure, 435, A24, A42
div, 51
division, 51
documentation, 37
doubly linked circular list, 494
doubly linked list, 478
doubly linked ring, 494
downto, 89
drunkard's walk problem, 176
dummy definition, 199
dynamic data structure, 429
dynamic variable, 429

E

EBCDIC, 16, 291, A1–A5
Eckert, J. P., 7
editing, 300–305
else, 111
empty set, 350
empty statement, 82
end, 72, 88–89, 120, 370
end-of-file mark, 223–227
end-of-line mark, 214–219, 295–299
ENIAC, 7
enumerated type, 246–253
eof function, 140, 224–227, 413
eoln function, 140, 294–299, 414–415
equality of sets, 352
equivalent type identifiers, 270
errors, 38
Euclidean Algorithm, 174–175, 207
exp function, 54, 140, A13
expanded form, 14
exponentiation, 194
expression, A19
  arithmetic, 52–53
  boolean, 95–98
  set, 353–355
external, 199

external file, 223, 402
external memory, 12, 222

F

factor, A20
factorial, 110, 161, 192
false, 48, 50, 95
Fibonacci numbers, 109, 208
field
    data, 436
    designator, 371
    key, 449
    link, 436
    list, A15
    output, 63
    of a record, 369 ff
    tag, 390 ff
FIFO structure, 290, 439
file, 222, 401, 403
    buffer variable, 406 ff
    component, 403
    declaration, 403
    external, 223, 402
    input, 211, 213–219
    internal, 402, 415
    list, A12
    opening for input, 223, 402
    opening for output, 228, 402
    output, 211
    as a parameter, 417
    permanent, 223, 402
    temporary, 402, 415
    text, 222–238, 402–403
    updating, 419–422
    variable, 223 ff, 403
    window, 406 ff
final value, 89
first generation, 9
fixed part of a record, 389 ff
flag, 102
floating point representation, 46
flowchart, 23
for statement, 89–95, A21
    nested, 93–95
formal parameter, 142 ff, 152 ff, 201 ff
format descriptor, 64–67
FORTRAN, 11
forward, 199
function, 141, 201
    abs, 54, 140
    arctan, 54, 140

arithmetic, 51, 53, 54, 140
chr, 248
cos, 54, 140
declaration part, 141, 145
definition, 141, A16
derivative of, 150
dummy definition of, 199
eof, 140, 224–227, 413
eoln, 140, 294–299, 414–415
exp, 54, 140
heading, 141–142, A16
ln, 54, 140
odd, 140
ord, 247
parameter, 200–204
pred, 247
predefined, 54, 140, A8
recursive, 192–196
round, 54, 140
sin, 54, 140
sqr, 54, 140
sqrt, 54, 140
standard (*see* predefined)
statement part, 143
succ, 247
trunc, 54, 140
user-defined, 141–148
zero of, 150
Fundamental Scope Principle, 161

G

get procedure, 413–415, A24
global variable, 163
goto statement, A22, A35–A40
greatest common divisor, 174–75, 207

H

Hangman, game of, 344
hardware, 9
harmonic series, 110
head node, 463
heading
    function, 141–142
    procedure, 152
    program, 31, 48, 62, 71–72
hexadecimal number system, 17
hierarchical records, 372
high-level language, 11
histogram, 310
Hollerith, Herman, 7

I

identifier, 48, 246, A12
  local, 162–163
  standard, 48, A7
  type, 243
if statement, 110–120, A22
  compound, 119
  nested, 111, 117, 119
in, 351
index, 260
index variable, 89
indirect recursion, 199
inductive step, 192
infinite series, 109, 110
infix notation, 468–477
initial value, 89
input, 22
input file, 62, 68 ff, 211, 213–219
input statement, 67–70
input/output, 61–70, 211–242
  devices, 12
  procedures, 211–219
insertion sort, 288
integer, 46
internal file, 402, 415
internal memory, 12
InventoryFile, A15
InventoryUpdate, A16

J

Jacquard, Joseph Marie, 4
Jensen, Kathleen, 45

K

key field, 449
keypunch, 33
knight's tour problem, 345

L

label section, 72, 244, A12, A36
leaf node, 479
least common multiple, 174
LeastSquaresFile, A27
Leibniz, Gottfried, 4
lexical analyzer, 361
Life, game of, 343
LIFO structure, 289, 438

linear search, 279
link field, 436
linked list, 430, 435
  deletion from, 448–449
  doubly, 478
  general, 444–458
  insertion into, 446–447
  multiply, 478
  ordered, 449–458
  searching, 449–450
  traversing, 446
list processing with one-dimensional arrays, 263–272
ln function, 54, 140, A23
local identifier, 162–163
local variable, 145–146
logarithms, 2
logical errors, 38
login, 33
loop, 89
Lukasiewicz, Jan, 468

M

machine language, 11
magic square, 342
magnetic disk, 222
magnetic tape, 222
Mark I, 7
matrix, 332
  adjacency, 343
  multiplication, 332–335
  sparse, 465–466
Mauchly, J. W., 7
maxint, 50
mean, 109
memory
  external, 12, 222
  internal, 12
  secondary, 12, 222
memory unit, 12
menu, 134
menu-driven program, 427
mergesort, 507–515
method of least squares, 240
microcomputer, 10
mod, 51
mode, 286
modular programming, 177
Monte Carlo technique, 176
Morse code, 340
multialternative selection structure, 119–125

multidimensional arrays, 313–345
multiplication, 51
multiply subscripted variable, 313 ff
mutual recursion, 199

N

n-dimensional arrays, 315
n-queens problem, 345
named constant, 49
Napier's bones, 2
negation, 96
nested
   for loops, 89–95
   if statements, 111, 117, 119
   records, 372
   with statements, 379–380
new procedure, 430–431, A24, A41–A42
Newton's method, 151
nil, 434
nil pointer, 434
Nim, game of, 344
node, 429, 478
   children of, 478
   head, 463
   leaf, 479
   parent, 479
   root, 478
not, 96
notation
   infix, 468–477
   postfix, 468
   prefix, 468
   reverse Polish (RPN), 468–477
Noyce, Robert, 10
number,
   abundant, 135
   cardinal, 367
   complex, 207, 399
   deficient, 135
   Fibonacci, 109, 208
   ordinal, 247
   perfect, 135
   prime, 150, 289, 358
   pseudorandom, 171
   random, 171
   rational, 400

O

object program, 11
octal number system, 17

odd function, 140
one-dimensional arrays, 262–312
opening a file
   for input, 223, 402
   for output, 228, 402
operating system, 11
operations, 353 ff, A9
   arithmetic, 51–53, A8
   assignment, 55, A9
   boolean, 96–97, A9
   relational, 97–98, 351–353, 355, A9
   set, 353 ff, A9
   unary, 53
operators (*see* operations)
or, 96
ord function, 247
ordinal number, 247
ordinal type, 243–256
out-of-range error, 254
output, 22
output file, 62, 211
output statement, 62–67
overflow, 16

P

pack procedure, 299, A14, A43–A44
packed, 263, 291
packed arrays, 291 ff
page procedure, 231, A24, A40
palindrome, 208, 310
parameter
   list, A16
   actual, 142 ff, 154 ff
   formal, 142 ff, 152 ff, 201 ff
   function, 200–204
   procedure, 200–204
   value, 155 ff
   variable, 153 ff
parent of a node, 479
partial sum, 109, 110
Pascal, Blaise, 2, 11
Pascal language, 11
Pascal User Manual and Report, 45
Pascal's triangle, 340
perfect number, 135
permanent file, 223, 402
personal mode, 14
pointer, 243, 429–435
polar coordinates, 156, 398
polynomial
   of degree *n,* 464
   derivative of, 464
   in two variables, 496

postfix notation, 468
Potential Problems, 81–83, 127–130, 173–174, 205–206
power series, 173–174
precedence levels of operators, 52, 98, 355
pred function, 247, A23
predefined constant, 50
predefined functions, 140–141
  abs, 54, 140
  arctan, 54, 140
  arithmetic, 140
  boolean-valued, 140
  chr, 248
  cos, 54, 140
  eof, 140, 224–227, 413
  eoln, 140, 294–299, 414–415
  exp, 54, 140
  ln, 54, 140
  odd, 140
  ord, 247
  pred, 247
  sin, 54, 140
  cos, 54, 140
  sqrt, 54, 140
  succ, 247
  trunc, 54, 140
predefined procedures, 141, 435, A24, A42
  dispose, 435, A24, A42
  get, 413–415, A24
  new, 430–431, A24, A41–A42
  pack, 299, A24, A34–A44
  page, 231, A40
  put, 405, 408–409, A24
  read, 216–221, 403, A24
  readln, 67–70, 211–222, 403, A24
  reset, 223, 402, 404–405, A24
  rewrite, 228, 402, 405 ff
  unpack, 299, A24, A43–A44
  write, 212–213
  writeln, 62–67, 211–213, 403, A24
prefix notation, 468
pretty-printer, 427
prime number, 150, 289, 358
procedure, 152, 504
  declaration part, 152
  definition, 152 ff, A17
  dispose, 435, A24, A42
  dummy, definition of, 199
  get, 413–415, A24
  heading, 152, A17
  input/output, 211–219
  new, 430–431, A24, A41–A42
  pack, 299, A24, A34–A44
  page, 231, A40

parameter, 200–204
  predefined, 141, 435, A24, A42
  put, 405, 408–409, A24
  read, 216–221, 403, A24
  readln, 67–70, 211–222, 403, A24
  reference statement, 152, 154, A22
  reset, 223, 402, 404–405, A24
  rewrite, 228, 402, 405 ff
  statement part, 152
  unpack, 299, A24, A43–A44
  user-defined, 152–159
  write, 212–213
  writeln, 62–67, 211–213, 403, A24
program, 31, 71, A11
  straight-line, 87
  structured, 87
program composition, 71–73
Program Design, 79–81, 126–127, 204
program heading, 31, 48, 62, 71–72, A11
Program Style, 37, 83–84, 131–132, 206–207
program testing and debugging, 37
program validation, 39
Programming Pointers, 79–84, 126–132, 204–207, 234–238, 255–256, 305–307, 336–337, 365–366, 393–397, 422–423, 458–462
pseudocode, 25
pseudorandom number, 171
put procedure, 405, 408–409, A24

Q

queue, 207, 290, 436, 440–444
  deletion from, 443
  insertion into, 443–444
  priority, 463
quicksort, 498–507
quipus, 2

R

random number, 171
random number generator, 171
range checking, 254
ranks of an array, 313
rational number, 400
read procedure, 216 ff, 403, A24
readln procedure, 67–70, 211–222, 304, A24
real, 46
record, 369

records, 369–400
  assignment of, 381
  fields of, 369 ff
  fixed part of, 389 ff
  hierarchical, 372
  nested, 372
  tag field of, 390 ff
  variant parts of, 389 ff, 541–542
  variant, 372, 389–393, 541–542
rectangular coordinates, 398
recursion, 192–200
  direct, 199
  indirect, 199
  mutual, 199
  simple, 199
refinement, 22
regression coefficients, 240
regression equation, 240
relational operator, 97–98, 351–353, 355
  <, 97, 525
  <=, 97, 352, A9
  <>, 97, 353, A9
  =, 97, 353, A9
  >, 97, A9
  >=, 97, 352, A9
  in, 351, A9
repeat statement, 95, 104–106, A22
repetition structure, 89–106
reserved words, 30, 48, A7
  and, 96
  array, 262, 315
  begin, 72
  case, 122
  const, 49, 72
  div, 51
  do, 89
  downto, 89
  else, 111
  end, 72, 88–89, 120, 370
  file, 401, 403
  for, 89
  forward, 199
  function, 141, 201
  goto, A35
  if, 111
  in, 351
  label, A36
  mod, 51
  nil, 434
  not, 96
  of, 120, 262, 315, 348, 403
  or, 96
  packed, 263, 291
  procedure, 152, 204

  program, 31, 71
  record, 369
  repeat, 104
  set, 348
  then, 111
  to, 89
  type, 244
  until, 104
  var, 29–30, 49, 72, 150
  while, 99
  with, 373
reset procedure, 223, 402, 404–405, A24
reverse Polish notation, 468–477
rewrite procedure, 228, 402, 405, A24
right-justified, 63, 66
root node, 478
round function, 54, 140, A23
rows of an array, 313
rowwise processing of arrays, 318 ff
RPN (*see* reverse Polish notation)
run-time errors, 38

S

same type, 270
scientific representation, 46
scope, 145, 161–171, 244–245
  Rule 1, 161, 244
  Rule 2, 163, 244
  Rule 3, 165, 244
  Rule 4, 168
  rules for labels, A38
search
  binary, 279–280
  linear, 279
searching, 279–284, 383–389
second generation, 9
secondary memory, 12, 222
section
  constant, 72, 244
  label, 72, 244, A36
  subprogram, 72, 141, 244
  type, 72, 244–245
  variable, 72, 244
selection structure, 110–125
  multialternative, 119–125
semantics, 76
sentinel, 102
sequential structure, 87–89
series
  harmonic, 110
  infinite, 109, 110
  power, 173–174

set, 348
  base type of, 348
  constant, 349–350
  declaration, 348
  difference, 353 ff, A9
  elements of a, 347
  empty, 350
  equality, 352
  intersection, 353 ff, A9
  members of a, 347
  operations, 353 ff, A9
  union, 353 ff, A9
  universal, 348
Shell sort, 288
Sieve of Eratosthenes, 289, 312, 358–361
simple data type, 243
simple expression, A19
simple recursion, 199
simple type, A14
sin function, 54, 140, A23
skewness, 287
slide rule, 2
sort
  bubble, 275–279, 385
  insertion, 288
  merge, 507–515
  quick, 498–507
  Shell, 288
sorted binary tree, 486–491
  deletion from, 496–497
  insertion into, 487
  searching, 487–488
sorting, 275–279, 383–389
  external, 507
  internal, 507
  stable, 506–507
source program, 11
sparse matrix, 465–466
sqr function, 54, 140, A23
sqrt function, 54, 140, A23
stack, 289, 436–442
  pop operation, 439
  push operation, 439
standard constants, A7
standard deviation, 109, 286
standard files, A7
standard functions, A8
standard identifiers, 48, A7
standard procedures, A8
standard types, A7
statement, A18
  assignment, 55–59, 269–270, 324, 350, 381, 433, A19
  case, 122–125, A21

compound, 88–89, A21
compound **if,** 119
empty, 82
for, 89–95, A22
goto, A22, A35–A40
if, 110–120, A22
input, 67–70
output, 62–67
procedure reference, 152, 154, A22
repeat, 95, 104–106, A22
while, 95, 99–104, A22
with, 373–382, A22
statement labels, A35–A40
statement part, 48, 71, A17
  function, 143
  procedure, 152
static variable, 429
Stonehenge, 2
straight-line program, 87
string constant, 47, 290
string type, 292 ff
string, 47, 290
structure
  multialternative selection, 119–125
  repetition, 89–106
  selection, 110–125
  sequential, 87–89
structure diagram, 23
structured data type, 243
structured program, 87
StudentFile, A28
StudentUpdate, A31
subprogram section, 72, 141, 244, A15
subprogram, 155
subrange type, 246, 253–255
subscript, 260 ff
subscripted variable, 260 ff
subset, 352
subtraction, 51
subtrees, 480–491
succ function, 247
sum-of-the-years-digits depreciation, 108
synonym, 156
syntax, 29, 76
syntax diagrams, 76–79, A11–A22
system software, 10

T

tag field, 390 ff
tape drive, 222
temporary file, 402, 415
term, A20

text editing, 300–305
text-editor, 426
text file, 222–238, 402–403
text-formatting, 426
then, 111
third generation, 10
three-dimensional arrays, 313
tic-tac-doe, 344
time-sharing, 13
to, 89
token, 361
top–down approach, 22
top–down design, 177–191
Towers of Hanoi problem, 196–198
tree, 478
  binary, 479–491
true, 48, 50, 96
trunc function, 54, 140, A23
truth table, 96
two-dimensional arrays, 313
type, 244, A14
  alfa, 292
  array, 262, 315
  base, 253, 348
  boolean, 46
  char, 46
  compatible, 254, 267
  enumerated, 246–253
  file, 401, 403
  integer, 46
  ordinal, 243–256
  pointer, 243
  real,
  record, 369
  same, 270
  set, 348
  simple, 243
  string, 292 ff
  structured, 243
  subrange, 246, 253–255
  text, 223, 402
type identifiers, 243
  equivalent, 270
type section, 244–245, A13

U

unary operator, 53
UNIVAC, 9

unpack procedure, 299, A24, A43–A44
unsigned constant, A21
unsigned integer, A12
unsigned number, A13
until, 104
updating a file, 419–422
user-defined function, 141–148
user-defined procedure, 152–159
UsersFile, A32

V

value parameter, 155 ff
var, 29–30, 49, 72, 153
variable, 29, 48, A19
  dynamic, 429
  file buffer, 406 ff
  file, 223 ff, 403
  global, 163
  index, 89
  local, 145–146
  multiply subscripted, 313 ff
  pointer, 429–435
  static, 429
  subscripted, 260 ff
variable parameter, 153 ff
variable section, 49, 72, 244, A15
variance, 109, 286
variant part, 389 ff
variant records, 372, 389–393, A41–A42
vertices, 478
von Neumann, John, 9

W

while statement, 95, 99–104, A22
Wirth, Niklaus, 11, 45
with statement, 373–382, A22
  nested, 379–380
word, 15
write procedure, 212–213, 403, 405 ff,
  A24
writeln procedure, 62–67, 211–213, 403,
  A24

Z

zero of a function, 150

Pascal Reference Chart (cont.)

STATEMENTS	EXAMPLE
Assignment (55–59,269,324, 350,381,433)	Count := 0; Wages := RoundCents (Hours * Rate); DeptCode := 'A'; OverTime := (Hours > 40); ProductName := 'Ford-Carburetor'; Letters := ['A'..'F', 'P', 'S']; EmpRec := InFile↑; EmpRec.Number := 12345; TempPtr := nil; FirstPtr↑.Data := ProductName;

Sequential (87–89)
　Compound (88)
	begin
	　Wages := RoundCents(Hours * Rate);
	　OverTime := false
	end;

Repetition (89–106)
　for (89)
	for I := 1 to Count do
	　writeln (Product[I]);
	for I := Count downto 1 do
	　writeln (Item[I]);

repeat (104)	repeat 　write ('Enter first initial : '); 　readln (FirstInit); until FirstInit in Letters;

while (99)	while not eof(InFile) do
	　begin
	　　readln (InFile, EmpRec.Number)
	　　writeln (EmpRec.Number)
	　end (* while *);

(handwritten annotation next to "until FirstInit in Letters;": UNTIL NOT (FIRSTINIT IN LETTERS))